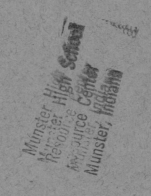

Microeconomic theory

THE IRWIN SERIES IN ECONOMICS

Consulting Editor   LLOYD G. REYNOLDS
Yale University

Microeconomic theory

C. E. FERGUSON
Late Professor, Texas A&M University

J. P. GOULD
Professor, University of Chicago

Fourth Edition 1975

RICHARD D. IRWIN, INC. Homewood, Illinois 60430

Irwin-Dorsey Limited, Georgetown, Ontario L7G 4B3

Fourth Edition

0 11 12 13 14 15 16 17 18 K 5 4 3 2 1 0 9

ISBN 0-256-01637-2
Library of Congress Catalog Card No. 74–24441
Printed in the United States of America

Preface

This fourth edition of *Microeconomic Theory*, like the three earlier editions, is a textbook on neoclassical price theory intended primarily for undergraduate students. The ultimate test of a textbook is provided by the market and the earlier editions did gratifyingly well by this criterion. In view of that success there has been a careful effort to retain much of the content and substance of the earlier editions in this book. There are, however, numerous changes in the fourth edition. As a general characterization, this edition places greater emphasis on the *analytical* aspects of economics while retaining the coverage of the theory found in earlier editions.

Specific changes include an expanded number of problems and exercises. Additional problems keyed to this text are in a Workbook that has been developed by Marcia Stigum. A major addition in this edition is a new chapter (Chapter 10) on the analytical uses of models of competition and monopoly, which replaces the chapter on Linear Programming. This new chapter is intended to illustrate how the theoretical tools of economics can be used to analyze the effects of such things as taxes, subsidies, and price controls on firm and industry price and output. Students have found this material useful in broadening their comprehension of the fundamental theoretical principles of firm and industry equilibrium.

In Chapter 3 the theory of consumer behavior is extended to decisions involving risk—an area of theoretical economics that has received increasing attention in recent years. There is also new material on consumption choices over time, showing how savings and intertemporal consumption behavior can be analyzed using simple modifications of the traditional indifference curves and budget lines. The material on risk and consumption over time is developed independently of the rest of the text and can be skipped at the instructor's option. There are also rather substantial revisions of the chapter on general economic equilibrium, showing how the basic concepts of general equilibrium apply in relatively simple economies.

Although the text is designed primarily for undergraduates, past experience shows that it has proved helpful to graduate students. The book continues to contain the by now well-known appendix "Comprehensive Examination in Micro-Economic Theory for Graduate Students." The questions in this appendix were developed by Fritz Machlup in conjunction with the two-semester course in microeconomic theory he taught while at Johns Hopkins. Professor Machlup's questions are indeed comprehensive (extending to topics not covered in the text) and provide a valuable perspective of the scope of neoclassical microeconomic theory.

Many users of earlier editions of this book, both teachers and undergraduate students, were kind enough to send letters to the late Professor Ferguson concerning errors of substance, and obscure points. These comments have been very helpful and I sincerely hope readers of the fourth edition will now direct their comments to me on any issue that arises.

Acknowledgments to all of those who have contributed helpful suggestions are too numerous to be listed, but I cannot fail to mention a thoughtful review of the Third Edition by Jerry Green of Harvard University which provided useful guidance for much of this revision and to thank Roy Ruffin of the University of Iowa for many valuable discussions on matters that arose during the revision. Ilene Haniotis and her coworkers at the University of Chicago provided exceptional cooperation and superb service in typing and preparing the manuscript. While the late Professor Ferguson did not participate directly in this revision, his is still the major contribution to this book. The final responsibility for errors that may remain is nonetheless mine.

January 1975   JOHN P. GOULD

Contents

Introduction
Scope and methodology of economics   1

Scope of Economics: *Economics in the Small and in the Large. Norms and Policy.* Methodology: *Model Analysis.* An Overview of this Book.

Advanced reading   7

part I
Theory of consumer behavior and demand   9

1. Theory of utility and preference   11

Introduction: *The Nature of Commodities. Full Knowledge. The Theory of Consumer Preference.* Utility and Preference: *The Utility Surface. The Indifference Curve. Summary.* Characteristics of Indifference Curves. Marginal Rate of Substitution. Conclusion.

2. Theory of consumer behavior   29

Introduction: *Maximization of Satisfaction. Limited Money Income. Shifting the Budget Line.* Consumer Equilibrium: *The Relevant Part of Commodity Space. Maximizing Satisfaction Subject to a Limited Money In-*

come. Changes in Money Income: *The Income-Consumption Curve. Engel Curves. Engel Curves and the Income Elasticity of Demand.* Changes in Price: *The Price-Consumption Curve. The Demand Curve. The Elasticity of Demand. Elasticity of Demand and the Price-Consumption Curve.*

3. Topics in consumer demand   52

Introduction. Substitution and Income Effects: *The Substitution Effect in the Case of a Normal or Superior Good. The Income Effect in the Case of a Normal Good. Normal or Superior Goods.* Inferior Goods: *Inferior Goods and Giffen's Paradox. Income and Substitution Effects for an Inferior Good.* Substitution and Complementarity: *Classification by Cross-Elasticities. Geometric Illustrations.* Application of Indifference Curve Analysis: The Economic Theory of Index Numbers: *Information from the Budget Map. Index Numbers as Indicators of Individual Welfare Changes.* Applications of Indifference Curve Analysis: The Choice between Leisure and Income: *The Income-Leisure Graph. Equilibrium between Income and Leisure. Overtime Rates. Demand for General Assistance Payments.* Time Preference—Consumption and Saving over the Life Cycle. Choices Involving Risk: *Probabilities and Expected Value. The Expected Utility Hypothesis. Indifference Curves and State Preference Analysis.* An Example of Decision Making In a Risky Situation.

4. Characteristics of market demand   90

Introduction. From Individual to Market Demand: *The Determinants of Demand. Determining Market Demand.* Elasticities of Demand: *Price Elasticity of Demand. Coefficient of Price Elasticity. Graphical Measurement of Point Elasticity. Factors Affecting Price Elasticity. Price Cross-Elasticity of Demand. Income Elasticity of Demand.* Marginal Revenue: *Calculation of Marginal Revenue. The Geometry of Marginal Revenue Determination.* Demand, Revenue, and Elasticity: *Elasticity and Total Revenue. Elasticity and Marginal Revenue. Demand Curve for a Firm in Perfect Competition.*

Advanced reading, part I   120

part II
Theory of production and cost   123

5. Production with one variable input   125

Introduction: *Fixed and Variable Inputs, the Short and Long Runs. Fixed or Variable Proportions.* The Production Function: *Total Output or Product. Average and Marginal Products. Law of Diminishing Marginal Physical Returns.* The Geometry of Average and Marginal Product Curves:

Geometry of Average Product Curves. Geometry of Marginal Product Curves. Total, Average, and Marginal Products. The Three Stages of Production. Linearly Homogeneous Production Functions.

6. **Production and optimal input proportions: Two variable inputs   144**

   Introduction: *Production Table. Input Substitution.* Production Surface: *Production Surface for Discrete Case. Production Surface for Continuous Case. Production Isoquants. Fixed-Proportions Production Functions.* Input Substitution: *Marginal Rate of Technical Substitution. Diminishing Marginal Rate of Technical Substitution. Economic Region of Production.* Optimal Combination of Resources: *Input Prices and Isocosts. Maximizing Output for a Given Cost. Minimizing Cost Subject to a Given Output.* The Expansion Path: *Isoclines. Changing Output and the Expansion Path. Expenditure Elasticity.* Changes in Input Price: *The Substitution and Output Effects. "Inferior Factors" and the Output Effect.* Analogies Between Consumer and Producer Behavior. Conclusion.

7. **Theory of cost   179**

   Introduction: *Social Cost of Production. Private Cost of Production. The Role of the Entrepreneur.* Short and Long Runs: *Long-Run Costs and the Production Function. Short-Run Costs and the Production Function. Fixed and Variable Costs in the Short Run.* Theory of Cost in the Short Run: *Total Short-Run Cost. Average and Marginal Cost. Geometry of Average and Marginal Cost Curves. Short-Run Cost Curves.* Long-Run Theory of Cost: *Short Run and the Long. Long-Run Average Cost Curve. Long-Run Marginal Cost. The Envelope Curve and the Expansion Path.* Cost Elasticity and the Function Coefficient: *The Function Coefficient. Cost Elasticity.* Shape of *LAC: Economies of Scale. Diseconomies of Scale.* Long-Run Cost and Changes in Factor Price: *Changes in Long-Run Average Cost. Changes in Long-Run Marginal Cost and Minimum Average Total Cost.* Conclusion.

   Advanced reading, part II   216

   **part III
   Theory of the firm and market organization**   219

8. **Theory of price in perfectly competitive markets   222**

   Introduction. Perfect Competition: *Price Taking Demanders and Suppliers. Homogeneous Product. Free Mobility of Resources. Perfect Knowledge.* Equilibrium in the Market Period: *Industry Equilibrium in the Market Period. Price as a Rationing Device.* Short-Run Equilibrium of a

Firm in a Perfectly Competitive Market: *Short-Run Profit Maximization, Total Revenue—Total Cost Approach. Short-Run Profit Maximization, the Marginal Approach. Proof of the Short-Run Equilibrium. Profit or Loss? Short-Run Supply Curve of a Firm in a Perfectly Competitive Industry.* Short-Run Equilibrium in a Perfectly Competitive Industry: *Short-Run Industry Supply Curve. Short-Run Market Equilibrium, Profit or Loss. Demand-Supply Analysis.* Long-Run Equilibrium in a Perfectly Competitive Market: *Long-Run Adjustment of an Established Firm. Long-Run Adjustment of the Industry. Long-Run Equilibrium in a Perfectly Competitive Firm. Constant Cost Industries. Increasing Cost Industries.* The Competitive Model in Practice. Conclusion.

9. **Theory of price under pure monopoly**   259

Introduction: *Definition. Bases of Monopoly.* Demand Under Monopoly. Cost and Supply Under Monopoly: *Cost with Monopoly in the Input Market. A Word on Monopoly Supply.* Short-Run Equilibrium Under Monopoly: *Total Revenue—Total Cost Approach. Marginal Revenue—Marginal Cost Approach. Short-Run Equilibrium. Monopoly Supply in the Short Run. Multiplant Monopoly in the Short Run.* Long-Run Equilibrium Under Monopoly: *Long-Run Equilibrium in a Single-Plant Monopoly. Comparison with Perfect Competition. Long-Run Equilibrium in a Multiplant Monopoly. Comparison with Perfect Competition.* Special Topics in Monopoly Theory: *Price Discrimination. Bilateral Monopoly.*

10. **Competition and monopoly: Some theoretical exercises**   292

Introduction: Excise Taxes in a Competitive Industry: *Short-Run Effects on Cost, Price, and Output. Long-Run Effects of the Tax. Ad Valorem Taxes.* Lump-Sum Taxes: *Short-Run Effects of a Lump-Sum Tax in a Competitive Industry. Long-Run Effects of a Lump-Sum Tax. Lump-Sum Taxes and the Size Distribution of Firms.* Price Controls: *Price Controls in a Competitive Industry. Price Controls in a Monopoly.* Price Supports and Output Restrictions: *Price Floors. Output Restrictions.* Suppression of Inventions in a Monopoly.

11. **Theory of price under monopolistic competition**   312

Introduction: *Historical Perspective. Product Differentiation. Industries and Product Groups.* A Different View of Perfect Competition: Short-Run Equilibrium in Monopolistic Competition: Long-Run Equilibrium in Monopolistic Competition: Characteristics of Monopolistic Competition: *"Ideal Output" and Excess Capacity. Nonprice Competition and Excess Capacity.* Comparisons of Long-Run Equilibria: *Equilibrium in the Firm. Long-Run Equilibria in Industries and Product Groups.* An Appraisal of Monopolistic Competition.

12. Theories of price in oligopoly markets   329

Introduction: *The Oligopoly Problem. Some Concepts and Assumptions.*
Some "Classical" Solutions to the Duopoly Problem: *Cournot Case. Edgeworth Case. Stability in Oligopoly Markets: Chamberlin Solution. Stability in Oligopoly Markets: Sweezy Solution. Theory of Games and Oligopoly Behavior.* Some "Market" Solutions to the Duopoly Problem:
*Cartels and Profit Maximization. Cartels and Market Sharing. Short and
Turbulent Life of Cartels—The Great Electrical Conspiracy. Price Leadership in Oligopoly.* Competition in Oligopoly Markets. Welfare Effects of
Oligopoly.

part IV
Theory of distribution   363

13. Marginal productivity theory of distribution in perfectly
    competitive markets   365

Introduction. Demand for a Productive Service: *Demand of a Firm for
One Variable Productive Service. Individual Demand Curves When Several Variable Inputs Are Used. Determinants of the Demand for a Produc-
tive Service. Market Demand for a Variable Productive Service.* Supply
of a Variable Productive Service: *General Considerations. Indifference
Curve Analysis of Labor Supply. The Market Supply of Labor.* Marginal
Productivity Theory of Input Returns: *Market Equilibrium and the Re-
turns to Variable Productive Services. Short Run and Quasi Rents. Clark-
Wicksteed Product Exhaustion Theorem.* Distribution and Relative Factor
Shares: *Least-Cost Combinations of Inputs and Linearly Homogeneous
Production Functions. The Elasticity of Substitution. Elasticity of Substitu-
tion and Changes in Relative Factor Shares. Classification of Technologi-
cal Progress. Biased Technological Progress and Relative Factor Shares.*
Appendix to Chapter 13: *The Clark-Wicksteed Theorem. The Output
Elasticity of Productive Services.*

14. Theory of employment in imperfectly competitive markets   397

Introduction. Monopoly in the Commodity Market: *Marginal Revenue
Product. Monopoly Demand for a Single Variable Service. Monopoly Demand for a Variable Productive Service When Several Variable Inputs Are
Used. Market Demand for a Variable Productive Service. Equilibrium
Price and Employment. Monopolistic Exploitation.* Monopsony: Monopoly
in the Input Market: *Marginal Expense of Input. Price and Employment
under Monopsony When One Variable Input Is Used. Price and Employment under Monopsony When Several Variable Inputs Are Used. Monopsonistic Exploitation. Monopsony and the Economic Effects of Labor
Unions.*

Advanced reading, part IV   421

part V
Theory of general equilibrium and economic welfare   423

15. Theory of general economic equilibrium   426

Introduction: *A Simple Two-Person Economy. The Farmer as Entrepreneur. The Farmer as Consumer-Laborer. General Equilibrium and Walras's Law.* General Equilibrium of Exchange: *Edgeworth Box Diagram. Equilibrium of Exchange. Deriving the Utility-Possibility Frontier.* General Equilibrium of Production and Exchange: *General Equilibrium of Production. General Equilibrium of Production and Exchange. Deriving the Production-Possibility Frontier or Transformation Curve.* General Competitive Equilibrium in a Two-Good Economy: *Production in a Two-Good Economy. Equilibrium in a Two-Good Economy. Factor Intensities and the Relationship Between Factor Prices and Commodity Prices.*

16. Theory of welfare economics   452

Introduction: *Marginal Conditions for Social Welfare. Welfare Maximization and Perfect Competition.* Input, Output, and Distribution: *General Assumptions. Retracing Some Steps: From Production Functions to the Production-Possibility Frontier. Production Possibilities and the Optimum Conditions of Exchange. Retracing Some Steps: From the Contract Curve to the Utility-Possibility Frontier. From a Utility-Possibility Point to the Grand Utility-Possibility Frontier. From the Utility-Possibility Frontier to the Point of "Constrained Bliss." Constrained Bliss and Efficiency. Inputs, Outputs, Distribution, and Welfare. From "Constrained Bliss" to Prices, Wages, and Rent. Minimum Wages and Pareto Efficiency: A Digression.* External Economies and Welfare Economics: A Final Word on Free Enterprise: *Social Benefits and Costs. Ownership Externalities. Technical Externalities. Public Good Externalities. Externalities and Free Enterprise.*

Advanced reading, part V   479

Appendix: A comprehensive examination in microeconomic
      theory for graduate students   485

Author index   521

Subject index   525

introduction

Scope and methodology of economics

I.1 SCOPE OF ECONOMICS

Economics is a social science that is concerned with the means by which scarce resources are used to satisfy competing ends. This standard but abstract definition often fails to convey just how pervasive the scope of economics really is. The idea of allocating limited resources to satisfy competing ends is familiar enough when one contemplates a household deciding how to budget its income for purchase of clothes, housing, insurance, entertainment, transportation, and other goods and services. It is also easy to see that businesses must make allocative decisions: General Motors has to decide how to allocate its production resources in the production of Chevrolets, Pontiacs, and Cadillacs. Universities must decide how much of tuition revenues and endowment should be spent on new buildings instead of books for the library or the hiring of additional faculty. Students have to allocate their studying time among the various courses they are taking and they also must decide how much of their time to spend in study rather than in other pursuits. Income earners must decide how much of their current earnings should be consumed now and how much should be saved for future consumption. On a broader scale, we often think of some resources as being so abundant that they can be used to satisfy *all* possible needs; air and water are examples. But even here an al-

1

locative decision must be made when it is recognized that certain activities pollute air and water. If we drive more cars or produce more steel we will have less clean air and water.

I.1.a Economics in the Small and in the Large

Economics is concerned both with the allocative decisions made by individuals, households, businesses, and other economic agents and with the broader question of how society as a whole allocates resources. Economists frequently assume that consumers attempt to maximize satisfaction and businessmen or entrepreneurs attempt to maximize profit. So defined, the goals of economic agents provide the economist with a frame of reference that permits systematic analysis of individual economic behavior. The behavior of one agent vis-à-vis another is likely to be, in some sense, competitive. But in a broader view, it is the mutual cooperation of agents with conflicting goals that is ultimately responsible for the production of economic goods and services.

When the principles of microeconomic behavior have been discovered, our attention can be focused on a macroeconomic problem that has beset economics from its inception as a science. Indeed, one might say it was the attempt to resolve this problem that caused economics to become a science. The problem may be stated as a question: Will the independent maximizing behavior of each economic agent eventually result in a social organization that, in a normative sense, maximizes the well-being of society as a whole? Adam Smith suggested an answer to this when he presented his doctrine of the "invisible hand." According to Smith, each individual, bent on pursuing his own best interest, is inevitably led, as if by an unseen hand, to pursue a course of action that benefits society as a whole. This is a happy and optimistic doctrine. It has, however, been increasingly questioned as the social and industrial milieu has undergone great change. If all economic agents are atomistic in size relative to the total economic society, either Smith's "invisible hand" or an IBM machine will seek out an optimal organization of economic activity. But, on the contrary, if all agents are not atomistic, one is compelled to ask if this optimum will be reached. Or will the very large agents play an economic game in which they achieve gains, but only at the expense of counterbalancing losses on the part of smaller units? The answers to these questions are not at all clear. But they are very important, both from the standpoint of theory and from that of policy.

Although the course for which this text has been prepared is primarily concerned with the analysis of microeconomic behavior, we must not lose sight of the dominant *quaesitum,* that is, social welfare. To this end, we shall assess each facet of individual behavior in terms of social welfare and finally conclude with a chapter devoted to welfare economics.

I.1.b Norms and Policy

The discussion of goals, especially in the last paragraph above, leads to a further discussion of *welfare norms* and economic policy (*positive economics*). Economists, in their role as economists, cannot establish normative objectives for a society. For example, an economist cannot say that free public education is desirable or that some minimum level of income should be received by each family unit. Of course, as a citizen he can vote for school bond issues and for legislators who favor income redistribution; but an economist *as an economist* cannot determine social goals.

The business of an economist is a positive, not a normative, one. That is, given a social objective, the economist can analyze the problem and suggest the most efficient means by which to attain the desired end. This book is accordingly devoted to the positive aspects of economic analysis, not to the normative decisions that a society must make.

I.2 METHODOLOGY

A person observing the real world of economic phenomena is confronted with a mass of data that is, at least superficially, meaningless. To discover order in this morass of facts and to arrange them in a meaningful way, it is necessary to develop theories to explain various aspects of human behavior, and thus to explain the otherwise meaningless data. By abstracting from the real world, it is possible to achieve a level of simplicity at which human action may be analyzed. But in the process of abstraction, the analyst must be careful to preserve the essential features of the real world problem with which he is concerned. That is to say, simplification is necessary; but at the same time a theory must capture the essence of the fundamental economic problem it is designed to solve.

I.2.a Model Analysis

Since this text is exclusively concerned with economic models and their use in analyzing real world economic problems, it is especially important to give attention to the use of model analysis in general before undertaking a study of specific economic models. It is convenient to do this schematically with the aid of the following diagram:[1]

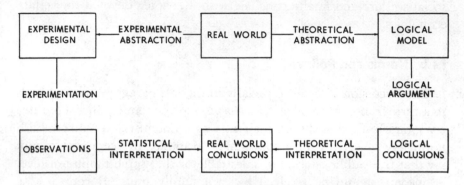

The real world is usually the starting point. A particular problem, or merely a desire to understand, motivates one to move from the complicated world of reality into the domain of logical simplicity. By means of theoretical abstraction, one hopefully reduces the complexities of the real world to manageable proportions. The result is a logical model presumably suited to explain the phenomena observed. By logical argument (i.e., deduction) one then arrives at logical or model conclusions. However, these must be transformed, by means of theoretical interpretation, into conclusions about the real world.

Let us summarize to this point. The economist, having begun with a portion of the real world, proceeds, through the use of completely theoretical means, to arrive at conclusions about the real world. His first step entails abstraction from the real world into a simplified logical model. His second step requires the use of logical argument to arrive at an abstract conclusion. His final step consists of a return to the real world by means of an interpretation that yields conclusions in terms of the concrete, sensible world of physical reality.

The same result may presumably be achieved by another method. Let us call it the *statistical method* to distinguish it from the *deductive method* previously discussed. Again starting from the real world, we may, by means of experimental abstraction, arrive at an experimental design. That is, we may, by a process of simplification, design a statistical model that is useful in analyzing the real world. In this instance, however, we obtain observations of real world data rather than theorems

---

[1] Adapted from a diagram appearing in C. H. Coombs, Howard Raiffa, and R. M. Thrall (eds.), "Mathematical Models and Measurement Theory," *Decision Processes* (New York: John Wiley & Sons, Inc., 1954), p. 22.

by logical deduction. These observations, given the proper statistical interpretation, yield conclusions concerning the real world.

Although there is some disagreement over the relative merit of the two methods, the tenor of present thinking is that they are complementary. That is to say, deductive and statistical methods are mutually reinforcing rather than alternative instruments of analysis. It is true, however, that professional opinion on methodology is still somewhat diverse.

1.3 AN OVERVIEW OF THIS BOOK

The authors of this book are sympathetic with the view that theory and empirical investigation are complementary: theory provides testable hypotheses about the real world, and statistical testing of these hypotheses helps to show the direction in which the theory should be further developed and refined. In this course, however, we are only concerned with economic theory and economic analysis—the right-hand side of the diagram in subsection I.2.a. Empirical testing is left to the specialized field called econometrics. It is worth noting, however, that econometricians have extensively examined, and generally validated, most of the fundamental theoretical principles presented here.

To reemphasize, this course is concerned first with developing well-established microeconomic theories and second with analyzing real world problems by means of these theories. To elucidate more, and perhaps give some warning to the student, we quote what Donald Dewey said of one of his own books but which applies equally well to this one: "This book employs the method of austere, sustained, and I regret, largely humorless abstraction that has served economics so well in the past. Given the excruciating complexity of so many of the problems . . . , I cannot see that any other method will allow us to cut through to first principles and deal with these problems according to their importance. Either we simplify drastically . . . , or we wander forever in the wilderness. . . ."[2]

Any society must accomplish four economic tasks: it must allocate resources, determine what is to be produced, distribute the product, and provide for growth. In the United States, as in many other countries, the price system is used extensively to accomplish these tasks; and we are primarily concerned in this course with how the price system works. At the same time, we cannot ignore the extent of governmental in-

---

[2] Donald J. Dewey, *Modern Capital Theory* (New York: Columbia University Press, 1965), p. vii.

volvement in the economy and we will have many occasions to consider how governmental regulations and other activities interact with the price system.

Part I of this book deals with consumer decision making and the underlying determinants of consumer demand. Part II deals with the theory of how entrepreneurs combine resources in the production of goods and services. Part III examines how the price system works to coordinate the decisions and behavior of consumers and entrepreneurs in the marketplace. Various forms of market organization are considered in this section. Part IV deals with the question of how prices of productive factors such as labor and capital are determined. This material is central to the problem of distribution in economic activity. Part V combines these various components to see how general equilibrium is achieved in the economy and then uses the results to consider how efficiently the economic system works and how well it achieves maximum social welfare.

SUGGESTED READINGS

Friedman, Milton. "The Methodology of Positive Economics," *Essays in Positive Economics,* pp. 1–43. Chicago: University of Chicago Press, 1953.

Machlup, Fritz. "The Problem of Verification in Economics," *Southern Economic Journal,* vol. 22 (1955), pp. 1–21.

Advanced reading

Buchanan, James M. *"Ceteris Paribus:* Some Notes on Methodology," *Southern Economic Journal,* vol. 24 (1958), pp. 259–70.

Harrod, R. F. "Scope and Method of Economics," *Economic Journal,* vol. 48 (1938), pp. 383–412.

Hurwicz, Leonid. "Mathematics in Economics: Language and Instrument," in *Mathematics and the Social Sciences* (ed. James C. Charlesworth), pp. 1–11. Philadelphia: The American Academy of Political and Social Science, 1963.

Knight, Frank H. "What Is Truth in Economics?" *Journal of Political Economy,* vol. 48 (1940), pp. 1–32.

Koopmans, T. C. "Measurement without Theory," *Review of Economics and Statistics,* vol. 29 (1947), pp. 161–72.

Krupp, Sherman Roy. "Equilibrium Theory in Economics and in Functional Analysis as Types of Explanation," in *Functionalism in the Social Sciences* (ed. Don Martindale), pp. 65–83. Philadelphia: The American Academy of Political and Social Science, 1965.

Morgenstern, Oskar. "Limits to the Uses of Mathematics in Economics," in *Mathematics and the Social Sciences* (ed. James C. Charlesworth), pp. 12–29. Philadelphia: The American Academy of Political and Social Science, 1963.

Theory of consumer behavior and demand

There are three sets of economic agents: consumers, entrepreneurs, and resource owners. Resource owners furnish the inputs used to produce whatever bill of goods is dictated by market forces. In return for the use of their resources, the resource owners receive money income. This money income, in turn, enables them to function as consumers.

Entrepreneurs organize production and, ultimately, determine the supply of goods and services in free markets. Those entrepreneurs who organize production efficiently and are successful in anticipating consumer desires are rewarded with money income in the form of profit. They are thereby also able to enter the market as consumers.

Some people earn money income by selling resources or the use of resources. Others earn income by using their special resource (entrepreneurial skill) to organize production. All people who earn money income belong to the set of economic agents called consumers. There are, of course, other members of this group. Family members who are dependent upon the income earner participate in the household budget decisions and are, therefore, consumers. People who are not able to earn money income receive money by some type of transfer payment and are also in the consumer category.

For our present purpose, the *source* of money income is not material. Only the fact that money is received by households and spent on consumer goods is of importance. Each household determines how to allocate its money income among the vast array of consumer goods available. In other words, each household decides upon its demand for every item (even though the quantity demanded at any price may be zero for many items). The aggregate of these demand decisions constitutes market demand, an expression of how society wants its resources allocated.

The fundamental purpose of Part I is to analyze the process by which market demand is formed—to find, in other words, the basic determinants of market demand.

1

Theory of utility and preference

1.1 INTRODUCTION

Each individual or household has a fairly accurate notion of what its money income will be for a reasonable planning period, say a year. It also has some notion—perhaps not too well defined—of the goods and services it wants to buy. The task confronting every household is to spend its limited money income so as to maximize its economic well-being. No individual or household, of course, actually succeeds in this task. To some extent this failure is attributable to the lack of accurate information; but there are other reasons as well, such as impulse buying. Yet in any event, the more or less conscious effort to attain maximum satisfaction from a limited money income determines individual demand for goods and services.

To analyze the formation of consumer demand more accurately, we use some simplifying assumptions that do not distort the crucial aspects of economic reality.

1.1.a The Nature of Commodities

The goods and services consumed by the household are generically called commodities. It is convenient to think of commodities as providing a flow of consumption services per unit of time. The objects of choice are then the services provided by the commodities rather than the commodities themselves. This allows us to handle durable goods

11

such as automobiles, television sets, and houses in a manner strictly analogous to nondurable goods and services such as food, haircuts, and theater tickets. What at first glance might appear to be problems arising from product indivisibilities are easily handled using this convention: it makes little sense to talk about an individual consuming half an automobile, but it is quite natural to think of using half (or any other fraction) of the services of an automobile per unit of time. Car pooling, rental, or any one of a number of other strategies can be used to adjust the service flow per unit of time.

There is nothing in the theory that severely limits the scope of what we call "commodities." Thus, the theory allows us to analyze choices involving where to live, the allocation of time between work and leisure, the amount of income given to charity, and many other dimensions of consumer behavior.

1.1.b Full Knowledge

We assume that each consumer or family unit has complete information on all matters pertaining to its consumption decisions. A consumer knows the full range of goods and services available in the market; he knows precisely the technical capacity of each good or service to satisfy a want. Furthermore, he knows the exact price of each good and service, and he knows these prices will not be changed by his actions in the market. Finally, the consumer knows precisely what his money income will be during the planning period.

In point of fact, the assumptions introduced above are unnecessarily restrictive so far as demand theory is concerned. In order to derive demand functions and indifference curves (see below), it is only necessary to assume that (*a*) the consumer is aware of the existence of some goods and services; (*b*) he has some reactions to them, that is, he prefers some goods to others; and (*c*) he has some money income so as to make these reactions significant in the market. Actually, the more rigid set of assumptions contained in the previous paragraph are necessary only when we come to the theory of welfare economics (at the end of the book). But since an assessment of economic welfare resulting from competitive markets is the central task of microeconomic theory, the more restrictive assumptions are introduced at this time.

1.1.c The Theory of Consumer Preference

A consuming unit—either an individual or a household—derives *satisfaction* or *utility* from the services provided by the commodities consumed during a given time period. In the given time period, the individual or household will consume a large variety of different commodities, and we will refer to this collection of different commodities as a *commodity bundle*. In order to attain its objective—maximization of satisfaction or utility for a given level of money income—the consuming unit must be able to rank different commodity bundles. That is, the consumer must be able to compare alternative commodity bundles and to determine his order of preference among them. To this end we assume that each consuming unit is able to make comparisons among alternative commodity bundles that satisfy the following conditions:

i. For any two commodity bundles *A* and *B* the consuming unit is able to determine which provides the most satisfaction. If *A* provides more satisfaction than *B*, then we say *A* is *preferred* to *B*, and if *B* provides more satisfaction than *A*, we say *B* is preferred to *A*. If both bundles provide the same satisfaction, we say the customer is *indifferent* between *A* and *B*.

ii. If *A* is preferred to *B* and *B* is preferred to *C*, then *A* is preferred to *C*. Preference is a *transitive* relation. Similarly, if *A* is indifferent to *B* and *B* is indifferent to *C*, then *A* is indifferent to *C*.

iii. If commodity bundle *A* is *strictly larger* than commodity bundle *B*, then *A* is preferred to *B*. One commodity bundle is said to be *strictly larger* than another if it contains more units of *every* commodity. If *A* contains as many units of every commodity as *B* and more units of at least one commodity, then *A* is said to be *larger* than *B* and *B* cannot be preferred to *A* (but in some instances the consumer may be indifferent between them).[1]

An example will help to illustrate these concepts.

Suppose there are only two goods, *X* and *Y*. The preferences of a given consumer are shown in Table 1.1.1 and illustrated in Figure 1.1.1. Commodity bundle *A* is clearly preferred to all other bundles (by (*iii*)) since it contains more of both commodities. Bundles *C* and *D* are, by assumption, indifferent to *B*. The consumer is willing to take less *Y* if

---

[1] This condition assumes that all commodities are "goods" and that satiation never obtains no matter how much the individual consumes. Condition (*iii*) is not really necessary for the theory of consumer behavior, and it is not always used. For example, we may wish to analyze consumption choices among bundles involving a "bad" and a "good" such as pollution and automobiles (see Question 5 at end of chapter), or we may wish to assume that too much of a "good" is a "bad" (see Question 6 at end of chapter). We have listed condition (*iii*) here because it holds in many situations of interest. To repeat, it is not really needed, and it in no way restricts the theory.

TABLE 1.1.1
Rank Ordering of Commodity Bundles

Bundle	Amount of X	Amount of Y	Rank Order*
A.................... 6	6	4
B.................... 3	5	3
C.................... 4	3	3
D.................... 5	2	3
E.................... 3	4	2
F.................... 1	4	1
G.................... 2	2	1
H.................... 3	1	1

* More preferred bundles are assigned a higher number.

he gets some more X in return. Bundle B, however, is preferred to E (the latter has less Y and the same quantity of X). Similarly, E is preferred to F (the latter has less X and the same quantity of Y). Finally, G and H are indifferent to F, the consumer being willing to substitute X for Y in his consumption pattern.

The assumptions necessary to analyze consumer behavior can be set out in the following compact form:

Assumptions: (a) Each consumer has exact and full knowledge of all information relevant to his consumption decisions—knowledge of the goods and services available and of their technical capacity to satisfy his wants, of market prices, and of his money income.

(b) Each consumer is able to make comparisons of commodity bundles such that (i) for any two bundles A is preferred to B, B is preferred to A, or the consumer is indifferent between A and B; (ii) if A is preferred (indifferent) to B and if B is preferred (indifferent) to C, then A is preferred (indifferent) to C; (iii) if bundle A is strictly larger than bundle B, then A is preferred to B.

1.2 UTILITY AND PREFERENCE

The analysis of consumer behavior is greatly facilitated by the use of a utility function which assigns a numerical value or utility level to commodity bundles. The reader may find it difficult to accept the idea that the highly subjective phenomenon of consumer preference, which obviously depends on each person's physiological and psychological makeup, can be so quantified. For most of our purposes, however, the particular numerical values assigned to commodity bundles are not of

FIGURE 1.1.1

Ordering of Bundles in Table 1.1.1

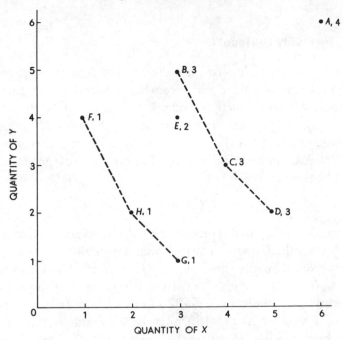

QUANTITY OF X

significance in their own right. All that is required of the utility function is that it reflect the same rankings that the consumer assigns to alternative commodity bundles. Thus, if the consumer prefers bundle A to bundle B the utility function has to assign a *larger* numerical value to bundle A than to bundle B, but the actual numerical values so assigned are themselves irrelevant. Similarly, if the consumer is indifferent between bundle A and bundle B the utility function must assign the *same* numerical value to each bundle, but the particular value so assigned is irrelevant. For example, the rank order assigned to commodity bundles A through H in Table 1.1.1. can be thought of as the numerical values assigned to these bundles by some utility function. Any other set of numbers, such as 20, 10, 10, 10, 8, 5, 5, 5, which preserved this ranking would do equally well for our purposes. A utility function that assigned the values 10, 9, 8, 7, 6, 5, 4, 3 to bundles A, B, C, D, E, F, G, H, respectively, would *not* apply, however, since such an assignment of numbers would indicate that bundle C is preferred to bundle B whereas the consumer is in fact indifferent between these bundles. In short, all we require of the utility function is that it provide an *ordinal* measurement of the utility provided by commodity bundles, not a *cardinal* measurement.[2]

1.2.a   The Utility Surface

Once it is recognized that only the ordinal properties of the utility function are important for our purposes, no harm is done by considering a specific utility function. Indeed, this is probably the most convenient way to gain an understanding of the ordinal properties in which we are interested. To illustrate with a concrete example suppose the utility that Smith obtains from consumption of goods X and Y is given by the function

$$U = XY.$$

In words, the utility is the product of the quantities of X and Y consumed by Smith. Using this utility function Smith derives 100 units of utility from a bundle consisting of 10 units of X and 10 units of Y $(100 = 10 \times 10)$. Smith also derives 100 units of utility from a bundle consisting of 5 units of X and 20 units of Y or from a bundle consisting of 1 unit of X and 100 units of Y. Smith is thus *indifferent* among these bundles. However, he prefers any of these bundles to a bundle consisting of 5 units of X and 5 units of Y since the latter has utility of only 25 according to the above function.

Since we are only concerned with the ordinal properties of the utility function (i.e., with the ranking assigned to the alternative bundles), there are many other utility functions that would represent Smith's preferences equally well. For example the utility function

$$V = (XY)^2$$

gives the same preference ranking of the above-mentioned bundles. The bundle consisting of 10 units of X and 10 units of Y has utility of 10,000 with this new utility function, but so do the bundles consisting of 5 X and 20 Y, and 1 X and 100 Y. Hence both U and V tell us that Smith is indifferent among these three bundles even though the

---

[2] The original approach to utility theory—atributable to Gossen (1854), Jevons (1871), and Walras (1874)—treated utility as *cardinally* measurable. The work of Pareto (1906), which had formal similarities to that of Edgeworth (1881), Antonelli (1886), and Irving Fisher (1892), among others, provided the foundation for the *ordinal* approach to utility theory.

FIGURE 1.2.1

Utility Surface

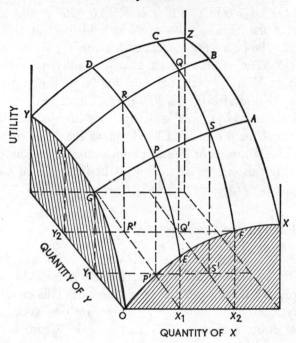

QUANTITY OF X

cardinal value of utility depends on the particular utility function (10,000 compared to 100).[3]

Utility functions can be represented geometrically by a utility surface such as the one shown in Figure 1.2.1. The utility surface is $OXZY$. Thus if OX_1 units of X and OY_1 units of Y are consumed per period of time, utility is the magnitude PP'. Similarly, if OX_2 and OY_2 are consumed per period of time, total utility is QQ'.

Suppose the rate of consumption of X is fixed at OX_1. The curve

---

[3] Once we have one utility function that correctly reflects the consumer's ordinal preferences we can construct an arbitrary number of alternative utility functions that reflect the same ordinal preferences. To see how, let $f(z)$ be any function such that $f(z_1) > f(z_0)$ whenever $z_1 > z_0$. Now consider any utility function U that correctly represents the consumer's ordinal preferences. Let $V = f(U)$. If bundle A is preferred to bundle B then $U(A) > U(B)$, but then $V(A) = f(U(A)) > f(U(B)) = V(B)$, so V also ranks A higher than B. Similarly if the consumer is indifferent between bundles C and D then $U(C) = U(D)$, but then $V(C) = f(U(C)) = f(U(D)) = V(D)$, so V also shows that the consumer is indifferent between C and D. Additional utility functions can easily be constructed by choosing different transformation functions like $f(z)$.

EPRD then shows the total utility associated with OX_1 units of X and variable amounts of Y. If consumption is OY_1, utility is PP'; if consumption is OY_2 ($>OY_1$), utility is RR' ($>PP'$), and so forth. In like manner, if the consumption of X is held fixed at OX_2 units per period of time, the curve *FSQC* relates total utility to the rate of consumption of Y. The same analysis can be applied to a fixed rate of consumption of Y and a variable rate for X. If the consumption of Y is fixed at OY_1, total utility is PP' if OX_1 units of X are consumed per period of time, SS' ($>PP'$) if the rate of consumption is OX_2 ($>OX_1$), etc. Thus the curve *GPSA* shows the level of total utility associated with OY_1 units of Y and various rates of consumption of X. Similarly, *HRQB* shows the same thing when the rate of consumption of Y is fixed at OY_2 units per period of time.

1.2.b The Indifference Curve

The utility surface helps us to focus on the important concept of a constant utility contour or *indifference curve* which is the basis of the modern (ordinal) theory of consumer behavior. This concept may be explained by means of Figure 1.2.2. There are two goods, X and Y, and the total utility surface is *OXZY*, just as in Figure 1.2.1. If OX_1 units of X and OY_3 units of Y are consumed per period of time, total utility is RR'. If the consumption of X is greater—at the rate OX_2, for instance—the consumption of Y remaining unchanged, the level of utility is greater. But an essential feature of utility theory is that one commodity may be *substituted* for another in consumption in such a way as to leave the level of total utility unchanged. For example, X_1X_2 units of X may be substituted for Y_3Y_2 units of Y without changing total utility. If the rates of consumption are OX_1 of X and OY_3 of Y, total utility is RR'. If the rates are OX_2 of X and OY_2 of Y, total utility is $PP' = RR'$. Similarly, OX_3 of X and OY_1 of Y yield total utility of $SS' = PP' = RR'$.

In other words, one may "slice" or intersect the utility surface at the level $RR' = PP' = SS'$ and determine all combinations of X and Y that will yield this constant level of utility. These combinations are shown by the dashed curve $R'P'S'$ in the X–Y plane. Since each combination of X and Y on $R'P'S'$ yields the same level of utility, a consumer would be indifferent to the particular combination he consumed. In like manner, all combinations of X and Y on the dashed curve $T'Q'V'$ yield the same total utility ($TT' = QQ' = VV'$). A consumer would thus be indifferent as to the particular combination consumed.

FIGURE 1.2.2

Utility Surface with Constant Utility Contours

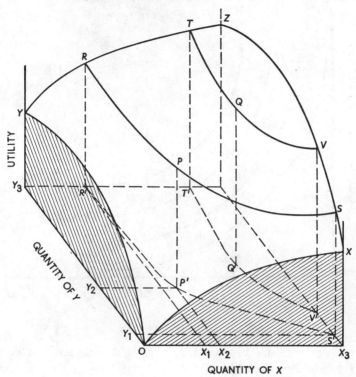

QUANTITY OF X

But a consumer would *not* be indifferent between a combination of X and Y lying on $R'P'S'$ and a combination lying on $T'Q'V'$. Each combination on $T'Q'V'$ is preferred to any combination on $R'P'S'$ because the former yields a higher level of total utility (for example, $TT' > RR'$).

Curves such as $R'P'S'$ and $T'Q'V'$ are called *indifference curves.*

Definition: An indifference curve is a locus of points—or particular combination of goods—each of which yields the same level of total utility, or to which the consumer is indifferent.

A partial set of indifference curves is shown in Figure 1.2.3. Graphs such as this are called *indifference maps.*[4]

---

[4] If the utility function is given by $U(X_1, X_2, \ldots, X_n)$ where X_1 is the amount of good 1 consumed, X_2 is the amount of good 2 consumed, and so forth, then an indifference curve is defined by the equation

$$U(X_1, X_2, \ldots, X_n) = c$$

where c is a constant representing the constant level of utility for that indifference curve. An indifference map is generated by choosing different values of c.

FIGURE 1.2.3

Indifference Curves

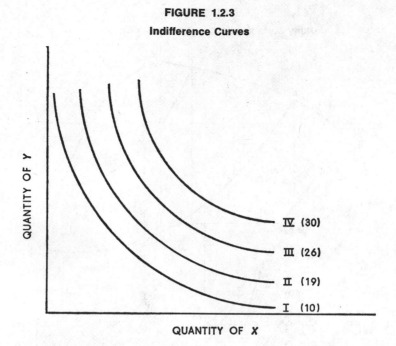

QUANTITY OF *X*

The curve labeled *I* in Figure 1.2.3 might represent all combinations of *X* and *Y* that yield 10 "utils" of utility to a certain person. Similarly *II, III,* and *IV* represent all combinations yielding 19, 26, and 30 utils respectively. The significance of the ordinal approach to utility is the recognition that the specific utility numbers attached to *I, II, III,* and *IV* are immaterial—the numbers could be 10, 19, 26, and 30, or 100, 190, 270, and 340, or any other set of numbers that *increase.* The salient point is that for the theory of consumer behavior, only the shape of the *indifference map* matters—the underlying *utility surface* is immaterial. The indifference map can be defined on a psychological-behavioristic basis without making use of the concept of measurable utility. The indifference curves and the concept of preference are all that are required—all bundles situated on the same indifference curve are equivalent; all bundles lying on a higher curve are preferred.

Relations: A consumer regards all bundles yielding the same level of utility as equivalent. The locus of such bundles is called an indifference curve because the consumer is indifferent as to the particular bundle he consumes. The higher, or further to the right, an indifference curve, the greater is the underlying level of utility (compare *R′P′S′* and *T′Q′V′* in

Figure 1.2.2). Therefore, the higher the indifference curve, the more preferred is each bundle situated on the curve.

1.2.c Summary

The cardinal measure of utility associated with each indifference curve is immaterial. The only requirement is that indifference curves rank bundles according to preference. Thus in Figure 1.2.3, all combinations on *IV* are most preferred; all bundles on *III* are preferred to those on *II* and *I* and are less desirable than those on *IV,* and so on. To repeat, cardinal measurement is not required. Ordinal measurement —ranking budgets first, second, third, and so forth—is sufficient.

1.3 CHARACTERISTICS OF INDIFFERENCE CURVES

Indifference curves have certain characteristics that reflect the three assumptions about consumer preferences discussed in subsection 1.1.c. For simplicity, assume that there are only two goods, *X* and *Y.* The *X–Y* plane is called the *commodity space.*

Now consider the three assumptions about consumer preferences. The first assumption is that the consumer can compare any two bundles and decide that he prefers one or is indifferent between them. This means that there is a point on the utility surface associated with each bundle in the commodity space or that *there is an indifference curve passing through each point in the commodity space.*[5] Assumption (*iii*) of subsection 1.1.c, that (strictly) larger commodity bundles are preferred to smaller bundles, implies that *indifference curves cannot be upward sloping.* Indifference curves are generally drawn downward sloping, but in some cases they may have horizontal or vertical segments.[6]

Third, *indifference curves cannot intersect.* This property is illustrated in Figure 1.3.1. In this graph *I* and *II* are indifference curves, and the points *P, Q,* and *R* represent three different bundles (or combinations of *X* and *Y*). *R* must clearly be preferred to *Q* because it contains

---

[5] Strictly speaking, in order to assure the existence of a continuous utility function that is suggested here, an additional assumption about the continuity of consumer preferences is needed. Readers interested in the conditions needed to establish the existence of a continuous utility function should consult Gerard Debreu, *The Theory of Value* (New York: John Wiley & Sons, Inc., 1959), chap. 4.

[6] When assumption (*iii*) is not made we can get cases when indifference curves are upward sloping in whole or in part (see Questions 5 and 6 at end of chapter).

FIGURE 1.3.1

Indifference Curves Cannot Intersect

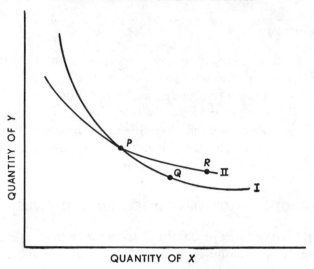

more of both goods (characteristic (*iii*) in subsection 1.1.c). *R* and *P* are equivalent because they are situated on the same indifference curve. In like manner, *P* and *Q* are indifferent. By characteristic (*ii*), subsection 1.1.c, indifference is a "transitive" relation—that is, if *A* is indifferent to *B* and *B* is indifferent to *C, A* must be indifferent to *C*. In our present case, *R* is indifferent to *P* and *P* is indifferent to *Q;* hence *R* must be indifferent to *Q*. But as previously shown, *R* is preferred to *Q* because it contains more of both goods. Hence intersecting indifference curves, such as those shown in Figure 1.3.1, are logically impossible given the assumptions about consumer preferences.

A fourth property of indifference curves, which is *not* implied by the assumptions about consumer preferences but is often used for expository convenience, is that indifference curves are convex. Convexity means that the indifference curve lies above its tangent at each point as illustrated in panel (b), Figure 1.3.2. The indifference curve in panel (a) of that figure is not convex (it is concave).

Properties: Indifference curves possess the following characteristics: (a) indifference curves are negatively sloped (or at least not positively sloped); (b) an indifference curve passes through each point in commodity space; (c) indifference curves cannot intersect. For expository convenience it is often assumed that indifference curves are convex.

FIGURE 1.3.2

Indifference Curves Are Convex

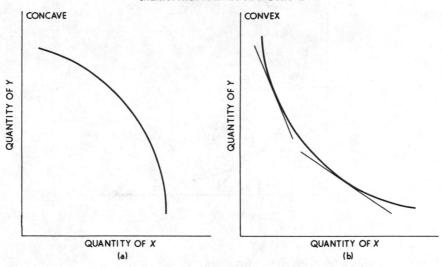

1.4 MARGINAL RATE OF SUBSTITUTION

As previously stressed, an essential feature of the subjective theory of value is that different combinations of commodities can yield the same level of utility.[7] In other words, the consumer is indifferent as to the particular combination he obtains. Therefore, as market prices might dictate, one commodity can be substituted for another in the right amount so the consumer remains just as well off as before. He will, in other words, remain on the same indifference curve. It is of considerable interest to know the *rate* at which a consumer is *willing* to substitute one commodity for another in his consumption pattern.

Consider Figure 1.4.1. An indifference curve is given by the curve labeled *I*. The consumer is indifferent between the bundle *R*, containing OX_1 units of *X* and OY_1 units of *Y*, and the bundle *P* containing $OX_2 > OX_1$ units of *X* and $OY_2 < OY_1$ units of *Y*. The consumer is willing to substitute X_1X_2 units of *X* for Y_1Y_2 units of *Y*. The rate at which he is willing to substitute *X* for *Y*, therefore, is

$$\frac{OY_1 - OY_2}{OX_2 - OX_1} = \frac{RS}{SP}.$$

---

[7] Some writers have questioned the existence of indifference loci on the grounds of the so-called psychological perception threshold. Notable among these is Professor Georgescu-Roegen. For references to some of his works, see the Advanced Readings at the end of this Part.

FIGURE 1.4.1

The Marginal Rate of Substitution

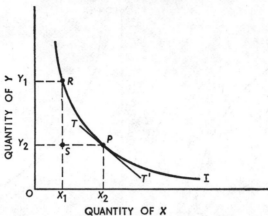

This ratio measures the average number of units of Y the consumer is willing to forego in order to obtain one additional unit of X (over the range of consumption pairs under consideration). Stated alternatively, the ratio measures the amount of Y that must be sacrificed per unit of X gained if the consumer is to remain at precisely the same level of satisfaction.

The rate of substitution is given by the ratio stated above. But as the point R moves along I toward P, the ratio RS/SP approaches closer and closer to the slope of the tangent TT' at point P. In the limit, for very small movements in the neighborhood of P, the slope of I or of its tangent at P is called the *marginal rate of substitution* of X for Y.

Definition: The marginal rate of substitution of X for Y measures the number of units of Y that must be sacrificed per unit of X gained so as to maintain a constant level of satisfaction. The marginal rate of substitution is given by the negative of the slope of an indifference curve at a point. It is defined only for movements along an indifference curve, never for movements among curves.[8]

---

[8] Let the utility function be $U(x, y)$. The change in utility arising from a small change in x (or y) is the *marginal utility* of x (or y). Hence the marginal utility of x is $\partial U/\partial x$ and the marginal utility of y is $\partial U/\partial y$. As in footnote 4, an indifference curve is given by $U(x, y) = c$ where c is a constant. Taking the total derivative, one obtains

$$\frac{\partial U}{\partial x}\, dx + \frac{\partial U}{\partial y}\, dy = 0 \,.$$

Solving for the slope of the indifference curve, dy/dx, we find that

FIGURE 1.4.2

The Diminishing Marginal Rate of Substitution

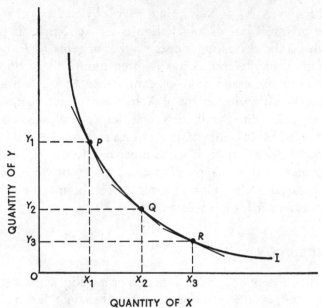

QUANTITY OF X

The convention that indifference curves are convex implies that the marginal rate of substitution of X for Y diminishes as X is substituted for Y along an indifference curve. This is illustrated in Figure 1.4.2.

I is an indifference curve; and P, Q, and R are three bundles situated on this curve. The horizontal axis is measured so that $OX_1 = X_1X_2 = X_2X_3$. Consider first the movement from P to Q. If P is very close to Q, or the amount X_1X_2 is very small, the marginal rate of substitution of X for Y at Q is

$$\frac{OY_1 - OY_2}{OX_2 - OX_1} = \frac{Y_1Y_2}{X_1X_2}.$$

Similarly, for a movement from Q to R, the marginal rate of substitution at R is

---

$$-\frac{dy}{dx} = MRS_{\text{ for } y} = \frac{\frac{\partial U}{\partial x}}{\frac{\partial U}{\partial y}}$$

The marginal rate of substitution of x for y is the ratio of the marginal utilities of x and y.

$$\frac{OY_2 - OY_3}{OX_3 - OX_2} = \frac{Y_2Y_3}{X_2X_3} \, .$$

By construction $X_1X_2 = X_2X_3$; but very obviously, $Y_1Y_2 > Y_2Y_3$. Hence the marginal rate of substitution is less at R than at Q. This is also shown by the decreasing slopes of the tangents at P, Q, and R.

Convexity of indifference curves is often intuitively justified on the grounds that as more and more of commodity X is taken away, the subjective value of an increment of X increases. Thus, as the quantity of X in the commodity bundle decreases, larger and larger increments of Y must be added to compensate the consumer for the loss of a given quantity of X. For example, if a consumer has 1,000 gallons of water a week he may be quite happy to trade an ounce of water for a crust of bread. If he has only a pint of water a week he may be reluctant to trade an ounce of it for a whole bakery.[9]

1.5 CONCLUSION

While the concept of a utility function or a utility surface sometimes aids one's intuition in explaining consumer behavior, we do not need such cardinal notions of utility to develop the fundamental theory. Instead of using the entire utility surface, only indifference curves are required. These curves are negatively sloped, pass through every point in commodity space, never intersect, and are convex. The last-mentioned property implies that the marginal rate of substitution of X for Y diminishes as X is substituted for Y so as to maintain the same level of satisfaction.

These concepts and relations are used in Chapter 2 to develop the modern theory of consumer behavior and to determine the shape of individual demand curves.

QUESTIONS AND EXERCISES

1. There are three commodities X, Y, and Z. The following table contains a list of commodity bundles composed of different combinations of these three goods. Determine the rank order of the bundles (in this problem, there are no bundles among which the consumer is indifferent) and list them on a separate sheet.

---

[9] The reader should be cautioned that decreasing marginal utility is neither a necessary nor sufficient condition for convexity of the indifference curves. However, if marginal utilities are decreasing and if an increment in X does not diminish the marginal utility of Y, then convexity of the indifference curves is assured.

| | *Amount of—* | | |
Bundle	X	Y	Z
A.....................	86	88	77
B.....................	86	87	76
C.....................	100	90	80
D.....................	79	80	69
E.....................	85	87	76
F.....................	79	79	68
G.....................	95	89	79
H.....................	80	80	70
I.....................	79	79	69
J.....................	86	87	77

2. In the following table, four commodity bundles each consisting of two commodities X and Y are listed. Also listed are six different "utility" functions U_1 to U_6. Which of these six utility functions, if any, are consistent with the assumptions about consumer preferences given in subsection I.1.c? When inconsistencies are found, indicate which assumption(s) is violated. (Hint: Plot the bundles on the X–Y commodity space.)

| | *Amount of—* | | *Utility Assigned by—* | | | | | |
Bundle	X	Y	U_1	U_2	U_3	U_4	U_5	U_6
A................	1	1	10	5	2	30	3	7
B................	2	3	30	10	2	60	6	7
C................	3	1	20	10	4	60	3	7
D................	1	4	30	10	4	30	3	7

3. What role do indifference curves play in economic theory and what economic principles do they illustrate? In what sense does this tool of analysis indicate the meaning of the basic economic problem of relating scarce resources to alternative goals?

4. Explain the following statement: The distance between two indifference curves is immaterial; the only relevant issue is which is higher and which is lower.

5. Assume that Jones thinks pollution is bad and automobiles are good. Draw a typical indifference curve in the pollution-automobile commodity space for Jones.

6. Suppose there are two commodities, each of which causes a reduction in total utility beyond a certain rate of consumption (i.e., marginal utility for each becomes negative beyond some point).[10] What would

---

[10] Marginal utility is defined in footnote 8.

be the shape of a typical indifference curve and how would the utility surface look?

7. What is the shape of a typical indifference curve for goods that must be consumed in fixed proportions (e.g., right- and left-hand gloves where two right gloves and one left presumably have no more utility than one right glove and one left glove)?

8. Consider a community of three individuals: Jones, Smith, and Brown. Three community projects are being considered, labeled *A, B,* and *C*. The table indicates the rank preference of each of the individuals.

Rank	Jones	Smith	Brown
1....................	A	C	B
2....................	B	A	C
3....................	C	B	A

Suppose community preferences are determined by a majority voting rule. Thus, in comparing project *A* and project *B* the community prefers *A* (Jones and Smith vote for *A*) to *B* (only Brown votes for *B*). Is this community preference rule consistent with the assumptions of subsection 1.1.c? [11]

SUGGESTED READINGS

Henderson, James M., and Quandt, Richard E. *Microeconomic Theory: A Mathematical Approach,* 2d ed. chap. 2, pp. 6–14. New York: McGraw-Hill Book Co., Inc., 1971. [Elementary math necessary.]

Hicks, John R. *Value and Capital,* pp. 1–25. 2d ed. Oxford: Oxford University Press, 1946.

Marshall, Alfred. *Principles of Economics,* Book III, chaps. 5–6, pp. 117–37. 8th ed. London: Macmillan & Co., Ltd., 1920.

Samuelson, Paul A. *Foundations of Economic Analysis,* chap. V, pp. 90–96. Cambridge, Mass.: Harvard University Press, 1947. [Advanced math necessary.]

Stigler, George J. "The Development of Utility Theory, I," *Journal of Political Economy,* vol. 58 (August, 1950), pp. 307–24.

---

[11] The problem of community or social choice has received substantial attention. It is interesting to note that majority ordering may be inconsistent even if individuals' preferences are consistent.

For a particularly important contribution, see Kenneth J. Arrow, *Social Choice and Individual Values* (New York: John Wiley & Sons, Inc., 1951).

2

Theory of consumer
behavior

2.1 INTRODUCTION

In this chapter, we will use the concepts of utility and indifference curves from Chapter 1 to explain the modern theory of consumer behavior. The fundamental work in the development of this theory was done by Slutsky (1915), Hicks and Allen (1934), Hotelling (1935), and Hicks (1939).

2.1.a Maximization of Satisfaction

The principal assumption upon which the theory of consumer behavior and demand is built is: a consumer attempts to allocate his limited money income among available goods and services so as to maximize his satisfaction. In short, a consumer arranges his purchases so as to maximize satisfaction subject to his limited money income. Given this assumption and the properties of indifference curves (developed in Chapter 1), individual demand curves can easily be determined. The usefulness of the theory lies in the fact that it can help us to understand how consumer demand responds to changes in prices and income.

2.1.b Limited Money Income

If each consumer had an unlimited money income—in other words, if there were an unlimited pool of resources—there would be no problems of "economizing," nor would there be "economics." But since this utopian state does not exist, even for the richest members of our society, people are compelled to determine their behavior in light of limited financial resources. For the theory of consumer behavior, this means that each consumer has a maximum amount he can spend per period of time. The consumer's problem is to spend this amount in the way that yields him maximum satisfaction.

Continue to assume that there are only two goods, X and Y, bought in quantities x and y. Each individual consumer is confronted with market-determined prices p_x and p_y of X and Y, respectively. Finally, the consumer in question has a known and fixed money income (M) for the period under consideration. Thus the maximum amount he can spend per period is M, and this amount can be spent only upon goods X and Y.[1] Thus the amount spent on X (xp_x) plus the amount spent on Y (yp_y) must not exceed the stipulated money income M. Algebraically,

$$M \geqq xp_x + yp_y .\qquad(2.1.1)$$

Expression (2.1.1) is an inequality that can be graphed in commodity space since it involves only the two variables X and Y. First consider the equality form of this expression:

$$M = xp_x + yp_y .\qquad(2.1.2)$$

This is the equation of a straight line. Solving for y—since y is plotted on the vertical axis—one obtains

$$y = \frac{1}{p_y} M - \frac{p_x}{p_y} x .\qquad(2.1.3)$$

---

[1] In more advanced cases, *saving* may be considered as one of the many goods and services available to the consumer. Graphical treatment limits us to two dimensions; thus we ignore saving. This does *not* mean that the theory of consumer behavior precludes saving—depending upon his preference ordering, a consumer may save much, little, or nothing. Similarly, spending may in fact exceed income in any given period as a result of borrowing or from assets acquired in the past. The "M" in question for any period is the total amount of money to be spent during the period. For a more sophisticated treatment of this problem, see Ralph W. Pfouts, "Hours of Work, Savings and the Utility Function," in Pfouts (ed.), *Essays in Economics and Econometrics in Honor of Harold Hotelling* (Chapel Hill: University of North Carolina Press, 1960), pp. 113–32.

FIGURE 2.1.1

The Budget Line

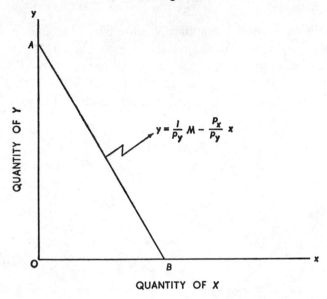

Equation (2.1.3) is plotted in Figure 2.1.1. The first term on the right-hand side of equation (2.1.3), $\frac{1}{p_y} M$, shows the amount of Y that can be purchased if X is not bought at all. This is represented by the distance OA in Figure 2.1.1; thus $\frac{1}{p_y} M$ is the *ordinate intercept* of the equation.

The second term on the right-hand side of equation (2.1.3), that is, $-\frac{p_x}{p_y}$, is the *slope* of the line. Consequently, the slope of the line is the negative of the price ratio. To see this, consider the quantity of X that can be purchased if Y is not bought. This amount is $\frac{1}{p_x} M$, shown by the distance OB in Figure 2.1.1. Since the line obviously has a negative slope, its slope is given by

$$-\frac{OA}{OB} = -\frac{\dfrac{1}{p_y} M}{\dfrac{1}{p_x} M} = -\frac{p_x}{p_y}.$$

The line in Figure 2.1.1 is called the *budget line*.

Definition: The budget line is the locus of commodity bundles that can be purchased if the entire money income is spent. Its slope is the negative of the price ratio.[2]

The budget line is the graphical counterpart of equation (2.1.3), but it is not the graph of the inequality in expression (2.1.1). The latter includes the budget line, but it also includes all commodity bundles whose total cost is not as great as M. Inequality (2.1.1) is shown graphically in Figure 2.1.2 by the triangular shaded area—it is the

FIGURE 2.1.2

Budget Space

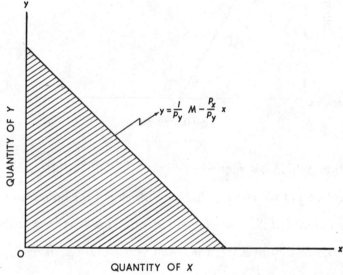

entire area enclosed by the budget line and the two axes. This area is called the *budget space*.[3]

Definition: The budget space is the set of all commodity bundles that may be purchased by spending some or all of a given money income. The budget space comprises only a part of (or is a subset of) commodity space.

---

[2] The prices p_x and p_y are the prices of X and Y in terms of money. They are commonly referred to as the *nominal* prices or the *money* prices of the goods. The price ratio p_x/p_y is the *relative* price of X in terms of Y—it tells how many units of Y must be given up to get one unit of X. Similarly, the ratio p_y/p_x is the relative price of Y.

[3] Mathematically, the budget space is defined by the following three inequalities:

$$M \geqq xp_x + yp_y ,$$
$$x \geqq 0 ,$$
$$y \geqq 0 .$$

2.1.c Shifting the Budget Line

In much of the analysis that follows, we are interested in *comparative static* changes in quantities purchased resulting from changes in price or money income. The latter changes are graphically represented by shifts in the budget line.

First consider an increase in money income from M to $M^* > M$, commodity prices remaining unchanged. The consumer can now purchase *more*—more of Y, more of X, or more of both. The maximum purchase of Y increases from $\dfrac{1}{p_y}M$ to $\dfrac{1}{p_y}M^*$, or from OA to OA' in Figure 2.1.3. Similarly, the maximum purchase of X increases from $\dfrac{1}{p_x}M$ to $\dfrac{1}{p_x}M^*$, or from OB to OB'. Since prices remain constant, the

FIGURE 2.1.3

Budget Lines When Money Income Increases, Prices Remaining Unchanged

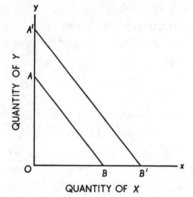

FIGURE 2.1.4

Budget Lines When Price of X Increases, Price of Y and Money Income Remaining Unchanged

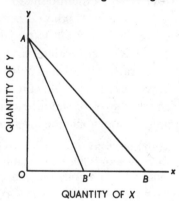

slope of the budget line does not change. Thus an increase in money income, prices remaining constant, is shown graphically by shifting the budget line upward and to the right. Since the slope does not change, the movement might be called a "parallel" shift. It readily follows that a decrease in money income is shown by a parallel shift of the budget line in the direction of the origin.

Figure 2.1.4 shows what happens to the budget line when the price of X increases, the money price of Y and money income remaining constant. Let the price of X increase from p_x to p_x^*. Since p_y and M are unchanged, the ordinate intercept does not change—it is OA in each case. But the slope of the line, the negative of the price ratio, changes from $-\dfrac{p_x}{p_y}$ to $-\dfrac{p_x{}^*}{p_y}$. Since $p_x{}^* > p_x$, $-\dfrac{p_x{}^*}{p_y} < -\dfrac{p_x}{p_y}$. In other words, the slope of the budget line becomes *steeper*.

Alternatively, the price change can be explained as follows. At the original price p_x, the maximum purchase of X is $\dfrac{1}{p_x} M$, or the distance OB. When the price changes to $p_x{}^*$, the maximum purchase of X is $\dfrac{1}{p_x{}^*} M$, or the distance OB'. Thus an increase in the price of X is shown by rotating the budget line *clockwise* around the ordinate intercept. A decrease in the price of X is represented by a *counterclockwise* movement.

Before summarizing these relations, it may be helpful to state the obvious and emphasize that *relative* prices are crucial. If money income remains constant and the nominal prices of both commodities change proportionately, there is no change in relative price; the change in this case is tantamount to an increase in income (if prices decline) or a decrease in income (if prices rise). Similarly, let money income and the nominal price of Y remain constant. An increase in the nominal price of X is equivalent to a decrease in the relative price of Y, and vice versa. As we shall subsequently see, given money income, only relative prices are relevant to a consumer's decision-making process. Hence the student should pay particular heed to the connections among nominal money income, nominal prices, and relative prices.

Relations: (*i*) An increase in money income, prices unchanged, is shown by a parallel shift of the budget line—outward and to the right for an increase in money income, and in the direction of the origin for a decrease in money income. (*ii*) A change in the price of X, the price of Y and money income constant, is shown by rotating the budget line around the ordinate intercept—to the left for a price increase, and to the right for a decrease in price.

2.2 CONSUMER EQUILIBRIUM

All bundles of goods in commodity space are available to the consumer in the sense that he *may* purchase them if he *can*. The consumer's indifference map establishes a rank ordering of all these bundles. The consumer's budget space is established by his fixed money income and relative commodity prices; it shows the bundles he *can* purchase. Our fundamental assumption that each consumer attempts to maximize satisfaction from a given money income simply means the following: that the consumer must select the most preferred bundle of goods in his budget space.

2.2.a The Relevant Part of Commodity Space

Graphically, the consumer's problem is depicted in Figure 2.2.1. The entire x–y plane is commodity space; his indifference map, represented by the five indifference curves drawn in that figure, indicates his preferences among all commodity bundles in this space. Similarly, the consumer's budget space—the line LM and the shaded area enclosed by LM and the two axes—shows the feasible bundles that the consumer can buy. Clearly, the consumer cannot purchase any bundles lying

FIGURE 2.2.1

Budget Space and the Indifference Map

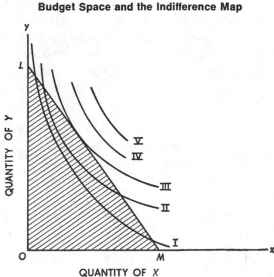

above and to the right of the budget line LM. He would prefer such a bundle if it were attainable; but his income is not sufficient to pay for it.

Thus his choice is limited to those bundles lying in the budget space. But again, we can eliminate most of these. In particular, no point in the interior of the budget space—below the budget line LM—can yield maximum satisfaction because a higher indifference curve can be reached by moving out to the budget line. Hence the only portion of commodity space relevant to the consumer's decision is the budget line.

2.2.b Maximizing Satisfaction Subject
to a Limited Money Income

The way in which a consumer maximizes satisfaction subject to a limited money income is illustrated in Figure 2.2.2. The budget line is *LM*, and the curves labeled *I, II, III,* and *IV* are a portion of an individual's indifference map. As already observed, the consumer cannot attain a position on any indifference curve, such as *IV,* that lies entirely beyond the budget line.

Three of the infinite number of attainable bundles on *LM* are represented by the points *Q, P,* and *R.* Each of these, and every other point on the budget line *LM,* is attainable with the consumer's limited money income.

Suppose the consumer were located at *Q.* Without experimenting, he cannot know for certain whether *Q* represents a maximum position for him. Thus let him experimentally move to a bundle just to the left and right of *Q.* Moving to the left from *Q* lowers his level of satisfaction to some indifference curve below *I.* But moving to the right brings him to a higher indifference curve; and continued experimentation will lead him to move at least as far as *P,* because each successive movement to the right brings the consumer to a higher indifference curve.

FIGURE 2.2.2

Consumer Equilibrium

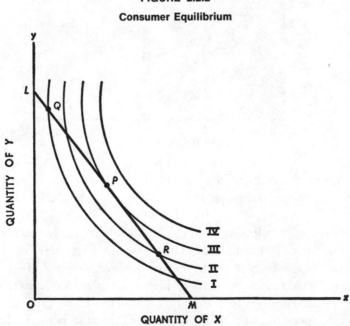

If he continued to experiment, however, by moving to the right of *P*, the consumer would find himself upon a lower indifference curve with its lower level of satisfaction. He would accordingly return to the point *P*.

Similarly, if a consumer were situated at a point such as *R*, experimentation would lead him to substitute *Y* for *X*, thereby moving in the direction of *P*. He would not stop short of *P* because each successive substitution of *Y* for *X* brings the consumer to a higher indifference curve. Hence the position of maximum satisfaction—or the point of consumer equilibrium—is attained at *P*, where an indifference curve is just tangent to the budget line.

As you will recall, the slope of the budget line is (the negative of) the price ratio, the ratio of the price of *X* to the price of *Y*. As you will also recall, the (negative of) slope of an indifference curve at any point is called the marginal rate of substitution of *X* for *Y*. Hence the point of consumer equilibrium satisfies the condition that the marginal rate of substitution equals the price ratio.

The interpretation of this proposition is very straightforward. The marginal rate of substitution shows the rate at which the consumer *is willing to substitute* *X* for *Y*. The price ratio shows the rate at which he *can substitute* *X* for *Y*. Unless these two are equal, it is possible to change the combination of *X* and *Y* purchased so as to attain a higher level of satisfaction. For example, suppose the marginal rate of substitution is two—meaning the consumer is willing to give up two units of *Y* in order to obtain one unit of *X*. Let the price ratio be unity, meaning one unit of *Y* can be exchanged for one unit of *X*. Clearly, the consumer will benefit by trading *Y* for *X*, since he is willing to give two *Y*'s for one *X* but only has to give one *Y* for one *X* in the market. Generalizing, unless the marginal rate of substitution and the price ratio are equal, some exchange can be made so as to push the consumer to a higher level of satisfaction.

Principle: The point of consumer equilibrium—or the maximization of satisfaction subject to a limited money income—satisfies the condition that the marginal rate of substitution of *X* for *Y* equals the ratio of the price of *X* to the price of *Y*.

This principle can be explained in more mathematical terms.[4] Let MU_x be the marginal utility of *X* and let MU_y be the marginal utility of *Y* (i.e., $MU_x = \partial U/\partial x$ and $MU_y = \partial U/\partial y$). If *X* and *Y* are changed

---

[4] Readers who are not mathematically inclined can skip to section 2.3 without loss of continuity.

by small amounts dx and dy, the resulting change in utility is the total derivative of the utility function or

$$dU = MU_x\, dx + MU_y\, dy. \tag{2.2.1}$$

The change in the budget caused by the changes dx and dy is

$$dM = p_x\, dx + p_y\, dy. \tag{2.2.2}$$

If the budget constraint is not to be violated, dx and dy must be chosen so that $dM = 0$ in (2.2.2). Thus, setting $dM = 0$ in (2.2.2) and solving for dy[5]

$$dy = -\frac{p_x}{p_y}\, dx. \tag{2.2.3}$$

Substituting (2.2.3) into (2.2.1) we obtain

$$dU = \left(MU_x - \frac{p_x}{p_y}\, MU_y \right) dx. \tag{2.2.4}$$

Now if $MU_x - \dfrac{p_x}{p_y} MU_y$ is positive, it follows from (2.2.4) that an increase in the quantity of X consumed (with the implicit reduction in the quantity of Y consumed necessitated by the requirement that total expenditures do not exceed M) will increase utility. That is, when $MU_x - \dfrac{p_x}{p_y} MU_y$ is positive then, from (2.2.4), $dx > 0$ implies $dU > 0$. Similarly, if $MU_x - \dfrac{p_x}{p_y} MU_y$ is less than zero a decrease in the consumption of X (and an increase in the consumption of Y) will increase utility. When utility is at its maximum subject to the budget constraint neither of these outcomes can hold and this means that $MU_x - \dfrac{p_x}{p_y} MU_y$ is zero. In other words, a necessary condition for maximum utility subject to the budget constraint is that X and Y be chosen such that

$$MU_x - \frac{p_x}{p_y} MU_y = 0$$

or

$$\frac{MU_x}{MU_y} = \frac{p_x}{p_y}. \tag{2.2.5}$$

---

[5] For purposes of the present argument, we could have equally well solved for dx.

We saw in footnote 8 of Chapter 1 that MU_x/MU_y is the marginal rate of substitution of X for Y so (2.2.5) says the point of consumer equilibrium requires

$$MRS_{x \text{ for } y} = \frac{p_x}{p_y} .$$

If there are several goods the same reasoning applies to get the consumer equilibrium conditions

$$\frac{MU_x}{p_x} = \frac{MU_y}{p_y} = \cdots = \frac{MU_z}{p_z} . \qquad (2.2.6)$$

2.3 CHANGES IN MONEY INCOME

Changes in money income, prices remaining constant, usually result in corresponding changes in the quantities of commodities bought. In particular, for so-called "normal" or "superior" goods an increase in money income leads to an increase in consumption and a decrease in money income to a decrease in consumption. It is of considerable interest to analyze the effects upon consumption of changes in income. To do so, we will hold nominal prices constant so as to observe the effects of income changes alone.[6]

2.3.a The Income-Consumption Curve

As explained in subsection 2.1.c, an increase in money income shifts the budget line upward and to the right, and the movement is a parallel shift because nominal prices are assumed to be constant. In Figure 2.3.1, the price ratio is given by the slope of LM, the original budget line, and remains constant throughout.

With money income represented by LM, the consumer comes to equilibrium at point P on indifference curve I, consuming Ox_1 units of X. Now let money income rise to the level represented by $L'M'$. The consumer shifts to a new equilibrium at point Q on indifference curve II. He has clearly gained. He also gains when money income shifts to the level corresponding to $L''M''$. The new equilibrium is at point R on indifference curve III.

As income shifts, the point of consumer equilibrium shifts as well. The line connecting the successive equilibria is called the income-consumption curve. This curve shows the *equilibrium combinations* of

---

[6] We assume throughout the discussion that the good is a "normal" or "superior" good. "Inferior" goods are treated in Chapter 3.

FIGURE 2.3.1

The Income-Consumption Curve

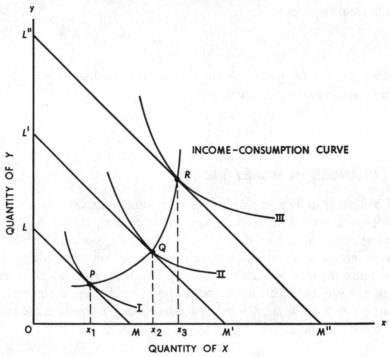

X and Y purchased at various levels of money income, nominal prices remaining constant throughout.

Definition: The income-consumption curve is the locus of equilibrium budgets resulting from various levels of money income and constant money prices. The income-consumption curve is positively sloped throughout its entire range when both goods are "normal" or "superior."

2.3.b Engel Curves

The income-consumption curve may be used to derive Engel curves for each commodity.

Definition: An Engel curve is a function relating the equilibrium quantity purchased of a commodity to the level of money income. The name is taken from Christian Lorenz Ernst Engel, a 19th-century German statistician.

Engel curves are important for applied studies of economic welfare and for the analysis of family expenditure patterns.

Engel curves relating the consumption of commodity X to income are constructed in Figure 2.3.2. Neither panel (a) nor panel (b) is directly based upon the particular income-consumption curve in Figure 2.3.1; but the process of deriving an Engel curve from an income-consumption curve should be clear.

At the original equilibrium point P in Figure 2.3.1, money income is $p_x \cdot OM$ (or $p_y \cdot OL$). At the income $p_x \cdot OM$, Ox_1 units of X are purchased. This income-consumption point can be plotted on a graph such as panel (a), Figure 2.3.2. When the budget line shifts from LM to $L'M'$ (Figure 2.3.1), money income increases to $p_x \cdot OM'$ and consumption to Ox_2 units. This income-consumption pair constitutes another point on the Engel curve graph. Repeating this process for all levels of money income generates a series of points on a graph such as panel (a), Figure 2.3.2. The Engel curve is formed by connecting these points by a line.

FIGURE 2.3.2

Engel Curves

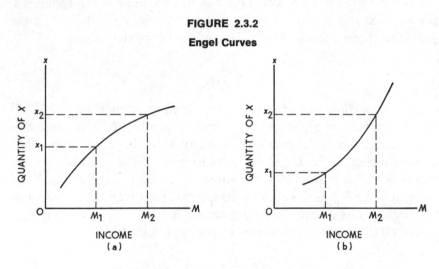

INCOME
(a)

INCOME
(b)

Two basically different types of Engel curves are shown in panels (a) and (b), Figure 2.3.2. In panel (a), the Engel curve slopes upward rather gently, implying that changes in money income do not have a substantial effect upon consumption. An Engel curve with this property indicates that the good is bought when income is low, but the quantity purchased does not expand rapidly as income increases. If "food" is treated as a single commodity, its Engel curve would look something like the curve in panel (a), even though the curve for "steak" as a separate commodity probably would not.

On the other hand, steak and many other types of goods give rise to

Engel curves more nearly represented by the curve in panel (b). The relatively steep upward slope indicates that the quantity bought changes markedly with income.[7]

2.3.c Engel Curves and the Income Elasticity of Demand

The income elasticity of demand, which is discussed much more throughly in Chapter 4, has the following

Definition: The income elasticity of demand is the proportional change in the consumption of a commodity divided by the proportional change in income.

Income elasticity may be related to the slope or curvature of an Engel curve and, in part, to the classification of commodities as superior, normal, or inferior.

Consider Figure 2.3.3. Our object is to determine the income elasticity of demand at any point on an Engel curve. As indicated in the definition above, income elasticity (η_m) is given by the formula

$$\eta_m = \frac{dx}{dM}\frac{M}{x}.\qquad(2.3.1)$$

Suppose a consumer of good X is situated at point B on the Engel curve. The tangent at B is given by the straight line EF. By the definition and formula (2.3.1), income elasticity is the reciprocal of the slope of the tangent to the Engel curve multiplied by the reciprocal of the proportion of income spent on commodity X. The slope of the Engel curve at point B is HB/EH, so its reciprocal is EH/HB. The amount of X bought is OH and the income spent on X is HB. Thus its reciprocal is HB/OH. Therefore, the income elasticity at point B is

$$\eta_m = \frac{EH}{HB}\cdot\frac{HB}{OH} = \frac{EH}{OH} < 1.\qquad(2.3.2)$$

It should thus be clear that if the tangent line to the Engel curve intersects the horizontal axis to the *right* of the origin, the income elasticity of demand is less than unity. Similarly, if the tangent line intersects the horizontal axis to the *left* of the origin, the income elasticity of demand is greater than unity. Finally, consider point J. If the

---

[7] If he likes, the reader may associate "necessities" and "luxuries" with commodities whose Engel curves look like those in panels (a) and (b) respectively. One should be warned, however, that such associations are very rough and highly sensitive to the particular definitions of the commodities in question.

FIGURE 2.3.3

Engel Curves and Income Elasticity of Demand

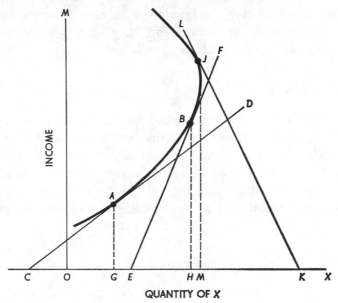

QUANTITY OF **X**

tangent to J intersects the horizontal axis to the right of M, the income elasticity is negative.

Definition: A good with a negative income elasticity is said to be inferior, a good with an income elasticity between zero and one is said to be normal, and a good with an income elasticity greater than one is said to be superior. Notice that the words "inferior," "normal," and "superior" are used here only to describe the income elasticity of a good, no more and no less. It is possible that a given good will be an inferior good for one consumer and a superior good for some other consumer.

If the income elasticity of a commodity is greater than one, then a consumer will increase the *fraction* of his income on that good when money income increases (prices remaining unchanged). Suppose at income M the individual consumes x and suppose that his consumption changes by dx when M increases by dM. Before the income change the fraction of income spent on x is $p_x x/M$ and after income changes this fraction is $p_x(x + dx)/(M + dM)$. The ratio of these fractions is

$$\frac{\frac{p_x(x + dx)}{M + dM}}{\frac{p_x x}{M}} = \left(\frac{x + dx}{x}\right)\left(\frac{M}{M + dM}\right) = \frac{1 + \frac{dx}{x}}{1 + \frac{dM}{M}} = \frac{\frac{M}{dM} + \frac{dx}{dM}\frac{M}{x}}{\frac{M}{dM} + 1}$$

and this last expression is greater than 1 if $\eta_m = \dfrac{dx}{dM}\dfrac{M}{x}$ is greater than 1. By the same reasoning the fraction of income spent on a good remains constant as income rises if income elasticity is unity, and the fraction decreases if income elasticity is less than unity.

2.4 CHANGES IN PRICE

The reaction of quantity purchased to changes in price is perhaps even more important than the reaction to changes in money income. In this section we will assume that money income and the nominal price of Y remain constant while the nominal price of X falls. We are thus able to analyze the effect of price upon quantity purchased without simultaneously considering the effect of changes in money income.

2.4.a The Price-Consumption Curve

In Figure 2.4.1 the price of X falls from the amount indicated by the slope of the original budget line LM to the amount indicated by the slope of LM' and then to the amount represented by the slope of LM''.

With the original budget line LM, the consumer reaches equilibrium at point P on indifference curve I. When the price of X falls, the budget line becomes LM' and the new equilibrium is attained at Q on indif-

FIGURE 2.4.1

The Price-Consumption Curve

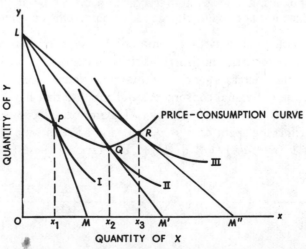

ference curve *II*. Finally, when the price falls again, the new equilibrium is point *R* on indifference curve *III* and budget line *LM''*. The line connecting these successive equilibrium points is called the price-consumption curve.

Definition: The price-consumption curve is the locus of equilibrium budgets resulting from variations in the price ratio, money income remaining constant. Nothing can be said a priori about the slope of the price-consumption curve.

2.4.b The Demand Curve

The individual consumer's demand curve for a commodity can be derived from the price-consumption curve, just as an Engel curve is derivable from an income-consumption curve.

Definition: The demand curve for a specific commodity relates equilibrium quantities bought to the market price of the commodity, nominal money income and the nominal prices of other commodities held constant.

When the price of *X* is given by the slope of *LM* in Figure 2.4.1, Ox_1 units of *X* are purchased. This price-consumption pair constitutes one point on the graph in Figure 2.4.2. Similarly, when the price of *X* falls to the level indicated by the slope of *LM'*, quantity purchased increases to Ox_2. This price-consumption pair is another point that can be plotted on Figure 2.4.2. Plotting all points so obtained and connect-

FIGURE 2.4.2

The Demand Curve

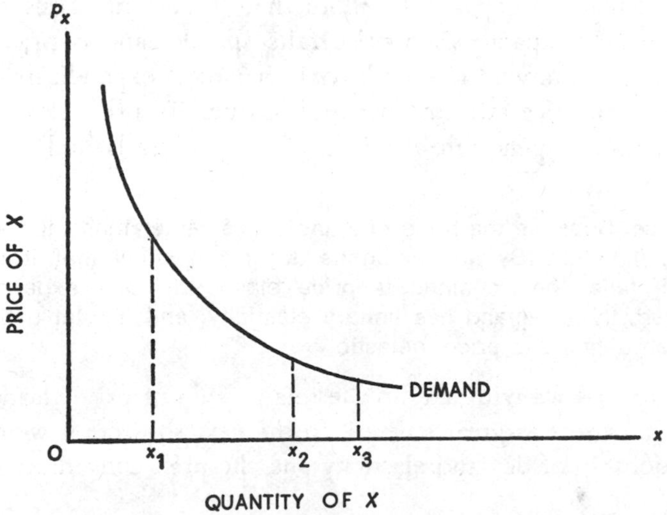

QUANTITY OF *X*

ing them with a line generates the consumer demand curve, as shown in Figure 2.4.2. Its shape indicates an important principle, called the Law of Demand.

Principle: Quantity demanded varies inversely with price, nominal money income and nominal prices of other commodities remaining constant.

(In the next chapter a minor exception to this principle is discussed.)

2.4.c The Elasticity of Demand

The elasticity of demand is an important concept. It is defined as follows:

Definition: Price elasticity of demand or elasticity of demand is the proportional change in the consumption of a good divided by the proportional change in the price of the good. It may also be determined from the changes in price and in the money income spent upon a good.

At this point it may be helpful briefly to review the relation between price elasticity of demand and changes in the total expenditure upon the good in question. First, suppose the nominal price of good X declines by 1 percent. The demand for X is said to be price elastic, of unitary price elasticity, or price inelastic according as the quantity of X demanded expands by more than 1 percent, by exactly 1 percent, or by less than 1 percent.

Next, recall that the total expenditure upon a good is the product of price per unit and the number of units purchased. Given an initial price and quantity bought, a unique initial total expenditure is determined. Now let price fall by 1 percent. If demand is price elastic, quantity demanded expands by more than 1 percent. Thus total expenditure must expand when price falls and demand is price elastic. By the same argument, one finds (*a*) that total expenditure remains constant when price falls and demand has unitary price elasticity, and (*b*) that total expenditure declines when price falls and demand is price inelastic.

Exercise: Suppose the price of X increases rather than falls as in the above explanation. By an analogous argument, show that if total expenditure falls, then demand is price elastic; if total expenditure is unchanged, then demand has unitary elasticity; and if total expenditure rises, then demand is price inelastic.

In Chapter 4 we will take up the relationship of price elasticity and the demand curve in greater detail. In the next subsection we examine the relationship of demand elasticity and the price-consumption curve.

2.4.d Elasticity of Demand and the Price-Consumption Curve

The elasticity of demand can be determined immediately from the slope of the price-consumption curve. Consider panel (a), Figure 2.4.3. Let Y represent "all other goods," or what is frequently called "Hicks-Marshall" money. This is plotted on the vertical axis and labeled "money," whose price is unity. Thus money income is fixed at OM, and its price is fixed at one. The original budget line is MN, and its slope is the price of $X(p_x/1 = p_x)$.[8]

FIGURE 2.4.3

Price-Consumption Curves and the Elasticity of Demand

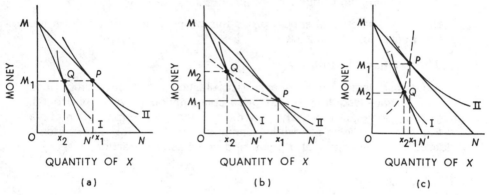

QUANTITY OF *X*   QUANTITY OF *X*   QUANTITY OF *X*

(a)   (b)   (c)

The original equilibrium is at point P on the indifference curve II. At this point $Ox_1 = M_1P$ units of X and OM_1 units of "money" are bought. The slope of MN is (the negative of) MM_1/M_1P, so the price of X is MM_1/M_1P. The total amount spent on X is accordingly $M_1P\,(MM_1/M_1P) = MM_1$. When the price of X increases to the level given by the slope of MN', the quantity of X purchased drops to Ox_2, the amount of "money" bought remains constant at OM_1, and the amount spent on X remains unchanged. Price increases to MM_1/M_1Q, quantity purchased declines to M_1Q, and total expenditure on X is $M_1Q\,(MM_1/M_1Q) = MM_1$. The proportionate increase in the price of X is exactly offset by the proportionate decrease in the quantity of X bought. Consequently, demand has unitary elasticity over this range.

---

[8] In microeconomic theory, a *price level* is not determined. That chore is left to macroeconomic theory. Thus we can take the "price" of Hicks-Marshall money to be whatever we wish it to be. Setting its price at unity is both logical and helpful. The determinants of the price level are determined and explained in courses in macroeconomic theory and monetary theory. Here we concentrate exclusively upon relative prices.

And notice: the price-consumption curve is QP. Thus when the price-consumption curve is horizontal, price elasticity of demand for X is unitary.

In panel (b), an increase in the price of X (from that given by the slope of MN to that given by the slope of MN') is accompanied by a decrease in expenditure on X from MM_1 to MM_2. The proportionate increase in the price of X is more than offset by the proportionate reduction in quantity demanded. Demand is therefore elastic. The price-consumption curve is $QP;$ hence when the price-consumption curve is negatively sloped, demand is elastic.

By the same reasoning, panel (c) illustrates the price-consumption curve when demand is inelastic.

Exercise: The student should prove this proposition for himself on the basis of panel (c), Figure 2.4.3.

Thus we have the following

Relations: Demand has unitary price elasticity, is price elastic, or is price inelastic according as the price-consumption curve is horizontal, negatively sloped, or positively sloped. Thus the price-consumption curve in Figure 2.4.1 reflects commodity demand that is first (at higher prices) elastic, becomes unitary at a point, and is inelastic thereafter.

2.5 CONCLUSION

The basic principles of consumer behavior and of individual demand have now been developed. In the following chapter various important, but subsidiary, topics are analyzed using the tools introduced in Chapters 1 and 2. The fundamental conclusion of this chapter is explained more fully and one special exception is noted, but this conclusion remains as fundamental as ever: if individual consumers behave so as to maximize satisfaction from a limited money income, individual quantities demanded will vary inversely with price.

QUESTIONS AND EXERCISES

1. One of the basic assumptions underlying the theory of consumer behavior states that increases in utility tend to diminish as the consumption of a good increases. (*a*) If you think this is true, show what role the assumption plays in the development of the theory and in its conclusions. (*b*) If you think it is false, demonstrate that the main results of the theory of consumer behavior can be obtained anyway.
2. Both the marginal utility approach and the indifference curve approach yield the same equilibrium position for a rational consumer. Compare

these explanations of equilibrium and discuss the relative advantage of the two approaches.

3. Comment on the following pair of statements: (*a*) consumer preferences are measured by relative prices; (*b*) consumer preferences are independent of relative prices.

4. A certain college student who is cramming for final exams has only six hours study time remaining. His goal is to get as high an *average* grade as possible in three subjects: economics, mathematics, and statistics. He must decide how to allocate his time among the subjects. According to the best estimates he can make, his grade in each subject will depend upon the time allocated to it according to the following schedule:

Economics		Mathematics		Statistics	
Hours of Study	*Grade*	*Hours of Study*	*Grade*	*Hours of Study*	*Grade*
0	20	0	40	0	80
1	45	1	52	1	90
2	65	2	62	2	95
3	75	3	71	3	97
4	83	4	78	4	98
5	90	5	83	5	99
6	92	6	86	6	99

How should the student allocate his time? How did you get the answer?

5. Consider a consumer in a two-commodity world whose indifference map is such that the slope of the indifference curves is everywhere equal to $-(y/x)$, where y is the quantity of good Y (measured along the vertical axis) and x is the quantity of good X (measured along the horizontal axis).

   a. Show that the demand for X is independent of the price of Y and that the price elasticity of demand for X is unitary. (Hint: Setting the marginal rate of substitution equal to the price ratio gives $(p_x/p_y) = (y/x)$, or $xp_x = yp_y$. Since $xp_x + yp_y = M$, where M is the given constant money income, one has $xp_x = (\frac{1}{2})M$. Thus the demand function is $x = (1/2p_x)M$. Go on from here.)

   b. Explain precisely the meaning of the term "marginal rate of substitution." What is the value of the equilibrium *MRS* for this consumer, given that the price of X is \$1, the price of Y is \$3, and the consumer's income is \$120?

   c. What does the Engel curve look like for X? What is the income elasticity of demand for X?

6. Suppose that a seller offers the following price policy for commodity
    X: The price of X is $2 a unit for the first 200 units and $1/2 a unit
    for all units purchased in excess of 200. Suppose commodity Y sells at
    a constant $1 a unit.
    a. Sketch the budget line when the consumer's income is $500.
    b. Is it possible to have more than one point of consumer equilibrium
          in this situation?

7. Suppose a consumer in a two-good world has linear indifference curves
    with a slope that is everywhere equal to $-$ 1/2; that is, the marginal rate
    of substitution is 1/2. What is the equilibrium consumption when $p_x =$
    1 and $p_y = 1$ and income is $1,000? What is the equilibrium con-
    sumption when $p_x = 1$ and $p_y = 2$?

8. In the modern theory of finance, portfolios of securities are constructed
    with various combinations of riskiness and rates of return.[9] Given a set
    of securities, it can be shown that the set of available combinations of
    riskiness and rate of return looks like the shaded area in the following
    figure:

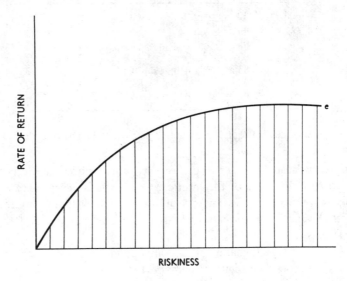

    The efficient frontier, *e,* shows the maximum rate of return that can
    be achieved at each level of riskiness. Portfolios on or below *e* are
    feasible, but not those above *e.*
    a. Assuming that investors like larger rates of return but do not prefer
          greater risk, what is the shape of a typical indifference curve in the
          rate of return-riskiness space?

---

b. Illustrate investor equilibrium graphically using indifference curves of the kind obtained in part (*a*) of this question and treating the efficient frontier as a "budget" line.

SUGGESTED READINGS

Henderson, James M., and Quandt, Richard E. *Microeconomic Theory: A Mathematical Approach* 2d ed. pp. 14–31. New York: McGraw-Hill Book Co., Inc., 1971. [Elementary math necessary.]

Hicks, John R. *Value and Capital,* pp. 26–30. 2d ed. Oxford: Oxford University Press, 1946.

Samuelson, Paul A. *Foundations of Economic Analysis,* pp. 96–100. Cambridge, Mass.: Harvard University Press, 1947. [Advanced math necessary.]

3

Topics in consumer demand

3.1 INTRODUCTION

The theory of consumer behavior was developed in Chapter 2, and it was shown that an individual consumer demand curve normally slopes downward to the right—that quantity demanded varies inversely with price. This chapter presents a closer analysis of consumer demand and of market demand for related commodities.

3.2 SUBSTITUTION AND INCOME EFFECTS

A change in the nominal price of a commodity actually exerts two influences on quantity demanded. In the first place, there is a change in *relative* price—a change in the terms at which a consumer *can* exchange one good for another. The change in relative price alone leads to a *substitution effect*. Second, a change in the nominal price of a good (nominal income remaining constant) causes a change in *real* income, or in the size of the bundle of goods and services a consumer can buy. If the nominal price of one good falls, all other nominal prices remaining constant, the consumer's real income rises because he can now buy more, either of the good whose price declined or of other goods. In other words, his level of satisfaction must increase. The change in the level of real income may or may not—depending upon the consumer's preference map—cause a significant change in his pattern of consumption. In any event, the change in real income leads to an *income effect* upon quantity demanded.

3.2.a The Substitution Effect in the Case of a Normal or Superior Good

When the price of one good changes, the prices of other goods and money income remaining constant, the consumer moves from one equilibrium point to another. In normal circumstances, if the price of a good diminishes, more of it is bought; if its price increases, fewer units are taken. The overall change in quantity demanded from one equilibrium position to another is referred to as the *total effect*.

Definition: The total effect of a price change is the total change in quantity demanded as the consumer moves from one equilibrium to another.

The total effect of a price change is illustrated in Figure 3.2.1. The original price ratio is indicated by the slope of the budget line *LM*. The consumer attains equilibrium at point *P* on indifference curve *II*, pur-

FIGURE 3.2.1

Substitution and Income Effects for a Normal or Superior Good in Case of a Price Rise

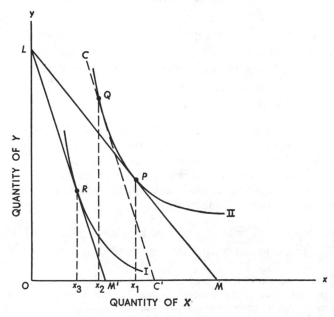

chasing Ox_1 units of X. When the price of X rises, as indicated by shifting the budget line from LM to LM', the consumer moves to a new equilibrium position at R on indifference curve I. At this point he purchases Ox_3 units of X. The total effect of the price change is indicated by the movement from P to R, or by the reduction in quantity demanded from Ox_1 to Ox_3. In other words, the total effect is $Ox_1 - Ox_3 = x_1x_3$. This is called a negative total effect because quantity demanded is reduced by x_1x_3 units.

The total effect of a price change, however, can be decomposed into two effects, the *substitution effect* and the *income effect*. Let us first examine the substitution effect. Consider Figure 3.2.1. When the price of X increases, the consumer suffers a decline in real income, as indicated by the movement from indifference curve II to indifference curve I. Suppose that coincident with the price rise the consumer were given an amount of (additional) money income just sufficient to compensate him for the loss in real income he would otherwise sustain. That is, he is given a compensatory payment just sufficient to enable him to remain on indifference curve II under the *new* price regime.

Graphically, this compensation is shown by constructing a fictitious budget line tangent to the *original* indifference curve, but whose slope corresponds to the *new* price ratio. The dashed line CC' in Figure 3.2.1 is the fictitious budget line for this example—it is tangent to the original indifference curve II at point Q; but it is parallel to the new budget line LM', thereby reflecting the new price ratio.

The substitution effect is represented by the movement from the original equilibrium position at P to the imaginary equilibrium position at Q, both points being situated on the original indifference curve. In terms of quantity, the substitution effect is the reduction in quantity demanded from Ox_1 to Ox_2, or by x_1x_2 units.

Definition: The substitution effect is the change in quantity demanded resulting from a change in relative price after compensating the consumer for his change in real income. In other words, the substitution effect is the change in quantity demanded resulting from a change in price when the change is restricted to a movement along the original indifference curve, thus holding real income constant.[1]

The substitution effect in the case of a price decline is illustrated in Figure 3.2.2. The original equilibrium is point P on indifference curve I,

---

[1] As this statement implies, we will use total consumer satisfaction as indicated by the indifference curve as the measure of real income. Hence all points on the same indifference curve represent the same real income, higher indifference curves represent greater real income, and lower indifference curves represent smaller real income.

FIGURE 3.2.2

Substitution and Income Effects for a Normal or Superior Good in Case of a Price Decrease

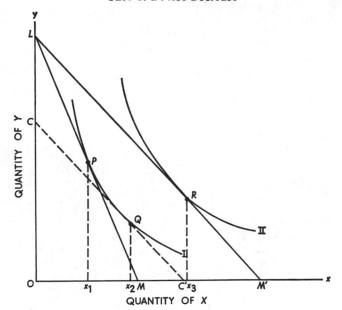

the price ratio being indicated by the original budget line *LM*. The price of *X* now declines to that indicated by the slope of *LM'*. In the absence of a compensatory payment, the consumer would enjoy an increase in real income, moving to equilibrium on indifference curve *II*. In this case, we compensate by imagining a decrease in money income by an amount just sufficient to maintain real income constant at the new price ratio. Graphically, this is illustrated by the dashed line *CC'*.

As a result of the price change alone, real income held constant, the consumer moves from the original equilibrium at *P* to the imaginary equilibrium at *Q*. The movement from *P* to *Q* along the original indifference curve represents the substitution effect. In quantity units, it is the expansion of quantity demanded from Ox_1 to Ox_2.

Comparing the cases in Figures 3.2.1 and 3.2.2, one readily sees that the *substitution effect always implies that quantity demanded varies inversely with price.* An increase in the price of *X* leads to a decrease in the quantity demanded of *X* if we keep real income constant (i.e., if we keep the consumer on the same indifference curve).

Some further insight may be gained into the proposition that income compensated price increases result in a reduction in the quantity demanded by considering the following argument that does not depend directly on the use of indifference curves. In Figure 3.2.3, the initial

FIGURE 3.2.3

**Substitution Effects with a Price Rise
and Income Compensation**

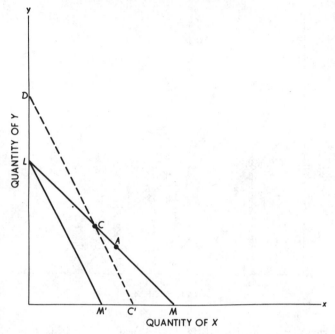

budget line is *LM*. By assumption (*iii*) of Chapter 1, we know the consumer will choose a point on (not below) *LM*. Suppose he chooses bundle *A*. Now let the price of *X* increase so the budget line is *LM'*. Once again by (*iii*) of Chapter 1, we know the consumer is worse off after this price increase. Next, assume we add money income until the consumer says he is as happy as he was before the price increase—that is, his satisfaction level is held constant. (By assumption (*i*) of Chapter 1 we know he will be able to make the comparisons necessary to do this.) Additions to money income cause parallel shifts in *LM'* to the northeast. We know that the consumer will be at least as happy as he was before the price increase if we shift the budget line until it intersects *LM* at *A,* because at that point he could, if he wished, consume *A* at the new prices. Accordingly, he will be as happy as he was before the price increase when the budget line has shifted to intersect *LM* at *A* or at some point to the left of *A*. Suppose the consumer says he is just as happy with the new budget line *DC'* as he was with the initial budget line *LM*. His new consumption bundle must be on the segment *DC* because any point on the segment *CC'* could have been consumed at the old budget line *LM* and we know he preferred *A* to any of these other consumption bundles. (This is the transitivity assumption (*ii*) of Chapter 1.) But all points on *DC* have less *X* than bundle *A,* so the quantity demanded of *X* decreases when there are income compensated increases in the price of *X* (i.e., when money income is raised just enough to offset the utility lost from the real income reduction caused by the increase in the price of *X*). This result is thus seen to follow directly from the assumptions about consumer behavior in Chapter 1 and does not require the explicit use of indifference curves.

3.2.b The Income Effect in the Case of a Normal Good

In determining the substitution effect, one is constrained to movements along the original indifference curve. However, the total effect of a price change, money income and the prices of other commodities held constant, always entails a shift from one indifference curve to another, or a change in real income.

Definition: The income effect of a change in the price of one commodity is the change in quantity demanded resulting exclusively from a change in real income, all other prices and money income held constant.

Consider Figure 3.2.1. When the price of *X* rises, as indicated by the shift of the budget line from *LM* to *LM',* the consumer attains his new equilibrium on indifference curve *I.* The movement from *P* to *Q* along indifference curve *II* represents the substitution effect. Now let the consumer's real income fall from the level represented by the fictitious budget line *CC'.* The movement from the imaginary equilibrium position *Q* on indifference curve *II* to the actual new equilibrium position *R* on indifference curve *I* indicates the income effect. Since *CC'* and *LM'* are parallel, the movement does not involve a change in relative prices. It is a real income phenomenon.

Real income declines as a result of the rise in the price of *X.* The reduction in quantity demanded from Ox_2 to Ox_3 measures the change in purchases attributable exclusively to the decline in real income, the change in relative price already having been accounted for by the substitution effect.

Similarly, in Figure 3.2.2, the decline in the price of *X* leads to an increase in real income. The substitution effect accounts for the movement from *P* to *Q,* and the income effect is represented by the movement from *Q* to *R.* Real income increases as a result of the price decrease, and quantity demanded increases from Ox_2 to Ox_3, *exclusively* as a result of the increase in real income.

From either graph one may readily see that the total effect of a price change is the sum of the substitution and income effects. In Figure 3.2.1, the total effect of the rise in the price of X is a reduction in quantity demanded from Ox_1 to Ox_3. The movement from Ox_1 to Ox_2 is attributable to the substitution effect, and the movement from Ox_2 to Ox_3 is the income effect. The same reasoning applies, *mutatis mutandis,* for the total effect shown in Figure 3.2.2.

3.2.c Normal or Superior Goods

As indicated by the subheadings above, our analysis has so far been restricted to the case of "normal" or "superior" goods, but a "normal" or "superior" good has not yet been defined except in terms of income elasticity of demand. We now have the tools necessary for a more refined definition.

Note from Figure 3.2.1 that when the price of a commodity rises, real income declines and the income effect causes a decrease in quantity demanded. On the other hand, a price decline (Figure 3.2.2) leads to an increase in real income and to an increase in quantity purchased attributable to the income effect. In both these cases the quantity demanded varies directly with real income: an increase in real income leads to an increase in quantity demanded and a decrease in real income reduces the quantity demanded.

Definition: A normal or superior good is one for which the quantity demanded varies directly with real income.

Principle: For a normal or superior good the income effect reinforces the substitution effect. A price decrease means real income has increased and, for a normal or superior good, this means the quantity demanded will increase. But a price decrease also increases the quantity demanded because of the substitution effect, so both the income and substitution effects work in the same direction. Thus for a normal or superior good quantity demanded always varies inversely with price.

3.3 INFERIOR GOODS

"Normal" or "superior" goods are given this name because in almost all cases the income effect is positive—this is the "normal" situation. In certain unusual cases, however, the income effect may cause a switch from margarine to butter, from dried to fresh beans. Thus an increase in real income may result in a decrease in the consumption of certain commodities. These commodities are called inferior goods.

Definition: An inferior good is one for which the quantity demanded varies inversely with real income—increases in real income reduce the quantity demanded and decreases in real income increase the quantity demanded of inferior goods.

3.3.a Inferior Goods and Giffen's Paradox

An increase in real income may be attributable to an increase in money income, commodity prices remaining constant, or to a decline in prices, money income remaining constant. Figure 3.3.1 shows an increase in income from the level given by the budget line *LM* to that given by *L'M'*. The two budget lines are parallel, so no change in relative price has occurred. The increase from *LM* to *L'M'* can come from an increase in money income, prices constant, or by uniform percentage reduction in both prices.

In the change, the position of consumer equilibrium shifts from point *P* on indifference curve *I* to point *Q* on indifference curve *II*. As a result of the *increase* in real income at the constant *relative* prices, the quantity demanded of good X falls from Ox_1 to Ox_2. The income-consumption curve, over this range of real income values, rises backward from *P* to *Q;* and the entire income-consumption curve might resemble the curve *APQB*.

FIGURE 3.3.1

Illustration of an Inferior Good

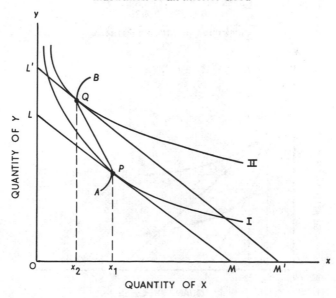

QUANTITY OF X

Figure 3.3.1 illustrates an indifference map involving one inferior good (*X*). The income effect is inverse, a rise in real income at a constant price ratio leading to a decline in quantity demanded. Similarly, if *L'M'* is regarded as the original income level, *LM* represents a lower real income. In this case, a decline in real income would be accompanied by an increase in the quantity of *X* demanded.

Generally, the substitution effect of a price change is great enough to offset a negative income effect. But in one case, called Giffen's Paradox, the income effect is so strong that it more than offsets the substitution effect. Thus a decline in price leads to a decline in quantity demanded and a rise in price induces a rise in quantity demanded. Figure 3.3.2 is an illustration of Giffen's Paradox. The original price of *X* is given by the slope of *LM*. With given money income and a constant price of *Y*, the price of *X* falls to the level indicated by the slope of *LM'*. The position of consumer equilibrium shifts from point *P* on indifference curve *I* to point *Q* on indifference curve *II*. Over this range, the price-consumption curve is *PQ*, and throughout the entire range it might look like the curve *APQB*. In the case of Giffen's Paradox, the price-consumption curve is *backward rising* over a certain range.

Definition: Giffen's Paradox refers to a good whose quantity demanded varies directly with price. A good must be an inferior good to belong in this category; but not all inferior goods conform to the conditions of Giffen's Paradox. The class of goods for which Giffen's Paradox holds constitutes the only exception to the law of demand.

FIGURE 3.3.2

Illustration of Giffen's Paradox

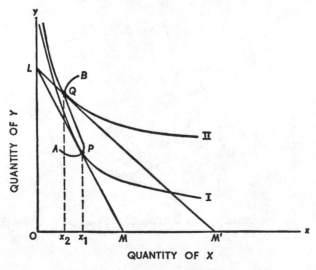

QUANTITY OF X

FIGURE 3.3.3

**Income and Substitution Effects for an Inferior Good Not
Subject to Giffen's Paradox**

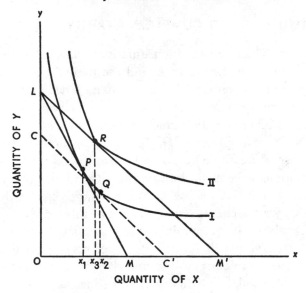

QUANTITY OF X

While the Giffen Paradox is a legitimate theoretical exception to the
law of demand, there is no persuasive empirical evidence that this phenomenon occurs to any measurable extent. There is evidence that some
goods, such as oleomargarine, may have negative income elasticities
and hence are inferior goods by our classification, but there is virtually
no evidence that the income effect is ever substantial enough in these
cases to lead to the Giffen Paradox.[2]

3.3.b   Income and Substitution Effects for an Inferior Good

The relations described in subsection 3.3.a are shown more clearly
by separating the total effect into its component parts. Figure 3.3.3 is an
illustration of the income and substitution effects for an inferior good
not subject to the conditions of Giffen's Paradox.

Exercise: Using Figure 3.3.3, show that X is an inferior good but is
not subject to the Giffen Paradox. (Hint: What are the income and sub-

---

[2] Frequently, one sees textbook "examples" of Giffen goods such as potatoes in
19th-century Ireland, but there does not appear to be any confirming evidence to
support these examples. The interested reader may wish to consult George J. Stigler,
"Notes on the History of the Giffen Paradox," *Journal of Political Economy,* vol.
55 (1947), pp. 152–56.

stitution effects when the price of X decreases and the budget line goes from *LM* to *LM'*?)

3.4 SUBSTITUTION AND COMPLEMENTARITY

When an individual's demand schedule is constructed, his preference pattern, his nominal money income, and the nominal prices of related commodities are held constant. Thus a demand schedule shows the relation between the nominal price of a commodity and the quantity of it demanded, all other demand influences held constant (or impounded in a *ceteris paribus* assumption). This partial equilibrium demand function is quite useful for some purposes, but much less useful for others. In some situations a general equilibrium view of the problem is required. So far as demand analysis is concerned, this means that one or more of the *ceteris paribus* assumptions must be relaxed.

More particularly, if the nominal prices of related commodities are allowed to vary, there will be definite repercussions on the quantity demanded of the commodity in question. By observing these repercussions, one is able to classify pairs of commodities as substitute or complementary goods. Historically, the first method of classification was based upon the *total effect* upon quantity demanded of good X resulting from a change in the price of good Y.

3.4.a Classification by Cross-Elasticities

If all prices are allowed to vary, the quantity of good X demanded depends not only upon its own price but upon the prices of related goods as well. Instead of a demand *curve* there is a demand *surface* such as shown in Figures 3.4.1 and 3.4.2.

For illustrative purposes suppose good X is related to only one other commodity, good Y. Schematically, the demand function can no longer be written as $q = h(p)$. Instead, one must write $q_x = f(p_x, p_y)$, where q and p represent quantity and price and the subscripts indicate the commodity in question.

The price elasticity of demand, or "own" elasticity, is

$$\eta_{xx} = -\left(\frac{\Delta q_x}{q_x} \div \frac{\Delta p_x}{p_x}\right),$$

where Δ means "the change in." The direct price elasticity, in other words, is the proportional change in quantity demanded of good X resulting from a given proportional change in the price of good X. The elasticity formula is applicable whether the demand function has the form shown in the first or second equation. When the price of a related good enters the demand function, however, it is possible to define the price cross-elasticity of demand:

$$\eta_{xy} = \frac{\Delta q_x}{q_x} \div \frac{\Delta p_y}{p_y} \ .$$

The price cross-elasticity of demand is the proportional change in the quantity of X demanded resulting from a given change in the price of the related good Y.

According to the cross-elasticity classification, goods X and Y are substitutes or complements according as the price cross-elasticity of demand is positive or negative. As trivial examples, consider the following. An increase in the price of pork, the price of beef remaining constant, will tend to augment the quantity of beef demanded; η_{xy} is positive, and beef and pork are said to be substitute goods. On the other hand, an increase in the price of gin will tend to reduce the quantity of vermouth demanded (the price of vermouth remaining constant); in this case η_{xy} is negative and gin and vermouth are said to be complementary goods.

3.4.b Geometric Illustrations

Linear demand surfaces for the two-good case are shown in Figures 3.4.1 and 3.4.2. In each graph, the quantity of X demanded is plotted on the vertical or "height" axis, while the prices of X and Y are plotted on the "width" and "length" axes. In each case, the plane $ABCD$ is the demand surface.

Figure 3.4.1 shows a linear demand surface in the case where goods X and Y are substitutes over the range of prices considered. First, notice that the law of demand holds: as the price of X increases, its quantity demanded falls. Thus if the price of Y is held fixed at Op_{y_1}, an increase in the price of X from Op_{x_1} to Op_{x_2} causes a decline in quantity demanded from RR' to TT'. Now hold the price of X constant at Op_{x_1}. As the price of Y increases from Op_{y_1} to Op_{y_2}, the quantity of X demanded rises from RR' to SS'—an increase in the price of good Y causes an increase in the quantity of X demanded. To put it differently, an increase in the price of Y causes the demand curve in the $Q_x - P_x$ plane to *shift* from EE' to FF'. Thus the coefficient η_{xy} is positive, and the goods are said to be substitutes.

Figure 3.4.2 shows the opposite relation over the range of prices

FIGURE 3.4.1

**Demand Surface for Good X When
X and Y Are Substitutes**

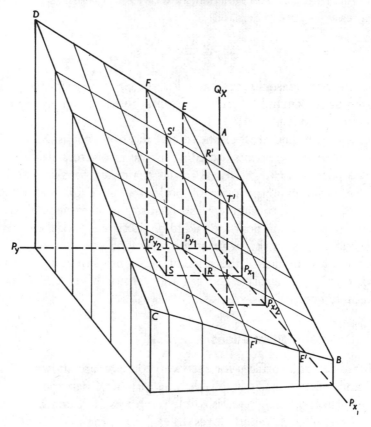

considered. Again, first note that the law of demand obtains. For a fixed price of Y, Op_{y_1}, an increase in the price of X from Op_{x_1} to Op_{x_2} causes a reduction in quantity demanded from RR' to TT'. But now hold the price of X constant at Op_{x_1}. An increase in the price of Y from Op_{y_1} to Op_{y_2} also causes a decline in the quantity of X demanded, from RR' to SS' in this case. Alternatively, one may say that the demand *curve* for X shifts from EE' to FF'. Accordingly, the coefficient of price cross-elasticity is negative and the commodities are said to be complementary goods.

The cross-elasticity approach to commodity classification directs attention to the change in quantity demanded resulting from a change in the price of a related good *without* compensating for the change in the level of real income. The *total effect* of a price change is thus the

FIGURE 3.4.2

**Demand Surface for Good X When
X and Y Are Complementary**

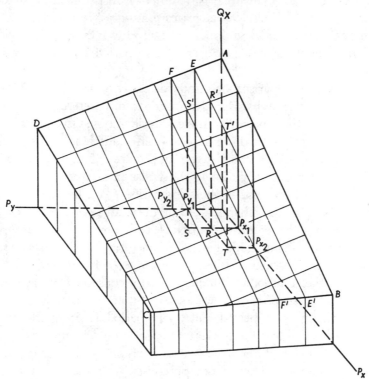

criterion used in this classification scheme. On an empirical level, this is the only feasible method of commodity classification because market demand functions can be computed while individual preference functions cannot (from readily available data).

Furthermore, in applied problems, one is usually interested in the *market* relation among commodities rather than the commodity relation as viewed by an individual consumer. Thus the cross-elasticity classification of commodity relations is the one most frequently encountered in applied studies. Indeed, reference to market cross-elasticities has even appeared in Supreme Court antitrust decisions.

3.5 APPLICATION OF INDIFFERENCE CURVE ANALYSIS: THE ECONOMIC THEORY OF INDEX NUMBERS

An interesting application of indifference curve analysis can be made in the field of index numbers. For simplicity, let us restrict our attention to a consumer who buys two commodities, X_1 and X_2, in two different time periods, 0 and 1. In time period 0 he buys x_1^0 units of X_1 at price p_1^0 and x_2^0 units of X_2 at price p_2^0. Similarly, in period 1 he purchases x_1^1 and x_2^1 units of X_1 and X_2 at prices p_1^1 and p_2^1 respectively. The essential problem of index numbers is as follows: has the individual's standard of living increased or decreased in period 1 as compared with period 0?

To make the comparison of standards of living at all meaningful, it is necessary to assume that the consumer's taste (preference map) does not change over the time period under consideration. Given this assumption, some information can be gained from indifference curve analysis.

Consider the budget lines given in Figure 3.5.1. In the original period (called the base period), the consumer's money income and prices p_1^0 and p_2^0 give rise to the budget line p_0p_0'. In period 1, prices (and possibly income) change so that the budget line becomes p_1p_1'. Is the consumer better off in period 1 compared to the base period in the sense of being on a higher indifference curve? The answer to this question, in the absence of direct knowledge of his indifference map, depends on the commodity bundles actually consumed in each period.

To see why, suppose first we observe that the consumer chooses bundle Q_0 in the base period and Q_1 in period 1. From the way the budget lines are drawn, it is clear that had the consumer wished, he could have purchased the base period bundle Q_0 in period 1. The reverse is not true; he could not purchase Q_1 at the base-year prices and income. Thus, since Q_0 is still available in period 1 but is not chosen, the consumer must be better off in period 1.

FIGURE 3.5.1

Theory of Index Numbers

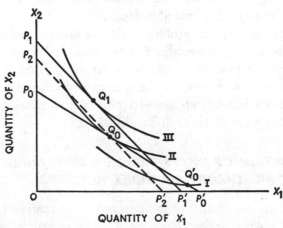

If, instead of Q_0, the consumer had chosen Q_0' in the base period, we would not be able to use this reasoning to conclude that Q_1 makes him better off. This is because Q_0' is not available to the consumer at the period 1 prices as Q_0 was. The reader should be able to convince himself of the ambiguity in this instance by imagining alternative sets of indifference maps imposed on Figure 3.5.1—one set of indifference curves that puts Q_0' on a higher indifference curve than Q_1 and an alternative set of indifference curves that puts Q_1 on a higher indifference curve than Q_0'. Thus, unless we know something about the indifference map, we are unable to determine which of the bundles Q_1 and Q_0' is preferred.

3.5.a Information from the Budget Map

What we do know is that if the total expenditure in period 1 exceeds the cost of the base period bundle in terms of period 1 prices, then the consumer is better off in period 1. Thus, if

$$p_1^1 x_1^1 + p_2^1 x_2^1 > p_1^1 x_1^0 + p_2^1 x_2^0 ,$$

then Q_1 is preferred to Q_0. Writing this expression as a sum and suppressing subscripts we know the individual is better off in period 1 when

$$\Sigma p^1 x^1 > \Sigma p^1 x^0 . \tag{3.5.1}$$

By the same reasoning, if

$$\Sigma p^0 x^0 > \Sigma p^0 x^1 , \tag{3.5.2}$$

then the individual is better off in the base period. This is because the inequality shows that the period 1 bundle was not chosen in the base period even though it could have been.

3.5.b Index Numbers as Indicators of Individual Welfare Changes

The analysis can be pushed somewhat further by introducing three index numbers. The first of these index numbers measures the change in the consumer's income from the base year to the given year. Since it is assumed that income equals expenditure, the incomes of the base year and the given year are $\Sigma p^0 x^0$ and $\Sigma p^1 x^1$, respectively. Consequently, the index of income change is

$$E = \frac{\Sigma p^1 x^1}{\Sigma p^0 x^0} . \tag{3.5.3}$$

The next index number to be introduced is called the Laspeyre index. This index number measures the cost, relative to the base period, of purchasing the base-year quantities at the given-year prices. Since the cost of the base-year quantities at given-year prices is $\Sigma p^1 x^0$, the Laspeyre index is[3]

$$L = \frac{\Sigma p^1 x^0}{\Sigma p^0 x^0} . \tag{3.5.4}$$

Finally, the Paasche index measures the cost of purchasing the given-year quantities at given-year prices relative to their cost at base-year prices. Since the cost of given-year quantities at base-year prices is $\Sigma p^0 x^1$, the Paasche index is

$$P = \frac{\Sigma p^1 x^1}{\Sigma p^0 x^1} . \tag{3.5.5}$$

Now from expression (3.5.1), the individual is better off in period 1 if $\Sigma p^1 x^1 > \Sigma p^1 x^0$. Dividing both sides of this inequality by $\Sigma p^0 x^0$, we have

$$\frac{\Sigma p^1 x^1}{\Sigma p^0 x^0} > \frac{\Sigma p^1 x^0}{\Sigma p^0 x^0} , \tag{3.5.6}$$

or

$$E > L . \tag{3.5.7}$$

Similarly, from expression (3.5.2), the individual is better off in the base period if $\Sigma p^0 x^0 > \Sigma p^0 x^1$. Dividing both sides of this inequality by $\Sigma p^1 x^1$, we have

$$\frac{\Sigma p^0 x^0}{\Sigma p^1 x^1} > \frac{\Sigma p^0 x^1}{\Sigma p^1 x^1} , \tag{3.5.8}$$

or

$$\frac{1}{E} > \frac{1}{P} , \tag{3.5.9}$$

or

$$E < P \tag{3.5.10}$$

From this analysis, especially expressions (3.5.7) and (3.5.10), four cases are possible.

---

[3] The familiar Consumer Price Index produced each month by the U.S. Bureau of Labor Statistics is an index of the Laspeyre form.

1. E is greater than either P or L. By expression (3.5.7), the individual's standard of living increases from period 0 to period 1. By (3.5.10) his standard of living does not fall. Hence the individual is definitely better off in period 1.

2. E is less than either P or L. By expression (3.5.10), the individual was better off in the base period. By (3.5.7) he was not better off in the given period. An unequivocal answer is again obtained: the individual's standard of living falls from period 0 to period 1.

3. $L > E > P$. In this case neither expression (3.5.7) nor (3.5.10) is satisfied. $L > E$ implies that the consumer is not better off in period 1. But $E > P$ implies that he was not better off in period 0 either. Consequently, no conclusion can be drawn.

4. $P > E > L$. This situation, though possible, is totally inconsistent. By expression (3.5.10), $P > E$ implies that the individual was better off in the base period. But $E > L$ implies, by (3.5.7), that he was better off in period 1. The individual's standard of living has both risen and fallen! Such a contradiction may be attributable to a change in the individual's preference pattern. In any event, it precludes an inference concerning the change in the individual's welfare.

In summary, it is sometimes possible to determine whether an individual's standard of living has increased or decreased by means of index number comparisons. In other situations, however, the results are inconclusive or contradictory. Therefore, in these cases the theory of index numbers has nothing to contribute to the analysis of individual welfare changes.

3.6 APPLICATIONS OF INDIFFERENCE CURVE ANALYSIS: THE CHOICE BETWEEN LEISURE AND INCOME

The theory of consumer behavior as formulated above is quite general, and it leads to many interesting and important propositions concerning demand and consumer choice. However, it is useful to simplify the theory and to introduce *leisure* into the preference function. To that end, let us aggregate expenditures on all goods and services into the simple term *income*. Since by our assumptions all income is spent on goods and services (which includes saving), this *income* is simply our familiar budget constraint.

At the same time, the amount of income received by a consumer depends upon the amount of time allocated to work. The more one works, the greater is his income. Yet the more one works, the less is the leisure time remaining to him. Leisure also has utility to most people; therefore, each consumer is confronted with a fundamental tradeoff between the consumption of goods and services and the consumption of leisure. The object of this section is to analyze this tradeoff in some very simple cases.

3.6.a The Income-Leisure Graph

Consider Figure 3.6.1. Income is plotted on the vertical axis, and leisure on the horizontal axis in the rightward direction. The unit of time in which leisure is measured is not relevant—it may be hours per day, weeks per year, or any other measurement unit. The essential point is that the total amount of time is fixed (say, 24 hours per day); and the sum of work time and leisure time must equal this fixed total time. Thus work time may be measured in a leftward direction along the horizontal axis. In Figure 3.6.1, OZ is the total time available. If OC hours per day are taken as leisure, then CZ hours are spent at work.

Let us now make two simplifying assumptions. First, the individual may work as many hours per day as he desires.[4,5] Second, the income per hour is the same irrespective of the number of hours worked. Thus if the individual works CZ hours per day and receives income of $CE = OG$, his hourly wage is CE/CZ. But since CEZ and OZA are similar triangles, $CE/CZ = OA/OZ$. Thus the slope of the straight line ZA represents the hourly wage rate.[6]

Exercise: Suppose an individual works CZ hours per day and receives income CF. Show that the slope of ZB represents the hourly wage rate.

3.6.b Equilibrium between Income and Leisure

Since income (or consumption) and leisure are competitive sources of utility, the consumer's preference pattern between them may be represented by an indifference map such as that shown in Figure 3.6.2.[7]

---

[4] Recall that the unit of measurement of time is irrelevant. For the sake of brevity, we speak of hours per day. Any other time measurement may be substituted.

[5] This is not an unrealistic assumption—individuals can find part-time employment and they also can hold more than one job by "moonlighting" and other means. In a problem at the end of the chapter, we ask the reader to analyze the effect of restrictions on the number of hours that can be spent working.

[6] ZA is a straight line because we have assumed that the hourly wage rate is constant.

[7] Note that this is exactly the same as saying that goods X and Y are alternative sources of utility and that there must be a tradeoff between them.

FIGURE 3.6.1

Income Constraint

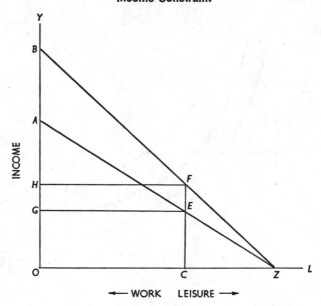

← WORK   LEISURE →

FIGURE 3.6.2

Tradeoff between Income and Leisure

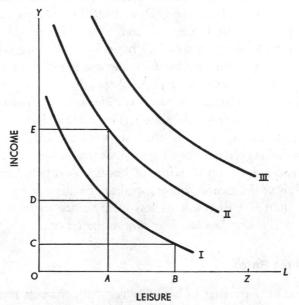

LEISURE

FIGURE 3.6.3

Consumer-Worker Equilibrium

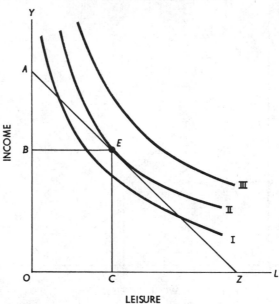

LEISURE

The indifference curves have all the properties of the usual indifference curves (see Chapter 1.3). Thus the consumer is indifferent between *OA* hours of leisure and income *OD,* and *OB* hours of leisure and income *OC.* Of course, the higher the indifference curve, the greater is utility. For example, suppose that *OA* hours of leisure are taken. Then the consumer gains greater utility if his income is *OE* than if it is *OD.*

Let us now put Figures 3.6.1 and 3.6.2 together, as shown in Figure 3.6.3. In the customary manner, we may determine the point of utility maximization (consumer equilibrium). The marginal rate of substitution is given by the (negative of the) slope of the indifference curve. The "price ratio" is given by the (negative of the) slope of *ZA.* Equilibrium is attained point *E* on *II,* with *CZ* hours of work and income *OB.* Indifference curve *III* cannot be attained at the given wage rate. Any curve lower than *II* will result in less utility since there is a possible tradeoff that will make the consumer-worker better off.

3.6.c Overtime Rates

It is now customary that union-management contracts require extra pay for "overtime" work. In the situation represented by Figure 3.6.4, "overtime" is any work in excess of *CZ* hours per day. Further assume that the "overtime" wage is half again as great as the "straight-time" wage. Thus the slope of *ZA* represents the regular wage and the slope of *ZFB* represents the straight-time and overtime wage (where *CZ* hours of work is straight time). Finally, assume that the worker can work overtime or not according to his choice.

It is clear from Figure 3.6.4 that the result of overtime pay for any

FIGURE 3.6.4

Overtime Rates

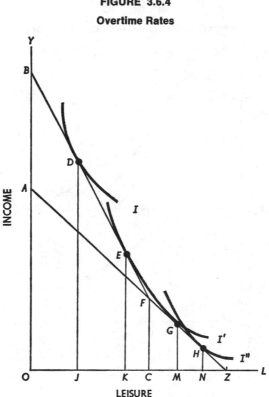

individual is uncertain. A person with an indifference map represented by *I* will clearly choose to work overtime, while an individual with an indifference map represented by *I″* will never voluntarily work overtime. An intermediate case is illustrated by the indifference curve *I′*. Such an individual is indifferent between working *KZ* hours for *KE* income or working *MZ* hours for *MG* income.

In the absence of auxiliary side agreements between union or individual worker and management, it is impossible to predict the effect of overtime wages.

3.6.d Demand for General Assistance Payments[8]

Among many of the social welfare programs that have been proposed for adoption by the federal government is one that would provide a minimum annual income per family. This program has not yet been adopted; nonetheless we may analyze some potential economic consequences of it.

Refer to Figure 3.6.5. Suppose the wage rate is represented by the

FIGURE 3.6.5

Demand for General Assistance Payments

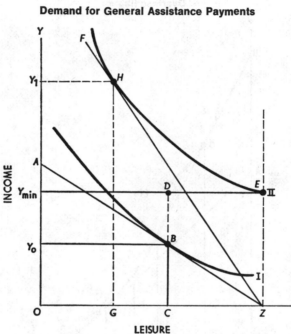

slope of ZA. In the absence of a guaranteed minimum income, an individual whose indifference map is given by I, II would attain equilibrium at B, working CZ hours and receiving income OY_0. If a minimum income of OY_{min} is guaranteed by the government, this individual might still work CZ hours, earn income of OY_0, and receive supplementary payment from the government of $BD = Y_0 - Y_{min}$. In this case, however, the individual can attain a greater level of satisfaction by doing no work at all—by moving to point E on indifference curve II and

---

[8] For a much more detailed discussion, see C. T. Brehm and T. R. Saving, "The Demand for General Assistance Payments," *American Economic Review*, vol. 54 (1964), pp. 1002–18.

receiving the minimum guaranteed income from the government.

From the point E the individual can be induced to work. In terms of Figure 3.6.5, if the wage rate should rise to ZF (or higher), he would forego his government payment, work GZ hours, and receive income of OY_1. From this example it is clear that a guaranteed minimum income can never lead to an increase in labor time. When all individuals in the society are considered, it will also surely lead to a reduction in labor time (and, consequently, in national output). The exact result, however, depends upon the leisure-income preferences of individuals, the level of the minimum income, and the wage rate available to each individual in question.

Exercise: Suppose an individual does not like to receive welfare payments. More specifically, assume that he regards $1 in welfare payments as equivalent to $0.50 of earned income. Analyze the effects of a guaranteed minimum income under these circumstances.

Exercise: There has recently been some policy discussion of a negative income tax. Under this scheme, a *base income* would be stipulated. A person earning more than the base income would pay a positive tax proportional to the difference between his earned income and the base income; one earning less than the base income would receive a subsidy proportional to the difference between the base income and his earned income. Suppose the factor of proportionality is 50 percent. (a) Analyze this welfare program by means of a graph such as Figure 3.6.5, and (b) compare the results of a negative income tax with the results of a guaranteed minimum income.

3.7 TIME PREFERENCE—CONSUMPTION AND SAVING OVER THE LIFE CYCLE

In the previous section, we investigated how a person might allocate his time between work (earning income) and leisure. A related question concerns how an individual might decide between present and future consumption. To introduce this, suppose we think of a person's life as being divided into two periods (e.g., working years and retirement years) and that he receives income of y_1 in the first period and income of y_2 in the second period.[9]

The individual can borrow or lend from a bank at a given interest rate, r, and by so doing he can transfer current income into future income or future income into current income. For example, if $y_1 = 100 and $y_2 = 50 and the interest rate is 5 percent, the individual can lend (save) the current $100 of income and have a total wealth in period 2 of $155 ($= 100(1.05) + 50$) or he can borrow against the

---

[9] This analysis easily can be extended to more than two periods.

collateral of his future income and have \$147.62 in period 1. In this last calculation, we use the fact that the \$47.62 the bank lends the individual in period 1 accrues interest of \$2.38 (at 5 percent) so the \$50 income in period 2 is just enough to pay back the principal of \$47.62 plus the accrued interest of \$2.38. Algebraically, the individual's period 1 wealth (or the maximum he can consume in period 1) is

$$y_1 + \frac{y_2}{(1+r)} \, .$$

By either borrowing or lending, the individual can have as much as \$155 to consume in period 2 (and nothing in period 1) or as much as \$147.62 in period 1 (and nothing in period 2) or any linear combination of these extremes. The relationship between first and second period consumption is given by

$$c_2 = y_2 + (y_1 - c_1)(1 + r) \tag{3.7.1}$$

or

$$c_2 = y_2 + y_1(1 + r) - c_1(1 + r) \tag{3.7.2}$$

where c_1 can have any value between 0 and $y_1 + y_2 / (1 + r)$. Equation (3.7.2) is the budget line between present and future consumption that is determined by the interest rate and the income in each of the two periods. As we have already seen, the individual moves along this budget line by either borrowing or lending (saving). If $y_1 - c_1$ is positive, then it represents the amount of saving the individual does in period 1 and $(y_1 - c_1)(1 + r)$ is the principal plus interest on this saving that is available for period 2 consumption. If $y_1 - c_1$ is negative, it represents the amount the individual borrows in period 1 and $(y_1 - c_1)(1 + r)$ is the principal plus interest he must pay back to the bank out of his period 2 income.

To find out how much the individual actually will save (or borrow) and consume, we simply introduce a utility function $U(c_1, c_2)$ representing the utility derived from consumption of c_1 in period 1 and c_2 in period 2. This utility function is represented in Figure 3.7.1 by indifference curves of the now familiar form. The budget line, BD, in Figure 3.7.1 is simply the linear equation (3.7.2) which has slope $- (1 + r)$. As shown, the individual has income of y_1 in period 1 and y_2 in period 2. He consumes OC in period 1 and saves Cy_1 $(= Oy_1 - OC)$. In period 2, he has income of y_2 plus the amount Ay_2 $(= Cy_1(1 + r))$ and consumes OA.[10]

---

[10] Because we have restricted the analysis to only two periods in this example, no saving for future consumption occurs in the second period.

FIGURE 3.7.1

**Time Preference—Consumption and Saving Decisions
over the Life Cycle**

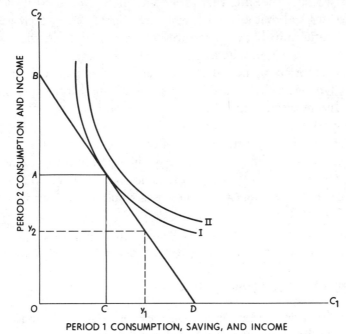

PERIOD 1 CONSUMPTION, SAVING, AND INCOME

As can be inferred from Figure 3.7.1, the equilibrium condition is that the marginal rate of substitution between current and future consumption should equal (the negative of) the slope of the budget line which is $1 + r$. The term $1 + r$ is the relative price of period 2 dollars in terms of period 1 dollars (i.e., a period 1 dollar will buy [by lending] $1 + r$ period 2 dollars). Thus, it is seen that interest rates act as prices at which income or assets can be transferred between different time periods.

Exercise: What do *OD* and *OB* represent in Figure 3.7.1?

To illustrate this theory with a specific case, assume that the marginal rate of substitution is always given by c_2/c_1. The equilibrium condition is then

$$\frac{c_2}{c_1} = 1 + r \cdot \tag{3.7.3}$$

Solving (3.7.3) for c_2 and substituting in (3.7.2), we obtain the equilibrium c_1

$$c_1 = \frac{1}{2}\left(y_1 + \frac{y_2}{1 + r}\right) \tag{3.7.4}$$

Equation (3.7.4) indicates that as income in *either* period increases, c_1 also increases and that as the interest rate r increases, c_1 decreases. The inverse relationship between the interest rate and c_1 in this example arises because a larger interest rate means savings in period 1 yield more consumption in period 2 than before the increase, or, to use different language, the higher interest rate means it now costs more to transfer future income into current consumption.

An increase in interest rates has both a substitution effect and a wealth effect (similar to the income effect discussed in section 3.2). The wealth effect occurs because an increase in interest rates means future income is worth less in present value. The wealth effect can, in theory, lead to cases where interest rate increases result in decreases in current saving.

Exercise: By use of indifference curves, show that it is possible that an increase in interest rates can reduce current savings (increase c_1).

3.8 CHOICES INVOLVING RISK

An assumption implicit in all we have done so far is that the consumer or decision maker is certain of the outcomes arising from alternative acts or decisions. For example, in section 3.7, we tacitly assumed that future income is known with certainty. This is clearly an unrealistic assumption, and one can think of many instances where risk is a major concern to the decision maker. This section provides an analytical method for dealing with such risky situations.

3.8.a Probabilities and Expected Value

Suppose someone offers to toss a six-sided die and pay you one dollar for each spot that appears on the face of the die. You know you will be paid from \$1 to \$6 depending on what the die shows, but you are uncertain as to exactly what payoff will obtain. If the die is fair, each side has an equal chance of showing and, since there are six sides, we say that the *probability* of any given side showing is one-sixth. You may find it convenient to think of probability in a long-run frequency sense. In other words, if a fair die were tossed a large number of times, it would show a 1 in one sixth of the tosses, a 2 in one sixth of the tosses, a 3 in one sixth of the tosses, and so on.

When we talk of a risky situation, we will mean one in which it is possible to assign a probability to each of the possible outcomes. In some situations, such as the die tossing example, the probability assignment is straightforward. In other situations, such probability assignments are somewhat ambiguous. For example, assessing the probability of rain in two weeks is a difficult task even for an experienced meteorologist. Despite such difficulties, we assume by using a combination of experience, objective evidence, and subjective intuition that decision makers are able to assign probabilities to the various outcomes in any given risky situation.[11] This kind of subjective calculation is exactly what is done when individuals set odds on prize fights, horseraces, and other betting situations. The statement that Bobby Riggs was a 5-to-2 favorite over Billie Jean King in their famous 1973 "Battle of the Sexes" tennis match meant that odds makers had assigned a probability of 5/7 to Riggs's winning and 2/7 to Ms. King's winning. The probability of any given outcome is a number between 0 and 1, and the sum of the probabilities of all possible outcomes is always 1.

By multiplying the payoff (or loss) of each outcome by its probability and summing, we get a number called the *expected value*. Intuitively, one can think of the expected value as the average payoff one would get by repeating the experiment a large number of times. In the die tossing example, the expected value is $3.50. Suppose there are n possible outcomes with probabilities $\pi_1, \pi_2, \ldots, \pi_n$, respectively, and payoffs $a_1, a_2, \ldots, a_n$; the expected value is then

$$E = \pi_1 a_1 + \pi_2 a_2 + \cdots + \pi_n a_n. \qquad (3.8.1)$$

As another example, suppose a fair coin is tossed and you are paid $1 if it comes up "heads" and you *lose* $1 if it comes up "tails." Because the coin is fair, each outcome has probability ½ and the expected value is

$$\frac{1}{2}(1) + \frac{1}{2}(-1) = 0.$$

Exercise: What is the expected value in the coin tossing example when the payoff for "heads" is $2 and you lose $1 if "tails" comes up?

---

[11] In recent years, there has been a good deal of work in Bayesian decision making which shows that individuals are able to quantify their subjective beliefs in this manner. See Ward Edwards, Harold Lindman, and Leonard J. Savage, "Bayesian Statistical Inference for Psychological Research," *Psychological Review*, vol. 70 (1963), pp. 193–242.

3.8.b The Expected Utility Hypothesis

In their landmark treatise, *The Theory of Games and Economic Behavior,* John von Neumann and Oskar Morgenstern provided a means of using the concept of probability in the analysis of decisions by individuals whose "payoffs" are in terms of subjective utility. In this work, von Neumann and Morgenstern were concerned with building a theory of individual preferences which would describe how an individual would choose among alternative risky situations. For example, how does an individual choose between two lottery tickets one of which pays \$5 with probability $\frac{1}{2}$ and one cent with probability $\frac{1}{2}$ and the other which pays \$10 with probability $\frac{1}{8}$ and \$1 with probability $\frac{7}{8}$? To answer questions like this, von Neumann and Morgenstern proposed certain axioms about individual behavior that described how such choices are made. These axioms imply the existence of a utility function that represents the individual's preferences among risky alternatives.[12]

The operational content of the von Neumann–Morgenstern results can be described as follows: Suppose the individual derives utility $U(X_1)$ from the certain payment of \$$X_1$ and that he derives utility $U(X_2)$ from a certain payment of \$$X_2$. Now suppose he were offered a lottery ticket paying \$$X_1$ with probability π_1 and \$$X_2$ with probability $\pi_2(= 1 - \pi_1)$. According to the von Neumann–Morgenstern theory, the utility of this ticket would be

$$\pi_1 U(X_1) + (1 - \pi_1)U(X_2) \qquad (3.8.2)$$

where (3.8.2) is the expected value of the utility of each outcome. If more than two outcomes are possible, the expected utility is simply

$$\pi_1 U(X_1) + \pi_2 U(X_2) + \pi_3 U(X_3) + \cdots + \pi_n U(X_n)$$

where π_i is the probability of the ith outcome and X_i is the payoff in the event of the ith outcome.

When choosing among alternative prospects, individuals will prefer the prospect that yields the largest expected utility. In other words, the theory says that individuals behave as if they maximize expected utility.

---

[12] A related set of axioms and a proof of the existence of such a utility function may be found in I. N. Herstein and John Milnor, "An Axiomatic Approach to Measurable Utility," *Econometrica,* vol. 23 (1953), pp. 291–97. The interested reader may also wish to consult Milton Friedman and L. J. Savage, "The Expected Utility Hypothesis and the Measurability of Utility," *Journal of Political Economy,* vol. 60 (1952), pp. 463–74.

It is important to emphasize that the expected value of utility is not the same as the utility of the expected value.[13]

Frequently it is assumed that the utility function is increasing and concave as shown by the curve *OA* in Figure 3.8.1. This figure helps

FIGURE 3.8.1

An Illustration of the Expected Utility Concept

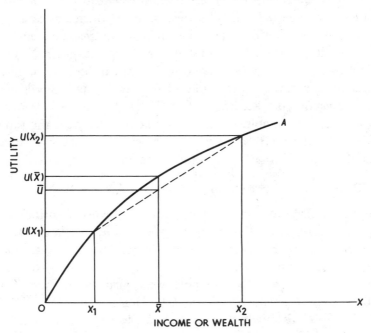

to illustrate the expected utility concept. The point $\bar{U}$ between $U(X_1)$ and $U(X_2)$ on the vertical axis is the expectation of the utilities associated with the payoffs X_1 and X_2 ($\bar{U} = \pi_1 U(X_1) + \pi_2 U(X_2)$). The reader will see that $U(\bar{X})$, where $\bar{X}$ ($= \pi_1 X_1 + \pi_2 X$) is the expected value of X_1 and X_2, is greater than $\bar{U}$. This phenomenon is called "risk aversion," and it says that the individual prefers a certain payment equal to the expected value $\bar{X}$ to any lottery ticket with expected value $\bar{X}$. Risk aversion holds whenever utility functions are concave.

---

[13] The only exception to this statement is the linear utility function where these two quantities are the same.

3.8.c Indifference Curves and State Preference Analysis

For simplicity, suppose there are only two outcomes or "states of nature". State 1 obtains with probability π_1, and state 2 obtains with probability $\pi_2 = 1 - \pi_1$. If the individual gets a payment of X_1 in state 1 and X_2 in state 2, his expected utility is simply expression (3.8.2).

The expected utility obviously depends on the values of X_1 and X_2 —if either is increased, the expected utility increases, and if either is decreased, the expected utility decreases. If X_1 increases and X_2 decreases, the expected utility may either increase, decrease, or remain constant depending on the relative magnitude of the changes in X_1 and X_2. This means that for a given change in X_1 we can find a change in X_2 that exactly offsets the effect of the change in X_1 and thus leaves expected utility constant. Because of this "tradeoff" it is possible to derive all of the possible combinations of X_1 and X_2 that yield the same expected utility. If we pick a given level of expected utility, k, then the values of X_1 and X_2 that satisfy the expression

$$k = \pi_1 U(X_1) + (1 - \pi_1)U(X_2) \tag{3.8.3}$$

lie on an indifference curve that has constant expected utility k. The geometrical derivation of such indifference curves is shown in Figure 3.8.2. There are four quadrants to the figure. The northeast quadrant shows the indifference curves (constant expected utility) for various combinations of X_1 and X_2. The northwest quadrant indicates (on the horizontal axis) the value $(1 - \pi_1)U(X_2)$ for each value of X_2. The curve OCC' in this quadrant is simply a plot of the function $(1 - \pi_1)U(X_2)$ which is rotated so the X_2 axis matches the X_2 axis in the northeast quadrant. The southwest quadrant is simply the linear relationship

$$\pi_1 U(X_1) = k - (1 - \pi_1)U(X_2) \tag{3.8.4}$$

implied by (3.8.3). By reading points along the line FG, we can find the value of $\pi_1 U(X_1)$ that keeps expected utility constant for each value of $(1 - \pi_1)U(X_2)$. By choosing larger values of k, this curve would shift parallel to itself in the southwest direction. The southeast quadrant is like the northwest quadrant but plots the function $\pi_1 U(X_1)$. The curve OHH' is the function $\pi_1 U(X_1)$ rotated so the X_1 axis matches the X_1 axis in the northeast quadrant.

To see how this geometry is used, we pick a value for X_2 along the vertical axis of the northeast quadrant—say the point OA. By moving to the left of the X_2 axis, we intersect the line in the northwest quadrant

FIGURE 3.8.2

The Derivation of Constant Expected Utility
Indifference Curves

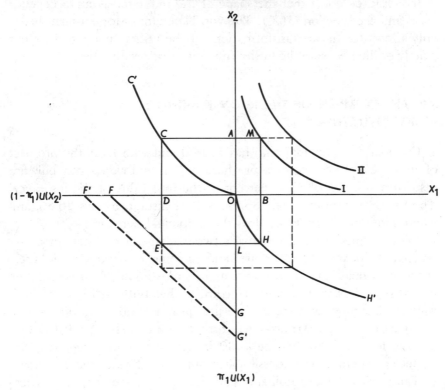

at C. Reading down from C to the horizontal axis, we find the distance
OD which is the value of $(1 - \pi_1)U(X_2)$ at the chosen X_2. Now
reading down to the point E on the line FG, turning a right angle and
reading over to the vertical axis, we find the point L that represents
the value of $\pi_1 U(X_1)$ needed to keep expected utility constant at the
chosen value k (see (3.8.4)). Reading horizontally over to H on the
curve OHH' representing $\pi_1 U(X_1)$ in the southeast quadrant, then
turning a right angle to the X_1 axis, we find the value of X_1 which
keeps expected utility equal to k when X_2 is equal to OA. Using OA
and OB as coordinates, we find the point M in the northeast quadrant.
Repeating this procedure for various values of X_2, we can trace out
the entire indifference curve I which represents all the combinations
of X_1 and X_2 that give the same expected utility.

   If the value of expected utility k is increased, the FG line shifts
parallel to itself in the southwest direction, forming $F'G'$, and a new,

higher indifference curve such as *II* can be traced out. The entire indifference curve map can, in principle, be found in this way.

It should be noted that the shape of the indifference curve depends on π_1 and the function $U(X)$. The von Neumann–Morgenstern theory only allows for linear transformations of the utility function. It is not strictly ordinal as were the utility functions discussed earlier.

3.9 AN EXAMPLE OF DECISION MAKING IN A RISKY SITUATION

Consider an individual who has $1,000 and who faces the prospect of losing $750 because of a fire hazard. The individual can buy fire insurance at a cost of 33⅓ percent of the face value of the insurance. Thus, $10 of insurance costs $3.33, $20 of insurance costs $6.66, and so on. How much insurance does the individual demand?

We can think of this decision as a two-outcome or two-state model—outcome 1 (or state 1) is "no fire" and outcome 2 (or state 2) is "fire." If the individual buys no insurance and there is no fire (outcome 1) he has $1,000; however, if there is a fire he has only $250. If he buys $300 of insurance and there is no fire he has $900 ($1,000 less the insurance cost of $100); however, if there is a fire he has $450 ($1,000 less the loss of $750 less the $100 insurance cost plus the $300 insurance payment). Other possible combinations of outcomes are shown in Table 3.9.1. The combinations of outcomes can be expressed algebraically as follows where X_1 is the amount of money the individual

TABLE 3.9.1

**Outcomes in the Case of No Fire and Fire
for Different Amounts of Insurance**

		Amount of Money in the Case of—	
Amount of Insurance	*Cost of Insurance*	*No Fire** (X_1)	*Fire†* (X_2)
$ 0	$ 0	$1,000.00	$250.00
100	33.33	966.67	316.67
200	66.66	933.34	383.34
300	100.00	900.00	450.00
400	133.33	866.67	516.67
500	166.66	833.33	583.33
750	250.00	750.00	750.00

* $1,000 less the cost of insurance.
† $1,000 less the loss of $750 less the cost of insurance plus the amount of insurance.

has in the event of no fire, X_2 is the amount of money he has in the event of fire, and I is the amount of insurance.

$$X_1 = \$1,000 - \tfrac{1}{3}I \qquad\qquad (3.9.1)$$

$$X_2 = \$1,000 - \$750 - \tfrac{1}{3}I + I \qquad\qquad (3.9.2)$$

Equation (3.9.1) says that when there is no fire the individual has $1,000 less the cost of insurance ($= \tfrac{1}{3}$ of the amount of insurance purchased). Equation (3.9.2) says that in the event of a fire the individual has $1,000 less the loss of $750 less the cost of insurance plus I, the insurance payment. If we solve (3.9.1) for I and substitute into (3.9.2) we get a linear equation relating the amount of dollars in state 2 (fire) to the amount of dollars in state 1 (no fire).

$$X_2 = \$2,250 - 2X_1 \qquad\qquad (3.9.3)$$

$$\$750 \leq X_1 \leq \$1,000$$

Equation (3.9.3) can be used directly to get the entries in the last two columns of Table 3.9.1. The inequality constraints on X_1 (money when

FIGURE 3.9.1

**Constant-Expected-Utility Indifference Curves
and the Demand for Insurance**

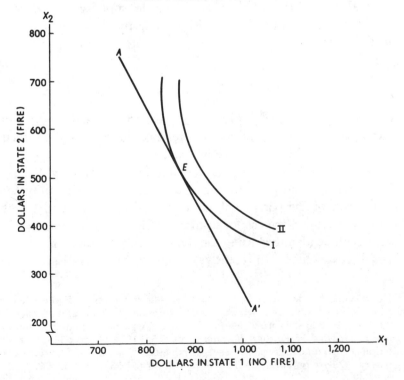

there is no fire) represent the $1,000 maximum the individual has with no insurance and the $750 minimum he has when he purchases full insurance coverage of $750 (we are assuming that he cannot insure more than 100 percent of the potential loss). Equation (3.9.3) can be viewed as a budget line showing the possible combinations of dollars in the two states that the individual can achieve by varying the amount of insurance he purchases.

To complete the analysis we construct constant expected utility indifference curves as in subsection 3.8.b. This can be done given the individual's utility function and the probabilities, π_1 and π_2, that he attaches to the outcome "no fire" and the outcome "fire" respectively. Combining the "budget" line (3.9.3) with the constant expected utility indifference curves from the northeast quadrant of Figure 3.8.3, we get a graph such as that shown in Figure 3.9.1. In Figure 3.9.1 the line AA' represents (3.9.3) and lines I and II are two representative indifference curves. The maximum expected utility is achieved at point E where AA' is tangent to an indifference curve. At this point X_1 is $875, so $125 is spent for insurance (this provides insurance coverage of $375) and X_2 is $500.

Figure 3.9.1 can be used to examine the effects of various changes in the conditions of the problem. For example, suppose the loss in the event of fire is $500 instead of $750. It is easily shown that the new "budget" line is

$$X_2 = \$2,500 - 2X_1 \tag{3.9.4}$$

$$\$833.34 \leq X_1 \leq \$1,000 .$$

This would be represented in Figure 3.9.1 as a shift in AA' to the northeast; and given the shape of the indifference curves I and II, such a shift would reduce the demand for insurance.

The analysis indicates that the demand for insurance will depend on the individual's attitude toward risk (reflected by his utility function), the size of the potential loss, his wealth or income, the probability of the loss, and the cost of insurance. The effects of these various influences can be identified using the modifications of indifference curve analysis discussed here.[14] In recent years economists have also used such

---

[14] For a more detailed analysis, see Isaac Ehrlich and Gary S. Becker, "Market Insurance, Self-Insurance, and Self-Protection," *Journal of Political Economy*, vol. 80 (1972), pp. 623–48. Also see Jan Mossin, "Aspects of Rational Insurance Purchasing," *Journal of Political Economy*, vol. 76 (1968), pp. 553–68. For an application to investment decisions, see J. Hirshleifer, "Investment Decisions under Uncertainty," *Quarterly Journal of Economics*, vol. 80 (1966), pp. 252–77.

models to examine questions of investment behavior and other decisions involving risk.

3.10 CONCLUSION

This chapter shows how the theory of consumer behavior developed in Chapters 1 and 2 can be applied to a wide variety of situations. Indifference curve analysis provides an important tool for the economist that can be used, and is used, in the analysis of many different problems. As we have seen, appropriate use of these tools permits us to deal with problems such as work-leisure choices, savings and consumption decisions over time, and even problems involving risk. In recent years, economists have applied these techniques to analyze questions such as racial discrimination, financial and portfolio decisions, the effects of law enforcement and punishment on crime rates, the resolution of legal conflicts, and the demand for medical care. The generality of the theory makes it useful in the analysis of a great many problems of interest. What is needed is ingenuity in building the appropriate models.

QUESTIONS AND EXERCISES

1. *a.* Suppose the price of apples increases 5 percent and the income elasticity for apples is 0.5. What will happen to the quantity of apples demanded?
   b. Suppose the price of flour increases by 1 percent and the income elasticity for flour is -0.36. What will happen to the quantity of flour demanded?

2. It has been observed that the amount of services of domestic servants consumed in the United States declined in the first half of the 20th century while per capita income was increasing. Does this mean that domestic servants are an inferior good?

3. The following table lists three situations for an individual who consumes two goods X_1 and X_2. The table lists the prices of the goods p_1 and p_2, the quantities consumed of the goods, the consumer's nominal income M, and his utility level.

Situation	p_1	p_2	Quantity of X_1	Quantity of X_2	M	Utility
1.........	$1	$1	50	40	90	10
2.........	1	½	48	84	90	15
3.........	1	½	40	70	75	10

   a. When the price of good 2 drops from $1 to $½, what is the change in the quantity demanded of X_2 when nominal income is constant at $90? What part of this change is due to the substitution effect and what part is due to the income effect? Is X_2 a normal or superior good or is it an inferior good?

   b. Fill in the blanks in the following table and answer the questions in part (*a*) for this table.

Situation	p_1	p_2	Quantity of X_1	Quantity of X_2	M	Utility
1........	$1	$1	50	—	70	10
2........	1	½	52	—	70	15
3........	1	½	—	36	60	10

4. Is it possible for all goods to be inferior goods? (Savings or cash balances are assumed to be goods.)

5. Mr. Jones spends all his income on two goods X_1 and X_2. The prices of these goods, p_1 and p_2, and the quantity Mr. Jones consumed of each are shown in the following table for three separate years:

Year	p_1	p_2	Quantity of X_1	Quantity of X_2
1..............	$6	$3	10	50
2..............	4	4	20	30
3..............	4	3	24	28

   a. What are the Laspeyre and Paasche indexes between years 1 and 2, between years 2 and 3, and between years 1 and 3?

   b. Is Mr. Jones better off in year 1 or year 2? Is he better off in year 2 or year 3? Is he better off in year 1 or year 3?

6. Is it true that if two goods are substitutes, a fall in the price of one will lead to a fall in the price of the other? Does it matter whether the initial decline in price is demand-led or supply-led?

7. Suppose that upon graduation from college a person has the option of taking a job paying $10,000 per year or borrowing money to go through medical school. Why would anyone become a medical doctor?

8. Suppose Miss Smith, who is 22 years old, learns that she has received an inheritance that will pay her $100,000 on her 35th birthday. Using indifference curve analysis, explain what happens to her current consumption behavior.

9. If $U(X) = \log X$, then expected utility is

$$\pi_1 \log X_1 + (1 - \pi_1) \log X_2$$

where X_1 and X_2 are money in state 1 and state 2, respectively, and π_1 and $1 - \pi_1$ are the respective state 1 and state 2 probabilities. The marginal rate of substitution can be shown to be

$$- \frac{dX_2}{dX_1} = \left(\frac{\pi_1}{1 - \pi_1} \right) \frac{X_2}{X_1}.$$

    a. Using the budget line (3.9.3) for the insurance problem discussed in the text and assuming $\pi_1 = 0.8$ how much money (X_1) will the individual have in state 1 and how much (X_2) will the individual have in state 2? How much insurance has been purchased?

    b. How much insurance will the individual purchase if $\pi_1 = 0.7$ (i.e., the probability of fire increases compared to part (a))?

    c. Suppose the loss in the event of fire is \$500 instead of \$750. When $\pi_1 = 0.8$ how much insurance will the individual purchase? Compare your answer to that in part (a) of this question.

10. *a.* Jeffrey, who is five years old, likes candy and hates spinach. He is allowed two candy bars a day, but his mother offers to give him one additional candy bar for every two ounces of spinach he eats each day. On these terms, Jeffrey eats three ounces of spinach and 3½ candy bars each day. Using indifference curves, analyze Jeffrey's equilibrium consumption of candy bars and spinach.

    b. Suppose Jeffrey's mother did not give him his two "free" candy bars each day but offered a candy bar for each two ounces of spinach. Would his spinach consumption be greater or smaller than in part (a)?

SUGGESTED READINGS

Ferguson, C. E. "Substitution Effect in Value Theory: A Pedagogical Note," *Southern Economic Journal,* vol. 24 (1960), pp. 310–14.

Georgescu-Roegen, Nicholas. "A Diagrammatic Analysis of Complementarity," *Southern Economic Journal,* vol. 19 (1952), pp. 1–20.

Henderson, James M., and Quandt, Richard E. *Microeconomic Theory,* 2d ed. pp. 32–49. New York: McGraw-Hill Book Co., Inc., 1971. [Elementary math necessary.]

Hicks, J. R. *Value and Capital,* pp. 42–52. 2d ed. Oxford: Oxford University Press, 1946.

Samuelson, Paul A. *Foundations of Economic Analysis,* pp. 100–107. Cambridge, Mass.: Harvard University Press, 1947. [Advanced math necessary.]

Staehle, Hans. "A Development of the Economic Theory of Price Index Numbers," *Review of Economic Studies,* vol. 2 (1935), pp. 163–88. [Elementary math necessary.]

4

Characteristics of market demand

4.1 INTRODUCTION

The analysis of Part I has firmly established the proposition that individual demand curves slope downward to the right—that quantity demanded varies inversely with price. The only exception is a truly insignificant one, Giffen's Paradox. But even if a few individuals are in a situation such that Giffen's Paradox applies, it is doubtful that the *market* demand curve would show the same properties.

This last chapter of Part I makes the transition from individual to market demand—from the demand of one individual for a particular commodity to the demand of all consumers taken together for that commodity. Having derived the market demand function, we can go on to describe many of its characteristics by means of such concepts as marginal revenue, direct price elasticity, price cross-elasticity, and income elasticity.

4.2 FROM INDIVIDUAL TO MARKET DEMAND

The demand function of one individual for a particular commodity is obtained by the process of maximizing satisfaction for a given level of money income. The process has been described in Chapter 2. From this discussion it is evident that the individual's preference function has an important role to play in determining his demand for each specific commodity. But it is not the only force. Indeed, there are four important determinants of quantity demanded.

4.2.a The Determinants of Demand

One of the four determinants of individual demand establishes quantity demanded given the *level* of the demand curve, while the others determine the level of demand itself.

The first determinant is the *price of the commodity* under consideration. According to the law of demand, quantity demanded varies inversely with price. Another way of expressing this principle is to say that the demand curve is negatively sloped; expressed in yet a different way, changes in nominal price cause movements *along* a given demand function, the movements representing the opposite changes in quantities demanded.

This familiar proposition is illustrated in panel a, Figure 4.2.1. As is *always* the case, price is plotted along the vertical axis and quantity demanded along the horizontal axis.[1] When price decreases from OP_1 to OP_2, quantity demanded increases from OQ_1 to OQ_2. This change represents a movement along the given demand curve DD' from E_1 to E_2. To reemphasize, changes in the price of a commodity lead to changes in *quantity demanded,* the demand curve remaining unchanged.

The remaining determinants establish the level or position of the entire demand curve. *Money income* is one of the important determinants. For almost all individuals and for almost all commodities, the greater the money income the greater the demand (meaning, the higher and further to the right the demand curve lies).[2] Consider panel b, Figure 4.2.1. DD' is the original demand curve. Let money income increase. Demand will also increase, shifting the demand curve outward to the right, to a position such as D_uD_u'. If money income should fall from its original level, on the other hand, demand would fall, or move downward and to the left. D_dD_d' represents such a shift.

Note that when demand increases, price remaining unchanged, quantity demanded increases as well. If price is OP and demand increases from DD' to D_uD_u', quantity demanded increases from OQ

---

[1] This manner of plotting is just the reverse of the accepted mathematical procedure of plotting the independent variable on the horizontal axis.

[2] Certain exceptions are discussed in section 4.3.

FIGURE 4.2.1

Shifting the Determinants of Demand

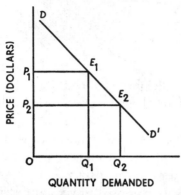

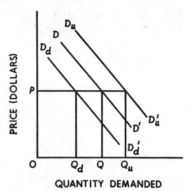

PANEL a--CHANGES IN QUANTITY
DEMANDED

PANEL b--CHANGES IN THE
DEMAND CURVE

to OQ_u. However, the important force in this situation is the change in money income that leads to the shift in demand.

The third determinant of demand is *taste*. The tastes or preference patterns of most individuals change from time to time. An increase in the intensity of one's desire for a commodity relative to other commodities naturally leads to an increase in his demand for the commodity. The opposite occurs, of course, if a person's taste for a commodity lessens.[3]

Finally, the *prices of related commodities* condition the level of demand for the commodity in question. In Chapter 3 the concepts of substitution and complementarity were discussed. Using the demand-function approach, two goods are said to be substitutes if an increase in the price of one leads to an increase in the consumption of the other. Let panel b, Figure 4.2.1, refer to the demand for beef. For a given price of pork, the original demand is DD'. If the price of pork increases, the *demand* for beef increases to D_uD_u'. If the price of beef remains unchanged (at OP), the quantity of beef demanded increases from OQ to OQ_u. Similarly, if the price of pork falls, the demand for beef would fall to D_dD_d' and the quantity demanded would decline to OQ_d.

The opposite relation holds for complementary goods. Let panel b

---

[3] Tastes often can be accounted for by observable phenomena such as weather conditions (that affect the demand for umbrellas or skiing), the age of the consumer, and the marital status of the consumer. Married consumers, for example, will tend to have a greater taste (and more demand) for furniture and children's clothing than unmarried consumers.

now represent the demand for golf clubs. A complementary good is a golf course. If the price of country club membership rises, fewer people will join the club and fewer will play golf. Thus the demand for golf clubs will decline. On the other hand, if the cost of playing golf declines, the demand for golf clubs is likely to expand.

These four factors—price, income, taste, and prices of related commodities—jointly determine the level of demand and the quantity demanded of every good by every individual. The next step is to aggregate individual demands to obtain a market demand for each commodity.

4.2.b Determining Market Demand

The market demand for a specific commodity is nothing more than the *horizontal summation* of the individual demands of each consumer. In other words, the market quantity demanded at each price is the sum of all individual quantities demanded at that price.

Table 4.2.1 and its accompanying diagram, Figure 4.2.2, provide an illustration when three consumers are in the market. Furthermore, it shows that even though Giffen's Paradox holds for individual *C's* demand, the derived market demand curve obeys the law of demand.

In the ordinary case a vast number of consumers are in each market; and they are not likely to have individual demands that differ as widely as those in Figure 4.2.2. Thus to depict the more usual situation, assume a market in which there are 75,000 consumers, each with identical

TABLE 4.2.1

**Individual and Aggregate Demand in a
Three-Consumer Market**

Price	Quantity Demanded by A	Quantity Demanded by B	Quantity Demanded by C	Market Quantity Demanded
$10	2	0	0	2
9	5	1	0	6
8	8	5	0	13
7	12	10	5	27
6	16	14	12	42
5	21	18	14	53
4	27	22	12	61
3	35	25	11	71
2	45	27	14	86
1	60	29	16	105

FIGURE 4.2.2

From Individual to Market Demand

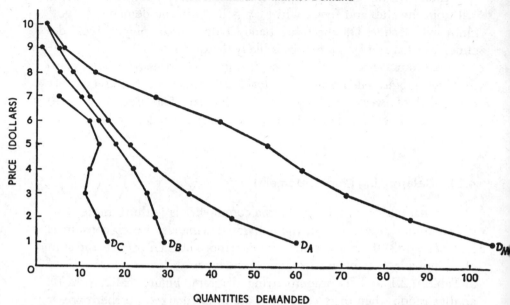

individual demands. Table 4.2.2 shows the demand of one individual and the aggregate market demand. Similarly, panel a, Figure 4.2.3, shows a plot of the individual demand curve; panel b shows the corresponding market demand.

At this point, it is worth reexamining the convexity assumption we have made about indifference curves. Suppose that an individual has concave indifference curves such as those labeled *I*, *II*, and *III* in Figure 4.2.4. If the budget line is *AB*, the individual will consume good *X* in the amount *OA* and *none* of good *Y*. When indifference curves are concave, such "corner" solutions are typical because at points of tangency, like *E* on curve *I*, the budget line will lie above the indifference curves and this means that higher indifference curves can be reached. If the price of *Y* decreases and the budget line shifts to *AC*, the individual can get the same utility from consuming *X* exclusively (in the amount *OA*) or *Y* exclusively (in the amount *OC*). The specific choice is ambiguous at this set of relative prices. However, if the price of *Y* declines further and the budget line shifts to *AD*, the individual unambiguously switches all his consumption to good *Y* (in this case to the amount *OD*). As the price of *Y* continues to decrease, the consumer will consume *Y* exclusively but in increasing quantity. The effect of

TABLE 4.2.2

Individual and Market Demand in a Large Market

Price	Quantity Demanded by a Typical Individual	Market Quantity Demanded
$8	3	225,000
7	8	600,000
6	13	975,000
5	18	1,350,000
4	23	1,725,000
3	28	2,100,000
2	33	2,475,000
1	38	2,850,000

concave indifference curves is thus to introduce a discontinuity or "jump" in the individual's demand curve. Such discontinuities are smoothed out by the horizontal summation of individual demand curves and the aggregate demand is "almost continuous." The convexity assumption used in Chapters 1 to 3 is a reasonable characterization of consumer behavior, but it is not critical to the development of the theory.

FIGURE 4.2.3

Aggregation of Individual Demand

PANEL a--INDIVIDUAL DEMAND.

PANEL b--MARKET DEMAND

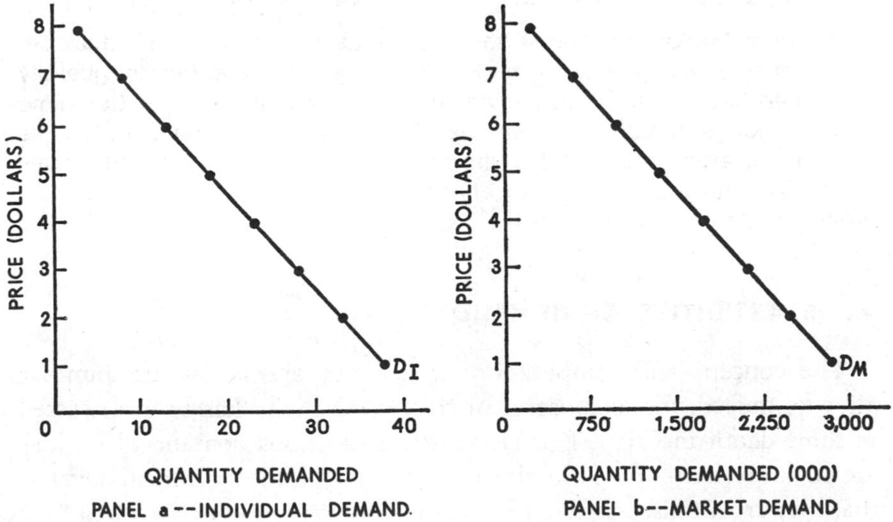

FIGURE 4.2.4

**Concave Indifference Curves and Individual
Demand Behavior**

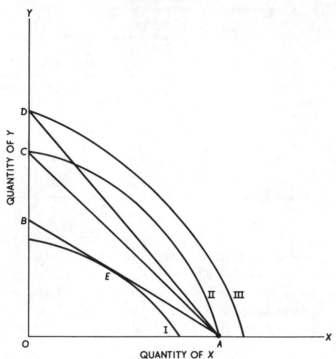

The results of this section may be summarized as follows:

Relation: Market demand is the horizontal sum of the individual demands of all consumers in the market. Thus at each price, market quantity
demanded is the sum of all individual quantities demanded at the same
price. Although some individuals may have demands subject to Giffen's
Paradox for a few commodities, the normal demands of other individuals
will usually outweigh the Giffen effect. Thus market demand curves will
ordinarily slope downward to the right.

4.3 ELASTICITIES OF DEMAND

The concept and computation of demand elasticities are familiar
already; indeed, the measure of price cross-elasticity has been discussed
in some detail in Chapter 3. However, the various demand elasticities
are so important—on both the theoretical and the empirical level—
that they are all discussed in this section.

4.3.a Price Elasticity of Demand

As noted above, the quantity of a commodity demanded depends upon its price. It is of interest to measure the relative change in quantity demanded ensuing upon a given proportional change in price. This measure is called the price elasticity of demand, which is given by the following

Definition: The price elasticity of demand is the relative responsiveness of quantity demanded to changes in commodity price; in other words, price elasticity is the proportional change in quantity demanded divided by the proportional change in price.

The coefficient of price elasticity is usually denoted by the lowercase Greek eta (η); when there is any danger of misinterpreting the elasticity under consideration, direct price elasticity is denoted by η_{xx}.

Since quantity demanded and price vary inversely, a positive change in price will be accompanied by a negative change in quantity demanded. Thus, in order to make the coefficient of price elasticity positive, a "minus" sign is introduced into the formula:[4]

$$\eta_{xx} = -\frac{\Delta q}{q} \div \frac{\Delta p}{p} = -\frac{\Delta q}{\Delta p}\frac{p}{q}. \qquad (4.3.1)$$

Equation (4.3.1) gives the formula for what is called "point" price elasticity of demand. This means that the coefficient computed is valid for very small movements only.

As an example, suppose we have the following information:

Price	Quantity Demanded
$29.001 ($p_1$)	2,999 (q_1)
29.000 (p_2)	3,000 (q_2)

Obviously, $\Delta p = -\$0.001$ and $\Delta q = +1$. In the formula for point elasticity, one must also use p and q; but a question could arise: should one use p_1 and q_1 or p_2 *and* q_2? For very small changes such as these, it

---

[4] Let the demand curve for commodity i be

$$q_i = f(p_1, p_2, \ldots, p_n, M)$$

where q_i is the quantity demanded, p_j is the price of the jth commodity, M is income, and we assume there are n commodities. By definition, the direct or "own" price elasticity of demand is

$$\eta_{ii} = -\frac{\partial q_i}{\partial p_i}\frac{p_i}{q_i} = -\frac{\partial \log q_i}{\partial \log p_i}$$

where log denotes logarithms to the base e.

is immaterial—either may be used, so the point elasticity formula is applicable. This may readily be seen from the following calculations:

$$\eta = - \frac{\Delta q}{\Delta p} \frac{p_1}{q_1} = - \frac{+1}{-0.001} \frac{29.001}{2,999} = +9.67022 \,,$$

$$\eta = - \frac{\Delta q}{\Delta p} \frac{p_2}{q_2} = - \frac{+1}{-0.001} \frac{29.000}{3,000} = +9.66667 \,.$$

The difference in the two computed elasticities is very small, only 0.00355 in a magnitude exceeding 9. For such cases, point elasticity is the appropriate calculation.

In many cases, however, observed changes in price and quantity are much larger. For example, one might have the following data:

Price	Quantity Demanded
$0.60 ($p_1$)	400,000 (q_1)
0.50 (p_2)	800,000 (q_2)

Again, the "changes" are not questionable: $\Delta p = -0.10$ and $\Delta q = +400,000$. Now let us compute the coefficient of price elasticity. Using original price and quantity figures, one finds

$$\eta = - \frac{\Delta q}{\Delta p} \frac{p_1}{q_1} = - \frac{400,000}{-0.10} \frac{0.60}{400,000} = +6.0 \,.$$

When the new price-quantity figures are used, however, the coefficient is vastly different:

$$\eta = - \frac{\Delta q}{\Delta p} \frac{p_2}{q_2} = - \frac{400,000}{-0.10} \frac{0.50}{800,000} = +2.5 \,.$$

In this case, the two calculations do not yield sufficiently similar results and we need to establish a convention or standard procedure for calculating elasticity in such situations. The convention we shall employ is the following: When price and quantity changes are not "small," the price figure used in the elasticity formula shall be the *lesser* of the two prices and the quantity figure used shall be the *lesser* of the two quantities. Thus, in the current example, the calculated price elasticity would be

$$\eta = - \frac{400,000}{-0.10} \frac{0.50}{400,000} = +5.0 \,.$$

The advantages of using this convention will be explained in detail later in the chapter.[5]

---

[5] A much more common convention is to use the average of the two price figures and the average of the two quantity figures in the elasticity calculation. Using this convention, we get the so-called "arc elasticity"

4.3.b Coefficient of Price Elasticity

Demand is classified as price elastic, of unitary price elasticity, or as price inelastic depending upon the value of η. If $\eta > 1$, demand is said to be *elastic*—a given percentage change in price will result in a greater percentage change in quantity demanded. Thus small price changes will result in much more significant changes in quantity demanded.

When $\eta = 1$, demand has unit elasticity, meaning that the percentage changes in price and quantity demanded are precisely the same. Finally, if $\eta < 1$, demand is inelastic. A given percentage change in price results in a smaller percentage change in quantity demanded.

These relations may be summarized in the following

Definition: Commodity demand is elastic or inelastic according as the coefficient of price elasticity is greater than or less than unity. If the coefficient is exactly one, demand is said to have unitary price elasticity.

4.3.c Graphical Measurement of Point Elasticity

The elasticity at a given point on a demand curve has a simple interpretation and measurement that can be illustrated graphically. Consider Figure 4.3.1. The demand curve is DD', and the problem is to determine price elasticity of demand at the point E (where price is OP_1 and quantity demanded is OQ_1). First construct the line CEF tangent to DD' at the point E. Tangency means that CEF has the same slope as DD' at the point E. The slope of CEF is the change in price divided by the change in quantity, and the inverse of this magnitude is hence the value $\Delta q/\Delta p$ for a small (infinitesmal) change in p at point E on DD'. The slope of CEF is simply $-CP_1/OQ_1$, so at point E,

$$-\frac{\Delta q}{\Delta p} = \frac{OQ_1}{CP_1}.$$

The price at E divided by the quantity demanded at E is OP_1/OQ_1, so the point elasticity at E is

$$\eta = -\frac{\Delta q}{\Delta p}\frac{p}{q} = \frac{OQ_1}{CP_1}\frac{OP_1}{OQ_1} = \frac{OP_1}{CP_1}. \tag{4.3.2}$$

$$\eta = -\frac{\Delta q}{\Delta p}\frac{\left(\dfrac{p_1 + p_2}{2}\right)}{\left(\dfrac{q_1 + q_2}{2}\right)} = -\frac{\Delta q}{\Delta p}\frac{(p_1 + p_2)}{(q_2 + q_1)}.$$

The convention used in the text has some distinct advantages over this more common usage as we shall see later.

FIGURE 4.3.1

Computation of Point Elasticity

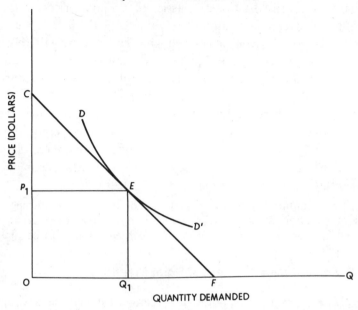

Since P_1CE, Q_1EF, and OCF are similar right triangles it can be seen that equivalent measures of the point elasticity at E are given by

$$\eta = \frac{FQ_1}{OQ_1}$$

and

$$\eta = \frac{EF}{CE}. \qquad (4.3.3)$$

Utilizing formula (4.3.3), it is easy to determine the ranges of demand elasticity for a linear demand curve. In Figure 4.3.2, DD' is a linear demand curve. Notice first from formula (4.3.3) that demand has unitary elasticity when $EF = CE$. Thus locate a point P on DD' such that $DP = PD'$. At this point, demand has unitary price elasticity, or $\eta = 1$. Next, consider *any* point to the left of P, such as P_1. At P_1, $\eta = (P_1D'/DP_1) > 1$. Thus for a linear demand curve, the coefficient of price elasticity is greater than unity at any point to the left of the midpoint on the demand curve. Demand is elastic in this region. Finally, at any point to the right of P, say P_2, the coefficient of price elasticity is $\eta = (P_2D'/DP_2) < 1$. Over this range, demand is inelastic.

FIGURE 4.3.2

Ranges of Demand Elasticity for Linear Demand Curve

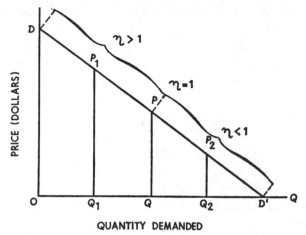

QUANTITY DEMANDED

These results may be summarized as follows:

Relations: Given any point *E* on a demand curve, construct the straight-line tangent to the curve at *E*. Call this line *CEF*. The coefficient of price elasticity at the point *E* is *EF/CE*. Furthermore, for a linear demand function: (*a*) demand is elastic at higher prices, (*b*) has unit elasticity at the midpoint of the demand curve, and (*c*) is inelastic at lower prices. Thus in case of linear demand, elasticity declines as one moves downward along the curve.

4.3.d Factors Affecting Price Elasticity

Whether demand is elastic or inelastic is an important consideration, especially for government policy in individual commodity markets. For example, suppose the demand for wheat were highly price elastic. An increase in the price of wheat would accordingly result in a proportionately greater reduction in quantity demanded. Total dollar expenditures on wheat would decline. Now suppose the government establishes a minimum wheat price above the market equilibrium price. Wheat sales would be reduced, and so too would farmers' incomes, unless the price support were accompanied by a minimum-sales guarantee.

This is but one example; a large book could be filled with similar ones. The policy importance of price elasticity has led to many statistical studies designed to estimate numerical values of price elasticity. Table 4.3.1 reproduces some of these estimates.

As you see from the table, price elasticities range quite widely. Two basic factors determine elasticity: availability of substitute goods and the number of uses to which a good may be put. These factors go a long way toward explaining the variations observed in Table 4.3.1.

The more and better the substitutes for a specific good the greater its price elasticity will tend to be. Goods with few and poor substitutes —wheat and salt, for example—will always tend to have low price elasticities. Goods with many substitutes—wool, for which cotton and man-made fibers may be substituted, for instance—will have higher elasticities.

Similarly, the greater the number of possible uses of a commodity the greater its price elasticity will be. Thus a commodity such as wool— which can be used in producing clothing, carpeting, upholstery, draperies and tapestries, and so on—will tend to have a higher price elasticity than a commodity with only one or a very few uses—butter, for example.

TABLE 4.3.1
Estimated Price Elasticity of Demand of Selected Commodities

Commodity	Elasticity Coefficient	Authority
Agricultural products at the farm level:		
Corn	0.77	Schultz
Cotton	0.51	"
Hay	0.78	"
Wheat	0.03	"
Potatoes	0.69	"
Oats	0.54	"
Barley	0.17	"
Buckwheat	1.50	"
Food:		
Beef	0.50	Wold
Pork	0.45	"
Butter	0.70	"
Milk	0.31	"
Goods other than food:		
Raw apparel wool	1.32	Ferguson
Furniture	3.04	Stone
Air transportation	1.10	Frisch

SOURCES: Henry Schultz, *The Theory and Measurement of Demand* (Chicago: University of Chicago Press, 1938); Herman Wold, *Demand Analysis* (New York: John Wiley & Sons, Inc., 1953); C. E. Ferguson and Metodey Polasek, "The Elasticity of Import Demand for Raw Apparel Wool in the United States," *Econometrica*, vol. 30 (1962), pp. 670–99; Richard Stone and D. A. Rowe, "The Durability of Consumers' Durable Goods," *Econometrica*, vol. 28 (1960), pp. 407–16; Ragnar Frisch, "A Complete Scheme for Computing All Direct Cross Demand Elasticities in a Model with Many Sectors," *Econometrica*, vol. 27 (1959), pp. 177–96.

4.3.e Price Cross-Elasticity of Demand

The measurement of price cross-elasticity of demand has been discussed in connection with the definition of substitute and complementary goods (Chapter 3, subsection 3.4.a). The definition is repeated at this point.

Definition: The price cross-elasticity of demand measures the relative responsiveness of quantity demanded of a given commodity to changes in the price of a related commodity. In other words, it is the proportional change in the quantity demanded of good X divided by the proportional change in the price of good Y.

Using this definition, the coefficient of price cross-elasticity of demand is defined as

$$\eta_{xy} = \frac{\Delta q_x}{q_x} \div \frac{\Delta p_y}{p_y} = \frac{\Delta q_x}{\Delta p_y} \frac{p_y}{q_x} . \qquad (4.3.4)$$

As you will recall, goods may be classified as substitutes or complements according as $\eta_{xy} \gtrless 0$.

The interrelations of demand have been investigated in some statistical studies. Schultz tested cross-elasticity for many agricultural commodities and found both substitute and complementary relations.[6] Unfortunately, he did not express his results in terms of price cross-elasticities. Various writers have provided estimates of price cross-elasticity, however. A few illustrative coefficients, taken from Wold, are presented in Table 4.3.2.

All the measured relations in Table 4.3.2 show the commodities to be substitute goods. In some cases the commodities are quite competi-

TABLE 4.3.2
Coefficients of Price Cross-Elastictiy of Demand

Commodity	Cross-Elasticity with Respect to Price of—	Coefficient of Price Cross-Elasticity
Beef............................	Pork	+0.28
Pork............................	Beef	+0.14
Butter..........................	Margarine	+0.67
Margarine......................	Butter	+0.81
Flour...........................	All animal foods	+0.56

SOURCE: Herman Wold, *Demand Analysis* (New York, John Wiley & Sons, Inc., 1953).

---

[6] Henry Schultz, *The Theory and Measurement of Demand* (Chicago: University of Chicago Press, 1938).

tive (butter and margarine), while in other cases the relation is relatively weak.

4.3.f Income Elasticity of Demand

The purchases of certain commodities are very sensitive to changes in nominal and real money income. Thus it is sometimes desirable to relax the assumption that money income is held constant. In a simple case, the demand function can then be written as

$$q = f(p, M), \tag{4.3.5}$$

where M is money income. Following the concepts of elasticity already developed, the income elasticity of demand is given by the following

Definition: The income elasticity of demand is the relative responsiveness of quantity demanded to changes in income. In other words, it is the proportional change in quantity demanded divided by the proportional change in nominal income.

Symbolically,

$$\eta_M = \frac{\Delta q}{q} \div \frac{\Delta M}{M} = \frac{\Delta q}{\Delta M} \frac{M}{q}. \tag{4.3.6}$$

Certain writers have suggested that commodities can be classified as "necessities" and "luxuries" on the basis of income elasticity. If income elasticity is very low (certainly less than one), quantity demanded is not very responsive to changes in income. Consumption remains about the same irrespective of income level. This suggests that the commodity in question is a "necessity." On the other hand, an income elasticity greater than one indicates that the commodity is more or less a luxury. Indeed, certain empirical "laws of consumption" were developed in the 19th century by the German statistician Christian Lorenz Ernst Engel. According to Engel, the income elasticity of demand for food is very low; those for clothing and shelter are about unity; while recreation, medical care, and other "luxury" goods have income elasticities in excess of unity. Therefore, according to Engel, the percentage of income spent on food by a family or a nation is a very good index of welfare—the poorer a family or a nation, the larger the percentage of expenditure that must go for food.

The latter generalization is somewhat crude; nonetheless, it does provide a rough measure of welfare. Some of Engel's specific statements regarding income elasticity, however, presumably no longer hold, as may be seen from the selected estimates of income elasticity presented in Table 4.3.3. Margarine and wheat flour have negative income

TABLE 4.3.3

Income Elasticity of Demand for Selected Commodities

Commodity	Estimated Income Elasticity of Demand	Authority
Milk and cream	0.07	Wold
Cream only	0.56	"
Butter	0.42	"
Margarine	−0.20	"
Cheese	0.34	"
Eggs	0.37	"
Meat	0.35	"
Flour	−0.36	"
Fruits and berries	0.70	"
Liquors	1.00	"
Tobacco	1.02	"
Restaurant consumption	1.48	"
Housing	0.38	Leser
Clothing	2.01	"
Durable goods (consumer)	2.90	"
Household goods	1.54	"

SOURCE: Herman Wold, *Demand Analysis* (New York: John Wiley & Sons, Inc., 1953); C. E. V. Leser, "Commodity Group Expenditure Functions for the United Kingdom, 1948–1957," *Econometrica*, vol. 29 (1961), pp. 24–32.

elasticities, indicating that the consumption of these goods declines as family income increases. This implies that they are inferior goods, because the latter is indicated by a negative income effect ensuing upon a price change.

4.4 MARGINAL REVENUE

Having developed the concept of market demand and of its price, cross, and income elasticities, our attention can be directed to a closely related concept: marginal revenue.

The market demand curve shows for each specific price the quantity of the commodity that buyers will take. For example, consider Figure 4.4.1. At the price *OP* per unit, *OQ* units are demanded and sold. From the standpoint of sellers, *OP* × *OQ,* or price times sales, is the *total revenue* obtainable when a price of *OP* per unit is charged. Thus total revenue is the area of the rectangle *OPRQ* in Figure 4.4.1.

Of perhaps greater importance than total revenue is the variation

FIGURE 4.4.1

The Measurement of Total Revenue

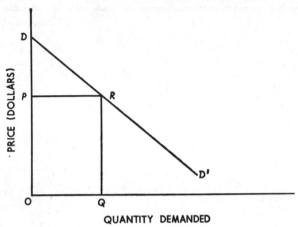

in total revenue incident to an expansion or contraction of sales. In the now familiar terminology of economics, this is called *marginal revenue.*

Definition: Marginal revenue is the change in total revenue attributable to a one-unit change in output. Marginal revenue is calculated by dividing the change in total revenue by the change in output.

4.4.a Calculation of Marginal Revenue

Consider carefully the definition of marginal revenue (MR); namely, the change in total revenue (TR) attributable to a one-unit change in output. For the first unit sold, total, average, and marginal revenue are identical; for a quantity sold of one, each is precisely equal to price. To expand sales to the rate of two units per period of time, price must be reduced. The marginal revenue of the second unit is equal to total revenue from the sale of two units *minus* total revenue from the sale of one unit. It follows, therefore, since $MR = TR$ for one unit, that TR for two units $= MR$ for one unit $+ MR$ for two units. Generalizing, total revenue is the sum of all marginal revenue figures. This point is illustrated by the hypothetical data presented in Table 4.4.1 and graphed in Figure 4.4.2.[7]

[7] The graph in Figure 4.4.2 contains a slight inaccuracy that may trouble the mathematically trained student. The example upon which the graph is based contains discrete data. The TR curve is obtained by plotting the points and connecting them by straight-line segments. The D and MR curves are obtained in the same manner. But here is where the inconsistency enters. Over any range of values for which total

TABLE 4.4.1

Demand, Total Revenue, and Marginal Revenue

Price	Quantity	Total Revenue	Marginal Revenue	Sum of MR Entries
$11	0	$ 0	—	—
10	1	10	$10	$10
9	2	18	8	18
8	3	24	6	24
7	4	28	4	28
6	5	30	2	30
5	6	30	0	30
4	7	28	−2	28
3	8	24	−4	24
2	9	18	−6	18
1	10	10	−8	10

The first two columns of this table contain price and quantity figures —the ingredients determining the demand curve (D) in Figure 4.4.2. The third column shows total revenue, the product of the corresponding entries in columns 1 and 2. The data in this column give rise to the TR curve in the figure. Column 4 contains the figures for marginal revenue calculated, according to the definition, as

$$MR_1 = \Delta TR_1 = TR_1 - TR_0 ,$$
$$MR_2 = \Delta TR_2 = TR_2 - TR_1 ,$$
$$\cdot \quad \cdot \quad \cdot \quad \cdot \quad \cdot \quad \cdot \quad \cdot$$
$$MR_{10} = \Delta TR_{10} = TR_{10} - TR_9 .$$

The final column is a check calculation to show that the sum of marginal revenue figures equals the associated total revenue. Using the notation employed above:

$$TR_1 = MR_1 ,$$
$$TR_2 = MR_1 + MR_2 ,$$
$$\cdot \quad \cdot \quad \cdot \quad \cdot \quad \cdot \quad \cdot \quad \cdot \quad \cdot \quad \cdot$$
$$TR_{10} = MR_1 + MR_2 + \cdots + MR_{10} .$$

This relation enters in an important way in the following subsection.

The data for marginal revenue are plotted in Figure 4.4.2 as the curve labeled MR. This curve has two crucial features. First, at the

---

revenue is linear, marginal revenue is constant; and when marginal revenue is constant, so too is the demand function. To be exactly correct, the D and MR curves should be drawn as step-decreasing functions rather than as continuous functions with continuous first derivatives. However, the example is *merely illustrative;* and it seems better to illustrate a more general situation.

FIGURE 4.4.2

Graph of Hypothetical Data in Table 4.4.1

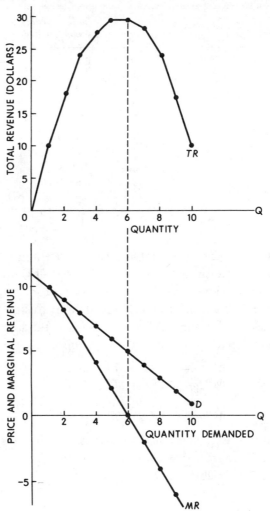

"outset" marginal revenue equals demand or average revenue. In this discrete example, $D = MR$ at quantity one and price $10. In a continuous case, the two are equal infinitesimally close to the vertical axis. Second, $MR = 0$ when total revenue is at its maximum. When marginal revenue is *positive,* total revenue increases; and when marginal revenue is *negative,* total revenue declines. Naturally enough, when the *addition* to total revenue is zero, total revenue must be at its maximum.

4.4.b The Geometry of Marginal Revenue Determination

Demand curves slope downward; and because of this, we know that an increase in quantity will be accompanied by a decrease in price. With this in mind, we can think of the revenue effect of an output increase in two parts. Suppose output increases by Δq and let $-b$ be the reduction in price per unit increase in output (i.e., let $-b = \Delta p / \Delta q$). Using this notation, the additional quantity sold yields a gain in revenue of

$$(p - b\Delta q)\Delta q \qquad (4.4.1)$$

where $(4.4.1)$ is the increase in output Δq multiplied by the new price $p - b\Delta q$. Because price has decreased there is also a revenue loss since all the earlier units are now sold at the new (lower) price. This revenue loss is the change in price multiplied by the old output or

$$[(p - b\Delta q) - p]q = -bq\Delta q . \qquad (4.4.2)$$

The net change in total revenue is the sum of these two changes or

$$p\Delta q - bq\Delta q - b(\Delta q)^2 . \qquad (4.4.3)$$

If Δq is very small, the term $-b(\Delta q)^2$ in $(4.4.3)$ is of "second-order" smallness and can be ignored. The change in revenue is then

$$\Delta TR = p\Delta q - bq\Delta q .$$

Marginal revenue is this change divided by the change in output Δq or

$$MR = \frac{\Delta TR}{\Delta q} = p - bq . \qquad (4.4.4)$$

This result can be illustrated geometrically as in Figure 4.4.3. Consider the point E on the demand curve DD'. The line UET is tangent to DD' at E. UET has slope $-b$ because it represents the decrease in price caused by a small increase in output in the neighborhood of E. If we shift this tangent line down until it intersects the price axis at point p, the distance ES along the line Eq must be the loss in revenue $-bq$ since it is the slope of UET times q.[8] Eq is simply the price p, so the distance qS ($= Eq - ES$) is the marginal revenue associated with a small increase in output at the point E on the demand curve.

---

[8] Note that (ignoring sign) $b = ES/pE$ and $q = pE$ so

$$bq = \left(\frac{ES}{pE}\right)pE = ES .$$

FIGURE 4.4.3

The Geometry of Marginal Revenue

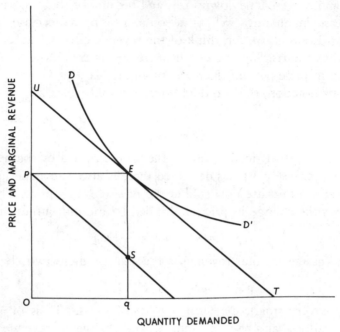

This technique can be used to trace out the entire marginal revenue curve.

When the demand curve is linear, the marginal revenue curve has a particularly simple algebraic form. Let the demand curve be represented by the linear expression[9]

$$p = a - bq .$$

The slope of this demand curve is clearly $-b$, so using (4.4.4) the marginal revenue curve is

$$MR = p - bq = a - 2bq . \tag{4.4.5}$$

Expression (4.4.5) says that when the demand curve is linear with intercept (on the price axis) a and slope $-b$, the marginal revenue curve is also linear with the same intercept and with twice as large a slope. A linear demand curve and its marginal revenue curve are shown in Figure 4.4.4.

Equation (4.4.5) suggests an alternative, and often easier way, to

---

[9] Actually this is the "inverse" demand curve of the linear demand curve

$$q = \frac{a}{b} - \frac{p}{b} .$$

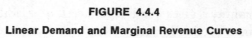

FIGURE 4.4.4

Linear Demand and Marginal Revenue Curves

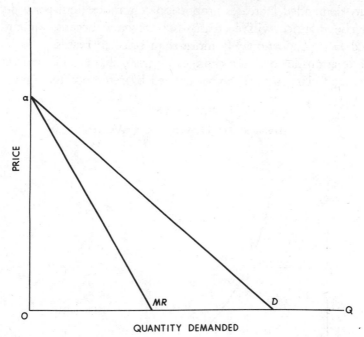

QUANTITY DEMANDED

construct marginal revenue curves. For example, in Figure 4.4.3 to find the marginal revenue at E first extend the tangent line at E until it intersects the price axis. Next drop the perpendiculars pE and Eq from E to the price and quantity axes. Divide the perpendicular pE in half and draw a straight line through U and the midpoint of pE. This line will intersect Eq at the marginal revenue point S.

4.5 DEMAND, REVENUE, AND ELASTICITY

After studying sections 4.3 and 4.4, you should be aware of a close relation between price elasticity of demand and the revenue function. Two types of relations are developed in this section.

4.5.a Elasticity and Total Revenue

If demand is elastic—that is, the coefficient of price elasticity exceeds unity—a decline in price will result in a proportionately greater expansion of quantity demanded and a rise in price will result in a proportionately greater decline in quantity demanded. Now, since "price times quantity" gives total revenue, it is readily seen that if demand is elastic a decline in price will increase total revenue because quantity demanded increases proportionately more than price declines, and a rise in price will decrease total revenue because quantity demanded falls proportionately more than price increases.

The relationship between changes in price, changes in total revenue, and demand elasticity can be formalized by reference to Figure 4.5.1.

FIGURE 4.5.1

Demand, Total Revenue, and Elasticity

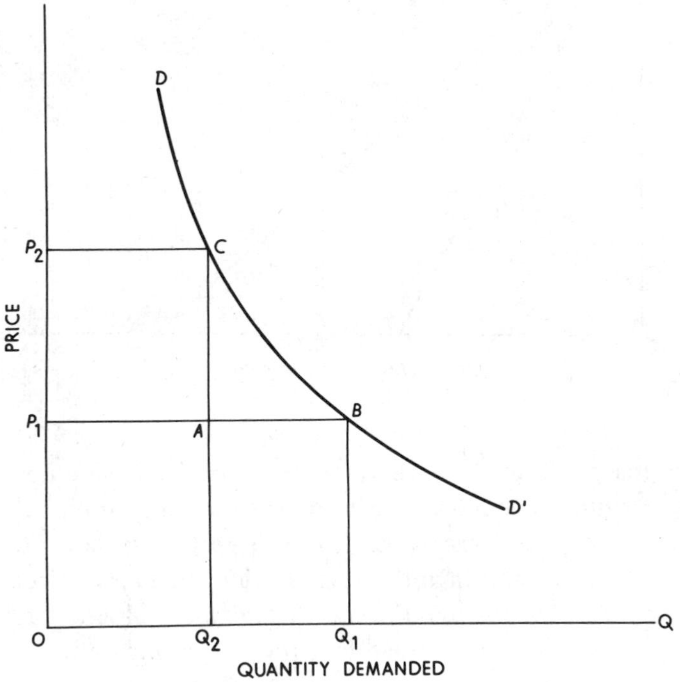

Suppose, initially, the price is OP_1 and quantity demanded is OQ_1. The total revenue is then the rectangle OP_1BQ_1. If price increases to P_2, quantity demand decreases to Q_2 and total revenue is the rectangle OP_2CQ_2. The change in total revenue is the difference in the areas of these two rectangles. The rectangle OP_1AQ_2 is common to both of these rectangles, so the change in total revenue is also given by the difference in the areas of the rectangles P_1P_2CA and Q_2ABQ_1. Let p_1 be the length of OP_1, let p_2 be the length of OP_2, let q_1 be the length of OQ_1 and let q_2 be the length of OQ_2.[10] The change in price is

---

[10] The lowercase letters are thus the numerical values of price and quantity.

$\Delta p = p_2 - p_1$, and the change in quantity is $\Delta q = q_2 - q_1$. Using this notation, the change in total revenue is

$$\Delta TR = q_2(p_2 - p_1) - p_1(q_1 - q_2)$$
$$= q_2 \Delta p + p_1 \Delta q . \tag{4.5.1}$$

Equation (4.5.1) can be written

$$\Delta TR = q_2 \Delta p \left(1 + \frac{p_1}{q_2} \frac{\Delta q}{\Delta p}\right) . \tag{4.5.2}$$

Notice that p_1 is the smaller of the two prices and q_2 is the smaller of the two quantities, so by our convention for computing elasticity,

$$-\eta = \frac{p_1}{q_2} \frac{\Delta q}{\Delta p} . \tag{4.5.3}$$

Substituting (4.5.3) in (4.5.2) we obtain

$$\Delta TR = q_2 \Delta p (1 - \eta) . \tag{4.5.4}$$

Here we see the advantage of the rule for computing elasticity that was introduced in subsection 4.3.a. By using the smaller price and smaller quantity in computing elasticity, we get an *exact* relationship between elasticity and the change in total revenue in (4.5.4).

From (4.5.4) we see that if elasticity is unity ($\eta = 1$), the price change does not cause a change in total revenue. This is because the proportional change in price is exactly offset by the proportional change in quantity. If demand is inelastic ($\eta < 1$), then total revenue rises when price rises ($\Delta p > 0$) and total revenue falls when price falls ($\Delta p < 0$). If demand is elastic ($\eta > 1$), then total revenue falls when price rises and total revenue rises when price falls.

Briefly, the results of this section may be summarized as follows.

Relations: When demand has unit elasticity, total revenue is not affected by changes in price. If demand is elastic, total revenue varies inversely with price; if demand is inelastic, total revenue varies directly with price.

These relations are given more explicitly in Table 4.5.1.

TABLE 4.5.1

Relations between Price Elasticity and Total Revenue

	Elastic Demand	Unitary Elasticity	Inelastic Demand
Price rises...............	TR falls	No change	TR rises
Price falls...............	TR rises	No change	TR falls

4.5.b Elasticity and Marginal Revenue

Since elasticity is related to total revenue it is necessarily related to marginal revenue as well. The precise relation follows from a comparison of Figure 4.4.2 and Table 4.5.1.

To review the important content of Figure 4.4.2, when total revenue rises, marginal revenue is positive; when total revenue declines, marginal revenue is negative; when total revenue is constant, marginal revenue is zero. Notice that marginal revenue is zero when total revenue is at its maximum point. On the basis of these relations, we are able to construct Table 4.5.2, which is very similar to Table 4.5.1 on page 113.

TABLE 4.5.2

**Relation between Marginal Revenue
and Price Elasticity of Demand**

Marginal Revenue Positive	*Marginal Revenue Zero*	*Marginal Revenue Negative*
Elastic demand	Unitary elasticity	Inelastic demand

An algebraic relationship among price, marginal revenue, and the coefficient of elasticity can be derived from equation (4.5.1). Note that equation (4.5.1) can be written

$$\Delta TR = p_1 \Delta q \left(1 + \frac{q_2}{p_1} \frac{\Delta p}{\Delta q} \right). \tag{4.5.5}$$

By our rule for calculating the coefficient of elasticity,

$$-\frac{1}{n} = \frac{q_2}{p_1} \frac{\Delta p}{\Delta q}. \tag{4.5.6}$$

Substituting (4.5.6) in (4.5.5) and dividing by Δq we obtain

$$MR = \frac{\Delta TR}{\Delta a} = p_1 \left(1 - \frac{1}{n} \right) \tag{4.5.7}$$

which is a precise relationship among price, the coefficient of elasticity, and marginal revenue. The relations between marginal revenue and elasticity described in Table 4.5.2 are seen to follow directly from equation (4.5.7).[11]

4.5.c Demand Curve for a Firm in Perfect Competition

All the relations thus far developed can be used to describe the demand curve facing an individual producer in a perfectly competitive market.

Suppose that panel a, Figure 4.5.2, depicts the equilibrium of a market in which there are a large number of sellers, each of approximately the same size. *DD'* and *SS'* are the market demand and market supply curves. Their intersection determines the equilibrium price *OP* and quantity demanded $O\overline{Q}$.

Let us now be more specific and stipulate that there are 25,000 sellers (say, wheat farmers) of approximately the same size in the market. If any one seller increases his output and sales by 100 percent, the total market sales will increase by only $\frac{1}{250}$ of 1 percent. Such a change is both graphically and *economically* so small as to have an imperceptible influence on price. Thus each individual seller may assume with confidence that variations in his *own* output and sales will have a negligible effect upon market price. Concerted action by a large number of sellers can influence market price; but one seller acting alone cannot. The individual seller may therefore assume that the demand curve facing *him* is a horizontal line at the level of price established by demand and supply equilibrium in the market.

The demand curve for a perfectly competitive producer is shown in panel b, Figure 4.5.2. The shape of the curve shows that the producer believes changes in his volume of output will have no perceptible effect upon market price. And if the producer is in fact in a perfectly competitive market, his belief is well founded. A change in his rate of

---

[11] This result holds for a differentiable demand function. By definition $TR = pq$ and $MR = dTR/dq$ where

$$\frac{dTR}{dq} = p + q\frac{dp}{dq} = p\left(1 + \frac{q}{p}\frac{dp}{dq}\right) = p\left(1 - \frac{1}{\eta}\right)$$

where η is the point elasticity

$$\eta = -\frac{dq}{dp}\frac{p}{q}.$$

FIGURE 4.5.2

Derivation of Demand for a Perfectly Competitive Firm

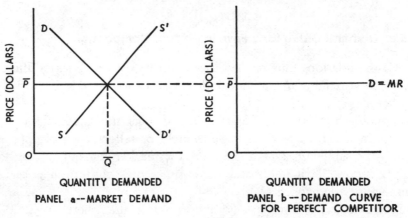

PANEL a--MARKET DEMAND

PANEL b -- DEMAND CURVE
FOR PERFECT COMPETITOR

sales per period of time will change his total revenue, but it will not affect market price.[12]

The producer in a perfectly competitive market, therefore, does not have to reduce his price in order to expand his rate of sales. Any number of units per period of time can be sold at the market equilibrium price. If he were to charge a higher price, he could sell nothing. A lower price would result in a needless loss of revenue. He thus charges the market price for whatever quantity he wishes to produce and sell.

Since price remains constant, each additional unit sold increases total revenue by its (constant) price. In this special case, therefore, price and marginal revenue are equal at every level of sales. Therefore, the demand curve and the marginal revenue curve are identical for a producer in a perfectly competitive market. For this reason, the curve in panel b is labeled $D = MR$.

When the demand curve is horizontal, demand is said to be perfectly elastic, meaning that the coefficient of price elasticity increases without bound as the percentage change in price becomes smaller and smaller. Take a numerical example. Suppose the market equilibrium price is $5 and a particular producer is selling 1,000 units at that price. If he increased his price to $5.01, his sales would fall to zero. Thus

---

[12] The rationale used here to argue that each producer has no effect on market price is commonly employed for expository convenience. Under certain reasonable conditions, in a general equilibrium context, the absence of the individual producer's influence on market price is not simply a close approximation, it is literally true. The details of the argument can be found in E. Fama and A. Laffer, "The Number of Firms and Competition," *American Economic Review*, vol. 63 (1972), pp. 670–74.

$$\frac{\Delta q}{q} = \frac{-1000}{1000} \quad \text{and} \quad \frac{\Delta p}{p} = \frac{1}{500}.$$

The coefficient of price elasticity would be

$$n = -\frac{\Delta q}{q} \div \frac{\Delta p}{p} = 1 \div \frac{1}{500} = 500.$$

If he increased the price to only $5.001, his sales would also fall to zero and η would be 5,000. Thus one generalizes by saying that for infinitesimally small price changes the coefficient of price elasticity approaches infinity under conditions of perfect competition.

The results of this section may be summarized as follows:

Relations: The demand for a producer in a perfectly competitive market is a horizontal line at the level of the market equilibrium price. The output decisions of the seller do not affect market price. In this case, the demand and marginal revenue curves are identical; demand is perfectly elastic and the coefficient of price elasticity approaches infinity.

QUESTIONS AND EXERCISES

1. The following table gives hypothetical data for a consumer. Compute all meaningful elasticity coefficients (price, cross, and income). Remember that income must be constant when price elasticities are computed, and prices must be constant when income elasticity is computed.

Year	Price of X	Quantity Purchased	Income	Price of Y
1..........	$1.00	100	$5,000	$0.50
2..........	1.01	95	5,000	0.50
3..........	1.01	100	5,500	0.51
4..........	1.01	105	5,500	0.52
5..........	1.00	100	5,500	0.50
6..........	1.00	105	5,500	0.51
7..........	1.00	100	5,000	0.51
8..........	1.02	105	5,500	0.51
9..........	1.02	95	5,500	0.50
10..........	1.03	90	5,500	0.50
11..........	1.03	100	6,500	0.51
12..........	1.03	105	7,000	0.51

2. The following table gives hypothetical data for market demand. Compute total revenue, marginal revenue, and the price elasticity of demand on a separate sheet. Plot the demand, total revenue, and marginal revenue curves.

Price	Quantity Demanded	Price	Quantity Demanded
$70.00	1	$23.33	7
50.00	2	20.00	8
40.00	3	17.50	9
35.00	4	15.00	10
30.00	5	12.50	11
26.67	6	10.00	12

3. Answer "true," "false," or "uncertain," and give a defense of your answer:

   a. If the income elasticity of demand for a commodity exceeds one, the relative price of that commodity will rise as real per capita income increases, that is, will rise relative to the goods whose income elasticity is less than one.

   b. If the utility of each good is independent of the quantities of all other goods consumed, then all goods must have positive income elasticities (i.e., all goods are normal goods).

   c. If total consumer expenditures are the same before and after a tax, then an excise tax on a consumer good with elastic demand will lead to an increase in consumption spending on other consumer goods, while an excise tax on a good whose demand is inelastic will lead to a decrease in consumption spending on other goods.

   d. An individual spends all his income on two goods, x and y. He spends one fourth of his income on good x, and the income elasticity for this good is 5. Thus, good y is now an inferior good to him. (Additional exercise: Determine the exact income elasticity for y)

   e. If each of 100 buyers has an elasticity of demand for a commodity equal to 3, then the elasticity of demand by the 100 buyers taken together is 0.03.

   f. Two consumers each buy positive amounts of commodities x and y at given market prices. In equilibrium they will have the same marginal rate of substitution between goods x and y even if they consume different amounts of these goods.

4. If half of the total quantity demanded of a good is purchased by 75 consumers each of whom has demand elasticity of 2 and the other half is purchased by 25 consumers each of whom has demand elasticity of 3, what is the elasticity of the 100 buyers taken together?

5. An individual spends all his income on two goods, x and y. If a $2 increase in the price of x does not change the amount consumed of y, what is the price elasticity of good x?

6. The following statement is taken from the *Wall Street Journal*, March 30, 1966: "A retired Atlanta railroad conductor complains that he can

no longer visit his neighborhood tavern six times a week. Since the price of his favorite beer went up to 30 cents a glass from 25 cents, he has been dropping in only five times a week." Assuming the man in question consumed the same amount of beer *per visit* before and after the price change, calculate the elasticity of his demand for tavern-dispensed beer.

7. "The experience with rail passenger transport indicates that traffic is negatively related to income—the richer one gets, the less he wants of the rails. For the trains that have survived, a mixture of the aged and low-income groups is the ideal combination; not surprisingly, the patronage on East Coast–Florida trains holds up better than on almost any others. The Illinois Central's *City of New Orleans,* running the length of Mississippi, is typically one of the strongest trains in the country, and passenger service in prosperous California is sick unto the death." (G. W. Hilton, "What Went Wrong," *Trains,* vol. 27 [January, 1967], p. 39.)

   a. From this statement, what can you say about the income elasticity of demand for rail passenger service? What type of good is rail passenger service?

   b. If (say) the Grand Trunk Western lowers its passenger fares, can you say anything about the income and substitution effects?

   c. Suppose a person gets a salary increase and accordingly uses the trains less. Using his indifference curves, show this response to his increased income.

SUGGESTED READINGS

Marshall, Alfred. *Principles of Economics,* pp. 92–113. 8th ed. New York: The Macmillan Co., 1920.

Robinson, Joan. *The Economics of Imperfect Competition,* pp. 29–40. London: Macmillan & Co., Ltd., 1933.

Advanced reading,
part I

I. THEORY OF CONSUMER BEHAVIOR, GENERAL

Georgescu-Roegen, Nicholas. "The Pure Theory of Consumer Behavior," *Quarterly Journal of Economics,* vol. 50 (1935–36), pp. 545–93.

Hicks, John R. *Value and Capital,* pp. 11–41, 305–11. 2d ed. Oxford: Clarendon Press, 1946.

Hotelling, Harold. "Edgeworth's Taxation Paradox and the Nature of Demand and Supply Functions," *Journal of Political Economy,* vol. 40 (1932), pp. 577–616.

———. "Demand Functions with Limited Budgets," *Econometrica,* vol. 3 (1935), pp. 66–78.

Samuelson, Paul A. *Foundations of Economic Analysis,* pp. 90–117. Cambridge, Mass.: Harvard University Press, 1947.

Schultz, Henry. *The Theory and Measurement of Demand,* pp. 5–58. Chicago: University of Chicago Press, 1938.

Wold, Herman O. A., with Jureen, Lars. *Demand Analysis,* pp. 81–139. New York: John Wiley & Sons, Inc., 1953.

II. COMPLEMENTARITY AND RELATED GOODS

Ferguson, C. E. "Substitution Effect in Value Theory: A Pedagogical Note," *Southern Economic Journal,* vol. 26 (1960), pp. 310–14.

Georgescu-Roegen, Nicholas. "A Diagrammatic Analysis of Complementarity," *Southern Economic Journal,* vol. 14 (1952), pp. 1–20.

Hicks, John R. *Value and Capital,* pp. 42–52, 311–14, 2d ed. Oxford: Clarendon Press, 1946.

Ichimura, S. "A Critical Note on the Definition of Related Goods," *Review of Economic Studies,* vol. 18 (1950–51), pp. 179–83.

Morishima, M. "A Note on Definitions of Related Goods," *Review of Economic Studies,* vol. 23 (1955–56), pp. 132–34.

Samuelson, Paul A. *Foundations of Economic Analysis,* pp. 183–89. Cambridge, Mass.: Harvard University Press, 1947.

Schultz, Henry. *The Theory and Measurement of Demand,* pp. 569–85, 607–28. Chicago: University of Chicago Press, 1938.

III. SPECIAL TOPICS IN DEMAND THEORY

A. Income-Compensated Demand Curves

Bailey, Martin J. "The Marshallian Demand Curve," *Journal of Political Economy,* vol. 42 (1954), pp. 255–61.

Friedman, Milton. "The Marshallian Demand Curve," *Journal of Political Economy,* vol. 57 (1949), pp. 463–95.

Knight, Frank H. "Realism and Relevance in the Theory of Demand," *Journal of Political Economy,* vol. 52 (1944), pp. 289–318.

Yeager, Leland B. *"Methodenstreit* over Demand Curves," *Journal of Political Economy,* vol. 48 (1960), pp. 53–64.

B. Revealed Preference and Index Numbers

Frisch, Ragnar. "Annual Survey of General Economic Theory: The Problem of Index Numbers," *Econometrica,* vol. 4 (1936), pp. 1–38.

Georgescu-Roegen, Nicholas. "Choice and Revealed Preference," *Southern Economic Journal,* vol. 21 (1954), pp. 119–30.

Hicks, John R. *A Revision of Demand Theory.* Oxford: Clarendon Press, 1956.

Houthakker, H. S. "Revealed Preference and the Utility Function," *Economica,* N.S. vol. 17 (1950), pp. 159–74.

Samuelson, Paul A. "A Note on the Pure Theory of Consumer Behavior," *Economica,* N.S. vol. 5 (1938), pp. 61–71.

————. *Foundations of Economic Analysis,* pp. 144–63. Cambridge, Mass.: Harvard University Press, 1947.

Staehle, Hans. "A Development of the Economic Theory of Price Index Numbers," *Review of Economic Studies,* vol. 2 (1935), pp. 163–88.

C. Cardinal Utility of Analysis of Choice under Risk

Alchian, A. A. "The Meaning of Utility Measurement," *American Economic Review,* vol. 42 (1953), pp. 26–50.

Baumol, W. J. "The Neumann-Morgenstern Utility Index—An Ordinalist View," *Journal of Political Economy,* vol. 59 (1951), pp. 61–66.

————. "The Cardinal Utility Which Is Ordinal," *Economic Journal,* vol. 67 (1958), pp. 665–72.

Ferguson, C. E. "An Essay on Cardinal Utility," *Southern Economic Journal,* vol. 25 (1958), pp. 11–23.

Friedman, Milton, and Savage, L. J. "The Utility Analysis of Choices Involving Risk," *Journal of Political Economy,* vol. 56 (1948), pp. 279–304.

————, and Savage, L. J. "The Expected-Utility Hypothesis and the Measurability of Utility," *Journal of Political Economy,* vol. 60 (1952), pp. 463–74.

Georgescu-Roegen, Nicholas. "Choice, Expectations and Measurability," *Quarterly Journal of Economics,* vol. 68 (1954), pp. 503–34.

Markowitz, Harry. "The Utility of Wealth," *Journal of Political Economy,* vol. 60 (1952), pp. 151–58.

Ozga, S. A. "Measurable Utility and Probability—A Simplified Rendering," *Economic Journal,* vol. 66 (1956), pp. 419–30.

Strotz, Robert H. "Cardinal Utility," *American Economic Review, Papers and Proceedings,* vol. 62 (1953), pp. 384–97.

Von Neumann, John, and Morgenstern, Oskar. *Theory of Games and Economic Behavior,* pp. 15–31, 617–32. Princeton, N.J.: Princeton University Press, 1944.

IV. MARKET STABILITY

Henderson, James M., and Quandt, Richard E. *Microeconomic Theory: A Mathematical Approach,* 2d ed. pp. 132–36, 191–201. New York: McGraw-Hill Book Co., Inc., 1971.

Hicks, John R. *Value and Capital,* pp. 62–77, 245–82, 315–19, 333–37. 2d ed. Oxford: Clarendon Press, 1946.

Kuenne, Robert E. "Hicks's Concept of Perfect Stability in Multiple Exchange," *Quarterly Journal of Economics,* vol. 73 (1959), pp. 309–15.

Metzler, Lloyd A. "Stability of Multiple Markets: The Hicks Conditions," *Econometrica,* vol. 13 (1945), pp. 277–92.

Samuelson, Paul A. *Foundations of Economic Analysis,* pp. 17–19, 260–65, 269–76. Cambridge, Mass.: Harvard University Press, 1947.

part II

Theory of production
and cost

In older textbooks it was conventional to define production as "the creation of utility" where utility meant "the ability of a good or service to satisfy a human want." In one respect this definition is too broad to have much specific content. On the other hand, it definitely points out that "production" embraces a wide range of activities and not *only* the fabrication of material goods. Rendering legal advice, writing a book, showing a motion picture, and servicing a bank account are all examples of "production." It is rather difficult to specify the inputs used in producing the outputs of these illustrative cases. Nevertheless, most people would probably agree that some kinds of technical and intellectual skills are required to perform the services.

Thus while "production" in a general sense refers to the creation of any *good or service* people will buy, the concept of production is much clearer when we speak only of *goods*. In this case it is simpler to specify the precise inputs and to identify the quantity and quality of output. Producing a bushel of wheat requires, in addition to suitable temperature and rainfall, a certain amount of arable land, seed, fertilizer, the services of agricultural equipment such as plows and combines, and human labor.

Even in our presently advanced state of automation, every act of production requires the input of human resources. Other inputs are

123

usually required as well. In particular, production normally requires various types of capital equipment (machines, tools, conveyors, buildings) and raw or processed materials. The theory of production consists of an analysis of *how* the businessman—given the "state of the art" or technology—combines various inputs to produce a stipulated output in an economically efficient manner.

Since the concept of production is clearer when applied to goods rather than services, our discussion will be restricted to production in agricultural and manufacturing industries. The student should be aware, nevertheless, that problems of resource allocation in service trades and government are not less serious because they are less discussed in this text. Indeed, as the population becomes more and more concentrated in the under 20 and over 65 age groups, the importance of services relative to goods increases. The principles of production studied here are as applicable to the output of services as to the output of goods, even though the application may be more difficult in the former case.

The same statement applies to the theory of cost. It is simpler to study a manufacturing business engaged in producing a specific good. Even then both costing and pricing are difficult matters—but not nearly so difficult as in service trades and government. Thus our discussion is restricted to producers of goods.

The theory of cost consists of an analysis of the costs of production —how costs are determined from a knowledge of the production function, the effects of diminishing returns, cost in the short and long runs, the "four cost curves," and so on. But more importantly, it establishes the basis for studying the pricing practices of business firms, which occupies Part III.

5

Production with one
variable input

5.1 INTRODUCTION

Production processes typically require a wide variety of
inputs. These are not as simple as "labor," "capital," and "materials";
many qualitatively different types of each input are normally used to
produce an output. To clarify the analysis, this chapter introduces some
simplifying assumptions whose purpose is to cut through the complexities of dealing with hundreds of different inputs. Thus our attention can
be focused upon the essential principles of production.

More specifically, we assume that there is only one *variable input*.
In subsequent discussion, this variable input is usually called "labor,"
although any other input could just as well be used. Second, we assume
that this variable input can be combined in different proportions with
one *fixed input* to produce various quantities of output. The fixed input
is called "land"; our discussion is thus principally concerned with one
specific example of production: agricultural output.

Finally, note that three assumptions are actually embodied in the
two propositions stated above: (*a*) there is only one variable input;
(*b*) there is only one fixed input; and (*c*) inputs may be combined in
various proportions to produce the commodity in question.

5.1.a Fixed and Variable Inputs, the Short and Long Runs

In analyzing the process of physical production and the closely related costs of production, it is convenient to introduce an analytical fiction: the classification of inputs as fixed and variable. Accordingly, a *fixed input* is defined as one whose quantity cannot readily be changed when market conditions indicate that an immediate change in output is desirable. To be sure, no input is ever *absolutely* fixed, no matter how short the period of time under consideration. But frequently, for the sake of analytical simplicity, we hold some inputs fixed, reasoning perhaps that while these inputs are in fact variable, the cost of immediate variation is so great as to take them out of the range of relevance for the particular decision at hand. Buildings, major pieces of machinery, and managerial personnel are examples of inputs that cannot be rapidly augmented or diminished. A *variable input,* on the other hand, is one whose quantity may be changed almost instantaneously in response to desired changes in output. Many types of labor services and the inputs of raw and processed materials fall in this category.

Corresponding to the fiction of fixed and variable inputs, economists introduce another fiction, the short and long runs. The *short run* refers to that period of time in which the input of one or more productive agents is fixed. Therefore, changes in output must be accomplished exclusively by changes in the usage of variable inputs. Thus if a producer wishes to expand output in the short run, he must usually do so by using more hours of labor service with the existing plant and equipment. Similarly, if he wishes to reduce output in the short run, he may discharge certain types of workers; but he cannot immediately "discharge" a building or a diesel locomotive, even though its usage may fall to zero.

In the long run, however, even this is possible, for the *long run* is defined as that period of time (or planning horizon) in which all inputs are variable. The long run, in other words, refers to that time in the future when output changes can be achieved in the manner most advantageous to the businessman. For example, in the short run a producer may be able to expand output only by operating his existing plant for more hours per day. This, of course, entails paying overtime rates to workers. In the long run, it may be more economical for him to install additional productive facilities and return to the normal work day.

In this chapter we are mostly concerned with the short-run theory of production, combining different quantities of variable inputs with a specific quantity of fixed input to produce various quantities of output. The long-run organization of production is largely determined by the relative cost of producing a desired output by different input combinations. Discussion of the long run is thus postponed until Chapters 6 and 7.

5.1.b Fixed or Variable Proportions

As already indicated, our discussion focuses largely upon the use of a *fixed* amount of one input and a *variable* amount of another to produce *variable* quantities of output. This means our attention is restricted mainly to production under conditions of *variable proportions.* The *ratio of input quantities* may vary; the businessman, therefore, must determine not only the level of output he wishes to produce but also the optimal proportion in which to combine inputs (in the long run).

There are two different ways of stating the principle of variable proportions. First, variable-proportions production implies that output can be changed in the short run by changing the amount of variable inputs used in cooperation with the fixed inputs. Naturally, as the amount of one input is changed, the other remaining constant, the *ratio* of inputs changes. Second, when production is subject to variable proportions, the *same* output can be produced by various combinations of inputs—that is, by different input ratios. This may apply only to the long run, but it is relevant to the short run when there is more than one variable input.

Most economists regard production under conditions of variable proportions as typical of both the short and long run. There is certainly no doubt that proportions are variable in the long run. When making an investment decision, a businessman may choose among a wide variety of different production processes. As polar opposites, an automobile can be almost handmade or it can be made by assembly-line techniques. In the short run, however, there may be some cases in which output is subject to fixed proportions.

Fixed-proportions production means there is one, and only one, ratio of inputs that can be used to produce a good. If output is expanded or contracted, all inputs must be expanded or contracted so as to maintain the fixed input ratio. At first glance this might seem the usual condition: one man and one shovel produce a ditch; two parts hydrogen and one part oxygen produce water. Adding a second shovel or a second part of oxygen will not augment the rate of production.

But in actuality examples of fixed-proportions production are hard to come by. Even the production of most chemical compounds is subject to variable proportions. It is true, for example, that hydrogen and nitrogen must be used in the fixed ratio 3:1 to produce ammonia gas. But if three volumes of hydrogen and one volume of nitrogen are mixed in a glass tube and heated to 400° C., only minute traces of ammonia will be found (and that only after heating for a very long time). However, if finely divided iron is introduced into the tube under the same conditions, almost the entire amount of hydrogen and nitrogen are converted to ammonia gas within minutes. That is to say, the *yield* of ammonia for any given amount of hydrogen and nitrogen depends upon the amount of the catalyst (finely divided iron) used. Proportions are indeed variable from the standpoint of the catalyst, not only in this instance but in the production of almost every chemical compound.

The hydrogen-nitrogen-ammonia illustration serves as a convenient introduction to a general view of production processes. One might say that in the short run there are three classes of productive inputs. First, there are certain fixed inputs whose quantity cannot be varied in the short run. Second, there are variable inputs whose usage may be changed. Finally, there are "ingredient" inputs whose quantities may be readily changed but must bear fixed proportions to one another and to output.

It is not difficult to find examples of "ingredient" inputs. Each brand of cigarettes contains its own special blend of tobaccos. That is, various tobaccos are blended in fixed proportions. And a fixed amount of tobacco blend must be used in each cigarette produced. But the production of cigarettes requires more than the fixed-proportions ingredient inputs. Certain capital equipment—rolling machines, packaging machines, and the like—must be used and human labor services are necessary. In the short run, the building and capital equipment are fixed inputs and most labor services are variable.

In the discussion of production the fixed and variable inputs are stressed. Ingredient inputs are necessary; and they must be used in fixed or relatively fixed proportions or else the quality or character of the output will change. The businessman has little or no choice in this regard. Hence our attention is directed to those aspects of production over which a businessman can exert control.

5.2 THE PRODUCTION FUNCTION

The discussion so far, especially in subsection 5.1.b, has emphasized that the quantity of output depends upon, or is a function of, the quantities of the various inputs used. This relation is more formally described by a *production function* associating physical output with input.

Definition: A production function is a schedule (or table, or mathematical equation) showing the maximum amount of output that can be produced from any specified set of inputs, given the existing technology or "state of the art." In short, the production function is a catalog of output possibilities.

5.2.a Total Output or Product

The production function may be shown as a table or, alternatively, as a mathematical equation. In either case the short-run production function gives the total (maximum) output obtainable from different amounts of the variable input, given a specified amount of the fixed input and the required amounts of the ingredient inputs.

As an example, consider an experiment in the production of wheat on 10 acres of land. The fixed input is land, the ingredient input is seed, the variable input is man-years of labor time, and the output is bushels of wheat. An agricultural experiment station blocks off 8 tracts of land, each containing 10 acres. The first tract is worked for a producing season by one man; the second tract is worked by two men; and so on until the eighth tract is worked by eight men. Total output on the various tracts of land might be as shown in Table 5.2.1.

The hypothetical data in Table 5.2.1 are graphed in Figure 5.2.1. Since output is a function of input, the former—output or total product —is plotted on the vertical axis. The independent variable—number of workers—is plotted on the horizontal axis. Joining the successive points by straight-line segments, one obtains the total product curve. It is important to note that the curve first rises slowly, then more rapidly, and

TABLE 5.2.1

**Output of Wheat in Bushels on
Ten-Acre Tracts of Land**

Tract No.	Number of Workers	Total Output
1	1	10
2	2	24
3	3	39
4	4	52
5	5	61
6	6	64
7	7	65
8	8	64

FIGURE 5.2.1

**Total Product Curve Obtained from Hypothetical
Data in Table 5.2.1**

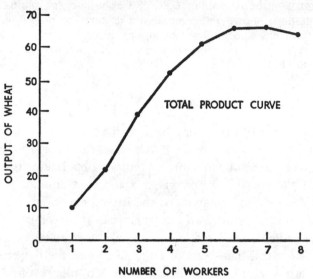

then more slowly again until it finally reaches a maximum and begins
to decrease. This curvature reflects the principle of diminishing marginal physical returns to be discussed in subsection 5.2.c.

5.2.b Average and Marginal Products

Two important relations between inputs affect the level of output
and the relation between output and input. The first of these is the
ratio in which the inputs are used (in the present illustration, the land-
labor ratio). Second, for any given input ratio the *scale* of inputs, or
the absolute magnitude of input quantities, is important. To analyze
scale effects there must be two or more variable inputs; so our attention
in this chapter is confined to the effects incident to changes in the
input ratio.

Table 5.2.2 is an expanded version of Table 5.2.1, with some change
in the *Total Output* column. The first two columns still indicate the
tract number and the number of workers on each tract. The third
column shows the input ratio for each tract, or the average number of
acres of land per worker. The fourth column reports the total output
for each tract of land, while the fifth column shows the average output
per worker, or the output-labor ratio. Finally, the sixth column contains
the entries for marginal product.

TABLE 5.2.2

**Average and Marginal Products and the Input Ratio
for Ten-Acre Tracts**

Tract Number	*Number of Workers*	*Land- Labor Ratio*	*Total Output*	*Average Product of Labor*	*Marginal Product of Labor*
1...............	1	10.0	10	10.0	—
2...............	2	5.0	24	12.0	14
3...............	3	3.33	39	13.0	15
4...............	4	2.50	52	13.0	13
5...............	5	2.00	61	12.2	9
6...............	6	1.67	66	11.0	5
7...............	7	1.43	66	9.4	0
8...............	8	1.25	64	8.0	−2

Definition: The average product of an input is total product divided by the amount of the input used to produce this output. Thus average product is the output-input ratio for each level of output and the corresponding volume of input.

Definition: The marginal product of an input is the addition to total product attributable to the addition of one unit of the variable input to the production process, the fixed input remaining unchanged.[1]

Table 5.2.2 and its accompanying graph, Figure 5.2.2, illustrate several important features of a typical production process. First, both average and marginal products initially rise, reach a maximum, and then decline. In the limit, average product could decline to zero because total product itself could conceivably decline to this point. Marginal product, on the other hand, may actually become negative—indeed, many economists suggest that the marginal product of agricultural workers in some underdeveloped countries is in fact negative. In the present example, the marginal product of labor becomes negative because the variable input is used too intensively with the fixed input (land).

A second feature of significance is that marginal product exceeds

---

[1] Consider the production function $f(x|y)$ where x is the variable input and y is the fixed input and where the vertical bar means "given." The average product of the variable input x is

$$\frac{q}{x} = \frac{f(x|y)}{x}$$

and the marginal product is the derivative,

$$\frac{dq}{dx} = \frac{df(x|y)}{dx} .$$

FIGURE 5.2.2

Average and Marginal Products Obtained from Data in Table 5.2.2

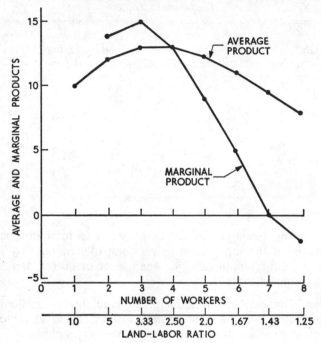

average product when the latter is rising, equals average product when the latter is a maximum, and lies below average product when the latter is falling. This proposition follows readily from the definitions of marginal and average product. So long as the *addition* to a total is greater than the previous average, the average must increase. If the *addition* to the total is less than the previous average, the newly computed average must be less. Thus, since the *additions* first rise and then decline so also must the averages; and the two curves must intersect at the point where the average curve reaches its maximum.

The third feature to note is that as the input (land-labor) ratio declines, the output-labor ratio first rises and then declines indefinitely. The marginal product of labor behaves in a similar manner, as will be explained below.

These results may be summarized in the following

Relations: Both average and marginal products first rise, reach a maximum, and decline thereafter. When average product attains its maximum, average and marginal products are equal. These relations apply only to variable-proportions production functions.

5.2.c   Law of Diminishing Marginal Physical Returns

The shape of the marginal product curve in Figure 5.2.2 graphically illustrates an important principle: the "law" of diminishing marginal physical returns.

When the outputs of tracts 1 and 2 are compared (Table 5.2.2), one sees that using two workers rather than one increases output by 14 bushels, the marginal product of labor when there are two workers. Similarly, comparing tracts 2 and 3, the use of a third worker augments output by 15 bushels. The marginal physical product of labor increases as the number of workers increases. This may well happen when the land-labor ratio is very high.

Ultimately, however, as the input ratio declines so also must the marginal product of the variable input. When the number of units of the variable input increases, each unit, so to speak, has on the average fewer units of the fixed input with which to work. At first, when the fixed input is relatively plentiful, more intensive utilization of fixed inputs by variable inputs may increase the marginal output of the variable input. Nonetheless, a point is quickly reached beyond which an increase in the intensity of use of the fixed input yields progressively less and less additional returns. Psychologists have even found that this holds true for consecutive study time.

Principle (the law of diminishing marginal physical returns): As the amount of a variable input is increased, the amount of other (fixed) inputs held constant, a point is reached beyond which marginal product declines. It might be well at this point to emphasize that the "law of diminishing returns" is actually an *empirical assertion about reality*. It is not a theorem derived from an axiom system; it is not a logical proposition that is susceptible of mathematical proof or refutation. It is a simple statement concerning physical relations that have been observed in the real economic world.

5.3 THE GEOMETRY OF AVERAGE AND MARGINAL PRODUCT CURVES

This study of production has so far focused attention upon one specific, discrete production function given in tabular form. We turn now to a more general formulation in which both discrete and continuous production functions are used.

5.3.a Geometry of Average Product Curves

A typical form of the (continuous) total product curve is shown in Figure 5.3.1. In this, as in all other one-variable-input product

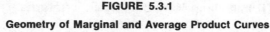

FIGURE 5.3.1

Geometry of Marginal and Average Product Curves

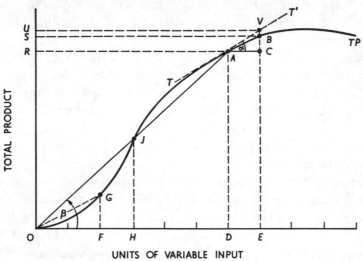

graphs, units of the variable input are plotted on the abscissa and total product is plotted on the ordinate.

Given the total product curve *TP*, we wish to find average product. First, from its definition average product is total product divided by the number of units of the variable input used to produce it, or the output–variable input ratio. Producing total output $OR = DA$ requires OD units of the variable input. Thus the average product of OD units of variable input is DA/OD. Similarly, the average product of OF units of variable input is FG/OF and of OH units is HJ/OH. In each case, to obtain the average product corresponding to a given point on the total product curve, we found the slope of the line joining the origin with the point in question. In other words, we found the tangent of the angle formed by the abscissa and the line from the origin to the given point on the total product curve.

As we have seen, the average product corresponding to point A is DA/OD, but this is precisely the slope of the line OA, or the tangent of the angle β. Notice also that average product must be the same for OH as for OD units of the variable input because the slopes of OJ and of OA are identical (in each case, average product is the tangent of angle β). Since average product is rising for movements along TP from the origin to point J, and since it is obviously falling for movements from A to B, there is reason to suspect that average product reaches its maximum at a point between *J* and *A* on the total product curve.

Average product does, in fact, attain its maximum at an intermediate point, as may be seen more clearly in Figure 5.3.2. Points *Q* and *R* in Figure 5.3.2 correspond to points *J* and *A*, respectively, in Figure 5.3.1, in that each pair of points lies on a common ray from the origin. Thus the average product at point *Q* is equal to the average product at point *R*. Since average product is the slope of a ray from the origin to a point on the curve, average product is a maximum when the slope of the line is steepest. This occurs, of course, when the line from the origin is just tangent to the total product curve, at point *P* with angle *θ* in Figure 5.3.2.

FIGURE 5.3.2

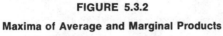

Maxima of Average and Marginal Products

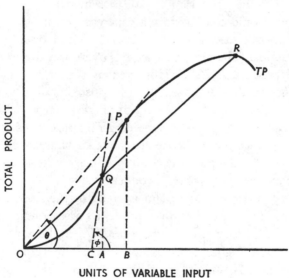

As one moves from the origin through point *Q* toward point *P*, the line from the origin to the curve becomes steeper. Similarly, as one moves from point *P* toward point *R*, the line moves downward, becoming less steep. Thus we have proved the following important points:

Relations: Average product corresponding to any point on the total product curve is given by the slope of a ray from the origin to the point in question. Average product attains its maximum value when this line is tangent to the total product curve.

5.3.b   Geometry of Marginal Product Curves

Using Figures 5.3.1 and 5.3.2 again, similar qualitative and quantitative relations may be found for the marginal product curve.

Turn first to Figure 5.3.1. By definition, marginal product is the addition to total product attributable to the addition of one unit (or a small amount) of the variable input to a given amount of the fixed input. Let the amount of variable input increase from OD to OE, or by the amount $DE = AC$. Output consequently increases from OR to OS, or by the amount $RS = BC$. Marginal product is, therefore, BC/AC. In this discrete case, there is no convenient slope measurement because the arc AB is not linear. That is, a unique slope measure cannot be obtained because the slope of the angle formed by arc AB and line AC changes over the interval $DE = AC$.

But let us suppose for a minute that the total product curve were linear from A to the point V. Then an increment of amount DE in the variable input would cause output to increase from OR to OU, or by $RU = CV$. In this case, marginal product would be CV/AC, or the tangent of angle a. The measure CV/AC overstates the true magnitude of marginal product, BC/AC. However, as the increment of variable input becomes smaller and smaller the approximation becomes better and better. In the limit, for a very tiny increase in variable input the slope of the tangent to point A, labeled TT', approaches the true slope of the total product curve. Hence for sufficiently small changes in the variable input, the slope of the total product curve at any point is a good approximation of marginal product.[2]

The slope of a curve at any point is given by the slope of its tangent at that point. Thus the marginal product corresponding to point Q in Figure 5.3.2 is the slope of the line CQ, or the tangent of angle $\phi = AQ/CA$. As Figure 5.3.2 is constructed, marginal product is a maximum when OA units of variable input are used. This is true be-

---

[2] Let $q = f(x)$ be the production function. If the increment of variable input is denoted Δx, the new output is $f(x + \Delta x)$. Thus, by definition, marginal product is

$$MP = \frac{f(x + \Delta x) - f(x)}{\Delta x}.$$

But also by definition, the derivative of $f(x)$ is

$$\frac{dq}{dx} = \lim_{\Delta x \to 0} \frac{f(x + \Delta x) - f(x)}{\Delta x}.$$

Hence in the limit, marginal product *is* the slope (dq/dx) of the total product curve. For finite changes, the slope is an approximation of marginal product.

cause the slope of the tangent to the total product curve is steeper at point Q than at any other point.

Other interesting relations can be determined from Figure 5.3.2. First, recall that maximum average product is associated with OB units of variable input and corresponds to point P. Hence marginal product attains its maximum at a lower level of variable input usage than does average product. Second, notice that the tangent to the total product curve at point P—the line whose slope gives marginal product corresponding to point P—is the line OP. We have already seen in subsection 5.3.a that the slope of OP also gives average product associated with point P and that average product attains its maximum value at that point. Hence, as we have seen previously, marginal product equals average product when the latter is at its maximum.

The principal information contained in this subsection can be summarized as follows:

Relations: Marginal product corresponding to any point on the total product curve is given by the slope of the tangent to the curve at that point. Marginal product attains its maximum value when the slope of the tangent is steepest. The point of maximum marginal product occurs at a smaller level of variable input usage than does maximum average product; and marginal product equals average product when the latter attains its maximum value.

5.3.c Total, Average, and Marginal Products

The relations discussed in the two preceding subsections are illustrated in Figure 5.3.3.[3] In this figure one can see not only the relation

---

[3] This graph is constructed under the assumption that output is zero if the input of the variable factor is zero. Thus if the production function is $q = f(x|y)$, we assume that $f(0|y) = f(x|0) = f(0|0) = 0$. For an alternative approach, see Frank Knight, *Risk, Uncertainty, and Profit,* Reprints of Economic Classics (New York: Augustus M. Kelley, 1964), p. 100.

It might be well to point out that not all production functions give rise to product curves such as those shown in Figure 5.3.3. For example, the celebrated Cobb-Douglas and CES functions do not have regions in which marginal and average products increase, nor do they have a region in which marginal product is negative. Further, the CES function with $y > 0$ has a positive ordinate intercept.

One form of a linearly homogeneous function that would give rise to the curves in Figure 5.3.3. is

$$q = a \left[\frac{bx^3y^2 + cx^2y^3}{ex^4 + gy^4} \right], \tag{5.3.1}$$

where a, b, c, e, and g are positive constants. For a more detailed treatment of the general case and a numerical example of equation (5.5.1), see C. E. Ferguson, *The Neoclassical Theory of Production and Distribution* (London and New York: Cambridge University Press, 1969), pp. 122–24.

between marginal and average products but also the relation of these two curves to total product.

Consider first the total product curve. For very small amounts of the variable input, total product rises gradually. But even at a low level of input it begins to rise quite rapidly, reaching its maximum slope (or rate of increase) at point 1. Since the slope of the total product curve equals marginal product, the maximum slope (point 1) must correspond to the maximum point on the marginal product curve (point 4).

After attaining its maximum slope at point 1, the total product curve continues to rise. But output increases at a decreasing rate, so the slope is less steep. Moving outward along the curve from point 1, soon the point is reached at which a ray from the origin is just tangent to the curve (point 2). Since tangency of the ray to the curve defines the condition for maximum average product, point 2 lies directly above point 5.

As the quantity of variable input is expanded from its value at point 2, total product continues to increase. But its rate of increase is progressively slower until point 3 is finally reached. At this position total product is at a maximum; thereafter it declines until it (conceivably) reaches zero again. Over a tiny range around point 3, additional input does not change total output. The slope of the total product curve is zero. Thus marginal product must also be zero. This is shown by the fact that points 3 and 6 occur at precisely the same input value. And since total product declines beyond point 3, marginal product becomes negative.

Most of the important relations have so far been discussed with reference to the total product curve. To emphasize certain relations, however, consider the marginal and average product curves in Figure 5.3.3. Marginal product at first increases, reaches a maximum at point 4 (the point of diminishing marginal physical returns), and declines thereafter. It eventually becomes negative beyond point 6, where total product is at its maximum.

Average product also rises at first until it reaches its maximum at point 5, where marginal and average products are equal. It subsequently declines, conceivably becoming zero when total product itself becomes zero. Finally, one may observe that marginal product exceeds average product when the latter is increasing and is less than average product when the latter is decreasing.

5.3.d The Three Stages of Production

Using Figure 5.3.3 we can identify three stages of production. The first stage corresponds to usage of the variables input to the left of

FIGURE 5.3.3

Total, Average, and Marginal Products

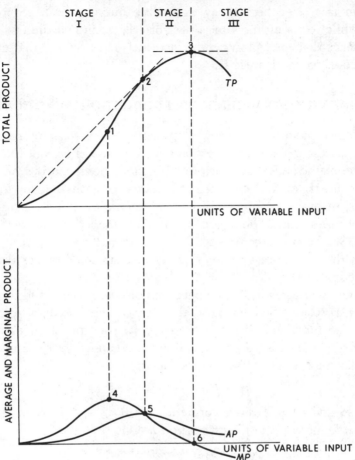

point 5 where average product achieves its maximum. Stage II corresponds to usage of the variable input between point 5 and point 6, where the marginal product of the variable input is zero. Finally, stage III corresponds to usage of the variable input to the right of point 6 where the marginal product of this input is negative.

Clearly, the producer would never produce in stage III, since when he is in this stage he can get more output by using less of the variable input. Such inefficiencies in the use of scarce production factors will always be avoided. In stage I, average product of the variable factor is increasing. As we shall see in Chapter 7, when the unit cost of the variable factor (e.g., the wage rate) is a constant, increasing average product of the variable factor implies that the unit cost of producing output decreases as output is increased. If the firm is in a competitive industry (see the discussion in subsection 4.5.c.), it would never produce in this stage because by expanding output it can reduce unit costs while receiving the same price for each additional unit sold, and this means that total profits must increase.[4] Thus we see that efficient production occurs in stage II.[5]

5.4 LINEARLY HOMOGENEOUS PRODUCTION FUNCTIONS

Whether production functions typically reflect constant returns to scale is at best an empirical question and at worst a moot one. Nonetheless, the mathematical simplicity of functions homogeneous of degree one frequently causes economists to assume constant returns to scale. That is, many of the more advanced economic models are simply not soluble unless linear homogeneity of the production function is assumed. Since constant-returns-to-scale production functions are so prevalent in the literature, some of their chief characteristics are discussed here and in Chapter 6.

"Linear homogeneity," "homogeneous of degree one," and "constant returns to scale" are interchangeable terms when used to describe a production function. All get at the essential concept: if all inputs are expanded in the same proportion, output is expanded in that proportion. Consider the simple Cobb-Douglas function:

$$q = f(x, y) = Ax^{\alpha}y^{1-\alpha}, \tag{5.4.1}$$

where A and α are positive constants and $0 < \alpha < 1$. Now let both x and y be increased in the proportion λ. One then has

$$
\begin{aligned}
f(\lambda x, \lambda y) &= A(\lambda x)^{\alpha}(\lambda y)^{1-\alpha} = A\lambda^{\alpha}\lambda^{1-\alpha}x^{\alpha}y^{1-\alpha} \\
&= A\lambda x^{\alpha}y^{1-\alpha} = \lambda(Ax^{\alpha}y^{1-\alpha}) = \lambda f(x, y) = \lambda q .
\end{aligned}
\tag{5.4.2}
$$

Thus if the usage of all inputs is expanded in the same proportion, output expands in that proportion. This is precisely what is meant by "constant returns to scale."

The other essential feature of linearly homogeneous production functions is as follows: the average and marginal products depend upon the *ratio* in which the inputs are combined, but their values are *independent* of the absolute magnitudes of the inputs. Again consider the

---

[4] An even stronger statement can be made when the production function exhibits constant returns to scale (see section 5.4): in this case, the marginal product of the fixed factor will be negative in stage I.

[5] As we shall see, however, a monopolist may decide, in some cases, to produce in stage I.

Cobb-Douglas function. Divide both sides of equation (5.4.1) by x to obtain the average product of X:

$$AP_x = \frac{q}{x} = Ax^{\alpha-1}y^{1-\alpha} = A\left(\frac{y}{x}\right)^{1-\alpha}. \tag{5.4.3}$$

This clearly shows that the average product of x depends upon the factor input ratio or factor proportions. For example, suppose $A = 100$ and $\alpha = \frac{1}{2}$. If $y = 4$ and $x = 1$, the average product of X is 200. If $y = 400$ and $x = 100$, the ratio is the same and so is the magnitude of the average product.

The same relation may be shown for the marginal product. Let y be constant and let the input of X increase from x to $x + \Delta x$. The difference in output is

$$\Delta q = A(x + \Delta x)^{\alpha}y^{1-\alpha} - Ax^{\alpha}y^{1-\alpha} = Ay^{1-\alpha}[(x + \Delta x)^{\alpha} - x^{\alpha}]. \tag{5.4.4}$$

Using the binomial theorem, we can expand the term $(x + \Delta x)^{\alpha}$ as follows:

$$(x + \Delta x)^{\alpha} = x^{\alpha} + \alpha x^{\alpha-1}\Delta x + \frac{\alpha(\alpha-1)x^{\alpha-2}(\Delta x)^2}{2!} + \cdots. \tag{5.4.5}$$

Now for small values of Δx, we may ignore the terms that involve higher powers of Δx, that is, $(\Delta x)^2$, $(\Delta x)^3$, and so forth. Thus $(x + \Delta x)^{\alpha}$ is approximately equal to $x^{\alpha} + \alpha x^{\alpha-1}\Delta x$. Substituting this in equation (5.4.4), we obtain

$$\Delta q = Ay^{1-\alpha}[x^{\alpha} + \alpha x^{\alpha-1}\Delta x - x^{\alpha}] = \alpha Ay^{1-\alpha}x^{\alpha-1}\Delta x. \tag{5.4.6}$$

Hence the marginal product of X can be written as

$$\frac{\Delta q}{\Delta x} = \alpha A\left(\frac{y}{x}\right)^{1-\alpha}, \tag{5.4.7}$$

which shows that the marginal product depends upon the input ratio only.

The essential features of linearly homogeneous production functions may be summarized as follows:

Relations: If the production function is homogeneous of degree one, (*i*) there are constant returns to scale, that is, to proportional expansions of all inputs; and (*ii*) the marginal and average product functions depend only upon the ratio in which the inputs are combined and, in particular, they are independent of the absolute amounts of the inputs employed.

QUESTIONS AND EXERCISES

Below are hypothetical data for a manufacturer possessing a fixed plant who produces a commodity that requires only one variable input. Total product is given. Compute and graph the average and marginal product curves. Make your basic calculations and set them up in tabular form using the following information for the stub and column (1) entries and your calculations for Average Product in column (2) and Marginal Product in column (3). Save them as they form the basis for a subsequent problem in Chapter 7.

Units of Variable Input	Total Product (1)
1.....................	100
2.....................	250
3.....................	410
4.....................	560
5.....................	700
6.....................	830
7.....................	945
8.....................	1,050
9.....................	1,146
10....................	1,234
11....................	1,314
12....................	1,384
13....................	1,444
14....................	1,494
15....................	1,534
16....................	1,564
17....................	1,584
18....................	1,594

After completing the table and graph, answer the following questions:

1. When marginal product is increasing, what is happening to average product?

2. Does average product begin to fall as soon as marginal product does? That is, which occurs first, the point of diminishing marginal or average returns?

3. When average product is at its maximum, is marginal product less than, equal to, or greater than average product?

4. Does total product increase at a decreasing rate: (*a*) When average product is rising? (*b*) When marginal product is rising? (*c*) When average product begins to fall? (*d*) When marginal product passes its maximum value?

5. When average product equals zero, what is total product?

6. What is the precise relation between a two-factor production function and the marginal product curve for one factor?

7. Beginning with a production function or schedule involving two inputs, explain how one derives the total, average, and marginal products for a single factor.

8. Comment on the following statement: If the production of wheat requires only land and labor, if there are constant returns to scale, and if labor has an increasing average product, then the world's wheat supply could be grown in a flower pot, provided the pot were small enough.

SUGGESTED READINGS

Clark, J. M. "Diminishing Returns," *Encyclopaedia of the Social Sciences,* vol. 5, pp. 144–46. New York: The Macmillan Co., 1931.

Ferguson, C. E. *The Neoclassical Theory of Production and Distribution,* chaps. 1–6. London and New York: Cambridge University Press, 1969. [Advanced math necessary.]

Henderson, James M. and Quandt, Richard E. *Microeconomic Theory: A Mathematical Approach,* 2d ed., pp. 52–58. New York: McGraw-Hill Book Co., Inc., 1971. [Elementary math necessary.]

Knight, Frank H. *Risk, Uncertainty, and Profit,* pp. 94–104. Boston: Houghton Mifflin Co., 1921.

Machlup, Fritz. "On the Meaning of the Marginal Product," *Explorations in Economics,* pp. 250–63. New York: McGraw-Hill Book Co., Inc., 1936. Reprinted in AEA, *Readings in the Theory of Income Distribution,* pp. 158–74. Philadelphia: Blakiston Co., 1951.

6

Production and optimal input proportions: Two variable inputs

6.1 INTRODUCTION

The fundamental physical relations of production were discussed in Chapter 5 under the assumption that there is only one variable input. The analysis is continued in this chapter for a more general case. Graphically, production is studied under the assumption that there are two variable inputs. One may regard these inputs either as cooperating with one or more fixed inputs or as the only two inputs. The latter situation, of course, is relevant only for the long run. In either case, however, the results of the two-input model are easily extended to cover multiple inputs.

6.1.a Production Table

The land-labor example used in Chapter 5 may be expanded to introduce the theory of production with two variable inputs. In the illustration we considered an agricultural experiment in which 10-acre tracts of land comprised the fixed input. Labor was the variable input, and we obtained eight sample observations corresponding to the cultivation of the 10-acre tracts by one worker, two workers, and so on. In the present example the agricultural experiment is pushed further so as to

144

obtain 64 sample observations. Land is, in a sense, still the fixed input; but now we suppose there are eight 1-acre tracts, eight 2-acre tracts, and so on up to eight 8-acre tracts. Each of the sets of 8 constant-acre tracts is cultivated by one worker, two workers, etc., up to eight workers. Thus we have samples ranging from one worker on 1 acre to eight workers on 8 acres. The hypothetical data are listed in Table 6.1.1.

The entries in the row corresponding to 3-acre tracts of land are exactly the same as the entries in Table 5.2.2. Indeed, in every respect this table is just a "larger" example of the hypothetical experiment in Chapter 5.

In the spirit of Chapter 5, consider land as the fixed input. The entries in each row show the total outputs produced on the stipulated acreage when different numbers of workers cultivate the land. By successive subtractions along each row, the marginal product of labor is obtained. Next, by going to successively higher rows one sees that the total, average, and marginal products of labor increase as larger and larger tracts of land are used—that is, as the fixed input is expanded relative to the variable input.

Up to a point! But just as too many workers per acre of land make cultivation too intensive, too many acres of land per worker make cultivation too extensive. Instead of viewing acres per tract as the fixed input, we can regard workers per tract as fixed and the number of acres per tract as variable. We then read up the columns rather than across the rows; but the same fundamental physical relations are exhibited.

With one worker per tract, output increases as the size of the tract

TABLE 6.1.1

Data from Hypothetical Agricultural Experiment*

					Output in Bushels				
	8	9	46	69	92	109	124	136	144
	7	13	46	69	91	108	123	134	140
	6	16	42	66	88	106	120	128	132
Acres of Land per Tract	5	15	37	60	80	100	113	120	121
	4	13	30	54	72	85	93	95	95
	3	10	24	39	52	61	66	66	64
	2	6	12	17	21	24	26	$25\frac{1}{2}$	$24\frac{1}{2}$
	1	3	6	8	9	10	10	9	7
		1	2	3	4	5	6	7	8

Workers per Tract of Land

*Notice that this production schedule does not represent a production function homogeneous of degree one.

increases until 6 acres per tract is reached. Thereafter total output declines and the marginal product of land is negative. As the number of workers per tract is expanded, thus diminishing the land-labor ratio for each given acreage, total product expands continuously beyond 3-acre tracts. Total product in these cases does not reach a maximum in the range shown in this example. But in each case the point of diminishing marginal returns is reached; thereafter output expands at a decreasing rate.

6.1.b Input Substitution

Table 6.1.1 shows that the basic principles of physical production hold whether workers per tract are varied with acres per tract constant or whether acres per tract are varied with workers per tract constant. It also illustates another very important physical relation between inputs: the same amount of total output may be produced by different input combinations. For example, an output of 66 bushels can be produced by using six workers on 3 acres of land or by using three workers on 6 acres. Similarly, 120 bushels can be produced either by seven workers on 5 acres or by six workers on 6 acres.

In this example no more than two different input combinations can be used to produce the same output. In a more general, continuous case, however, a given level of output can be produced by a wide variety of different input combinations. In other words, one input may be *substituted* for another in producing a specified volume of output. One of the important tasks of a businessman is to select the particular input combination that minimizes the cost of producing any given level of output. The chief purpose of this chapter is to show how this is done.

6.2 PRODUCTION SURFACE

Selection of the least-cost input combination requires knowledge of substitution possibilities and of relative input prices. For an individual producer, we assume that the input prices are given by market forces of supply and demand. Input substitution is the center of our interest. To get at an explanation requires the use of a device much like the one used in Part I to describe a consumer's preference surface. In the theory of consumer behavior we used equal-satisfaction contour lines, or indifference curves. Here we use equal-output contours, or *isoquants*.

6.2.a Production Surface for Discrete Case

As an introduction, first look at the total production surface. Figure 6.2.1 is a graph of the discrete production function given in Table 6.1.1. The height of the rectangular blocks indicates the volume of output. By following the heights visually in either "horizontal" direction, one may see how the total product curve is shaped for a fixed amount of one input and variable amounts of the other. But as we have already

FIGURE 6.2.1

Physical Production Surface for Example in Table 6.1.1

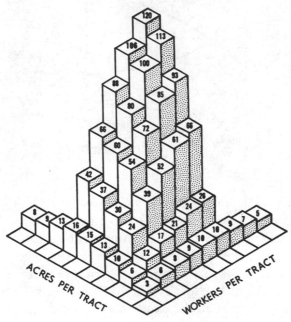

observed in this example, substitution possibilities are very limited. In certain cases two different input combinations yield the same output. However, this example is *too* discrete to illustrate a wide range of production possibilities.

6.2.b Production Surface for Continuous Case

For this purpose a *continuous* production function is required. Let us imagine a manufacturing process that requires two inputs—labor and capital—to produce a specific commodity. The production function for this good is continuous; it cannot, therefore, be shown conveniently in tabular form. However, either a mathematical or a graphical representation is suitable.[1] The production function for this particular example is shown in Figure 6.2.2., a three-dimensional diagram in which

FIGURE 6.2.2

Physical Production Surface for a Continuous Production Function

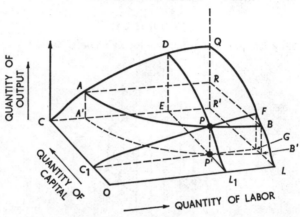

height measures quantity of output and the two "flat" or "horizontal" dimensions measure quantities of the two inputs.[2]

The production surface is $OCQL$. Any point on this surface represents a particular quantity of output. Dropping perpendiculars from the point to the axes shows the quantities of inputs required. For example, P is a point on the surface and PP' is the associated volume of output. Drawing perpendiculars to the axes, $OL_1 (=C_1P')$ units of labor and $OC_1 (=L_1P')$ units of capital are required to produce the amount PP' at this particular point.

The production surface may be viewed in a different manner. Hold the capital input constant at the amount OC_1. The total product curve for OC_1 units of capital and variable inputs of labor is C_1PF. At labor input OL_1, total output is PP'; and at labor input OL, total output is FG. The total product curve C_1PF rises rapidly for small quantities of labor input, reaches a point of maximum slope (the point of diminishing

---

[1] Let Q, K, and L represent the quantities of output, capital, and labor, respectively. The production function may be written $Q = f(K, L)$, where $\partial Q/\partial K$ and $\partial Q/\partial L$ are the marginal products of capital and labor respectively.

[2] In constructing Figure 6.2.2 we have assumed that $f(K, 0) = f(0, L) = f(0, 0) = 0$.

marginal physical returns to labor for the given capital input OC_1), and thereafter increases at a decreasing rate.

The same statement applies to a typical total product curve for a fixed labor input and variable capital usage. Hold the input of labor constant at OL_1 units. L_1PD is the curve of total output resulting from variable inputs of capital. For example, when OC_1 units of capital are used, output is PP'; when OC units are employed, output is DE.

6.2.c Production Isoquants

Still using Figure 6.2.2, let us determine all the different input combinations capable of producing PP' units of output. To do this, we slice (or "intersect") the production surface $OCQL$ at the height $PP' = AA' = BB'$. This slicing process generates the curve APB, a locus of points equidistant ($AA' = PP' = BB'$) from the $C–L$ plane. By dropping perpendiculars from each point on the APB curve to the $C–L$ plane, one obtains the input combinations associated with each point. In other words, the curve APB is projected onto the $C–L$ plane, generating the curve $A'P'B'$. The latter is a locus of points each of which represents a combination of inputs capable of producing the stipulated quantity of output $PP' = AA' = BB' = RR'$. For examples, the following three combinations of capital and labor are points on the curve $A'P'B'$: OC, CA'; OC_1, OL_1; LB', OL.

The curve $A'P'B'$ is called an *isoquant*.

Definition: An isoquant is a curve in input space showing all possible combinations of inputs physically capable of producing a given level of output. The entire three-dimensional production surface can be exactly depicted by a two-dimensional isoquant map.

A portion of an isoquant map, derived from a production surface such as $OCQL$ in Figure 6.2.2, is shown in Figure 6.2.3.[3] The two axes measure the quantities of inputs, and the curves show the different input combinations that can be used to produce 100, 200, 300, and 400 units of output respectively. As is obvious, the further northeast a curve lies the greater is the output associated with it.

Consider first the isoquant for 100 units of output. Each point on this curve shows a capital-labor combination that can produce 100 units of output. For example, OC_1 units of capital and OL_1 units of labor may be used, or OC_3 units of capital and OL_3 units of labor, or any other input combination found by dropping perpendiculars to the axes from a point on the curve.

---

[3] The excluded portion of the isoquant map is discussed in subsection 6.3.d.

FIGURE 6.2.3

Typical Set of Isoquants

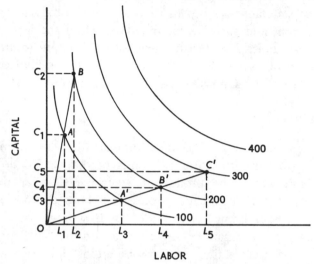

A ray from the origin, such as OAB or $OA'B'C'$, defines a constant capital-labor input ratio. In particular, the slope of the ray is the input ratio. For example, at points A and B, 100 and 200 units of output, respectively, are produced at the capital-labor ratio $OC_1/OL_1 = OC_2/OL_2$. Similarly, at points A', B', and C', 100, 200, and 300 units of output, respectively, are produced at the capital-labor ratio $OC_3/OL_3 = OC_4/OL_4 = OC_5/OL_5$.

Along the ray OAB, various levels of output are producible by the same input ratio; the magnitude of the inputs increases as one moves out along the ray but the capital-labor ratio remains unchanged. This contrasts clearly with movements along an isoquant. In this case the level of output remains unchanged and the capital-labor ratio changes continuously.

These points may be summarized as follows.

Relations: An isoquant represents different input combinations, or input ratios, that may be used to produce a specified level of output. For movements *along an isoquant,* the level of output remains constant and the input ratio changes continuously. A ray from the origin defines a specific, constant input ratio. For movements *along a ray,* the level of output changes continuously and the input ratio remains constant.

6.2.d Fixed-Proportions Production Functions

Using the isoquant device, it is easy to illustrate the case of fixed-proportions production functions, briefly mentioned in Chapter 5. As

FIGURE 6.2.4

Isoquant Map for Fixed-Proportions Production Function

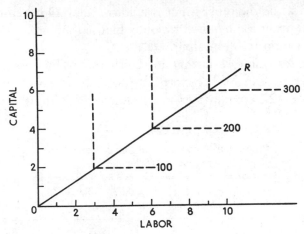

you will recall, production is subject to fixed proportions when one, and only one, combination of inputs can produce a specified output.[4] For example, consider the hypothetical production process illustrated in Figure 6.2.4. Two inputs, capital and labor, must be used in the fixed ratio 2:3. That is, 2 units of capital and 3 units of labor are required to produce 100 units of output. Thus 4 units of capital and 6 units of labor can produce 200 units of output; 6 units of capital and 9 units of labor can produce 300 units; and so on.

The required capital-labor ratio is shown by the slope of the ray *OR* in Figure 6.2.4. Isoquants are constructed for 100, 200, and 300 units of output. Rather than taking the more conventional shape shown in Figure 6.2.3, the isoquants for fixed-proportions processes are L-shaped curves. This illustrates, for example, that if 3 units of labor and 2 units of capital are employed, 100 units of output are obtainable. However, if the quantity of capital is expanded, labor input held constant, no additional output can be obtained. Similarly, if capital input

---

[4] A fixed-proportions production function, which is frequently called a Leontief function, may be represented by

$$Q = \text{minimum} \left(\frac{K}{\alpha}, \frac{L}{\beta} \right),$$

where α and β are constants and "minimum" means that Q equals the smaller of the two ratios. For a detailed treatment of the fixed-proportions case, see C. E. Ferguson, *The Neoclassical Theory of Production and Distributions* (London and New York: Cambridge University Press, 1969), chaps. ii–iii.

is held constant and labor expanded, output is unchanged. In other words, the marginal product of either labor or capital is zero if its usage is expanded while the other input is held constant. On the other hand, doubling inputs at the required ratio doubles output; trebling inputs at the required ratio trebles output, etc.[5]

A rather realistic case is that in which many, but not an infinite number of, different fixed-proportions processes are available. For example, Table 6.2.1 contains hypothetical data regarding the production

TABLE 6.2.1

**Production When Several Fixed-Proportions
Processes Are Available**

Ray	Capital–Labor Ratio	Capital Input	Labor Input	Total Output
OA	11:1	11	1	100
		22	2	200
OB	8:2	8	2	100
		16	4	200
OC	5:4	5	4	100
		10	8	200
OD	3:7	3	7	100
		6	14	200
OE	1:10	1	10	100
		2	20	200

of a commodity for which five different fixed-proportions processes are available. The 100-output isoquants, together with the capital-labor ratio rays, are plotted in Figure 6.2.5.

Heavily shaded straight lines have been drawn to connect the different possible input combinations. Each of the points on this kinked line represents an input combination capable of producing 100 units of output. The kinked line *ABCDE* looks very much like the "normal" isoquant shown in Figure 6.2.3. It is different, however, in that no input combination lying on the arc between *A* and *B, B* and *C,* etc., is itself *directly* a feasible input combination. For example, it is not possible to produce 100 units of output by *one* process using 7.25 units of capital and 2.5 units of labor.

On the other hand, if input units are sufficiently divisible, any particular input ratio—represented by a point on the kinked line—can

---

[5] It is readily seen from the Leontief function in footnote 4 that fixed-proportions production functions are homogeneous of degree one, that is, such functions reflect constant returns to scale.

FIGURE 6.2.5

Isoquant Map When Five Fixed-Proportions Processes Are Available

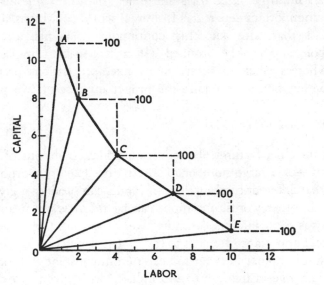

be achieved. All that is required is the proper combination of the two fixed-proportions processes with which it is most closely associated. For example, suppose a producer wished to obtain 100 units of output by using 7.25 units of capital and 2.5 units of labor. He could do so by producing 75 units of output by the process represented by the ray OB and 25 units by the process OC. To produce 75 units at the 8:2 ratio requires 6 units of capital and 1.5 units of labor. Producing 25 units at the 5:4 ratio requires 1.25 units of capital and 1 unit of labor. Thus 100 units of output can be produced at the desired ratio 7.25:2.5 by combining the two processes represented by the rays OB and OC.

Finally, suppose there are many fixed-proportions processes by which a given level of output can be produced. Instead of the five points in Figure 6.2.5 there would be many points. Similarly, there would be many straight-line facets of the type AB, BC, etc. As the number of processes increases, the kinked line looks more and more like a typical isoquant. Indeed, an isoquant depicting a variable-proportions production function is just the limiting case of fixed-proportions processes as the number of processes increases without bound.

This argument, in fact, constitutes one rationale for the use of smooth isoquants and variable-proportions production functions in economic theory. Many manufacturing processes may be characterized by fixed, or almost fixed, proportions; however, usually many different fixed-proportions processes are available. Constructing smooth isoquants rather than multiple facet lines simplifies analysis while leading to relatively unimportant departures from real world conditions. The chief difference is that with smoothly continuous isoquants, any desired capital-labor ratio can be attained (if it is feasible) by using one process, whereas when there are many fixed-proportions processes, a desired combination may require the proper mixture of two processes.

6.3 INPUT SUBSTITUTION

One of the chief features of production under conditions of variable proportions—or a large number of alternative fixed-proportions processes—is that different combinations of inputs can produce a given level of output. In other words, one input can be *substituted* for another in such a way as to maintain a constant level of output. Great theoretical and practical importance attaches to the *rate* at which one input must be substituted for another in order to keep output constant and to the proportionate change in the input ratio induced by a given proportionate change in the rate of substitution.

6.3.a Marginal Rate of Technical Substitution

Consider the representative isoquant I_1 in Figure 6.3.1. P and R are two of the many different input combinations that may be used to

FIGURE 6.3.1

Marginal Rate of Technical Substitution

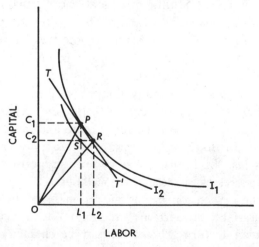

produce the I_1 level of output. If production occurs at P, OC_1 units of capital and OL_1 units of labor are required. OC_2 units of capital and OL_2 units of labor are required for production at R. Thus P is associated with the capital-labor ratio given by the slope of $OP = OC_1/OL_1$ and R with the capital-labor ratio given by the slope of $OR = OC_2/OL_2$.

If there is a change from P to R, the same level of output is produced by using *more* labor and less capital—labor can be substituted for capital by moving from P to R, and *vice versa*. The rate at which labor can be substituted for capital over the arc PR is given by

$$-\frac{OC_1 - OC_2}{OL_1 - OL_2} = \frac{PS}{SR},$$

where the minus sign is affixed so as to yield a positive number. Stated alternatively, the rate of substitution is the change in capital usage divided by the change in labor usage, or the slope of the curvilinear angle PRS.

As the distance from P to R diminishes, the slope of the curvilinear segment PR approaches the slope of the tangent TT' at point P. In the limit, for a very tiny movement in the neighborhood of P the slope of the tangent at P measures the rate of substitution. In this case—for small movements along I_1—it is called the *marginal rate of technical substitution*, just as the slope of a consumer's indifference curve is called the marginal rate of substitution in consumption.

Next, suppose labor input is held constant at the OL_1 level while the input of capital is increased from OC_2 to OC_1. Output would increase from the I_2 level (say Q_2) to the I_1 level (say Q_1). The marginal product of capital is, of course, the increase in output per unit increase in input, or

$$\frac{Q_1 - Q_2}{OC_1 - OC_2}.$$

Since $OC_1 - OC_2 = PS$, the marginal product of capital is

$$\frac{Q_1 - Q_2}{PS}.$$

Now return to the I_2 level and hold capital input constant at OC_2 while increasing labor input from OL_1 to OL_2, or by the amount SR. The marginal product of labor for this change is

$$\frac{Q_1 - Q_2}{SR}.$$

The ratio of the marginal product of labor to that of capital is

$$\frac{Q_1 - Q_2}{SR} \div \frac{Q_1 - Q_2}{PS} = \frac{PS}{SR},$$

the rate of substitution of capital for labor.[6] Thus in the limit, as the distance from P to R becomes very small, the marginal rate of technical substitution of capital for labor is equal to the ratio of the marginal product of labor to the marginal product of capital.

These results may be summarized as follows:

Relations: The marginal rate of technical substitution measures the reduction in one input per unit increase in the other that is just sufficient to maintain a constant level of output. The marginal rate of technical substitution of input X for input Y at a point on an isoquant is equal to the negative of the slope of the isoquant at that point. It is also equal to the ratio of the marginal product of input Y to the marginal product of input X.

6.3.b Diminishing Marginal Rate of Technical Substitution

As already defined, the marginal rate of technical substitution is the ratio of the marginal product of labor to the marginal product of capital. As labor is substituted for capital, the marginal product of labor declines and the marginal product of capital increases.[7] Hence the marginal rate of technical substitution of capital for labor declines as

---

[6] The standard terminology in the theory of production differs slightly from that in the theory of consumer behavior. Let X and Y be commodities and I an indifference curve. In keeping with standard terminology, we defined the marginal rate of substitution of X for Y as the number of units by which Y consumption must be decreased when X consumption is increased by one unit while maintaining the same level of satisfaction. In symbols:

$$MRS_{X \text{ for } Y} = - \left.\frac{\Delta Y}{\Delta X}\right]_{\text{utility constant}} = - \left.\frac{dY}{dX}\right]_{du=0}.$$

In the theory of production, the concept of the marginal rate of technical substitution is entirely analogous to the marginal rate of substitution in the theory of consumer behavior. However, there is a change in terminology. Let K and L be inputs and I an isoquant. The marginal rate of technical substitution, just as the marginal rate of substitution in consumption, is defined as (the negative of) the slope of the isoquant. But it is called the marginal rate of technical substitution of K for L. That is,

$$MRTS_{K \text{ for } L} = - \left.\frac{\Delta K}{\Delta L}\right]_{\text{output constant}} = - \left.\frac{dK}{dL}\right]_{dq=0}.$$

To emphasize: the concepts are analogous, the terminology reversed.

[7] This is not universally true but it will typically be the case in the economic region of production as will be seen shortly.

labor is substituted for capital so as to maintain a constant level of output. This may be summarized as follows:

Relation: As labor is substituted for capital along an isoquant (so that output is unchanged), the marginal rate of technical substitution declines.

The fact that the marginal rate of technical substitution falls as labor is substituted for capital means that isoquants must be convex (that is, in the neighborhood of a point of tangency, the isoquant must lie above the tangent line). This is illustrated in Figure 6.3.2.

Q, R, S, and T are four input combinations lying on the isoquant I. Q has the combination OC_1 units of capital and one unit of labor; R has OC_2 units of capital and two units of labor; and so on. For the movement from Q to R, the marginal rate of technical substitution of capital for labor is, by formula,·

$$-\frac{OC_1 - OC_2}{1 - 2} = OC_1 - OC_2 .$$

Similarly, for the movements from R to S and S to T, the marginal rates of technical substitution are $OC_2 - OC_3$ and $OC_3 - OC_4$, respectively.

Since the marginal rate of technical substitution of capital for labor diminishes as labor is substituted for capital, it is necessary that $OC_1 - OC_2 > OC_2 - OC_3 > OC_3 - OC_4$. Visually, the amount of capital replaced by successive units of labor will decline if, and only if, the isoquant is convex. Since the amount *must* decline, the isoquant must be convex.

Relation: Isoquants must be convex at every point in order to satisfy the principle of diminishing marginal rate of technical substitution.

FIGURE 6.3.2

Diminishing Marginal Rate of Technical Substitution

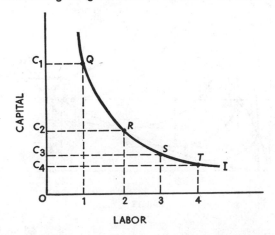

6.3.c Economic Region of Production

Many production functions lead to initial isoquant maps such as shown in Figure 6.2.3. Others, however, generate an isoquant map such as that shown in Figure 6.3.3. It is like the map in Figure 6.2.3 in that the isoquants do not intersect; the higher the isoquants the greater the level of output; and over a range of input values they are negatively sloped. The only difference lies in the fact that the isoquants in Figure 6.3.3 "bend back upon themselves," or have positively sloped segments.

The parallel dashed lines in Figure 6.3.3 indicate the points at which the isoquants bend back upon themselves. The lines OC and OL join these points and form, as we will see, the boundaries for the economic region of production (or the stage II region).

Suppose the quantity represented by isoquant I_4 is to be produced. Producing this amount requires a *minimum* of OC_4 units of capital, inasmuch as any smaller amount would not permit one to attain the I_4 level of output. With OC_4 units of capital, OL_4 units of labor must be used. Beyond this level of input, additional units of labor in combination with OC_4 units of capital would yield a smaller level of output. To maintain the I_4 level of output with a greater labor input would require

FIGURE 6.3.3

Full Isoquant Map and the Relevant Range of Production

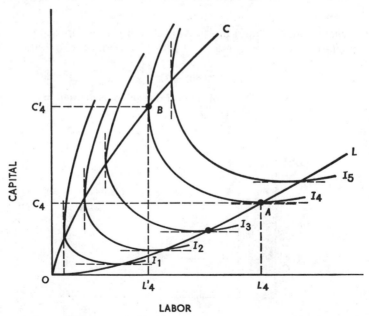

a greater input of capital as well—a palpably uneconomic use of resources.

Since an expansion of labor input beyond OL_4, in the face of the constant capital input OC_4, reduces total output, point A on I_4 represents the intensive margin for labor. Its marginal product is zero, and hence the marginal rate of technical substitution of capital for labor is zero. This is shown by the horizontal tangent at point A. At this point labor has been substituted for capital to the maximum extent consistent with the level of output I_4.

Similarly, producing at the I_4 level requires a certain minimum input of labor, OL'_4 in Figure 6.3.3. The I_4 level cannot be attained without at least this much labor; and with this minimum amount additions to capital input beyond OC'_4 would reduce rather than augment output. Thus the marginal product of capital is zero at point B and negative for quantities in excess of OC'_4 units (in combination with OL'_4 units of labor). Since the marginal product of capital is zero, the marginal rate of technical substitution of capital for labor is infinite or undefined at this point; capital is used to its intensive margin.

By connecting the points of zero marginal labor product, the line OL is formed. Similarly, OC is the locus of points for which the marginal product of capital is zero. Production must take place within this range. Hence the "ridge" lines OL and OC separate the economic from the uneconomic regions of production. To summarize:

Relations: If the production function is such that the total isoquant map is like the one in Figure 6.3.3, then only those portions of the isoquants lying between the ridge lines (the loci of zero marginal products) are relevant to production. These economic portions of the isoquants are uniquely associated with stage II production of each input.

Stage I production for any input conforms to the region of rising average product; and if average product rises, marginal product must exceed average product. Since a stage I area must be present to generate the isoquant map shown in Figure 6.3.3, the "normal" set of product curves—as shown in Figure 5.3.3—must be associated with the production function giving rise to this isoquant map. This "normal" set of product curves is reproduced in panel a, Figure 6.3.4.[8]

Some production functions, however, generate isoquant maps such

---

[8] We "superimpose" total product, average product, and marginal product curves on the same graph for purposes of comparison. Since these are measured differently (total product is units of output while average and marginal product are units of output per unit of input of the productive factor), we are using different scales on the vertical axis.

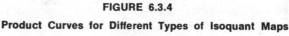

FIGURE 6.3.4

Product Curves for Different Types of Isoquant Maps

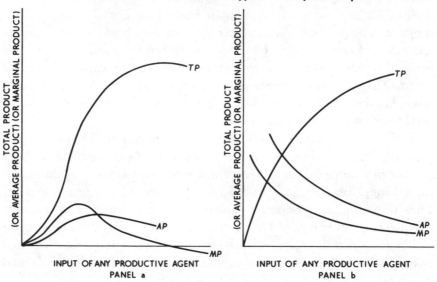

as that in Figure 6.2.3. There is neither a stage I nor a stage III range for either input. The entire production function represents stage II, or the economic region. Marginal and average products decline continuously, but neither reaches zero because there is not a maximum point on the total product curve. Such a production function is shown in panel b, Figure 6.3.4. The average and marginal product curves begin some distance from the origin. This is a mere convenience. They are both defined for infinitesimally small amounts of input; but at input levels less than unity, average and marginal products exceed total product.

The importance of production functions giving rise to the product curves of panel b is an empirical question. For expository purposes, production functions of the type shown in panel a are generally used. In empirical, statistical, and econometric applications, however, a broad class of production functions such as shown in panel b are most often used. The distinction, in fact, is relevant only in theory because observed production relations are always those of stage II.

6.4 OPTIMAL COMBINATION OF RESOURCES

So far the theory of production has been analyzed from the standpoint of an individual entrepreneur. However, nothing has been said regarding the *optimal* way in which he should combine resources. Any desired level of output can normally be produced by a number of different combinations of inputs. Our task now is to determine the specific combination a producer should select.

6.4.a Input Prices and Isocosts

Inputs, just as outputs, bear specific market prices. In determining his *operating* input combination, a producer must pay heed to relative input prices if he is to minimize the cost of producing a given output or maximize output for a given level of cost. In the long run the producer must do this to obtain the *maximum* attainable profit.

Input prices are determined, just as the prices of goods, by supply and demand in the market. For producers who are not monopsonists or oligopsonists, input prices are given by the market, and his rates of purchase do not change them. Let us now concentrate upon a producer who is a perfect competitor in the input market, even though he may be a monopolist or an oligopolist in his output market. (Consideration of monopsony and oligopsony is deferred to Chapter 14.)

Let us continue to assume that the two inputs are labor and capital, although the analysis applies equally well to any two productive agents. Denote the quantity of capital and labor by K and L, respectively, and their unit prices by r and w. The total cost C of using any volume of K and L is $C = rK + wL$, the sum of the cost of K units of capital at r per unit and of L units of labor at w per unit.[9]

To take a more specific example, suppose capital costs $1,000 per unit ($r = \$1,000$) and labor receives a wage of $2,500 per man-year ($w = \$2,500$). If a total of $15,000 is to be spent for inputs, the following combinations are possible: $\$15,000 = \$1,000\,K + \$2,500\,L$, or $K = 15 - 2.5\,L$. Similarly, if $20,000 is to be spent on inputs, one can purchase the following combination: $K = 20 - 2.5\,L$. More generally, if the fixed amount $\bar{C}$ is to be spent, the producer can choose among the combinations given by

$$K = \frac{\bar{C}}{r} - \frac{w}{r}\,L.$$

---

[9] The w, L measurement should be clear. L is the number of man-hours, and w is the wage per hour. The r, K measurement may not be so clear. Various interpretations may be used. One simple interpretation is to suppose that capital is rented and r is the rental price. Even if capital is owned rather than rented, this interpretation is useful because the entrepreneur must "charge" himself rK if he could earn this amount by renting the capital to someone else. This concept of "opportunity" cost will be discussed in Chapter 7.

This is illustrated in Figure 6.4.1. If $15,000 is spent for inputs and no labor is purchased, 15 units of capital may be bought. More generally, if $\bar{C}$ is to be spent and r is the unit cost, $\bar{C}/r$ units of capital may be purchased. This is the vertical-axis *intercept* of the line. If one unit of labor is purchased at $2,500, two and five-tenths units of capital must be sacrificed; if two units of labor are bought, five units of capital must be sacrificed; and so on. Thus as the purchase of labor is increased, the purchase of capital must be diminished. For each additional unit of labor, w/r units of capital must be foregone. In Figure 6.4.1, $w/r = 2.5$. Attaching a negative sign, this is the *slope* of the straight lines constructed in this graph.

The solid lines in Figure 6.4.1 are called *isocost curves* because they

FIGURE 6.4.1

Isocost Curves for $r = \$1,000$ and $w = \$2,500$

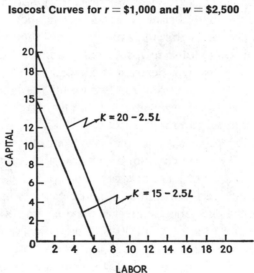

show the various combinations of inputs that may be purchased for a stipulated amount of expenditure. In summary:

Relation: At fixed input prices r and w for capital and labor, respectively, a fixed outlay $\bar{C}$ will purchase any combination of capital and labor given by the following linear equation:

$$K = \frac{\bar{C}}{r} - \frac{w}{r}L.$$

This is the equation for an isocost curve, whose intercept $(\bar{C}/r)$ is the amount of capital that may be purchased if no labor is bought and whose slope is the negative of the input-price ratio (w/r).

6.4.b Maximizing Output for a Given Cost

Suppose at given input prices *r* and *w*, a producer can spend only $\overline{C}$ on production. Subject to this input cost, he only operates efficiently if he maximizes the output attainable. To do this he must select the proper input combination. That is, among all input combinations he can purchase for the fixed amount $\overline{C}$, he must select the one that results in the greatest level of output.

Let the given level of cost $\overline{C}$ be represented by the isocost curve *KL* in Figure 6.4.2. The slope of *KL* is therefore equal to the (negative)

FIGURE 6.4.2

**Optimal Input Combination to Maximize Output
Subject to a Given Cost**

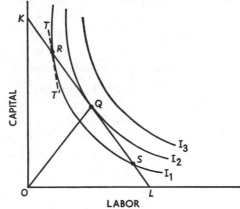

ratio of the price per unit of labor to the price per unit of capital. I_1, I_2, and I_3 are isoquants representing various levels of output. First, observe that the I_3 level of output is not obtainable because the *available* input combinations are limited to those lying on or beneath the isocost curve *KL*.

Next, the producer could operate at points such as *R* and *S*. At these two points, the input combinations *required* to produce the I_1 level of output are *available* for the given cost represented by the isocost *KL*. In this case, however, output can be increased without incurring additional cost by the selection of a more appropriate input combination. Indeed, output can be expanded until the I_2 level is reached—the level at which an isoquant is just tangent to the specified isocost curve. A greater output is not obtainable for the given level of expenditure; a lesser output is inefficient because production can be expanded at no additional cost. Hence the input combination represented by the slope of the ray *OQ* is optimal because it is the combination that maximizes output for the given level of cost.

After studying the theory of consumer behavior, this proposition should be more or less obvious. However, a sound reason lies behind it. For a moment suppose the entrepreneur contemplated producing at point *R*. The marginal rate of technical substitution of capital for labor —given by the slope of the tangent *TT′*—is relatively high. Suppose it is 3:1, meaning that one unit of labor can replace three units of capital at that point. The relative input price, given by the slope of *KL*, is much less, say 1:1. In this case, one unit of labor costs the same as one unit of capital but it can replace three units of capital in production. The producer would obviously be better off if he substituted labor for capital. The opposite argument holds for point *S*, where the marginal rate of technical substitution is less than the input-price ratio.

Following this argument, the producer reaches equilibrium (maximizes output for a given level of cost) only when the marginal rate of technical substitution of capital for labor is equal to the ratio of the price of labor to the price of capital. The market input-price ratio tells the producer the rate at which he *can substitute* one input for another *in purchasing*. The marginal rate of technical substitution tells him the rate at which he *can substitute in production*. So long as the two are not equal, a producer can achieve either a greater output or a lower cost by moving in the direction of equality.[10]

---

[10] Let MP_K be the marginal product of K and let MP_L be the marginal product of L. If capital is changed by a small amount ΔK, the resulting change in output will be

$$MP_K \Delta K$$

and capital costs will change by $r\Delta K$. If total cost is to remain constant, the change in labor costs must exactly offset this change in capital costs or

$$w\Delta L = -r\Delta K .$$

The change in output resulting from this change in labor input will be

$$MP_L \Delta L = -\frac{r}{w} MP_L \Delta K .$$

The net change in output is the sum of these two changes or

$$\Delta Q = \left(MP_K - \frac{r}{w} MP_L \right) \Delta K .$$

If the bracketed expression is positive, an increase in K will increase output; and if the bracketed expression is negative, a decrease in K will increase output. Hence, at maximum output, the bracketed expression must be zero or

Principle: To maximize output subject to a given total cost and given input prices, the producer must purchase inputs in quantities such that the marginal rate of technical substitution of capital for labor is equal to the input-price ratio (the price of labor to the price of capital). Thus

$$MRTS_{K \text{ for } L} = \frac{MP_L}{MP_K} = \frac{w}{r} \, .$$

6.4.c Minimizing Cost Subject to a Given Output

As an alternative to maximizing output for a given cost, an entrepreneur may seek to minimize the cost of producing a stipulated level of output. The problem is solved graphically in Figure 6.4.3. The

FIGURE 6.4.3

Optimal Input Combination to Minimize Cost Subject to a Given Level of Output

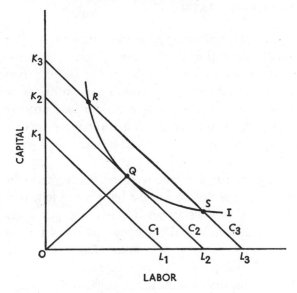

isoquant I represents the stipulated level of output, while C_1, C_2, and C_3 are isocost curves with the same slope (input-price ratio).

First notice that the level of cost represented by C_1 is not feasible because the I level of output is not physically producible by any input combination available for this outlay. Next, the I level could be pro-

$$\frac{MP_L}{MP_K} = \frac{w}{r} \, .$$

By definition, the left side of this expression is $MRTS_{K \text{ for } L}$ as stated in the text.

duced, for example, by the input combinations represented by the points R and S, both at the cost level C_3. But by moving either from R to Q or from S to Q, the entrepreneur can obtain the same output at lower cost.

By the very same arguments used in subsection 6.4.b, a position of equilibrium is attained only at point Q where the isoquant is just tangent to an isocost curve. Thus in equilibrium the marginal rate of technical substitution of capital for labor must equal the ratio of the price of labor to the price of capital. The previous principle may thus be elaborated.

Principle: In order either to maximize output subject to a given cost or to minimize cost subject to a given output, the entrepreneur must employ inputs in such amounts as to equate the marginal rate of technical substitution and the input-price ratio.

6.5 THE EXPANSION PATH

The object of an entrepreneur is to maximize profit. But to do this, he must organize production in the most efficient or economical way. This involves, as we have now seen, adjusting factor proportions until the marginal rate of technical substitution equals the factor-price ratio —or what is the same, adjusting factor proportions until the marginal product of a dollar's worth of each input is the same. When this task is accomplished, equilibrium is attained at a point such as Q in Figures 6.4.2 and 6.4.3.

Now let us digress for a moment to recall the procedure we used when studying the theory of consumer behavior. First, the position of consumer equilibrium was established. Then we posed and answered the following question: how will the combination of goods be changed when price or income changes? We must now pose the same type of question from the standpoint of a producer: how will factor proportions change when output or the factor-price ratio changes?

6.5.a Isoclines

Consider panel a, Figure 6.5.1. The curves *I, II,* and *III* are isoquants depicting a representative production function. T_1, T_2, and T_3 are tangents to *I, II,* and *III,* respectively; and the tangents have been constructed so that they are parallel to one another. That is, the marginal rate of technical substitution of capital for labor is the same at points *A, B,* and *C.* These points have been connected by a smooth curve labeled *OS,* which is called an *isocline.*

FIGURE 6.5.1

Isoclines

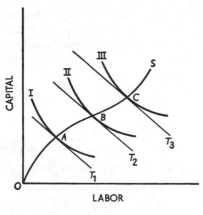

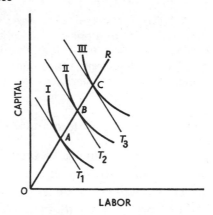

| PANEL a--GENERAL PRODUCTION | PANEL b--LINEARLY HOMOGENEOUS |
| FUNCTION | PRODUCTION FUNCTION |

Definition: An isocline is a locus of points along which the marginal rate of technical substitution iş constant.

In general, isoclines may have almost any shape. The one in panel a has been constructed so as to ramble through the isoquant map. The *special* isoclines in Figure 6.3.3 have a very regular shape. We may now pause to point out the following

Relation: The "ridge lines" defining the economic region of production are isoclines inasmuch as the marginal rate of technical substitution is constant along the lines. In particular (see Figure 6.3.3), *OC* is the isocline along which the marginal rate of technical substitution of capital for labor is infinite, *OL* is the isocline along which it is zero.

Now turn to panel b, Figure 6.5.1, in which the labeling corresponds to that of panel a—with one important exception: the *curve OS* has become the *ray OR*. This is always true when the production function is homogeneous of degree one. In that case, all marginal products are functions of the input ratio only. Thus the marginal rate of technical substitution, which is the ratio of the marginal products, is itself a function of the input ratio and of nothing else. Therefore, whenever the input ratio is constant—for example, 200:100, 400:200, etc.—the marginal rate of technical substitution is constant and independent of the absolute magnitude of the inputs. Since a ray from the origin (such as *OR* in panel b) defines a constant input ratio, the ray must intersect the successive isoquants at points (such as *A, B,* and *C*) where the marginal rates of technical substitution are the same. Hence we may state the following

Relations: The isoclines associated with production functions homogeneous of degree one are straight lines. Therefore, since ridge lines are special isoclines, the ridge lines associated with linearly homogeneous production functions are straight lines (providing, of course, that the function under consideration gives rise to an uneconomic region).

6.5.b Changing Output and the Expansion Path

Turn now to panel a, Figure 6.5.2. Given the input prices, the output corresponding to isoquant *I* can be produced at least cost at point *A*, where the isoquant is tangent to the isocost curve *KL*. This is the position of producer equilibrium. With input prices remaining constant, suppose the entrepreneur wishes to expand output to the level corresponding to the isoquant *II*. The new equilibrium is found by shifting the isocost curve until it is tangent to *II*. Since factor prices remain constant, the slope of the isocost curve does not change. Hence it shifts from *KL* to *K′L′*. Similarly, if the entrepreneur wished to expand output to the amount corresponding to the isoquant *III*, he would produce at point *C* on *III* and *K″L″*.

Connecting all points such as *A*, *B*, and *C* generates the curve *OE*. Now let us assemble some facts. First, factor prices have remained constant. Second, each equilibrium point is defined by equality between the

FIGURE 6.5.2

Expansion Paths

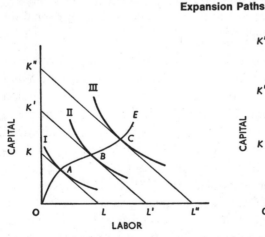

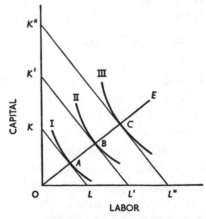

PANEL a-- GENERAL PRODUCTION
FUNCTION

PANEL b-- LINEARLY HOMOGENEOUS
PRODUCTION FUNCTION

marginal rate of technical substitution and the factor-price ratio. Since the latter has remained constant, so has the former. Therefore, *OE* is an isocline, a locus of points along which the marginal rate of technical substitution is constant. But it is an isocline with a special feature. Specifically, it is the isocline along which output will expand when factor prices are constant. We may accordingly formulate this result as a

Definition: The *expansion path* is the particular isocline along which output will expand when factor prices remain constant. The expansion path thus shows how factor proportions change when output or expenditure changes, input prices remaining constant throughout.

Turn now to panel b. Since the isoclines of a linearly homogeneous production function are straight lines, the expansion path is also. Let us state this as the following

Relation: The expansion path corresponding to a production function homogeneous of degree one is a straight line. This reflects the fact that under constant returns to scale, factor proportions depend only upon the factor-price ratio (the slope of the isocost curve); and in particular, factor proportions are independent of the level of output.

As we shall see in Chapter 7, the expansion path is crucial in determining the long-run cost of production.

6.5.c   Expenditure Elasticity[11]

In Chapters 2 and 4 the income elasticity of commodity demand was discussed. In particular, income elasticity was related to the income-consumption curve; and commodities were classified as superior, normal, or inferior according as income elasticity exceeds unity, lies in the unit interval, or is negative. The expenditure elasticity of a factor of production is an analogous concept: its measurement is restricted to the expansion path; and factors are classified as superior, normal, or inferior according as the corresponding expenditure elasticity exceeds unity, lies in the unit interval, or is negative.

Let us begin with the following

Definition: Consider a well-defined factor *X*. The expenditure elasticity of *X* is the relative responsiveness of the usage of *X* to changes in total expenditure. In other words, the expenditure elasticity of *X* is the proportional change in the usage of *X* divided by the proportional change in

---

[11] For a mathematical elaboration of this subsection, see C. E. Ferguson and Thomas R. Saving, "Long-Run Scale Adjustments of a Perfectly Competitive Firm and Industry," *American Economic Review,* vol. 59 (1969), pp. 774–83.

total expenditure. In this definition changes in total expenditure *are restricted to movements along the expansion path.*

Symbolically, the formula for the expenditure elasticity is

$$\eta_x = \frac{dx}{x} \div \frac{dc}{c} = \frac{dx}{dc} \frac{c}{x} \, ,$$

where x is the usage of factor X and c is total expenditure on factors of production.

Next we introduce another

Definition: A factor of production is said to be superior, normal, or inferior according as its expenditure elasticity exceeds unity, lies in the unit interval, or is negative.

This definition is illustrated schematically in Figure 6.5.3. Consider the expansion path and concentrate on factor X. Along ray OR both inputs expand proportionally. At points such as A the usage of factor X expands proportionally more than total expenditure along the expansion path. At all such points the factor is superior. At points such as B factor usage expands proportionally less than total expenditure. Expenditure elasticity lies in the unit interval, and the factor is said to be normal. At D the change in usage of both inputs is proportional and the expenditure elasticity is unity. Analysis is the same along any ray from the origin.

In certain—presumably unusual—cases, the usage of a factor may

FIGURE 6.5.3

Expenditure Elasticity and Factor Classification

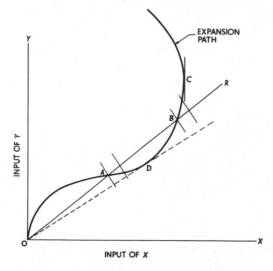

decline when output and resource expenditure are increased. At point C in Figure 6.5.3 the expenditure elasticity of X is instantaneously zero. Beyond point C, the expansion path "bends back" on itself. The usage of X diminishes as expenditure is increased beyond point C. Over this range of expenditure and output, X is an inferior factor. There is a further discussion of inferior factors in section 6.6, and the concept of expenditure elasticity is used in Chapter 7 to analyze the changes in cost curves that result from changes in factor price.

6.6 CHANGES IN INPUT PRICE

From Part I you know a change in the price of a good has two theoretically discernible effects: the substitution effect and the income effect. The substitution effect is always negative; and the income effect is normally positive and reinforces it. Much the same type of effects may be isolated for changes in input price.

First consider Figure 6.6.1. This graph illustrates increases in the price of labor inputs, the price of the capital input remaining constant. The original factor-price ratio is given by the slope of the isocost curve KL_1. As this isocost curve shifts leftward to KL_2 and KL_3, the price of labor increases because the same total expenditure on labor will at first purchase OL_1 units, then OL_2 units, and finally only OL_3 units.

FIGURE 6.6.1

Shifting Isocost Curves to Show an Increase in the Price of Labor

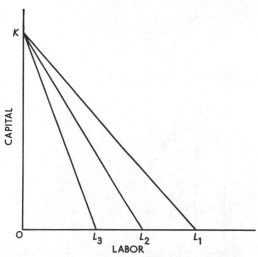

6.6.a The Substitution and Output Effects

The substitution and output effects are shown in Figure 6.6.2. The original point of equilibrium is Q. The level of output is indicated by the isoquant I_1, and the input-price ratio by the slope of the isocost curve KL_1; and Ok_1 units of capital and Ol_1 units of labor are used. Now let the price of labor increase, the price of capital remaining unchanged. This shifts the isocost curve to KL_2. If the producer maximizes the output attainable for this given cost, the equilibrium point changes from Q to S, the level of output falling to that indicated by the isoquant I_2. In the ultimate equilibrium position, Ok_3 units of capital and Ol_3 units of labor are used. The total effect of the wage rate change on labor usage is, therefore, a decrease from Ol_1 to Ol_3, or a reduction of l_1l_3 units of labor.

The total effect may be decomposed into two components. The change in labor usage attributable *exclusively* to the change in the relative input price is called the *substitution effect.* To determine this effect graphically, construct the fictitious isocost line $K'L'$. This line is constructed so there is a fictitious equilibrium at the *old* output level and the *new* input prices. In other words, the rise in input prices has been compensated by an increase in expenditure sufficient to maintain the old level of output. A fictitious equilibrium is reached at point R, and the

FIGURE 6.6.2

**Output and Substitution Effects of a Rise
in the Price of Labor**

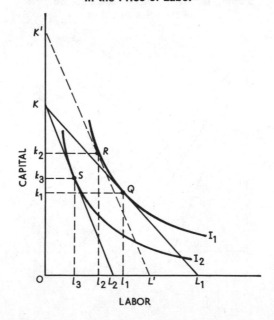

movement from Q to R represents the substitution effect, the change in input usage attributable only to the change in relative input prices, the level of output remaining constant. In input units, the substitution effect reduces labor input from Ol_1 to Ol_2, or by the amount l_1l_2. Capital is substituted for labor, increasing capital usage from Ok_1 to Ok_2, or by k_1k_2.

When an input price increases, however, there must be a decrease in output if the level of expenditure does not increase. The *output* effect is represented by the shift from the fictitious equilibrium point R on I_1 to the ultimate equilibrium point S on I_2. The output effect leads to a reduction in labor input from Ol_2 to Ol_3, or by the amount l_2l_3. Capital usage is also reduced by the output effect, from Ok_2 to Ok_3, or by k_2k_3.

The effect upon labor usage attributable to the rise in the price of labor is simply the sum of the two effects:

$$l_1l_3 \quad = \quad l_1l_2 \quad + \quad l_2l_3$$
$$(Effect) \quad (Substitution\ effect) \quad (Output\ effect)$$

Summarizing, we have the following

Relation: The effect of a change in the price of an input upon the usage of this input may be decomposed into two components. The substitution effect shows the change in input usage attributable exclusively to the change in relative input prices, output held constant. This effect is always negative in that a rise in input price leads to a reduction, and a fall in input price to an increase, in the usage of the input. The output effect shows the change in input usage attributable exclusively to a change in the level of output, input prices remaining constant. It should be emphasized that these adjustments are for a fixed total expenditure. They do not allow for adjustment to a point of profit maximization.

6.6.b "Inferior Factors" and the Output Effect[12]

Just as there may be inferior goods, there may be inferior factors of production; and just as the former is associated with a negative income effect, the latter is associated with a negative output effect. The case of factor inferiority is illustrated in Figure 6.6.3, which is, for all practical purposes, the same as Figure 6.5.3.

The initial equilibrium is at Q on I_1, where the slope of the isocost KL_1 indicates the factor-price ratio and Ol_1 units of labor are employed. Now let the wage rate rise so as to rotate the isocost curve to KL_2. The point of equilibrium shifts to S on I_2, and the usage of labor *expands* to

---

[12] For a detailed treatment of factor inferiority, upon which this section is based, see C. E. Ferguson, *The Neoclassical Theory of Production and Distribution* (London and New York: Cambridge University Press, 1969), chap. 9.

FIGURE 6.6.3

Optimal Input Combination to Maximize Output

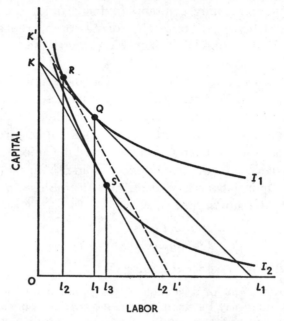

Ol_3. To see the components of the change, construct the fictitious isocost curve $K'L'$ so that it is tangent to the original isoquant but has a slope reflecting the new price ratio. The tangency occurs at R, and it shows the combination of inputs that would be used if the *old* level of output were produced at the *new* input-price ratio. The movement from Q to R, or the decrease from Ol_1 to Ol_2, is the substitution effect; and, as in all cases, it is negative. That is, the quantity of an input demanded varies inversely with its price for movements along an isoquant.

The movement from the fictitious equilibrium at R to the proper equilibrium at S, or the increase from Ol_2 to Ol_3, represents the output effect of the wage rate change. In this case it is negative: the *reduction* in output from the I_1 level to the I_2 level causes an *increase* in the usage of the factor. Whenever this relation occurs, the factor under consideration is said to be an inferior factor.

Definition: An inferior factor of production is one that has a negative output effect or a negative expenditure elasticity.[13]

---

[13] Professor Hicks calls this a "regression relation" and suggests that an inferior factor is one that is particularly suited for small-scale production of the product in question. See John R. Hicks, *Value and Capital* 2d ed. (Oxford: Clarendon Press, 1946), pp. 93–96, esp. p. 96.

We are now treading dangerously close to drawing a mistaken analogy between consumers and producers. It might be well to recount the analogies that can and cannot be drawn between the theories of consumer and producer behavior.

6.7 ANALOGIES BETWEEN CONSUMER AND PRODUCER BEHAVIOR

We have seen that there are many analogies between the theories of consumer and producer behavior. Despite these technical similarities, however, there is an important difference that should not be overlooked. The theory of consumer behavior explains the nature of the consumer's equilibrium. The theory of producer behavior, on the other hand, does not represent a final equilibrium. What the theory tells us is how the producer will combine inputs to produce a *given output* at the lowest possible cost. It does not explain which output the producer will decide on. That decision depends on considerations of profit maximization that will be taken up in later chapters. For example, in Figure 6.6.2 the effect of the increase in the price of labor is to shift the quantity demanded of labor from l_1 to l_3 assuming the producer spends the same amounts on inputs after the price of labor changes as he did before. In fact, as we shall see in the next two chapters, a profit maximizing entrepreneur typically will not spend the same amount after a change in factor prices. It is important to emphasize that the demand for a factor of production *cannot be derived* solely from a graph such as Figure 6.6.2, because more information is needed to determine the profit maximizing output.

6.8 CONCLUSION

Chapters 5 and 6 contain an explanation of the theory of production and of the optimal combination of inputs when input prices are constant. We turn next to the theory of cost, which relies upon the physical laws of production and upon the prices an entrepreneur must pay for his inputs.

QUESTIONS AND EXERCISES

1. Suppose that Transport Service must produce a certain output of cargo and passenger service per year. The Service is confronted with the·following combinations of HC100 aircraft and mechanics which can be

used to yield this required output over its route pattern and meet schedule requirements.

Combination Number	Number of Aircraft	Number of Mechanics
1	60	1,000
2	61	920
3	62	850
4	63	800
5	64	760
6	65	730
7	66	710

    a. If Transport Service is using 60 aircraft and 1,000 mechanics, how many men can it dispense with and still maintain its output if it acquires an additional HC100?

    b. Your answer in (1) is called the _____ _____ of _____ in economic theory.

    c. If the additional annual cost resulting from the operation of another HC100 is $250,000 and if mechanics cost Transport Service $6,000 each annually, should the Service acquire a 61st HC100?

    d. Which combination of aircraft and mechanics should Transport system use to minimize its costs?

    e. Suppose the *annual* cost of an HC100 drops to $200,000 and the cost of mechanics rises to $7,000 per year. What combination should now be employed to minimize annual costs?

    f. Can the data presented above be used to illustrate the law of diminishing returns? Why or why not?

2. Suppose that a product requires two inputs for its production. Then is it correct to say that if the prices of the inputs are equal, optimal behavior on the part of producers will dictate that these inputs be used in equal amounts?

3. The Norfolk and Western Railway did not change from steam to diesel locomotives until nearly all other railroads had done so. This was probably because: (*a*) the N & W wanted to conserve national oil reserves for future generations; (*b*) since the railroad ran through the heart of the Appalachians, coal was cheap relative to diesel fuel; (*c*) N & W management—like some economics professors—couldn't bear to part with the "Iron Horse"; (*d*) all of the above.

4. A railroad would be most likely to substitute expensive signaling systems for multiple track operation if: (*a*) second and third tracks were heavily taxed by the counties through which they passed; (*b*) signaling equipment was produced by a monopolist; (*c*) all railroad officers took Principles of Economics; (*d*) none of the above.

5. Answer true or false and explain your choice.

    a. Two factors of production, say A and B, have the same price. The least-cost combination of A and B for producing a given output will be at the point where the isoquant has a slope of minus 1.

    b. Assume only two factors A and B are used to produce output X. A decrease in the price of A leads to less of B being used.

    c. If the marginal product of A is 5 and its price is \$2, then the additional cost of one more unit of output obtained by employing more of factor A is \$2.

    d. At current levels of employment of factors A and B, the marginal product of A is 3 and the marginal product of B is 2. The price of A is \$5 a unit, and the price of B is \$4 a unit. Because B is the less expensive factor of production, the firm can produce the same output at lower cost by reducing the employment of A and increasing the employment of B.

6. *a.* If the marginal product of L is $MP_L = 100K - L$ and the marginal product of K is $MP_K = 100L - K$, then what is the maximum possible output when the total amount that can be spent on K and L is \$1,000 and the price of K is \$5 and the price of L is \$2?

    b. Answer part (a) when the price of K is \$5 and the price of L is \$5.

    c. (Advanced) When the price of K is P_K and the price of L is P_L, what is the expenditure elasticity for K? For L? (Hint: Use the marginal productivity equilibrium conditions to derive a relationship that expresses L in terms of K, P_K, P_L and the parameters of MP_K and MP_L. Use this expression to substitute for L in the cost equation $C = P_K K + P_L L$.)

    d. (Advanced) If total output is zero when K and L are zero, what is the production function $F(K, L)$?

SUGGESTED READINGS

Borts, George H., and Mishan, E. J. "Exploring the 'Uneconomic Region' of the Production Function," *Review of Economic Studies*, vol. 29 (1962), pp. 300–312.

Cassels, John M. "On the Law of Variable Proportions," *Explorations in Economics,* pp. 223–36. New York: McGraw-Hill Book Co., Inc., 1936.

Ferguson, C. E. *The Neoclassical Theory of Production and Distribution*, chaps. 1–6. London and New York: Cambridge University Press, 1969. [Advanced math necessary.]

———, and Saving, Thomas R. "Long-Run Scale Adjustments of a Perfectly Competitive Firm and Industry," *American Economic Review*, vol. 59 (1969), pp. 774–83. [Advanced math necessary.]

Henderson, James M., and Quandt, Richard E. *Microeconomic Theory: A Mathematical Approach,* 2d ed., pp. 58–67. New York: McGraw-Hill Book Co., Inc., 1971. [Elementary math necessary.]

Hicks, John R. *Value and Capital,* pp. 78–98. 2d ed. Oxford: Oxford University Press, 1946.

Samuelson, Paul A. *Foundations of Economic Analysis,* pp. 57–76. Cambridge, Mass.: Harvard University Press, 1947. [Advanced math necessary.]

7

Theory of cost

7.1 INTRODUCTION

The physical conditions of production, the price of resources, and the economically efficient conduct of an entrepreneur jointly determine the cost of production of a business firm. The production function furnishes the information necessary to trace out the isoquant map. Resource prices establish the isocost curves. Finally, efficient entrepreneurial behavior dictates the production of any level of output by that combination of inputs which equates the marginal rate of technical substitution and the input-price ratio. Each position of tangency therefore determines a level of *output* and its associated *total cost*. From this information, one may construct a table, a schedule, or a mathematical function relating total cost to the level of output. This is the cost schedule or cost function that is one of the subjects of this chapter.

It is not the only subject, however, because in the short run, by definition, all inputs are not variable. Some are fixed, and the entrepreneur cannot instantaneously achieve the input combination that corresponds to economic efficiency (i.e., the one that equates the marginal rate of technical substitution with the input-price ratio). He will operate as efficiently as possible; but in the short run, a point on the expansion path will generally not be attained. We must thus analyze not only long-run cost but short-run cost as well.

Before turning to the mechanics of cost analysis, however, we need to pause for a somewhat broader view and to pose the question, "Just *what* constitutes the legitimate costs of production?" There are two answers to this question which, under ideal circumstances, happen to become one and the same. At present we must be content with the two; but in Chapter 16 we set out the conditions under which the answers are the same.

7.1.a Social Cost of Production

Economists are principally interested in the social cost of production, the cost a society incurs when its resources are used to produce a given commodity. At any point in time a society possesses a pool of resources either individually or collectively owned, depending upon the political organization of the society in question. From a social point of view the object of economic activity is to get as much as possible from this existing pool of resources. What is "possible," of course, depends not only upon the efficient and full utilization of resources but upon the specific list of commodities produced. A society could obviously have a greater output of automobiles if only small compact cars were produced. Larger, more luxurious cars require more of almost every input. But in their private evaluation schemes, some members of the society may attach much greater significance to luxury cars than to compact cars.

Balancing the relative resource cost of a commodity with its relative social desirability entails a knowledge of both social valuations and social cost. This broad problem is deferred to Chapter 16 so that our attention can now be directed exclusively to social cost.

The social cost of using a bundle of resources to produce a unit of commodity X is the number of units of commodity Y that must be sacrificed in the process. Resources are used to produce both X and Y (and all other commodities). Those resources used in X production cannot be used to produce Y or any other commodity. To illustrate with a simple example, think of Robinson Crusoe living alone on an island and sustaining himself by fishing and gathering coconuts. The cost to Crusoe of an additional fish is measured by the number of coconuts he has to forego because he spends more time fishing.

The concept of social cost, or as it is more frequently called, the *alternative* or *opportunity* cost of production, captures much of the essence of what economics is about. Unfortunately, this concept of cost is often overlooked in popular discussions of public and private policy issues. For example, congressional spokesmen often argue against the policy of an all volunteer armed force on the grounds that it "costs" too much relative to a policy of conscription. The error in this reasoning is that the cash payments by the government to individuals who are drafted into military service are not the appropriate measure of the social cost of the draft. The individuals drafted into military service are often taken out of civilian jobs where they are producing goods and services like health care, houses, automobiles, and educational services. By drafting people into the armed services, society must give up some of these goods and services and this foregone production is the appropriate measure of the cost of conscription.

Definition: The *alternative* or *opportunity cost* of producing one unit of commodity X is the amount of commodity Y that must be sacrificed in order to use resources to produce X rather than Y. This is the social cost of producing X.

7.1.b   Private Cost of Production

There is a close relation between the opportunity cost of producing commodity X and a calculation the producer of X must make. The use of resources to produce X rather than Y entails a social cost; there is a private cost as well because the entrepreneur must pay a price to get the resources he uses.

Suppose he does. The entrepreneur pays a certain amount to purchase resources, uses them to produce a commodity, and sells the commodity. He can compare the receipts from sales with the cost of resources and, roughly speaking, determine whether he has made an accounting profit or not. But an economist would be quick to tell the entrepreneur he should make some further calculations. He has invested his time and money in producing commodity X. If he had not undertaken this line of business, he could have invested his time and money elsewhere—in another line of business, perhaps, or by purchasing securities with his money and using his time as an employee of another entrepreneur.

The producer of X incurs certain *explicit costs* by purchasing resources. He incurs some *implicit costs* also, and a full accounting of profit or loss must take these implicit costs into consideration. The pure economic profit an entrepreneur earns by producing commodity X may be thought of as his accounting profit minus what could be earned in the best alternative use of his time and money. These two elements are called the implicit cost of production.

Definition: The implicit costs incurred by an entrepreneur in producing a specific commodity consist of the amounts he could earn in the best alternative use of his time and money. He earns a *pure economic profit* from producing X if, and only if, his total receipts exceed the sum of his explicit and implicit costs.

Implicit costs are thus a fixed amount (in the short run) that must be added to explicit costs in a reckoning of pure economic profit.

7.1.c The Role of the Entrepreneur

The cost concepts discussed in subsections 7.1.a and 7.1.b are useful in understanding the role that the entrepreneur plays in the economic system. To take a simple example, suppose there are two towns that are geographically separated. In one of these towns there is an abundance of apples but very little bread. The reverse is true in the other town. Accordingly, apples are cheap and bread expensive in the first town, and bread is cheap and apples are expensive in the second town. An enterprising businessman who observes these differences stands to profit by purchasing apples from the first town at low prices and selling them at high prices in the second town. At the same time, he can purchase bread at low prices in the second town and sell it at high prices in the first town. The businessman will continue to engage in such trading until he drives the prices in the two towns so close together that transportation costs, the opportunity cost of his money, plus the value of his time are no longer covered by gains from further transactions. In this process, both the businessman and the townspeople have gained. For example, the people in the first town got more bread, which they valued highly, for apples which were relatively less valuable to them.

This simple illustration helps us see the importance of measuring costs as *alternative* costs as in subsection 7.1.a or measuring implicit as well as explicit costs as in subsection 7.1.b. When costs are so measured, the existence of a pure *economic* profit is a signal that individuals value the use of resources more highly in the activity where economic profits exist than in the activities where those resources are currently employed.[1] Entrepreneurs' efforts to maximize pure economic profits provide the mechanism by which scarce resources are directed into activities or uses which the individuals in the society value most highly.

---

[1] It is interesting to note that the symmetry of the definition of opportunity cost means that when a pure economic profit exists in one activity, there is necessarily a pure economic loss in one or more other activities.

7.2 SHORT AND LONG RUNS

In Chapter 5 a convenient analytical fiction was introduced, namely the *short run,* defined as a period of time in which certain types of inputs cannot be increased or decreased. That is, in the short run there are certain inputs whose usage cannot be changed regardless of the level of output. Similarly, there are other inputs, variable inputs, whose usage can be changed. In the long run, on the other hand, all inputs are variable—the quantity of all inputs can be varied so as to obtain the most efficient input combination.

The definition of the long run is reasonably clear-cut; it is a period of time sufficiently long, such that all factors of production can be fully adjusted. The short run is a more nebulous concept. In one nanosecond virtually nothing can be changed in the production process. In a day it may be possible to intensify the usage of certain machines; in a month the entrepreneur may be able to rent some additional equipment; and in a year it may be feasible to have a new plant built. There are obviously many "short runs," and the longer the time the greater the possibilities for factor substitution and adjustment. Costs of producing a given output will clearly depend on the time available to make adjustments in amounts used of the productive factors. Before going into detail about long- and short-run costs, we provide a general overview by examining the relationship between production functions and costs.

7.2.a Long-Run Costs and the Production Function

The tools of Chapter 6 allow us to relate costs to outputs. That is, for any given output, we can determine the minimum cost at which that output can be produced given factor prices and the production function. This is illustrated in panel (a) of Figure 7.2.1 for three different output levels. At output level Q_1, the minimum total cost is determined by the isocost line C_1. At output level Q_2, the minimum total cost is determined by isocost line C_2. The isocost line for Q_2 is above and to the northeast of the isocost line for Q_1, which means, as we expect, that costs increase with output.

It is easily seen that by repeating this procedure at all isoquants along the expansion path E, it is possible to derive the long-run cost schedule for the firm—that is, the schedule which shows the cost of producing each output after all factors of production have been fully adjusted. This is illustrated in panel (b) of Figure 7.2.1. From panel

FIGURE 7.2.1

Long-Run Costs and the Production Function

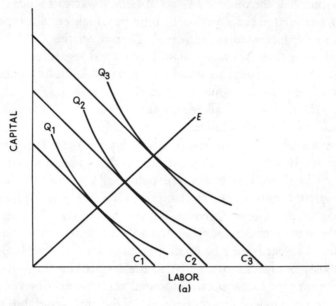

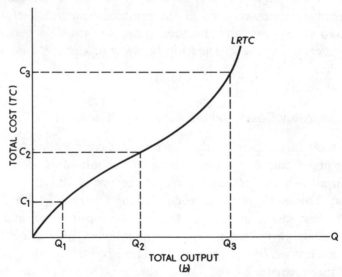

(a) we see that output Q_1 is produced at total cost C_1, and these two values are used as coordinates to plot a point on the total output–total cost graph of panel (b). Similarly Q_2 is produced at total cost C_2, and Q_3 is produced at total cost C_3. These points are also plotted on the panel (b) graph. Repeating this procedure for all other outputs, the long-run total cost schedule *LRTC* of panel (b) is derived.

Relation: The long-run total cost schedule is directly related to the expansion path; indeed, the long-run total cost schedule or function is simply the cost-output equivalent of the expansion path.

7.2.b Short-Run Costs and the Production Function

We have observed that there are really a large number of "short" runs depending on the time period involved. Each such short run is characterized by the fact that not all factors of production can be fully adjusted in the given time period. To see the significance of this, suppose a firm wishes to increase output and must acquire 150 more milling machines to do so at lowest cost (i.e., the long-run optimum requires 150 more machines). To be concrete we assume there are four "short" runs each of which is three months longer than the previous one. Because of delivery lags, no new milling machines can be added in the first 3 months but delivery schedules permit the delivery of 50 additional machines in each of the next 3-month periods. Hence, the long-run adjustment (1 year in this case) involves an addition of 150 milling machines, but these are added in three steps. In the shortest run (3 months) no new machines are available, in the 6-month "run" there are 50 new milling machines, in the 9-month "run" there are 100 new milling machines, and in the long run (12 months) there are 150 new machines. To produce at the new output level, different amounts of labor are needed in each three-month period. We assume by use of overtime and part-time employment that man-hours can be freely adjusted at all times. (For simplicity of exposition we also assume here that the wage rate does not increase for overtime hours.) This situation is illustrated in Figure 7.2.2.

In this figure, initial output is given by the isoquant Q_0 and the new higher output is shown by the isoquant Q_1. During the first three-month period (the "shortest" run) the output Q_1 is produced with the current stock of milling machines ($K_1 = K_0 = 30$) and L_1 man-hours. Total cost to the entrepreneur in this period is given by the isocost line C_1. Note that the isocost line is *not* tangent to Q_1 at point A. This is because of the inability of the firm to get any additional milling machines in the first three months. Given the existing stock of 30 milling machines, the cheapest way to get output Q_1 is by a substantial increase in man-hours (from L_0 to L_1).[2]

During the next 3 months, 50 new milling machines are delivered

---

[2] The entrepreneur would not want to operate with less than 30 milling machines in the short run because to produce Q_1 even more labor than L_1 then would be needed, and this would shift the isocost line further to the northeast.

FIGURE 7.2.2

Short-Run Costs and the Production Function

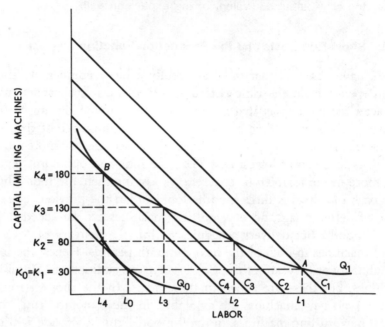

so the total stock of milling machines rises to K_2 ($K_2 = 80 = K_1 +$ 50). This allows the entrepreneurs to cut overtime and part-time labor hours to L_2. It also reduces his cost of producing output Q_1 because, as may readily be seen in Figure 7.2.2, the C_2 isocost line is to the southwest of isocost line C_1. Because capital stock is below the long-run optimum of 150 machines, however, it is still true that the C_2 isocost line is not tangent to Q_1. The next 3 months bring 50 more milling machines and a further shift in the isocost line to C_3.

Equilibrium is finally reached in 1 year when 180 milling machines are available. At this level, the isocost line C_4 is tangent to Q_1, and Q_1 is being produced at the lowest possible total cost given factor prices and the production function.

This example illustrates the key point that the shorter the run the more costly it is to produce outputs other than the output for which the current capital stock is optimal (i.e., the output given by Q_0 in this example). Long-run costs for producing a given output will never exceed short-run costs of producing that output.

The dynamic theory of short- and long-run costs can be derived several ways. For example, it is possible to introduce adjustment costs explicitly and obtain models of optimal capital accumulation.[3] However, in order to concentrate on important comparative static results, we will adhere to the traditional dichotomy between the short run and the long run. *In other words, while we recognize that there are many short runs, we will focus our attention on a given short-run period for expository convenience.*

7.2.c Fixed and Variable Costs in the Short Run

Corresponding to fixed inputs are short-run fixed costs. The various fixed inputs have unit prices; the fixed explicit cost is simply the sum of unit prices multiplied by the fixed number of units used. In the short run, implicit costs are also fixed; thus it is an element of fixed cost. In the example of subsection 7.2.b, the fixed costs in the short run are the costs of the given stock of milling machines. In more complicated examples there will be many such fixed inputs with corresponding fixed costs.

Definition: Total fixed cost is the sum of the short-run explicit fixed cost and the implicit cost incurred by an entrepreneur.

Inputs that are variable in the short run give rise to short-run variable cost. Since input usage can be varied in accordance with the level of output, variable costs also vary with input. If there is zero output, no units of variable input need be employed. Variable cost is accordingly zero, and total cost is the same as total fixed cost. When there is a positive level of output, however, variable inputs must be used. This gives rise to variable costs, and total cost is then the sum of total variable and total fixed cost.

Definition: Total variable cost is the sum of the amounts spent for each of the variable inputs used.

Definition: Total cost in the short run is the sum of total variable and total fixed cost.

7.3 THEORY OF COST IN THE SHORT RUN

Our analysis of cost begins with the theory of short-run cost; we then move to the "planning horizon" in which all inputs are variable and study the theory of cost in the long run, when the optimal input combination can be obtained.

---

[3] See for example, J. P. Gould, "Adjustment Costs in the Theory of Investment of the Firm," *The Review of Economic Studies,* vol. 35 (1968), pp. 47–55.

7.3.a   Total Short-Run Cost

Analysis of total short-run cost depends upon two propositions already discussed in this chapter: (*a*) the physical conditions of production and the unit prices of inputs determine the cost of production associated with each possible level of output; and (*b*) total cost may be divided into two components, fixed cost and variable cost.

Suppose an entrepreneur has a fixed *plant* that can be used to produce a certain commodity. Further suppose this plant cost $100. Total fixed cost is, therefore, $100—it does not change in magnitude irrespective of the level of output. This is reflected in Table 7.3.1 by the column of $100 entries labeled "Total Fixed Cost." It is furthermore shown by the horizontal line labeled *TFC* in Figure 7.3.1. Both table and graph emphasize that fixed cost is indeed fixed.

Variable inputs must also be used if production exceeds zero. In the spirit of Chapter 5, you might suppose there is only one variable input; alternatively, the multiple-input approach of Chapter 6 may be adopted. The choice is really not material, because an increase in the level of output requires an increase in the usage of inputs—whether this be

TABLE 7.3.1

Fixed, Variable, and Total Cost

Quantity of Output	Total Fixed Cost	Total Variable Cost	Total Cost
0	$100	–0–	$ 100.00
1	100	$ 10.00	110.00
2	100	16.00	116.00
3	100	21.00	121.00
4	100	26.00	126.00
5	100	30.00	130.00
6	100	36.00	136.00
7	100	45.50	145.50
8	100	56.00	156.00
9	100	72.00	172.00
10	100	90.00	190.00
11	100	109.00	209.00
12	100	130.40	230.40
13	100	160.00	260.00
14	100	198.20	298.20
15	100	249.50	349.50
16	100	324.00	424.00
17	100	418.50	518.50
18	100	539.00	639.00
19	100	698.00	798.00
20	100	900.00	1,000.00

one variable input or many variable inputs used in the optimal combination. In either case, the greater the level of variable input the greater the variable cost of production. This is shown in column 3 of Table 7.3.1 and by the curve labeled *TVC* in Figure 7.3.1.

Summing total fixed and total variable cost gives total cost, the entries in the last column of Table 7.3.1 and the curve labeled *TC* in Figure 7.3.1. From the figure, one may see that *TC* and *TVC* move together and are, in a sense, parallel. That is to say, the slopes of the

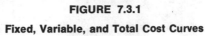

FIGURE 7.3.1

Fixed, Variable, and Total Cost Curves

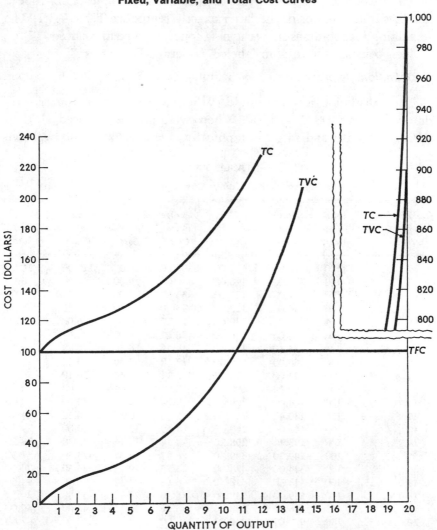

two curves are the same at every output point; and at each point, the two curves are separated by a vertical distance of $100, the total fixed cost.

7.3.b Average and Marginal Cost

The total cost of production, including implicit cost, is very important to an entrepreneur. However, one may obtain a deeper understanding of total cost by analyzing the behavior of various average costs and of marginal cost.

The illustration of Table 7.3.1 is continued in Table 7.3.2. Indeed the first four columns of the latter exactly reproduce Table 7.3.1. The remaining four columns show the new concepts to be introduced.

First consider the column labeled "Average Fixed Cost."

Definition: Average fixed cost is total fixed cost divided by output.

The calculation is very simple. When one unit of output is produced, AFC is $100/1 = $100. When two units are produced, $AFC = $100/2 = $50; and so on. Graphically, average fixed cost is shown

TABLE 7.3.2

Average and Marginal Cost Calculations

Quantity of Output	Total Fixed Cost	Total Variable Cost	Total Cost	Average Fixed Cost	Average Variable Cost	Average Total Cost	Marginal Cost
1..........	$100	$ 10.00	$ 110.00	$100.00	$10.00	$110.00	$ 10.00
2..........	100	16.00	116.00	50.00	8.00	58.00	6.00
3..........	100	21.00	121.00	33.33	7.00	40.33	5.00
4..........	100	26.00	126.00	25.00	6.50	31.50	5.00
5..........	100	30.00	130.00	20.00	6.00	26.00	4.00
6..........	100	36.00	136.00	16.67	6.00	22.67	6.00
7..........	100	45.50	145.50	14.29	6.50	20.78	9.50
8..........	100	56.00	156.00	12.50	7.00	19.50	10.50
9..........	100	72.00	172.00	11.11	8.00	19.10	16.00
10..........	100	90.00	190.00	10.00	9.00	19.00	18.00
11..........	100	109.00	209.00	9.09	9.91	19.00	19.00
12..........	100	130.40	230.40	8.33	10.87	19.20	21.40
13..........	100	160.00	260.00	7.69	12.31	20.00	29.60
14..........	100	198.20	298.20	7.14	14.16	21.30	38.20
15..........	100	249.50	349.50	6.67	16.63	23.30	51.30
16..........	100	324.00	424.00	6.25	20.25	26.50	74.50
17..........	100	418.50	518.50	5.88	24.62	30.50	94.50
18..........	100	539.00	639.00	5.56	29.94	35.50	120.50
19..........	100	698.00	798.00	5.26	36.74	42.00	159.00
20..........	100	900.00	1000.00	5.00	45.00	50.00	202.00

by the curve designated *AFC* in Figure 7.3.2. Cost in dollars is plotted on the vertical axis and output on the horizontal axis. The *AFC* curve is negatively sloped throughout because as output increases the ratio of fixed cost to output must decline.[4] Mathematically, the *AFC* curve is a rectangular hyperbola.

Next move to column 6, Table 7.3.2. This column is labeled "Average Variable Cost," a concept that is entirely analogous to average fixed cost.

Definition: Average variable cost is total variable cost divided by output.

Again the calculation is simple and gives rise to the curve labeled *AVC* in Figure 7.3.2. But now there is a great difference between *AVC* and *AFC*: the former does not have a negative slope throughout its entire range. Indeed, in this illustration *AVC* first declines, reaches a minimum, and rises thereafter.

The reason for this curvature lies in the theory of production. Total variable cost equals the number of units of variable input used (V) multiplied by the unit price of the input (P). Thus in the one-variable-input case, $TVC = PV$.

Average variable cost is TVC divided by output Q, or

$$AVC = \frac{TVC}{Q} = P\frac{V}{Q}.$$

Consider the term V/Q, the number of units of input divided by the number of units of output. In Chapter 5, average product (AP) was defined as total output (Q) divided by the number of units of input (V). Thus

$$AVC = P\left(\frac{1}{AP}\right),$$

or price per unit of input multiplied by the reciprocal of average product. Since average product normally rises, reaches a maximum, and then declines, average variable cost normally falls, reaches a minimum, and rises thereafter.

Relation: A production function such as that shown in Figure 5.2.1 gives rise to the average product curve shown in Figure 5.2.2. This type of production function also determines a total variable cost curve such as that in Figure 7.3.1 and the average variable cost curve shown in Figure 7.3.2.

---

[4] Let the cost function be $C = A + g(q)$, where A is total fixed cost and $g(q)$ gives the total variable cost associated with each level of output. Thus average fixed cost is A/q and its slope is $-A/q^2$.

FIGURE 7.3.2

Average and Marginal Cost Curves

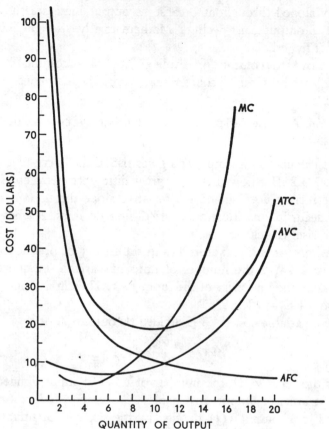

Column 7, Table 7.3.2, contains the entries for average total cost, which may also be called average cost or unit cost.

Definition: Average total cost is total cost divided by output.

In light of this definition, ATC may be computed by dividing the entries in column 4 by the corresponding entries in column 1.

However, since

$$TC = TFC + TVC \, ,$$
$$ATC = \frac{TC}{Q} = \frac{TFC}{Q} + \frac{TVC}{Q} = AFC + AVC \, .$$

Thus one may calculate average cost as the sum of average fixed and average variable cost.

This method of calculation also explains the shape of the average total cost curve in Figure 7.3.2. Over the range of values for which both *AFC* and *AVC* decline, *ATC* must obviously decline as well. But even after *AVC* turns up, the marked decline in *AFC* causes *ATC* to continue to decline. Finally, however, the increase in *AVC* more than offsets the decline in *AFC*; *ATC* therefore reaches its minimum and increases thereafter.

Finally, column 8 of Table 7.3.2 contains the entries for marginal cost.

Definition: Marginal cost is the addition to total cost attributable to the addition of one unit to output.

Marginal cost is thus calculated by subtracting successively the entries in the Total Cost column.[5] For example, the marginal cost of the second unit produced is $MC_2 = TC_2 - TC_1$. Since only variable cost changes in the short run, however, marginal cost may be computed by successive subtraction of the entries in the Total Variable Cost column. Thus the marginal cost of the second unit is also $MC_2 = TVC_2 - TVC_1$.

As shown in Figure 7.3.2, *MC*—like *AVC*—first declines, reaches a minimum, and rises thereafter. The explanation for this curvature also lies in the theory of production. Let Δ denote "the change in." As shown just above, $MC = \Delta(TVC)$ for a unit change in output. More generally, if output does not change by precisely one unit, $MC = \Delta(TVC)/\Delta Q$. In our previous notation, $TVC = PV$. Thus $\Delta TVC = P(\Delta V)$ for an entrepreneur who is a perfect competitor in the input market (input price is given by market demand and supply and changes in his purchases do not affect the price).

Using the two relations,

$$MC = P\frac{\Delta V}{\Delta Q} \, .$$

In Chapter 5, marginal product (*MP*) was defined as the change in output attributable to a change in input, or $MP = \Delta Q/\Delta V$. Thus

$$MC = P\left(\frac{1}{MP}\right) \, .$$

Since marginal product normally rises, reaches a maximum, and declines, marginal cost normally declines, reaches a minimum, and rises thereafter.

---

[5] Let the cost function be defined as in footnote 4. For infinitesimally small changes in output,

$$MC = \frac{dC}{d} = g'(q) \, .$$

Relation: A production function such as that shown in Figure 5.2.1 gives rise to the marginal product curve shown in Figure 5.2.2. This type of production function also determines a total cost curve such as that in Figure 7.3.1 and the marginal cost curve shown in Figure 7.3.2.

7.3.c Geometry of Average and Marginal Cost Curves

In Chapter 5, the average and marginal product curves were derived geometrically from the total product curve. In like manner, the average and marginal cost curves may be derived from the corresponding total cost curve.

Figure 7.3.3 illustrates the derivation of average fixed cost. (Note:

FIGURE 7.3.3

Derivation of the Average Fixed Cost Curve

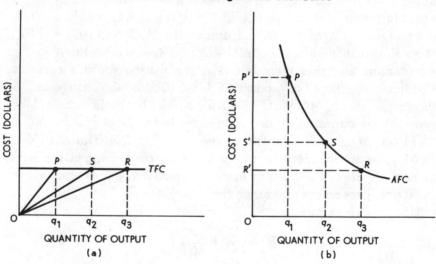

vertical axes of panels (a) and (b) have different scales.) In panel (a), total fixed cost is plotted and the outputs Oq_1, Oq_2, and Oq_3 are measured so that $Oq_1 = q_1q_2 = q_2q_3$. Since $AFC = TFC/Q$, average fixed cost is given by the slope of a ray from the origin to a point on the TFC curve. For output Oq_1, AFC is the slope of the ray OP, or q_1P/Oq_1. Similarly, for output Oq_2, AFC is q_2S/Oq_2, and so on. Since TFC is always the same, $q_1P = q_2S = q_3R$. By construction, $Oq_2 = 2Oq_1$, and $Oq_3 = 3Oq_1$. Thus AFC for output Oq_2 is $q_2S/Oq_2 = q_1P/2Oq_1 = 1/2 \ (q_1P/Oq_1) = 1/2 \ AFC$ for output Oq_1. This is shown in panel (b) by the difference in OP' and OS'—more specifically, $OS' = 1/2$

FIGURE 7.3.4

Derivation of the Average Variable Cost Curve

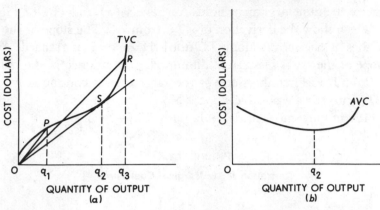

QUANTITY OF OUTPUT
(a)

QUANTITY OF OUTPUT
(b)

OP'. Similarly, as you can demonstrate for yourself, $OR' = 1/3 \ OP'$. The remaining points on AFC are determined in the same way.

Figure 7.3.4 shows how AVC is derived from TVC. As is true of all "average" curves, the average variable cost associated with any level of output is given by the slope of a ray from the origin to the corresponding point on the TVC curve. As may easily be seen from panel (a), the slope of a ray from the origin to the curve steadily diminishes as one passes through points such as P; and it diminishes until the ray is just tangent to the TVC curve at point S, associated with output Oq_2. Thereafter the slope increases as one moves from S toward points such as R. This is reflected in panel (b) by constructing AVC with a

FIGURE 7.3.5

Derivation of the Average Total Cost or Unit Cost Curve

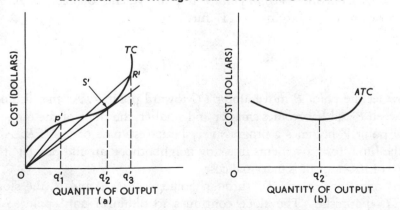

QUANTITY OF OUTPUT
(a)

QUANTITY OF OUTPUT
(b)

negative slope until output Oq_2 is attained. After that point, the slope becomes positive and remains positive thereafter.

Exactly the same argument holds for panels (a) and (b) of Figure 7.3.5, which show the derivation of ATC from TC. The slope of the ray diminishes as one moves along TC until the point S' is reached. At S' the slope of the ray is least, so minimum ATC is attained at the output level Oq'_2. Thereafter the slope of the ray increases continuously, and the ATC curve has a positive slope. (Note: The output level Oq_2 does not represent the same quantity in Figures 7.3.3–7.3.6.)

FIGURE 7.3.6

Derivation of the Marginal Cost Curve

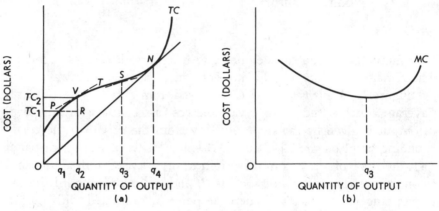

QUANTITY OF OUTPUT
(a)

QUANTITY OF OUTPUT
(b)

Finally, the derivation of marginal cost is illustrated in Figure 7.3.6. Panel (a) contains the total cost curve TC. As output increases from Oq_1 to Oq_2, one moves from point P to point V, and total cost increases from TC_1 to TC_2. Marginal cost is thus

$$MC = \frac{TC_2 - TC_1}{Oq_2 - Oq_1} = \frac{VR}{PR}.$$

Now let the point P move along TC toward point V. As the distance between P and V becomes smaller and smaller, the slope of the tangent T at point V becomes a progressively better estimate of VR/PR. And in the limit, for movements in a tiny neighborhood around point V the slope of the tangent is marginal cost.

As one moves along TC through points such as P and V, the slope of TC diminishes. The slope continues to diminish until point S is reached at output Oq_3. Thereafter the slope increases. Therefore, the

FIGURE 7.3.7

Typtical Set of Cost Curves

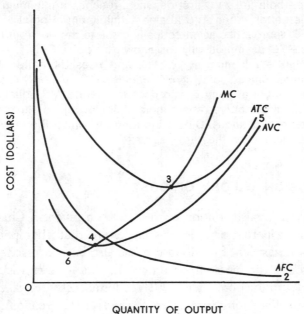

QUANTITY OF OUTPUT

MC curve is constructed in panel (b) so that it decreases until output Oq_3 is attained and increases thereafter.

One final point should be noted about Figures 7.3.4 and 7.3.6. As already shown, TC and TVC have the same slope at each output point; TC is simply TVC displaced upward by the constant amount TFC. Since the slopes are the same, MC is given by the slope of either curve. In panel (a), Figure 7.3.4, the slope of the ray OS gives minimum AVC. But at this point the ray OS is just tangent to TVC; hence it also gives MC at this point. Thus $MC = AVC$ when the latter attains its minimum value. Similarly, in panel (a), Figure 7.3.6, the slope of the ray ON gives minimum ATC. But at this point the ray is tangent to TC; thus its slope also gives MC. Consequently $MC = ATC$ when the latter attains its minimum value.

7.3.d Short-Run Cost Curves

The properties of the average and marginal cost curves, as derived in subsection 7.3.c, are illustrated by the "typical" set of short-run cost curves shown in Figure 7.3.7. The properties may be summarized as follows:

Relations: (*i*) AFC declines continuously, approaching both axes asymptotically, as shown by points 1 and 2 in the figure. AFC is a rectangular hyperbola. (*ii*) AVC first declines, reaches a minimum at point 4, and rises thereafter. When AVC attains its minimum at point 4, MC equals AVC. As AFC approaches asymptotically close to the horizontal axis, AVC approaches ATC asymptotically, as shown by point 5. (*iii*) ATC first declines, reaches a minimum at point 3, and rises thereafter. When ATC attains its minimum at point 3, MC equals ATC. (*iv*) MC first declines, reaches a minimum at point 6, and rises thereafter. MC equals both AVC and ATC when these curves attain their minimum values. Furthermore, MC lies below both AVC and ATC over the range in which the curves decline; it lies above them when they are rising.

7.4 LONG-RUN THEORY OF COST

The conventional definition of the long run given in Chapter 5 and elsewhere is "a period of time of such length that all inputs are variable." Another aspect of the long run has also been stressed—an aspect that is, perhaps, the most important of all. The long run is a *planning horizon*. All production, indeed all economic activity, takes place in the short run. The "long run" refers to the fact that economic agents— consumers and entrepreneurs—can plan ahead and choose many aspects of the "short run" in which they will operate in the future. Thus in a sense, the long run consists of all possible short-run situations among which an economic agent may choose.

As an example, *before* an investment is made an entrepreneur is in a long-run situation. He may select any one of a wide variety of different investments. After the investment decision is made and funds are congealed in fixed capital equipment, the entrepreneur operates under short-run conditions. Thus perhaps the best distinction is to say that an economic agent *operates* in the short run and *plans* in the long run.

7.4.a Short Run and the Long

To begin with a highly simplified situation, suppose technology is such that plants in a certain industry can have only three different sizes. That is, the fixed capital equipment comprising the "plant" is available in only three sizes—small, medium, and large.

The plant of smallest size gives rise to the short-run average cost curve labeled SAC_1 in Figure 7.4.1; the medium-size plant has short-run average cost given by SAC_2; and the large plant has an average cost given by SAC_3. In the long run, an entrepreneur has to choose among

FIGURE 7.4.1

Short-Run Average Cost Curves for Plants of Different Size

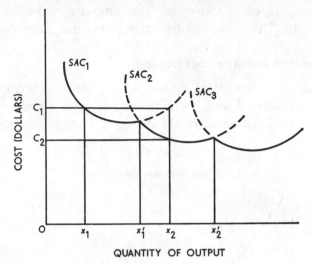

QUANTITY OF OUTPUT

the three investment alternatives represented by the three short-run average cost curves. If he expects his most profitable output to be Ox_1, he will select the smallest plant. If he expects Ox_2 to be most profitable, he will select the medium plant; and so forth. Such decisions would be made because the entrepreneur chooses the plant capable of producing the expected output at the lowest unit cost.

If he expected to produce either Ox_1' or Ox_2', his decision would be more difficult. At each of these points, two plants give rise to the same average cost. An entrepreneur might choose the smaller plant because it requires a smaller investment. On the other hand, he might select the larger plant in order to meet a possible expansion of demand. In these two examples the entrepreneur's decision would be based upon considerations other than least-cost output.

In all other cases his decision is determined by unit cost. Suppose he expects to produce output Ox_1. He accordingly builds the plant represented by SAC_1. Now suppose he actually finds it desirable to produce Ox_2 units. He can do this with his plant, at an average cost of OC_1 per unit. In the short run this is all he can do; he has no option. But he can plan for the future. Once his old plant has "worn out" he can replace it with a new one—and it will be a medium-size plant because the output Ox_2 can be produced for an average cost of OC_2 per unit, substantially less than with the small plant.

In the short run, an entrepreneur must operate with SAC_1, SAC_2, or SAC_3. But in the long run, he can plan to build the plant whose size leads to the least average cost for any given output. Thus as a planning device he regards the heavily shaded curve as his long-run average cost curve because this curve shows the least unit cost of producing each possible output. This curve is frequently called the "envelope curve."

7.4.b Long-Run Average Cost Curve

The illustration above is, as we said, highly simplified. An entrepreneur is normally faced with a choice among quite a wide variety of plants. In Figure 7.4.2, six short-run average cost curves are shown: but

FIGURE 7.4.2

Long-Run Average Cost Curve

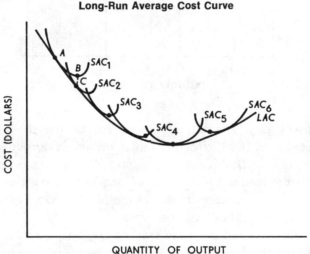

this is really far from enough. Many curves could be drawn between each of those shown. These six plants are only representative of the wide variety that could be constructed.

These many curves, just as the three in subsection 7.4.a, generate *LAC* as a planning device. Suppose an entrepreneur thinks the output associated with point *A* will be most profitable. He will build the plant represented by SAC_1 because it will enable him to produce this output at the least possible cost per unit. With the plant whose short-run average cost is given by SAC_1, unit cost could be reduced by expanding output to the amount associated with point *B*, the minimum point on SAC_1. If demand conditions were suddenly changed so this larger output were desirable, the entrepreneur could easily expand—and he would add to his profitability by reducing unit cost. Nevertheless, when setting his future plans the entrepreneur would decide to construct the plant represented by SAC_2 because he could reduce unit costs even more. He would operate at point C, thereby lowering his unit cost from the level at point B on SAC_1.

The long-run planning curve, LAC, is a locus of points representing the least unit cost of producing the corresponding output. This curve is the long-run average cost curve. The entrepreneur determines the size of plant by reference to this curve. He selects that short-run plant which yields the least unit cost of producing the volume of output he anticipates.[6]

7.4.c Long-Run Marginal Cost

A marginal cost curve may be constructed for the planning curve or the long-run average cost curve. This is illustrated in Figure 7.4.3.

FIGURE 7.4.3

Long-Run and Short-Run Marginal Cost

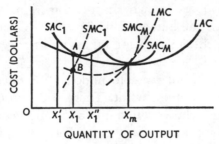

Consider the plant represented by the short-run average cost curve SAC_1 with the associated short-run marginal cost curve SMC_1. At point A, corresponding to output Ox_1, SAC and LAC are equal. Hence short-run and long-run total cost are also equal.

For smaller outputs, such as Ox_1', SAC_1 exceeds LAC, so short-run total cost is greater than long-run total cost. Thus for an expansion of output toward Ox_1, long-run marginal cost—whatever it may be—must exceed the known short-run marginal cost. That is, we have moved from a point where short-run total cost exceeds long-run total cost to

[6] It is important to recall that we are operating under the assumption that the "short" run is a well-defined period of time. That is, for expository purposes, we have adopted the analytical fiction that there is only *one* short run. If we were to account for the more realistic case of many short runs each corresponding to a different length of time (as in subsection 7.2.b), we would have to replace each SAC curve in Figure 7.4.2. with a nested set of short-run average cost curves.

a point where they are equal. The addition to total cost, or marginal cost, must consequently be smaller for the short-run curve than for the long-run curve. Therefore LMC is greater than SMC to the left of point A.[7]

For an expansion of output from Ox_1 to Ox_1'', the opposite situation holds. SAC_1 is greater than LAC at Ox_1'', so short-run total cost exceeds long-run total cost at this point. Now we have moved from a point where short-run and long-run total cost are equal (Ox_1) to a point where short-run total cost exceeds long-run total cost (Ox_1''). Therefore, the addition to total cost, or marginal cost, must be greater for the short-run curve than for the long-run curve. Whatever LMC might be, it must be less than SMC_1 to the right of Ox_1.

Now we have the information to find one point on the LMC curve. LMC must exceed SMC_1 to the left of Ox_1 and it must be less than SMC_1 to the right of Ox_1. Therefore, LMC must equal SMC_1 at output Ox_1. This gives us point B on the LMC curve. To find all the other points, this process is repeated. Take the next short-run average cost curve, together with its known short-run marginal cost. LMC must equal this SMC for the output at which the SAC curve is tangent to LAC. Performing this process for all plant sizes generates the LMC curve.

There is one important point to notice. LMC intersects LAC when the latter is at its minimum point. There will be one, and only one, short-run plant size whose minimum short-run average cost coincides with minimum long-run average cost. This plant is represented by SAC_M and SMC_M in Figure 7.4.3. SMC_M equals SAC_M at the minimum point on the latter curve. SAC_M is tangent to LAC at their common minimum; and as we have shown, LMC equals SMC at the point where SAC and LAC are tangent. Therefore, LMC must pass through the minimum point on LAC.

At the risk of belaboring the obvious, let us emphasize that *optimal* adjustment is always preferable to *suboptimal* adjustment. This leads to a slightly different view of LAC and LMC. This is stated as a

Definition: The long-run average cost curve shows the *minimum unit cost* of producing every feasible level of output; the long-run marginal cost curve shows the *minimum amount* by which cost is increased when output is expanded and the *maximum amount* that can be saved when output is reduced.

---

[7] It might be well to emphasize this point by means of a simple numerical example. Refer to Figure 7.4.3. At output Ox_1', since $SAC_1 > LAC$, let short-run total cost be \$100 and long-run total cost be \$90. At output Ox_1, they are equal, say \$110. Thus over the range Ox_1' to Ox_1, short-run marginal cost is \$10 while long-run marginal cost is \$20.

7.4.d   The Envelope Curve and the Expansion Path

We have just discussed the concept of the long-run average cost curve as the envelope of a set of short-run curves. Earlier, in subsection 7.2.a, the relationship between the expansion path and the long-run total cost curve was explained. Since long-run average costs are simply long-run total costs divided by output, these two approaches to long-run costs are really one and the same. In subsection 7.2.b, we saw that producing a given output with factor combinations other than those along the expansion path always meant that short-run total costs were higher than long-run total costs. This means, of course, that short-run average costs must exceed long-run average costs except at points corresponding to factor usage along the expansion path. The points on the expansion path are thus related on a one-to-one basis with the points of tangency of the short-run average cost curves and the long-run average cost curve in Figure 7.4.2.

This situation is illustrated in Figure 7.4.4. Suppose the short-run capital stock is fixed at K_0. The long-run equilibrium output for this capital stock obtains at point B where the isocost line C is tangent to isoquant Q at the given (fixed) capital stock K_0. This is a point on

FIGURE 7.4.4

The Expansion Path and Suboptimal Adjustment

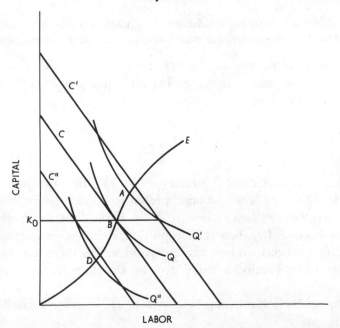

the expansion path E. To produce output Q' with capital stock K_0, the isocost line is shifted to C'. Note that point A, where the isoquant Q' intersects the expansion path E, is the long-run equilibrium for output Q'. In the short run, with K_0 fixed, the entrepreneur is on a higher isocost line than he would be if capital stock could be adjusted. Thus, short-run costs (average and total costs) are greater than the long-run costs of producing Q'.

The same reasoning applies to the output Q'' where short-run costs are given by the isocost line C''. When capital stock can be fully adjusted (downward in this case), equilibrium will occur at point D on the expansion path, and this will be on a lower isocost line. Once again short-run costs exceed long-run costs. Only on the expansion path is $SAC = LAC$.

7.5 COST ELASTICITY AND THE FUNCTION COEFFICIENT

A very important relationship between the production function and the long-run total cost curve may now be established. We begin by introducing the concept of the function coefficient.

7.5.a The Function Coefficient

The function coefficient is defined for every production function as follows:

Definition: The *function coefficient* (ϵ) shows the proportional change in output that results when all inputs are expanded in the same proportion.

The function coefficient may be expressed as a formula. The proportional change in output is $\Delta q/q$. Let all inputs be expanded in the proportion λ. Then, by definition

$$\epsilon = \frac{\left(\dfrac{\Delta q}{q}\right)}{\lambda}. \tag{7.5.1}$$

If the function coefficient is unitary ($\epsilon = 1$), then the proportional change in inputs leads to the same proportional change in output and we say there are *constant returns to scale*. If the function coefficient is less than 1 ($\epsilon < 1$), then the proportional change in output is less than the proportional change in inputs and we say there are *decreasing returns to scale*. Finally, when $\epsilon > 1$ we say there are *increasing returns to scale*.

Let the production function be $q = f(x, y)$; then for a small change in x, denoted Δx, output will change by $MP_x \Delta x$ which is the marginal product of x times the change in x. Similarly, for a small change in y, output will change by $MP_y \Delta y$ where MP_y is the marginal product of y. For small changes in x and y, then, the output change is

$$\Delta q = MP_x \Delta x + MP_y \Delta y .\qquad(7.5.2)$$

Simple algebra shows that (7.5.2) is equivalent to

$$\frac{\Delta q}{q} = \frac{x}{q} MP_x \frac{\Delta x}{x} + \frac{y}{q} MP_y \frac{\Delta y}{y} .\qquad(7.5.3)$$

Now suppose x and y increased in the same proportion λ (i.e., let $\Delta x/x = \Delta y/y = \lambda$) and we have from (7.5.3):

$$\frac{\Delta q}{q} = \left(MP_x \frac{x}{q} + MP_y \frac{y}{q} \right) \lambda \qquad(7.5.4)$$

or

$$\epsilon = \frac{\frac{\Delta q}{q}}{\lambda} = MP_x \frac{x}{q} + MP_y \frac{y}{q} .\qquad(7.5.5)$$

This result is useful in the following subsection.

7.5.b Cost Elasticity

The results of interest require some *tedious but straightforward* manipulation of symbols that is relegated to a footnote.[8] This symbol manipulation leads to the following

---

[8] Start with (7.5.5) in the text and let the prices of the two imputs be p_x and p_y. Multiply and divide the first term on the far right-hand side of (7.5.5) by p_x, the second term by P_y. One thus obtains

$$\epsilon = \frac{MP_x}{p_x} \frac{x p_x}{q} + \frac{MP_y}{p_y} \frac{y p_y}{q} .\qquad(7.8.1)$$

In Chapter 6 we found that the expansion path is defined by equality between the marginal rate of technical substitution and the input-price ratio. Further, we saw that this may always be expressed by saying that the marginal product of a dollar's worth of each input must be the same. Symbolically,

$$\frac{MP_x}{p_x} = \frac{MP_y}{p_y} .\qquad(7.8.2)$$

Substituting equation (7.8.2) in (7.8.1), write

$$\epsilon = \frac{MP_x}{p_x} \left(\frac{x p_x}{q} + \frac{y p_y}{q} \right) = \frac{MP_x}{p_x} \left(\frac{x p_x + y p_y}{q} \right) \qquad(7.8.3)$$

Relation: The function coefficient is equal to the ratio of long-run average cost to long-run marginal cost; in symbols,

$$\epsilon = \frac{LAC}{LMC} . \tag{7.5.6}$$

File this result for the moment and consider the elasticity of total cost. By definition, it is the proportional change in cost resulting from a given proportional change in output. In symbols, the formula is

$$\kappa = \frac{\Delta C}{C} \div \frac{\Delta q}{q} = \frac{\Delta C}{\Delta q} \frac{q}{C} = \frac{LMC}{LAC} . \tag{7.5.7}$$

As with all elasticities, it is the ratio of the marginal to the average. Let us emphasize this

Relation: The elasticity of total cost equals the ratio of marginal cost to average cost.

Comparing equations (7.5.6) and (7.5.7), we find that

$$\kappa = \frac{1}{\epsilon} , \tag{7.5.8}$$

which is the important relation we set out to find.

Finally, we need some information from this chapter. First, by definition, total cost (C) is the sum of the payments to all inputs, that is, the price of each input multiplied by the number of units employed and summed over all inputs. Thus

$$C = xp_x + yp_y . \tag{7.8.4}$$

Further, we defined average cost as $AC = C/q$. Substitution in equation (7.8.3) gives

$$\epsilon = \frac{MP_x}{p_x} (AC) . \tag{7.8.5}$$

The other bit of information we need from this chapter is that marginal cost (LMC) is equal to the input price divided by its marginal product:

$$LMC = \frac{p_x}{MP_x} . \tag{7.8.6}$$

Substituting in equation (7.8.5) completes our "busy work":

$$\epsilon = \frac{LAC}{LMC} , \tag{7.8.7}$$

the relation stated in the text.

It is worthwhile to emphasize one point. When we substituted equation (7.8.2) in (7.8.1), we eliminated MP_y/p_y. We could just as easily have eliminated MP_x/p_x. The results would be the same because marginal cost is equal to the input price divided by its marginal product. The result to emphasize is as follows: for movements along the expansion path, marginal cost is the same irrespective of the input for which it is calculated. This is just another way of stating the familiar proposition that "at the *margin,* all things are equally dear."

Relation: The elasticity of total cost is equal to the reciprocal of the function coefficient; specifically, the elasticity of total cost is less than, equal to, or greater than unity according as the function coefficient is greater than, equal to, or less than unity.

The implications of this relation are worth exploring in some detail. First, recall that there are increasing, constant, or decreasing returns to scale according as the function coefficient exceeds, equals, or is less than one. For example, suppose $\epsilon > 1$. This implies that a proportional expansion of inputs causes output to expand in greater proportion. Now if $\epsilon > 1$, $\kappa < 1$. This implies that a proportional increase in output causes cost to expand in smaller proportion. The reason is clear: since there are increasing returns to scale, the given proportional expansion of output can be achieved by a smaller proportional increase in input usage. At constant input prices, cost therefore increases by proportionately less than output.

Exercise: Carry out this type of argument for the case in which $\epsilon < 1$.

Now continue to assume that $\epsilon > 1$ and $\kappa < 1$. If total cost increases in smaller proportion than output, average cost declines. Thus over the range in which the production function exhibits increasing returns to scale, the long-run average cost curve declines (see Figure 7.5.1). On the other hand, when there are decreasing returns to scale ($\epsilon < 1$), the total cost function is elastic ($\kappa > 1$). This means that

FIGURE 7.5.1

Long-Run Average Cost and the Function Coefficient

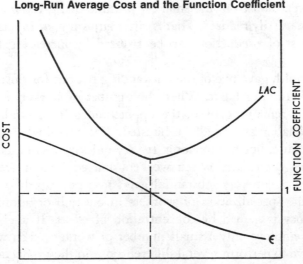

cost increases by proportionately more than output, so that average cost rises. Again the reason is clear: when $\epsilon < 1$, a given proportional increase in output requires inputs to be increased in greater proportion. At constant factor prices, total cost expands by proportionately more than output and average cost increases.

These results may be summarized as the following

Relation: Long-run average cost decreases or increases according as there are increasing or decreasing returns to scale; this relation holds if, and only if, factor prices are constant throughout.

7.6 SHAPE OF *LAC*

The short- and long-run average cost curves are alike in that each has been drawn with a U shape. The reasons for this shape, however, are quite different. *SAC* is U-shaped because the decline in average fixed cost is ultimately more than offset by the rise in average variable cost— the latter occurring because average product reaches a maximum and declines. But this has nothing at all to do with the curvature of *LAC*. Increasing or decreasing returns to scale in the production function and certain financial economies and diseconomies of scale are the factors governing the shape of *LAC*.

7.6.a Economies of Scale

As the size of plant and the scale of operation become larger, considering expansion from the smallest possible plant, certain economies of scale are usually realized. That is, after adjusting *all* inputs optimally the unit cost of production can be reduced by increasing the size of plant.

Adam Smith gave one of the outstanding reasons for this: specialization and division of labor. When the number of workers is expanded, fixed inputs remaining fixed, the opportunities for specialization and division of labor are rapidly exhausted. The marginal product curve rises, to be sure, but not for long. It very quickly reaches its maximum and declines thereafter. When workers and equipment are expanded together, however, very substantial gains may be reaped by division of jobs and the specialization of workers in one job or another.

Proficiency is gained by concentration of effort. If a plant is very small and employs only a small number of workers, each worker will usually have to perform several different jobs in the production process. In doing so he is likely to have to move about the plant, change tools, and so on. Not only are workers not highly specialized but a part of their work time is consumed in moving about and changing tools. Thus important savings may be realized by expanding the scale of operation. A larger plant with a larger work force may permit each worker to specialize in one job, gaining proficiency and obviating time-consuming interchanges of location and equipment. There naturally will be corresponding reductions in the unit cost of production.

Technological factors constitute a second force contributing to economies of scale. If several different machines, each with a different rate of output, are required in a production process, the operation may have to be quite sizable to permit proper "meshing" of equipment. Suppose only two types of machines are required, one that produces and one that packages the product. If the first machine can produce 30,000 units per day and the second can package 45,000, output will have to be 90,000 units per day in order fully to utilize the capacity of each machine.

Another technological element is the fact that the cost of purchasing and installing larger machines is usually proportionately less than the cost of smaller machines. For example, a printing press that can run 200,000 papers per day does not cost 10 times as much as one that can run 20,000 per day—nor does it require 10 times as much building space, 10 times as many men to work it, and so forth. Again, expanding size tends to reduce the unit cost of production.

Thus two broad forces—specialization and division of labor and technological factors—enable producers to reduce unit cost by expanding the scale of operation.[9] These forces give rise to the negatively sloped portion of the long-run average cost curve.

But why should it ever rise? After all possible economies of scale have been realized, why does the curve not become horizontal?

7.6.b Diseconomies of Scale

The rising portion of *LAC* is usually attributed to "diseconomies of scale," which essentially means limitations to efficient management. Managing any business entails controlling and coordinating a wide variety of activities—production, transportation, finance, sales, etc. To

---

[9] This discussion of economies of scale has concentrated upon physical and technological forces. There are financial reasons for economies of scale as well. Large-scale purchasing of raw and processed materials may enable the buyer to obtain more favorable prices (quantity discounts). The same is frequently true of advertising.

perform these managerial functions efficiently, the manager must have accurate information; otherwise the essential decision making is done in ignorance.

As the scale of plant expands beyond a certain point, top management necessary has to delegate responsibility and authority to lower echelon employees. Contact with the daily routine of operation tends to be lost and efficiency of operation to decline. Red tape and paper work expand; management is generally not as efficient. This increases the cost of performing the managerial function and, of course, the unit cost of production.

It is very difficult to determine just when diseconomies of scale set in and when they become strong enough to outweigh the economies of scale. In businesses where economies of scale are negligible, dis-

FIGURE 7.6.1

Various Shapes of *LAC*

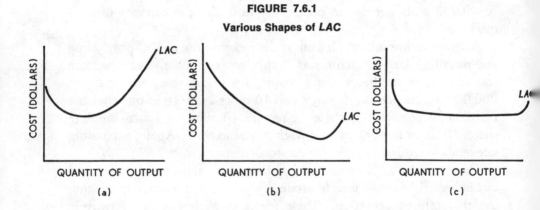

economies may soon become of paramount importance, causing *LAC* to turn up at a relatively small volume of output. Panel (a), Figure 7.6.1, shows a long-run average cost curve for a firm of this type. In other cases, economies of scale are extremely important. Even after the efficiency of management begins to decline, technological economies of scale may offset the diseconomies over a wide range of output. Thus the *LAC* curve may not turn upward until a very large volume of output is attained. This case, typified by the so-called natural monopolies, is illustrated in panel (b), Figure 7.6.1.

In many actual situations, however, neither of these extremes describes the behavior of *LAC*. A very modest scale of operation may enable a firm to capture all of the economies of scale; however, diseconomies may not be incurred until the volume of output is very great. In this case, *LAC* would have a long horizontal section, as shown in panel (c). Many economists and businessmen feel that this type of *LAC* curve describes most production processes in the American economy.

7.7 LONG-RUN COST AND CHANGES IN FACTOR PRICE[10,11]

Given the production function, costs change when factor prices change. In particular, total and average cost increase when a factor price increases, fall when a factor price declines. For simplicity, in this section we assume that only *one* factor price changes, and this change is represented by an increase in factor price.

7.7.a Changes in Long-Run Average Cost

Long-run total cost of any given output must increase when the price of any factor increases. Factor substitution may occur, but the cost of producing the given output at the new prices and new set of inputs must be greater than the cost of producing the output at the old prices and at the old set of inputs. Were this not so, cost could have been reduced before the factor price change by using the new set of inputs (at the original factor prices). This reasoning holds for all output levels, so long-run average cost must increase after the factor price increases. In particular, the new level of minimum average cost must be higher than the old level of minimum average cost.

7.7.b Changes in Long-Run Marginal Cost and Minimum Average Total Cost

As explained in footnotes 10 and 11, the results of this section are based upon mathematical analysis that is not readily susceptible of verbal explanation. For that reason the following relations are stated without proof (but see Figure 7.7.1).

Relation: When the price of a factor of production increases, long-run average cost increases. The new point of minimum long-run average cost corresponds to a greater output if the factor under consideration is normal

---

[10] This section contains a verbal summary of the mathematical and economic results presented in C. E. Ferguson and Thomas R. Saving, "Long-Run Scale Adjustments of a Perfectly Competitive Firm and Industry," *American Economic Review*, vol. 59 (1969), pp. 774–83.

[11] This section may be omitted without loss in continuity. It is based upon mathematical results contained in Ferguson and Saving, "Long-Run Scale Adjustments." Unfortunately, these results do not have a simple verbal or graphical interpretation.

FIGURE 7.7.1

**Schematic Illustration of Shifts in *AC* and *MC*
When Factor Price Increases**

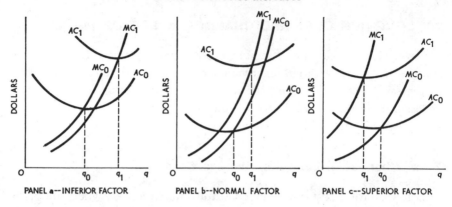

or inferior. It corresponds to a smaller output if the factor is superior. The opposite relation holds if the price of the factor decreases.

Relation: If the price of a factor of production increases, long-run marginal cost decreases if the factor under consideration is inferior. Otherwise, long-run marginal cost increases. The opposite relation holds for a decrease in factor price.

7.8 CONCLUSION

The physical conditions of production and resource prices jointly establish the cost of production. This is very important to individual business firms and to the economy as a whole. But it is only half the story. Cost gives one aspect of economic activity: to the individual businessman it comprises his obligations to pay out funds; to the society as a whole it represents the resources that must be sacrificed to obtain a given commodity. The other aspect is revenue or demand. To the individual businessman, revenue constitutes the flow of funds from which his obligations may be met. To society, demand represents the social valuation placed on a commodity.

Thus both demand and cost must be taken into consideration. It is to the demand side that we turn in Part III.

QUESTIONS AND EXERCISES

Return to the problem at the end of Chapter 5. Total product column (1) is given; and you have computed average product column (2) and marginal product column (3). You are also given the following information:

1. Total fixed cost (total price of fixed inputs) is $220 per period.

2. Units of the variable input cost $100 per unit per period. Using this information, add to your table entries for the new categories shown below in columns 4 through 10.

Units of Variable Input (1)	Total Product (2)	Average Product (2)	Marginal Product (3)	Total Fixed Cost (4)	Total Variable Cost (5)	Total Cost (6)	Average Fixed Cost (7)	Average Variable Cost (8)	Average Total Cost (9)	Marginal Cost (10)

I. Graph the total cost curves on one sheet and the average and marginal curves on another.

II. By reference to table and graph, answer the following questions.

   1. When marginal product is increasing, what is happening to—
      a. Marginal cost?
      b. Average variable cost?

   2. When marginal cost first begins to fall, does average variable cost begin to rise?

   3. What is the relation between marginal cost and average variable cost when marginal and average products are equal?

   4. What is happening to average variable cost while average product is increasing?

   5. Where is average variable cost when average product is at its maximum? What happens to average variable cost after this point?

   6. What happens to marginal cost after the point where it equals average variable cost?
      a. How does it compare with average variable cost thereafter?
      b. What is happening to marginal product thereafter?
      c. How does marginal product compare with average product thereafter?

   7. What happens to total fixed cost as output is increased?

   8. What happens to average fixed cost as:
      a. Marginal product increases?
      b. Marginal cost decreases?
      c. Marginal product decreases?
      d. Marginal cost increases?
      e. Average variable cost increases?

   9. How long does average fixed cost decrease?

10. What happens to average total cost as:
    a. Marginal product increases?
    b. Marginal cost decreases?
    c. Average product increases?
    d. Average variable cost decreases?

11. Does average total cost increase:
    a. As soon as the point of diminishing marginal returns is passed?
    b. As soon as the point of diminishing average returns is passed?

12. When does average cost increase? Answer this in terms of—
    a. The relation of average cost to marginal cost.
    b. The relation between the increase in average variable cost and the decrease in average fixed cost.

1. Consider the point where $SAC = LAC$. Explain precisely why LMC exceeds SMC for a decrease in output. (Hint: Both MC's show the reduction in cost attributable to the reduction in output.)

2. Comment on the following statement: long-run average cost is a meaningless concept since in this period most conditions underlying the cost function will probably change in unpredictable ways.

3. Beginning with a production function or schedule involving two variable inputs, explain how one derives both the short- and long-run average cost curves and the short-run marginal cost curve.

4. Given constant input prices and completely divisible and adaptable inputs, are the customary U-shaped short-run average variable cost curves consistent with a constant-returns-to-scale production function? Answer the same question for long-run average cost.

5. What are the relations between increasing returns to scale and decreasing long-run average cost? More generally, what relations, if any, exist between "returns to scale" and the shape of the long-run average cost curve?

6. The Southern Railway's lines from East St. Louis (Ill.) and Evansville (Ind.) to grain-consuming destinations in Georgia had substantial excess trackage capacity. In deciding whether to invest in a sizable fleet of giant cars for carrying grain to these destinations and in setting rates for this traffic, Southern would rationally consider (a) fully allocated costs of the trackage, crew and fuel costs; (b) fully allocated cost of the trackage, extra equipment costs, crew and fuel costs; (c) cost of the new equipment, crew and fuel costs; (d) none of the above.

7. In the late 1950s, the development of trilevel railroad "rack" cars for carrying new automobiles substantially lowered the costs of hauling such traffic. This represented (a) a change in demand for railroad ser-

vices, (*b*) a change in supply of railroad services, (*c*) a change in supply of trucking services for new automobiles, (*d*) all of the above.

8. Forty years ago, several trains used the Monon Railroad Station in Lafayette, Indiana, each day; eight years ago (and today), the station was used by one train per day in each direction. In deciding whether to tear down its older large station and to replace it with a smaller building, the Monon probably considered whether (*a*) the total cost of the old building was greater than the total cost of the new building, (*b*) the variable cost of operating the old building was greater than the total cost of the new building, (*c*) the variable cost of the old building was greater than the variable cost of the new building, (*d*) the total cost of the old building was greater than the variable cost of the new building.

9. Suppose that the employees of a certain firm establish a labor union and are able to negotiate an *effective* featherbedding contract (i.e., the firm must employ more workers than dictated by the conditions of optimal resource utilization). Determine how this featherbedding contract changes the short-run cost curves of the firm. Hold your answer to this exercise for a related exercise in Chapter 9.

SUGGESTED READINGS

Clark, J. M. *The Economics of Overhead Costs,* chaps. 4–6. Chicago: University of Chicago Press, 1923.

Ferguson, C. E. *The Neoclassical Theory of Production and Distribution,* chap. 7. London and New York: Cambridge University Press, 1969. [Advanced math required.]

————, and **Saving, Thomas R.** "Long-Run Scale Adjustments of a Perfectly Competitive Firm and Industry," *American Economic Review,* vol. 59 (1969), pp. 774–83.

Henderson, James M., and Quandt, Richard E. *Microeconomic Theory: A Mathematical Approach,* 2nd ed., pp. 70–79. New York: McGraw-Hill Book Co., Inc., 1971. [Elementary math required.]

Viner, Jacob. "Cost Curves and Supply Curves," *Zeitschrift für Nationalökonomie,* vol. 3 (1931), pp. 23–46. Reprinted in AEA, *Readings in Price Theory,* pp. 198–232. Homewood, Ill.: Richard D. Irwin, Inc., 1952.

Advanced reading, part II

I. THE THEORY OF PRODUCTION

Arrow, Kenneth J.; Chenery, Hollis B.; Minhas, Bagicha; and Solow, Robert M. "Capital-Labor Substitution and Economic Efficiency," *Review of Economics and Statistics,* vol. 43 (1961), pp. 225–50.

Borts, George H., and **Mishan, E. J.** "Exploring the 'Uneconomic Region' of the Production Function," *Review of Economic Studies,* vol. 29 (1962), pp. 300–12.

Carlson, Sune. *A Study on the Pure Theory of Production,* Stockholm Economic Studies, No. 9. London: P. S. King & Sons, Ltd., 1939.

Cassels, John M. "On the Law of Variable Proportions," *Explorations in Economics,* pp. 223–36. New York: McGraw-Hill Book Co., Inc., 1936.

Ferguson, C. E. "Transformation Curve in Production Theory: A Pedagogical Note," *Southern Economic Journal,* vol. 29 (1962), pp. 96–102.

———. *The Neoclassical Theory of Production and Distribution,* chaps. 2–6. London and New York: Cambridge University Press, 1969.

———, and **Saving, Thomas R.** "Long-Run Scale Adjustments of a Perfectly Competitive Firm and Industry," *American Economic Review,* vol. 59 (1969), pp. 774–83.

Machlup, Fritz. "On the Meaning of the Marginal Product," *Explorations in Economics,* pp. 250–63. New York: McGraw-Hill Book Co., Inc., 1936.

Samuelson, Paul A. *Foundations of Economic Analysis,* pp. 57–89. Cambridge, Mass.: Harvard University Press, 1947.

Shephard, Ronald W. *Cost and Production Functions.* Princeton, N.J.: Princeton University Press, 1953.

Stigler, George J. *Production and Distribution Theories.* New York: The Macmillan Co., 1946.

Walters, A. A. "Production and Cost Functions: An Econometric Survey," *Econometrica,* vol. 31 (1963), pp. 1–66, with extensive bibliography.

II. THE THEORY OF COST

Viner, Jacob. "Cost Curves and Supply Curves," *Zeitschrift für Nationalökonomie,* vol. 3 (1931), pp. 23–46. This is the classic reference in the field. In addition, see Ferguson, *The Neoclassical Theory of Production and Distribution* (chaps. 7 and 8); Samuelson, *Foundations of Economic Analysis;* Shephard, *Cost and Production Functions;* and Walters, "Production and Cost Functions: An Econometric Survey," as listed above.

part III

Theory of the firm and
market organization

The theory of business operation within an organized but uncontrolled market brings together the topics covered in Parts I and II. Demand, the broad topic of Part I, establishes the *revenue side* of business operation. Product demand determines either the quantity a firm can sell at any price it selects or the price a firm can obtain for any quantity it wishes to market. Market demand also helps to determine the type of industry structure that is likely to emerge in response to market conditions—whether the industry is likely to be competitive, monopolistic, or what have you.

The technical conditions of production and their reflection in business operating costs, the subject of Part II, establish the *cost side* of business operation and the *supply conditions* of the industry. Brought together, revenue and cost for the individual business concern and demand and supply for the entire market determine the market price and output of the firm and the industry. These forces accordingly determine the allocation of resources among industries as well.

The general purpose of Part III is to discover how the price-output decisions of individual entrepreneurs and the structure of the market jointly determine the allocation of resources. This inquiry inevitably entails an appraisal of the *efficiency* with which resources are allocated.

Given the conditions of demand and supply, or of revenue and cost, our analysis is based upon two fundamental assumptions.

Free Market. First, we assume that each market is free and operates freely in the sense that there is no external control of market forces. One form of external control is government intervention. The federal government (and upon occasion state and local governments as well) imposes various types of regulations that condition the economic milieu in which firms operate and to which they must ultimately adjust. The regulation of so-called public utilities by both federal and state governments is one example—perhaps the most well-known example, but still only one. Parity-price programs and acreage controls are examples of regulations applied largely to agricultural markets. Tariffs and certain antitrust regulations are examples of controls principally applicable to industrial markets. President Nixon's wage-price freeze of 1971 and subsequent Phase I to Phase IV policies represent an attempt at multisector economic controls.

Another type of government control, at times more subtle than the explicit regulations mentioned above, is "moral suasion." By "moral suasion" one generally means the more or less effective control of business (and sometimes labor union) activity by means of appeal to "social conscoiusness," "social responsibility," or "regard for public welfare." Incidences of moral suasion have run the gamut from President Dwight D. Eisenhower's rather weak appeal to all businessmen to resist price increases to President John F. Kennedy's forceful threat to steel producers.

Irrespective of their nature, all these controls establish artificial market conditions to which business firms must adjust—they help to establish the economic environment in which business decisions are made. So also does another type of external control somewhat more amorphous than government regulation. To set the stage for explanation, let us quote Adam Smith: "People of the same trade seldom meet together, even for merriment and diversion, but the conversation ends in a conspiracy against the public, or in some contrivance to raise prices."[1] Simply, when only a small number of producers are in a certain field there is a strong incentive for them to act collusively to fix a monopoly or near monopoly price.

Such collusive behavior imposes an external control upon the market and thereby limits the free exercise of market forces. It is perhaps for this reason that the Sherman Antitrust Act was passed in 1890, declaring it illegal to (*a*) enter into a contract, combination, or con-

---

[1] Adam Smith, *Wealth of Nations* (Cannan ed.; London: Methuen, 1904), vol. 1, p. 130.

spiracy in restraint of trade (sec. 1); and (*b*) to monopolize, attempt to monopolize, or combine or conspire to monopolize trade (sec. 2).

While many markets are not "free" in the sense used here, a vast number are. The object is to analyze the efficiency of resource allocation in free markets. In case a market is not free, one is able to draw important inferences concerning the relative efficiency of free as against controlled markets.

Profit Maximization.   The second fundamental assumption underlying Part III is that entrepreneurs try to maximize profit.[2] The discussion of implicit and explicit costs and economic profit in Chapter 7 indicates the important role of profit maximization as a mechanism for allocating resources in a market economy. While the proximate causes for profit maximization may be inglorious motives such as greed and avarice, the result of such behavior is the socially desirable movement of resources into activities where maximum benefits are generated. This is not to say that all efforts directed to profit maximization have socially desirable consequences. We have just noted that successful efforts of entrepreneurs to form cartels or monopolies limit the freedom of market forces. Such undesirable aspects of profit-maximizing behavior can be attenuated through appropriate legislation such as the antitrust laws.

Whether profit maximization is a reasonable assumption is a question long debated in economics. Several important criticisms have been brought to bear. However, these criticisms do not overcome the supremely important fact that the assumption of profit maximization is the only one providing a general theory of firms, markets, and resource allocation that is successful both in explaining and predicting business behavior.

---

[2] For the purpose of *explaining* business behavior it is sufficient to assume that entrepreneurs act *as if* they tried to maximize profit. For the purpose of predicting business behavior the *as if* assumption is the only justifiable one.

8

Theory of price in perfectly competitive markets

8.1 INTRODUCTION

"Perfect competition" is an exacting concept forming the basis of the most important model of business behavior. The essence of the concept, to be defined more fully below, is that the market is entirely *impersonal*. There is no "rivalry" among suppliers in the market, and buyers do not recognize their competitiveness vis-à-vis one another. Thus in a sense perfect competition describes a market in which there is a complete absence of direct competition among economic agents. As a theoretical concept of economics, it is the diametrical opposite of the businessman's concept of competition.

In ordinary conversation the market for automobiles, say, or for razor blades would be described as highly competitive; each firm competes vigorously with its rivals, who are few in number. The principal area of competition is in advertising. The advertisement of one firm will state that its product is superior to those of its rivals, which it will virtually name. Firms also strive to attract customers by means of style features, method of packaging, claims of durability, and such. More generally, there is active, if sometimes spurious, quality competition. In fact, firms compete in almost every conceivable way except by means of price reduction.

The type of market just described, however, is far from what the economist means when he speaks of perfect competition. When this austere concept is used, no traces of personal rivalry can appear. All relevant economic magnitudes are determined by impersonal market forces.

8.2 PERFECT COMPETITION

An understanding of concepts of perfect competition and equilibrium in a perfectly competitive market is facilitated by the following scenario or parable. Consider the market for a given commodity and suppose that participants in this market are divided into two groups: one group consists of consumers or demanders of the commodity and the other group consists of producers or suppliers of the commodity. Exchange between these groups is accomplished through an auctioneer in the following manner. The auctioneer announces a price for the commodity, and each consumer decides how much of the commodity he wishes to purchase at that price. Similarly, each producer decides how much of the commodity he wishes to supply at the announced price. The auctioneer adds up the demands of all the consumers and also adds up the supply offers of all the producers. If the aggregate demand equals the aggregate supply, the announced price is said to be the equilibrium price, and transactions are consummated at this price. If, at the currently announced price, the quantity that consumers wish to purchase is not the same as the quantity that producers wish to supply, a new price is announced by the auctioneer. This process is repeated until an equilibrium price is found.

Four important conditions are used by economists to define perfect competition. We will discuss these conditions in turn and show how each is related to the "auctioneer" parable.

8.2.a Price Taking Demanders and Suppliers

In the above parable, every market participant, be he demander or supplier, regards price as given. While it is true that the aggregate behavior of demanders and suppliers affects the price, no economic agent takes the effect of its behavior on price into account when making a consumption or production decision. Frequently, economists try to capture the essence of the price-taker assumption by stipulating that in a competitive market, every economic agent is so small, relative to the market as a whole, that it cannot exert a perceptible influence on price.

The critical ingredient, however, is not the assumption of a large number of small economic agents but rather the assumption that each economic agent acts as if prices are given.[1]

8.2.b   Homogeneous Product

A closely related provision is that the product of any one seller in a perfectly competitive market must be identical to the product of any other seller. This ensures that buyers are indifferent as to the firm from which they purchase.

The relationship of this assumption to the auctioneer parable is obvious: in that parable, consumers make no distinctions among the outputs of different producers.

8.2.c   Free Mobility of Resources

A third condition for perfect competition is that *all* resources are perfectly mobile—that each resource can move in and out of the market very readily in response to pecuniary signals.

The condition of perfect mobility is an exacting one. First, it means that labor must be mobile, not only geographically but among jobs. The latter, in turn, implies that the requisite labor skills are few, simple, and easily learned. Next, free mobility means that the ingredient inputs are not monopolized by an owner or producer. Finally, free mobility means that new firms (or new capital) can enter and leave an industry without extraordinary difficulty. If patents or copyrights are required, entry is not free. Similarly, if average cost declines over an appreciable range of output, established producers will have cost advantages that make entry difficult. In short, free mobility of resources requires free entry and exit of new firms into and out of an industry—a condition very difficult to realize in practice.

In terms of the earlier parable, the assumption of free mobility of resources means that during the auction process, individual producers can decide to offer no output if they so desire and also that new producers can enter and make supply offers when they wish.

8.2.d   Perfect Knowledge

Consumers, producers, and resource owners must possess perfect knowledge if a market is to be perfectly competitive. If consumers are

---

[1] In footnote 12 of Chapter 4, we noted that the absence of any economic agent's influence on market price could be rigorously argued in a general equilibrium context.

not fully cognizant of prices, they might buy at higher prices when lower ones are available. There will then not be a uniform price in the market. Similarly, if laborers are not aware of the wage rates offered, they may not sell their labor services to the highest bidder. Finally, producers must know their costs as well as price in order to attain the most profitable rate of output.

But this is only the beginning. In its fullest sense, perfect knowledge requires complete knowledge of the future as well as the present. In the absence of this omniscience, perfect competition cannot prevail.

In the auctioneer parable, this assumption means that all producers and consumers, including potential entrants, are informed about the price in the market. Moreover, the assumption implies that producers are able to correctly assess the costs of labor and other inputs when they make their supply offers.

The discussion to this point can be summarized by the following:

Definition: Perfect competition is an economic model of a market possessing the following characteristics: each economic agent acts as if prices are given, that is, each acts as a price-taker; the product is homogeneous; there is free mobility of all resources, including free entry and exit of business firms; and all economic agents in the market possess complete and perfect knowledge.

Even in basic agricultural markets, where the first three requirements are frequently satisfied, the fourth is obviated by vagaries of weather conditions. One might therefore reasonably ask why such a palpably unrealistic model should be considered at all.

The answer can be given in as much or as little detail as desired. For our present purposes, it is brief. First, generality can be achieved only by means of abstraction. Hence no theory can be perfectly descriptive of real world phenomena. Further, the more accurately a theory describes one specific real world case the less accurately it describes all others. In any area of thought a theoretician does not select his assumptions on the basis of their realism; the conclusions, not the assumptions, are tested against reality.

This leads to a second point of great, if pragmatic, importance. The conclusions derived from the model of perfect competition have, by and large, permitted accurate explanation and prediction of real world phenomena. That is, perfect competition frequently *works* as a theoretical model of economic processes. The most persuasive evidence supporting this assertion is the fact that despite the proliferation of more "sophisticated" models of economic behavior, economists today probably use the model of perfect competition in their research more than ever before.

8.3 EQUILIBRIUM IN THE MARKET PERIOD

The short run and the long run were defined in Chapter 5. In the short run, some inputs are fixed—they are not instantaneously augmentable. Changes in the quantity of output per unit of time can be achieved only by changes in the usage of the instantaneously variable inputs. In the long run, on the other hand, all inputs are variable. Changes in the volume of output can be achieved by changes in the usage of any input.

These two "runs," however, do not cover all cases. In certain instances the quantity of a commodity available for sale is absolutely fixed for a short period of time. For example, after the harvest of an agricultural crop the quantity of the commodity cannot be increased until the next harvest. As another example, merchants hold inventories of goods. The quantity available for sale cannot be increased instantly because the order and delivery process inevitably entails some delay. Finally, in some cases quantity can be increased virtually instantaneously; but the cost of rapid production is so great as to preclude very quick changes. In all these cases, the short period of time in which supply is absolutely fixed is called the *market period.*

8.3.a Industry Equilibrium in the Market Period

Definition: An industry is a collection of firms producing a homogeneous product.

In both the short run and long run each individual firm can adjust its output. Thus one must analyze equilibrium adjustments for the firm as well as the industry. In the market period, however, the individual business concerns cannot adjust at all. By definition, output cannot be changed in the market period. Hence the behavior of individual firms need not be studied—each firm has a fixed supply that it sells for the market-established price.

Since the supply of each firm is absolutely fixed in the market period, the market supply curve is simply the horizontal sum of all firms' supply curves. And again, since supply is fixed, the market supply curve is a straight line parallel to the vertical axis, as shown in Figure 8.3.1. The fixed quantity available for sale is $O\bar{q}$, and the market supply curve is the straight line labeled S.

Market equilibrium is attained, of course, at that price which exactly clears the market. If market demand is given by the curve labeled D in Figure 8.3.1, the market equilibrium price is $O\bar{p}$. If demand were

FIGURE 8.3.1

Equilibrium in the Market Period

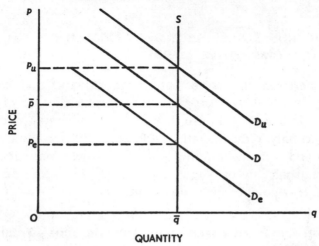

QUANTITY

greater, say D_u, the equilibrium price would also be greater, Op_u. But the market equilibrium quantity would be the same as before because supply is absolutely fixed. Similarly, if demand were less, D_e, the equilibrium price would be lower, Op_e. Thus in the market period demand *alone* determines the market equilibrium price, given the fixed supply, while supply *alone* determines the market equilibrium quantity. This result differs markedly from the corresponding result for the short and long runs in which demand and supply *jointly* determine *both* the equilibrium price and quantity.

8.3.b   Price as a Rationing Device

The price a commodity bears may play various roles. It may be a signal to producers to expand or contract their rate of production. It may reflect the marginal social value of the commodity. And, among other things, it is always a rationing device.

In the market period, rationing the existing supply among prospective buyers is the chief function performed by market price. Since supply is not related to the cost of production when the former is fixed, price is exclusively a demand phenomenon. When the market equilibrium price is established, it rations the fixed supply of goods among those individuals who are willing and able to pay a unit price equal to or greater than the market equilibrium price. While this is true of an equilibrium price in any market in any "run," it is dramatically true in the market period.

8.4 SHORT-RUN EQUILIBRIUM OF A FIRM IN A PERFECTLY COMPETITIVE MARKET

In the short run, the rate of output per period of time can be increased or decreased by increasing or decreasing the use of variable inputs. The individual firm can adjust its rate of output over a wide range subject only to the limitations imposed by its fixed inputs (generally, plant and equipment). Since each firm adjusts until it reaches a profit-maximizing rate of output, the market or industry also adjusts until it reaches a point of short-run equilibrium.

8.4.a Short-Run Profit Maximization, Total Revenue—Total Cost Approach

As already noted, we assume that each firm adjusts its rate of output so as to maximize the profit obtainable from its business operation. Since profit is the difference between the total revenue from sales and the total cost of operation, profit is a maximum for the rate of output that maximizes the excess of revenue over cost (or minimizes the excess of cost over revenue).

Consider the example contained in Table 8.4.1 and shown graphically in Figure 8.4.1. The first two columns of the table give the demand curve for the perfectly competitive producer. Market price is $5

TABLE 8.4.1
Revenue, Cost, and Profit for a Hypothetical Firm

Market Price	Rate of Output and Sales	Total Revenue	Total Fixed Cost	Total Variable Cost	Total Cost	Profit
$5.00..............	1	$ 5.00	$15.00	$ 2.00	$17.00	−$12.00
5.00.............	2	10.00	15.00	3.50	18.50	− 8.50
5.00.............	3	15.00	15.00	4.50	19.50	− 4.50
5.00.............	4	20.00	15.00	5.75	20.75	− 0.75
5.00.............	5	25.00	15.00	7.25	22.25	+ 2.75
5.00.............	6	30.00	15.00	9.25	24.25	+ 5.75
5.00.............	7	35.00	15.00	12.50	27.50	+ 7.50
5.00.............	8	40.00	15.00	17.50	32.50	+ 7.50
5.00.............	9	45.00	15.00	25.50	40.50	+ 4.50
5.00.............	10	50.00	15.00	37.50	52.50	− 2.50

FIGURE 8.4.1

Profit Maximization by the Total Revenue–Total Cost Approach

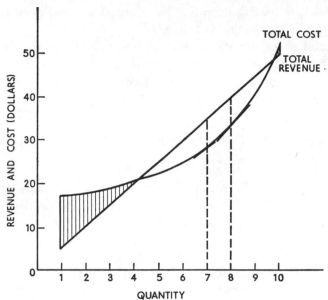

per unit; the producer can sell as many units as he chooses at this price. The product of columns 1 and 2 gives total revenue, the entries appearing in column 3. The straight line in Figure 8.4.1 is a graphical representation. Notice that the total revenue curve is always a straight line in the case of perfect competition because unit price does not change when quantity sold changes.

Columns 4, 5, and 6 give total fixed, total variable, and total cost respectively. Total cost is graphed as the curved line in Figure 8.4.1. Profit—the difference between total revenue and total cost—is shown in the last column of Table 8.4.1, and it is represented by the positive or negative distance between the total revenue and total cost curves in Figure 8.4.1. Profit is first negative, becomes positive, and is ultimately negative again. In Figure 8.4.1, the shaded areas denote the range of output over which profit is negative (a loss is incurred).

It is clear from either the table or the figure that maximum profit is $7.50, achieved with an output of either seven or eight units. The seeming indeterminacy of the rate of output is attributable to the discrete data used in this hypothetical example. If continuous data were used, it would be obvious that the profit-maximizing output is eight units per period of time. This is because the maximum distance separating the two curves occurs at the point where the tangents to the curves have the same slope. From the two tangents constructed in Figure 8.4.1, it is easily seen that the slopes are equal only at the output of eight units per period of time.

The total revenue–total cost approach is a useful one from some standpoints; however, it does not lead to an analytical interpretation of business behavior. To get at this, the familiar marginal approach must be adopted.

8.4.b Short-Run Profit Maximization, the Marginal Approach

The definitions of marginal revenue and marginal cost are familiar from Chapters 4 and 7 respectively. Similarly, the method of calculating each has been learned. Applying these methods to the data in Table 8.4.1, we obtain the information in Table 8.4.2.

TABLE 8.4.2

Marginal Revenue, Marginal Cost, and Profit

Output and Sales	Marginal Revenue or Price	Marginal Cost	Average Total Cost	Unit Profit	Total Profit
1	$5.00	$ 2.00	$17.00	−$12.00	−$12.00
2	5.00	1.50	9.25	− 4.25	− 8.50
3	5.00	1.00	6.50	− 1.50	− 4.50
4	5.00	1.25	5.19	− 0.19	− 0.75
5	5.00	1.50	4.45	+ 0.55	+ 2.75
6	5.00	2.00	4.04	+ 0.96	+ 5.75
7	5.00	3.25	3.93	+ 1.07	+ 7.50
8	5.00	5.00	4.06	+ 0.94	+ 7.50
9	5.00	8.00	4.50	+ 0.50	+ 4.50
10	5.00	12.00	5.25	− 0.25	− 2.50

Columns 1 and 2 show the demand or marginal revenue curve, identical for the firm in a perfectly competitive market (as explained in Chapter 4). Column 3 contains the marginal cost figures, while average total or unit cost has been computed from column 6, Table 8.4.1, and entered in column 4. Unit profit, the difference between price and average total cost, is shown in column 5. Finally, total profit, the difference between total revenue and total cost, is contained in column 6.

As in the previous case, maximum profit corresponds to either seven or eight units of output and sales per period of time. Unit profit is a

FIGURE 8.4.2

Profit Maximization by the Marginal Approach

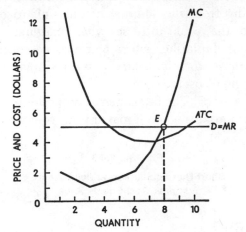

maximum at seven units of output, but this is immaterial inasmuch as the entrepreneur is concerned with total profit.

The data in Table 8.4.2 are plotted in Figure 8.4.2. The short-run equilibrium of the firm is clearly attained at point E, where marginal cost equals marginal revenue. Alternatively stated, since marginal revenue equals price for a perfectly competitive producer, short-run equilibrium occurs at the output point for which marginal cost equals price.

8.4.c Proof of the Short-Run Equilibrium

To prove the proposition that a firm in perfect competition attains its profit-maximizing equilibrium at the rate of output for which marginal cost equals price, the hypothetical example of Figure 8.4.2 has been converted to the general representation in Figure 8.4.3. The theorem follows immediately from the definitions of marginal revenue and marginal cost.[2]

---

[2] Let $p = f(q)$ represent the inverse demand function. Hence $qf(q)$ is total revenue. Further, let $C = A + g(q)$ be the total cost function. Profit (π) is thus $\pi = qf(q) - A - g(q)$. Profit is a maximum when $d\pi/dq = 0$ and $d^2\pi/dq^2 < 0$. Taking the first derivative and equating with zero,

$$\frac{d\pi}{dq} = f(q) - g'(q) = 0 \qquad (8.2.1)$$

or

$$f(q) = g'(q), \qquad (8.2.2)$$

because $p = f(q)$ is a given constant. Marginal cost is $g'(q)$; see Chapter 7. Marginal revenue and price are both given by $f(q)$. Hence equation (8.2.2) states that

Marginal revenue is the addition to total revenue attributable to the addition of one unit to sales, while marginal cost is the addition to total cost resulting from the addition of one unit to output. Thus it should be evident that profit increases when marginal revenue exceeds marginal cost and diminishes when marginal cost exceeds marginal revenue. Profit must, therefore, attain its maximum when marginal revenue and marginal cost are equal.

Consider Figure 8.4.3. The fundamental proposition is that at market price $O\bar{p}$, the firm attains a profit-maximizing equilibrium at point E,

FIGURE 8.4.3

**Short-Run Equilibrium at Point Where
Marginal Cost Equals Price**

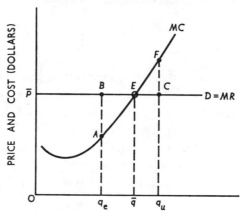

corresponding to the output of $O\bar{q}$ units per period of time. If the rate of output were less than $O\bar{q}$, say Oq_e, marginal revenue q_eB would exceed marginal cost q_eA. Adding a unit to output and sales would increase total revenue by more than total cost. Profit would accordingly increase, and it would continue to increase so long as marginal revenue exceeds marginal cost.

On the other hand, suppose the rate of output exceeded $O\bar{q}$—say

---

marginal revenue or price must equal marginal cost. This is the necessary condition for profit maximization. From equation (8.2.1) the second-order condition is that $d^2\pi/dq^2 = -g''(q) < 0$ or

$$g''(q) > 0 . \tag{8.2.3}$$

Hence stability of equilibrium, by inequality (8.2.3), requires a *positively sloped* marginal cost curve.

Oq_u. At this point, marginal cost q_uF exceeds marginal revenue q_uC. This unit of output causes total cost to increase by more than total revenue, thereby reducing profit (or increasing loss). As is evident from the graph, profit must be reduced by adding a unit to output and sales whenever marginal cost exceeds marginal revenue.

Therefore, since profit increases when marginal revenue exceeds marginal cost and declines when marginal revenue is less than marginal cost, it must be a maximum when the two are equal. Furthermore, since price equals marginal revenue for a firm in perfect competition, the following theorem has been proved.

Proposition: A firm in a perfectly competitive industry attains its short-run, profit-maximizing equilibrium by producing the rate of output for which marginal cost equals the given, fixed market price of the commodity.

8.4.d Profit or Loss?

The equality of price and marginal cost guarantees either that profit is a maximum or that loss is a minimum. Whether a profit is made or a loss incurred can be determined only by comparing price and average total cost corresponding to the equilibrium rate of output. If price exceeds unit cost, the entrepreneur will enjoy a profit in the short run. On the other hand, if unit cost exceeds price a loss must be incurred.

Figure 8.4.4 illustrates this. MC and ATC represent marginal cost and average total cost respectively. First, suppose short-run market

FIGURE 8.4.4

Profit or Loss in the Short Run

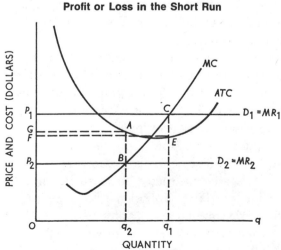

equilibrium establishes the price Op_1 per unit. The demand and marginal revenue curves for the firm are, therefore, given by the horizontal line labeled $D_1 = MR_1$. Short-run equilibrium is attained when output is Oq_1 units per period of time. At this rate of output, total revenue (price times quantity) is given by the area of the rectangle Oq_1Cp_1. Similarly, total cost (unit cost times quantity) is the area Oq_1EF. Total revenue exceeds total cost, and profit is represented by the area of the rectangle $CEFp_1$.

On the other hand, suppose the market price-quantity equilibrium established the price Op_2. In that case the optimum rate of output would be Oq_2 units per period of time. Total revenue is the area of Oq_2Bp_2, while total cost is Oq_2AG. Since total cost exceeds total revenue, a loss is incurred in the amount represented by the area of p_2BAG.

When demand is $D_2 = MR_2$, there is no way the firm can earn a profit. If output were either smaller or greater than Oq_2 units per period of time, the loss would simply be greater. One might therefore ask why the firm does not go out of business since a loss is incurred at any rate of output.

8.4.e Short-Run Supply Curve of a Firm in a Perfectly Competitive Industry

The basic answer to this question is that an entrepreneur incurring a loss will continue to produce in the short run if, and only if, he loses less by producing than by closing the plant entirely. As you will recall from Chapter 7, there are two types of costs in the short run: fixed costs and variable costs. The fixed costs cannot be changed and are incurred whether the plant is operated or not. Fixed costs, that is, are the same at zero output as at any other.

Therefore, so long as total revenue exceeds the total variable cost of producing the equilibrium output, a smaller loss is suffered when production takes place. Figure 8.4.5 is a graphical demonstration of this.

As previously explained, the business decision regarding production in the short run is not affected by fixed costs. Therefore, only the average total cost, average variable cost, and marginal cost curves are shown in Figure 8.4.5. Since our discussion involves only a loss situation, the price lines are constructed so as to lie entirely beneath the average total cost curve. First, suppose market price is Op_1, so the firm's demand–marginal revenue curve is given by $D_1 = MR_1$. Profit maximization (or loss minimization) leads to producing the output for which marginal cost equals price—production occurs at point B, or at the rate

FIGURE 8.4.5

Ceasing Production in the Short Run

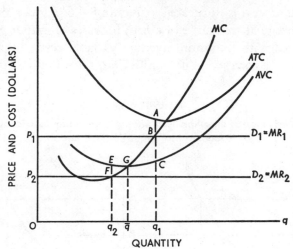

of Oq_1 units per period of time. At this rate of output the firm loses AB dollars per unit produced. However, at the price Op_1 average variable cost is not only covered but there is an excess of BC dollars per unit. The average cost of the variable inputs is q_1C dollars per unit of output. The price obtained per unit is q_1B. The excess of price over average variable cost, BC, can be applied to the fixed costs. Thus not all of the fixed costs are lost, as would be the case if production were discontinued. Although a loss is sustained, it is smaller than the loss associated with zero output.

This is not always the case, however. Suppose market price were as low as Op_2, so that demand is given by $D_2 = MR_2$. If the firm produced at all, its equilibrium output would be Oq_2 units per period of time. Here, however, the average variable cost of production exceeds price. The firm producing at this point would not only lose its fixed costs, it would lose EF dollars per unit on its variable costs as well. Thus when price is below average variable cost, the short-run equilibrium output is zero.

As shown in Chapter 7, average variable cost reaches its mimimum at the point where marginal cost and average variable cost intersect— point G in Figure 8.4.5. If price is less than $\bar{q}G$ dollars per unit, equilibrium output is zero. For a price equal to or greater than $\bar{q}G$ dollars per unit, equilibrium output is determined by the intersection of marginal cost and the price line.

Using the proposition just discussed, it is possible to derive the short-run supply curve of an individual firm in a perfectly competitive market. The process is illustrated in Figure 8.4.6. Panel a of the figure shows the marginal cost curve of a firm for rates of output greater than that associated with minimum average variable cost. Suppose market price is Op_1. The corresponding equilibrium rate of output is Oq_1. Now

FIGURE 8.4.6

Derivation of the Short-Run Supply Curve of an Individual Producer in Perfect Competition

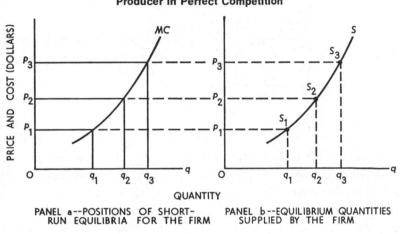

PANEL a--POSITIONS OF SHORT-   PANEL b--EQUILIBRIUM QUANTITIES
RUN EQUILIBRIA FOR THE FIRM   SUPPLIED BY THE FIRM

on panel b find the point associated with the coordinates Op_1, Oq_1. Label this point S_1; it represents the quantity supplied at the price Op_1.

Next, suppose price is Op_2. In this case, equilibrium output is Oq_2. Plot the point associated with the coordinates Op_2, Oq_2 on panel b—it is labeled S_2. Similarly, other equilibrium quantities supplied can be determined by postulating other market prices (for example, price Op_3 leads to output Oq_3 and point S_3 on panel b). Connecting all of the S points so generated one obtains the short-run supply curve of the firm, the curve labeled S in panel b. But by construction, the S curve is precisely the same as the MC curve. The following is therefore established:

Proposition: The short-run supply curve of a firm in perfect competition is precisely its marginal cost curve for all rates of output equal to or greater than the rate of output associated with minimum average variable cost. For market prices lower than minimum average variable cost, equilibrium quantity supplied is zero.

8.5 SHORT-RUN EQUILIBRIUM IN A PERFECTLY COMPETITIVE INDUSTRY

In Part I it was shown that market demand is simply the horizontal sum of individual demand curves. Deriving the short-run industry supply curve may not be such an easy matter as deriving the market demand.

8.5.a Short-Run Industry Supply Curve

As you will recall from Chapter 7, the short-run marginal cost curve of a firm is derived from its marginal product curve under the assumption that the unit price of the variable input is fixed. For most firms and inputs this is a reasonable assumption because one firm is usually so small, relative to all users of the resource taken together, that variations in its rate of purchase will not affect the market price of the resource. In other words, many resource markets are more or less perfectly competitive, at least on the *buying* side. Thus production and resource use can frequently be expanded in any one firm without affecting the market price of the resource.

But when *all* producers in an industry simultaneously expand output, there may be a marked effect upon the resource market. As an example, consider farming as an industry. One single farmer can doubtless double his output and, therefore, materially increase his inputs, without affecing the market price of fertilizer, tractors, etc. But if all farmers double output there will inevitably be a marked upward pressure on the prices of these inputs.

As a consequence, the industry supply curve usually cannot be obtained by summing horizontally the marginal cost curves of each producer. As industry output expands, input prices normally increase, thereby shifting each marginal cost curve upward.[3] A great deal of information would be required to obtain the exact supply curve. However, one may generally presume that the industry supply curve is somewhat more steeply sloped and somewhat less elastic when input prices increase in response to an increase in output. In this case, the concept of a competitive industry supply curve is less precise. Nonetheless, doubt is not cast upon the basic fact that in the short run, quantity supplied

---

[3] If the only input whose price increases is an inferior input, each firm's marginal cost curve will shift downward to the right. This does not affect the argument in the text—the horizontal sum of all firms' marginal cost curves would still not yield the industry supply curve.

varies directly with price. The latter is all one needs to draw a positively sloped market supply curve.

The explanation above may be summarized in the following

Relation: If factor prices change in response to a change in *industry* factor usage, the industry supply curve is not the horizontal summation of all firms' marginal cost curves. Each firm's marginal cost curve shifts when factor prices change. However, the industry supply curve is perfectly determinate—it is the sum of the quantities supplied by all firms, which is determined from the marginal cost curve corresponding to the prevailing set of factor prices.

8.5.b Short-Run Market Equilibrium, Profit or Loss

Given the market demand and supply curves, a short-run market price-quantity equilibrium is attained when quantity demanded and quantity supplied are equal. This proposition is so familiar that a proof

FIGURE 8.5.1

Short-Run Market Equilibrium and Profit or Loss in the Firm

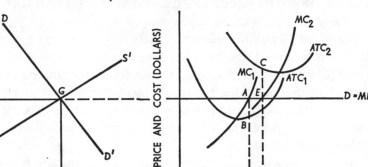

| PANEL a--MARKET PRICE-QUANTITY EQUILIBRIUM | PANEL b--PROFIT OR LOSS IN SHORT-RUN EQUILIBRIUM |

is not given here, although the equilibrium is illustrated in panel a, Figure 8.5.1. DD' is market demand and SS' is market supply.[4] The price-quantity equilibrium is attained at point G, with equilibrium price $O\overline{P}$ and equilibrium quantities demanded and supplied $O\overline{Q}$.

---

[4] The equilibrium may be explained in terms of the auctioneer parable discussed earlier. At prices above $\overline{P}$, supply offers exceed demand, signaling the need for a downward revision in price. When price is below $\overline{P}$, demand exceeds supply and this calls for an upward revision in price.

The market equilibrium price $O\overline{P}$, which establishes the horizontal demand or marginal revenue curve $D = MR$ for a typical firm in the industry, is shown in panel b. First, suppose the firm has cost represented by ATC_1 and MC_1. It then attains its profit-maximizing equilibrium at point A, producing Oq_1 units per period of time and earning a pure economic profit of AB dollars per unit. On the other hand, if cost is given by ATC_2 and MC_2, equilibrium is reached at point E. The firm produces Oq_2 units and incurs a pure loss of CE dollars per unit.

A perfectly competitive firm is merely a *quantity adjuster*. Price is given by the market; the firm produces the rate of output that maximizes profit or minimizes loss for its established plant. In the short run, no other alternative is available. In the long run, however, there is.

8.5.c Demand-Supply Analysis

The analysis of market equilibrium is simple, but it is not simple-minded. Indeed, this type of analysis offers significant qualitative, if not quantitative, insight into the functioning of real world markets. Let us consider an example.

Suppose that the demand for coal at the retail level is elastic over the relevant price range. Further, suppose the government feels that the price of coal is too high. It therefore places a price ceiling or maximum on coal at the mine. What will happen to the price of coal at the retail level? Will total receipts of retailers increase or decrease?

As a first step let us consider what happens at the mine (or mining area). Assume for analytical purposes that coal mining is a perfectly competitive, increasing cost industry. Assume also that before the imposition of the ceiling price, the industry was in equilibrium; each firm produced the quantity at which $P = LAC$ and therefore enjoyed no pure profit. Figure 8.5.2 shows the market demand and supply for coal at the mine. Demand $(D_m D_m')$ is the demand curve of retailers for coal at the mine. It is derived holding the demand for coal from retailers and other factors constant (we assume that individual consumers cannot purchase coal directly from the mine).

The long-run industry supply curve is $S_m S_m'$. It is the locus of long-run equilibria for the mining industry. Since we assume an increasing-cost industry, $S_m S_m'$. is upward sloping. The equilibrium price at the mine is OW_c and equilibrium quantity is OQ_c.

Figure 8.5.3 shows demand and supply conditions at retail. $D_r D_r'$ is the consumers' demand for coal. $S_r S_r'$, based upon a given cost of coal at the mines to retailers (OW_c), is the retailers' supply curve. Since

FIGURE 8.5.2

Supply and Demand at the Mine

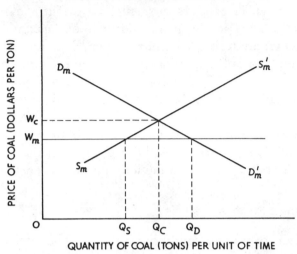

coal is an input for the retailers, the supply curve for coal at retail should shift when the price of coal at the mine changes, just as a change in the price of any factor of production changes the supply of the product produced. Specifically, when the price at the mine falls, other things remaining the same, the retail supply curve should shift to the

FIGURE 8.5.3

Demand and Supply at Retail

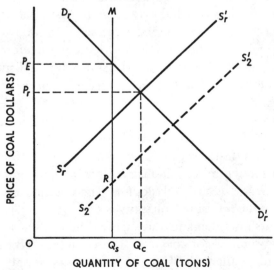

right. That is, if retailers can buy coal cheaper, they would be willing and able to supply more retail coal at every retail price. Equilibrium in the retail market occurs at a price of OP_r (given a price at the mine of OW_c) and a quantity sold of OQ_c, obviously the same as OQ_c in Figure 8.5.2 because the retailers sell all that they buy.

Returning to Figure 8.5.2, assume that the government sets the ceiling price OW_m. Quantity demanded by retailers at the new price is OQ_D. The new price is below OW_c (the price at which neither profit nor loss occurs); thus firms begin to make losses and some leave the industry. Since we assume that mining is an increasing-cost industry, the exit of firms and the decrease in quantity produced lowers factor prices and hence lowers the long-run average and marginal cost curves of the remaining firms in the industry. Figure 8.5.4 shows the process.

FIGURE 8.5.4

Cost Curves of an Individual Firm

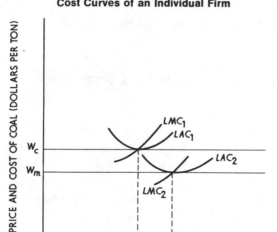

Long-run average and marginal costs fall from LAC_1 and LMC_1 to LAC_2 and LMC_2. The minimum point on LAC_2 equals the ceiling price OW_m. Each remaining firm now produces Oq_m (the new equilibrium output) rather than Oq_c, but there are fewer firms, none of which makes pure profit. The new quantity supplied by the industry, indicated in Figure 8.5.2, is OQ_S. Thus a shortage (excess demand) of Q_SQ_D occurs at the mines since retailers now wish to purchase OQ_D but the mines are only willing to sell OQ_S. The mining industry must find some method of allocation (rationing, first come first served, favoritism, and so on) in order to determine which retailers get the available supply. In any case only OQ_S is available to the retailers.

Now according to our analysis the lower price of coal at the mine should cause supply at retail to shift to S_2S_2' (Figure 8.5.3). Retail price should fall, and the quantity of coal sold should increase as determined by the intersection of D_rD_r' and S_2S_2'. But remember that only OQ_S is produced, so only OQ_S can be sold. The curve S_2S_2' specifies the quantities that retailers are *willing* to sell at the mine price of OW_m; the vertical line MQ_S indicates the maximum amount retailers are *able* to sell at that price. Therefore, the curve S_2RM shows the quantities that retailers are *willing and able* to sell at each retail price when the mine price is fixed at OW_m.

The intersection of supply and demand now occurs at the price OP_E, clearly higher than the old price. The quantity sold is OQ_S. After the ceiling price at the mine is imposed, consumers pay a higher price for less coal. Since demand was assumed to be elastic, retailers receive less total revenue.

8.6 LONG-RUN EQUILIBRIUM IN A PERFECTLY COMPETITIVE MARKET

Since all inputs are variable in the long run, an entrepreneur has the option of adjusting his plant size, as well as his output, to achieve maximum profit. In the limit, he can liquidate his business entirely and transfer his resources and his command over resources into a more profitable investment alternative. But just as established firms may leave the industry, new firms may enter the industry if profit prospects are brighter there than elsewhere. Indeed, adjustment of the number of firms in the industry in response to profit motivation is the key element in establishing long-run equilibrium.

8.6.a Long-Run Adjustment of an Established Firm

In the long run, an entrepreneur adjusts his plant size, and therefore his rate of output, in order to attain maximum profit. The adjustment process is illustrated in Figure 8.6.1.

Let market price be $O\overline{P}$ and suppose the firm has a plant whose costs are represented by SAC_1 and SMC_1 (short-run average total and marginal cost, respectively). With this plant, short-run equilibrium is reached at point A, corresponding to output of Oq_1 units per period of

FIGURE 8.6.1

Long-Run Adjustment of Plant Size

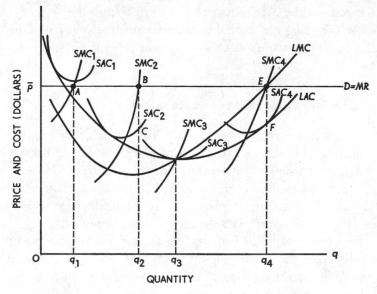

time. At this point the firm sustains a small loss on each unit of output produced and sold.

In looking to the long run, or the planning horizon, the entrepreneur has two options: he can go out of business or he can construct a plant of more suitable size. For example, he could decide upon the plant size represented by SAC_2 and SMC_2. At price $O\overline{P}$, he would produce Oq_2 units per period of time and make a pure profit of BC dollars per unit. However, with perfect knowledge, the plant represented by SAC_4 and SMC_4 would be constructed.

With this plant, operated so as to produce Oq_4 units per period of time, the maximum attainable profit is realized. The logical basis of this proposition is the same as in the case of short-run profit maximization. Long-run marginal cost shows the addition to total cost attributable to the addition of one unit to output, *after plant size has been adjusted so as to produce that rate of output at minimum achievable unit cost.* Marginal revenue, or demand, shows the increase in revenue attributable to the addition of one unit to sales. By the familiar argument, therefore, maximum profit is obtained by producing that rate of output in the plant of such size that long-run marginal cost equals price at the point where the relevant short-run marginal cost equals price.

In Figure 8.6.1, the optimum-size plant is larger than the plant for which unit cost reaches its minimum—the plant given by SAC_3. However, at the optimum rate of output, Oq_4, unit cost is smaller in the plant represented by SAC_4 than in a plant of any other size. So long as price is $O\overline{P}$, long-run equilibrium adjustment dictates building the plant SAC_4 and operating it so as to produce Oq_4 units per period of time.

8.6.b   Long-Run Adjustment of the Industry

If all firms in the industry originally had plants of size represented by SAC_1, the simultaneous expansion of plant size by all firms would shift the industry supply curve materially to the right. Market price would be reduced, and each firm would then possess a plant that is too large. Further adjustment of plant size by established firms would be necessary before long-run equilibrium could be attained.

On the other hand, if all firms except one originally possessed plants of optimum size, the expansion by one plant would not have a perceptible effect upon market price. All firms would be in a temporarily optimal situation, earning a pure economic profit of EF dollars per unit (Figure 8.6.1).

As you will recall from Chapter 7, economic cost and economic profit are somewhat different from the corresponding accounting concepts. In particular, economic cost includes the returns that could be obtained from the most profitable alternative use of the invested resources. Hence a *pure economic profit* represents a return on investment in excess of that obtainable elsewhere. The appearance of such profit naturally attracts new firms into the industry, expanding industry supply and reducing market price. When this occurs, all firms—both old and new—must adjust; and the adjustment process must continue until a position of long-run equilibrium is attained.

The process of long-run equilibrium adjustment is illustrated by Figure 8.6.2. Suppose each firm in the industry is identical. The original size is represented by SAC_1 and SMC_1 in panel b. The market demand curve is given by DD' in panel a, and the market supply is S_1S_1'. Market equilibrium establishes the price of OP_1 dollars per unit and total output and sales of OQ_1 units per period of time. At price OP_1, each firm attains a point of short-run equilibrium where SMC_1 equals price. Each firm produces Oq_1 units per period of time and reaps a pure economic profit of AB dollars per unit. As panel b is constructed, this position could be one of long-run equilibrium inasmuch as LMC equals price at this point.

FIGURE 8.6.2
Long-Run Equilibrium Adjustment in a Perfectly Competitive Industry

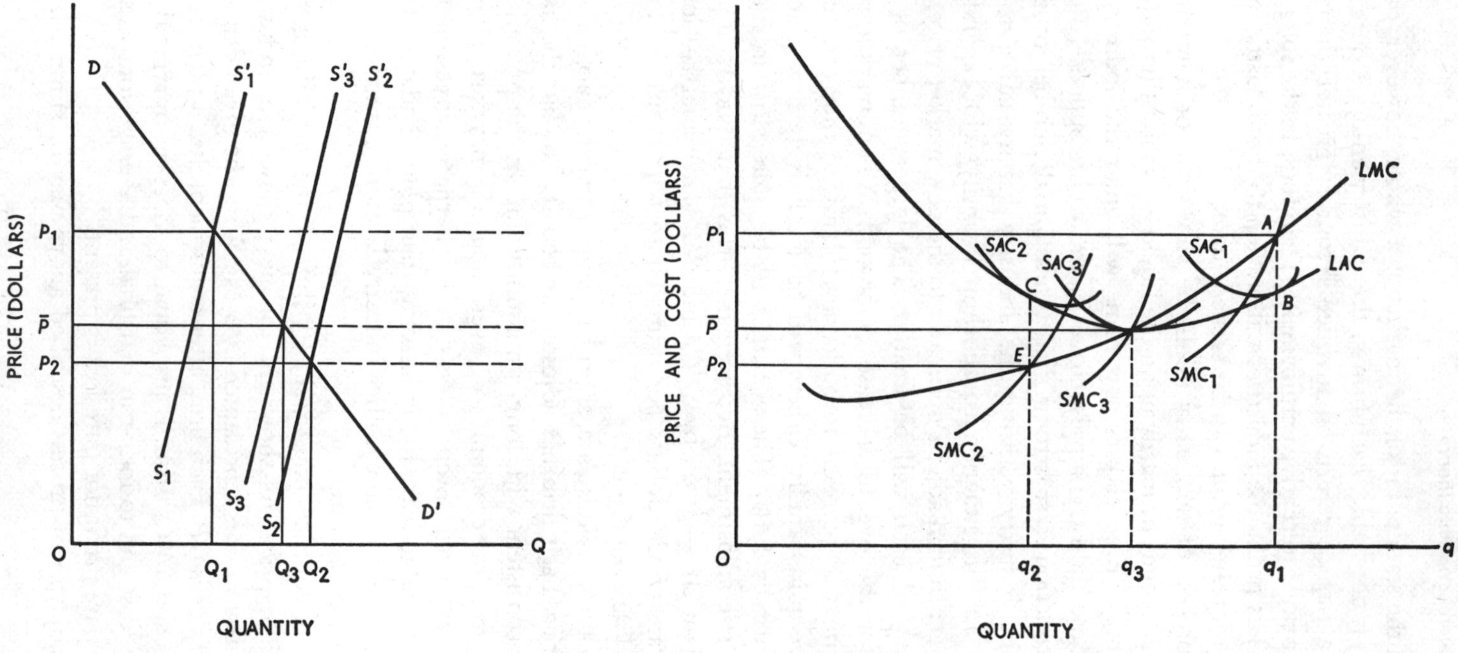

PANEL a—LONG-RUN MARKET EQUILIBRIUM

PANEL b—LONG-RUN EQUILIBRIUM ADJUSTMENT IN A TYPICAL FIRM

From the standpoint of the market as a whole, however, the present situation is not stable. Each firm in the industry enjoys a pure economic profit—a rate of return on invested resources greater than could be earned in any alternative employment. Therefore, in the long run some firms in less profitable industries will switch to the industry in question because a greater profit can be earned there.

The process of new entry might be very slow, or it might be very fast; this depends primarily upon the liquid assets in other industries. In any event, as time elapses new firms will enter the industry, thereby shifting the industry supply curve to the right. Suppose, indeed, the profit attraction is so strong that a substantial number of new firms enters the industry, shifting the industry supply curve to $S_2 S_2'$ in panel a. In this situation equilibrium quantity will expand to OQ_2.

When each firm adjusts optimally to the new market price, however, the output of each will be smaller. The larger number of firms accounts for the overall increase in output. When market price falls some firms will be ready to build new plants, so they can adjust their plant size quite rapidly. Others will have relatively new plants of size represented by SAC_1. These firms will be quite slow in making the optimal size adjustment. But even the firms that quickly adjust to optimal plant size—given by SAC_2 and SMC_2 in panel b—lose money at the rate of CE dollars per unit. Those whose size is not quickly adapted lose even more.

As in the previous case, short-run and long-run marginal cost both equal price. Each firm has adjusted as best it can; but the situation is still not consistent with long-run equilibrium. In the present case each firm incurs a pure economic loss, even though it may earn an accounting profit. In any event, profit is less than in alternative investments. Hence firms will tend to leave the industry as their plants and equipment wear out. Investment in some other industry is more attractive because the profit outlook is better.

As a consequence industry supply shifts to the left, raising the market equilibrium price. As shown in the next subsection, industry supply must shift until it is represented by $S_3 S_3'$. With the given demand curve, market price is $O\overline{P}$. Each firm, after adjustment, has a plant represented by SAC_3 and SMC_3. Price is just equal to short-run marginal and average total cost and to long-run marginal and average total cost as well. Neither pure profit nor pure loss is present.

The adjustment process described above may be summarized by the following

Proposition: In perfect competition there is a tendency for firms to enter or exit until each existing firm earns neither pure profit nor pure loss.

8.6.c Long-Run Equilibrium in a Perfectly Competitive Firm

The proposition of long-run equilibrium is inevitable from and is embodied in the assumptions of profit maximization and free entry. Each firm strives to achieve the maximum possible profit. In the short run a firm in perfect competition can do nothing more than adjust its output so that marginal cost equals price. In the long run it can adjust the size of its plant and it can select the industry in which it operates—both with an eye to profit.

The long-run equilibrium of a firm in a perfectly competitive industry is explained by means of Figure 8.6.3. If price is above the level $O\bar{P}$,

FIGURE 8.6.3

Long-Run Equilibrium of a Firm in a Perfectly Competitive Industry

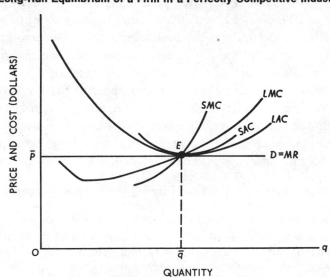

each established firm in the industry earns a pure profit. New firms are attracted into the industry, shifting the market supply curve to the right. Market equilibrium price declines, and the horizontal demand curve confronting each firm falls to a lower level. On the other hand, if price is below $O\overline{P}$, each firm in the industry incurs a pure economic loss. As their plants and equipment depreciate, some firms will leave the industry, thereby causing the market supply curve to shift to the left. Market price and, accordingly, the horizontal individual demand curves rise.

The only conceivable point of long-run equilibrium occurs at point E in Figure 8.6.3. Here firms in the industry receive neither pure profit nor pure loss. There is no incentive for further entrance because the rate of return in this industry is the same as in the best alternative. But for the same reason there is no incentive for a firm to leave the industry. The number of firms stabilizes, each firm with a short-run plant represented by SAC and SMC.

The position of long-run equilibrium is actually determined by the horizontal demand curve confronting each firm. Since the industry is perfectly competitive by assumption, firms will enter or leave the industry if there is either pure profit or pure loss. Therefore, since the position of long-run equilibrium must be consistent with *zero* profit (and zero loss), it is necessary that price equal average total cost. For a firm to attain its individual equilibrium, price must be equal to marginal cost. Therefore, price must equal both marginal and average total cost. This can only occur at the point where average total and marginal cost are equal, or at the point of minimum average total cost.

The statement, so far, could conceivably apply to any SAC and SMC. However, unless it applies *only* to the short-run plant that coincides with minimum long-run average cost, a change in plant size would lead to the appearance of pure profit, and the wheels of adjustment would be set in motion again. These arguments establish the following

Proposition: Long-run equilibrium for a firm in perfect competition occurs at the point where price equals minimum long-run average cost. At this point minimum short-run average total cost equals minimum long-run average total cost, and the short- and long-run marginal costs are equal. The position of long-run equilibrium is characterized by a "no profit" situation—the firms have neither a pure profit nor a pure loss, only an accounting profit equal to the rate of return obtainable in other perfectly competitive industries.

8.6.d   Constant Cost Industries

The analysis of subsections 8.6.b and 8.6.c was based upon the tacit assumption of "constant cost," in the sense that expanded resource usage does not entail an increase in resource prices. To carry the analysis further, and to make it more explicit, both constant and increasing cost industries are examined in this subsection.[5]

Long-run equilibrium and long-run supply price under conditions of constant cost are explained by means of Figure 8.6.4. Panel a shows

FIGURE 8.6.4

Long-Run Equilibrium and Supply Price in a Perfectly Competitive Industry Subject to Constant Cost

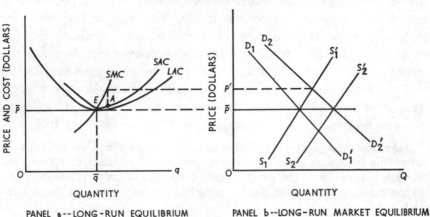

PANEL a--LONG-RUN EQUILIBRIUM OF THE FIRM

PANEL b--LONG-RUN MARKET EQUILIBRIUM

the long- and short-run conditions of a typical firm in the industry, while panel b depicts the market as a whole. D_1D_1' and S_1S_1' are the original market demand and supply curves, establishing a market equilibrium price of $O\overline{P}$ dollars per unit. Assume that the industry has attained a position of long-run equilibrium, so the position of each firm in the industry is depicted by panel a—the price line is tangent to the long- and short-run average total cost curves at their minimum points.

Now suppose demand increases to D_2D_2'. Instantaneously, with the number of firms fixed, the price will rise to OP' and each firm will move to equilibrium at point A. However, at point A each firm earns a pure economic profit, thereby attracting new entrants into the industry and shifting the industry supply curve to the right. In this case we assume that all resources used in the industry are *unspecialized;* so increased usage does not affect the market price of the resources. As a consequence, the entrance of new firms does not increase the costs of existing firms; the *LAC* curve of established firms does not shift and

[5] The phenomenon of decreasing cost involves some additional problems of industry equilibrium. For a discussion, see Milton Friedman, *Price Theory: A Provisional Text* (Chicago: Aldne Publishing Co., 1962), chap. 5.

new firms can operate with an identical LAC curve. Long-run equilibrium adjustment to the shift in demand is accomplished when the number of firms expands to the point at which S_2S_2' is the industry supply curve.

In other words, since output can be expanded by *expanding the number of firms* producing $O\bar{q}$ units per period of time at average cost $O\bar{P}$, the industry has a *constant long-run supply price* equal to $O\bar{P}$ dollars per unit. If price were above this level, firms of size represented by SAC would continue to enter the industry in order to reap the pure profit obtainable. If price were less than $O\bar{P}$, some firms would ultimately leave the industry to avoid the pure economic loss. Hence in the special case in which an expansion of resource usage does not lead to an increase in resource price, the long-run industry supply price is constant. This is precisely the meaning of a "constant-cost" industry.

Let us now summarize and emphasize. First, we need the following

Definition: The long-run industry supply price shows for each level of output the *minimum* price required to induce this industry output after (a) each firm in the industry has made the optimal internal adjustment and (b) the number of firms in the industry has, by entry or exit, been optimally adjusted.

Exercise: What are the precise relations and analogies between long-run supply price for a perfectly competitive industry and long-run average cost for a perfectly competitive firm?

Long-run industry supply price will be constant if, and only if, the industry output can be expanded or contracted by expanding or contracting the number of firms without affecting minimum long-run average cost. This condition, in turn, will exist if, and only if, all resources used by the industry are unspecialized—which means that the prices the firms must pay for all resources do not change with the level of resource use. To put it another way, the supply curve of each resource used in the industry must be perfectly elastic so far as the firms in *that* industry are concerned. This means that the industry *as a whole* must be a perfect competitor in each resource market—the industry must have a position vis-à-vis each resource market that is exactly like the position of a consumer vis-à-vis each commodity market.

In Chapters 5 and 6 there was a discussion of "returns to scale," and in Chapter 7 this was related to the shape of a firm's long-run average cost curve. The relations merit further comment. First, suppose all resource prices are constant. If the firm's production function first shows increasing and then decreasing returns to scale, its long-run average cost curve will have a U shape; *but* the long-run industry supply price will be constant because resource prices are constant (the number of firms producing at minimum *LAC* can be changed without affecting the *LAC* of any firm.). On the other hand, if the production function exhibits constant returns to scale, the long-run average cost curve will rise if resource prices vary directly with resource usage. As we will now see, industry supply price also rises in this case. Before reading further, however, think through the *important* exercise that follows.

Exercise: Suppose all resource prices are constant and that the production function of each firm in an industry exhibits constant returns to scale. Samuelson (*Foundations,* pp. 78–80) refers to this as the "indeterminacy of purest competition." Explain the meaning of this phrase.

8.6.e   Increasing Cost Industries

Increasing cost or increasing industry supply price is depicted by Figure 8.6.5. The original situation is the same as in Figure 8.6.4. The industry is in a position of long-run equilibrium. D_1D_1' and S_1S_1' are the market demand and supply curves respectively. Equilibrium price is OP_1. Each firm operates at point E_1, where price equals minimum average cost, both long- and short-run cost. Thus each firm is also in a position of long-run equilibrium.

Let demand shift to D_2D_2', so price instantaneously rises to a much higher level. The higher price is accompanied by pure economic profit; new firms are consequently attracted into the industry. The usage of resources expands and now, we assume, resource prices expand with

FIGURE 8.6.5

Long-Run Equilibrium and Supply Price in a Perfectly Competitive Industry Subject to Increasing Cost

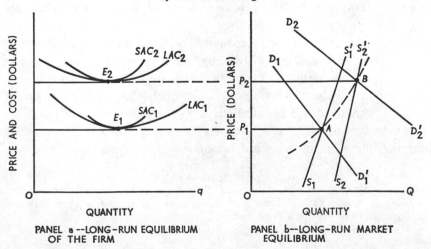

PANEL a --LONG-RUN EQUILIBRIUM
OF THE FIRM

PANEL b--LONG-RUN MARKET
EQUILIBRIUM

resource usage. The cost of inputs therefore increases for the established firms as well as for the new entrants. As a result the entire set of cost curves shifts upward, say to a position represented by LAC_2 in panel a.

Naturally, the process of equilibrium adjustment is not instantaneous. The LAC curve gradually shifts upward as new entrants gradually join the industry. The marginal cost curve of each firm shifts to the left, thereby tending to shift the industry supply curve to the left. However, more firms are producing and this tends to shift industry supply to the right. The latter tendency must dominate, for otherwise new firms would have obtained resources *only* by bidding them away from established firms in the industry. Total output could not expand as dictated by the increase in market price. New resource units must have entered the industry, so the supply curve shifts to the right, though not by as much as it would in a constant-cost industry.

The process of adjustment must continue until a position of full long-run equilibrium is attained. In Figure 8.6.5, this is depicted by the intersection of D_2D_2' and S_2S_2', establishing an equilibrium price of OP_2 dollars per unit. Each firm produces at point E_2, where price equals minimum average total cost. The important point to emphasize is that in constant-cost industries new firms enter until price returns to the unchanged level of minimum, long-run average cost. For industries subject to increasing long-run supply price, new firms enter until minimum long-run average cost shifts upward to equal the new price. The number of firms and the industry output increase. However, there is no way to predict what will happen to the equilibrium output per firm. It may decrease, as shown in Figure 8.6.5, or it may remain constant or increase. But these items are certain: industry output, the number of firms, and long-run supply price will all increase.

In the transition from one long-run equilibrium to the other, the long-run supply price increases from OP_1 to OP_2. This is precisely what is meant by an "increasing-cost industry" or increasing long-run industry supply price. In keeping with this, the long-run industry supply curve is given by a line joining such points as A and B in panel b. Thus an increasing-cost industry is one with a positively sloped long-run supply curve. Alternatively stated, after all long-run equilibrium adjustments are made, an increasing-cost industry is one in which an increase in output requires an increase in the long-run supply price.[6]

---

[6] Notice that in the short run an increase in output will be induced only by an increase in price, regardless of the nature of the industry. In the special case of constant cost an increase in output can be achieved at a constant price after *all* long-run equilibrium adjustments have been made.

The result of this section can be summarized as follows:

Relations: Constant or increasing cost in an industry depends entirely upon the way in which resource prices respond to expanded resource usage. If resource prices remain constant, the industry is subject to constant cost; if resource prices increase, the industry is one of increasing cost.

The long-run supply curve for a constant-cost industry is a horizontal line at the level of the constant long-run supply price. The long-run industry supply curve under conditions of increasing cost is positively sloped, and the long-run supply price increases as long-run equilibrium quantity supplied expands.

8.7 THE COMPETITIVE MODEL IN PRACTICE

We noted above that despite the abstract and apparently unrealistic assumptions underlying the model of perfect competition, this model has proved very useful in predicting and explaining real world phenomena. For example, according to the theory, policies that restrict entry into industries can be expected to lead to persistent economic profits for those firms that are lucky enough to be in the industry. Taxicabs are licensed in many cities such as Chicago and New York. The number of taxicabs licensed tends to remain constant for long periods of time, and it is possible to enter the industry only by purchasing a license or "medallion" from someone who currently owns one. It follows that the price of the medallion should represent the value of the economic profits arising from restricted entry. The price of a medallion in Chicago was about $25,000 in 1973.[7]

Another implication of the theory is that when price ceilings are imposed in an industry, demand will exceed supply and shortages will develop.

An interesting example of shortages arising from price controls is the natural gas industry. Natural gas prices are controlled by the Federal Power Commission, and the FPC has kept these prices below market clearing levels for quite some time. It is well known that for many years there were long waiting lists of consumers wishing to obtain natural gas service for home heating, cooking, and air conditioning. The situation became especially acute by 1970. According to reports of the FPC, the shortages were so severe that gas had to be shut off with increasing

---

[7] When the price of the medallion is included in costs, the taxis earn only a competitive rate of return. The gain accrues solely to those people who were lucky enough to be given a medallion in the initial distribution of medallions.

frequency and for longer periods of time in the winters of 1970 to 1972.

In 1973, Professors Paul MacAvoy and Robert Pindyck published a study of the natural gas industry which provided estimates of the shortages that would arise under various pricing policies that the FPC might follow in the 1970s.[8] MacAvoy and Pindyck describe the natural gas industry as a "mixed" set of markets exhibiting both competitive and noncompetitive characteristics. Nonetheless, their conclusions are exactly what one would expect under the assumption that natural gas is a competitive industry of the kind discussed in this chapter.

The MacAvoy-Pindyck estimates are derived from a complex set of statistical equations describing field market behavior, production out of reserves, wholesale price markups, wholesale demand for gas, and interregional flows of gas. The equations in the model are estimated by standard econometric techniques using time-series and cross-sectional data covering the period from the early 1960s to the early 1970s. Using these equations, MacAvoy and Pindyck simulated the behavior of the natural gas industry for the period 1972–80 under three different pricing policies. The pricing policies they simulated were:

a. Annual price increases that average about 1.8 cents per Mcf of natural gas. This is called the *cost of service* policy because it represents the price increases that presumably would be allowed if "cost justification" criteria were applied by the FPC.

b. Annual price increases that average about 2.6 cents per Mcf of natural gas. This policy is called the *regulatory status quo* because it represents a continuation of the FPC policy of the early 1970s.

c. Annual price increases that average about 4 cents per Mcf of natural gas. This is called the *deregulation* policy. The policy would allow a 15-cent increase per Mcf for all new contracts in 1974 followed by a 3 cents per year increase in 1975 and all subsequent years.

The salient demand, supply, and price data from these simulations are shown in Table 8.7.1 for 1975 and 1980.

The simulations show that the effects of the different price policies are exactly what one would predict from the model of perfect competition. The "cost of service" policy has the most restrictive price

---

[8] Paul W. MacAvoy and Robert S. Pindyck, "Alternative Regulatory Policies for Dealing with the Natural Gas Shortage," *The Bell Journal of Economics and Management Science,* vol. 4 (1973), pp. 454–98.

TABLE 8.7.1

**Estimated Demand and Supply of Natural Gas
for Different Price Policies**

Price Policy	Total Reserves (trillions of cu. ft.)		Supply (trillions of cu. ft.)		Demand (trillions of cu. ft.)		Shortage (demand less supply)		Average Wholesale Price (cents per Mcf)	
	1975	1980	1975	1980	1975	1980	1975	1980	1975	1980
Cost of service.....	214	198	23.4	28.0	26.9	36.9	3.5	8.9	40.1	48.0
Status quo.........	213	197	23.9	30.2	26.9	35.5	3.0	5.3	41.5	54.6
Deregulation.......	209	200	26.0	32.8	26.4	32.4	0.4	−0.4	45.8	64.9

SOURCE: Paul W. MacAvoy and Robert S. Pindyck, "Alternative Regulatory Policies for Dealing with the Natural Gas Shortage," *The Bell Journal of Economics and Management Science*, vol. 4 (1973), pp. 454–98.

ceiling and leads to the largest shortage by 1980. The "deregulation" policy has the least restrictive price ceiling, and under this policy there are virtually no shortages from 1974 on. It is also interesting to note that total reserves of natural gas in 1980 are as large under the deregulation policy as in the alternative policies. In short, both the supply and demand response are in accordance with the predictions of the competitive model even though the assumptions underlying the competitive model are not strictly met in the natural gas industry.

8.8 CONCLUSION

Up to this point the salient feature of perfect competition is that in long-run market equilibrium, market price equals minimum average total cost. This means that each unit of output is produced at the lowest possible cost, either from the standpoint of money cost or of resource usage. The product sells for its average (long-run) cost of production; each firm accordingly earns the "going" rate of return in competitive industries, nothing more or less.

But so far we have seen only one side of perfect competition—the operation of firms within a perfectly competitive industry. The pricing of productive services under conditions of perfect competition is also an important feature, as is the question of general economic welfare in a perfectly competitive economy. While all of these studies are based upon a highly stylized set of assumptions, they ultimately provide criteria by which to evaluate actual market operation and practice.

QUESTIONS AND EXERCISES

Use the output-cost data computed for the first question in Chapter 7.

1. Suppose the price of the commodity is $1.75 per unit.
    a. What would net profit be at each of the following outputs? (*i*) 1,314; (*ii*) 1,384; (*iii*) 1,444; (*iv*) 1,494; and (*v*) 1,534.
    b. What is the greatest profit output?
    c. Is there any output that will yield a greater profit at any price?
    d. How much more revenue is obtained by selling this number of units than by selling one fewer? What is the relation between marginal revenue and selling price?
    e. If you are given selling price, how can you determine the optimum output by reference to marginal cost?

2. Suppose price is 70 cents.
    a. What would net profit be at each of the following outputs? (*i*) 410; (*ii*) 560; (*iii*) 700; (*iv*) 830; (*v*) 945; (*vi*) 1,234; (*vii*) 1,444.
    b. Is there any output that will earn a net profit at this price?
    c. When price is 70 cents, what is the crucial relation between price and average variable cost?
    d. Consider any price for which the corresponding marginal cost is equal to or less than 70 cents. At such a price, what is the relation between marginal cost and average variable cost?
    e. When the relation in (*d*) exists, what is the relation between average and marginal product?
    f. What will the producer do if faced with a permanent price of 70 cents?
    g. Why is it not socially desirable to have a producer operating when price is 70 cents?

3. Suppose price is 80 cents.
    a. What will the optimum output be?
    b. Can a profit be made at this price?
    c. Will the producer operate at all at this price?
    d. How long?

4. Determine the supply schedule of this individual producer listing the quantity supplied at the following prices: $0.60, 0.70, 0.80, 0.90, 1.00, 1.10, 1.20, 1.30, 1.40, 1.50, 1.60, 1.70, 1.80, 1.90, and 2.00.

5. The following report appeared in the *Wall Street Journal:* "The world's first plant for the manufacture of gasoline from natural gas will be shut down as uneconomical, it was announced today by the Amoco Chemical Corp.

    "The plant, at Brownsville, Texas, will be closed within the next few months, with a reduction of the work force to begin Oct. 1.

"J. A. Forrester, president of Amoco, a subsidiary of the Standard Oil Co. (Indiana) said: 'We have determined that the Brownsville plant cannot make gasoline and chemicals from natural gas at present market prices as cheaply as they can be made by other processes . . .'

"Mr. Forrester declared: 'We have proved the technical soundness of the process. However, results indicate that the units are more costly to operate and maintain than we had anticipated.' "

Consider whether it was wasteful to close down the plant (*a*) from the point of view of the firm, and (*b*) from the point of view of society.

6. New York City licenses taxicabs in two classes: for operation by companies with fleets and for operation by independent driver-owners each having only one cab. The city also fixes the rates the taxis may charge. For many years now, no new licenses have been issued in either class. There is an unofficial market for the "medallions" that signify the possession of a license. A medallion for an independent cab sold in 1959 for about $17,000.

   a. Discuss the factors determining the price of a medallion.

   b. What factors would determine whether a change in the fare fixed by the city would raise or lower the price of a medallion?

   c. Cab drivers, whether hired by companies or owners of their own cabs, seem unanimous in opposing any increase in the number of cabs licensed. They argue that an increase in the number of cabs, by increasing competition for customers, would drive down what they consider as an already unduly low return to drivers. Is their economics correct? Who would benefit and who would lose from an expansion in the number of licenses issued at a nominal fee?

7. Comment on the following quotation: "The orthodox tools of supply and demand assume that sellers and buyers are free to buy or sell any quantity they wish at the prices determined by the market. This assumption cannot validly be made when price controls or rationing are imposed by the government. It follows that these tools are useless in analyzing the effects of such governmental action. Economists should free themselves from slavish adherence to outmoded concepts and fashion new tools of analysis for the new problems raised by the modern Leviathan."

8. Assume that the demand for shoes at the retail level is elastic. Further assume that a ceiling price below the current market price is placed on shoes at the factory (i.e., a maximum price the shoe manufacturer can charge the retail dealer). The total revenue received from the sale of shoes at the retail level will increase because of the imposition of the ceiling price at the factory level. *Problem:* Decide whether the conclusion above is true, false, or uncertain and defend your answer.

9. Suppose a frost kills a large portion of the orange crop, with a resulting higher price of oranges. It has been said that such an increase in the

price benefits no one since it cannot elicit a supply response; the higher price, it is said, simply "lines the pockets of profiteers." Analyze this position. (Hint: Be sure to focus on the rationing function of market price.)

10. Assume that crab packing is a perfectly competitive industry on a national scale, or at least along the Eastern seaboard and Gulf Coast. The North Carolina crab packers have insisted that if the minimum wage is increased to $1.60 an hour, they will have to close their plants. Assume that they are correct. State the assumptions that must (implicitly) underlie their analysis and explain the situation graphically.

SUGGESTED READINGS

Henderson, James M., and Quandt, Richard E. *Microeconomic Theory: A Mathematical Approach,* 2d ed., pp. 103–18. New York: McGraw-Hill Book Co., Inc., 1971. [Elementary math required.]

Knight, Frank H. *Risk, Uncertainty and Profit,* chaps. 1, 5, 6. London School Reprints of Scarce Works, No. 16, 1933.

Machlup, Fritz. *Economics of Sellers' Competition,* pp. 79–125, esp. pp. 79–85 and pp. 116–25. Baltimore: The Johns Hopkins Press, 1952.

Stigler, George J. "Perfect Competition, Historically Contemplated," *Journal of Political Economy,* vol. 65 (1957), pp. 1–17.

9

Theory of price under pure monopoly

9.1 INTRODUCTION

"Perfect competition" provides the economist with a very useful analytical model, even though the exacting conditions of the model never exist in the real world. The same statement almost applies to the model of pure monopoly, to which we now turn. The conditions of the model are exacting; and it is difficult, if not impossible, to pinpoint a pure monopolist in real world markets. On the other hand, many markets closely approximate monopoly organization, and monopoly analysis often explains observed business behavior quite well.

9.1.a Definition

A pure monopoly is said to exist if there is one, and only one, seller in a well-defined market. Thus from the sales or revenue side pure monopoly and perfect competition are polar opposites. The perfectly competitive firm has so many "rivals" in the market that competition becomes impersonal; and rivalry, or "competition" in the popular sense, does not exist at all. Rivalry does not exist in the case of pure monopoly either, for the simple reason that there are no rivals. There is no "competition" in the popular sense; and there is no competition in the technical sense either.

Yet this may overstate the case somewhat, for two types of *indirect competition* and one source of *potential competition* tend to moderate the price-output policies of pure or near-pure monopolies. The first source of indirect competition is the general struggle for the consumer's dollar. *All* commodities compete for a place in the consumer's budget— the products of monopolists as well as the products of perfectly competitive firms. Unless a monopolist can secure a market for his product, his monopoly position is worthless. For example, the files of the U.S. Patent Office would reveal many patents (and therefore output monopoly) for products that were never produced or were produced for only a short period of time. Monopoly does not guarantee success; it only guarantees that the monopolist can make the most of whatever demand conditions exist.

A second source of indirect competition lies in the existence of substitute goods. Needless to say, there are no *perfect* substitutes for a monopoly product; otherwise a monopoly would not exist. However, imperfect substitutes exist; and the true market power of a monopolist depends upon the extent to which other commodities may be used as substitutes in consumption. For example, whale oil lamps and gaslights, candles and Coleman Lanterns are very poor substitutes for electricity in residential and commercial lighting. Therefore, electricity for lighting purposes closely approximates pure monopoly. On the other hand, there are quite good substitutes for electrical heating. Fuel oil and natural gas are strong competitors in the residential heating market; coal-fired steam heat, in addition to oil and gas, competes in the commercial market. As a consequence, the "monopoly" position of electrical power companies is very weak in these markets.

As has been said, the presence of indirect competition tends to moderate the price-output policies of monopolists. The threat of potential competition does so as well. Various reasons explain the establishment of a monopoly position (see subsection 9.1.b). An entrepreneur can sometimes maintain his monopoly position, however, only if he does not fully exploit it. In many cases potential competitors will be attracted into the market if profit prospects are bright. This is particularly true when the price-output policy of the existing monopolist is such that potential competitors feel they can readily capture a substantial portion of the market. While this situation is especially applicable to local or regional markets served by only one firm, it applies in broader situations as well. Whenever entry is possible, the position of an existing monopoly is perilous. To protect it the monopolist must serve his market well; otherwise new entrants will be attracted and the monopoly broken.

To summarize:

Definition: A pure monopoly exists when there is only one producer in a market. There are no direct competitors or rivals in either the popular or technical sense. However, the policies of a monopolist may be constrained by the indirect competition of all commodities for the consumer's dollar and of reasonably adequate substitute goods, and by the threat of potential competition if market entry is possible.

9.1.b Bases of Monopoly

Since the business of businessmen is profit, one might wonder why a monopoly ever arises, that is, why other firms do not enter the industry in an attempt to capture a part of the monopoly profit. Many different factors may lead to the establishment of a monopoly or near monopoly. Thus, on a local level the personal characteristics of the owner-monopolist may bring all the trade to him. Other seemingly trivial reasons may explain monopoly; but monopolies so established are destined for a short life. Permanent monopoly must rest on firmer ground.

One of the most important bases for monopoly lies in the control of raw material supplies. Suppose input x is required to produce output y. If one person has exclusive control over or ownership of x, he can easily establish a monopoly over y by refusing to sell x to any potential competitors. An interesting example of input-control monopoly can be taken from the economic history of the United States. Bauxite is a necessary ingredient in the production of aluminum. For many years the Aluminum Company of America (Alcoa) owned almost every source of bauxite in the United States. The control of resource supply, coupled with certain patent rights, provided Alcoa with an absolute monopoly in aluminum; it was only after World War II that the federal courts effectively broke Alcoa's monopoly of the aluminum market.

The discussion of Alcoa brings to light another important source of monopoly. The patent laws of the United States make it possible for a person to apply for and obtain the exclusive right to produce a certain commodity or to produce a commodity by means of a specified process. The patent lasts for 17 years, and it may be renewed after that time. Obviously, such exclusive rights can easily lead to monopoly. Alcoa is an example of a monopoly based upon both resource control and patent rights. E. I. du Pont de Nemours & Co. has enjoyed patent monopolies over many commodities, cellophane being perhaps the most notable. The Eastman Kodak Company enjoyed a similar position (by lease from a German company); the Minnesota Mining and Manufacturing Company ("Three M") has enjoyed patent monopoly or near monopoly with products such as their Scotch Tape and Thermofax Copier.

Despite these notable examples, patent monopoly may not be quite what it seems in many instances. A patent gives one the exclusive right to produce a particular, meticulously specified commodity or to use a particular, meticulously specified process to produce a commodity others can produce. But a patent does not preclude the development of closely related substitute goods or closely allied production processes. International Business Machines has the exclusive right to produce IBM machines; but other millisecond digital computers are available and there is keen competition in the computer market. The same is true of production processes. Thus while patents may sometimes establish pure monopolies, at other times they are merely permits to enter highly—but not perfectly—competitive markets.

A third source of monopoly lies in the cost of establishing an efficient production plant, especially in relation to the size of the market. The situation we are now discussing is frequently called "natural" monopoly. It comes into existence when the minimum average cost of production occurs at a rate of output sufficient, almost sufficient, or more than sufficient to supply the entire market at a price covering full cost.

Suppose a situation such as this exists but two firms are in the market. If the market is split between the two, each must necessarily produce at a relatively high average cost. Each has an incentive to lower price and increase output because average cost will also decline. But if both act in this fashion, price will surely fall more rapidly than average cost. Economic warfare ensues, and the ultimate result is likely to be the emergence of only one firm in a monopoly position.[1] The term "natural" monopoly simply implies that the "natural" result of market forces is the development of a monopoly organization.

Examples of natural monopoly are not hard to come by. Virtually all public utilities are natural monopolies and vice versa. Municipal waterworks, electrical power companies, sewage disposal systems, telephone companies, and many transportation services are examples of natural monopolies on both local and national levels.

The final source of monopoly to be discussed here is the market franchise. Use of a market franchise is frequently associated with natural monopolies and public utilities, but it need not be. A market franchise is actually a contract entered into by some governmental body (for instance, a city government) and a business concern. The governmental unit gives a business firm the exclusive right to market a good or service within its jurisdiction. The business firm, in turn, agrees to permit the

---

[1] For the classical treatment of this situation, see F. Zeuthen, *Problems of Monopoly and Economic Warfare* (London: Routledge, 1930).

governmental unit to control certain aspects of its market conduct. For example, the governmental unit may limit, or attempt to limit, the firm to a "fair return on fair market value of assets." In other cases the governmental unit may establish the price and permit the firm to earn whatever it can at that price. There are many other ways in which the governmental unit can exercise control over the firm. The essential feature, however, is that a governmental unit establishes the firm as a monopoly in return for various types of control over the price and output policies of the business.

9.2 DEMAND UNDER MONOPOLY

The most important object of Part I was to show that market demand curves are negatively sloped (except for the truly insignificant case of Giffen's Paradox). Now, since a monopoly constitutes a one-firm market, the market demand curve *is* the monopoly demand curve. As explained in section 4.4 of Chapter 4, when demand is negatively sloped average and marginal revenue are different, and for marginal profit calculations the latter is the relevant concept.[2]

Consider a hypothetical situation given by the data in Table 9.2.1. Market demand is indicated by the first two columns and is plotted graphically in Figure 9.2.1. Total revenue, the product of price and quantity, is given in column 3 and depicted graphically in Figure 9.2.1. (*Note:* The right-hand ordinate refers to total revenue while the customary left-hand ordinate refers to price and marginal revenue.) Finally, marginal revenue is shown in column 4.

TABLE 9.2.1
Demand and Marginal Revenue under Monopoly

Quantity	Price	Total Revenue	Marginal Revenue
5	$2.00	$10.00	—
13	1.10	14.30	$0.54
23	0.85	19.55	0.52
38	0.69	26.22	.44
50	0.615	30.75	0.35
60	0.55	33.00	0.23
68	0.50	34.00	0.13
75	0.45	33.75	−0.03
81	0.40	32.40	−0.23
86	0.35	30.10	−0.46

---

[2] The remainder of this section is a brief review of section 4.4 in Chapter 4. Students thoroughly familiar with the content of this section may proceed immediately to section 9.3.

As you will recall, marginal revenue is the addition to total revenue attributable to the addition of one unit to output (or sales). In this

FIGURE 9.2.1

Demand and Revenue under Monopoly

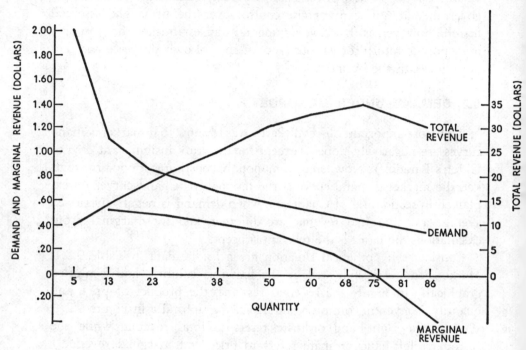

example, quantity does not increase by single units. Thus marginal revenue must be calculated as the *average* marginal revenue over the corresponding quantity range. Thus[3]

$$MR = \frac{\Delta TR}{\Delta} = \text{(for example)} \ \frac{\$14.30 - \$10.00}{13 - 5} = \$0.54 \ .$$

The corresponding plot is shown in Figure 9.2.1.

[3] For continuous cases, the demand function in inverse form may be written

$$p = f(q) \ , \qquad f'(q) < 0 \ , \tag{9.3.1}$$

where p and q denote price and quantity respectively. Thus total revenue is

$$pq = qf(q) \ , \tag{9.3.2}$$

and marginal revenue is

$$MR = \frac{d(pq)}{dq} = f(q) + qf'(q) \ . \tag{9.3.3}$$

FIGURE 9.2.2

Relations among Demand, Total Revenue, and Marginal Revenue

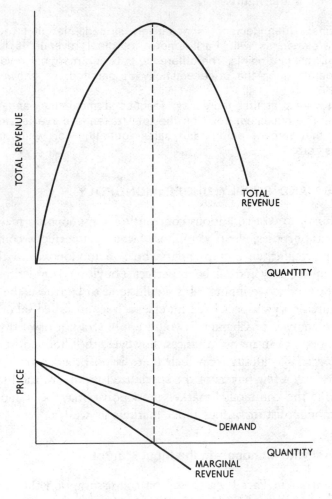

As you will recall from section 4.4 in Chapter 4, price elasticity of demand is

$$\eta = -\frac{dq}{dp}\frac{p}{q} \qquad -\frac{1}{f'(q)}\frac{p}{q} = -\frac{p}{qf'(q)}. \tag{9.3.4}$$

Now, factor $p = f(q)$ from the right-hand side of expression (9.3.3), obtaining

$$MR = p\left(1 + \frac{qf'(q)}{p}\right). \tag{9.3.5}$$

Thus from expression (9.3.4),

$$MR = p\left(1 - \frac{1}{\eta}\right). \tag{9.3.6}$$

The highly discrete case in Figure 9.2.1 is generalized in Figure 9.2.2. The important relations, already discussed, are immediately apparent from the figure.

Relations: When demand is negatively sloped, marginal revenue is negatively sloped as well. Furthermore, marginal revenue is less than price at all relevant points. The difference between marginal revenue and price depends upon the price elasticity of demand, as shown by the formula $MR = p(1 - 1/\eta)$.

Total revenue at first increases, reaches a maximum, and declines thereafter. The maximum point on the total revenue curve is attained at precisely that rate of output and sales (quantity) for which marginal revenue is zero.

9.3 COST AND SUPPLY UNDER MONOPOLY

The short-run cost conditions confronting a monopolist may be, for all practical purposes, identical to those faced by a perfectly competitive firm. In particular, an entrepreneur who is a monopolist in the commodity market may indeed be a perfect (buying) competitor in the market for productive inputs. This would tend to be true if the monopolist required only unspecialized inputs, such as unskilled labor. In this event, the analysis of Chapter 7 would apply straightforwardly to cost under monopoly. In many instances, however, the monopolist requires certain *specialized* inputs for which there is no broad general market. There are only a few buyers of the specialized input (in the limit, only one). Thus the commodity-market monopolist may be a monopolist or near monopolist in various input markets as well.[4]

9.3.a Cost with Monopoly in the Input Market

The analysis in Part I was based on the assumption that each consumer is a perfect competitor in the *buying* market. That is, each consumer is such a small purchaser, relative to the entire market, that he may buy any quantity he wishes without affecting market price. The same type of assumption was used in Chapter 7: each producer employs such a small quantity of each input, relative to the entire market for that input, that he may employ any amount he desires without affecting input price. But if a producer is a monopolist or near monopolist in an

---

[4] In this case the monopolist is called a monopsonist or an oligopsonist. The use of this terminology is deferred until Chapter 14, where the present case is analyzed more intensely.

input market, the price of that input will depend in part upon the purchases of the producer in question.

This is a simple matter of demand and supply analysis. If the commodity-market monopolist is a monopolist in the input market, his individual input demand is the *market* input demand as well. Given a (positively sloped) input supply curve, input price is determined and is, among other things, a function of input demand.

To get at this another way, consider Table 9.3.1 and the associated

TABLE 9.3.1

Cost under Monopoly in the Input Market

Units of Variable Input	Total Product	Fixed Cost	Price of Variable Input	Total Variable Cost	Marginal Expense of Input	Total Cost	Average Variable Cost	Average Total Cost	Marginal Cost
0............	0	$10	$2.00	$ 0	—	$10.00	—	—	—
1............	5	10	2.25	2.25	—	12.25	$0.45	$2.45	$0.45
2............	13	10	2.50	5.00	$2.75	15.00	0.39	1.15	0.34
3............	23	10	2.75	8.25	3.25	18.25	0.36	0.80	0.33
4............	38	10	3.00	12.00	3.75	22.00	0.32	0.58	0.25
5............	50	10	3.25	16.25	4.25	26.25	0.33	0.53	0.35
6............	60	10	3.50	21.00	4.75	31.00	0.35	0.52	0.48
7............	68	10	3.75	26.25	5.25	36.25	0.39	0.53	0.66
8............	75	10	4.00	32.00	5.75	42.00	0.43	0.56	0.82
9............	81	10	4.25	38.25	6.25	48.25	0.47	0.60	1.04
10............	86	10	4.50	45.00	6.75	55.00	0.52	0.64	1.35

Figure 9.3.1. Assume that only one variable input is required in the production process, as shown in columns 1 and 2. The remaining columns contain cost data. Total fixed cost is $10, given in column 3. Under present assumptions, the commodity monopolist is a monopolist in the input market as well. He thus faces a rising supply curve for the input. Columns 1 and 4 give the supply of input curve, which is shown graphically in Figure 9.3.1. Given the supply of input curve, total variable cost (column 5) is obtained by multiplying the number of units of the variable input used by the supply price of that number of units.

Column 6 introduces a new concept. When a producer is a perfect competitor in the input market he can purchase any quantity of the input he desires without affecting market price. Thus the price of the input is equal to the marginal expense of the input, just as price of out-

FIGURE 9.3.1

Supply and Marginal Expense of Input

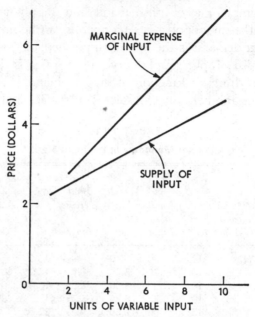

put equals marginal revenue in a perfectly competitive selling market. Implicit in the above statement is the following

Definition: The marginal expense of a variable input is the addition to total variable cost attributable to the addition of one unit of the variable input to the production process.

The marginal expense of the variable input is computed in the same manner as any other "marginal" quantity: the difference in total variable cost is divided by the difference in the number of units of the variable input. Thus the first entry in column 6 is

$$\frac{\$5.00 - \$2.25}{2 = 1} = \$2.75 .$$

The marginal expense of input is shown graphically in Figure 9.3.1. Using this figure, provide a nonmathematical, but logical, answer to the following

Exercise: Given a positively sloped supply of variable input curve, prove that the marginal expense of input curve lies above, and rises more rapidly than, the associated supply curve (the latter will not hold if the supply curve is concave). Also, compare and contrast the relations between demand and marginal revenue and supply and the marginal expense of input.[5]

The last four columns of Table 9.3.1 follow by the calculations developed in Chapter 7. Two important elements are to be gleaned from this analysis. First, a rising supply price of a variable input causes an input-market monopolist to be confronted with a higher and also rising marginal expense of input curve. The significance of this relation will become quite clear in Chapter 14.

Second, the rising supply price of the variable input causes the cost curves to rise more rapidly than if the supply price of input were constant. Thus, for example, marginal cost of output rises not only because

---

[5] A mathematical answer is as follows:
The supply of input curve in inverse form is given by

$$p = g(q), \qquad g'(q) > 0, \qquad (9.5.1)$$

where p and q represent price and quantity supplied of the variable input respectively. The condition $g'(q) > 0$ implies that the supply curve is positively sloped. Total variable cost is

$$TVC = pq = qg(q), \qquad (9.5.2)$$

so the marginal expense of input is

$$\frac{d[qg(q)]}{dq} = g(q) + qg'(q). \qquad (9.5.3)$$

In light of expression (9.5.1), $g(q) + qg'(q) > g(q)$. Hence the marginal expense of input curve must lie above the supply of input curve. Further, from expression (9.5.1) the slope of the supply curve is $g'(q)$, while from expression (9.5.3) the slope of the marginal expense curve is $2g'(q) + qg''(q)$. For linear curves, $g''(q) = 0$; so the marginal expense curve has a steeper slope than the supply curve. If the supply curve is convex, $g''(q) > 0$, and the conclusion holds *a fortiori*. However, if the supply curve is positively sloped but concave, $g''(q) < 0$. In this case the marginal expense curve lies above the supply curve but approaches it asymptotically as q increases without bound.

Next, the elasticity of supply is the relative responsiveness of quantity supplied to a change in supply price. In the present notation, this may be written

$$\theta = \frac{p}{q}\frac{dq}{dp} = \frac{p}{q}\frac{1}{\dfrac{dp}{dq}} = \frac{p}{q}\frac{1}{g'(q)}. \qquad (9.5.4)$$

Equation (9.5.3) may be written

$$MEI = p\left(1 + \frac{q}{p}g'(q)\right), \qquad (9.5.5)$$

since $p = g(q)$. Substituting expression (9.5.4) in expression (9.5.5), one obtains

$$MEI = p\left(1 + \frac{1}{\theta}\right). \qquad (9.5.6)$$

The analogy with demand-marginal revenue is obtained from this last expression.

of diminishing marginal physical productivity of the input but also because the price of the input rises as its use expands.

9.3.b A Word on Monopoly Supply

Short-run monopoly supply is discussed in some detail in subsection 9.4.d. However, since cost conditions have been introduced, a word of caution is in order. The marginal cost curve is *not* the monopolist's supply curve. In fact, as you will see below, "supply" generally has a much less-precise meaning in monopoly than in perfect competition.

9.4 SHORT-RUN EQUILIBRIUM UNDER MONOPOLY

The analysis of perfect competition was based upon two important assumptions: each entrepreneur attempts (or acts as though he attempts) to maximize profit; and the firm operates in an environment not subject to outside control. Monopoly analysis rests upon the same two assumptions; accordingly, the results must be modified when applied to franchise monopoly or to monopolies subject to some form of government regulation and control.

9.4.a Total Revenue—Total Cost Approach

The monopolist, just as the perfect competitor, attains maximum profit by producing and selling at that rate of output for which the positive difference between total revenue and total cost is greatest. (Or,

TABLE 9.4.1

Profit Maximization by the Total Revenue–Total Cost Approach

Output and Sales	Price	Total Revenue	Total Cost	Profit
5	$2.00	$10.00	$12.25	$ −2.25
13	1.10	14.30	15.00	−0.70
23	0.85	19.55	18.25	+1.30
38	0.69	26.22	22.00	+4.22
50	0.615	30.75	26.25	+4.50
60	0.55	33.00	31.00	+2.00
68	0.50	34.00	36.25	−2.25
75	0.45	33.75	42.00	−8.25
81	0.40	32.40	48.25	−15.85
86	0.35	30.10	55.00	−24.90

he minimizes loss when the negative difference is least.) To illustrate
the total revenue-total cost approach, the hypothetical revenue and cost
data from Tables 9.2.1 and 9.3.1 are reproduced in Table 9.4.1. These
data are illustrated graphically in Figure 9.4.1.

The table and graph are almost self-explanatory. One should note
that maximum profit ($4.50) is attained at 50 units of output and sales.

FIGURE 9.4.1

Profit Maximization by the Total Revenue–Total Cost Approach

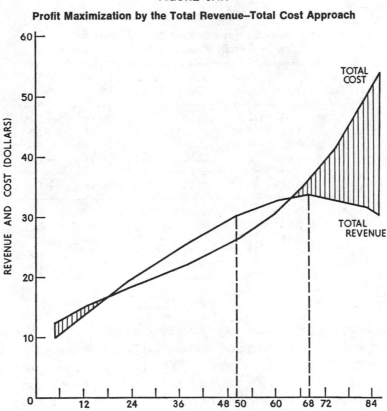

By reference to Table 9.3.1, this rate of output is less than that associated with minimum unit cost. Similarly, it is less than the maximum
revenue output; and it is also less than the rate of output (somewhat
greater than 60) for which price equals marginal cost. The latter
condition is the "rule" for profit maximization under perfect competition. But it does not hold for monopoly, as the *marginal* approach
makes clear.

9.4.b   Marginal Revenue–Marginal Cost Approach

Since all underlying concepts have been introduced, this section begins with a continuation of the example previously used. Table 9.4.2
provides the relevant data, shown graphically in Figure 9.4.2.

Under monopoly, maximum profit is attained at that rate of output
and sales for which marginal cost equals marginal revenue. The hypothetical data in Table 9.4.2 clearly illustrate this proposition. For a

TABLE 9.4.2

**Marginal Revenue–Marginal Cost Approach to
Profit Maximization**

Output and Sales	Price	Total Revenue	Total Cost	Marginal Revenue	Marginal Cost	Profit
5	$2.00	$10.00	$12.25	—	$0.45	$−2.25
13	1.10	14.30	15.00	$0.54	0.34	−0.70
23	0.85	19.55	18.25	0.52	0.33	+1.30
38	0.69	26.22	22.00	0.44	0.25	+4.22
50	0.615	30.75	26.25	0.35	0.35	+4.50
60	0.55	33.00	31.00	0.23	0.48	+2.00
68	0.50	34.00	36.25	0.13	0.66	−2.25
75	0.45	33.75	42.00	−0.03	0.82	−8.25
81	0.40	32.40	48.25	−0.23	1.04	−15.85
86	0.35	30.10	55.00	−0.46	1.35	−24.90

proof, however, the continuous case represented by Figure 9.4.3 is used.

Marginal cost and marginal revenue are given by curves of customary shape, intersecting at point E. We wish to prove that producing
output $O\overline{q}$ associated with this intersection leads to maximum profit
or minimum loss. The method of attack is "proof by contradiction."
Suppose $O\overline{q}$ were not the profit-maximizing output. First, assume that
it is less than $O\overline{q}$—say, Oq_l. At that point marginal cost is OA and
marginal revenue is $OB > OA$. Hence adding a unit to output and
sales will increase total revenue by more than it increases total cost.
Therefore profit can be expanded, or loss reduced, by expanding output
from the rate Oq_l. And this statement must hold for *any* output less
than $O\overline{q}$ since $MR > MC$ over the entire range from O to $O\overline{q}$.

Next, suppose the profit-maximizing output were greater than $O\overline{q}$
—say, Oq_h. At this point marginal revenue is OC and marginal cost is

FIGURE 9.4.2

Profit Maximization by the Marginal Revenue–Marginal Cost Approach

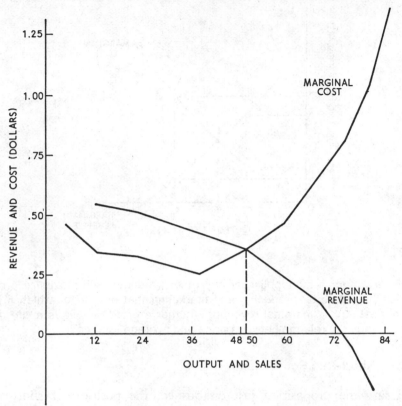

$OD > OC.$ At this rate of output an additional unit of output and sales adds more to total cost than to total revenue. Profit is accordingly diminished or loss augmented. Further, this must hold for *any* output greater than $O\bar{q}$ because $MC > MR$ over than entire range of output.

Since the profit-maximizing output can neither exceed nor be less than $O\bar{q}$, the following proposition is established:[6]

---

[6] Let the monopolist's demand function in inverse form be $p = f(q)$ and let his cost be $C = C(q)$. Thus profit (π) is

$$\pi = qf(q) - C(q) .\qquad(9.6.1)$$

The first-order condition for profit maximization requires that the first derivative of expression (9.6.1) equal zero, or

$$d\pi/dq = f(q) + qf'(q) - C'(q) = 0 .\qquad(9.6.2)$$

Marginal revenue is $d[qf(q)]/dq = f(q) + qf'(q)$. Similarly, marginal cost is

FIGURE 9.4.3

Proof of $MC = MR$ Theorem for Profit Maximization

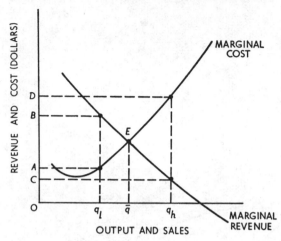

OUTPUT AND SALES

Proposition: A monopolist, or any other producer, will maximize profit or minimize loss by producing and marketing that output for which marginal cost equals marginal revenue. Whether a profit or loss is made depends upon the relation between price and average total cost.

9.4.c Short-Run Equilibrium

Using the proposition just established, the position of short-run equilibrium under monopoly is easily described. Figure 9.4.4 is a graphical representation. The revenue side is given by the demand and marginal revenue curves, D and MR respectively. Costs are depicted by the average total cost and marginal cost curves, ATC and MC respectively.

$dC/dq = C'(q)$. Hence expression (9.6.2) gives the profit-maximization rule stated in the text.

For a true local maximum, the second derivative of expression (9.6.1) must be less than zero. That is, the second-order condition requires that

$$d^2\pi/dq^2 = 2f'(q) + qf''(q) - C''(q) < 0 . \qquad (9.6.3)$$

The first two terms give the slope of the marginal revenue curve while $C''(q)$ is the slope of the marginal cost curve. The second-order condition requires that the slope of the marginal revenue curve be less than the slope of the marginal cost curve (with respect to the quantity axis). Given a negatively sloped marginal revenue curve, the condition is obviously satisfied when marginal cost is positively sloped. However, monopoly differs from perfect competition in that the marginal cost curve may be negatively sloped at the profit-maximizing point provided its slope is less steep (absolute value of slope is less) than that of marginal revenue.

FIGURE 9.4.4

Short-Run Equilibrium under Monopoly

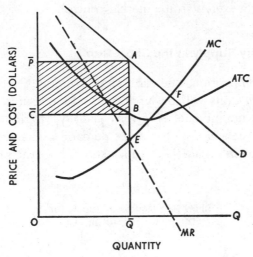

The profit-maximization "rule" states that short-run equilibrium occurs at point E where marginal cost equals marginal revenue. The associated price and output are $O\overline{P}$ and $O\overline{Q}$. At the rate of output $O\overline{Q}$, average total or unit cost is $O\overline{C}$ ($= \overline{Q}B$). Profit per unit is $O\overline{P} - O\overline{C} = \overline{PC}$. Thus short-run monopoly profit is $\overline{PC} \times O\overline{Q} = \overline{P}AB\overline{C}$. It is thus represented by the area of the shaded rectangle in Figure 9.4.4.

In the example of Figure 9.4.4, the monopolist earns a pure profit in the short run, just as a perfect competitor may. If demand is sufficiently low relative to cost he may also incur a loss, just as a perfect competitor may. In the short run the primary difference between monolopy and perfect competition lies in the slope of the demand curve. Either may earn a pure economic profit; either may incur a loss. Other comparisons are difficult. If it happened that Figure 9.4.4 also exactly represented a perfect competitor with horizontal demand curve intersecting *MC* at point *F,* one could say that price would be lower and the output greater under perfect competition than under monopoly.

This type of comparison is very risky, however, because it involves all sorts of assumptions concerning the behavior of cost as plant size expands or contracts. In particular, one must assume that *MC* somehow represents competitive supply. But as we have already seen, the competitive supply curve usually cannot be taken as the sum of individual marginal cost or supply curves. As a consequence, short-run comparisons are fraught with danger. About the best that can be said is that a monopolist is more likely to earn a pure profit in the short run because he can effectively exercise some market control.

9.4.d Monopoly Supply in the Short Run

In perfect competition, one can define a unique "supply price" for each quantity: q units will be supplied for $\$x$ per unit. In monopoly, supply price is not unique. A given quantity would be supplied at different prices, depending on market demand and marginal revenue. This is illustrated in Figure 9.4.5 which shows how the price a monopo-

FIGURE 9.4.5

**Short-Run Monopoly Supply for
Different Demand Curves**

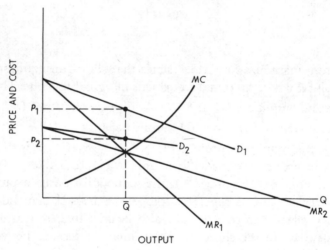

list will charge depends on the demand curve given the marginal cost curve MC. When demand is D_1 and marginal revenue is MR_1, the quantity $\overline{Q}$ would be sold at a price of P_1 per unit. If, however, the demand curve is D_2 and the marginal revenue curve is MR_2, the same quantity, $\overline{Q}$ would be sold at P_2.

Relations: Monopoly supply depends on the shape and location of the demand curve and does not have the clear and exact meaning that competitive supply has. It is meaningless to ask in general what price a monopolist will charge for a given output since the answer is not unique.

9.4.e Multiplant Monopoly in the Short Run

The discussion has so far been based upon the implicit assumption that a monopolist owns and produces by means of only one plant. This, however, is not necessarily the case. The monopolist may operate more than one plant, and cost conditions may differ from one plant to another. A hypothetical two-plant example is given in Table 9.4.3 and illustrated graphically in Figure 9.4.6.

TABLE 9.4.3

Profit Maximization in a Multiplant Monopoly

Output and Sales	Price	Marginal Revenue	Marginal Cost Plant 1	Marginal Cost Plant 2	Monopoly Marginal Cost
1..........	$5.00	—	$1.92	$2.04	$1.92
2..........	4.50	$4.00	2.00	2.14	2.00
3..........	4.10	3.30	2.08	2.24	2.04
4..........	3.80	2.90	2.16	2.34	2.08
5..........	3.55	2.55	2.24	2.44	2.14
6..........	3.35	2.35	2.32	2.54	2.16
7..........	3.20	2.30	2.40	2.64	2.24
8..........	3.08	2.24	2.48	2.74	2.24
9..........	2.98	2.18	2.56	2.84	2.32
10..........	2.89	2.08	2.64	2.94	2.34

The first three columns of Table 9.4.3 provide the revenue data, while the last three contain the relevant cost data. The marginal costs of plants 1 and 2 are shown in columns 4 and 5, and they are plotted in panel a, Figure 9.4.6. Similarly, demand and marginal revenue are plotted in panel b. The final column, "Monopoly Marginal Cost," is derived from the marginal cost curves of the individual plants.

If output is expanded from zero to one, the one unit should clearly be produced in plant 1, whose marginal cost is $1.92 ($<$\$2.04$ in plant 2). Hence marginal cost for the multiplant monopoly is $1.92. If output is to be two units, both should be produced in plant 1 because its marginal cost for the second unit ($2) is less than the marginal cost of producing one unit in plant 2. Hence monopoly marginal cost for two units is $2. If three units of output are to be produced, however, plant 2 should enter production because its marginal cost for the first unit ($2.04) is less than the marginal cost of the third unit in plant 1.

FIGURE 9.4.6

Short-Run Profit Maximization for a Multiplant Monopoly

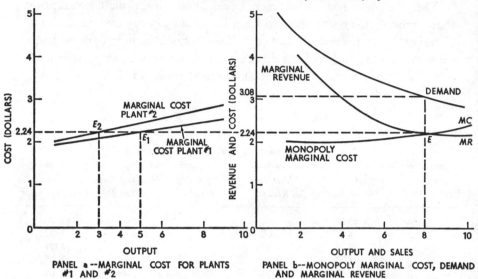

PANEL a--MARGINAL COST FOR PLANTS #1 AND #2

PANEL b--MONOPOLY MARGINAL COST, DEMAND AND MARGINAL REVENUE

By producing two units in plant 1 and one unit in plant 2, the multiplant monopoly has a marginal cost of $2.04 for the third unit. Column 6, "Monopoly Marginal Cost," is derived by continuing this line of reasoning for each successive unit of output.

Monopoly marginal cost is plotted in panel b, Figure 9.4.6. It intersects marginal revenue at point E, corresponding to eight units of output and market price of $3.08. By the $MC = MR$ rule, this price-output combination is the one for which monopoly profit is a maximum. The problem faced by the monopolist is the allocation of production between plants 1 and 2.

First, observe that $MC = MR = \$2.24$ at the equilibrium point. A horizontal dashed line at the $2.24 level has been extended from panel b to panel a. The line intersects the plant marginal cost curves at E_1 and E_2, the points at which $MC_1 = MC_2 = MC = MR$. The associated outputs are five units for plant 1 and three units for plant 2; their combined quantity is precisely eight units, the profit-maximizing output. Thus the monopolist allocates production to his plants by equating plant marginal cost with the common value of monopoly marginal cost and marginal revenue at the equilibrium output.

Generalizing, we obtain the following

Proposition: A multiplant monopolist maximizes profit by producing that output for which monopoly marginal cost equals marginal revenue.

Optimal allocation of production among the various plants requires each plant to produce that rate of output for which the plant marginal cost is equal to the common value of monopoly marginal cost and marginal revenue at the monopoly equilibrium output.

9.5 LONG-RUN EQUILIBRIUM UNDER MONOPOLY

A monopoly exists if, and only if, there is only one firm in the market. Among other things this statement implies that *entrance* into the market is not possible. Thus whether or not a monopolist earns a pure profit in the short run, no other producer can enter the market in the hope of sharing whatever pure profit exists. Therefore, pure economic profit is not eliminated in the long run, as it is in the case of perfect competition.[7]

9.5.a Long-Run Equilibrium in a Single-Plant Monopoly

Long-run equilibrium adjustment in a single-plant monopoly must take one of two possible courses. First, if the monopolist incurs a short-run loss and if there is no plant size that will result in pure profit (or at least, no loss), the monopolist goes out of business. Second, if he earns a short-run profit with his original plant, he must determine

---

[7] Certain economists prefer to say that in the long run pure profit does not exist irrespective of the type of market organization (whether perfectly competitive, monopolistic, etc.). They contend that the monopoly position or the monopoly-causing "ingredient" should be capitalized, thereby increasing total cost by the amount of the pure profit that would otherwise exist (in the absence of capitalization). This is a perfectly defensible argument; however, the interpretation used in the text is retained to facilitate comparisons among long-run equilibria under various types of market organization. If the no-profit approach is preferred by the student, he should compare long-run equilibria in terms of differential returns to the same inputs.

The way in which *LAC* changes when monopoly profit is capitalized may be illustrated graphically. In the figure, *LAC* is the "regular" envelope curve. Suppose revenue conditions are such that the monopolist earns only the competitive rate of profit at OQ_1 and OQ_2. For outputs less than OQ_1 or greater than OQ_2, the monopolist incurs a pure economic loss. Then *LAC'* indicates the "monopoly profit capitalized" long-run average cost curve. Note that it must lie *below* the usual long-run average cost curve when the monopolist incurs a pure loss, and it must lie above when the monopolist reaps a pure long-run profit. Thus it must equal the usual *LAC* at the points where the monopolist earns the going rate of profit that prevails in competitive industries.

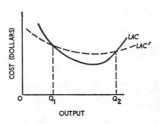

whether a plant of different size (and thus a different price and output) will enable him to earn a larger profit.

The first situation requires no comment. The second is illustrated by Figure 9.5.1. *DD′* and *MR* show the market demand and marginal

FIGURE 9.5.1

Long-Run Equilibrium for a Single-Plant Monopolist

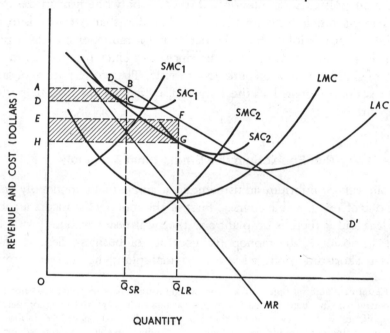

revenue confronting a monopolist. *LAC* is his long-run envelope cost curve (see Chapter 7), and *LMC* is the associated long-run marginal cost curve. Suppose in the initial period the monopolist builds the plant represented by SAC_1 and SMC_1. Equality of short-run marginal cost and marginal revenue leads to the sale of $O\overline{Q}_{SR}$ units at the price *OA*. At this rate of output, unit cost is $OD = \overline{Q}_{SR}C$; short-run monopoly profit is represented by the area of the shaded rectangle *ABCD*.

Since a pure economic profit can be reaped, the monopolist would not consider going out of business. However, he would search for a more profitable long-run organization. To this end, long-run marginal cost becomes the relevant consideration. By an argument analogous to the one used in subsection 9.4.b to establish the $MC = MR$ rule, the profit-maximum *maximorum* is attained when long-run marginal cost equals marginal revenue. The associated rate of output is $O\bar{Q}_{LR}$, and price is OE.

By reference to LAC, the plant capable of producing $O\bar{Q}_{LR}$ units per period at the least unit cost is the one represented by SAC_2 and SMC_2. Unit cost is accordingly OH, and long-run maximum monopoly profit is given by the area of the shaded rectangle $EFGH$. This profit is obviously (visually) greater than the profit obtainable from the original plant.

Generalizing, we have the following

Proposition: A monopolist maximizes profit in the long run by producing and marketing that rate of output for which long-run marginal cost equals marginal revenue. The optimal plant is the one whose short-run average total cost curve is tangent to the long-run average cost curve at the point corresponding to long-run equilibrium output. At this point short-run marginal cost equals marginal revenue.

The organization described by the proposition above is the best the monopolist can attain; and he *can* attain it because in the long run his plant size is variable and the market is effectively closed to entry.

9.5.b Comparison with Perfect Competition

The long-run equilibrium positions of a monopolist and a perfect competitor are somewhat more comparable than their short-run equilibria. The comparison is based upon the graphical illustrations of long-run equilibrium in Figures 8.6.3 and 9.5.1.

First, under perfect competition production occurs at the point of minimum long- and short-run average cost. While the monopolist utilizes the plant capable of producing his long-run equilibrium output at the least unit cost, this plant is not the one associated with absolute minimum unit cost (for any output).[8] Thus in a sense to be described more fully in Chapter 16, society's limited resources are used relatively more efficiently in perfectly competitive markets than in monopoly markets.[9]

---

[8] Of course, the demand curve *could* be such that marginal revenue intersects long-run marginal cost at the point where the latter intersects the long-run average cost curve. In this instance the single-plant monopolist would produce at minimum long-run unit cost. Such a case would indeed be rare, and the slightest change in demand would upset it.

[9] This statement is concerned with relative economic efficiency and ignores the fact that cost comparisons between monopoly and perfect competition are *generally impossible*. Comparison is possible if the industry in question is truly a constant-cost industry, for minimum long-run average cost is attained at the same level irrespective

Second, the perfect competitor produces at the point where marginal cost and price are equal. For the monopolist, price exceeds marginal cost by a substantial amount. Under certain conditions,[10] demand represents the marginal *social* valuation of a commodity by the members of the society. Similarly, long-run marginal cost usually represents the marginal *social* cost of production. Under monopoly, the marginal *value* of a commodity to society exceeds the marginal cost of its production to society. The society as a whole would therefore benefit by having more of its resources used in producing the commodity in question. The profit-maximizing monopolist will not do so, however, for producing at the point where price equals marginal cost would eliminate all, or almost all, of his profit. Indeed, he might incur a loss. Therefore, all other things equal, social welfare tends to be promoted more by competitive than by monopolistic market organization.

9.5.c Long-Run Equilibrium in a Multiplant Monopoly

In the long run a multiplant monopolist adjusts the number of plants to attain equilibrium. The process is illustrated in Figure 9.5.2.

The adjustment of each individual plant is shown in panel a. Irrespective of original plant size, in the long run the monopolist can construct *each* plant of such size that short-run average cost coincides with long-run average cost at the minimum point on the latter curve. In other words, he can construct each plant of such size that the desired rate of output per plant can be produced at the irreducible minimum unit cost. But as he expands output by expanding the number of plants operating at minimum long-run average cost, the cost curves for each plant shift upward. This must be true because input prices increase with input usage (that is, one must presume that if *all* resources used were unspecialized, there would be a competitive market organization).

In Chapter 8 this type of situation was discussed. In that case we said the competitive industry was an increasing cost industry, and we showed how to construct the long-run supply curve (or curve showing the long-run supply price). A similar curve can be constructed for the multiplant monopolist; but it does *not* relate to long-run supply or long-run supply price (long-run supply, as well as short-run supply, is not well defined in the case of monopoly). To the monopolist this curve is his long-run marginal cost curve because it shows the *minimum*

---

of the scale of operation. On the other hand, comparisons are not valid for long-run decreasing- or increasing-cost industries.

[10] The exceptions are noted in Chapter 16.

FIGURE 9.5.2

Long-Run Equilibrium in a Multiplant Monopoly

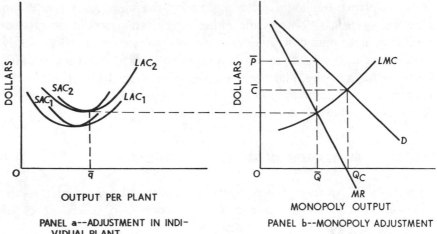

OUTPUT PER PLANT

PANEL a--ADJUSTMENT IN INDI-
VIDUAL PLANT

MONOPOLY OUTPUT

PANEL b--MONOPOLY ADJUSTMENT

increase in cost attributable to an expansion of output by expanding the number of optimally adjusted plants (i.e., plants operating at minimum long-run average cost).

The long-run marginal cost curve thus derived is labeled LMC in panel b. The revenue conditions are shown by D and MR. Invoking the $LMC = MR$ rule, long-run profit maximizing equilibrium is attained at an output of $O\overline{Q}$ units per period and a price of $O\overline{P}$. The optimum output per plant is $O\overline{q}$. The number of plants n_m the monopolist constructs and utilizes is $n_m = O\overline{Q}/O\overline{q}$.

9.5.d Comparison with Perfect Competition

In the long run both perfectly competitive firms and multiplant monopolists operate their plants at minimum long- and short-run unit cost. In this respect they are alike. Their differences will become clear by considering a hypothetical case.

Suppose each firm in a perfectly competitive industry is represented by panel a, Figure 9.5.2. Then long-run industry equilibrium would occur at OQ_c in panel b, where demand equals long-run supply. The associated market price is $O\overline{C}$, and the equilibrium number of firms n_c is presumably greater than n_m, the number of plants operated by the multiplant monopolist.

Next, suppose all firms are bought by the same individual, who creates an effective monopoly. As shown before, the monopolist will produce $O\bar{Q}$ units and sell them at $O\bar{P}$ each. He would require only $n_m < n_c$ plants; he would accordingly scrap the superfluous plants (in number, $n_c - n_m$). Thus while either organization would be characterized by minimum-cost production, in comparison with the perfectly competitive industry, the multiplant monopolist would sell fewer units, charge a higher price, and operate fewer plants. In this case, as in the case of a single-plant monopoly, social welfare tends to be promoted to a greater extent by competition than by monopoly.

9.6 SPECIAL TOPICS IN MONOPOLY THEORY

Sections 9.1 through 9.5 comprise the theory of price under conditions of monopoly. In this concluding section two special types of monopoly organization are discussed.

9.6.a Price Discrimination

Certain commodities are purchased by two or more distinct types of buyers. For example, commercial and residential purchasers of electric power can usually be sharply divided on the basis of demand elasticity. Similarly, tourists and traveling salesmen constitute two different types of markets for motel accommodations. If a monopolist possesses a market divisible in this manner and if he can effectively separate it, he may practice *discriminatory pricing* to augment his monopoly profit.

Price discrimination occurs when different prices are charged for the same commodity in different markets. The analysis of discriminatory pricing is a straightforward application of the $MR = MC$ rule; but in a sense it is diametrically opposite to the application of the rule to multiplant monopoly. In the latter, plant marginal cost curves are aggregated to obtain the monopoly marginal cost, which is equated to marginal revenue. In price discrimination, submarket marginal revenue curves are aggregated to obtain the monopoly marginal revenue, to which marginal cost is equated.

For simplicity, consider the case in which a general market can be separated into two distinct submarkets. Panel a, Figure 9.6.1, shows demand (D_1D_1', D_2D_2') and marginal revenue (MR_1, MR_2) for submarkets one and two respectively. Aggregating the demand and marginal revenue curves horizontally yields the market demand and

FIGURE 9.6.1

Market Conditions Leading to Price Discrimination

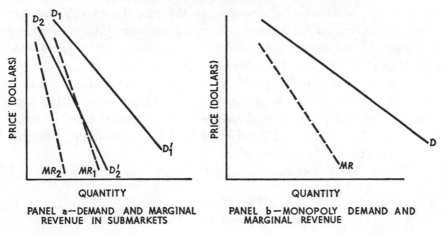

PANEL a—DEMAND AND MARGINAL   PANEL b—MONOPOLY DEMAND AND
REVENUE IN SUBMARKETS   MARGINAL REVENUE

marginal revenue curves shown in panel b. The allocation of sales between the two markets is the basic problem encountered by the price-discriminating monopolist.

Suppose, for the moment, that the monopolist has somehow correctly allocated the sale of q units. Next, suppose he decides to expand output and sales to $q + 1$ units. In which market should the additional unit be sold? The answer should be obvious: the additional unit should be sold so as to increase total revenue by the greatest possible amount. This will occur, of course, if the unit is sold in the market with the higher marginal revenue corresponding to the prior allocation of the q units.

Generalizing, the total output to be sold should be allocated between the two markets in such a way that marginal revenue is the same in both markets. If marginal revenue were higher in market 1 than in market 2, for example, the monopolist could augment his profit by shifting some units from market 2 to market 1. Maximum profit is obtained only when marginal revenue is the same in both markets.

This argument establishes the basis of allocating a given volume of sales between two markets. It also permits an easy explanation of the fundamental market condition required for profitable and meaningful price discrimination. Recall that marginal revenue may be expressed in the following way:

$$MR = p\left(1 - \frac{1}{\eta}\right),$$

where p is price and η is the elasticity of demand. As just shown, MR must be the same in each market. If η were also the same in each market, p would necessarily be the same. In this case the two submarkets would be indistinguishable since all revenue-connected magnitudes are the same. Consequently, profitable price discrimination requires that the elasticity of demand differ between the two markets.

As has been said, the first problem confronting a price-discriminating monopolist is the allocation of a given level of sales between his markets. The second problem is determining the optimal level of sales and, therefore, the level of price in each of the submarkets. For this calculation cost data are required.

In Figure 9.6.2, AC and MC represent the (aggregate) unit and

FIGURE 9.6.2

Profit Maximization with Price Discrimination

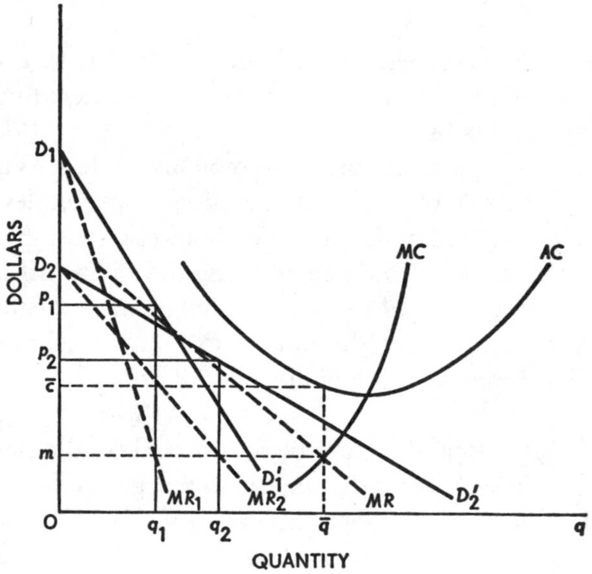

marginal cost of producing the monopolized output. $D_1 D_1'$ and $D_2 D_2'$ are the submarket demand curves; MR_1 and MR_2 are the corresponding marginal revenue curves. Aggregating the two marginal revenue curves, just as we previously aggregated plant marginal costs, the monopoly marginal revenue curve MR is obtained. Next, invoking the $MC = MR$ rule, the profit-maximizing output is $O\bar{q}$ units. The marginal revenue associated with this output is Om.

The market allocation rule, previously determined, requires that marginal revenue be the same in each submarket. Thus Oq_1 units are sold in market 1 and Oq_2 units in market 2 $(Oq_1 + Oq_2 = O\bar{q})$. Furthermore, given the submarket demand curves, the price in each submarket is determined. A price of Op_1 per unit is charged in market 1, and Op_2 per unit is charged in market 2.

At any given output it is visually apparent that demand is more elastic in market 2 than in market 1. Using this information in conjunction with the results above brings out an interesting, albeit rather obvious, point: the more elastic the submarket demand the lower the equilibrium price in the submarket.[11] Among other things, this principle accounts for the price differential favoring commercial, as against residential, users of electrical power.

Summarizing these results:

Proposition: If the aggregate market for a monopolist's product can be divided into submarkets with different price elasticities, the monopolist can profitably practice price discrimination. Total output is determined by equating marginal cost with aggregate monopoly marginal revenue. The output is allocated among the submarkets so as to equate marginal revenue in each submarket with aggregate marginal revenue at the $MR = MC$ point. Finally, price in each submarket is determined directly from the submarket demand curve, given the submarket allocation of sales.

---

[11] This proposition is easily proved. First, recall that marginal revenue may always be written as

$$MR = p\left(1 - \frac{1}{\eta}\right).$$
(9.11.1)

Next, since marginal revenue must be equal in both markets, we have

$$MR_1 = MR_2,$$
(9.11.2)

where subscripts denote the market. Using expression (9.11.1) in expression (9.11.2), we obtain

$$p_1\left(1 - \frac{1}{\eta_1}\right) = p_2\left(1 - \frac{1}{\eta_2}\right).$$
(9.11.3)

Let market one be characterized by the higher price elasticity of demand. Hence,

$$\eta_1 > \eta_2,$$

and thus

$$\left(1 - \frac{1}{\eta_1}\right) > \left(1 - \frac{1}{\eta_2}\right).$$

Using the latter inequality in expression (9.11.3), equality between the left- and right-hand sides requires $p_2 > p_1$.

9.6.b Bilateral Monopoly

The final special topic, bilateral monopoly, is analyzed chiefly to explain the meaning of *indeterminacy* in economics. Our general conclusion is that price and quantity is *indeterminate* in cases of bilateral monopoly. This does not mean that the market collapses or that the parties fail to reach a definite agreement on price and quantity. Rather it means the information the economist has is not sufficient to determine the precise market solution. The solution, in other words, is based not only upon conditions of demand and cost, with which the economist can deal, but also upon bargaining skills and other personal characteristics anterior to the realm of economic analysis.

A bilateral monopoly is said to exist when one producer has an output monopoly and there is only one buyer for the product (a purchase monopoly). Thus a bilateral monopoly would exist if there were only one copper-mining firm and one brass manufacturer in the world. This example is somewhat fanciful; however, the situation is sometimes approximated quite closely in the real world. A "one-mill" town with

FIGURE 9.6.3

Bilateral Monopoly

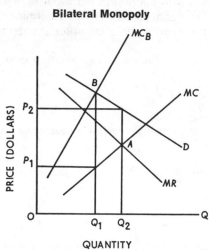

an effective labor union, while not exactly a bilateral monopoly situation, is very close to being one.

Bilateral monopoly is analyzed by means of Figure 9.6.3. *D* is the demand curve of the single buyer in the market; hence *D* and *MR* are the demand and marginal revenue curves confronting the monopolistic seller. Similarly, *MC* is the marginal cost curve of the single producer.

MC and MR intersect at point $A;$ hence the output monopolist wishes to sell OQ_2 units at a price of OP_2 per unit. If he could do so, his profit from operation would be maximized.

If the output monopolist could force the single buyer to behave as though he were a buyer in a large and impersonal market, he could do so. But in this situation the single buyer realizes his potential power as a buying monopolist. In the limit, if the single buyer could control the market completely, he could make the output monopolist behave as if he were a perfect competitor. Then MC would be the supply curve as well as the marginal cost curve. If it were, the curve marginal to MC, labeled MC_B, would be the *marginal cost of buying* an additional unit.[12]

Optimally, the single buyer would like to equate his marginal valuation of the product (given by his demand curve) with the marginal cost of purchasing. He would strive to attain point B with the purchase of OQ_1 units at a price of OP_1 (determined by the MC equals potential supply curve) per unit. If a large number of producers were in the market, or if he could get the monopolist to act as if he were a perfect competitor, he could do so.

However, the single buyer can no more induce the output monopolist to act as a perfectly competitive producer than the single seller can induce the purchase monopolist to act as a perfectly competitive buyer. Each realizes the situation that exists and tries to do his best. The economist cannot determine the solution. He can say the "best" the output monopolist can do is to sell OQ_2 units at OP_2 per unit. Similarly, the "best" the purchase monopolist can do is to buy OQ_1 units at OP_1 per unit. Neither extreme is likely to materialize. Output will lie somewhere between OQ_1 and OQ_2 and price somewhere between OP_1 and OP_2. The precise result is determined by factors beyond the purview of economic analysis.

Exercise: In Chapter 7 there was an exercise concerning the short-run effect of featherbedding on the cost curves of a firm. Now suppose a monopolist is suddenly confronted with a featherbedding contract and, merely for simplicity, assume that there is no change in the wage rate (only in the number of union workers employed). (*i*) Assuming profit maximization by the monopolist, what will be the direction of change in his price and output? (*ii*) Assume that the monopolist expects the featherbedding contract to be permanent. What type of long-run changes is he likely to make?

---

[12] With necessary verbal changes to allow for the difference between buying products and hiring inputs, MC_B in Figure 9.6.3 is entirely analogous to the marginal expense of input curve in Figure 9.3.1.

QUESTIONS AND EXERCISES

1. Federal Milk Marketing Orders, covering most metropolitan areas, impose a specified price to be paid dairy farmers for milk used for industrial purposes (e.g., in making cheese, ice cream, etc.) and a higher price for milk used for direct consumption (i.e., drinking).

   a. Does such an arrangement affect the returns to the dairy farming industry?

   b. How do the Marketing Orders affect the allocation of resources and economic welfare of the community?

2. In a Consent Decree signed in the mid-1950s, IBM agreed to sell, as well as rent, various business machines. IBM also agreed to dispose of the facilities used to produce punch cards that were required to operate the machines and agreed further that IBM would no longer sell punch cards. Firms renting IBM machines formerly had to buy their punch cards from IBM. At this time IBM owned 90 percent of all machines in its field. What effect would prohibiting the producing and selling of punch cards have on IBM's pricing policy for machines?

3. On its leased duplicating machines, Xerox has used a pricing policy which involves a lower charge per copy the larger the number of copies of a given original. In other words, one copy of each of five separate originals costs more than five copies of a single original. What similarities does this pricing policy have with the IBM policy in Question 2?

4. In a number of university towns, college professors receive discounts from the local bookstores, usually about 10 percent. Students are generally not given similar discounts. Assuming that this practice constitutes price discrimination, what conditions make it feasible and desirable for the stores?

5. Some time ago, most of the major airlines issued student travel cards at a nominal price. These cards permit college students to fly "space available" (i.e., no reservations allowed) at substantial discounts. When this practice was in effect some older nonstudents were using the cards, and some students were insuring themselves available space by reserving seats for fictitious passengers who then do not show up for the flight.

   a. Did the discounts represent price discrimination?

   b. Did the conditions necessary for successful discrimination exist?

6. From 1923 to 1946, Du Pont was virtually the sole American producer of "moistureproof Cellophane," a product for which it held the key patents. In its opinion, which exonerated Du Pont of possessing any economically meaningful monopoly, the Supreme Court held "an appraisal of the 'cross-elasticity' of demand in the trade" to be of considerable importance to the decision. Why?

SUGGESTED READINGS

Allen, R. G. D. *Mathematical Analysis for Economists,* chap. 18. London: Macmillan & Co., Ltd., 1956. [Elementary math required.]

Hicks, J. R. "Annual Survey of Economic Theory: The Theory of Monopoly," *Econometrica,* vol. 3 (1936), pp. 1–20. [Elementary math required.]

Machlup, Fritz. *The Political Economy of Monopoly.* Baltimore: Johns Hopkins Press, 1952.

————. *The Economics of Sellers' Competition,* pp. 543–66. Baltimore: Johns Hopkins Press, 1952.

Robinson, Joan. *The Economics of Imperfect Competition.* pp. 47–82. London: Macmillan & Co., Ltd., 1933.

Samuelson, Paul A. *Foundations of Economic Analysis,* pp. 57–89. Cambridge, Mass.: Harvard University Press, 1947. [Advanced math required.]

Simkin, C. G. F. "Some Aspects and Generalizations of the Theory of Discrimination," *Review of Economic Studies,* vol. 15 (1948–49), pp. 1–13. [Advanced math required.]

10

Competition and monopoly:
Some theoretical
exercises

10.1 INTRODUCTION

The models of Chapers 8 and 9 have played a central role in the economists' tool bag for many years. This is not because they appear "realistic" on a priori grounds, but because they are capable of providing interesting hypotheses that have held up rather well in empirical tests.

The aim of this chapter is to illustrate the use of these models as hypothesis "generators." We will use the competitive industry model and the model of pure monopoly to analyze the impact of certain governmental and industrial policies such as taxes and price controls. The specific analyses presented are meant to be illustrative, not definitive. What we wish to do is show how the models can be used as analytical tools, and we have chosen some relatively simple examples and assumptions for this purpose. A more complete analysis would include a refinement of the assumptions, a more detailed consideration of secondary and tertiary affects, and at least some recognition of the general equilibrium aspects of the problem. Despite these simplifications, however, the discussion ought to help the reader develop a deeper understanding of how the models work.

10.2 EXCISE TAXES IN A COMPETITIVE INDUSTRY

We begin with an analysis of the impact of a governmentally imposed excise tax in a competitive industry. We assume that the tax is imposed on a per unit basis, that is, for each unit sold a tax of say 10 cents must be paid.[1] The tax is paid to the government by the producer rather than the buyer, but this has no effect on the conclusions so long as we assume that collection costs are essentially the same for producers and buyers. We also assume a constant-cost industry so changes in total industry output do not affect technology or factor prices. The objective of the analysis is to determine what will happen to prices, industry output, firm output, and the number of firms in the industry when the tax is imposed. We will consider the effect on these magnitudes first in the short run and then in the long run.

10.2.a Short-Run Effects on Cost, Price, and Output

To facilitate the discussion assume that all firms in the industry are identical and that there are n_0 such firms before the tax is imposed. The initial equilibrium is shown in Figure 10.2.1. The left-hand graph is the short-run average total cost and the associated marginal cost curve for a typical firm. The firm is in equilibrium at a price of p_0 and an output of q_0. The right-hand graph in Figure 10.2.1 is the industry supply curve and the demand curve. Given the constant-cost industry assumption, the supply curve is simply the horizontal summation of the marginal cost curves of the firms. Because we assume there are n_0 firms (all the same as the "typical" firm), the total quantity supplied and demanded is $n_0 q_0$.

When the tax is imposed on producers, marginal cost increases by the amount of the tax because the tax is paid on each unit sold. Hence, the marginal cost curve shifts up vertically by the amount of the tax. For the same reason the average cost curve also shifts up vertically by the amount of the tax.[2] Notice that this means the post-tax minimum

---

[1] Such taxes apply to cigarettes, for example. A more familiar tax is an *ad valorem* tax where the tax is stated as a given *percentage* of the selling price. The *ad valorem* tax is analyzed in a manner similar to the unit tax, but the analysis differs in certain details.

[2] If the total cost of the firm is $C(q)$ before the tax, then before-tax marginal cost is $C'(x)$ and before-tax average cost is $C(q)/q$. After the tax is imposed, total cost is $C(q) + tq$ where t is the tax. After-tax marginal cost is $C'(q) + t$, and after-tax average cost is $C(q)/q + t$. Observe that the minimum pre-tax average cost occurs at the same output as post-tax average cost because these two functions differ only by the constant per unit tax.

FIGURE 10.2.1

Initial Equilibrium in a Competitive Industry

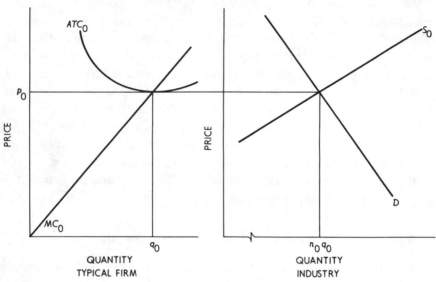

average cost occurs at the same output as the pre-tax minimum average cost. The new cost curves are shown by MC_1 and ATC_1 in the left-hand graph of Figure 10.2.2.

Recall that short-run profits will be maximized (or losses minimized) by a competitive firm if output is chosen so as to equate price and marginal cost (given that this price is above average variable cost). The tax shifts the marginal cost curve so when firms equate price to marginal cost the post-tax output of the firm will be lower at each price than pre-tax output at that price. In a constant-cost industry this means the industry supply curve will shift. In particular, for a per unit tax the industry supply curve will shift up vertically by the amount of the tax. This is shown by the post-tax supply curve S_1 in the right-hand panel of Figure 10.2.2.

The short-run equilibrium (i.e., market clearing price) will obtain where the short-run post-tax supply curve intersects the demand curve. If the demand curve were completely inelastic, the new price would have to be greater than the old price by exactly the amount of the tax. However, when the demand curve is not perfectly inelastic, the new price will be above the old price but by *less* than the amount of the tax. This is because increases in price reduce the quantity demanded and the market will not clear at a new price equal to the old price plus the tax because at that price producers would be willing to supply the *old*

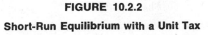

FIGURE 10.2.2

Short-Run Equilibrium with a Unit Tax

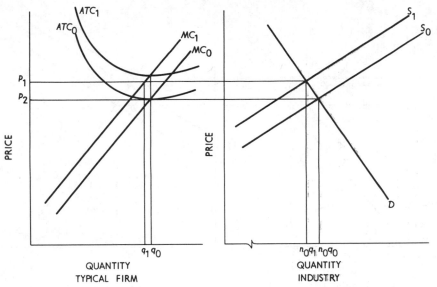

quantity but consumers would demand less than the old quantity. Thus, the new market price shown by p_1 in Figure 10.2.2 is above the old but by less than the tax.[3]

At p_1 each firm reduces its output from q_0 to q_1 and short-run industry output is n_0q_1. It was noted above that the minimum of the average cost curve including the tax is at the same output, namely q_0, as the minimum of the pre-tax average cost curve. This means that p_1 is below the minimum average total cost and that firms are suffering short-run economic losses. The presence of losses in the short run sets in motion the forces that lead to the new long-run equilibrium.

10.2.b Long-Run Effects of the Tax

The short-run losses that result from the tax cause firms to leave the industry.[4] The actual process by which this occurs is a dynamic question not answered by the comparative static models of Chapter 8. Thus we are not able to tell precisely which firms will leave or how fast this

---

[3] We assume that the new price, p_1, is above average variable cost including the tax.

[4] This analysis assumes that the tax is not applied to all other industries. If it were, the alternative costs would be affected and the cost curves of the industry would be shifted.

FIGURE 10.2.3
Long-Run Equilibrium with a Unit Tax

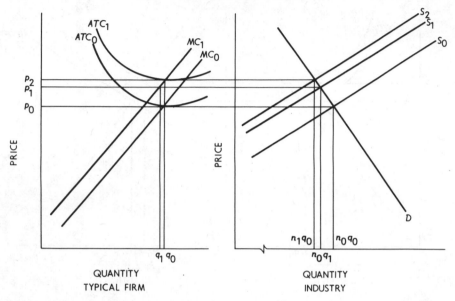

QUANTITY
TYPICAL FIRM

QUANTITY
INDUSTRY

will happen. We know, however, that firms will exit so long as losses exist.

Of course the losses will not continue indefinitely as firms leave. Remember that the supply curve is the *sum* of the marginal cost curves of the firms. As firms leave this sum will involve a smaller number of firms and thus the industry supply curve shifts upward and to the left. The shift will stop when economic profits are back to zero which is, of course, at the price which exceeds the initial price by exactly the amount of the tax. (This is because the new average cost curve has a minimum that is equal to the minimum of the old average cost curve plus the tax.)

As the supply curve shifts upward, price will rise and hence output of each firm will increase. The process will terminate at the point where each remaining firm is producing the same output, q_0, that it produced before the tax. The number of firms has decreased, however, and so has total industry output. The post-tax long-run equilibrium is shown by price p_2, firm output q_0, and industry output n_1q_0 in Figure 10.2.3. Note that n_1 is less than n_0. These effects are summarized in Table 10.2.1.[5]

---

[5] These results depend on the constant-cost industry assumption. One of the questions for this chapter asks the reader to do the analysis for the increasing-cost industry case.

TABLE 10.2.1

**The Effects of a Unit Tax on a Constant
Cost Competitive Industry**

Effect on—	*Short Run*	*Long Run*
Price	Increased but less than tax	Increased by amount of tax
Firm output	Decreased	Unchanged
Industry output	Decreased	Decreased (by more than short-run decrease)
Number of firms	Unchanged	Decreased

10.2.c *Ad Valorem* Taxes

Ad valorem taxes are imposed as a fixed percentage of the price of a commodity. The analysis is quite similar to the unit tax but it is somewhat easier to explain it by assuming that the tax is collected from consumers rather than suppliers.[6] In view of these strong similarities, we will refer only to the industry curves in the graphs.

When an *ad valorem* tax is imposed, a fraction of the price paid by consumers is taken by the government and the price net of tax is received by producers. In Figure 10.2.4, the curve labeled D is the demand curve. This curve represents the gross amount consumers are willing to pay per unit for any given output. Before the tax is imposed, producers receive all that consumers pay and, assuming a supply curve S_0, the equilibrium price and quantity are p_0 and n_0q_0.

After the tax is imposed producers do not receive all that consumers pay because some fixed fraction of the price goes to the government. Accordingly, we add an auxiliary curve, labeled D_T in Figure 10.2.4, which shows the price net of taxes received by producers.[7] For each quantity, the associated price on the demand curve D is reduced by the fixed tax percent and the resulting "net of tax" price is the point on D_T associated with that quantity. The D_T curve is the relevant one for determining the quantity at which the market clears. In Figure 10.2.4 the short-run market clearing quantity after the tax is n_0q_1

---

[6] The same analysis could be applied in the case of a unit tax with no change in the conclusions.

[7] It is inappropriate to add the tax to D since the demand curve depends only on the gross price paid for the good. The consumer decides how much to demand given the gross price; he is unconcerned about what the tax authority or the producer receives.

FIGURE 10.2.4

Ad Valorem Taxes

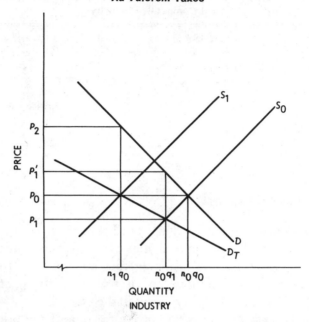

where the price received by producers is p_1 and the price paid by consumers is p_1'. The difference $p_1' - p_1$ is the tax per unit. Since the minimum average cost before the tax was equal to p_0 (remember there are zero economic profits in competitive equilibrium), the after-tax price p_1 is below this minimum average cost.[8] This means there are economic losses in the industry and, as in the unit tax case, firms begin to leave.

The reduction in the number of firms drives the supply curve up and to the left because we are summing over fewer firms to get this curve. When the supply curve finally shifts to S_1, the net-of-tax price is p_0, so firms are again making zero economic profit. In this post-tax long-run equilibrium, each firm produces q_0, the output before the tax, but there are fewer firms so industry output, $n_1 q_0$, is less than both initial output and short-run output. Price has risen so that the new equilibrium price exceeds the old by the amount of the tax.[9]

---

[8] We are accounting for the tax by the auxiliary curve D_T so the cost curves of the firm are not affected.

[9] We have treated the tax as if it were deducted from the price paid by the consumer. Let λ be the tax; then $p_T = p - \lambda p$ is the price received by the producer where p is the price paid by the consumer. This tax is equivalent to a tax of $\lambda/(1 - \lambda)$ *added* to the price received by the producer. Hence a 5 percent sales tax added to the producer's price can be treated as a 4.76 percent tax deducted from the price paid by the consumer for analytical purposes.

10.3 LUMP-SUM TAXES

Lump-sum taxes differ from unit taxes or *ad valorem* taxes in that they do not vary with output or price. The lump-sum tax, as its name suggests, is simply a fixed dollar tax obligation, that is, a fixed cost rather than a variable cost. It is a "long-run" fixed cost in the sense that it cannot be avoided except by going out of business. Annual operating license fees for retail stores are an example of lump-sum taxes.

10.3.a Short-Run Effects of a Lump-Sum Tax in a Competitive Industry

Using the assumptions of section 10.2 we can analyze the effect of a lump-sum tax on a competitive industry. We note first that lump-sum taxes do not affect either marginal cost or average variable cost because they do not vary with output. They do affect average total cost just as any fixed cost would. Figure 10.3.1, like the figures in section 10.2, shows the cost curves for the typical firm and the supply and demand curves for the industry. Before the tax is imposed, the industry is in equilibrium at a price of p_0 and an industry output of $n_0 q_0$. Each of the n_0 firms produces an output of q_0.

The imposition of the lump-sum tax raises the average total cost

FIGURE 10.3.1

Lump-Sum Taxes

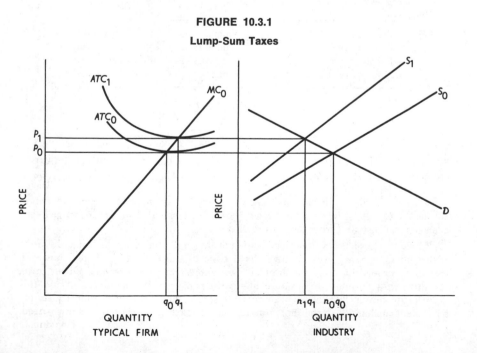

curve of each firm but does not affect marginal cost. After the tax is imposed the average cost curve shifts from ATC_0 to ATC_1. The marginal cost curve does not change, and this means that it must intersect ATC_0 at its minimum point *and* ATC_1 at its minimum point. The minimum of ATC_1 must be above and to the right of the minimum of ATC_0.[10]

The marginal cost curve determines the industry supply function in the constant cost industry case, and because there is no change in the marginal cost function, the lump-sum tax does not affect the short-run supply schedule. This means that in the short run there is no change in price, firm output, or industry output.[11] The short-run situation will not persist indefinitely, however, because all firms are experiencing economic losses equal to the amount of the lump-sum tax.

10.3.b Long-Run Effects of a Lump-Sum Tax

The economic losses caused by a lump-sum tax in the short run result in an exodus of firms from the industry. As firms leave, the sup-

TABLE 10.3.1

Effects of a Lump-Sum Tax in a Constant-Cost Competitive Industry

	Short Run	Long Run
Price	Unchanged	Increased
Firm output	Unchanged	Increased
Industry output	Unchanged	Decreased
Number of firms	Unchanged	Decreased

ply curve shifts up and to the left because we are summing over a smaller number of firms. This causes price to rise (and industry output to fall) until the firms remaining in the industry return to zero eco-

---

[10] Let T be the lump-sum tax. Then if $C(q)$ is the total cost function before the tax, $C(q) + T$ is total cost after the tax. Marginal cost is unchanged, but average total cost goes from $C(q)/q$ to $C(q)/q + T/q$.

[11] Students sometimes find this result puzzling and they tend to think the firms will want to increase price to cover fixed costs. It must be remembered, however, that in a competitive industry firms are *price-takers* not price setters. Given price, the firms will continue to produce along their marginal cost curve because this decision maximizes profits (or minimizes losses). Hence, since the industry supply schedule is unchanged in the short run, the market clearing price remains unchanged.

nomic profits. As shown in Figure 10.3.1, the new equilibrium obtains
at a price of p_1 equal to the minimum of the post-tax average cost curve.
At the new equilibrium firms remaining in the industry are producing
a larger output than before the tax. Post-tax industry output is smaller.
These results are summarized in Table 10.3.1.[12]

10.3.c Lump-Sum Taxes and the Size Distribution of Firms

The analysis of subsection 10.3.b suggests that lump-sum taxes tend
to have the long-run effect of decreasing the number of firms in an
industry and increasing their size. In other words, lump-sum taxes tend
to concentrate output among a smaller number of larger firms, and the·
bigger the tax the more pronounced will be this effect.

This is not to say that lump-sum taxes necessarily favor firms that
are relatively larger before the tax is imposed. To illustrate this suppose
that an industry contains firms of two sizes. Smaller sized firms achieve
minimum average total cost at three units of output, and larger firms
achieve minimum average total cost of five units of output. The two
sizes of firms can coexist in the industry so long as both have the same
minimum average cost. Table 10.3.2 presents the relevant data for a
lump-sum tax of $10. Column 1 of the table is output, column 2 is
the average lump-sum tax, column 3 is pre-tax average total cost for
a typical small firm, column 4 is post-tax ATC for a small firm, column
6 is pre-tax ATC for a typical large firm, and column 7 is post-tax ATC
for a large firm. Before the tax small and large firms each have a minimum ATC of $100. After the tax the minimum ATC for small firms
is $101.70 and $101.91 for large firms. Hence the large firms cannot
exist in the industry after the tax is imposed, and those firms which
were small before the tax survive. It is true, of course, that the pre-tax
small firms produce a larger output after the tax than the large firms
did before the tax, so our earlier conclusion that lump-sum taxes increase the average firm size is still true.[13]

The disadvantage of the pre-tax large firms in this example arises
because the ATC of large firms rises much more rapidly than that of
small firms as output deviates from the output associated with minimum
ATC. It is easy to construct alternative examples in which the large
firms survive the lump-sum tax and the small firms leave. The example

---

[12] See footnote 5.

[13] This increase in the size of the firm always holds when small and large firms
have the same pre-tax minimum cost.

TABLE 10.3.2

**Example of the Effect of Lump-Sum Taxes in an
Industry with Firms of Different Sizes**

Output (units)	Average Cost of Lump-Sum Tax $\left(\dfrac{\$10}{q}\right)$	Small Firm		Large Firm	
		Average Cost before Tax	Average Cost after Tax	Average Cost before Tax	Average Cost after Tax
1	$10.00	$100.20	$110.20	$101.00	$111.00
2	5.00	100.10	105.10	100.75	105.75
3	3.33	(100.00)	103.33	100.50	103.83
4	2.50	100.10	102.60	100.25	102.75
5	2.00	100.20	102.20	(100.00)	102.00
6	1.66	100.30	101.96	100.25	(101.91)
7	1.42	100.40	101.82	100.50	101.92
8	1.25	100.50	101.75	100.75	102.00
9	1.11	100.60	101.71	101.00	102.11
10	1.00	100.70	(101.70)	101.25	102.25
11	0.909	100.80	101.709	101.50	102.40
12	0.83	100.90	101.73	101.75	102.58
13	0.76	101.00	101.76	102.00	102.76
14	0.71	101.10	101.81	102.25	102.96
15	0.66	101.20	101.86	102.50	103.16

is intended to show that this depends on the shape as well as the location of the ATC curve.

10.4 PRICE CONTROLS

Efforts by the government to put ceilings (and in some cases floors) on prices are fairly common. Major efforts of this kind were made during World War II, and more recently in the Phase I to Phase IV policies of the Nixon administration. Other examples such as rent controls in New York City and foreign cities have been around for many years. In this section we examine the effect of price ceilings in competitive and monopolistic industries.

10.4.a Price Controls in a Competitive Industry

Figure 10.4.1 shows the industry supply curve S_0 and the industry demand curve D for a competitive constant-cost industry of the kind discussed in sections 10.2 and 10.3. Before controls are imposed the market clears at a price of p_0 and an indsutry output of $n_0 q_0$. (There are n_0 firms each producing q_0.

FIGURE 10.4.1

Price Controls in a Competitive Industry

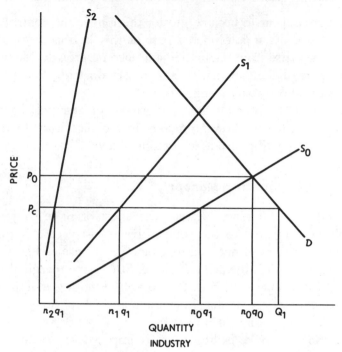

Now suppose the government imposes a price ceiling of p_c (where $p_c < p_0$). At this lower price consumers demand Q_1 units but firms each cut back their output to q_1. The shortage created by the ceiling price is thus $Q_1 - n_0q_1$ initially. Because p_c is below the minimum ATC $(= p_0)$ of firms there is an exodus of firms from the industry. This causes a shift of the supply curve, say, to S_1. The shortage grows to $Q_1 - n_1q_1$ because there are fewer firms in the industry.[14] The reduction in the number of firms does not affect the controlled price, so the exodus continues. As time goes on and more firms leave, the supply curve shifts to S_2 and the shortage grows to $Q_1 - n_2q_1$. Ultimately all firms will leave the industry.[15]

---

[14] We do not change the demand curve in this example. In fact, the inconveniences caused by the shortage are like an added cost that may lead consumers to switch to other goods and this would change the position of the demand curve in the controlled industry.

[15] This exodus of *all* firms depends on the constant-cost assumption. The case of an increasing-cost industry is left to the reader as an exercise at the end of this chapter.

As simple as this analysis is, it captures two interesting features of price control programs that are frequently observed in the real world:

a. Shortages appear to become greater the longer the controls are in effect. In a dynamic economy part of this is because of demand shifts that arise from population and income growth. Nonetheless, a big part of the explanation also has to do with dwindling supply as the above analysis suggests.
b. The longer the controls are in effect the greater will be the rise in price needed to clear the market in the short run. In the long run the price will return to its precontrol level.[16]

10.4.b Price Controls in a Monopoly

An interesting difference between the effect of price controls in a monopoly as compared to the competitive industry case is that in a monopoly controls need not lead to a shortage. Consider Figure 10.4.2 where the line EAD is the demand curve, EBC is the marginal revenue curve, and MC is marginal cost. Before a price ceiling is imposed, the monopolist chooses the output Q_0 where marginal revenue equals marginal cost. The output is sold at price p_0.

Now suppose a price ceiling of p_c is imposed on the monopolist. Given the demand curve the most he can sell at this price is output Q_c. If he wants to sell more than Q_c, he must reduce the price below p_c. This means that for outputs up to Q_c the monopolist has marginal revenue equal to p_c. Marginal revenue drops to B when output is increased slightly beyond Q_c. This is because the reduction in price needed to sell additional output must also be applied to the output Q_c which was previously sold at the ceiling price p_c. For further output increases the marginal revenue is given by the segment BC of the original marginal revenue curve.

The effect of the ceiling price is thus to change marginal revenue from EBC to the broken line p_cABC. The segment AB is actually a discontinuity in the post-control marginal revenue curve. Marginal cost, as drawn in Figure 10.4.2, passes through the discontinuous segment AB of the new marginal revenue curve. Hence for outputs less than Q_c, marginal revenue $(= p_c)$ is greater than marginal cost and the monopolist increases profit by increasing output over this region. For outputs greater than Q_c, marginal cost is greater than marginal revenue

---

[16] In the comparative static analysis used here we assume that no dynamic shifts in supply or demand conditions occur during the period of controls.

FIGURE 10.4.2

Price Controls in a Monopoly

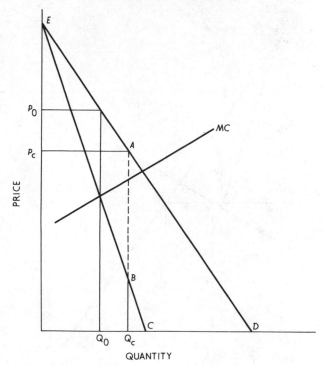

so profits are increased by reducing output over this range. It follows that after the price ceiling is imposed the profit maximizing output is Q_c which is sold at the ceiling price p_c. The price ceiling has led the monopolist to increase his output, and no shortage occurs—at least for the particular price ceiling shown in Figure 10.4.2.[17]

Price ceilings can cause shortages in a monopoly as shown in Figure 10.4.3. When the price ceiling is pushed down far enough, the marginal revenue curve becomes p_cAQ_D. The marginal cost curve intersects this marginal revenue curve at the point B in the horizontal segment p_cA. The monopolist produces Q_c after the ceiling is imposed because this is the point at which marginal revenue $(= p_c)$ equals marginal cost. At the ceiling price p_c consumers demand Q_D and a shortage of $Q_D - Q_c$ obtains.

---

[17] This phenonemon is often used to justify regulation of monopolists' prices. In reality it is hard to pick the right price and errors can be made that do lead to shortages as we shall soon see. A better policy would be to break up the monopoly with antitrust action.

FIGURE 10.4.3

Shortages in a Monopoly

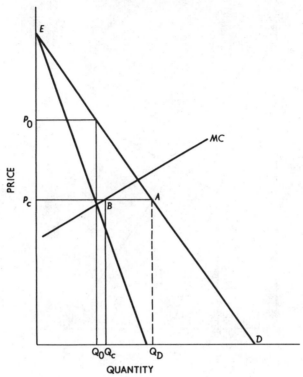

10.5 PRICE SUPPORTS AND OUTPUT RESTRICTIONS

Governments put floors under some prices just as they put ceilings on others. Agricultural price supports are a well-known example in the United States. For many years political pressures have led the Congress and the Executive to provide legislation that keeps farm prices above market clearing levels. In this section we examine two common ways in which this is done.

10.5.a Price Floors

Figure 10.5.1 is the supply and demand curve for a competitive industry. Before price supports are introduced, the market clears at price p_0 and quantity Q_0. If the government supports the price at p_s (where $p_s > p_0$) supply will increase to Q_2 and demand will decrease to Q_1. The government buys and stores the surplus $Q_2 - Q_1$. The

FIGURE 10.5.1

Price Supports

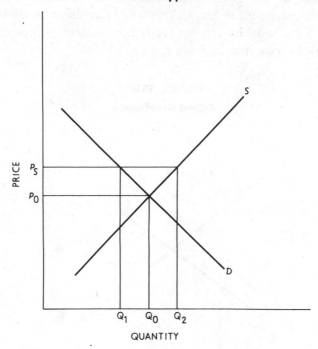

monetary cost to the government is $p_s \times (Q_2 - Q_1)$. The cost to society would be measured by the inefficient shift of resources to the farm sector and the loss of consumer welfare arising from the increased price.[18] The price support programs in the United States have led the government to hold substantial stocks of farm products. For the period 1961–65 annual carryover stocks of wheat averaged 1,129 million bushels, and for 1966–70 the annual average carryover stock was 641 million bushels of wheat. Farm income support programs in 1971–72 cost the government over $5 billion and represented more than 35 percent of net farm income.

10.5.b Output Restrictions

Another way of sustaining farm prices at greater than competitive levels is to use output restrictions. The "soil bank" programs which

---

[18] The surplus and associated costs could be even larger if we account for entry into the industry (or the failure of inefficient firms to exit) that arises because of the price supports.

limit the amount of acreage that farmers plant are an example of such policies. Assume the government restricts the amount of land that farmers can use to grow crops. The short-run effect is illustrated in Figure 10.5.2 where the acreage restriction reduces output to Q_1 and results in an increase in price from p_0 to p_s.

FIGURE 10.5.2

Output Restrictions

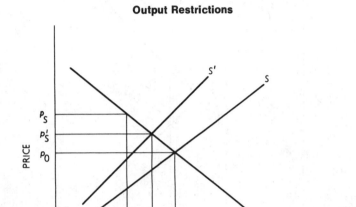

A major difficulty with acreage restriction programs is that farmers are encouraged to increase other inputs to get more output. For example, they may use more fertilizer, plant crops closer together, and so on. This is an inefficient alternative to using more land and it leads to an increase in costs. Because of these cost increases, the supply curve shifts upward to S' in Figure 10.5.2. Farmers are able to expand output along this curve because they are meeting the government's acreage restriction while substituting other inputs for land. The result is a reduction in market price to p_s' and a greater cost of producing the corresponding output (namely, Q_2) than would obtain in the absence of the acreage restrictions.[19]

---

[19] This point has been made by Professor Arnold Harberger of The University of Chicago.

10.6 SUPPRESSION OF INVENTIONS IN A MONOPOLY[20]

It is frequently asserted, especially in popular discussion, that monopolists will suppress inventions and decrease the durability of a good in order to increase sales. To analyze this question we consider the following problem: Suppose a monopolist can produce two different qualities of a good with the same total cost function for each. The better quality good provides a greater flow of services per unit of time than the lower quality good.[21] Which quality will the monopolist produce?

The interesting answer to this question is that the monopolist will always produce the better quality good. To show why, we begin by looking at the consumer's behavior. Let K be the amount of the good the consumer purchases, and let p_k be the price of the good. The service flow per unit of the good will be given by a constant u. Thus the consumer who has K units of the good has a total service flow of uK. The consumer also consumes another good X which has price p_x. If the consumer's money income is M then his utility maximization problem is

$$\text{maximize} \quad U(X, uK)$$

$$\text{subject to} \quad M = p_x X + p_k K \,.$$

Denote the total service flow by $Y = uK$ and rewrite the maximization problem as

$$\text{maximize} \quad U(X, Y)$$

$$\text{subject to} \quad M = p_x X + \frac{p_k}{u} Y \,.$$

Let X^* and Y^* be the values of X and Y that solve this problem. Next suppose that the service flow per unit of K is increased by λ where $\lambda > 1$. If the price of K were simultaneously increased by λ, the new maximization problem would be

$$\text{maximize} \quad U(X, Y)$$

$$\text{subject to} \quad M = p_x X + \frac{\lambda p_k}{\lambda u} Y \,.$$

---

[20] This section is somewhat more technical than the rest of the chapter and can be skipped without loss of continuity.

[21] The approach taken here is the same as that given by Jack Hirschleifer, "Suppression of Inventions," *Journal of Political Economy,* vol. 79 (1971), pp. 382–83. By using a more complicated model, Professor P. L. Swan has established analogous results for the problem of product durability. See P. L. Swan, "Durability of Consumption Goods," *The American Economic Review,* vol. 60 (1970), pp. 884–94.

In the new problem the λ cancels in the numerator and denominator of the fraction in the budget constraint so the new problem is *identical* to the old. This means that if X^*, Y^* solved the initial problem then X^*, Y^* also solve the new problem. It is important to note however that the optimal K for the old problem is $K^* = Y^*/u$ and the optimal K for the new problem is the smaller quantity $K^{**} = Y^*/\lambda u$ because $Y = \lambda u K$ in the new problem.

This result says that the demand curve for K shifts when u is increased. The specific shift can be determined as follows: pick a K on the old demand curve, increase the associated price by a factor of λ, then K/λ is the quantity associated with this price on the new demand

FIGURE 10.6.1

Product Quality and Monopoly

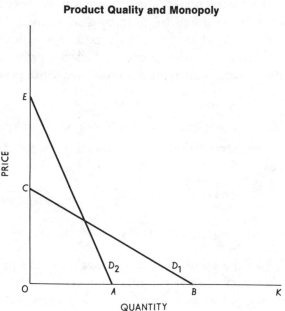

curve.[22] The shift is illustrated in Figure 10.6.1 for the case of a linear demand curve with $\lambda = 2$. The old demand curve is D_1, and the new curve (after u is doubled) is D_2. Because $\lambda = 2$ the distance OA is one half of OB and the distance OE is twice OC.

It is now easy to answer the original question. If the monopolist can offer two goods, one with a service flow per unit of u and the other with a service flow of λu (where $\lambda > 1$), he will prefer the latter if pro-

---

[22] If the old demand curve is $p_k = h(K)$, *the new one is* $p_k = \lambda h(\lambda K)$.

duction costs are the same. This is because, given the demand curve shift, he could raise his price from p_k to λp_k and get the same revenue since consumers will then demand $1/\lambda$ of their original quantity of K. The monopolist's costs are reduced, however, since the quantity of output has dropped. Thus profits are increased. Of course the actual change in price need not be an increase by a factor of λ, but the preceding argument shows that the profits at the optimum price with the new demand curve must be greater than the optimum profits for the old demand curve since we have shown at least one way to increase profits over the old optimum.

QUESTIONS AND EXERCISES

1. Using the format of Table 10.2.1, show the effects of a unit tax on price, firm output, industry output, and the number of firms both in the short run and the long run for an increasing-cost industry.

2. Using the format of Table 10.3.1, show the effects of a lump-sum tax on price, firm output, industry output, and the number of firms both in the short run and the long run for an increasing-cost industry.

3. Discuss the effects of price controls in a competitive increasing-cost industry.

4. What are the short-run and long-run effects of a lump-sum subsidy (in a constant-cost industry) on price, firm output, industry output, and the number of firms when—
   a. The subsidy is given to all firms in the industry including those that decide to enter after the subsidy program is established;
   b. The subsidy is given only to firms in the industry at the time the subsidy is established and not to any new entrants to the industry.

5. What are the short-run and long-run effects of a unit tax on a monopolist?

6. What are the short-run and long-run effects of an *ad valorem* tax on a monopolist?

11

Theory of price under monopolistic competition

11.1 INTRODUCTION

Chapters 8 and 9 dealt with the "pure" and "extreme" cases of perfect competition and monopoly. The two models are pure in that the analytical results are completely independent of personal influences, especially entrepreneurial expectations and speculation concerning the behavior of rivals. Indeed, there are no *rivals* in either perfect competition or monopoly. They are "extremes" from the standpoint of numbers and profit. In perfect competition the number of firms in an industry is indefinitely large, while at the opposite end of the "numbers" spectrum, monopoly is a one-firm industry. Similarly, zero economic profit per firm is the central characteristic of long-run equilibrium in perfect competition. In contrast, monopolization of a market guarantees the single firm a greater long-run pure profit than it could earn under any other organization of the market (that is, than if there were one or more rival firms in the market).

11.1.a Historical Perspective

With the exception of a few "naïve" duopoly theories, discussed in Chapter 12, the theories of perfect competition and monopoly constituted "classical" microeconomic theory from Marshall to Knight. In point of fact, the theory of perfect competition was not perfectly developed until the publication of Knight's *Risk, Uncertainty, and Profit.*[1] Stigler even argued that Knight's meticulous discussion of perfect competition, clearly pointing out the austere nature of the rigorously defined concept, caused a widespread reaction against the use of perfect competition as a model of economic behavior.[2] This is probably true; but whatever the cause, in the late 1920s and early 1930s there was definitely a reaction against the use both of perfect competition and of pure monopoly as analytical models of business firms and market behavior.

A Cambridge economist, Piero Sraffa, was among the first to point out the limitations of "competition-or-monopoly" analyis;[3] he was soon followed by others. Hotelling emphasized that "the difference between the Standard Oil Company in its prime and the little corner grocery is quantitative rather than qualitative. Between the perfect competition and monopoly of theory lie the actual cases."[4] Similarly, Zeuthen urged that "neither monopoly nor competition are ever absolute, and the theories about them deal only with the outer margins of reality, which is always to be sought between them."[5]

In the late 1920s and early 1930s economists began turning their attention to the middle ground between monopoly and perfect competition. Two of the most notable achievements were attributable to an English economist, Joan Robinson,[6] and to an American, Edward Chamberlin.[7] Our attention in this chapter is directed toward Chamberlin's unique achievement.

11.1.b Product Differentiation

Chamberlin based his theory of "monopolistic competition" on a solid, empirical fact: there are very few monopolists because there are

---

[1] London School Reprints of Scarce Works, No. 16 (1933).

[2] George J. Stigler, "Perfect Competition, Historically Contemplated," *Journal of Political Economy,* vol. 65 (1957), pp. 1–17.

[3] Piero Sraffa, "The Laws of Returns under Competitive Conditions," *Economic Journal,* vol. 36 (1926), pp. 535–50.

[4] Harold Hotelling, "Stability in Competition," *Economic Journal,* vol. 29 (1929), pp. 41–57; citation from p. 44.

[5] F. Zeuthen, *Problems of Monopoly and Economic Warfare* (London: Routledge, 1930), p. 62.

[6] Joan Robinson, *The Economics of Imperfect Competition* (London: Macmillan & Co., Ltd., 1933).

[7] E. H. Chamberlin, *The Theory of Monopolistic Competition* (6th ed.; Cambridge, Mass.: Harvard University Press, 1950).

very few commodities for which close substitutes do not exist; similarly, there are very few commodities that are entirely homogeneous among producers. Instead, there is a wide range of commodities, some of which have relatively few good substitutes and some of which have many good, but not perfect, substitutes.

Let us begin with an example. The American Tobacco Company has an absolute monopoly in the manufacture and sale of Lucky Strike cigarettes. To be sure, another concern could manufacture identically the same cigarette; but it could *not* label the cigarette Lucky Strike. However, other concerns can manufacture cigarettes and call them Chesterfield, Camel, and so forth. Just as American Tobacco has an absolute monopoly of Lucky Strikes, Liggett and Myers has an absolute monopoly of Chesterfields, and Reynolds Tobacco has an absolute monopoly of Camel. Each concern has a monopoly over its own product; but the various brands are closely related goods and there is intense, *personal* competition among the firms.

Two important points are to be gleaned from the example. First, the products are *heterogeneous* rather than homogeneous; hence perfect, and *impersonal,* competition cannot exist. Second, although heterogeneous, the products are only slightly differentiated. Each is a very close substitute for the other; hence competition exists but it is a *personal* competition among rivals who are well aware of each other.

This general type of market is characterized by product differentiation; and product differentiation, in turn, characterizes most American markets. There is not one homogeneous type of automobile; nor, for that matter, are there homogeneous types of soap, men's suits, television sets, grocery stores, magazines, or motels. Each producer tries to differentiate his product so as to make it unique; yet to be in the market at all, his particular product must be closely related to the general product in question.

There are many ways of differentiating products, some quite real and others very spurious. In case of real product differentiation one can usually catalog the differences in terms of chemical composition, services offered by the sellers, horsepower, cost of inputs, and so on. In other cases—which many regard as spurious—product differentiation is based upon advertising outlays, difference in packaging material or design, brand name only (consider the aspirin market), and others.

In any event, when products are differentiated each product is unique and its producer has some degree of monopoly power he can exploit. But usually it is very little, because other producers can market a closely related commodity. It is not by chance that the selling price of cigarettes is almost uniform from brand to brand.

11.1.c Industries and Product Groups

In Chapter 8, an industry was defined as a collection of firms producing a homogeneous good. For example, by specifying clip, denier, and other characteristics of raw apparel wool, we can define the "raw apparel wool" industry. But when products are differentiated one cannot define an industry in this narrow sense. There is no "automobile" industry or "furniture" industry. Each firm having a distinct product is, in a sense, an industry in itself, exactly as a monopoly was described in Chapter 9. Nonetheless, one can usefully lump together firms producing very closely related commodities and refer to them as a *product group*. Thus hand soap, ready-to-eat cereal, or automobiles, for example, comprise instantly recognizable product groups, even though in our terminology they cannot be called industries.

Naturally enough, combining firms to make product groups is somewhat arbitrary. It is not possible to state precisely how "good" the substitutes must be. Chewing gum is a substitute for cigarettes, at least to people who are trying to quit smoking. But it is doubtful that anyone would place the Wrigley Company in the "cigarette" product group. On the other hand, decaffeinated coffee is not a substitute for regular coffee for many people. Yet few would not place Sanka in the "coffee" product group.

Fortunately, at our level of abstraction precise distinction is not material. When "industry" is used, perfect competition or monopoly is implied. When product differentiation is an important feature of the market, "product group" is used to denote the collection of firms, however combined, that produce some variety of the "product."

11.2 A DIFFERENT VIEW OF PERFECT COMPETITION

To set the stage for the exposition of monopolistic competition, it is helpful to review the model of perfect competition from a slightly different viewpoint. Suppose there are n identical firms in the industry and also suppose that consumers distribute their purchases so that each firm sells $1/n$ of total market demand when all firms charge the same price. Given these assumptions, we can analyze the behavior of the industry using Figure 11.2.1. In this figure the curves LAC and MC are the average total cost and the marginal cost curves, respectively, for a representative or typical firm. The curve D is the amount of demand going to a typical firm when all firms are charging the same price. This curve is constructed by taking $1/n$ of total market quantity demanded at each price. We will refer to this curve as the *proportional* demand curve.

FIGURE 11.2.1

Equilibrium in Perfect Competition

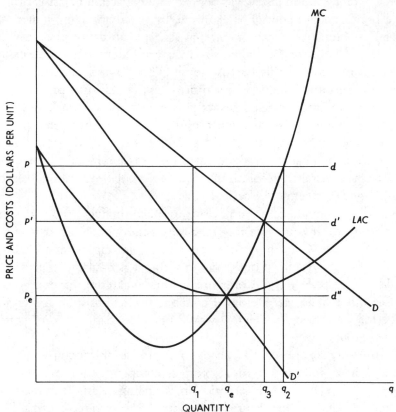

Assume first that the market price is p and each firm is getting $1/n$ of the total market (equal to q_1 in Figure 11.2.1). In perfect competition each firm thinks it can sell all it wishes at the market price, and thus the demand curve perceived by the *individual* firm is the horizontal line d. Each firm will therefore wish to sell q_2 units of output since at this output marginal cost is equal to price. Thus at price p the market supply ($= nq_2$) will exceed market demand ($= nq_1$) and the market is not in equilibrium.[8]

The efforts of all firms to sell more output than the market demands at the price p causes the price to be driven down. Equilibrium occurs only when the price is such that the horizontal demand curve

---

[8] Recall that market equilibrium requires supply to equal demand at the market price.

perceived by each firm intersects MC at exactly the point where the proportional demand curve D intersects the curve MC. In Figure 11.2.1 equilibrium is at the price p'. This is the equilibrium because each firm has precisely the sales quantity q_3 it desires, given its perceived demand curve d'; and since D intersects d' at this price, market supply equals market demand.

This equilibrium is only short run, however, because at p' each firm is making a positive economic profit. As more firms are attracted to the industry by this profit, the market demand is divided among a larger number of competing firms. The larger number of firms causes D to move down and to the left because at each price the representative firm has a smaller proportion of the market. Long-run equilibrium exists when D has shifted to D' and the price is p_e.[9] At p_e the horizontal "demand" curve d'' perceived by the individual firm is tangent to the minimum point of LAC and economic profits are zero. The proportional demand curve D' intersects LAC at its minimum so each firm is able to sell q_e, which is exactly the output it wishes.[10]

11.3 SHORT-RUN EQUILIBRIUM IN MONOPOLISTIC COMPETITION

It is an easy step from the discussion of perfect competition in section 11.2 to Chamberlin's model of monopolistic competition. The proportional demand curve D has the same meaning as in section 11.2, and it is also assumed that all firms have identical costs.[11] The key difference is that each firm perceives its own demand curve (i.e., the one that would obtain if it changed its price while all other firms left their price unchanged) to be less than perfectly elastic because its output is not a perfect substitute for the output of other firms. This is illustrated in Figure 11.3.1 where the demand curve perceived by the representative firm, d, is downward sloping instead of horizontal as in Figure 11.2.1. If every firm charged p, each would sell q_1 units of output.

[9] We assume a constant-cost industry. Long-run equilibrium could also be obtained if factor prices, and hence the ATC and MC curves, rose as entry occurs.

[10] At prices below p_e firms would produce less output than is required to meet market demand so price would rise.

[11] Chamberlin clearly intended this definition of D at least for expositional purposes. In his words, "Such a curve will, in fact, be a fractional part of the demand curve for the general class of product, and will be of the same elasticity. If there were 100 sellers, it would show a demand at each price which will be exactly 1/100 of the total demand at that price (since we have assumed all markets to be of equal size)" Chamberlin, *Theory of Monopolistic Competition,* (5th ed.), p. 90.

FIGURE 11.3.1

The Firm in Monopolistic Competition

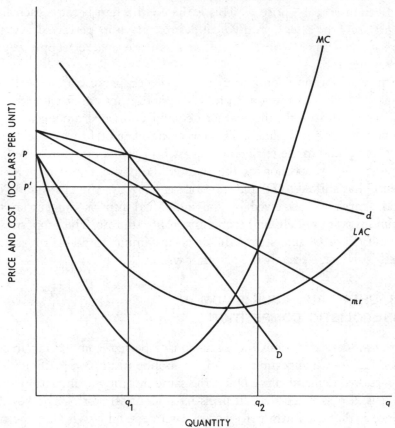

QUANTITY

As in section 11.2 the typical firm, acting on the assumption that the other firms will keep price at p, finds it profitable to reduce price to p' and sell an output of q_2. (Note that p' and q_2 are on the perceived demand curve d.) The important difference between this case and that in section 11.2 is that the downward slope of d means that the firm perceives that it must reduce price to get more customers. Accordingly, the curve mr, which is the marginal revenue curve for d, will be equated with the marginal cost curve MC to find the profit maximizing output and price p' and q_2, respectively. This is the "monopolistic" aspect of monopolistic competition.

Just as in section 11.2 the assumption that all firms are identical means that what looks good to one looks good to all. When every firm cuts its price, a new d curve is established for every firm. The new

FIGURE 11.3.2

Short-Run Equilibrium in Monopolistic Competition

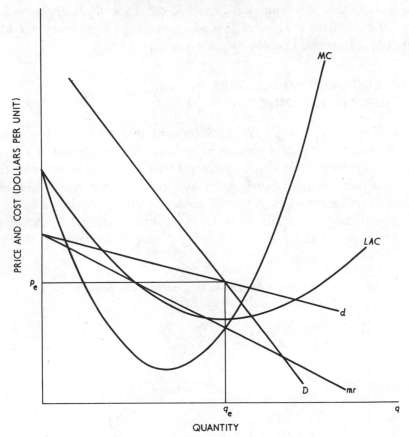

d curve intersects *D* at a lower price than the former *d* curve, and the firm's attempt to get to output q_2 is frustrated. Such price cutting will continue so long as each firm finds it advantageous to expand output by reducing its price below the current market price.

In strict analogy to section 11.2 the short-run equilibrium must have the characteristic that at the current market price no firm has an incentive to change its own price.[12] This means that in equilibrium the *mr* curve of each firm must equal marginal cost at an output such that the market price at that output is on *D*. This is illustrated in Figure 11.3.2.

---

[12] If the market price were too low, each firm would be motivated to raise its price to equate *mr* and *MC*. When all firms do this there is an upward movement of *d* along *D* until the short-run equilibrium defined in the text is reached.

When firms equate *mr* with *MC*, the output q_e is exactly that required for a market price of p_e as indicated by the intersection of *d* and *D* at p_e. *In summary, short-run equilibrium in monopolistic competition has two characteristics:* (a) *each firm picks output to equate* mr *and* MC *and* (b) d *intersects* D *at the output chosen by the firm.*

11.4 LONG-RUN EQUILIBRIUM IN MONOPOLISTIC COMPETITION

The equilibrium in Figure 11.3.2 shows that each firm is making positive economic profits because price is above average cost at output q_e. Monopolistic competition assumes that entry of new firms to the product group is uninhibited. As firms enter, the proportional demand curve *D* will move to the left until economic profits are driven to zero. A typical long-run equilibrium (zero economic profit) is shown in Figure 11.4.1. This equilibrium has the short-run characteristic that no

FIGURE 11.4.1

Long-Run Equilibrium in Monopolistic Competition

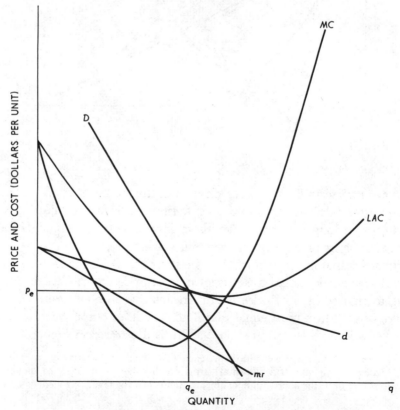

firm has an incentive to alter its price or output since $mr = MC$ at q_e. Moreover, at the market price p_e, the proportional demand curve D intersects the average cost curve so no economic profits are being made and no firm has a motivation to enter or leave the product group.

Long-run equilibrium is defined by the two conditions: (a) d *must be tangent to the average total cost curve and* (b) *the proportional demand curve* D *must intersect both* d *and average cost at the point of tangency. The conditions are the same as short-run equilibrium with the additional requirement that* d *be tangent to* ATC *at the equilibrium output.*

11.5 CHARACTERISTICS OF MONOPOLISTIC COMPETITION

In this section we examine some of the characteristics of the model of monopolistic competition that have attracted the attention of a number of economists.

11.5.a "Ideal Output" and Excess Capacity

The concept of ideal output and the associated concept of excess capacity refer only to the long run. In the short run, under any type of market organization, there can be all sorts of departures from the ideal, reflecting incomplete adjustment to existing market conditions.

From Marshall to such later writers as Kahn, Harrod, and Cassels,[13] the ideal output of a firm was generally regarded as that output associated with minimum long-run average cost, the output corresponding to the points labeled E_c in Figure 11.5.1. Consequently, the ideal plant size is the one giving rise to the short-run average cost curve that is tangent to the long-run average cost curve at the latter's minimum point. Excess capacity, therefore, is the difference between ideal output and the output actually attained in long-run equilibrium. In Figure 11.4.1 excess capacity is measured by the distance between the output associated with the minimum point on *LAC* and q_e.

Following Cassels, excess capacity is composed of two parts, as illustrated in Figure 11.5.1. Suppose in a monopolistically competitive market, a typical firm attains long-run equilibrium at the point E_p, with

---

[13] R. F. Kahn, "Some Notes on Ideal Output," *Economic Journal,* vol. 45 (1935), pp. 1–35; R. F. Harrod, "Doctrines of Imperfect Competition," *Quarterly Journal of Economics,* vol. 49 (1934–35), pp. 442–70; and J. M. Cassels, "Excess Capacity and Monopolistic Competition," *Quarterly Journal of Economics,* vol. 51 (1936–37), pp. 426–43.

FIGURE 11.5.1

Ideal Output and Excess

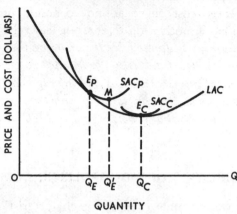

output OQ_E. From the standpoint of the *firm,* long-run optimal plant size is given by SAC_p. According to the present view of ideal output, the socially optimal plant size is represented by SAC_c, and excess capacity (negative, notice) is measured as Q_EQ_C units of output.

The measure of excess capacity may be divided in two parts. First, given the plant SAC_p, the firm operates at point E_p rather than at the point of minimum unit cost M. From a social point of view, the resources used by the firm would be more efficiently utilized if OQ_E', rather than OQ_E, units were produced. Thus a portion of excess capacity, represented by Q_EQ_E', is attributable to socially inefficient utilization of the resources actually used. The second portion of excess capacity, $Q_E'Q_C$, arises because socially and individually optimal sizes differ. The monopolistically competitive firm does not employ enough of society's resources to attain minimum unit (dollar and resource) cost.

The view of ideal output just expounded rests, fundamentally, upon the horizontal demand curve faced by a perfect competitor. But if individual demand curves are negatively sloped, if active price competition characterizes the market, and if entry is free into the product group, Chamberlin argues that E_c does not correspond to ideal output. Product heterogeneity is desired per se; and, according to Chamberlin, it inevitably gives rise to negatively sloped individual demand curves.

"Differentness" is considered a quality of the product and entails a cost just as any other quality. The cost of differentness is represented by production to the left of minimum average cost. The difference between actual (long-run equilibrium) output and output at minimum cost is, then, a measure of the "cost" of producing "differentness" rather than a measure of excess capacity. But this is true only so long as there is effective price competition in the market. The presence of price competition guarantees that buyers can select the "amount" of differentness they wish to purchase. In the case of price competition, Chamberlin regards E_p as a "sort of ideal" for a market in which there is product differentiation.[14]

11.5.b Nonprice Competition and Excess Capacity

According to Chamberlin, long-run equilibrium under monopolistic competition does not give rise to excess capacity so long as the market is characterized by active price competition. In his view, excess capacity arises when free entry is coupled with the absence of price competition. This brand of excess capacity is illustrated by Figure 11.5.2.

LAC, as usual, represents long-run average cost. If there is free entry and price competition, long-run equilibrium is attained at E_p, where the perceived demand curve $d_p d_p'$ is tangent to *LAC*. As noted, E_p must lie to the left of the competitive equilibrium E_c; but with active price competition it will tend to lie rather close to the competitive point.

For many reasons, active price competition may not characterize certain markets. A "live and let live" outlook on the part of sellers, tacit agreements, open price associations, price maintenance, customary prices, and professional ethics are a few causes of nonaggressive price policies. If price competition is, in fact, lacking, individual entrepreneurs will have no regard for the existence of curves such as dd'. They will be concerned only with the effects of a general price rise or decline, or with the DD' curve.

With free entry in the absence of price competition, long-run equilibrium is attained (pure profit eliminated) only when enough firms have entered the industry to push the demand curve to $D_N D_N'$. Equilibrium is attained at E_N, with output OQ_N and price OP_N per unit. In Chamberlin's opinion, $Q_N Q_P$ represents excess capacity: it is the difference in output attributable to the absence of effective price competition. If the latter prevails, the firm attains a "sort of ideal" output.

Chamberlin then concludes that by nonaggressive price policies sellers

. . . protect, over short periods, their profits, but over longer periods, their numbers, since when prices do not fall costs rise, the two being equated by the development of excess productive capacity . . . for which there is no

---

[14] Chamberlin, *Theory of Monopolistic Competition,* p. 94.

FIGURE 11.5.2

Long-Run Equilibrium with Nonprice Competition and Excess Capacity

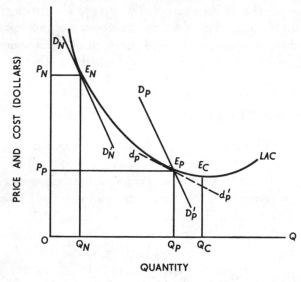

QUANTITY

automatic corrective. . . . It may develop over long periods with impunity, prices always covering costs, and may . . . become permanent and normal through a failure of price competition to function. The result is high prices and waste . . . [attributable to] the monopoly element in monopolistic competition.[15]

11.6 COMPARISONS OF LONG-RUN EQUILIBRIA

A comparison of long-run equilibria is rather difficult inasmuch as it must rest essentially upon statements pertaining to cost curves. Conditions giving rise to monopoly probably lead to noncomparable differences between competitive and monopolistic costs; for similar reasons, noncomparability is also likely between either of these two and monopolistic competition. However, a few generalizations are possible if one bears in mind that the statements are relative, not absolute. The relevant points follow immediately from a comparison of Figures 8.6.3, 9.5.1, and 11.4.1.

11.6.a Equilibrium in the Firm

For emphasis, it may be well to note the "competitive" and "monopolistic" aspects of monopolistic competition. A monopolistically competitive firm is like a monopoly in that it faces negatively sloped

[15] Ibid., pp. 107, 109.

demand and marginal revenue curves; it therefore determines its price-output policy by equating marginal cost with marginal revenue rather than with price as in perfect competition. At the same time, the monopolistically competitive firm is like a perfectly competitive one in that it faces direct market competition. The long-run result is the absence of pure profit, just as in the competitive case. While all three types may enjoy economic profit in the short run, freedom of entry eliminates it in the long run, except under conditions of pure monopoly. The qualitative nature of rivalry is also different. In perfect competition rivalry is completely impersonal. At the opposite extreme, there is no direct (only indirect and potential) rivalry under monopoly. The case of monopolistic competition is somewhat different, but it lies closer to perfect competition. The monopolistic competitor, at least in abstract, is aware of the slightly differentiated, highly substitutable products of other firms. There would be personal rivalry except for the condition of large numbers—so large that each entrepreneur believes his actions will go unnoticed by his competitors (because they are so numerous that his actions will not have a readily perceptible effect upon any *one* of them).

11.6.b Long-Run Equilibria in Industries and Product Groups

In long-run competitive equilibrium, total industry output is produced in a group of plants each of which operates at (long-run) minimum average cost. The product is sold at a price equal to minimum average cost, and it is significant to note that long-run marginal cost equals both price and average cost at this point.

Under monopoly the long-run equilibrium situation is substantially different. The industry output is produced by one firm which may operate one or more plants. If the monopolist operates one plant, it is very unlikely to be of such size as to produce at (long-run) minimum average cost; if multiple plants are used, however, each will operate a minimum cost. In neither case will price equal minimum average cost or marginal cost. Indeed, price will exceed both so that in long-run equilibrium, the marginal social valuation of the commodity exceeds the marginal cost of its production.

In the competitive case, each firm operates a plant of ideal size and the industry produces the ideal output. Thus, according to the Marshall-Kahn-Cassels version, there is no excess capacity in long-run competitive equilibrium. In a multiplant monopoly each plant is of ideal size; however, there are not enough plants to produce the ideal industry output. As a consequence there is long-run (negative) excess capacity under monopoly market organization.

Monopolistic competition is somewhat more difficult to analyze in these terms. In large-group equilibrium with active price competition, price is above marginal cost, although it equals average cost. The latter is not minimum average cost; but Chamberlin argues that the difference between cost at E_p and E_c is itself the "cost" of product differentiation. Since product heterogeneity is apparently desired per se, the cost of differentiation is a valid social cost. Hence, according to Chamberlin's argument, E_p actually represents the minimum attainable average cost when *all* relevant social costs are included. Each firm, and the product group as a whole, produces the "sort of ideal" output, and excess productive capacity does not appear in long-run equilibrium.

If Chamberlin's argument is accepted (and it is *not,* universally), one difficulty remains. Suppose E_p does represent minimum attainable unit cost, including the "cost" attributable to the "ideal" amount of product differentiation. Even then long-run price exceeds short-run marginal cost for the plant in question. The marginal social valuation of the product exceeds its marginal cost for the established level of differentiation. Socially, output should be expanded and price reduced until $P = MC$. Given the plant size, plant MC intersects $D_p D_p{}'$ somewhere below both SAC and LAC. Hence the socially desirable output would cause each firm to sustain a long-run pure loss, a situation incompatible with private enterprise.

In short, the social welfare aspects of monopolistic competition are ambiguous. From a very microscopic standpoint, each firm produces less than the socially optimal output. On the other hand, if each firm were somehow forced to produce this seemingly desirable level of output at marginal cost price, private enterprise would no longer represent a viable economic system. Finally, the abolition of private enterprise would violate a macroscopic welfare criterion that apparently transcends microscopic considerations, at least in the United States and most industrially advanced Western nations. Thus while the theoretical analysis of monopolistic competition is quite clear, the welfare implications of this analysis are not. Micro- and macroeconomic welfare criteria are not consistent and/or reconcilable. The economist *qua* economist can only indicate the dilemma; establishing definitive social goals and welfare standards is beyond his professional capacity.

11.7 AN APPRAISAL OF MONOPOLISTIC COMPETITION

Economists have been aware of the model of monopolistic competition since the early 1930s, but the model has not played a very central role in economic analysis. In part, this is because many situations that economists wish to analyze are explained quite well by the models of perfect competition or pure monopoly. Those situations that do not seem to fit these models well often fall into the broad class of oligopoly models (small numbers of sellers) discussed in Chapter 12.

The model of monopolistic competition also has met with some strong challenges on theoretical grounds. Professor George Stigler has criticized Chamberlin's definition of the product group. Stigler noted that every product has many "close" substitutes that do not fit easily into any systematic definition of a product group. Stigler gives the example of housing of people who live in New York City. He observes that housing facilities range from incredible estates to unbelievable slums. The housing facilities are geographically diverse extending directly to several states and ultimately to the whole world. It is perfectly possible that the product group contains only one firm or, on the contrary, all the firms of the economy. This makes it likely that the products of the group are heterogeneous from the technological viewpoint. The problem in defining the product group makes it difficult to provide any rigorous explanation for the downward sloping d curve in monopolistic competition.[16]

R. F. Harrod has criticized the excess capacity findings of the monopolistically competitive model. He finds it inconsistent that the firm equates a long-run marginal cost curve and a short-run marginal revenue curve to determine output. If the long-run marginal revenue curve were used, the output of the firm would be greater because long-run demand is assumed to be more elastic.[17]

Cohen and Cyert have raised an important objection to the behavioral assumptions underlying Chamberlin's model.[18] They find it puzzling that firms do not eventually learn that their actions induce predictable reactions from other firms. Firms cannot continue to believe that their perceived d curve provides real price-output opportunities when they find themselves continually frustrated in their efforts to move along this curve. If the firms do learn from experience, then the market is appropriately analyzed using a model of monopoly, oligopoly, or perfect competition according to the conditions of entry.

---

[16] George J. Stigler, *Five Lectures on Economic Problems* (London: Longmans, Green & Co., 1949).

[17] R. F. Harrod, *Economic Essays* (New York: Harcourt Brace & Co., 1952).

[18] K. J. Cohen and R. M. Cyert, *Theory of the Firm* (Englewood Cliffs, N.J.: Prentice-Hall, Inc., 1965).

QUESTIONS AND EXERCISES

1. Explain the difference between short-run equilibrium and long-run equilibrium in monopolistic competition.
2. Given the market demand curve $Q = 100 - \frac{1}{2} p$, what is the proportional demand curve when there are 20 firms in the industry? Show that the proportional demand curve has the same elasticity at any price as the market demand curve.
3. Show that the model of monopolistic competition is the same as the model of pure monopoly when there is only one firm in the industry and entry is prohibited.
4. Given the long-run equilibrium proportional demand curve $p = 51 - 2q$ and the ATC curve $ATC(q) = q^2 - 16q + 100$ for a firm in monopolistic competition:
    a. What is the long-run equilibrium price and quantity?
    b. What is the slope of the perceived demand curve d at the equilibrium quantity?
    c. What is the marginal revenue perceived by the firm at the equilibrium output?

SUGGESTED READINGS

Chamberlin, E. H. *The Theory of Monopolistic Competition,* esp. chap. 5, pp. 71–116. 6th ed. Cambridge, Mass.: Harvard University Press, 1950.

Ferguson, C. E. "A Social Concept of Excess Capacity," *Metroeconomica,* vol. 8 (1956), pp. 84–93.

Machlup, Fritz. *The Economics of Sellers' Competition,* pp. 135–241. Baltimore: Johns Hopkins Press, 1952.

Robinson, Joan. *The Economics of Imperfect Competition,* pp. 133–76. London: Macmillan & Co., Ltd., 1933.

Smithies, Arthur. "Equilibrium in Monopolistic Competition," *Quarterly Journal of Economics,* vol. 55 (1940), pp. 95 ff. [Advanced math required.]

Triffin, Robert. *Monopolistic Competition and General Equilibrium Theory,* pp. 17–96. Cambridge, Mass.: Harvard University Press, 1949.

12

Theories of price in oligopoly markets

12.1 INTRODUCTION

Oligopoly, or its limiting form duopoly, is a market situation intermediate between the cases previously studied. In monopoly only one seller is in the market; competition, in either the technical or the popular sense, does not exist. Perfect competition and large-group monopolistic competition represent the opposite. So many firms are in the market that the actions of each are expected to be imperceptible to the others. There is competition in the technical sense, but little or none in the popular sense. The reverse tends to be true in oligopoly; technically competition is lacking but sometimes there is intense rivalry or competition in the popular sense.

Oligopoly is said to exist when more than one seller is in the market, but when the number is not so large as to render negligible the contribution of each. If only two sellers are in the market, the special case of duopoly exists. For simplicity the duopoly market organization will be discussed rather than the more general oligopoly; since the fundamental problem is the same, generality is not sacrificed.

12.1.a The Oligopoly Problem

The discussion so far may seem to indicate that there is primarily a quantitative difference among the various types of market organizations. In monopoly there is one seller; in duopoly two; and so on. To be sure, a quantitative difference does exist; and it is convenient to classify markets according to this difference. Yet there is a qualitative difference of transcending importance. Briefly, when numbers are few each seller must be acutely conscious of the actions of his rivals and of their re-actions to changes in his policies.

Consider a duopoly market. Each seller must almost surely recognize that his actions affect his rival; and the latter will almost surely react to any measures that affect him adversely. Since the market is divided be-tween the two, most courses of action benefiting one firm will be harm-ful to the other; hence action by one rival will have its counterpart in a maneuver by the other. Thus many different courses of action may result.

The rivals may spend their lives trying to "second guess" each other; they may tacitly agree to compete by advertising but not by price changes; or, recognizing their monopoly potential, they may form a coalition and cooperate rather than compete. In fact, there are just about as many different results as there are oligopolies; to examine each would carry taxonomy too far. Thus we concentrate our attention on two sets of oligopoly theories. First, a few "classical" solutions to the duopoly problem are analyzed. Next, some theoretical "market" solutions are examined. But our investigation cannot be complete, for that would re-quire one or more volumes in itself. Nonetheless, the principal feature of oligopoly markets should be clear. The firms are interdependent; the policies of one directly and perceptibly affect the others. Hence competi-tion cannot be impersonal.

12.1.b Some Concepts and Assumptions

First, for analytical convenience we assume that the products within an oligopoly market are homogeneous. As a practical matter, most oligopolies are characterized by product differentiation; yet the distinc-tion is not of paramount importance because the firms are interde-pendent whether they produce identical commodities or not. Second, we assume that oligopolistic firms purchase inputs in perfectly competi-tive markets. This may or may not be true; it may hold for some inputs but not for others. However, when the assumption does great violence to reality, a small modification of the cost curves is all that is required. Finally, for the present we assume that the firms behave independently even though they are interdependent in the market. That is, the case of collusive oligopoly is ruled out even though to the firms concerned it is a highly desirable and sometimes realized solution. Since the Sherman Act, this is more a legal than an economic matter.

12.2 SOME "CLASSICAL" SOLUTIONS TO THE DUOPOLY PROBLEM

Formal speculation about the duopoly problem is sometimes dated from the work of a French economist, A. A. Cournot. Beginning with his famous "mineral springs" case, some of the outstanding theories of oligopoly behavior will be analyzed. Except for game-theory models and the Hotelling case, little credence is today accorded these solutions. However, as Machlup put it, "Familiarity with the classical models has become a kind of hallmark of the education of an economic theorist, even if it helps him more in the comprehension of the traditional lingo than in the analysis of current economic problems."[1]

12.2.a Cournot Case[2]

Assume, with Cournot, that two mineral springs, furnishing identical mineral water, are situated side by side. One is owned by **A**, the other by **B**. The springs are actually artesian wells to which purchasers must bring their own containers. Consequently the only costs are the fixed costs of sinking the wells; in particular, marginal cost is zero for each producer. The duopoly market so constructed is illustrated in Figure 12.2.1. DQ is the market demand for mineral water, and MR is the marginal revenue curve.

Suppose **A** is initially the only seller in the market. To maximize his profit he sells OQ_1 units of mineral water, so that marginal revenue equals the zero marginal cost. Price is OP_1 per unit, and profit is OQ_1CP_1. Now **B** enters the market and Cournot's crucial assumption comes into the picture.

To get at an analytical solution of a duopoly situation one must make a behavioral assumption concerning each entrepreneur's expectations of his rival's policies. Cournot's assumption is that each entrepreneur expects his rival *never* to change his output. Thus when **B** enters the mar-

---

[1] Fritz Machlup, *The Economics of Sellers' Competition* (Baltimore: Johns Hopkins Press, 1952), p. 369.

[2] Augustin Cournot, *Recherches sur les principes mathématiques de la théorie des richesses* (Paris, 1838). English translation by Nathaniel T. Bacon entitled *Researchers into the Mathematical Principles of the Theory of Wealth* (New York: Macmillan & Co., 1897; reprinted 1927).

FIGURE 12.2.1

Cournot Solution

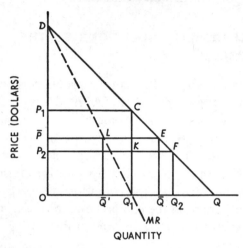

ket, he expects **A** always to market OQ_1 units of mineral water. He accordingly views the segment CQ as that portion of total demand from which his demand curve is derived—that portion of the market remaining after **A** sells OQ_1 units. To maximize his profit, **B** decides to sell Q_1Q_2 units at price OP_2.[3] His anticipated profit is Q_1Q_2FK, and **A's** anticipated profit falls to OQ_1KP_2.[4]

Now **A**, in his turn, expects **B** always to market $Q_1Q_2 = Q_2Q$ units of mineral water. Hence, according to his belief OQ_2 represents the total market available to him. With straight-line demand and marginal revenue curves, the best he can do is to market $1/2\ OQ_2$ units. Thus he reduces his output somewhat and market price rises accord-

---

[3] Recall the method of deriving marginal revenue from demand and the fact that marginal cost equals zero.

[4] The dynamics of transition from an initial monopoly position to an ultimate duopoly equilibrium can be explained in various ways, none of which is particularly satisfactory. The presentation in the text is adopted because it is the one most frequently found in the literature and because if one ignores certain minor points, it is the most easily understood. But the "minor points" may cause the serious student some concern. For example, when **B** enters the market, he charges a price of OP_2 per unit. Price for both **A** and **B** is accordingly OP_2, and total sales are OQ_2. But since the products of **A** and **B** are homogeneous, OQ_2 would be evenly divided between **A** and **B**, not divided two thirds for **A** and one third for **B**, as the analysis in the text assumes. With some considerable graphical difficulty, the analysis can be revised to allow for market sharing subsequent to price changes. The same conclusion, however, ultimately emerges. Mathematical treatment of the Cournot case is not encumbered by this difficulty.

ingly. **B** views the situation anew and sees more of the market now available, specifically $OQ - 1/2\ OQ_2$. Consequently, **B** increases his output to $1/2\ (OQ - 1/2\ OQ_2)$, price falls somewhat, and **A** must reappraise the situation.

Believing **B** will forevermore sell $1/2\ (OQ - 1/2\ OQ_2)$ units, the available market for **A** appears to be $OQ - 1/2\ (OQ - 1/2\ OQ_2)$. His profit-maximizing output is thus $1/2[OQ - 1/2\ (OQ - 1/2\ OQ_2)$, somewhat less than previously. And so the process continues, **A** gradually decreasing his sales and **B** increasing his. But there is a limit; the adjustment mechanism converges.

To see the ultimate result, concentrate first on **B**. He initially sells $Q_1Q_2 = Q_2Q = \frac{1}{4}\ OQ$ units. In other words, he has one fourth of the market. Then he increases his output to $\frac{1}{2}(OQ - \frac{1}{2}\ OQ_2) = \frac{1}{2}\ (OQ - \frac{3}{8}\ OQ) = OQ(\frac{1}{2} - \frac{3}{16}) = \frac{5}{16}\ OQ$. He thus expands by $\frac{5}{16} - \frac{1}{4} = \frac{1}{16}$. His next expansion is by $\frac{1}{64}$; the next by $\frac{1}{256}$; and so on. His final output is $OQ(\frac{1}{4} + \frac{1}{16} + \frac{1}{64} + \ldots) = \frac{1}{3}\ OQ$.

A, on the other hand, initially had one half of the market, $OQ_1 = \frac{1}{2}\ OQ$. His output first falls to $\frac{1}{2}OQ_2 = \frac{1}{2}(\frac{3}{4}\ OQ) = \frac{3}{8}\ OQ$. Hence he loses $\frac{1}{8}$ of the market in the first round. Next, his output falls to $\frac{1}{2}[OQ - \frac{1}{2}(OQ - \frac{3}{8}\ OQ)] = \frac{11}{32}\ OQ$. In this round he loses $\frac{1}{32}$ of the market; in the next he loses $\frac{1}{128}$, and so on. His final output is $OQ(\frac{1}{2} - \frac{1}{8} - \frac{1}{32} - \frac{1}{128} - \ldots) = \frac{1}{3}\ OQ$.

Graphically, **A** produces $O\overline{Q}'$ units, **B** produces $\overline{Q}'\overline{Q}$ units, and market price is $O\overline{P}$. **A**'s profit is $O\overline{Q}'L\overline{P}$. **B**'s is $\overline{Q}'\overline{Q}EL$, and the total profit is $O\overline{Q}E\overline{P}$. If price were set equal to (zero) marginal cost, OQ units would be sold, and profit would be zero. This is the perfectly competitive solution. Under monopoly, output would be $1/2\ OQ$ and profit would be OQ_1CP_1. Thus duopoly output $(2/3\ OQ)$ is smaller than the competitive output but somewhat larger than monopoly output. The duopoly price (OP) is two thirds of the monopoly price; total duopoly profit is two thirds of potential monopoly profit.

The Cournot case is one possible solution to the duopoly problem. However, it is based upon an extraordinarily naïve assumption: each entrepreneur believes his rival will never change his volume of sales, even though he repeatedly observes such changes. The next duopoly model is based upon a similarly naive assumption.[5]

---

[5] The mathematically trained reader may wish to show that when the market demand curve is given by $p = a - bQ$ where Q is total output of all producers, then, when there are n firms, each acting as a Cournot oligopolist, the output of each firm in equilibrium is $a/[2b + b(n-1)]$. If $n = 2$, $q = a/3b$ and

12.2.b Edgeworth Case

Although written in 1838, Cournot's work received little attention until a much later date. Indeed, it was 1883 before a review of his book appeared. This review was written by a French mathematician, Joseph Bertrand, who criticized Cournot for having his entrepreneurs assume that quantity is held constant. Instead, said Bertrand, a solution should be based on the assumption that entrepreneurs believe their rivals will maintain a constant price.[6] This suggestion was developed by Edgeworth into the duopoly solution that bears his name.[7]

As in the Cournot situation, suppose two firms are selling a homogeneous product at zero marginal cost. Edgeworth assumes that each seller has a capacity limitation and that every consumer has an identical demand curve for the product. Suppose one of the sellers sets a price, say p_1. The other seller can do one of two things: (*a*) set a slightly lower price than p_1 taking most of the market from the first seller or (*b*) set a monopoly price for those customers who could not purchase from the first seller because he sold all of his output at p_1 to the first arrival customers on a first-come-first-served basis. The situation can be illustrated best with a numerical example. Suppose there are 1,000 consumers each with a demand curve $q = 1 - p$ where p is price and q is quantity. Each seller has a capacity of 400 units. If the first seller chooses price p_1, the demand per consumer will be $1 - p_1$. The number of consumers that are able to purchase from this seller before capacity is exhausted is $N_1 = 400/(1 - p_1)$. If N_1 is less than 1,000, then there are $1,000 - N_1$ consumers that are unable to purchase the good at price p_1 and these "residual" consumers are a captive market for the second seller. To maximize profits in the residual market, the price is set at $p = 1/2$. At $p = 1/2$, each consumer in the residual market demands $1/2$ unit and total revenue for the residual market is $p(1,000 - N_1)(1 - p) = 1/4(1,000 - N_1)$. Since the monopoly

---

$Q = 2a/3b$. If $n = 1$, the monopoly solution obtains, and as n approaches infinity, output per firm approaches zero and total industry output approaches the competitive solution $Q = a/b$. This tendency toward the competitive solution as $n \rightarrow \infty$ does not hold unless there are no scale economies in production as shown by Roy J. Ruffin, "Cournot Oligopoly and Competitive Behavior," *The Review of Economic Studies*, vol. 38 (1971), pp. 493–502.

[6] Joseph Bertrand, "Theorie Mathématique de la Richesse Sociale," *Journal des Savants* (Paris, 1883), pp. 499–508.

[7] F. Y. Edgeworth, "La teoria pura del monopolio," *Giornale degli Economisti,* vol. 15 (1897), pp. 13–31. The article was reprinted in English as "The Pure Theory of Monopoly," in Edgeworth, *Papers Relating to Political Economy* (London: Macmillan & Co., Ltd., 1925), vol. 1, pp. 111–42.

TABLE 12.2.1

Edgeworth Oligopolists

| | Low Price Seller | | | | | Residual Market | |
p_1 ($/unit)	Demand per Consumer (units)	Total Demand (units)	Total Revenue ($)	Total Consumers Served	Residual Consumers	Total Demand of Residual Consumers (units)	Total Revenue of Residual Consumers ($)
0.50	0.50	500	$200	800.00	200.00	100.00	$ 50.00
0.45	0.55	550	180	727.27	272.73	136.37	68.18
0.40	0.60	600	160	666.66	333.33	166.66	83.33
0.35	0.65	650	140	615.38	384.62	192.31	96.16
0.30	0.70	700	120	571.43	428.57	214.28	107.14
0.25	0.75	750	100	533.33	466.67	233.33	116.66
0.20	0.80	800	80	500.00	500.00	250.00	125.00
0.15	0.85	850	60	470.59	529.41	264.70	132.35
0.10	0.90	900	40	444.44	555.56	277.78	138.89
0.05	0.95	950	20	421.05	578.95	289.48	144.74
0	1.00	1,000	0	400.00	600.00	300.00	150.00

price for the residual market is $1/2$, it follows that the primary (low-price) market must have a price that is no greater than $1/2$ (i.e., $p_1 \leq 1/2$). The situation is tabulated in Table 12.2.1 for p_1 between 0.50 and 0 in steps of 0.05. In Table 12.2.1, column 1 is p_1, column 2 is the demand per consumer at price p_1, column 3 is total demand at p_1 ($= 1{,}000 \times$ column 2), column 4 is total revenue for the low-price seller ($= p_1 \times 400$), and column 5 is N_1, the number of customers served by the low-price seller. These five columns represent the situation for the low-price seller. Column 6 is the number of customers unable to buy from the low-price seller ($= 1{,}000 -$ column 5), column 7 is total demand of these residual customers at a price of $1/2$ ($= 1/2 \times$ column 6), and column 8 is the total revenue of the residual customers at the monopoly price of $1/2$ ($=$ column $6 \times 1/4$).

Suppose to start, seller **A** sets a price of $1/2$. His total revenue will be $200, and there will be 200 residual customers. The maximum revenue in the residual market is $50 which is less than the $200 earned by seller **A**. Thus seller **B** will cut price below $1/2$ to capture the majority of the market. Suppose seller **B** cuts price to $0.45. His revenue is then $180 and he leaves 272.73 customers for the residual market.[8] When seller **B** is at $0.45, the best **A** can do in the residual market is a total revenue of $68.18. Thus **A** responds by cutting **B**'s price to get the major part of the market back.

This process of bidding prices down will continue so long as making a price cut to capture the low-price market yields more total revenue than the residual market. Comparing columns 4 and 8 of Table 12.2.1 we see that total revenue in the low-price market exceeds the revenue in the residual market for all prices from $0.50 down to $0.30. At a price of $0.25 in the low-price market, total revenue in this market ($100) is less than the total revenue in the residual market ($116.66). In fact, at a price of $0.2785 in the low-price market, total revenue is the same ($111.40) in both markets. Thus, when the price gets bid down to $0.2785 (or lower), one of the sellers will have an incentive to raise his price to $0.50.

Suppose one seller is charging $0.2785 per unit and the other $0.50 per unit. We have just seen that each has the same total revenue ($111.40) at these prices. Does this mean that equilibrium has been achieved? Given the assumption that each rival assumes the other's price will never change, the answer is no. This is because the low-price

---

[8] Of course, it makes no literal sense to speak of a fractional consumer as the 0.73 in this sentence indicates. Nonetheless, carrying such fractions facilitates computation in the example.

seller, seeing his rival's price at $0.50, believes he can do better by raising his price to just under $0.50. For example, if he charges $0.49, he thinks he can earn $196 compared to his present $111.40. However, by raising his price, he upsets the residual market and another round of price cutting would ensue.

And so it goes, price continually moving between $0.50 and $0.2785. The duopoly situation, according to Edgeworth, is unstable and indeterminate (in the same sense that the solution to the bilateral monopoly problem is indeterminate). The Edgeworth case, just as the Cournot case, requires no further comment because it is based upon a naive hypothesis that is itself continually shown to be wrong by market results.[9]

12.2.c Stability in Oligopoly Markets: Chamberlin Solution

Chamberlin proposed a stable duopoly solution that depends upon mutual recognition of market interdependence.[10] Chamberlin's case is exactly that of Cournot except for the final result (see Figure 12.2.2). DQ is the linear demand for mineral water. **A** first enters the market and sells OQ_1 units at price OP_1, thereby reaping monopoly profit. **B** next enters the market. Seeing that **A** produces OQ_1 units, **B** regards CQ as his demand function. The best he can do is to market Q_1Q_2 units. Price falls to OP_2, and total profit for both entrepreneurs is OQ_2FP_2.

The difference between Cournot and Chamberlin now arises. According to the latter, **A** will survey the market situation after **B**'s entry, recognize their mutual interdependence, and recognize also that sharing monopoly profit OQ_1CP_1 is the best either he or **B** can do. **A** consequently reduces his output to $OQ_2' = \frac{1}{2}\, OQ_1$. **B** also recognizes the best solution; he therefore maintains his output at $Q_1Q_2 = Q_2'Q_1 = \frac{1}{2}\, OQ_1$. Hence total output is OQ_1, price is OP_1, and **A** and **B** share equally the monopoly profit OQ_1CP_1.

---

[9] Edgeworth implicitly assumes that price differentials will not lead to arbitrage among consumers who buy at different prices. This is a highly questionable assumption, and it does not obtain in the Cournot model where the prices of the two firms are always the same. It is also worth noting that the oscillatory prices in Edgeworth's model depend on the assumption of fixed capacity. If capacities were unlimited, the assumption by each firm that the rival will not cut his price would lead to a bidding down of the price to zero.

[10] E. H. Chamberlin, *The Theory of Monopolistic Competition* (Cambridge, Mass.: Harvard University Press, 1933), pp. 46–51. An earlier model of stability in oligopolistic markets was provided by Harold Hotelling, "Stability in Competition," *Economic Journal,* vol. 39 (1929), pp. 41–57.

FIGURE 12.2.2

Chamberlin Solution

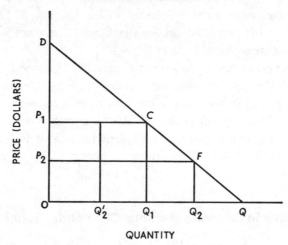

Chamberlin's solution has much to recommend it. Most important, his entrepreneurs take their rival's behavior into account in a sophisticated way when making their decisions.

12.2.d Stability in Oligopoly Markets: Sweezy Solution

Another model of stable oligopoly price that was at one time popular is the "kinked demand-curve hypothesis" of Sweezy,[11] illustrated in Figure 12.2.3. Suppose the demand curve confronting an oligopolist is given by the "kinked" curve CEF. The slope of the curve changes drastically at the point E, corresponding to price $O\overline{P}$. The kink in the demand curve causes a finite discontinuity in the marginal revenue curve, which is given by the dashed line $CABD$. CA is the segment corresponding to the CE portion of the demand curve; BD corresponds to the less elastic EF segment. At point E, however, there is a finite discontinuity represented by the segment AB.

The principal feature is the absolutely vertical section AB. Marginal cost can intersect marginal revenue at any point from A to B and nonetheless result in the same market price $O\overline{P}$ and sales $O\overline{Q}$. For example, suppose initial cost conditions give rise to the plant represented by SAC_2 and SMC_2. SMC_2 intersects marginal revenue in the vertical segment AB, so price is $O\overline{P}$. If costs rise appreciably, so that SAC_1 and

[11] Paul Sweezy, "Demand under Conditions of Oligopoly," *Journal of Political Economy,* vol. 47 (1939), pp. 568–73.

FIGURE 12.2.3

Sweezy Solution

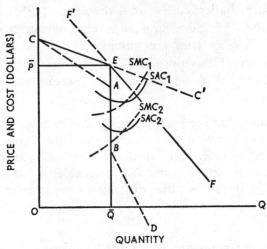

QUANTITY

SMC_1 now represent the plant operating costs, price does not change. Or going the other way around, cost could fall from SMC_1 to SMC_2 without affecting market equilibrium price and quantity. Thus, according to Sweezy, oligopoly price tends to be very sticky, changing only infrequently and as the result of very significant changes in cost.[12]

The question on which the Sweezy thesis falls is *why* the kink occurs at a specific point E and remains there. One approach is to regard CC' as Chamberlin's *d* curve, $F'F$ as his *D* curve. This would set a temporary price at E. Then one must assume that each entrepreneur believes (*a*) his competitors will not match a price increase, so CE is relevant for price increases, but (*b*) they will match any price decreases, so the proportional market demand curve EF is relevant for price declines. This analysis explains *how* a kink occurs but it does not explain *where*. If one knows the equilibrium price ($O\overline{P}$) he can rationalize it by means of the Sweezy hypothesis. But the purpose of price theory is to explain how the interaction of demand and cost establishes a unique price-quantity equilibrium. The kinked demand theory does not do this because market equilibrium is consistent with a wide variety of cost situations. The Sweezy thesis, accordingly, must be regarded as an ex-

---

[12] For a variety of recent views concerning oligopoly price, consult the papers by Ackley, Alderson, Bailey, Baumol, Lanzillotti, Lerner, and Weston, in *The Relationship of Prices to Economic Stability and Growth, Compendium of Papers Submitted by Panelists appearing before the Joint Economic Committee* (Washington, D.C.: U.S. Government Printing Office, 1958).

post rationalization rather than as an ex-ante explanation of market equilibrium.

George Stigler challenged Sweezy's theory on both theoretical and empirical grounds.[13] Stigler found in several industries with a small number of sellers (cigarettes, automobiles, anthracite, steel, dynamite, gasoline, and potash) that price *increases* by one firm were often followed by rivals and that in potash a price decrease was not followed. In Stigler's words:

This indicates only that not every oligopoly has reason to believe that it has a kinky demand curve and most adherents of the theory would readily concede this. On the other hand, there are seven industries in which the existence of the kinky demand curve is questionable—a list which is longer by seven than the list of industries for which a prima facie case has been made for the existence of the kink.[14]

12.2.e Theory of Games and Oligopoly Behavior

For a time one of the most exciting new developments in economic theory was John von Neumann and Oskar Morgenstern's *Theory of Games and Economic Behavior*.[15] After 15 or 20 years' experience with game theory models, the consensus seems to be that game theory is more relevant to the study of specific business problems than to general theory. Nonetheless, it represents a unique approach to the analysis of business decisions; and these decisions comprise the ultimate raw material with which economic theorists must work.

The general object of game theory is to determine standards of rational behavior in situations in which the outcomes depend upon the actions of interdependent "players." Indeed, von Neumann and Morgenstern had, as their purpose, ". . . to find the mathematically complete principles which define 'rational behavior' for the participants in a social economy, and to derive from them the general characteristics of that behavior. . . . The immediate concept of a solution is plausibly a set of rules for each participant which tell him how to behave in every situation which may conceivably arise."[16]

---

[13] George J. Stigler, "The Kinky Oligopoly Demand Curve and Rigid Prices," *Journal of Political Economy,* vol. 55 (1947), pp. 432–49.

[14] Ibid., p. 441.

[15] John von Neumann and Oskar Morgenstern, *Theory of Games and Economic Behavior* (Princeton, N.J.: Princeton University Press, 1953). Even the non-mathematical student can read with profit pp. 1–45. The mathematical reader should first try the Shubik volume cited at the end of this chapter.

[16] Ibid., p. 31.

Initially, it will be helpful not to restrict ourselves to an economic context. A "game" is any situation in which two or more people compete. Tennis and poker are good examples, but so also are Russian roulette and duopoly markets. For simplicity, we restrict our discussion to games in which there are two participants, called "players." Whatever data are initially available comprise the "rules of the game," such as the dimensions of a tennis court, the ranking of poker hands, exact specification of commodities, and so forth. In a game one assumes that all possible courses of action for each player are known. Each particular course of action is called a "strategy" which, by definition, is a complete specification of the action to be taken by a player under every possible contingency in the playing of the game. Obviously, this information requirement is satisfied in few, if any, real world situations because each player must know the full set of strategies available not only to him but to his opponent as well.

In certain cases the information required is even greater. In a wide variety of games (games of chance), the outcome is not known with certainty; it depends upon a chance variable. When chance enters the picture one must assume perfect knowledge of the probability of each possible outcome corresponding to every possible combination of strategies by the players. The necessary information is readily available for the game of matching pennies; but in more interesting games such as bridge or duopoly the probability that the probabilities are known is negligible.

The simplest class of games, and the only class to be discussed here, are "strictly adversary" games in which the possible outcomes are ranked in opposite order by the players. Among the games of this class the most prevalent are "constant-sum" games, which means that the sum of the winnings of the players is the same regardless of its distribution among participants. A market in which demand is completely inelastic is illustrative of constant-sum games. Finally, in a case of constant-sum games is the "zero-sum" game, perhaps best illustrated by the game of matching pennies. Briefly, in a zero-sum game the winnings of one player are matched exactly by the losses of another. The constant to which the winnings sum, in other words, is zero.

With these preliminaries out of the way let us turn to a constant-sum, strictly adversary, "strictly determined" game. In this case the von Neumann–Morgenstern "minimax" solution is most readily explicable. Assume that player **A** can choose among three strategies (a, b, c), while player **B** has four possible strategies (a', b', c', d'). Any two-person, constant-sum game of this nature can be completely described by a "payoff" matrix, as represented in Table 12.2.2.

TABLE 12.2.2

Payoff Matrix for a Two-Person, Constant-Sum Game

A's Strategies	*B's Strategies*				*Row Min.*
	a'	b'	c'	d'	
a..................	10	9	14	13	9
b..................	11	8	4	15	4
c..................	6	7	15	17	6
Col. Max..............	11	9	15	17	$9 = 9$

A's alternative strategies are listed in the column stub and B's in the row stub. A's payoff for each possible combination of strategies is given by an element in the matrix. For example, if A chooses strategy c and B chooses strategy d', A wins six. B wins the constant value of the game minus A's winnings. If the constant value is 20, B wins 14. In summary, each element e_{ij} in the matrix represents the amount obtained by A if he chooses the strategy corresponding to the ith row and B chooses the strategy corresponding to the jth column.

Initially, assume A is allowed to select his strategy first and he chooses c. B, who selects next, would immediately choose d' to maximize his winnings, given the strategy adopted by A. On the other hand, suppose B chooses first and selects c'. A would choose strategy c to obtain maximum winnings for B's chosen strategy. In actuality, with full knowledge assumed (each player knows the precise entries in the payoff matrix), the choices indicated above would never be made.

A realizes that for any strategy (row) he selects, B will select the strategy (column) which minimizes A's winnings (or maximizes B's return). Thus A is really interested in the row minima, shown in the last column of Table 12.2.2. He chooses strategy a because it guarantees him the largest return. In all cases, A adopts the strategy that corresponds to the maximum of the row minima. He "maximins." Similarly, B is only interested in the column maxima, or more precisely, in the constant sum minus the column maxima. He knowns, for example, if he selects strategy d', A will choose strategy b. Hence B's return would be $20 - 11$, or 9. Consequently, to assure his maximum payoff B selects the strategy corresponding to the minimum of the column maxima; he "minimaxes."

The strategy pair a, b' is determined; A wins 9 and B wins $20 - 9$, or 11. This game is strictly determined because each player selects and pursues a unique, pure strategy; when these two strategies are adopted, the maximum of the row minima equals the minimum of the column maxima. Neither player could possibly accomplish more.

The case of unique or "pure" strategies is an interesting one from the standpoint of economic theory. The more sophisticated treatments of duopoly using the older tools of analysis stress the importance of recognizing mutual interdependence. But in a strictly determined game this is irrelevant so long as each participant behaves rationally. So long as one of the rivals pursues a minimax strategy the other cannot improve upon a minimax strategy himself. Furthermore, advanced knowledge of the opponent's strategy does not aid one in determining his own plan of action. Thus the Chamberlin duopolist sets monopoly price.

Unfortunately, both the more common games of chance and game theoretic models of economic behavior are not strictly determined. In

FIGURE 12.2.4

A Nonstrictly Determined Game

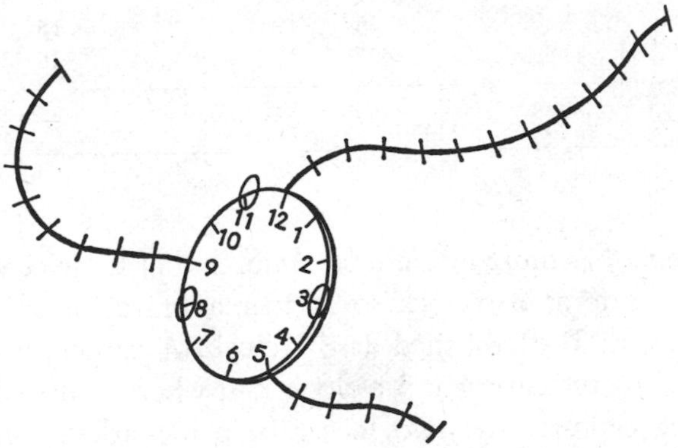

essence this means that if pure strategies are selected by the participants, the maximum value of the row minima is less than the minimum value of the column maxima. Such a game is illustrated by Figure 12.2.4 and Table 12.2.3.[17]

The diagram in Figure 12.2.4 represents a market in which demand is completely inelastic. Twelve customers are located in the circular portion of the market and are numbered like hours on a clock. At 5, 9, and 12 o'clock there are branch markets containing 5, 9, and 12 buyers each. Each buyer purchases one unit of commodity per unit of

[17] This example is due to William Vickrey, "Theoretical Economics," Part III-A (mimeograph manuscript).

time. There are two sellers, **A** and **B**, of a homogeneous commodity; they can choose among three different locations: 3, 8, and 11 o'clock. Both may situate at the same location. Since the commodities are identical and we now assume zero transportation cost, price must be the same for each seller. Buyers purchase from the nearer seller.

This market game is represented by the payoff matrix in Table 12.2.3. The entries show **A**'s sales per unit of time as a function of the locations (strategies) selected by **A** and **B**. The game has a constant value of 38. **B**'s sale for any pair of strategies is found by subtracting **A**'s sales from the constant value of the game.

TABLE 12.2.3

Payoff Matrix for a Nonstrictly Determined Game

A's Location	**B**'s Location			
	3	8	11	Row Min.
3................	19	23	11	11
8................	15	19	20	15
11...............	27	18	19	18
Col. Max...........	27	23	20	$20 \neq 18$

Let us suppose **A** must locate first. Assume that he selects 11 o'clock. **B** will then locate at 8 o'clock so as to maximize his sales (or minimize **A**'s). With **B** established at 8 o'clock, **A** can increase his sales from 18 to 23 by relocating at 3 o'clock. But when he does so, **B** moves to 11 o'clock, captures the two larger branch markets, and **A**'s sales decline to 11 units. But with **B** at 11 o'clock, **A** moves to 8 o'clock, expanding his sales to 20 units. Then **B** moves to 3 o'clock, **A** moves to 11 o'clock, and we are right back where we started. The process of continuous relocation goes on because there is no unique minimax: the minimum of the column maxima exceeds the maximum of the row minima. As this game is constructed there is no unique stable solution.

There is a way out of the impasse in many games, however. To illustrate, consider the game of matching pennies, represented by the payoff matrix in Table 12.2.4 **A** tries to match **B**; if so, he wins 1 cent, losing 1 cent otherwise. As in the market game, the minimum of the column maxima exceeds the maximum of the row minima. To this stage there is no formal equilibrium solution. von Neumann and Morgenstern provided a solution, however, by introducing the concept of

TABLE 12.2.4

A Nonstrictly Determined Game: Matching Pennies

A's Strategy	B's Strategy		
	Heads	Tails	Row. Min.
Heads......................	1	−1	−1
Tails.......................	−1	1	−1
Col. max....................	1	1	$1 \neq -1$

mixed strategies, defined as ". . . an assignment of probabilities to the feasible pure strategies in such manner that the sum of the probabilities is unity for each participant."[18]

Since probability elements are now present in the analysis of a game, the object of each participant can no longer be stated as the maximization or minimization of a particular value. One must look to the *expected value* of the game, which is determined by performing two simple operations on the payoff matrix: (a) multiply each element in the matrix by the compound probability that it is selected and (b) sum these products for all elements in the payoff matrix.

To illustrate further, let p_i be the probability that **A** selects the strategy corresponding to the ith row. Similarly, q_j is the probability that **B** chooses the strategy corresponding to the jth column. Thus $p_i q_j$ is the compound probability that the strategy pair i, j is selected. If a_{ij} is the associated element in the payoff matrix, step (a) above involves computing $p_i q_j a_{ij}$ for all i and j. Step (b) simply requires summing, so the expected value of the game ($\bar{v}$) is

$$\bar{v} = \sum_i \sum_j p_i q_j a_{ij} \, ,$$

where, by requirement,

$$p_i \geq 0, q_j \geq 0, \quad \sum_i p_i = 1, \quad \text{and} \quad \sum_j q_j = 1 \, .$$

In the game of matching pennies suppose each player chooses heads with probability one half. Thus each must also choose tails with probability one half. Consequently, the expected value of the game is

$$\bar{v} = (\tfrac{1}{2})(\tfrac{1}{2})(1) + (\tfrac{1}{2})(\tfrac{1}{2})(-1) + (\tfrac{1}{2})(\tfrac{1}{2})(-1) + (\tfrac{1}{2})(\tfrac{1}{2})(1) = 0 \, \cdot$$

[18] von Neumann and Morgenstern, *Theory of Games and Economic Behavior*, p. 145.

von Neumann and Morgenstern showed that if mixed strategies are allowed every constant-sum game has a unique minimax solution. That such a minimax strategy actually exists for the game of matching pennies can easily be shown. Compute the expected value of the game from A's standpoint for all possible probability assignments by A, assuming B always selects the probability combination most advantageous to himself, given A's selection. As an example, try the following probabilities for A: one-third heads, two-thirds tails. Then B can set probabilities as nine-tenths heads, one-tenth tails. The expected value of the game is minus four-fifteenths to A.[19] Assuming B always selects his best strategy, given A's selection, the maximum expected value of the game for A is zero, obtained when he sets probabilities one-half heads, one-half tails. Thus the *optimal mixed strategy* for A is $p_H = p_T = \frac{1}{2}$. When A plays this strategy, the best B can do is set $q_H = q_T = \frac{1}{2}$; the expected value of the game to B is also zero.

In contrast to strictly determined games, advanced knowledge of the opponent's plans is very important in games requiring mixed strategies for a minimax solution. As von Neumann and Morgenstern wrote:

. . . It constitutes a definite disadvantage for each player to have his intentions found out by his opponent. Thus one important consideration for a player in such a game is to protect himself against having his intentions found out by his opponent. Playing several different strategies at random, so that only their probabilities are determined, is a very effective way to achieve a degree of such protection: By this device, the opponent cannot possibly find out what the player's strategy is going to be, since the player does not know it himself. Ignorance is obviously a very good safeguard against disclosing information directly or indirectly.

In other words, the best way of deciding whether to show heads or tails is to flip a coin and let the toss decide.

Having sketched the outlines of game theory, we can now turn to some more general considerations. The heart of game theory is the minimax principle; and there are numerous criticisms of applying this principle to decision making in economics and business. Essentially, the minimax principle requires the player to maximize his payoff (or minimize his rival's) under the assumption that his rival always takes the

---

[19] The probabilities for B were limited to small numbers. B can gain more the closer he sets the probability of heads to unity. In the limit, given A's choice of one-third heads, two-thirds tails, B can gain one third (that is, the expected value of the game to A is minus one third). More generally, if A sets probability $p_H < p_T$, B always wins by setting probabilities $q_H = 1$, $q_T = 0$. If A sets probabilities $p_H > p_T$, B always wins by setting $q_H = 0, q_T = 1$.

least desirable course of action from the former's standpoint. Slightly less precisely, the minimax principle requires the player (or entrepreneur) to adopt the plan of action that will make the best of the worst possible situation. But this plan of action will not be the best if the worst possible situation does not arise. It does not allow the entrepreneur to exploit favorable changes in the market or, in any sense, to be "dynamic."

Many economists believe the minimax principle is an unnecessarily conservative standard. Furthermore, it is frequently asserted that minimax strategy is not compatible with the dominant entrepreneurial psychology. The object of most entrepreneurs is not to make the best of a bad situation. Indeed, it appears that many entrepreneurs attempt to maximize their objective under the assumption that very favorable conditions will prevail. And, of course, they generally expend considerable effort to influence the market so as to make the assumption correct.

If mixed strategies are required, the minimax principle is subject to another criticism. Specifically, random choice among strategies introduces uncertainty, which many entrepreneurs—perhaps almost all—go to great lengths to avoid. Thus entrepreneurs may not adopt a minimax strategy even if it is available.

On a more theoretical level, game theory requires more information than is likely to be available. Also, game theoretic models are absolutely static, seldom permitting even comparative static analysis. Furthermore, and of particular relevance to oligopoly markets, collusion cannot be introduced in a constant-sum game.

A final conclusion as to the value of game theory in economics is not possible at this time. On the technical or engineering side, the contributions of mathematical programming are unquestionable. But in theoretical economics it seems that success must await further refinements, if, indeed, it is achieved at all.[20]

12.3 SOME "MARKET" SOLUTIONS TO THE DUOPOLY PROBLEM

The classical treatments of duopoly, with the possible exception of Chamberlin's, are based upon the assumption that entrepreneurs act independently of one another even though they are interdependent in

---

[20] One aspect of game theory called the *theory of the core* has received increasing attention as a useful tool in theoretical economics. The interested reader may wish to consult E. Malinvaud, *Lectures on Microeconomic Theory* (Amsterdam-London/New York: North-Holland Publishing Company/American-Elsevier Co., Inc., 1972), chap. 6; and L. G. Telser, *Competition, Collusion, and Game Theory* (Chicago: Aldine Atherton, Inc., 1972).

the market. We turn now to some theories based upon explicit or implicit collusion among firms.

12.3.a Cartels and Profit Maximization

A *cartel* is a combination of firms whose object is to limit the scope of competitive forces within a market. It may take the form of open collusion, the member firms entering into an enforceable contract pertaining to price and possibly other market variables. This is perhaps best illustrated by the German *Kartelle;* but the NRA codes of our Great Depression years fall into this category as well. On the other hand, a cartel may be formed by secret collusion among sellers; many examples of this exist in American economic history. Most tend to date to the early years of the 20th century.[21]

The cases of open and secret collusion offer the best examples of cartels. However, in a broad sense trade associations, professional organizations, and the like perform many functions usually associated with a cartel.

Of the wide variety of services a cartel may perform for its members, two are of central importance: price fixing and market sharing. In this section, we will examine price fixing in an "ideal" cartel.

Suppose a group of firms producing a homogeneous commodity forms a cartel. A central management body is appointed, its function being to determine the uniform cartel price. The task, in theory, is relatively simple, as illustrated by Figure 12.3.1. Market demand for the homogeneous commodity is given by DD', so marginal revenue is given by the dashed line MR. The cartel marginal cost curve must be determined by the management body. If all firms in the cartel purchase all inputs in perfectly competitive markets, the cartel marginal cost curve (MC_c) is simply the horizontal sum of the component marginal

---

[21] As a matter of fact, government prosecution of collusive price-fixing activities in violation of Section 1 of the Sherman Act are filed regularly.

In fiscal 1970, the Antitrust Division filed 19 price-fixing cases and 23 in the preceding fiscal year. It should be noted that vertical price-fixing agreements, that is, those agreements not exempt from prosecution under Fair Trade exemptions, constituted about 75 percent of those cases filed in 1970 and roughly 40 percent of those filed in 1969.

The Federal Trade Commission, under Section 5 of the Federal Trade Commission Act, may file civil suits against price-fixing conspirators. However, this would be rare since under present liaison arrangements with the Antitrust Division all hardcore price-fixing cases, of the type discussed in "Cartels and Profit Maximization," are prosecuted by the Antitrust Division.

Mr. William J. Curran provided helpful advice regarding this point.

FIGURE 12.3.1

Cartel Profit Maximization

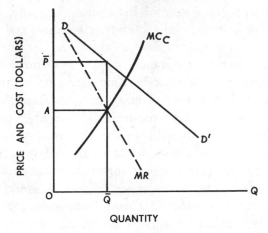

QUANTITY

cost curves of the member firms. Otherwise, allowance must be made for the increase in input price accompanying an increase in input usage; MC_c will stand further to the left than it would if all input markets were perfectly competitive.

In either case the management group determines cartel marginal cost, MC_c. The problem is the simple one of determining the price that maximizes cartel profit—the monopoly price. From Figure 12.3.1 marginal cost and marginal revenue intersect at the level OA; thus the market price $O\overline{P}$ is the one the cartel management will establish. Given the demand curve DD', buyers will purchase $O\overline{Q}$ units from the members of the cartel. The second important problem confronting the cartel management is *how* to distribute the total sales of $O\overline{Q}$ units among the member firms.

12.3.b Cartels and Market Sharing

Fundamentally there are two methods of sales allocation: nonprice competition and quotas. The former is usually associated with "loose" cartels. A uniform price is fixed, and each firm is allowed to sell all it can at that price. The only requirement is that firms do not reduce price below the cartel price. There are many examples of this type of cartel organization in the United States today. For instance, in most localities both medical doctors and lawyers have associations whose Code of Ethics is frequently the basis of price agreement. All doctors, for example, will charge the same rate for office and house calls. The patient market is divided among the various doctors by nonprice competition: each patient selects the doctor of his choice. Similarly, the generally uniform prices of haircuts, major brands of gasoline, and movie tickets do not result from perfect competition within the market. Rather, they result from tacit, and sometimes open, agreement upon a price; the sellers compete with one another but *not* by price variations.

The so-called fair-trade laws of many states establish loose, but very legal, cartels. Under these laws the manufacturer of a commodity may set its retail price. The retail sellers of the commodity (the sometimes reluctant members of the cartel) are forbidden by law to charge a lower price. The various retailers compete for sales by advertising, customer credit policies, repair and maintenance services, delivery, and such.

The second method of market sharing is the *quota* system, of which there are several variants. Indeed, there is no uniform principle by which quotas can be determined. In practice, the bargaining ability of a firm's representative and the importance of the firm to the cartel are likely to be the most important elements in determining a quota. Beyond this there are two popular methods. The first of these has a statistical base, either the relative sales of the firm in some precartel base period or the "productive capacity" of the firm. As a practical matter, the choice of base period or of the measure of capacity is a matter of bargaining among the members. Thus, as said above, the most skillful bargainer is likely to come out best.

The second popular basis for the quota system is geographical division of the market. Some of the more dramatic illustrations involve international markets. For example, an agreement between Du Pont and Imperial Chemicals divided the market for certain products so that the former had exclusive sales rights in North and Central America (except for British possessions) and the latter had exclusive rights in the British Empire and Egypt. Another example is an agreement between the American company Rohm and Haas and its German counterpart Roehm und Haas. The former was given exclusive rights in North, Central and South America, and in Australia, New Zealand, and Japan; the latter was given Europe and Asia, except for Japan. The illustrations can be multiplied many times over, but these should serve to indicate the quota by geographical division.

While quota agreement is quite difficult in practice, in theory some guidelines can be laid down. Consider the "ideal" cartel represented by Figure 12.3.1. A reasonable criterion for the management group would be "minimize total cartel cost." This is identical to the short-run problem of allocating monopoly output among plants in a multiplant monopoly (see Figure 9.4.6). Minimum cartel cost is achieved when each firm produces the rate of output for which its marginal cost equals the common value of cartel marginal cost and marginal revenue. Thus each firm would produce the amount for which its marginal cost equals OA (Figure 12.3.1); by the summing process to obtain MC_c, total cartel output will be $O\overline{Q}$. The difficulty involved with this method is that the lower cost firms obtain the bulk of the market and the bulk of profits. To make this method of allocation acceptable to all members, a profit-sharing system more or less independent of sales quota must be devised.

In certain cases the member firms may be able to agree upon the share of the market each is to have. This is illustrated in Figure 12.3.2 for an "ideal" situation. Suppose only two firms are in the market and they decide to divide the market evenly. The market demand curve is DD', so the half-share curve for each firm is Dd. The curve marginal to Dd is the dashed line MR, the half-share marginal revenue for each firm. Suppose each firm has identical costs, represented by SAC and SMC. Each will decide to produce $O\overline{Q}$ units with price $O\overline{P}$, corresponding to the intersection of marginal revenue and marginal cost. A uniform price of $O\overline{P}$ is established and $OQ_c = 2\ O\overline{Q}$ units are supplied. This happens, in our special case, to be a tenable solution because the market demand curve is consistent with the sale of OQ_c units at the price $O\overline{P}$.

To see this, let us go the other way around. Suppose a cartel man-

FIGURE 12.3.2

Ideal Market-Sharing in a Cartel

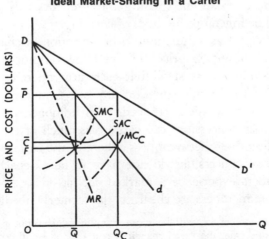

agement group is formed and given the task of maximizing cartel profit. With the demand curve DD', the management group views Dd as marginal revenue. Next, summing the identical SMC curves it obtains cartel marginal cost MC_c.[22] The intersection of cartel marginal cost and cartel marginal revenue occurs at the level OF, corresponding to output OQ_c and price $O\overline{P}$. The same is true for the individual firms, so the firms' decision to share the market equally is consistent with the objective market conditions. But this is a rare condition; cost differences between the firms would have created a situation inconsistent with market conditions and the voluntary market-sharing agreement would have collapsed. That, as we shall see, is what is most likely to happen to cartels anyhow.

12.3.c Short and Turbulent Life of Cartels—The Great Electrical Conspiracy

Unless backed by strong legal provisions, cartels are very likely to collapse from internal pressure (before being found out by the Antitrust Division of the Department of Justice). A few large, geographically concentrated firms producing a homogeneous commodity may form a very successful cartel and maintain it, at least during periods of prosperity. But the greater the number of firms, the greater the scope for product differentiation, and the greater the geographical dispersion of firms the easier is it to "cheat" on the cartel's policy. In times of marked prosperity profit may be so great that there is little incentive to cheat. But when profits are low or negative there is a marked incentive; and when the incentive exists enterprising entrepreneurs will discover what they believe to be ingenious methods of cheating.

The typical cartel as a functioning organization is characterized by high (perhaps monopoly) price, relatively low output, and a distribution of sales among firms such that each firm operates at less than minimum unit cost. In this situation any one firm can profit greatly from secret price concessions. Indeed, with homogeneous products, a firm offering price concessions can capture as much of the market as it desires, providing the other members adhere to the cartel's price policy. Thus secret price concessions do not have to be extensive before the obedient members experience a marked decline in sales. Recognizing that one or more members are cheating, the formerly obedient members

---

[22] The problem, of course, will be more complicated if input prices vary with input usage. In this case, the cartel marginal cost cannot be directly obtained by summing the members' marginal cost curves.

must themselves reduce price in order to remain viable. The cartel accordingly collapses. Without effective *legal* sanctions, the life of a cartel is likely to be brief, ending whenever a business recession occurs.

One of the most notorious examples of a market-sharing cartel occurred in the electrical equipment industry between 1950 and the early 1960s when it was finally broken up by the federal government. During the days of the Office of Price Administration, major suppliers of electrical switchgear began to get together to decide pricing strategies. After the abolishment of the OPA, the electrical equipment suppliers continued to meet regularly, if secretly, at the Penn-Sheraton Hotel in Pittsburgh. Between 1951 and 1958 the cartel split $75 million of annual sales in electrical switchgear by agreeing in advance which company would be the "low" bidder on upcoming contracts. In 1951 the market was split as follows: General Electric, 45 percent; Westinghouse, 35 percent; Allis-Chalmers, 10 percent; and Federal Pacific, 10 percent. There was constant chiseling among the cartel members especially on sealed bid business where policing was difficult. In 1954–55 there was a severe breakdown of the cartel known as the "white sale" when prices were discounted by 40 to 45 percent in a very short period of time. The cartel was reconstituted in 1956; but within about a year, Westinghouse gave one customer, Florida Power and Light Company, a price break on circuit breakers by hiding the discount in its transformer order. This triggered another breakdown of the cartel, and between 1957 and 1958 prices dropped by 60 percent. When the cartel was reformed in 1958, the entry of ITE resulted in a new sharing agreement: General Electric, 40.3 percent; Westinghouse, 31.3 percent; Allis-Chalmers, 8.8 percent; Federal Pacific, 15.6 percent; and ITE, 4 percent. The fascinating history of this cartel is strewn with episodes of breakdowns in its agreements and devious schemes of cartel members to capture business in violation of the cartel rules.[23]

12.3.d Price Leadership in Oligopoly

Another type of market solution of the oligopoly problem is *price leadership* by one or a few firms. This solution does not require open collusion but the firms must tacitly agree to the solution. Price leadership has in fact been quite common in certain industries. For example, Clair Wilcox lists, among others, the following industries as character-

---

[23] Richard Austin Smith has detailed the history of this cartel in "The Incredible Electrical Conspiracy," *Fortune,* vol. 63 (April and May 1961), pp. 132 ff. (April) and pp. 161 ff. (May).

FIGURE 12.3.3

Price Leadership by the Lower Cost Firm

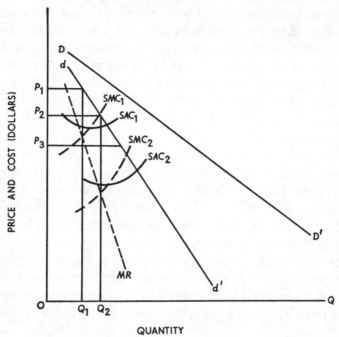

ized by price leadership: nonferrous alloys, steel, agricultural implements, and newsprint.[24] Similarly, in their interview study Kaplan,
Dirlam, and Lanzillotti found that Goodyear Tire and Rubber, National
Steel, Gulf Oil, and Kroger Grocery follow the price leadership of
other firms in the market.[25]

To introduce the price-leadership model, consider the simple illustration in Figure 12.3.3 an extension of the market-sharing cartel model
of Figure 12.3.2. Two firms produce a homogeneous commodity whose
market demand is given by DD'. By either explicit collusion or tacit
agreement the firms decide to split the market evenly. Thus each views
dd' as his demand curve and MR as his marginal revenue curve. In
this case, however, the costs of the two producers are different; firm 1
has substantially higher costs than firm 2, as shown by $SAC_1 - SMC_1$
and $SAC_2 - SMC_2$, respectively.

---

[24] Clair Wilcox, *Competition and Monopoly in American Industry,* Temporary
National Economic Committee, Monograph No. 21 (Washington, D.C.: U.S. Government Printing Office, 1940), pp. 121–32.

[25] A. D. H. Kaplan, Joel B. Dirlam, and Robert F. Lanzillotti, *Pricing in Big
Business* (Washington, D.C.: The Brookings Institution, 1958), pp. 201–7.

Other things equal, firm 1 would like to charge OP_1 per unit, selling OQ_1 units. This price-output constellation would lead to maximum profit for firm 1; but firm 2 can do much better since its marginal cost is substantially below its marginal revenue at this point. In this situation, firm 2 has an effective control. Being a lower cost producer, entrepreneur 2 can set the lower price OP_2 that maximizes his profit. Entrepreneur 1 has no choice but to follow; if he tries to retain OP_1, his sales will be zero. Hence the higher cost firm must be content to accept the price decision of the lower cost firm.

The particular solution shown here is not a very likely one. If this situation existed in a market, entrepreneur 2 would hardly agree, tacitly or otherwise, to split the market evenly. But given the antitrust laws in the United States he would not drive entrepreneur 1 out of the market. He has the power to do so. By setting a price such as OP_3, he can earn a pure profit and ultimately drive firm 1 out of the market. But then he would face the legal problems of monopoly. A better solution, from the viewpoint of the lower cost firm, is to tolerate a "competitor." Thus while not sharing the market equally, as in this illustration, entrepreneur 2 would nevertheless set a price high enough for entrepreneur 1 to remain in the market.

A much more typical example of price leadership is illustrated by Figure 12.3.4. The model is a somewhat exaggerated representation of a situation which, some say, exists in several American industries. There is one (or a small number of) dominant firm(s) and numerous small ones. As shown by the marginal cost curves in Figure 12.3.4, the dominant firm is almost as large as all the small firms combined.

The dominant firm could possibly eliminate all its rivals by a price war. But this would establish a monopoly with its attendant legal problems. A more desirable course of action for the dominant firm is to establish the market price and let the small firms sell all they wish at that price. The small firms, recognizing their position, will behave just as perfectly competitive firms. That is, they will regard their demand curve as a horizontal line at the prevailing price and sell that amount for which marginal cost equals price. Notice this does not entail the long-run zero profit solution because price may be set far above (minimum) unit cost.

The problem confronting the dominant firm is to determine the price that will maximize its profit while allowing the small firms to sell all they wish at that price. To do this it is necessary to find the demand curve for the dominant firm. Suppose DD' is the market demand curve and MC_s is the horizontal summation of the marginal cost curves of the

FIGURE 12.3.4

Price Leadership by the Dominant Firm

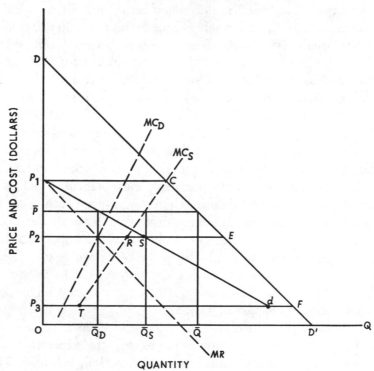

small firms. Since the small firms equate marginal cost and price, MC_S is also the collective supply curve of the small firms.[26]

First, suppose the dominant firm sets the price OP_1. The small firms would sell P_1C units, exactly the market quantity demanded. Hence sales by the dominant firm would be zero, and P_1 would be a point on its demand curve. If price OP_2 were set by the dominant firm, the small firms would sell P_2R units and the dominant firm would sell $RE = P_2S$ units; thus S is also a point on its demand curve. Finally, suppose the price were set at OP_3. The small firms would sell P_3T units and the dominant firm $TF = P_3d$ units. For a price below OP_3, only the dominant firm would sell. Hence its demand curve is P_1dFD', and its marginal revenue is given by the dashed line MR.

---

[26] Again, for simplicity, we ignore the problem created by rising input prices. In principle, the solution is determinate if input prices rise as input usage increases; however, the case cannot be analyzed graphically.

Equating marginal revenue and marginal cost (MC_D), the dominant firm sets the price $O\overline{P}$ and sells $O\overline{Q}_D$ units. At this price the small firms sell $O\overline{Q}_S$ units; and by construction of the demand curve P_1dFD', $O\overline{Q}_D + O\overline{Q}_S$ must equal $O\overline{Q}$, the total quantity sold at price $O\overline{P}$.

Many variations of this basic price-leadership model can be constructed by changing the assumptions. One may allow for two or more dominant firms, for product differentiation, for geographically separated sellers and transportation cost, and so on. Nonetheless, the basic results are much the same; and they may help to explain price-output policies in a variety of oligopoly markets.

12.4_ COMPETITION IN OLIGOPOLY MARKETS

Practically speaking, active price competition is seldom if ever observed in oligopolistic markets. To be sure, price wars occasionally erupt; but this really does not indicate price competition. A price war indicates that the (probably implicit) communication channels among firms in the market are temporarily out of repair. In the normal course of events, the pre–price-war situation is quickly restored.

Absence of price competition, as we have said, is what one typically observes in the real world. It is also the inference to be drawn from almost every model of oligopoly behavior analyzed so far. With the exception of the Edgeworth model, the normal prediction is stable price with competition for market sales taking some form other than active price competition. The alternative forms of nonprice competition are as diverse as the minds of inventive entrepreneurs can make them. Yet there is one central feature: an entrepreneur attempts to attract customers to himself (and, therefore, away from rivals) by some means other than a price differential. Nonprice competition accordingly involves the differentiation of a product fundamentally more or less homogeneous among producers. The ways of differentiating are diverse, but three principal methods deserve mention.

Perhaps the most important technique of nonprice competition is advertising. In the United States, and increasingly in European countries, advertising is the uniformly most accepted and acceptable method of attracting customers, at least to businessmen if not to economists. The "pros and cons" of advertising expenditure have been argued at length; the argument is likely to continue because the question at stake is a moot one. But for good or not, advertising is an established practice that is presumably considered worthwhile, for otherwise businessmen would not continue to spend billions of dollars annually on this type of nonprice competition.[27]

Another important type of nonprice competition consists in creating bona fide (and sometimes spurious) quality differentials among products. The general effect of quality differentiation is to divide a broad market into a group of submarkets among which there is usually a relatively large price differential. The automobile market offers a good example. There are definite, physically specifiable differences between a Ford Pinto and the Ford Motor Company's Continental. There is also a substantial price difference; no one buyer is likely to be a potential customer in both markets, except perhaps for automobiles to perform two fundamentally different services (family car and business runabout).

Ford is not alone in creating quality differentials, however. General Motors and Chrysler do the same; and they engage in active nonprice competition within each of the submarkets. Further, the automobile market example brings to light a social criticism of quality competition. Too many quality differentials may be created so that items supposedly in one class overlap with items in another. Thus within the broad market not only is there competition to create new quality classes and gain the competitive edge of being the first in the market; there is also competition within quality classes.

Finally, a third major technique of nonprice competition is design differences. This type could also be illustrated by the automobile market; but the market for golf clubs serves just as well. MacGregor, Wilson, Spaulding, and other producers now "change models" annually, just as do the automobile manufacturers. They also create (possibly spurious) quality differentials as between sporting-goods stores and pro shops. But within, say, the pro-shop market, the competition among companies is strictly a matter of club design.

These three types of nonprice competition far from exhaust the possible methods but they do illustrate the ways in which entrepreneurs can spend resources in an effort to attract customers to their particular "brands."

---

[27] The reader should be careful not to fall into the trap of assuming that advertising implies oligopolistic structure of the industry. Advertising can be viewed as consistent with competition in many respects. See L. G. Telser, "Advertising and Competition," *Journal of Political Economy*, vol. 72 (December 1964), pp. 537–62; and P. Nelson, "Information and Consumer Behavior," *Journal of Political Economy*, vol. 78 (March–April 1970), pp. 311–29.

12.5 WELFARE EFFECTS OF OLIGOPOLY

Since there are many models of oligopoly behavior, each predicting somewhat different results, it is impossible to be precise about the welfare effects of oligopolistic market organization. Furthermore, any set of static welfare criteria one applies to the situation may be relatively insignificant in a dynamic context. Nonetheless, a few things may be said.

First, whatever the model, two characteristics common to all oligopoly markets can be isolated. Firms in an oligopoly presumably produce their output at the minimum attainable unit cost. But there is no reason to believe their output uniquely corresponds to minimum long-run unit cost. Hence oligopoly organization requires more units of resources per unit of commodity produced than absolutely necessary. Furthermore, since pure economic profit normally accompanies oligopolistic market organization, price is higher than both unit and marginal cost. In whatever equilibrium is reached the marginal valuation of buyers is greater than the marginal cost of output. If the commodity were priced at either marginal or average cost, buyers would like to purchase more than producers would be willing to sell.

A second consideration is also important. Vast amounts of resources are devoted to advertising and to creating quality and design differentials. The allocation of some resources for these purposes is doubtless justifiable. For example, to the extent that advertising merely reports price and seller location, it helps keep buyers better informed. Similarly, certain quality and design differentials may be socially desirable. Nonetheless, there is a strong presumption (based upon purely empirical grounds) that oligopolists push all forms of nonprice competition beyond the socially desirable limits. In absence of evidence to the contrary, it is reasonable to conclude that buyers in oligopoly markets would be better off if there were more active price competition and less nonprice competition.

As noted, the welfare criteria imposed so far are *static;* and from the standpoint of these criteria oligopoly fares rather badly. However, dynamic considerations should not be entirely ignored. Industrial research and development, the now-famous R. & D., was essential to the evolution of our modern industrial society and is now essential to its continued viability and growth. Many argue, with considerable persuasiveness, that R. & D. usually thrives only in oligopolistic markets. Neither perfect competitors nor pure monopolists have the incentive to undertake industrial research; and perfect competitors are usually not large enough to support research departments. Oligopolistic firms, on the other hand, always have the incentive: improve the product or reduce its cost so as to increase profit. Furthermore, such firms are typically large enough to absorb the short-run cost of R. & D. in order to reap its long-run payoff. In short, all sorts of static welfare criteria may be violated more or less with impunity if the dynamic rate of growth is sufficiently rapid. Some economists, and all oligopolists, hold that oligopolistic market organization is essential for the dynamic growth of the economy.

QUESTIONS AND EXERCISES

1. Assume that the skilled laborers in a competitive industry are represented by a strong union that is able to fix the wage at its monopoly level. Also assume that the firms are effectively prevented from colluding by strong antitrust laws, but unions are free to collude.
   a. Is it in the interest of the firms to have the union enforce an output restriction on behalf of the employers, assuming that the union would not change the wage rate for skilled labor or otherwise make new demands on the firms?
   b. Would the above output restriction be in the union's interest?
   c. If your answer to (a) is *yes* and (b) is *no,* could the firms make the output restriction attractive both to themselves and the union by offering a higher wage?
   d. If your answer to (c) is *no,* is there any arrangement that would make output restriction mutually beneficial?

2. Explain the nature of the harm, if any, done to the efficiency of the economy when the firms in an industry—
   a. Organize to prevent other firms from entering the industry;
   b. Agree to charge a uniform price;
   c. Restrict the output of the firms so as to increase the total profit earned by all firms together;
   d. Sell all their output through a cooperative selling agency;
   e. Establish different selling prices for two different markets.

3. Discuss the following statement: "In oligopoly there is a tendency toward the maximization of aggregate industry profits. . . . But this tendency is counteracted by other forces." (Fellner, *Competition among the Few,* p. 142.)

4. "The problem of bilateral monopoly is obviously one of negotiating and bargaining in order to reach an agreement between certain limits of feasibility. . . . [it] is useful to consider the oligopoly problem as being

'essentially' of this character" (Fellner, *Competition among the Few*, p. 23).

   a.   What are the aspects of oligopoly behavior that Fellner views as equivalent to "negotiating and bargaining"?

   b.   Why is such behavior to be expected in an oligopoly situation?

5.   Assume that the bituminous coal industry is a competitive industry and that it is in long-run equilibrium. Now assume that the firms in the industry form a cartel.

   a.   What will happen to the equilibrium output and price of coal and why?

   b.   How should the output be distributed among the individual firms?

   c.   After the cartel is operating, are there incentives for the individual firms to cheat, and why or why not?

   d.   Does the possibility of entry by other firms make a difference in the behavior of the cartel

SUGGESTED READINGS

Chamberlin, E. H. *The Theory of Monopolistic Competition,* pp. 30–55, pp. 221–29. Cambridge, Mass.: Harvard University Press, 1933 (8th ed., 1962). [Elementary math required.]

Fellner, William. *Competition among the Few: Oligopoly and Similar Market Structures.* New York: Alfred A. Knopf, Inc., 1949.

Hicks, J. R. "Annual Survey of Economic Theory: The Theory of Monopoly," *Econometrica,* vol. 3 (1935), pp. 1–20. [Elementary math required.]

Hotelling, Harold. "Stability in Competition," *Economic Journal,* vol. 39 (1929), pp. 41–57. [Elementary math required.]

Machlup, Fritz. *The Economics of Sellers' Competition,* pp. 347–514, esp. pp. 368–413. Baltimore: Johns Hopkins Press, 1952.

Malinvaud, E. *Lectures on Microeconomic Theory,* pp. 144–62. New York: American-Elsevier Co., Inc., 1972.

Rothchild, K. W. "Price Theory and Oligopoly," *Economic Journal,* vol. 57 (1947), pp. 299–320.

Shubik, Martin. *Strategy and Market Structure,* esp. pp. 1–18 and pp. 59–78. New York: John Wiley & Sons, Inc., 1959. [Advanced math required.]

Stigler, George J. "The Kinked Oligopoly Demand Curve and Rigid Prices," *Journal of Political Economy,* vol. 55 (1947), pp. 432–49.

———. "Notes on a Theory of Duopoly," *Journal of Political Economy,* vol. 48 (1940), pp. 521–41.

Sweezy, Paul. "Demand under Conditions of Oligopoly," *Journal of Political Economy,* vol. 47 (1939), pp. 568–73.

part IV

Theory of distribution

Parts I and III, together with the tools developed in Part II, present the modern or neoclassical theory of *value*—a theory explaining the origin of demand, supply, and market price. Hopefully, the market price so determined represents the marginal social valuation of the commodity. If so, some theoretical statements concerning economic welfare can be made (Part V).

A central part of this theory of value is the marginal cost of production and its possible reflection in the supply curve. Costs and supply, in turn, depend upon the technological conditions of production and the cost of productive services. So far we have assumed that both are given; and we will continue to assume that the physical conditions of production are technologically given and do not change over the time period relevant to our analysis. But now we must determine the prices of productive services, the *distribution* half of "Value and Distribution," or modern microeconomic theory. The theories of value and distribution are then brought together in Part V, first to discuss the general economic equilibrium and second to analyze economic welfare in a competitive society.

Broadly speaking, the theory of input pricing does not differ from the theory of pricing goods. Both are fundamentally based upon the interaction of demand and supply. In the present case, demand arises from business firms (rather than consumers) and supply, at least the supply of labor services, arises from individuals who are not only sellers of labor time but also consumers. Furthermore, for the most interesting cases of capital and labor, one determines the price of using the resource for a stipulated period of time, not the price of purchasing the resource. In other respects, however, the theory of distribution is the theory of value of productive services.

The previous level of abstraction is maintained throughout Part IV. This is certainly to be expected in Chapter 13, which presents the marginal productivity theory of distribution in perfectly competitive input and output markets. When imperfections appear in either market, however, the situation changes appreciably. This is especially true when large employers bargain directly with representatives of powerful labor organizations. When market imperfections arise, labor unions tend to arise as well. The theoretical discussion in Chapter 14 may seem far removed from the dramatic world of *GM* v. *UAW*. Indeed it is, in a certain sense. Yet the theoretical results obtained do set limits within which collective bargaining agreements are likely to occur.

Our point of view is that collective bargaining between management and union representatives constitutes bilateral monopoly, an indeterminate economic situation. Our analysis sets broad limits within which the solution lies. To push further requires one or more *courses,* not chapters. For example, there is a substantial body of theory concerning the collective bargaining process,[1] but an understanding of labor markets also requires an extensive knowledge of the institutional framework within which labor unions and business management operate.[2] This type of knowledge must be acquired in "applied" courses or contexts, just as "applied" courses supplement the other portions of microeconomic theory.

---

[1] For a taste of this body of theory, see Allan M. Cartter, *Theory of Wages and Employment* (Homewood, Ill.: Richard D. Irwin, Inc., 1959), pp. 77–133.

[2] For institutional setting, see John T. Dunlop and James J. Healy, *Collective Bargaining: Principles and Cases* (rev. ed.; Homewood, Ill.: Richard D. Irwin, Inc., 1953).

13

Marginal productivity
theory of distribution in
perfectly competitive
markets

13.1 INTRODUCTION

As indicated in the introduction to Part IV, this section
is not intended to be a practical man's guide to wage determination. Yet
the marginal productivity theory constitutes a framework in which
practical problems can be analyzed; thus it is a useful analytical tool for
economic theorists.

The origin of marginal productivity theory is more or less dim.[1]
Perhaps John Bates Clark is most widely associated with its development;[2] however, earlier hints appeared in Von Thünen's *Der isolierte
Staat* (1826), Longfield's *Lectures on Political Economy,* and Henry
George's *Progress and Poverty* (1879). Indeed, George presented a
"universal law of wages" that clearly indicates marginal productivity
analysis:

Wages depend upon the margin of production, or upon the produce
which labor can obtain at the highest point of natural productiveness open
to it without the payment of rent. . . . Thus the wages which an employer
must pay will be measured by the lowest point of natural productiveness to

---

[1] For a survey of its development, see Allan M. Cartter, *Theory of Wages and
Employment* (Homewood, Ill.: Richard D. Irwin, Inc., 1959), pp. 11–32.

[2] John Bates Clark, *The Distribution of Wealth* (New York: The Macmillan
Co., 1902).

which production extends, and wages will rise or fall as the point rises or falls.[3]

In the preface to his important work, Clark acknowledged his indebtedness to George and summarized his theory simultaneously:

It was the claim advanced by Mr. Henry George, that wages are fixed by the product which a man can create by tilling rentless land, that just led me to seek a method by which the product of labor everywhere may be disentangled from the product of cooperating agents and separately identified; and it was this quest which led to the attainment of the law that is here presented, according to which the wages of all labor tend, under perfectly free competition, to equal the product that is separately attributable to labor.[4]

But in the 1880s and 1890s, Clark was not alone in developing the marginal productivity concept. Jevons, Wicksteed, Marshall, Wood, Walras, Barone, and others made important contributions.[5] Indeed, during this period an important distinction between views of marginal productivity theory arose.

First, to state the *marginal productivity principle* (developed in subsection 13.2.a) : there is a direct functional relation between wages and the level of employment; each profit-maximizing entrepreneur will attempt to adjust employment so that the marginal product of labor equals the wage rate.

From Clark's point of view, this principle, slightly embellished, constituted the theory of wages. Marshall strongly disagreed:

This doctrine [the marginal productivity principle] has sometimes been put forward as a theory of wages. But there is no valid ground for any such pretension. . . . Demand and supply exert equally important influences on wages; neither has a claim to predominance; any more than has either blade of a scissors, or either pier of an arch . . . [but] the doctrine throws into clear light the action of one of the causes that govern wages.[6]

According to Clark, the marginal productivity principle determines wages. Marshall, and later Hicks, and most other theorists, regard the principle as determining only the *demand* for labor. The supply of

---

[3] Henry George, *Progress and Poverty* (1879), p. 213.

[4] Clark, *Distribution of Wealth,* p. viii.

[5] W. Stanley Jevons, *The Theory of Political Economy;* Philip Wicksteed, *An Essay on the Coordination of the Theory of Distribution;* Alfred Marshall, *Principles of Economics;* Stuart Wood, "The Theory of Wages," AEA Publications, IV (1889); Leon Walras, *Elements d'économie politique pure;* Enrico Barone, "Studi sulla distribuzione," *Giornale degli economisti,* vol. 12 (1896).

[6] Marshall, *Principles of Economics,* pp. 518, 538.

labor, or any other productive service, must enter before a full theory of wage determination is developed. This modern, or neoclassical, view is adopted here.

13.2 DEMAND FOR A PRODUCTIVE SERVICE[7]

Following the Marshall-Hicks approach, one must pay heed both to the demand for and supply of a productive service. In this section the theory of input demand, based upon the marginal productivity principle, is developed. The theory is applicable to any productive service although the most natural application, and the bulk of literary treatments, refers to the demand for labor. Thus we shall usually speak of "the demand for labor," but "the demand for a productive service of any sort" is implied.

13.2.a Demand of a Firm for One Variable Productive Service

Before embarking on a formal analysis it may be useful to point out the direct analogy between the behavior of the firm in determining its profit-maximizing output and its profit-maximizing combination of resources. In the former study, we assumed that market demand and supply determine market equilibrium price, without first explaining the origin of market supply. Next, since each firm is too small to affect price by changes in its output, the demand curve confronting each producer is a perfectly elastic horizontal line at the level of market price. Our problem in this case was to determine marginal cost, and thus supply, given the state of technology and input prices. The analysis was completed by obtaining market supply from the individual supply curves.

The procedure in the present case is completely analogous, but reversed. First, we assume that the market demand for and supply of labor determine the market equilibrium wage rate, without initially explaining the origin of the demand for labor curve.[8] Next, since each firm is too small to affect the wage rate by changes in its labor input, the supply of labor curve confronting each producer is a perfectly elastic horizontal line at the level of the market wage rate. Our problem now is to determine the individual demand for labor curve, given the state of

---

[7] The analysis of sections 13.2 and 13.4 relies heavily upon the tools developed in Chapters 5 and 6. The student should review these chapters unless he is thoroughly familiar with them.

[8] The supply curve, in this instance, has not been explained either. It is analyzed in section 13.3.

technology and the market price of the output produced. The analysis is then completed by obtaining market demand from the individual demand curves.

Let us begin with an example, given in Table 13.2.1 and graphically illustrated in panels a and b, Figure 13.2.1. We consider a production process involving fixed inputs, and thus fixed costs, but only *one* variable input, labor. Thus total labor cost equals total variable cost. The product sells for $5 per unit, and labor costs $20 per unit. The produc-

TABLE 13.2.1

Value of the Marginal Product and Individual Demand for Labor

Units of Labor Input	Total Product	Marginal Product	Product Price	Total Revenue	Value of Marginal Product	Wage per Unit of Labor	Total Variable Cost	TR Minus TVC
0.......	0	—	$5.00	$ 0	—	$20	$ 0	$ 0
1.......	10	10	5.00	50	$50	20	20	30
2.......	19	9	5.00	95	45	20	40	55
3.......	27	8	5 00	135	40	20	60	75
4.......	34	7	5.00	170	35	20	80	90
5.......	40	6	5.00	200	30	20	100	100
6.......	45	5	5.00	225	25	20	120	105
7.......	49	4	5.00	245	20	20	140	105
8.......	52	3	5.00	260	15	20	160	100
9.......	54	2	5.00	270	10	20	180	90
10.......	55	1	5.00	275	5	20	200	75

tion function is specified by the first three columns. Column 5 shows total revenue (total product multiplied by commodity price), and column 8 lists total variable cost (units of labor input multiplied by the price per unit). Finally, the last column shows total revenue minus total variable cost, a proxy for profit inasmuch as it (profit) differs from column 9 only by the constant fixed cost.[9] The difference between total revenue and total variable cost is greatest when seven units of labor are used; this solution accordingly corresponds to the profit-maximizing organization of production. The total revenue–total variable cost approach is illustrated in panel a, Figure 13.2.1. The maximum distance between the two curves occurs when their slopes are equal, or

---

[9] For example, if total fixed cost is $50, profit is column 9 minus $50. Thus maximum profit corresponds to the maximum entry in column 9.

FIGURE 13.2.1

Graphical Illustration of Profit Maximization by Two Approaches

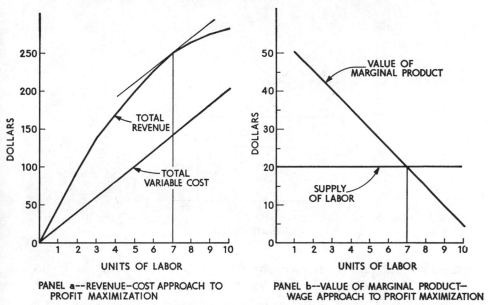

PANEL a--REVENUE–COST APPROACH TO
PROFIT MAXIMIZATION

PANEL b--VALUE OF MARGINAL PRODUCT–
WAGE APPROACH TO PROFIT MAXIMIZATION

when marginal revenue per unit of labor equals marginal cost per unit of labor.

From the standpoint of input analysis it is more useful to approach the profit-maximization problem in a different way. First, note that the supply of labor curve (panel b) is given by the entries in column 7, Table 13.2.1. It is a horizontal line at the $20 level, indicating the addition to total cost attributable to the addition of one unit of labor. The marginal product of successive additional units of labor is shown in column 3. Multiplying these entries by commodity price, one obtains the value of the marginal product, shown in column 6.

Definition: The value of the marginal product of a variable productive service is equal to its marginal product multiplied by the market price of the commodity in question.

From panel b, Figure 13.2.1, it is easily seen that the value of the marginal product curve intersects the supply of labor curve at a point corresponding to seven units of labor input. As we have previously seen, this is precisely the profit-maximizing labor input.

To get more directly to the proposition we seek, consider the generalization of panel b shown in Figure 13.2.2. Suppose the value of

FIGURE 13.2.2

Proof of *VMP* = *w* Theorem

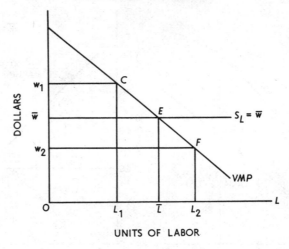

UNITS OF LABOR

the marginal product is given by the curve labeled *VMP* in Figure 13.2.2. The market wage rate is $O\overline{w}$, so the supply of labor to the firm is the horizontal line S_L. First, suppose the firm employed only OL_1 units of labor. At that rate of employment, the value of the marginal product is $L_1C = Ow_1 > O\overline{w}$, the wage rate. At this point of operation an additional unit of labor adds more to total revenue than to total cost (inasmuch as it adds the value of its marginal product to total revenue and its unit wage rate to cost). Hence a profit-maximizing entrepreneur would add additional units of labor; and indeed, he would continue to add units so long as the value of the marginal product exceeds the wage rate.

Next, suppose OL_2 units of labor were employed. At this point the value of the marginal product $L_2F = Ow_2$ is less than the wage rate. Each unit of labor adds more to total cost than to total revenue. Hence a profit-maximizing entrepreneur would not employ OL_2 units, or any number for which the wage rate exceeds the value of the marginal product. These arguments show that neither more nor fewer than $O\overline{L}$ units of labor would be employed and that to employ $O\overline{L}$ units leads to profit maximization. The statements are summarized as follows:

Proposition: A profit-maximizing entrepreneur will employ units of a variable productive service until the point is reached at which the value of the marginal product of the input is exactly equal to the input price.

In other words, given the market wage rate or the supply of labor curve to the firm, a perfectly competitive producer determines the quantity of labor to hire by equating the value of the marginal product to the wage rate. If the wage rate were Ow_1 (Figure 13.2.2), the firm would employ OL_1 units of labor to equate the value of the marginal product to the given wage rate. Similarly, if the wage rate were Ow_2, the firm would employ OL_2 units of labor. By definition of a demand curve, therefore, the value of the marginal product curve is established as the individual demand for labor curve.[10]

Definition: The individual demand curve for a single variable productive service is given by the value of the marginal product curve of the productive service in question.

13.2.b Individual Demand Curves When Several Variable Inputs Are Used

When a production process involves more than one variable productive service, the value of the marginal product curve of an input is not its demand curve. The reason lies in the fact that the various inputs are interdependent in the production process, so that a change in the price of one input leads to changes in the rates of utilization of the others. The latter, in turn, shifts the marginal product curve of the input whose price initially changed.[11]

Consider Figure 13.2.3. Suppose an equilibrium initially exists at point A. The market wage rate is Ow_1, the value of the marginal product

----

[10] The results of this section can be developed mathematically. Let the production function be

$$q = f(x) , \qquad (13.10.1)$$

where x is the single variable productive service. Marginal product is accordingly given by $f'(x)$. Under the assumptions of this chapter, the producer is a perfect competitor in both commodity and factor markets. Hence the market price of the commodity (p) and the market price of the input (w) are given.

The profit function is

$$\pi = pq - wx - F = pf(x) - wx - F , \qquad (13.10.2)$$

where F represents fixed cost and wx is the variable cost. The entrepreneur adjusts his input usage so as to maximize profit. Mathematically, this is represented by

$$\frac{d\pi}{dx} = pf'(x) - w = 0 , \qquad (13.10.3)$$

or

$$pf'(x) = w , \qquad (13.10.4)$$

the theorem stated in the text.

[11] For a review, see Chapter 5, subsection 5.2.d, especially Figures 5.2.3 and 5.2.4.

FIGURE 13.2.3

Individual Input Demand When Several Variable Inputs Are Used

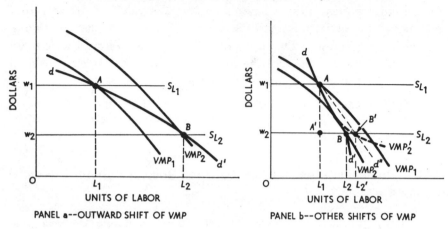

PANEL a--OUTWARD SHIFT OF VMP   PANEL b--OTHER SHIFTS OF VMP

curve for labor is VMP_1 when labor is the only input varied, and OL_1 units of labor are employed. Now let the equilibrium wage rate fall to Ow_2, so that the perfectly elastic supply curve of labor to the firm is S_{L_2}.

The change in the wage rate *in general* has three effects that are admittedly difficult to explain because they do not lend themselves conveniently to graphical analysis. Two effects —the substitution effect and

FIGURE 13.2.4

**Substitution and Output
Effects of a Change
in Input Price**

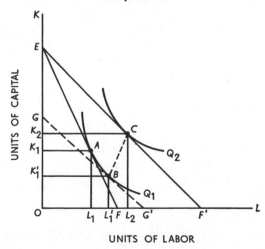

UNITS OF LABOR

the output effect—were explained in Chapter 6. These two effects are reexamined here by means of Figure 13.2.4. For convenience, assume that there are only two variable inputs, capital (K) and labor (L). Q_1 and Q_2 are production isoquants, and the initial input price ratio (when the wage rate is Ow_1 in Figure 13.2.3) is given by the slope of EF. As explained in Chapter 6, equilibrium is attained at point A, with inputs of OL_1 units of labor and OK_1 units of capital. Now let the wage rate fall to Ow_2, the cost of capital remaining constant. The new input price ratio is represented by the slope of the new isocost curve EF'. Equilibrium is ultimately attained at point C on the higher isoquant Q_2, with OL_2 units of labor and OK_2 units of capital employed.

The movement from A to C can be decomposed into two separate "effects." The first is a *substitution effect,* represented by the movement along the original isoquant from A to B. To understand this movement, construct the fictional isocost curve GG' with the following characteristics: (a) it is parallel to EF', thus representing the new input price ratio, but (b) it is tangent to Q_1, thus restricting output to the initial level. The movement from A to B is a pure substitution of labor for capital as a result of the decrease in the relative price of labor. The movement *would* occur if the entrepreneur were restricted to his original level of output at the new input price ratio.

The movement from B to C represents the *output effect*. First, recall that Figure 13.2.4 depicts the maximization of output for a *given* expenditure on resources. When the price of labor falls, more labor, more capital, or more of both may be bought at the given, constant expenditure. The movement from B to C represents this, and position C indicates the ratio in which the inputs will be combined if expenditure on resources remains unchanged.[12]

In summary, the substitution effect resulting from a reduction in the wage rate causes a substitution of labor for capital. This effect alone, therefore, shifts labor's marginal product curve to the left because there is less of the cooperating factor (capital) with which to work. The output effect generally[13] results in an increased usage of both inputs. Thus the output effect alone tends to shift labor's marginal product curve to the right because there is usually more of the cooperating factor with which to work.

Let us now reemphasize that point C, Figure 13.2.4, indicates the optimal input *ratio* for the given expenditure on resources; but it does

---

[12] The analysis is not affected if either of the inputs is "inferior" (see Chapter 6).

[13] There can be exceptions, but they are unusual. See the references in footnote 14.

not show the profit-maximizing *amounts* of the inputs. When the wage rate falls, the marginal cost of production is reduced for every level of output unless labor is an inferior factor. The marginal cost curve shifts to the right, and the profit-maximizing output of the perfectly competitive firm increases. This is a separate effect that may be called the *profit maximizing effect*. In terms of Figure 13.2.4, the isocost curve EF' shifts outward and to the right, remaining parallel to itself, as it were. The profit maximizing effect normally leads, via an expansion of output, to an increase in the usage of both inputs. Hence this effect also shifts labor's marginal product curve to the right.

Now return to Figure 13.2.3. When the wage rate falls from Ow_1 to Ow_2, the usage of labor expands. However, the expansion does not take place along VMP_1. When the quantity of labor used and the level of output change, the usage of other inputs changes as well. The substitution effect of the change causes a leftward shift of labor's marginal product curve. But the output and profit maximizing effects cause a reverse shift to the right unless labor is an inferior factor.

Panels a and b, Figure 13.2.3, illustrate the ways in which the VMP curve may shift. In panel a, the value of the marginal product curve shifts uniformly outward to the right, from VMP_1 to VMP_2. The equilibrium usage of labor at wage rates Ow_1 and Ow_2 correspond to the points A and B respectively. Generating a series of points such as A and B by varying the wage rate also generates the labor demand curve dd'. Panel b illustrates that the value of the marginal product curve may shift uniformly inward to the left (VMP_2) or that it may "twist" (VMP_2'). In either case, connecting points such as A and B or A and B' generates factor demand functions such as dd' or dd'' respectively. The only requirement is that the new VMP curve intersect S_{L_2} at a point to the right of A in panel b. The factor demand curve, that is, *must* be negatively sloped.[14]

Thus the input demand curve, while more difficult to derive, is just

---

[14] Unfortunately this assertion, which is essential for the results of this section, cannot be proved graphically and the mathematical proof is long and tedious. For detailed treatments of the general case, see C. E. Ferguson, "Production, Prices, and the Theory of Jointly Derived Input Demand Functions," *Economica,* N.S. vol. 33 (1966), pp. 454–61; C. E. Ferguson, " 'Inferior Factors' and the Theories of Production and Input Demand," *Economica,* N.S. vol. 35 (1968), pp. 140–50; C. E. Ferguson, *The Neoclassical Theory of Production and Distribution* (London and New York: Cambridge University Press, 1969), chaps. 6 and 9; and C. E. Ferguson and Thomas R. Saving, "Long-Run Scale Adjustments of a Perfectly Competitive Firm and Industry," *American Economic Review,* vol. 59 (1969), pp. 774–83.

as determinate in the multiple-input case as in the single-input situation. The results of this section may be summarized in the following important

Proposition: An entrepreneur's demand curve for a variable productive agent can be derived when more than one variable input is used. The demand curve must be negatively sloped because, on balance, the three effects of an input price change *must* cause quantity demanded to vary inversely with price.

13.2.c Determinants of the Demand for a Productive Service

The determinants of the demand for a variable productive service by an individual firm, while embodied in our derivation of the demand curve, have not been stated explicitly. It may serve well to enumerate them now.

First, the greater the quantity of cooperating services employed, the greater the demand for a given quantity of the variable service in question. This proposition follows immediately from the facts that (a) the product price is fixed for our analysis and (b) the greater the quantity of cooperating inputs the greater the marginal product of the input in question.

Second, the demand price for a variable productive service will be greater the higher the selling price of the commodity it is used to produce. Fixing marginal product, the greater the commodity price the greater the value of the marginal product.

Third, the demand price for a variable productive service will be lower the greater the quantity of the service currently in use. For a given commodity price, this proposition follows immediately from the law of diminishing marginal physical returns.

Finally, the demand for a variable productive service depends upon "the state of the art," or technology. Given the production function, marginal product and the value of the marginal product for each commodity price are known and do not change except for the first point above. However, technology does change; and it should be apparent that technological progress changes the marginal productivity of all inputs. Thus a technological change that makes a variable input more productive also makes the demand for any given quantity of it greater, and vice versa.[15]

---

[15] For more explanation, see Alfred Marshall, *Principles of Economics* (8th ed.; New York: The Macmillan Co., 1920), pp. 381–93.

13.2.d Market Demand for a Variable Productive Service

The market demand for a variable productive service, just as the market demand for a commodity, is the horizontal sum of the constituent individual demands. However, in the case of productive services the process of addition is considerably more complicated because when all firms expand or contract simultaneously, the market price of the commodity changes.[16] Nonetheless, the market demand curve can be obtained, as illustrated in Figure 13.2.5.

FIGURE 13.2.5

Derivation of the Market Demand for a Variable Productive Service

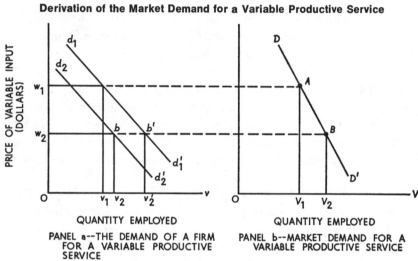

PANEL a--THE DEMAND OF A FIRM FOR A VARIABLE PRODUCTIVE SERVICE

PANEL b--MARKET DEMAND FOR A VARIABLE PRODUCTIVE SERVICE

A typical employing firm is depicted in panel a. For the going market price of the commodity produced, $d_1 d_1'$ is the firm's demand curve for the variable productive service, as derived in Figure 13.2.3. If the market price of the resource is Ow_1, the firm uses Ov_1 units. Aggregating over all employing firms, OV_1 units of the service are used. Thus point A in panel b is one point on the market demand curve for the variable productive service.

Next, suppose the price of the service declines to Ow_2 (because, for example, the supply curve of the variable service shifts to the right). Other things being equal, the firm would move along $d_1 d_1'$ to point b',

---

[16] An algebraic analysis of the derivation of market demand is simple but lengthy. For one version, see George J. Stigler, *The Theory of Price* (New York: The Macmillan Co., 1949), pp. 184–86.

employing Ov_2' units of the service. But other things are not equal.[17] When all firms expand their usage of the input, total output expands. Or stated differently, the market supply curve for the commodity produced shifts to the right because of the decline in the input's price. For a given commodity demand, commodity price must fall; and when it does the individual demand curves for the variable productive service also fall.[18]

In panel a, the decline in individual input demand attributable to the decline in commodity price is represented by the shift leftward from d_1d_1' to d_2d_2'. At input price Ow_2, b is the equilibrium point, with Ov_2 units employed. Aggregating for all employers, OV_2 units of the productive service are used and point B is obtained in panel b. Any number of points such as A and B can be generated by varying the market price of the productive service. Connecting these points by a line, one obtains DD', the market demand for the variable productive service.

13.3 SUPPLY OF A VARIABLE PRODUCTIVE SERVICE

All variable productive services may be broadly classified into three groups: natural resources, intermediate goods, and labor. Intermediate goods are those produced by one entrepreneur and sold to another who, in turn, utilizes them in his productive process. For example, cotton is produced by a farmer and (after middlemen) sold as an intermediate good to a manufacturer of damask; the damask, in turn, becomes an intermediate good in the manufacture of upholstered furniture. The supply curves of intermediate goods are positively sloped because they are the *commodity outputs* of manufacturers, even if they are variable inputs to others; and, as shown in Part III, commodity supply curves are positively sloped.

Natural resources may be regarded as the commodity outputs of (usually) mining operations. As such, they also have positively sloped supply curves.[19] Thus our attention can be restricted to the final, and most important, category: labor.

---

[17] Compare the following to the derivation of market commodity supply by summing individual supply curves.

[18] Let p_1 and p_2 be the original and the new commodity prices respectively. Thus $VMP_1 = p_1MP$, $VMP_2 = p_2MP$, and $VMP_1 > VMP_2$ since $p_1 > p_2$.

[19] There is some difficulty involving the optimal time for marketing natural resources; but this generally does not affect the slope of their supply curves. For an elegant treatment, see Harold Hotelling, "The Economics of Exhaustible Resources," *Journal of Political Economy,* vol. 39 (1931), pp. 137–75.

13.3.a General Considerations

As population increases and its age composition changes, as people migrate from one area to another, and as education and reeducation enable people to shift occupations, rather dramatic changes can occur in the supply curves of various types of labor at various locations throughout the nation. These changes represent *shifts* in the supply curve and are quite independent of its slope. To get at the supply curve for a well-defined market, assume that the following are constants (they are temporarily impounded in *ceteris paribus*): the size of the population, the labor force participation rate, and the occupational and geographic distribution of the labor force. Thus one first asks, what induces a person to forego leisure for work?

13.3.b Indifference Curve Analysis of Labor Supply

The supply of labor offered by one individual can, in principle, be determined by indifference curve analysis, as shown in Figure 13.3.1. Hours of leisure are measured along the horizontal axis, OM representing the maximum, or the total number of potential work hours in the week. The total money income from work is measured along the vertical axis. The slope of a line connecting M and any point on the vertical axis represents a wage per hour. For example, if OY_1 is the money income that would be received for OM hours of work, the hourly wage rate is OY_1/OM, or the slope of MY_1. Finally, curves I, II, and III represent indifference curves between income and leisure. For example, along the lowest shown level of indifference I, an individual is indifferent between OC hours of leisure (he works CM hours) and income CF, and OG hours of leisure (GM hours of work) and income GH.

When the wage rate is given by the slope of MY_1, the tangency condition for maximization[20] establishes equilibrium at point F on curve I. The individual works CM hours for income CF. His leisure, therefore, is OC. Let the wage rate increase, as given by the slope of MY_2. The new equilibrium is E on curve II. Hours of work expand from CM to BM as a result of the increase in the wage rate; they would further expand to AM if the wage line changed to MY_3. The equilibrium points $F, E, D, \ldots$ can be connected by the dashed line S, showing the supply of labor offered by one individual. In this case the supply

---

[20] Utility is regarded as a function of income and leisure. The problem is to maximize utility for a given hourly wage rate.

FIGURE 13.3.1

Indifference Curve Analysis of Labor Supply

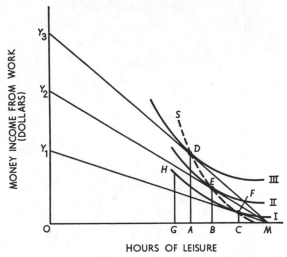

curve is positively sloped since an increase in the wage rate results in an increase in the number of hours worked.

Figure 13.3.2 illustrates the opposite case. Individual labor supply curves can behave in a variety of ways; the crucial question is how their *sum* behaves—what is the shape of the market supply curve of any specified type of labor?

13.3.c The Market Supply of Labor

In fact, considerably more can be said about the *sum* than about the constituent parts. First, consider the situation in which one industry uses exclusively a specialized type of labor (obviously, technically skilled). In the short run nothing can be said about the slope or shape of the labor supply curve. It may be positive, it may be negative, or it may have segments of positive and negative slope. But now let us relax our assumption concerning occupational immobility; and in the long run, one must. The master baker can become an apprentice candlestick maker if the financial inducement is sufficient. But more to the point, young people planning their education and career must surely be affected by current returns in various professions. Thus in the long run the supply of specialized labor is likely to have a positive slope.

The other case, in which labor is not specialized to one particular

FIGURE 13.3.2

**Indifference Curve Analysis of Labor Supply,
Negatively Sloped Curve**

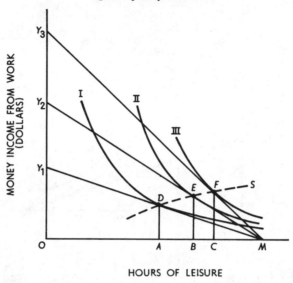

HOURS OF LEISURE

industry, is even more clear. In particular, if more than one industry uses a particular type of labor, the labor supply curve to any one industry must be positively sloped. Suppose any one industry increases its employment; the wage rate must rise for two reasons. First, to expand employment workers must be obtained from the other industries, thereby increasing the demand price of labor. Second, the industries that lose labor must reduce output; hence commodity prices in these industries will tend to rise, causing an additional upward pressure on the demand price of labor. Thus the industry attempting to expand employment must face a positively sloped supply of labor curve.[21]

In summary, we have the following

Relation: The supply curves of raw materials and intermediate goods are positively sloped, as are the supply curves of nonspecialized types of

---

[21] There are two possible exceptions, each of which leads to a horizontal industry supply of labor curve. First, if the industry is exceedingly small or if it uses only very small quantities of labor, its effect upon the market may be negligible. That is, the industry may stand to the market as a perfectly competitive firm does to the industry. Second, if there is unemployment of the particular type of labor under consideration, the supply of labor to all industries may be perfectly elastic up to the point of full employment. Thereafter the supply curve would rise.

labor. In the very short run the supply of specialized labor may take any shape or slope; but in the long run it too tends to be positively sloped.

13.4 MARGINAL PRODUCTIVITY THEORY OF INPUT RETURNS

The currently accepted version of marginal productivity theory follows immediately from the tools developed above. Indeed, it is merely another application of demand and supply analysis.

13.4.a Market Equilibrium and the Returns to Variable Productive Services

The demand for and supply of a variable productive service jointly determine its market equilibrium price; this is precisely marginal productivity theory. In Figure 13.4.1, DD' and SS' are the demand and supply curves. Their intersection at point E determines the stable[22] market equilibrium price $O\overline{W}$ and quantity demanded and supplied $O\overline{V}$. The only features unique to this analysis are the methods of determining the demand for variable productive services and the supply of labor services. The fact that input demand is based upon the value of the marginal product of the input gives rise to the label "marginal productivity theory."

13.4.b Short Run and Quasi Rents

Up to this point we have not been very specific about the short run and the long. Indeed it has not been necessary, because marginal productivity theory is concerned with the price of *variable* productive services. In the long run all inputs are variable; so marginal productivity theory covers all resources in the long run. However, in the short run certain inputs are *fixed;* they cannot be varied and hence a "marginal product" cannot readily be generated. The return to short-run fixed inputs therefore requires another explanation. Following Marshall, this return is denoted "quasi rent."[23]

---

[22] *Exercise:* Prove graphically that this is a stable equilibrium. Next, let the SS' curve bend back upon itself. Can you generate an unstable case?

[23] In classical usage, "rent" is the return to a resource whose supply is absolutely fixed and nonaugmentable (that is, whose supply curve is a line perpendicular to the quantity axis). The return to short-run fixed inputs is called quasi rent because their quantities are variable in the long run.

The definition of quasi rent used in the text, which is the customary modern

FIGURE 13.4.1

**Market Equilibrium Determination of the Price of a Variable
Productive Service**

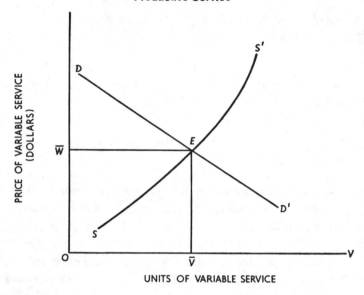

UNITS OF VARIABLE SERVICE

The explanation of quasi rents requires the customary cost curve graph, illustrated in Figure 13.4.2. In that figure, *ATC, AVC,* and *MC* denote average total cost, average variable cost, and marginal cost respectively. Suppose market price is $O\overline{P}$. The profit-maximizing firm produces $O\overline{Q}$ units of output and incurs variable costs which, on average, amount to $OA = \overline{Q}D$ dollars per unit of output. Thus the total expenditure required to sustain the necessary employment of variable productive services is represented by $OAD\overline{Q}$. Total revenue is $O\overline{P}E\overline{Q}$; thus the difference between total revenue and total variable cost is $A\overline{P}ED$. Similarly, if market price were OA per unit, the difference between total revenue and total variable cost would be *HAFG*.

This difference *is* quasi rent, which must always be nonnegative (if price fell to *OJ,* total revenue and total variable cost would be equal; if price fell below *OJ,* production would cease and total revenue and total variable cost would both equal zero). Notice that quasi rent is the

definition, differs slightly from Marshall's original definition (see his *Principles of Economics* [8th ed.; London: Macmillan & Co., Ltd., 1920], footnote on pp. 426–27). Marshall defined quasi rent as the return to a temporarily fixed input *minus* the cost of maintenance and replacement. Quasi rent as defined by Marshall cannot be illustrated by means of conventional cost diagrams. In particular, Marshall's definition is *not* equivalent to the text definition minus the area *ABCD* in Figure 13.4.2.

FIGURE 13.4.2

Determination of Quasi Rent

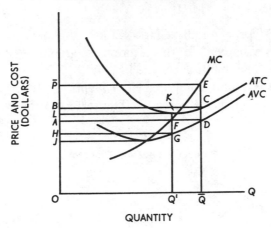

total return ascribable to the fixed inputs. If price is $O\bar{P}$, quasi rent can be divided into two components: the amount $ABCD$, representing their opportunity cost; and the amount $B\bar{P}EC$, representing the pure economic profit attributable to their use in this industry rather than in their best alternative use. Similarly, if market price is OA, quasi rent ($HAFG$) has two components: the amount $HLKG$, the opportunity cost of using the fixed inputs in this industry; and the (negative) amount $ALKF$, representing the pure economic loss incurred as a penalty for using the resources in their current employment.

Finally, a rather obvious point should be noted: the sum of (total) variable cost and quasi rent as imputed above precisely equals the dollar value of the total product. This is simply a matter of definition and arithmetic; but it has a logical foundation, as we shall now see.

13.4.c Clark-Wicksteed Product Exhaustion Theorem

In short-run equilibrium the sum of total variable cost and quasi rent definitionally equals the dollar value of output. As has been said, this is a simple and obvious matter of arithmetic. It is not obvious, however, that in long-run competitive equilibrium the total physical product will be exactly sufficient to pay each input its marginal product. This is an important theorem attributable to Clark, Wicksteed, and other pioneers of marginal productivity theory.

To repeat:

Proposition: In long-run competitive equilibrium, rewarding each input according to its marginal physical product precisely exhausts the total physical product.

A mathematical proof of the Clark-Wicksteed theorem is in the appendix to this Chapter; in this section a graphical demonstration attributable to Chapman is presented.[24]

Consider an economy composed of *n* identical farms, each worked by an identical number of laborers. In Figure 13.4.3 the horizontal axis

FIGURE 13.4.3

Product-Exhaustion Theorem

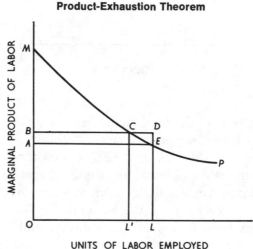

UNITS OF LABOR EMPLOYED

represents the number of workers per farm and the curve *MP* is the marginal product of labor. Suppose *OL* workers are employed per farm and that each is paid his marginal physical product. The real wage is *OA = LE*, and total wages are *OAEL*. The total physical product per farm is *OMEL*, so rent per farm is *AME*. Rent so computed is merely a residual; our problem is to prove that *AME* is also the marginal product of land.

First, observe that the total product of the economy is *n × OMEL*. Next, suppose another farm is added to the economy, the number of workers remaining unchanged. If we can determine total output with

---

[24] S. J. Chapman, "The Remuneration of Employers," *Economic Journal,* vol. 16 (1906), pp. 523–28. This is a problem in long-run analysis. In terms of Figure 13.4.3, in the short run there is an excess rent or profit equal to the area of triangle *CDE*. In the long run the number of farms must adjust so that area *CDE* approaches zero.

$n + 1$ farms, the difference in total output when there are $n + 1$ and n farms is the marginal product of land.

When the $(n + 1)$-st farm is added, each existing farm must supply its proportional share of workers to the new farm. There are $n \times OL$ workers available; each farm now employs a number of workers, say OL', such that $(n + 1) \times OL' = n \times OL$. When each farm employs OL' workers, output per farm is $OMCL'$ and the total output of the economy is

$$(n + 1) \times OMCL' = n \times OMCL' + OMCL' .$$

The total product with n farms is

$$n \times OMEL = n \times OMCL' + n \times L'CEL .$$

The marginal product of land, therefore, is the difference, or

$$n \times OMCL' + OMCL' - n \times OMCL' - n \times L'CEL$$
$$= OMCL' - n \times L'CEL = BMC + OBCL' - n \times L'CEL .$$

Now consider the last term above:

$$n \times L'CEL = n \times L'CDL - n \times CDE .$$

Since $n \times L'L = OL'$ by the equal division of workers, it follows that $n \times L'CDL = OBCL'$, the total return to labor per farm when OL' workers are employed on each farm. Therefore, the marginal product of the $(n + 1)$-st farm is

$$BMC + OBCL' - OBCL' + n \times CDE = BMC + n \times CDE .$$

The last term, $n \times CDE$, approaches zero as n increases without bound —that is, as the size of each farm decreases. Thus for an infinitesimally small increase in land the marginal product of land is BMC. But BMC is also the rent per farm computed by the residual method when OL' workers are on each farm. Consequently, the marginal product of land is the same as the residual, proving the Clark-Wicksteed theorem.

13.5 DISTRIBUTION AND RELATIVE FACTOR SHARES

The basic elements of marginal productivity theory have been known since the time of Marshall, Clark, and Wicksteed. However a fully systematic exposition, together with a theory of relative factor shares, was not presented until Hicks published his important *Theory of Wages.*[25] This may be regarded as the foundation of the modern neo-

---

[25] John R. Hicks, *The Theory of Wages* (2d ed.; London: Macmillan & Co., Ltd., 1932, 1963).

classical theory of distribution and relative factor shares. Before we get into concepts, however, a bit of review is in order.

13.5.a Least-Cost Combination of Inputs and Linearly Homogeneous Production Functions

The present section is a brief review of the topics developed in Chapter 6, especially subsections 6.3.c and 6.4.c. First recall that the least-cost combination of inputs is obtained when the marginal rate of technical substitution equals the input-price ratio. This proposition is

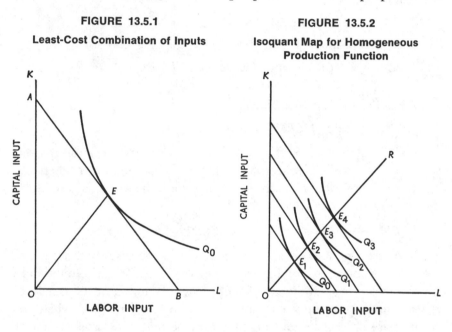

FIGURE 13.5.1

Least-Cost Combination of Inputs

FIGURE 13.5.2

Isoquant Map for Homogeneous Production Function

illustrated in Figure 13.5.1, in which Q_0 is an isoquant and the slope of AB represents the wage-rent ratio. The slope of the isoquant at any point is the ratio of the marginal product of labor to that of capital. Least-cost input proportions are attained only when the ratio of marginal products (the marginal rate of technical substitution) equals the input-price ratio. This occurs at point E, and the slope of the ray OE defines the optimal input (capital-labor) ratio.

The capital-labor ratio is important in any circumstance; but when the production function is homogeneous of degree one it plays an even more vital role. To say a production function is linearly homogeneous implies that the marginal product of each input, and hence the marginal rate of technical substitution, is a function of the input ratio exclusively. Or, in terms of Figure 13.5.2, the marginal rate of technical substitution of capital for labor is a function of the capital-labor ratio only. In particular, the marginal rate of technical substitution is *not* a function of the scale of output.[26]

An isoquant map for a linearly homogeneous production function is shown in Figure 13.5.2. Consider any ray from the origin, say *OR*, which specifies a capital-labor ratio. This ray intersects all isoquants in points (such as E_1, . . . , E_4) such that the slopes of the isoquants are identical; in other words, the marginal rate of technical substitution is the same at E_1, E_2, E_3, and E_4. This is true not only of the ray *OR* but of *any* other ray as well. Hence a single isoquant fully describes the isoquant map when the production function is homogeneous of degree one.

13.5.b The Elasticity of Substitution

At the heart of neoclassical theory is the *elasticity of substitution,* a concept introduced by Hicks in 1932.[27] Just as every elasticity, it measures the relative responsiveness of one variable to proportional changes in another.

Definition: The elasticity of substitution measures the relative responsiveness of the capital-labor ratio to given proportional changes in the marginal rate of technical substitution of capital for labor.

Thus by formula, the elasticity of substitution (σ) is

----

[26] Let the production function be

$$Q = F(K, L) , \qquad (13.26.1)$$

where $F(K, L)$ is homogeneous of degree one in K and L. By its homogeneity property, equation (13.26.1) may be written

$$q = f(k) , \qquad (13.26.2)$$

where $q = Q/L$ and $k = K/L$. It is a simple matter to show that the marginal products $\partial Q/\partial K$ and $\partial Q/\partial L$ are given by

$$\frac{\partial Q}{\partial K} = f'(k) \qquad (13.26.3)$$

and

$$\frac{\partial Q}{\partial L} = f(k) - kf'(k) . \qquad (13.26.4)$$

These last two equations show that the marginal products are functions of the capital-labor ratio only.

[27] Hicks, *Theory of Wages,* p. 117.

$$\sigma = \frac{\Delta\left(\dfrac{K}{L}\right)}{\left(\dfrac{K}{L}\right)} \div \frac{\Delta(MRTS)}{MRTS} = \frac{\Delta\left(\dfrac{K}{L}\right)}{\Delta(MRTS)} \cdot \frac{MRTS}{\left(\dfrac{K}{L}\right)} \cdot \qquad (13.5.1)$$

The formula expressed above, however, can be made more meaning-ful. Recall that the marginal rate of technical substitution of capital for labor is the ratio of the marginal product of labor to that of capital. Let w, r, and p denote the prices of labor, capital, and output respectively. Rearranging the "VMP rule," we have

$$MRTS = \frac{MP_L}{MP_K} = \frac{(w/p)}{(r/p)} = \frac{w}{r} \cdot$$

Hence in equilibrium, the elasticity of substitution may be written as

$$\sigma = \frac{\Delta\left(\dfrac{K}{L}\right)}{\Delta\left(\dfrac{w}{r}\right)} \cdot \frac{\left(\dfrac{w}{r}\right)}{\left(\dfrac{K}{L}\right)} = \frac{\Delta\left(\dfrac{K}{L}\right)}{\left(\dfrac{K}{L}\right)} \div \frac{\Delta\left(\dfrac{w}{r}\right)}{\left(\dfrac{w}{r}\right)} \qquad (13.5.2)$$

In this form, the elasticity of substitution shows the proportional change in the capital-labor ratio induced by a given proportional change in the factor-price ratio.

13.5.c Elasticity of Substitution and Changes in Relative Factor Shares

In the notation introduced just above, the relative share of labor in output—that is, the total payment to labor divided by the total value of output—is

$$\frac{wL}{pQ} \cdot$$

Similarly, the relative share of capital is

$$\frac{rK}{pQ},$$

thus the ratio of relative shares is

$$\frac{wL}{rK} \cdot \quad [28]$$

Now consider the right-most expression in (13.5.2). Suppose the

----

[28] Consider the expression for labor's relative share. The real marginal product of labor is w/p, and L/Q is the reciprocal of labor's average product. Hence

$$\text{labor's relative share} = \frac{MP_L}{AP_L} = \epsilon_L,$$

the output elasticity of labor (see the appendix to this chapter). This is always true when labor is paid its real marginal product. Thus we may state the following

Relation: The relative share of an input is equal to its output elasticity.

wage-rent ratio increases by 10 percent. An increase in the relative price of labor will, of course, lead to a substitution of capital for labor and, thereby, to an increase in the capital-labor ratio. Suppose it increases by 5 percent. Then the elasticity of substitution is less than one. Knowing this allows us to infer the behavior of relative factor shares. In the case above, w/r increases by 10 percent and K/L increases by only 5 percent. It therefore follows that wL/rK increases.

Let us look briefly at the cause. By assumption, the wage-rent ratio increases—because, perhaps, the supply of capital increases proportionately more than the supply of labor. As labor becomes relatively more expensive, entrepreneurs substitute capital for labor to the extent permitted by the production function. Now if the production function is characterized by inelastic substitutability, entrepreneurs cannot substitute capital for labor in the same proportion as the wage rate has risen relative to capital rent. Thus the relative share of labor must rise.

The same sort of reasoning applies when the elasticity of substitution is equal to or greater than unity. Hence we may summarize the relation between the elasticity of substitution and the behavior of relative factor shares in the following

Proposition: Consider a two-factor model in which the absolute return to one factor increases relative to the absolute return to the other; the relative share of the former will increase, remain unchanged, or decrease according as the elasticity of substitution is less than, equal to, or greater than unity.[29]

Whether the elasticity of substitution is greater than, less than, or equal to unity is an empirical question; but it is one of great importance to various socioeconomic groups. For the American economy and for the manufacturing sector as a whole, there is strong evidence that the elasticity of substitution is substantially less than unity.[30] This is in keeping with the increases in the relative wage rate and in the relative share of labor. On the other hand, however, many specific industries and product groups apparently have production functions whose elasticities of substitution exceed unity.[31] In such industries the share of capital increases even though its relative return diminishes.

---

[29] *Exercise:* Explain this same proposition as stated by Hicks (*Theory of Wages,* p. 117): "An increase in the supply of any factor will increase its relative share if its 'elasticity of substitution' is greater than unity."

[30] As only one example, see J. W. Kendrick and Ryuzo Sato, "Factor Prices, Productivity, and Growth," *American Economic Review,* vol. 53 (1963), pp. 974–1003.

[31] See C. E. Ferguson, "Cross-Section Production Functions and the Elasticity of Substitution in American Manufacturing Industry," *Review of Economics and Statistics,* vol. 45 (1963), pp. 305–13; and "Time-Series Production Functions

13.5.d Classification of Technological Progress

So far we have operated under the tacit assumption that a production function is both given and unchanging over the period of analysis; our case has been strictly static. Technological progress does occur; and it is of some interest to classify the nature of technological change.

Many years ago Hicks defined technological progress as capital-using, neutral, or labor-using according as the marginal rate of technical substitution of capital for labor diminishes, remains unchanged, or increases at the originally prevailing capital-labor ratio. In other words, if technological change increases the marginal product of capital more than the marginal product of labor (at a given capital-labor ratio), progress is capital-using because a producer now has an incentive to use

FIGURE 13.5.3

Neutral Technological Progress

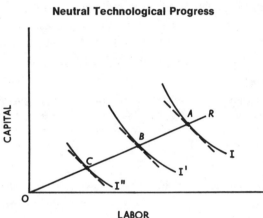

more capital relative to labor because its (capital's) marginal product has increased relative to that of labor. The same type of statement holds, *mutatis mutandis,* for neutral and for labor-using technological progress.

Basically, technological progress consists of any change (graphically, shift) of the production function that either permits the same level of output to be produced with less input or enables the former level of inputs to produce a greater output.

Technological progress is shown graphically in Figures 13.5.3 and 13.5.4. The figures are constructed with uniform notation. The level of output is *I,* and the various isoquants (*I, I',* and *I''*) show the combina-

and Technological Progress in American Manufacturing Industry," *Journal of Political Economy,* vol. 73 (1965), pp. 135–47.

FIGURE 13.5.4
Biased Technological Progress

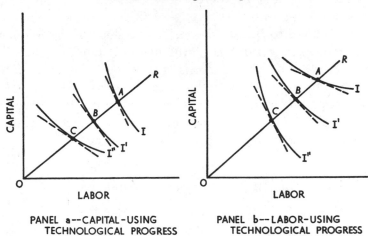

PANEL a--CAPITAL-USING
TECHNOLOGICAL PROGRESS

PANEL b--LABOR-USING
TECHNOLOGICAL PROGRESS

tions of inputs capable of producing this given level of output. *OR* is the ray whose slope gives a constant capital-labor ratio. The points *A, B,* and *C* show the points of production at the given capital-labor ratio as technological progress occurs.

Technological progress is shown graphically by a shift of an isoquant in the direction of the origin. In Figure 13.5.3, the three isoquants— *I, I',* and *I''*—all represent the same level of output. As technological progress takes place *I'* shows that the given level of output can be produced by smaller quantities of inputs than at *I*. Similarly, as technological progress continues *I''* shows that still smaller input combinations can produce the same level of output.

Figure 13.5.3 illustrates neutral technological progress. Recalling the definition, technological progress is neutral if at a constant capital-labor ratio the marginal rate of technical substitution of capital for labor is unchanged. The constant capital-labor ratio ray *OR* intersects the three isoquants at points *A, B,* and *C* respectively. At these points, the slope of the isoquant—or the marginal rate of technical substitution of capital for labor—is the same. Hence it represents a shifting production function characterized by neutral technological progress.

Panels a and b, Figure 13.5.4, illustrate capital-using and labor-using technological progress respectively. Capital-using technological progress occurs when at a constant capital-labor ratio, the marginal product of capital increases relative to the marginal product of labor. In other words, since the marginal rate of technical substitution of capital for labor is the ratio of the marginal product of labor to that of capital, capital-using technological progress occurs when the marginal rate of technical substitution declines along a constant capital-labor ray. As one moves from A to B to C in panel a, the slope of the isoquant diminishes, representing a decline in the marginal rate of technical substitution. Hence this panel depicts a shifting production function characterized by capital-using technological progress.

By the same line of reasoning, panel b illustrates labor-using technological progress because the marginal rate of technical substitution increases as one moves from A to B to C.

13.5.e Biased Technological Progress and Relative Factor Shares

Observed changes in relative shares depend upon changes in relative input prices and in the responsiveness of input proportions to these changes. Over time, changes in relative shares depend upon the nature of technological progress as well. Indeed, this is evident from the definition of biased technological progress introduced in the subsection above.[32]

First consider neutral technological progress. By definition, the capital-labor ratio and the marginal rate of technical substitution of capital for labor remain unchanged. Next, recall that in equilibrium, the marginal rate of technical substitution of capital for labor must equal the input-price ratio. Therefore the wage-rent ratio also remains unchanged. That is, both (K/L) and (w/r) are unchanged by neutral technological progress. Consequently, relative shares are not affected by technological progress when the latter is neutral.

Now suppose technological progress is capital-using. This implies that at a constant capital-labor ratio the marginal rate of technical substitution, and hence the wage-rent ratio, declines. This is tantamount to saying that r increases relative to w while K/L is constant. The relative share of capital accordingly increases and that of labor declines.

By a similar line of reasoning, one may show that labor-using tech-

---

[32] The relations among relative shares, changes in relative factor supplies, the elasticity of substitution, and the nature of technological progress can readily be developed mathematically. However, a mathematical treatment requires more space than is here available. For details, see C. E. Ferguson, "Neoclassical Theory of Technical Progress and Relative Factor Shares," *Southern Economic Journal,* vol. 34 (1968), pp. 490–504; and Ferguson, *The Neoclassical Theory of Production and Distribution,* chaps. 11 and 12.

nological progress causes a decrease in the relative share of capital with a corresponding increase in the relative share of labor. Summarizing, we have the following

Relations: The relative share of labor increases, remains unchanged, or decreases according as technological progress is labor-using, neutral, or capital-using; the opposite relation holds for the relative share of capital.

As a final empirical note, there is some evidence that the American economy has been characterized by labor-using technological progress over the postwar years.[33]

QUESTIONS AND EXERCISES

1. The United States has a law that requires equal pay for women who perform the same job as men in a given plant. What is the effect of this law on the wage and employment of men and women?

2. "An increase in the income tax rate will induce laborers to work more since their net incomes will decline." Discuss.

3. "The completion of the marginal productivity theory of distribution was achieved only with the development of the proof that if all productive agents are rewarded in accord with their marginal products, then the total product will be exhausted." Explain.

4. Consider a model that rationalizes a person's choice between income and leisure. If leisure is a normal good, the resulting supply of labor curve may be negatively sloped. Derive such a labor-supply function. How would the analysis be affected if we were to introduce a progressive income tax? If the wage rate for overtime work is 150 percent of the basic wage rate?

5. How do the elasticity of substitution and the change in relative factor supply relate to changes in relative factor shares?

6. "If the production function in a particular industry exhibits constant returns to scale, a tax imposed on the employment of one factor will in the short run increase that factor's marginal product and in the long run will have no effect." Discuss.

7. "Inputs A and B are used in the production of the same product. An increase in the price of A (due to a shift in A's supply curve) will result in a decline in the price of B." Discuss.

---

[33] See Murray Brown and John S. de Cani, "Technological Changes in the United States, 1950–1960," *Productivity Measurement Review*, No. 29 (May 1962), pp. 26–39; and C. E. Ferguson, "Substitution, Technical Progress, and Returns to Scale," *American Economic Review, Papers and Proceedings*, vol. 55 (1965), pp. 296–305.

8. "*A* is a product used in the production of *B*. Price control is imposed on the production of *A* but not *B*. The ceiling price imposed on *A* is less than the equilibrium price. This will result in a fall in the price of *B*." Discuss.

9. "Increasing the minimum wage to $2.75 per hour would have no effect outside the South if all workers earning less than $2.75 are located in the South." Discuss.

10. Part of the following statement follows directly from price theory, part not. Separate into the components: "Southern wages are lower than wages in the North (even in the same industry) because Southern workers have less education and the Southern climate causes everybody to work at a slower pace. Southern plants typically employ less capital per man. So, all in all, Southern workers are less efficient. They get paid less because they deserve less."

SUGGESTED READINGS

Cartter, Allan M. *Theory of Wages and Employment,* pp. 11–74. Homewood, Ill.: Richard D. Irwin, Inc., 1959.

Douglas, Paul H. *The Theory of Wages.* New York: The Macmillan Co., 1934.

Ferguson, C. E. " 'Inferior Factors' and the Theories of Production and Input Demand," *Economica,* N.S. vol. 35 (1968), pp. 140–50. [Advanced math necessary.]

————. *The Neoclassical Theory of Production and Distribution,* chaps. 6 and 9. London and New York: Cambridge University Press, 1969. [Advanced math necessary.]

————. "Production, Prices, and the Theory of Jointly-Derived Input Demand Functions," *Economica,* N.S. vol. 33 (1966), pp. 454–61. [Advanced math necessary.]

————, and Saving, Thomas R. "Long-Run Scale Adjustments of a Perfectly Competitive Firm and Industry," *American Economic Review,* vol. 59 (1969), pp. 774–83. [Advanced math necessary.]

Hicks, John R. *The Theory of Wages.* London: Macmillan & Co., Ltd., 1932.

————. *Value and Capital,* pp. 78–111. 2d ed. Oxford: Clarendon Press, 1946.

Samuelson, Paul A. *Foundations of Economic Analysis,* pp. 57–89. Cambridge, Mass.: Harvard University Press, 1947. [Advanced math necessary.]

Stigler, George J. *Production and Distribution Theories,* pp. 296–387. New York: The Macmillan Co., 1941. [Elementary math necessary.]

APPENDIX

I. THE CLARK-WICKSTEED THEOREM

The proof of the theorem used here is attributable to Erich Schneider in his *Theorie der Produktion* (Vienna: Springer Verlag, 1935), pp. 19–21. Let the production function be

$$q = f(x_1, x_2, \cdots, x_n) \tag{1}$$

where q is physical output and x_i is the input of the ith productive service. Denote $\partial f/\partial x_i$ by f_i. Then from (1) we have

$$dq = \sum_i f_i \, dx_i. \tag{2}$$

Increase all inputs by the constant proportion λ. Thus

$$\lambda = \frac{a x_1}{x_1} = \frac{a x_2}{x_2} = \cdots = \frac{a x_n}{x_n}. \tag{3}$$

Substitute (3) into (2), multiply by q and divide by λq obtaining

$$q \frac{dq}{\lambda a} = \sum_i f_i x_i. \tag{4}$$

Consider the term $dq/\lambda q$, which shows the relative change in output attributable to the same relative change in all inputs. This term may be called the *function coefficient* or the *elasticity of the production function*. (Schneider's term [*Theorie der Produktion*, p. 10] is "ergiebigkeitsgrad." The term "elasticity of production" is attributable to W. E. Johnson, "The Pure Theory of Utility Curves," *Economic Journal*, vol. 23 [1913], p. 507. The term "function coefficient" is used by Sune Carlson, *A Study on the Pure Theory of Production*, Stockholm Economic Studies, No. 9, 1939, p. 17.) Denote the function coefficient by ϵ. Thus from (4) we have:

$$q\epsilon = \sum_i f_i x_i. \tag{5}$$

Thus competitive imputations (paying each input its marginal product) precisely exhaust the total product if, and only if, $\epsilon = 1$. If there are constant returns to scale $\epsilon = 1$; in this case average cost is also constant. But this is precisely the condition of long-run competitive equilibrium, in which output is expanded or contracted by the exit and entry of firms each producing at the point of minimum long-run average cost. Thus, the Clark-Wicksteed theorem holds at the point of long-run competitive equilibrium—that is,

$$q = \sum_i f_i x_i \tag{6}$$

is an equation holding only for the precise set of equilibrium inputs, not an identity holding for any set of values of the variables.

II. THE OUTPUT ELASTICITY OF PRODUCTIVE SERVICES

Using the production function (1), the output elasticity of the ith productive service is defined as:

$$\epsilon_i = \frac{\partial q}{\partial x_i} \frac{x_i}{q} = f_i \frac{x_i}{q}. \tag{7}$$

The marginal product of x_i is f_i, and its average product is q/x_i; hence, from (7)

$$\epsilon_i = \frac{MP_i}{AP_i}$$

or, in words, the output elasticity of a productive service is the ratio of its marginal product to its average product.

14

Theory of employment in imperfectly competitive markets

14.1 INTRODUCTION

The analytical principles underlying the theory of resource price and employment are the same for perfectly and imperfectly competitive markets. Demand and supply determine market equilibrium resource price and employment; and marginal productivity considerations are the fundamental determinants of demand. To be sure, some adjustments must be made to allow for the fact that commodity price and marginal revenue are different in imperfectly competitive markets. Thus the value of the marginal product of a variable service is not the relevant guide. Furthermore, imperfect competition in the resource buying market must be introduced. Hence two additions to marginal productivity theory are presented in this chapter.

14.2 MONOPOLY IN THE COMMODITY MARKET

The first situation is that of a monopolist in the commodity market, or more generally an oligopolist or a monopolistic competitor, purchasing variable productive services in perfectly competitive input markets. Since the principle is precisely the same for all types of imperfect competition in the selling market, our attention is restricted to monopoly, except for subsection 14.2.d.

14.2.a Marginal Revenue Product

When a perfectly competitive seller employs an additional unit of, say, labor, his output is augmented by the marginal product of that unit. In like manner, his total revenue is augmented by the value of its marginal product inasmuch as market (selling) price remains unchanged. When a monopolist employs an additional unit of labor, his output is also increased by the marginal product of the worker. However, to sell his larger output, market price must be reduced for all units sold; hence total revenue is not augmented by the value of the marginal product of the additional worker. A numerical example is given in Table 14.2.1.

TABLE 14.2.1

Marginal Revenue Product for a Monopolistic Seller

Units of Variable Service	Total Product	Marginal Product	Selling Price per Unit	Total Revenue*	Marginal Revenue	Marginal Revenue Product
0....................	0	—	—	—	—	—
1....................	10	10	$10.00	$100	$10	$100
2....................	19	9	9.05	172	8	72
3....................	27	8	8.45	228	7	56
4....................	34	7	7.94	270	6	42
5....................	40	6	7.50	300	5	30
6....................	45	5	7.11	320	4	20
7....................	49	4	6.78	332	3	12
8....................	52	3	6.44	335	1	3
9....................	54	2	6.20	335	0	0
10....................	55	1	6.05	333	−2	−2

* Rounded to nearest even dollar.

The first three columns of the table give the production function. Column 4 shows the price at which the total product can be sold; hence columns 2 and 4 give the demand function. Columns 5 and 6 contain the figures for total and marginal revenue respectively. Finally, column 7 shows marginal revenue product, whose meaning and derivation must be explained.

Suppose the monopolist is producing and selling 27 units of the commodity at $8.45 per unit. This rate of output and sales requires three units of the variable productive service. Now consider what happens if a fourth unit of the variable service is used. Output increases to 34, or the marginal physical product of the fourth unit is 7. To sell 34 units per period of time, the monopolist must decrease his price to \$7.94 per unit. His total revenue expands, but *not* by 7 × \$8.45 or 7 × \$7.94. Total revenue expands by only \$42; so on average, marginal revenue is \$6. The addition of a unit of the variable service expands revenue, therefore, by the product of marginal revenue and marginal product, or by the increase in total revenue attributable to the addition of the marginal product (not one unit) to output and sales. This magnitude is called the *marginal revenue product* of the variable service.

An alternative arithmetic derivation of marginal revenue product may be helpful. When labor input expands from 3 to 4 units, output and sales expand by 7 units (from 27 to 34). Consequently, one might say that the *gross* increase in revenue attributable to the fourth unit of labor is 7 × \$7.94 which, rounded, equals \$56. That is, the gross increase equals the increase in output multiplied by the new market price per unit of output. However, when output expands, market price falls by 51 cents, from \$8.45 to \$7.94. Therefore, the 27 units that had been selling at \$8.45 must now be sold at \$7.94; thus 27 × 51 cents, or, rounded, \$14 must be deducted from the gross increase in revenue. As a result the *net* increase in revenue, or the marginal revenue product of the fourth unit of labor, is \$56 — \$14, or \$42.[1]

---

[1] A simple algebraic demonstration that marginal revenue product equals marginal revenue multiplied by marginal physical product is also revealing. Let *MRP, TR, TP, MPP*, and *L* denote marginal revenue product, total revenue, total product, marginal physical product, and labor input respectively. Also, as customary, let Δ denote "the change in."

By definition (in the text)

$$MRP = \frac{\Delta TR}{\Delta L}.$$ (14.1.1)

From the definition of marginal revenue ($MR = \Delta TR/\Delta TP$), one may write

$$\Delta TR = MR \times \Delta TP.$$ (14.1.2)

Similarly, from the definition of marginal physical product ($MPP = \Delta TP/\Delta L$), the change in labor input may be expressed as

$$\Delta L = \frac{\Delta TP}{MPP}.$$ (14.1.3)

Substituting expressions (14.1.2) and (14.1.3) in (14.1.1), the definition of marginal revenue product is obtained:

$$MRP = \frac{MR \times \Delta TP}{\dfrac{\Delta TP}{MPP}} = MR \times MPP.$$ (14.1.4)

A more directly mathematical derivation may be given. Let the demand function in inverse form be

Definition: Marginal revenue product equals marginal revenue multiplied by the marginal physical product of the variable productive service; or, marginal revenue product is the net addition to total revenue attributable to the addition of one unit of the variable productive service.

Before utilizing marginal revenue product to determine the monopolist's demand for a variable productive service, it may be well to show a graphical derivation of marginal revenue product. Panel a, Figure 14.2.1, shows a smooth production function for a certain commodity whose production requires the input of only one variable service. Suppose the monopolistic seller initially uses 24 units of the variable service, thereby producing 100 units of output. At that point, marginal product is five units.

Panel b shows the demand and marginal revenue curves that confront the monopolist. When 100 units are sold, price is $6 per unit

$$p = h(q) , \qquad h' < 0 . \tag{14.1.5}$$

Thus total revenue is

$$TR = qh(q) , \tag{14.1.6}$$

and marginal revenue is

$$MR = h(q) + qh'(q) . \tag{14.1.7}$$

The production function, assuming only one variable input x, is

$$q = f(x) , \qquad f' > 0 . \tag{14.1.8}$$

By definition, marginal revenue product is the change in total revenue attributable to a small (say, unit) change in input. Thus

$$MRP = \frac{d(TR)}{ax} . \tag{14.1.9}$$

From (14.1.6), we find

$$MRP = h(q)\frac{dq}{dx} + qh'(q)\frac{dq}{dx} . \tag{14.1.10}$$

From (14.1.8), $dq/dx = f'(x)$. Hence we have

$$MRP = [h(q) + qh'(q)]f'(x) . \tag{14.1.11}$$

By (14.1.7) and (14.1.8),

$$MRP = MR \cdot MP . \tag{14.1.12}$$

If there is a multi-input production function, $f'(x)$ is replaced by $\partial f/\partial x_i$ for the ith input. Equation (14.1.10) becomes

$$MRP_i = [h(q) + qh'(q)]\frac{\partial f}{\partial x_i} , \tag{14.1.13}$$

or

$$MRP_i = MR \cdot MP_i . \tag{14.1.14}$$

FIGURE 14.2.1

**Derivation of the Marginal Revenue Product Curve
for a Single Productive Service**

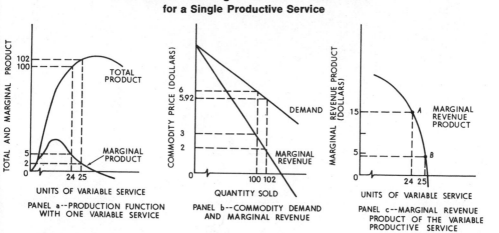

PANEL a--PRODUCTION FUNCTION WITH ONE VARIABLE SERVICE

PANEL b--COMMODITY DEMAND AND MARGINAL REVENUE

PANEL c--MARGINAL REVENUE PRODUCT OF THE VARIABLE PRODUCTIVE SERVICE

and marginal revenue is $3. Hence marginal revenue product of the 24th unit of the variable service is 5 × $3 or $15, plotted as point A in panel c. Now let the monopolist add an additional unit of the variable service. Output increases to 102 units per period, and the marginal physical product of the 25th unit of variable service is 2. When output expands to 102 units per period, the monopolist must reduce his selling price to $5.92 per unit to clear the market. Hence marginal revenue declines to $2 per unit. As a consequence, when 25 units of the variable service are employed, marginal revenue product becomes 2 × $2, or $4, plotted as point B in panel c.

Performing this operation for all feasible levels of employment generates the marginal revenue product curve. It must quite obviously slope downward to the right because two forces are working to cause marginal revenue product to diminish as the level of employment increases: (*a*) the marginal physical product declines (over the relevant range of production) as additional units of the variable service are added, and (*b*) marginal revenue declines as output expands and market price falls.

14.2.b Monopoly Demand for a Single Variable Service

Under the present assumption the monopolist purchases the variable service in a perfectly competitive input market. Hence, just as a perfectly competitive producer, he views his supply (of variable service)

FIGURE 14.2.2

Monopoly Demand for a Single Variable Service

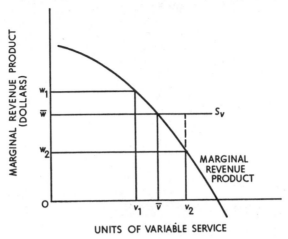

UNITS OF VARIABLE SERVICE

curve as a horizontal line at the level of the prevailing market price. Such a supply curve is illustrated by S_v in Figure 14.2.2, where the market price of the output is $O\overline{w}$.

The marginal revenue product curve is also shown in the figure; our task is to prove the following

Proposition: An imperfectly competitive producer who purchases a variable productive service in a perfectly competitive input market will employ that amount of the service for which marginal revenue product equals market price. Consequently, the marginal revenue product curve is the monopolist's demand curve for the variable service when only one variable input is used.

Given the market price $O\overline{w}$, our task is to prove that equilibrium employment is $O\overline{v}$. Suppose the contrary, in particular, that Ov_1 units of the variable service are used. At the Ov_1 level of utilization the last unit adds Ow_1 to total revenue but only $O\overline{w}$ to total cost. Since $Ow_1 > O\overline{w}$, profit is augmented by employing that unit. Furthermore, profit increases when additional units are employed so long as marginal revenue product exceeds the market equilibrium price of the input. Thus a profit-maximizing monopolist would never employ fewer than $O\overline{v}$ units of the variable service. The opposite argument holds when more than $O\overline{v}$ units are employed, for then an additional unit of the variable service adds more to total cost than to total revenue. Therefore, a profit-maximizing monopolist will adjust employment so that marginal revenue product equals market equilibrium input price. If only one variable productive service is used, the marginal revenue product curve is the monopolist's demand curve for the variable service in question.[2]

14.2.c Monopoly Demand for a Variable Productive Service When Several Variable Inputs Are Used

When more than one variable input is used in the production process, the marginal revenue product curve is not the demand curve for the reasons discussed in Chapter 13. However, the demand curve can be derived just as it was derived in that chapter.

Suppose, as in Figure 14.2.3, that at a given moment the market input price of a particular variable service is Ow_2 and that its marginal

---

[2] In the notation of footnote 1, let the demand and production functions be given, respectively, by

$$p = b(q), \qquad b' < 0; \qquad q = f(x), \qquad f' > 0. \qquad (14.2.1)$$

Let the competitively given price of the input be w. Thus total profit (π) may be written

$$\pi = pq - wx - F, \qquad (14.2.2)$$

where F is fixed cost. Using $(14.2.1)$, we may rewrite $(14.2.2)$ as

$$\pi = b[f(x)]f(x) - wx - F. \qquad (14.2.3)$$

Maximizing profit, one obtains

$$\frac{d\pi}{dx} = f(x)\frac{dp}{dq}\frac{dq}{dx} + p\frac{dq}{dx} - w = 0, \qquad (14.2.4)$$

or

$$\left(q\frac{dp}{dq} + p\right)\frac{dq}{dx} - w = 0. \qquad (14.2.5)$$

This may be written as

$$[b(q) + qb'(q)]f'(x) = w. \qquad (14.2.6)$$

This establishes the relation in the text, that is, $MRP = w$. It is further interesting to note that using the expression for marginal revenue developed in Part III, we may write

$$p\left(1 - \frac{1}{\eta}\right)f'(x) = w, \qquad (14.2.7)$$

showing the relations among commodity price, factor price, elasticity of demand, and the production function.

FIGURE 14.2.3

**Monopoly Demand for a Variable Productive Service
When Several Variable Services Are Used**

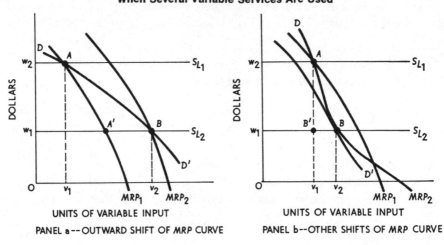

PANEL a--OUTWARD SHIFT OF *MRP* CURVE   PANEL b--OTHER SHIFTS OF *MRP* CURVE

revenue product is given by MRP_1. The monopolist attains equilibrium employment at point *A,* using Ov_1 units of the variable service. Next, let the price of the service fall to Ow_1 (because, for example, the market supply curve for the input shifts to the right). Other things being equal, the monopolist would expand along MRP_1 to A' in panel a. But other things are not equal.

Substitution, output, and profit maximizing effects exist, as explained in Chapter 13. Exactly the same analysis applies to a monopolist or set of oligopolists as applies to a set of perfectly competitive producers. The substitution, output, and profit maximizing effects, on balance, cause a shift of the marginal revenue product curve, which may be outward, inward, or twisted. Panel a, Figure 14.2.3, illustrates the first mentioned; panel b illustrates the last mentioned. In any event, as in Chapter 13, the fall in marginal revenue cannot completely offset the expansive forces. The factor demand function must be negatively sloped.[3]

---

[3] For proofs, see C. E. Ferguson, "Production, Prices, and the Theory of Jointly-Derived Input Demand Functions," *Economica,* N.S. vol. 33 (1966), pp. 454–61; C. E. Ferguson, " 'Inferior Factors' and the Theories of Production and Input Demand," *Economica,* N.S. vol. 35 (1968), pp. 140–50; C. E. Ferguson and Thomas R. Saving, "Long-Run Scale Adjustments of a Perfectly Competitive Firm and Industry," *American Economic Review,* vol. 59 (1969), pp. 774–83. The mathematical analysis contained in these papers is presented in greater detail in C. E. Ferguson, *The Neoclassical Theory of Production and Distribution* (London and New York: Cambridge University Press, 1969), chaps. 6 and 9.

The results of this section may be clearly summarized in the following:

Proposition: Input demand curves are negatively sloped regardless of the market organization in the product market.

14.2.d Market Demand for a Variable Productive Service

If a group of monopolists uses a variable productive service, the market demand for the service is simply the sum of the individual demands of the various monopolists. There are no *external* effects of expanded output on price; the effect of expansion is internal to each monopolist and has already been considered in obtaining his individual demand curve. Similarly, if all sorts of producers use the variable service, the market demand curve is the sum of the various component *industry* demand curves, where the industries may be composed of any number of firms. However, a minor qualification is required in cases of oligopoly and monopolistic competition. Since the situation is the same in both cases, only monopolistic competition is considered.

The demand curve for a variable service on the part of any one monopolistically competitive producer is derived in the same way as a monopolist's demand curve. But when all sellers in the product group expand output, market price diminishes (along Chamberlin's DD' curve), just as in a perfectly competitive industry. Thus to obtain the market demand from individual demand curves one must allow for the decrease in market price and marginal revenue. Graphically, the derivation is exactly like that in Figure 13.2.5, except that the individual demand curves are based upon marginal revenue product rather than the value of the marginal product.

14.2.e Equilibrium Price and Employment

The analysis of market equilibrium price and employment of a variable agent is no different whether the employers are monopolists or perfectly competitive producers. The determination of quasi rents is also the same; thus the discussion of Chapter 13, subsections 13.4.a and 13.4.b, applies equally well in the present context.

While the *analysis* does not change, there is one important difference to bear in mind: in cases of monopoly the demand curve is based upon the marginal revenue product of the variable productive service rather than upon the value of its marginal product. This gives rise to what is sometimes called monopolistic exploitation.[4]

---

[4] This term is apparently attributable to Joan Robinson. See her *Economics of Imperfect Competition* (London: Macmillan & Co., Ltd., 1933), pp. 281–91.

14.2.f Monopolistic Exploitation

According to Mrs. Robinson's definition, a productive service is exploited if it is employed at a price that is less than the value of its marginal product.[5] As we have seen in Chapter 13 and in the foregoing portion of this chapter, it is to the advantage of any individual producer (whether monopolist or competitor) to hire a variable service until the point is reached at which an additional unit adds precisely the same amount to total cost and total revenue. This is simply the input market implication of profit maximization.

When a perfectly competitive producer follows this rule, a variable service receives the value of its marginal product because price and marginal revenue are the same. This is not true, however, when the commodity market is imperfect. Marginal revenue is less than price, and marginal revenue product is correspondingly less than the value of the marginal product. Profit-maximizing behavior of imperfectly competitive producers causes the market price of a productive service to be less than the value of its marginal product.

If the market price of the commodity reflects its social value, the productive service receives less than its contribution to social value. Raising the input price is not a remedy, however, because producers would merely reduce the level of employment until marginal revenue product equaled the higher input price. The trouble initially lies in the fact that imperfectly competitive producers do not use as much of the resource as is socially desirable and do not attain the correspondingly desirable level of output. The fundamental difficulty rests in the difference between price (marginal social valuation) and marginal (social) cost at the profit-maximizing output. Thus so long as imperfectly competitive producers exist there must be some "monopolistic exploitation" of productive agents.

The significance of this "exploitation" can easily be exaggerated. Following Chamberlin, product differentiation is desired per se; and whenever there is differentiation, price and marginal revenue diverge so that "exploitation" is inevitable. Furthermore, the alternatives to "exploitation" are not attractive. Either there must be state ownership and operation of all nonperfectly competitive industries or else there must be rigid price control by the state. For a variety of reasons, either alternative is likely to raise more problems than it solves.[6]

---

[5] Ibid., p. 281.

[6] Cf. C. E. Ferguson, *A Macroeconomic Theory of Workable Competition* (Durham, N.C.: Duke University Press, 1964).

14.3 MONOPSONY: MONOPOLY IN THE INPUT MARKET

The analysis of pricing and employment of productive services has so far rested upon the assumption that each producer (buyer of the service in question) cannot affect the market price of the service by changes in his utilization of it. This assumption obviously does not hold in all situations. There are sometimes only a few, and in the limit one, purchasers of a productive service. Where there is a single buyer of an input a *monopsony* is said to exist; if there are several buyers *oligopsony* is the proper designation.

A wide variety of categories can be classified. Broadly speaking, commodity markets may be perfectly competitive, monopolistically competitive, oligopolistic, or monopolistic. For each of these four types of commodity market organizations the input market can be either a monopsony or an oligopsony. However, the analytical principle is the same irrespective of the organization of the commodity and input markets (so long as there is not perfect competition in the input market). Thus we restrict our attention to the case in which there is monopoly in the commodity market combined with monopsony in the input market.

14.3.a Marginal Expense of Input

The supply curve for most productive services or production agents is positively sloped. A buyer in a perfectly competitive input market views the supply of input curve as a horizontal line because his purchases are so small, relative to the market, that changes on his part do not perceptibly affect market price. A monopsonist, however, being the only buyer in the market, faces a positively sloped market supply of input curve. As a result, changes in his volume of purchases do affect input price; as he expands input usage, input price increases. The monopsonist, therefore, must consider the *marginal expense* of purchasing an additional unit of a variable productive agent.

Computation of the marginal expense of input is shown in Table 14.3.1, and the supply and marginal expense of input curves are illustrated in Figure 14.3.1. Columns 1 and 2 show the supply curve, plotted as the right-most curve in Figure 14.3.1. When only one unit of the variable agent is employed its cost is $2; thus the total cost of the input, and total variable cost when only one agent is used, is also $2. If two units are used the supply price per unit is $2.50; total cost of the input is $5, an increase of $3 over the previous total cost, even though the

TABLE 14.3.1

Monopsony and the Marginal Expense of Input

Units of Variable Input	Price per Unit	Total Cost of Input	Marginal Expense of Input
1........................	$2.00	$ 2.00	—
2........................	2.50	5.00	$ 3.00
3........................	3.00	9.00	4.00
4........................	3.50	14.00	5.00
5........................	4.00	20.00	6.00
6........................	4.50	27.00	7.00
7........................	5.00	35.00	8.00
8........................	5.50	44.00	9.00
9........................	6.00	54.00	10.00
10........................	6.50	65.00	11.00

price per unit increased by only 50 cents. In other words, hiring an additional unit of input increases total cost by more than the price of the unit because all units employed receive the new, higher price.

The marginal expense of input, the left-most curve in Figure 14.3.1, is calculated by successive subtraction in the "total cost of input" column. Since the price per unit rises as employment increases, the marginal expense of input exceeds its price at all employment levels; and the marginal expense of input curve is positively sloped, lies to the left of the supply of input curve, and typically rises more rapidly than the latter.[7]

___

[7] These statements can easily be proven. Let the input supply function in inverse form be

$$w = g(x),$$ (14.7.1)

where w is input price, x is the quantity of the input supplied, and $g'(x) = dw/dx > 0$ by assumption (i.e., the input supply curve is positively sloped). Total variable cost is

$$C(x) = wx = xg(x).$$ (14.7.2)

By definition, the marginal expense of input is

$$MEI = \frac{dC(x)}{dx} = g(x) + xg'(x) = w + x\frac{dw}{dx}.$$ (14.7.3)

Since $g'(x) > 0$ by assumption, a comparison of (14.7.1) and (14.7.3) shows that the marginal expense of input curve must lie above the input supply curve for each quantity supplied. Usually, the MEI curve is positive and rises more rapidly than the input supply curve. The slope of the latter is $g'(x)$, while the slope of the former is given by

$$\frac{dMEI}{dx} = 2g'(x) + xg''(x).$$ (14.7.4)

FIGURE 14.3.1

Marginal Expense of Input

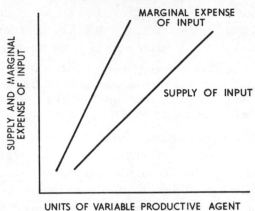

UNITS OF VARIABLE PRODUCTIVE AGENT

Definition: The marginal expense of input is the increase in total cost (and in total variable cost and in total cost of input) attributable to the addition of one unit of the variable productive agent.

14.3.b Price and Employment under Monopsony When One Variable Input Is Used

The market demand curve for a productive service is the demand curve of the single buyer under monopsony conditions. Furthermore, if

---

Thus *MEI* must be positive and have the steeper slope unless the input supply curve is *very* concave (i.e., $g'' < 0$ and large in absolute value).

Finally, we may relate the *MEI* to input price and input supply elasticity in the same way that marginal revenue is related to commodity price and the elasticity of commodity demand. By definition, the elasticity of input supply is

$$\theta = \frac{ax}{aw}\frac{w}{x}. \tag{14.7.5}$$

Now write (14.7.3) as

$$MEI = w + x\frac{dw}{dx} = w\left(1 + \frac{x}{w}\frac{dw}{dx}\right). \tag{14.7.6}$$

Using (14.7.5) in (14.7.6), one obtains

$$MEI = w\left(1 + \frac{1}{\theta}\right). \tag{14.7.7}$$

When the input supply curve is perfectly elastic, $\theta \to \infty$ and $MEI = w$, that is, monopsony does not exist.

Exercise: State and explain all of the relations between $MR = \left(1 - \frac{1}{\eta}\right)$ and $MEI = w\left(1 + \frac{1}{\theta}\right)$.

only one variable input is used in the production process, the demand curve is the monopsonist's marginal revenue product curve. Confronting the monopsonist is the positively sloped supply of input curve and the higher marginal expense of input curve. The situation is illustrated in Figure 14.3.2. Using this graph we will prove the following

Proposition: A profit-maximizing monopsonist will employ a variable productive service until the point is reached at which the marginal expense of input equals its marginal revenue product. The price of the input is determined by the corresponding point on its supply curve.

The proof of this proposition follows immediately from the definitions of marginal revenue product and marginal expense of input. Marginal revenue product is the addition to total revenue attributable to the addition of one unit of the variable input; the marginal expense of input is the addition to total cost resulting from the employment of an additional unit. Therefore, so long as marginal revenue product exceeds the marginal expense of input, profit can be augmented by expanding input usage. On the other hand, if the marginal expense of input exceeds its marginal revenue product, profit is less or loss greater than if fewer units of the input were employed. Consequently, profit is maximized by employing that quantity of the variable service for which marginal expense of input equals marginal revenue product.

This equality occurs at point E in Figure 14.3.2; $O\bar{v}$ units of the service are accordingly employed. At this point the supply of input curve becomes particularly relevant. $O\bar{v}$ units of the variable productive agent are associated with point E' on the supply of input curve. Thus $O\bar{v}$ units

FIGURE 14.3.2

Price and Employment under Monopsony

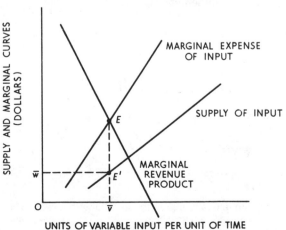

UNITS OF VARIABLE INPUT PER UNIT OF TIME

will be offered at $O\bar{w}$ per unit. Hence Ow is the market equilibrium input price corresponding to market equilibrium employment $O\bar{v}.$[8]

14.3.c Price and Employment under Monopsony When Several Variable Inputs Are Used

To secure the least-cost combination of variable inputs an entrepreneur must employ productive services in such proportion that the marginal rate of technical substitution equals the input-price ratio. But this proposition holds if, and only if, the inputs are purchased in perfectly competitive markets. Otherwise a change in input composition entails a change in relative input prices.

Let us illustrate this algebraically. Suppose there are two variable inputs, capital (K) and labor (L). Denote the marginal physical products by MP_K and MP_L and their market prices by r and w respectively. If the input markets are perfectly competitive, the least-cost combination rule requires that

$$\frac{MP_K}{MP_L} = \frac{r}{w} . \tag{14.3.1}$$

----

[8] This proposition may easily be proved by using footnotes 1 and 7. Summarizing,

$$p = b(q) , \qquad q = f(x) , \qquad \text{and} \qquad w = g(x) \tag{14.8.1}$$

are the commodity demand function, the production function, and the input supply function respectively. Ignoring fixed cost, the profit function is

$$\pi = pq - wx = qb(q) - xg(x) = f(x)b[f(x)] - xg(x) . \tag{14.8.2}$$

The entrepreneur determines the amount of the variable input so as to maximize profit:

$$\frac{d\pi}{dx} = b[f(x)]f'(x) + \frac{db(q)}{dq}f'(x)f(x) - g(x) - xg'(x) = 0 , \tag{14.8.3}$$

or

$$\left[b(q) + q\frac{db}{dq} \right] f'(x) = [g(x) + xg'(x)] . \tag{14.8.4}$$

By footnote 1, the left-hand side of (14.8.4) is marginal revenue product. By footnote 7, the right-hand side is the marginal expense of input. Thus the theorem is proved.

Also using footnotes 1 and 7, we may write this relation as

$$p\left(1 - \frac{1}{\eta}\right)f'(x) = w\left(1 + \frac{1}{\theta}\right) . \tag{14.8.5}$$

Exercise: State and explain the interesting relations implicit in equation (14.8.5).

Stated alternatively,

$$\frac{MP_K}{r} = \frac{MP_L}{w}. \tag{14.3.2}$$

Equation (14.3.2) implies that the marginal product per dollar spent on each input must be the same. The *reason* for this rule is that marginal physical product represents the additional revenue, and input price the additional cost attributable to the input. This holds for both competitive and monopolistic commodity markets; price changes as output changes in monopoly markets, but the price change is the same whether output is expanded by increasing the employment of capital, the employment of labor, or both.

The proposition stated in equation (14.3.2) is fairly obvious, but it might be well to discuss it some more. Suppose

$$\frac{MP_K}{r} > \frac{MP_L}{w}. \tag{14.3.3}$$

By inequality (14.3.3), a dollar's worth of capital contributes more to output than a dollar's worth of labor, at the *present* capital-labor ratio. If the input markets are perfectly competitive, rates of employment can be changed without affecting input prices. Therefore the entrepreneur would substitute capital for labor because he can obtain the same output for less cost. As he makes this substitution, the marginal product of capital declines and the marginal product of labor increases. With market determined r and w, the entrepreneur will continue the substitution until equality (14.3.2) is established.

If the input markets are monopsonistic, changes in the volume of employment cause corresponding changes in input prices. In particular, the entrepreneur must look to the marginal expense of input (MEI) rather than its market price when making employment decisions. Consider labor only, for the moment. An additional unit adds its marginal product to output, but it does not add w to total cost; instead, with a positively sloped input supply curve it adds its marginal expense MEI_L.

Suppose the capital-labor ratio in production at a given moment is such that

$$\frac{MP_K}{MEI_K} > \frac{MP_L}{MEI_L}. \tag{14.3.4}$$

Inequality (14.3.4) has the following meaning: at the prevailing input combination an entrepreneur can obtain a greater increase in output per additional dollar of cost by employing capital rather than labor. Consequently, he can maintain the same output but reduce cost by substituting capital for labor. As he does so, two forces work to bring about an equality: as the employment of capital expands and that of labor declines (a) the marginal product of capital declines and that of labor increases and (b) the marginal expense of input of capital rises and that of labor declines. Since the entrepreneur can reduce cost so long as the inequality in expression (14.3.4) prevails, he will substitute capital for labor until

$$\frac{MP_K}{MEI_K} = \frac{MP_L}{MEI_L} . \tag{14.3.5}$$

When equality (14.3.5) obtains, no change in input composition will reduce cost. Consequently, we have proved that:[9]

Proposition: A monopsonist who uses several variable productive inputs will adjust input composition until the ratio of marginal product to marginal expense of input is the same for all variable inputs used. The least-cost combination is accordingly obtained when the marginal rate of technical substitution equals the marginal expense of input ratio.

---

[9] The proof of this proposition is accomplished by an easy extension of footnote 8. Let

$$p = h(q) , \qquad q = f(K, L) , \qquad r = g(K) , \qquad w = m(L) \tag{14.9.1}$$

be the commodity demand function, the production function, the supply of capital function, and the labor supply function respectively. The profit function is, accordingly,

$$\pi = qh(q) - Kg(K) - Lm(L) . \tag{14.9.2}$$

The entrepreneur adjusts both inputs so as to maximize profit:

$$\frac{\partial \pi}{\partial K} = q\frac{dh}{dq}\frac{\partial f}{\partial K} + h(a)\frac{\partial f}{\partial K} - g(K) - Kg'(K) = 0 , \tag{14.9.3}$$

$$\frac{\partial \pi}{\partial L} = q\frac{dh}{dq}\frac{\partial f}{\partial L} + h(q)\frac{\partial f}{\partial L} - m(L) - Lm'(L) = 0 , \tag{14.9.4}$$

or

$$[qh'(q) + h(q)]\frac{\partial f}{\partial K} = g(K) + Kg'(K), \tag{14.9.5}$$

$$[qh'(q) + h(q)]\frac{\partial f}{\partial L} = m(L) + Lm'(L) . \tag{14.9.6}$$

The two equations just above state that the marginal revenue product of each input must equal its marginal expense of input. Taking the ratio of the two equations and canceling the marginal revenue term yields

$$\frac{MP_K}{MP_L} = \frac{MEI_K}{MEI_L} . \tag{14.9.7}$$

Transforming (14.9.7) yields the relation stated in the text.

In the two-input situation, we have

$$\frac{MP_L}{MP_K} = \frac{MEI_L}{MEI_K} .$$ (14.3.6)

Thus one sees that rule (14.3.1) for perfectly competitive input markets is a special case of rule (14.3.6); rule (14.3.1) is valid because in perfectly competitive input markets, the marginal expense of input is precisely equal to its market price.[10]

14.3.d Monopsonistic Exploitation

In subsection 14.2.f it was shown that monopoly in the commodity market leads to "monopolistic exploitation" in the input market. Monopolistic exploitation exists in the sense that each productive service is paid its marginal revenue product which, because of the negatively sloped commodity demand curve, is less than the value of its marginal product. Each unit of resource receives the amount which, on average, it contributes to the firm's total receipts; but the units of resources do not receive the values of their marginal products.

Monopsonistic exploitation is something in addition to this, as illustrated by Figure 14.3.3. The figure is constructed to cover a variety of cases; the curves would doubtlessly change as the type of market or-

---

[10] An important matter is here relegated to a footnote because even a graphical exposition requires some mathematics. *But note:* the student, whether mathematically trained or not, should read this footnote.

The relation in equation (14.3.6) in the text states that the marginal rate of technical substitution of capital for labor equals the ratio of their marginal expenses of input. This is the "rule" for optimum input proportions. As explained in the text and in footnote 9, the "rule" is based upon profit maximization. It can, of course, be so based. But the important point is that this rule can be established upon the much weaker assumption that entrepreneurs minimize the cost of producing a given output or maximize the output obtainable from a given expenditure upon resources.

Just as in Chapter 6, this may be shown graphically by use of isoquants and isocost curves. The mathematics enters in showing that the isocost curve is not a straight line. Everything else follows from the definitions introduced above.

Exercise: For mathematically trained students only. Suppose $\overline{C}$ is spent on resources. Thus the isocost curve is $Kg(K) + Lm(L) = \overline{C}$. Show the following relations: (a) the isocost curve is "usually" concave, but may be convex if an input supply function is negatively sloped: (b) the "rule" stated in equation (14.3.6) mathematically; (c) if an input supply function is negatively sloped, *economically* efficient operation may require the entrepreneur to produce in the *technologically* inefficient region (i.e., the region in which one marginal product is negative).

Exercise: Give an economically rational explanation of (c) above.

Reference for exercises: Ferguson, *The Neoclassical Theory of Production and Distribution*, chaps. 7 and 8.

FIGURE 14.3.3

Monopsonistic Exploitation

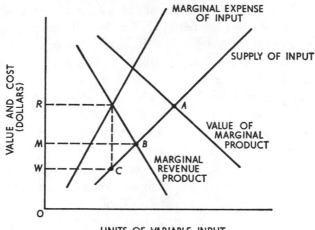

ganization changes. However, allowing for this, Figure 14.3.3 is a schematic device for illustrating monopolistic and monopsonistic exploitation.

First, suppose both the commodity and input markets are perfectly competitive. The value of the marginal product curve is the industry demand for input curve.[11] As you will recall, it is not the *direct* sum of the individual curves; however, it does represent the value of the input's marginal product to the industry as a whole. Demand and supply intersect at point *A*, each unit of input receiving the market value of its marginal product.

Next, let the commodity market be monopolistic, while the input market is perfectly competitive. The marginal revenue product curve represents the collection of monopoly demand curves (just as the value of the marginal product curve represents the collection of individual demand curves). Equilibrium is attained at point *B*. The difference between the wage rates corresponding to points *A* and *B* ($OR - OM = RM$) is the "monopolistic exploitation" of the input. Because of mo-

---

[11] The concept of a *VMP* curve for an industry is somewhat ambiguous. For a firm it is clear: it is the input's marginal product multiplied by the *constant* (to the firm) commodity price. For an industry it is somewhat different. For each level of employment and output, industry *VMP* is the marginal product of the input (efficient operation of firms assures equality among firms) multiplied by the market price associated with that level of output. Of course, market price decreases as output increases; and the various marginal products are multiplied by the relevant, *but changing*, market price.

nopolistic exploitation, fewer units of the input are employed and the unit price of each is less. Nonetheless, each unit of input receives an amount equal to what its employment adds to total receipts.

Finally, suppose there is monopoly in the commodity market and monopsony in the input market. Equilibrium is attained at C, at a still lower price and employment level. Monopsonistic exploitation is represented by the difference between points A and C, or by the difference in input prices between the competitive and monopsonistic equilibria ($OR - OW = RW$). The portion RM is attributable to monopoly in the commodity market; it is not unique to monopsony. The additional portion MW, however, is uniquely attributable to monopsony (or more generally, to oligopsony). The existence of the differential MW is caused by the fact that each unit of input contributes OM to total receipts but receives only OW in return. Thus the chief feature of monopsonistic exploitation is that each unit of input does not receive in pay an amount equal to its contribution to total receipts.

In subsection 14.2.f it was indicated that while monopolistic exploitation could be removed, the "cure" might be worse than the "disease." Indeed, within a free enterprise economic system monopolistic exploitation is bound to arise. Even bona fide product differentiation causes this type of "exploitation." The same is not true of monopsonistic exploitation. Countermeasures exist, and they are not fundamentally destructive to a free enterprise system.

14.3.e Monopsony and the Economic Effects of Labor Unions

A study of labor unions and of the collective-bargaining process, even on a purely theoretical level, is beyond the scope of this work.[12] However, the issue of monopsonistic exploitation allows one briefly to indicate the economic effects of labor unions. Consider any typical labor market with some kind of supply of labor curve; for simplicity, assume that it is positively sloped. If the workers in this market are unionized, the union bargaining representative fundamentally has one power to exert: he can make the effective supply of labor curve a horizontal line at any wage level he wishes, at least until the horizontal line reaches the existing supply curve. Thus the marginal expense of input is the same as the supply price of labor over the horizontal stretch of the

---

[12] For an excellent theoretical treatment, see Allan M. Cartter, *Theory of Wages and Employment* (Homewood, Ill.: Richard D. Irwin, Inc., 1959), pp. 77–133.

union supply curve. That is to say, the union representative can name a wage rate and guarantee the availability of workers at this price.[13]

To introduce this topic, let us suppose the labor market in question is perfectly competitive (large number of purchasers of this type of labor) and unorganized. The situation is depicted in panel a, Figure 14.3.4, where D_L and S_L are the demand for and supply of labor re-

FIGURE 14.3.4

Effects of a Labor Union in a Perfectly Competitive Labor Market

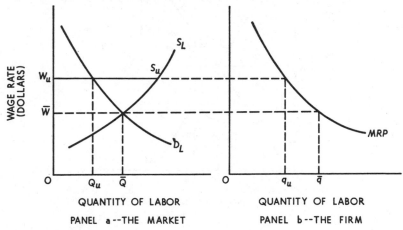

QUANTITY OF LABOR   QUANTITY OF LABOR

PANEL a--THE MARKET   PANEL b--THE FIRM

spectively. The market equilibrium wage rate is $O\overline{W}$, and $O\overline{Q}$ units of labor are employed. Each individual firm (panel b) accordingly employs $O\overline{q}$ units. Next, suppose the labor market is unionized. If the union does not attempt to raise wages the situation might remain as it is. However, scoring wage increases is the *raison d'être* of unions. Thus suppose the bargaining agency sets OW_u as the wage rate; in other words, the union supply of labor curve $W_u S_u S_L$ is established. OQ_u units of labor are employed, each firm taking Oq_u units. The result is a rise in wages and a decline in employment. In perfectly competitive input markets this is *all* unions can do.

This does not necessarily mean a union cannot benefit its members. If the demand for labor is inelastic, an increase in the wage rate will result in an increase in total wages paid to the workers, even though the number of workers employed is less. If the union can somehow equita-

---

[13] This is, of course, an heroic oversimplification, but it is a useful one for analytical purposes.

FIGURE 14.3.5

**Economic Effects of a Labor Union
in a Monopsonistic Labor Market**

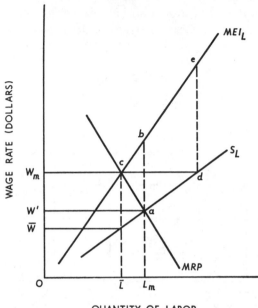

QUANTITY OF LABOR

bly divide the proceeds of OQ_u employed workers among the $O\bar{Q}$ potential workers, all will benefit. Such a division is easy to achieve. Suppose $OQ_u = \frac{1}{2}O\bar{Q}$ and that a 40-hour week characterizes the market. Then OQ_u units of labor can be furnished by having $O\bar{Q}$ units work a 20-hour week.

The other side of the coin is worth noting, however. If the demand for labor is elastic, total wage receipts will decline and the union cannot compensate the $Q_u\bar{Q}$ workers who are unemployed because of the increase in wage rates. Thus in perfectly competitive labor markets labor unions are not an unmitigated blessing.[14]

In monopsonistic or oligopsonistic markets, however, unions *must* benefit their members if they employ rational policies. Consider the monopsony labor market represented by Figure 14.3.5. If the labor force is not organized, equilibrium is attained at point *c*, where marginal

---

[14] ***Exercise:*** Suppose panel a, Figure 14.3.4, represents the market for unskilled labor in absence of a minimum-wage law. What are the market effects of the establishment of a minimum wage by some government agency? Is there any empirical evidence that the analytical result you obtain is descriptive of the real world?

revenue product equals the marginal expense of input (based upon the positively sloped supply of input curve S_L). The equilibrium wage is $O\overline{W}$, and equilibrium employment is $O\overline{L}$. Now suppose the workers establish a union that bargains collectively with the monopsonist.

At one extreme the union may attempt to achieve maximum employment for its members. To this end, it establishes the supply of labor curve $W'aS_L$. The associated marginal expense of input curve accordingly becomes $W'abMEI_L$. Marginal revenue product equals the marginal expense of input at point a; OL_m units of labor are therefore employed at the wage OW'. Consequently, as one alternative, the union can achieve a small increase in wages accompanied by an increase in the number of workers employed. Each unit of labor receives its contribution to the firm's total receipts; the exploitation uniquely attributable to monopsony is eliminated.

At another extreme, suppose the union decides to maintain the initial level of employment $O\overline{L}$. It accordingly establishes the supply curve $W_m dS_L$. The corresponding marginal expense of input curve is $W_m deMEI_L$. Marginal revenue product equals the marginal expense of input at point c; hence equilibrium employment is $O\overline{L}$ and the associated equilibrium wage is OW_m. This wage rate is the maximum attainable without a reduction in employment below the pre-union level. At the wage OW_m, however, the union can achieve a substantial wage increase without affecting employment. Again, the unique portion of monopsonistic exploitation is removed.

We have considered only two extremes. The union can, in fact, select intermediate policies, scoring increases in both employment and the wage rate. The union can harm its members only if the demand for labor is elastic, and it sets the supply of labor curve so that the equilibrium wage exceeds OW_m. But even then the unique portion of monopsonistic exploitation would be eliminated. Thus we have a general principle that broadly describes the economic effects of labor unions: labor unions can eliminate the portion of total monopsonistic exploitation that is uniquely attributable to monopsony in the labor market; however, the portion attributable to monopoly can in no way be eliminated by trade union activity.

QUESTIONS AND EXERCISES

1. Since monopolists do not pay factors of production the value of their marginal products, how do monopolists retain factors when perfect competitors use the same kind of resources in producing their output?

2. Provide an economic analysis of the U.S. minimum wage law. Do the same thing for a *state* (or county, or city) minimum wage law.

3. The government imposes a ceiling price on commodity A but not on the competing commodity B. C, D, and E are factors used in producing A, while D, E, and F are factors used in producing B. C is used in the production of A only and not in the production of any other commodity in the economy. Discuss the effects of this ceiling price on the product and factor markets.

4. "Without collective bargaining, the workers' market disadvantage would enable the owners of other productive agents to appropriate income that would otherwise go to labor." Discuss.

5. Assume that an industrial union's primary purpose is to raise the wages of its members above the competitive level. (*a*) Explain on a theoretical level how this increase might be accomplished; (*b*) what conditions would make the union's job easier?

6. Consider a trade union that is strong enough to prevent nonmembers from working at the trade in question. For simplicity, assume that membership is not affected by the level of returns to members. Finally, assume that there is immigration into the country of unskilled workers. What will be the effect of the immigration on the incomes of the union members? What factors tend to increase income, what factors tend to cause it to decline? Is there a clear balance in favor of either increase or decline?

7. "If a union succeeds in raising wages, it will cause the ratio of the cost of union labor to total cost to rise." Discuss.

SUGGESTED READINGS

Cartter, Allan M. *Theory of Wages and Employment,* pp. 77–133. Homewood, Ill.: Richard D. Irwin, Inc., 1959.

Hicks, John R. *The Theory of Wages.* London: Macmillan & Co., Ltd., 1932.

Robinson, Joan. *The Economics of Imperfect Competition,* pp. 218–28, 281–304. London: Macmillan & Co., Ltd., 1933.

Advanced reading, part IV

I. MARGINAL PRODUCTIVITY AND INPUT DEMAND

Chamberlin, E. H. "Monopolistic Competition and the Productivity Theory of Distribution," *Explorations in Economics,* pp. 237–49. New York: McGraw-Hill Book Co., Inc., 1936.

Douglas, P. H. *The Theory of Wages.* New York: The Macmillan Co., 1934.

Ferguson, C. E. " 'Inferior Factors' and the Theories of Production and Input Demand," *Economica,* May, 1968.

———. *The Neoclassical Theory of Production and Distribution,* chaps. 6 and 7. London and New York: Cambridge University Press, 1969.

———. "Production, Prices, and the Theory of Jointly Derived Input Demand Functions," *Economica,* November, 1966.

———, and Saving, Thomas R. "Long-Run Scale Adjustments of a Perfectly Competitive Firm and Industry," *American Economic Review,* vol. 59 (1969), pp. 774–83.

Hicks, John R. *The Theory of Wages.* London: Macmillan & Co., Ltd., 1932.

Mosak, Jacob L. "Interrelations of Production, Price and Derived Demand," *Journal of Political Economy,* vol. 46 (1938), pp. 761–87.

Pfouts, R. W. "Distribution Theory in a Certain Case of Oligopoly and Oligopsony," *Metroeconomica,* vol. 7 (1955), pp. 137–46.

Schultz, Henry. "Marginal Productivity and the General Pricing Process," *Journal of Political Economy,* vol. 37 (1929), pp. 505–51.

Stigler, George J. "Production and Distribution in the Short Run," *Journal of Political Economy,* vol. 47 (1939), pp. 305–27.

II. DISTRIBUTION AND RELATIVE SHARES

Ferguson, C. E. "Neoclassical Theory of Technical Progress and Relative Factor Shares," *Southern Economic Journal,* vol. 34 (1968), pp. 490–504.

————. *The Neoclassical Theory of Production and Distribution,* chaps. 11 and 12. London and New York: Cambridge University Press, 1969.

Robinson, Joan. "Euler's Theorem and the Problem of Distribution," *Economic Journal,* vol. 44 (1934), pp. 398–414.

Stigler, George J. *Production and Distribution Theories.* New York: The Macmillan Co., 1941.

part V

Theory of general equilibrium and economic welfare

Well over 100 years ago Frederic Bastiat, a noted French economist, wrote about the Paris of his day. Hundreds of thousands of people then lived in Paris, each consuming a wide variety of commodities, especially food products not produced in the city. The survival of the city required the constant influx of goods and services. No single agency planned the daily inflow of commodities; but each day goods did arrive in approximately correct quantities: Paris survived. "Imagination is baffled when it tries to appreciate the vast multiplicity of commodities which must enter tomorrow in order to preserve the inhabitants from falling prey to the convulsions of famine, rebellion, and pillage," Bastiat wrote. "Yet all sleep, and their slumbers are not disturbed for a single minute by the prospect of each a frightful catastrophe."

Paris survived because of the unplanned cooperation of many people, most of whom competed against each other. Not for altruistic motives, to be sure, but for the profit to be gained from selling in the Paris market. Even before the days of Bastiat, Adam Smith had observed the effects of cooperation in production. Smith visited a small pin factory, one doubtless primitive by modern standards. Yet Smith was so struck by the gain in productivity resulting from cooperation and the specialization of labor that he wrote an account now classic in economic literature:

One man draws out the wire, another straights it, a third cuts it, a fourth points it, a fifth grinds it at the top for receiving the head; to make the head requires two or three distinct operations; to put it on is a peculiar business; to whiten it is another; it is even a trade by itself to put them into paper. . . . I have seen a small factory of this kind where ten men only were employed and where some of them consequently performed two or three distinct operations. But though they were very poor and therefore but indifferently accommodated with the necessary machinery, they could, when they exerted themselves, make among them about twelve pounds of pins in a day. There are in a pound upwards of 4,000 pins of middling size. Those ten persons, therefore, could make among them upwards of 48,000 pins a day. . . . But if they had all wrought separately and independently . . . they could certainly not each of them make twenty, perhaps not one pin in a day. . . .

Specialization and division of labor make possible a larger output than if each person worked alone and were self-sufficient. But self-sufficiency does guarantee that the consumer gets what he wants, or what he wants most and what is within his ability to achieve. When each person is not self-sufficient, the economy either must be *planned* by some central agency or there must be some mechanism that accomplishes the same goal. Adam Smith chose to call this mechanism the "invisible hand"; in the terminology of today it might better be called a "great IBM machine in the sky." But whatever the terminology, a free enterprise price system generally functions so as to achieve the goals of state planning, usually much more efficiently than planned economies achieve them. Economic welfare under a free enterprise system is the topic of Chapter 16, after we analyze general economic equilibrium in Chapter 15.

To this point our discussion has focused only upon the economic behavior of single economic agents or of single industries or product groups. But there are millions of economic agents in the economy, and we have not yet seen how the behavior of each is coordinated to achieve a general equilibrium.

Looked at differently, the familiar graph in Figure V.1 illustrates the problem. On the one hand, households function both as consumers and resource suppliers. On the other hand, business firms use the resources, organize production, and sell the products of the process. There is a flow of *real* productive services from households to businesses and a return flow of *real* goods and services from business firms to households. If a barter system were feasible in an advanced industrial nation,

FIGURE V.1

Circular Flow of Economic Activity

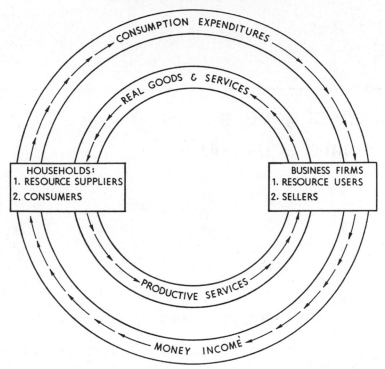

we should have to go no further. But it is not; money must be introduced.

Rather than trade output for input, business firms pay households money income for the productive services supplied. In their roles as consumers, households create a counterflow of consumption expenditures to business firms, exchanging their money income for the real goods and services supplied to them. Thus there is a monetary flow in one direction to offset each real flow in the opposite direction. The problem of general equilibrium analysis is to determine the process by which the various flows balance.

15

Theory of general
economic equilibrium

15.1 INTRODUCTION

According to the principle of maximization adhered to throughout the book, each economic agent attains an equilibrium position when *something* is maximized. A consumer maximizes satisfaction subject to a budget constraint; an entrepreneur maximizes profit, possibly subject to the constraint imposed by a production function; workers may determine their labor supply curves by maximizing satisfaction derived from leisure, subject to given wage rates. In terms of an old cliché, we have studied the trees fairly intensely but we have not yet seen the forest.

The problem of forests arises, however. Millions of economic agents pursue their own goals and strive for their own equilibrium without particular regard for others. The problem is to determine whether the more-or-less independent behavior of economic agents is consistent with each agent's attaining equilibrium. All economic agents, whether consumer, producer, or resource supplier, are *interdependent;* will *independent* action by each lead to a position in which equilibrium is achieved by all? This is the problem of general (static or stationary) economic equilibrium.

To get a handle on the concept of general economic equilibrium we will examine a variety of relatively simple cases. The concepts and

426

propositions that hold in these simple cases also apply to more complex economies albeit with a good deal of additional mathematical notation.

15.1.a   A Simple Two-Person Economy

Consider an economy consisting of two individuals, say two farmers. Each farmer owns a fixed amount of land which can be used to produce a homogeneous output. The output of each farm depends on the amount of labor put to work on the farm. We will think of each farmer in two separate roles. On the one hand each farmer is an entrepreneur who hires labor to work on his farm. He pays labor the market wage, which is denominated in terms of the output of the farm, and keeps the remaining output as a rent on his land. On the other hand each farmer can be viewed as a household which consumes farm output and supplies labor. The rental income earned by the farmer *qua* entrepreneur is part of the income the farmer spends *qua* consumer. In subsection 15.1.b, we examine the farmers in their role as entrepreneurs making output decisions and deciding how much labor to hire. In subsection 15.1.c, we examine the farmers in their role as householders deciding how much to consume and how much labor to supply. Finally, we bring both sides of the market together to show how a general equilibrium is achieved. The objective is to illustrate the circular flow of economic activity in Figure V.1.

15.1.b   The Farmer as Enterpreneur

The explanation of the farmer as an entrepreneur is based on the following assumptions:

*e*1:   Output of the farm is an increasing function of the amount of labor used on the farm, and since the amount of land is assumed to be constant, the law of diminishing returns applies to labor. This is the situation described in Chapter 5.

*e*2:   Each farmer acts as a price-taker both with respect to his sales of output and his hiring of labor. We use the output of the farm as *numeraire* or unit of account and hence set its price equal to one. The wage rate is given by w.[1]

---

[1] The reader will recall from earlier discussion that we are dealing with *relative* prices in this book. Thus, if p is the output price and w the wage rate, the equilibrium determines only w/p (or p/w) not p and w separately. Thus, we are justified in setting $p = 1$ for expositional purposes. Note that w is the *real* wage when this convention is used.

e3: Each farmer, when acting as entrepreneur, chooses output and employment, given the wage rate, to maximize the rental income of the land. The rental income will be the amount of output left after wages have been paid.

To see how the farmer behaves in his role as entrepreneur given these assumptions, we consider the case of the first farmer, called farmer 1. Farmer 1 has a production function that relates labor input to farm output as shown by the curved line $Q_{S_1} = f_1(L_{D_1})$ in Figure 15.1.1. Q_{S_1} refers to the output of farmer 1, L_{D_1} is the amount of labor demanded by farmer 1 for use on his farm, and $f_1(L_{D_1})$ is the production function of the first farmer. f_1 is written as a function of labor only since land is assumed fixed. The function $f_1(L_{D_1})$ is concave in accordance with the assumption *e1* that the law of diminishing returns applies to labor.

Now suppose the wage rate is *w*. The total wage bill for farmer 1 will be wL_{D_1}. This is shown in Figure 15.1.1 as a straight line with slope *w*. At any given use of labor on the farm (along the horizontal axis) output is given by the line $Q_{S_1} = f_1(L_{D_1})$, total wages are the corresponding point on the line wL_{D_1} and the difference between $f_1(L_{D_1})$ and wL_{D_1} is the output left for the entrepreneur after wages have been paid (i.e., the rent on the land). We know from Chapter 13 that rent on land will be maximized when the value of the marginal product of labor equals the wage rate. Since the price of output is set

FIGURE 15.1.1

Demand for Labor and Supply of Output

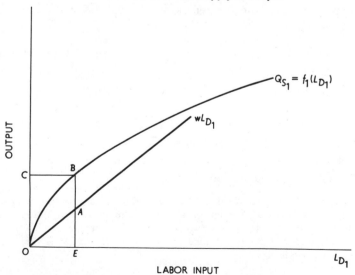

FIGURE 15.1.2

Aggregate Demand for Labor

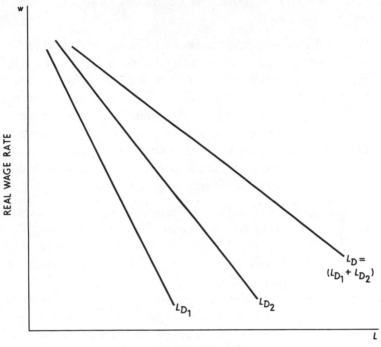

REAL WAGE RATE

L_{D_1}

L_{D_2}

$L_D = (L_{D_1} + L_{D_2})$

LABOR DEMANDED

L

at 1, this means that the distance between $f_1(L_{D_1})$ and wL_{D_1} is maximized when L_{D_1} is chosen so that the slope of $f_1(L_{D_1})$ is equal to the wage rate.[2] In Figure 15.1.1, when the wage rate is w the farmer hires OE units of labor, produces EB ($= OC$) units of output, pays EA in wages and keeps BA ($= EB - EA$) as rent on land. Since the slope of $f_1(L_{D_1})$ is decreasing as more labor is used, it follows that to maximize rental income the farmer will hire more labor as the wage rate decreases and less labor as the wage rate increases. Hence, we get a demand for labor function that is inversely related to the wage rate as shown by the line L_{D_1} in Figure 15.1.2.

By similar arguments for farmer 2, we can derive his demand for labor. This is shown by L_{D_2} in Figure 15.1.2. The total demand for labor at any given wage rate is the sum of the demands for labor by farmer 1 and farmer 2. In Figure 15.1.2, this is shown by the line L_D, which is the horizontal sum of L_{D_1} and L_{D_2} at each wage rate.

---

[2] The rent on the land is the residual $f_1(L_{D_1}) - wL_{D_1}$, and this is maximized when $f_1'(L_{D_1}) = w$. The slope, $f_1'(L_{D_1})$, is the marginal product of labor.

15.1.c   The Farmer as Consumer-Laborer

The explanation of the farmer as a consumer-laborer is based on the following assumptions.

$c1$:   Farmer 1 chooses consumption and the amount of labor he supplies so as to maximize a utility function $U_1(Q_{D_1}, L_{S_1})$. Q_{D_1} is the amount of consumption of farmer 1 and L_{S_1} is the amount of labor supplied by farmer 1. The utility function U_1 is increasing in Q_{D_1} and decreasing in L_{S_1}. In other words, the farmer gains utility from more consumption and loses utility from more labor (i.e., less leisure). Similarly farmer 2 acts to maximize $U_2(Q_{D_2}, L_{S_2})$ where Q_{D_2} is the amount of output demanded and L_{S_2} is the amount of labor supplied by farmer 2.

$c2$:   Rental income obtained by the farmer acting as an entrepreneur is treated as income by the farmer acting as consumer. We have seen in subsection 15.1.b that rental income depends on the wage rate and hence can be denoted by $R_1(w)$ for farmer 1 and $R_2(w)$ for farmer 2.[3]

$c3$:   The income of the farmer i consists solely of his labor income and his rental income. Accordingly, when the wage rate is w, he chooses Q_{D_i} and L_{S_i} to maximize his utility function subject to the budget constraint

$$Q_{D_i} = wL_{S_i} + R_i(w) .$$

$c4$:   Each farmer can work for himself, for the other farmer, or for himself part of the time and for the other farmer part of the time.

To see how the farmer acts in his role as consumer-laborer we modify Figure 15.1.1 slightly. Suppose the wage rate is w. In Figure 15.1.3, the slope of $f_1(L_{D_1})$ is equal to w when output is Q_{S_1} and labor demanded is L_{D_1}. The line $R_1(w)A$ has slope w and is drawn tangent to $f_1(L_{D_1})$ at L_{D_1}. Accordingly, this line intersects the vertical axis at $K_1(w)$ which is the maximum rent on land that farmer 1 can get when the wage is w.[4] The line $R_1(w)A$ is the budget line of the farmer acting as a labor supplier-consumer since when he provides no labor his income

---

[3] For farmer i ($i = 1, 2$) let $L^*_{D_i}(w)$ be the amount of labor demanded at wage rate w when the optimal output decision is made. Then $R_i(w) = Q^*_{S_i} - wL^*_{D_i}(w)$ where $Q^*_{S_i}$ is the rent-maximizing output for wage rate w.

[4] Since the wage rate is the slope of $R_i(w)A$ in Figure 15.1.3, the total wage paid to L_{D_1} units of labor is measured along the vertical axis by $Q_{S_1} - R_1(w) = wL_{D_1}$. The remaining output, $OR_1(w)$, is the rent on land.

is $R_1(w)$, and when he works, he adds w times the amount of labor he supplies to this rental income.

The indifference curves from the utility function $U_1(Q_{D_1}, L_{S_1})$ are shown by the curves marked *I, II,* and *III* in Figure 15.1.3. These in-

FIGURE 15.1.3

Consumption and Labor Supply

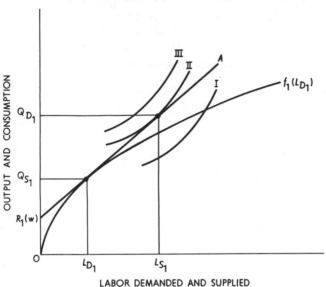

LABOR DEMANDED AND SUPPLIED

difference curves are upward-sloping because labor is considered a bad (i.e., more labor is less leisure or a reduction in a good).[5] To maximize utility the farmer finds the indifference curve which is tangent to the budget line.[6] This tangency occurs at L_{S_1} in Figure 15.1.3. Hence, when the wage rate is w the farmer hires L_{D_1} units of labor, produces Q_{S_1} units of output, supplies L_{S_1} units of labor, and consumes Q_{D_1} units of output.

By changing the wage rate w the line $R_1(w)A$ is made to move along $f_1(L_{D_1})$. As this is done, the labor supply function of the farmer is derived. In Figure 15.1.4 we illustrate the labor supply function so derived. The line L_{S_1} is the labor supplied by farmer 1 and L_{S_2} is the

---

[5] See Question 5 of Chapter 1.

[6] Given w the farmer's problem is max $U_1(Q_{D_1}, L_{S_1})$ subject to $Q_{D_1} = wL_{S_1} + R_1(w)$. The first-order condition is given by $-(\partial U_1/\partial L_{S_1})/(\partial U_1/\partial Q_{D_1}) = w$ which is the tangency indicated in Figure 15.1.3.

labor supplied by farmer 2. Summing these two curves horizontally we obtain the labor supply function, L_S, for the whole economy.

15.1.d General Equilibrium and Walras's Law

The equilibrium wage rate, that is, the wage rate that equates the supply and demand for labor, can be found by combining Figure 15.1.2 and Figure 15.1.4. This is done in Figure 15.1.5. The equilibrium wage

FIGURE 15.1.4

Aggregate Supply of Labor

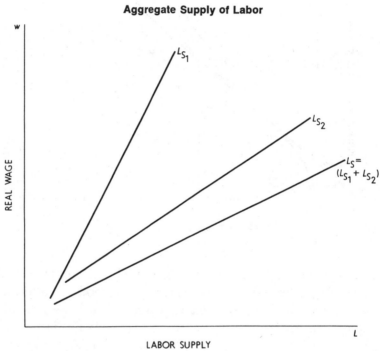

rate w^* is where L_S and L_D intersect. At this point farmer 1 supplies $L_{S_1}^*$ units of labor and demands $L_{D_1}^*$. Farmer 2 demands $L_{D_2}^*$ units of labor and supplies $L_{S_2}^*$. Farmer 1 is a net demander of labor (since $L_{D_1}^* > L_{S_1}^*$) and farmer 2 is a net supplier of labor (since $L_{D_2}^* < L_{S_2}^*$). Obviously $L_{D_1}^* - L_{S_1}^* = L_{S_2}^* - L_{D_2}^*$.[7]

It remains to show that the product market is in equilibrium when the labor market is in equilibrium. Let w^* be the equilibrium wage. Then we have the equations

---

[7] $L_S^* = L_{S_1}^* + L_{S_2}^*$ and $L_D^* = L_{D_1}^* + L_{D_2}^*$. Since in equilibrium $L_S^* = L_D^*$, it follows that $L_{D_1}^* - L_{S_2}^* = L_{S_1}^* - L_{D_2}^*$.

FIGURE 15.1.5

Equilibrium in the Labor Market

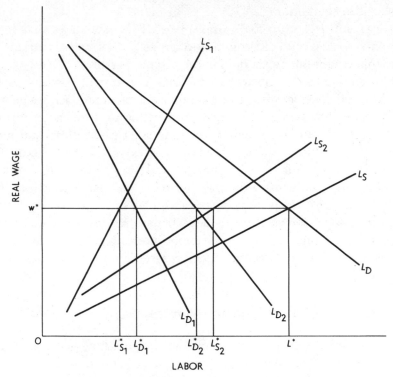

$$R_1(w^*) = Q^*_{S_1} - w^*L^*_{D_1}$$
$$R_2(w^*) = Q^*_{S_2} - w^*L^*_{D_2}$$

$$(15.1.1)$$

$$Q^*_{D_1} = w^*L^*_{S_1} + R_1(w^*)$$
$$Q^*_{D_2} = w^*L^*_{S_2} + R_2(w^*)$$

where the asterisks indicate the values of the variables at w^*. Solving the last two equations for $R_1(w^*)$ and $R_2(w^*)$ and substituting in the first two equations

$$Q^*_{D_1} - w^*L^*_{S_1} = Q^*_{S_1} - w^*L^*_{D_1}$$

$$(15.1.2)$$

$$Q^*_{D_2} - w^*L^*_{S_2} = Q^*_{S_2} - w^*L^*_{D_2}.$$

Adding these two equations

$$Q^*_{D_1} + Q^*_{D_2} - w^*(L^*_{S_1} + L^*_{S_2})$$
$$= Q^*_{S_1} + Q^*_{S_2} - w^*(L^*_{D_1} + L^*_{D_2}). \quad (15.1.3)$$

We know that w^* is such that the labor market is in equilibrium, so $L^*_{S_1} + L^*_{S_2} = L^*_{D_1} + L^*_{D_2}$. Hence, (15.1.3) becomes

$$Q^*_{D_1} + Q^*_{D_2} = Q^*_{S_1} + Q^*_{S_2}$$

which says that aggregate demand of output equals aggregate supply of output. Thus, the product market is in equilibrium when the labor market is in equilibrium.

This result is known as Walras's Law. That law states that in an economy with n markets, equilibrium in $n - 1$ of those markets assures that equilibrium must hold in the nth market also.[8]

This simple model illustrates how the price system coordinates the activities and decisions of diverse economic agents in producing a general equilibrium. The entrepreneur acting to maximize profits (in this example, the rent on land) ends up making a set of decisions that mesh perfectly with the consumption-labor choices of the household. The same kind of coordination of demand and supply decision occurs in more complex economies through virtually the same kind of price mechanisms. That the price system can achieve such coordination of the mind-boggling assortment of markets that we see in real world economies is truly astonishing. It is even more interesting, as we shall see in Chapter 16, that a competitive price system also maximizes social welfare.

15.2 GENERAL EQUILIBRIUM OF EXCHANGE

The model of section 15.1 is useful in showing how general equilibrium is achieved in an economy with one consumption good. In this section we develop a method for the analysis of equilibrium when there are two or more goods in the economy. In the next section we will see how the same apparatus can be applied in the analysis of allocating productive factors to the production of two or more goods.

15.2.a Edgeworth Box Diagram

The Edgeworth box diagram is a graphical technique for illustrating the interaction between two economic activities when their inputs are fixed in quantity. It is thus an ideal instrument for analyzing general equilibrium and economic welfare.

Two basic Edgeworth box diagrams are illustrated in Figure 15.2.2. Panel a shows the construction for a consumption problem whose inputs are types of, say, food; panel b refers to production activities whose inputs are factors of production.

First consider Figure 15.2.1. There are two consumption goods, X and $Y;$ these goods are available in absolutely fixed amounts. In

---

[8] Leon Walras was a pioneer in the analysis of general economic equilibrium. Leon Walras, *Elements d'economique pure* (Lausanne: F. Rouge, 1874).

FIGURE 15.2.1

Constructing the Edgeworth Box Diagram for a Consumption Problem

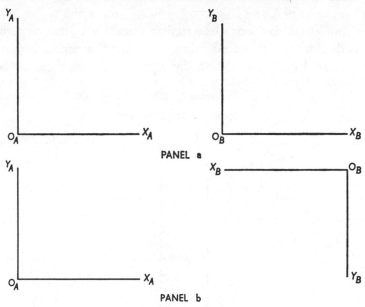

addition, there are only two individuals in the society, A and B; they initially possess an endowment of X and Y, but the endowment ratio is not the one either would choose if he were allowed to specify it. This general equilibrium problem is graphically illustrated by constructing an *origin* for A, labeled O_A, and plotting quantities of the two goods along the abscissa and ordinate. Thus from the origin O_A, the quantity of X held by $A(X_A)$ is plotted on the abscissa and the quantity of $Y(Y_A)$ on the ordinate. A similar graph for B, with origin O_B, may be constructed beside the graph for A. These two basic graphs are illustrated in panel a, Figure 15.2.1.

Next, rotate the B graph $180°$ to the left, so that it is actually "upside down" when viewed normally, as shown in panel b. The Edgeworth box diagram is formed by bringing the two graphs together. There could conceivably be a problem involving the lengths of the axes; if the X axes meshed, the Y axes might not. The problem does not in fact exist, however, because of our assumption concerning fixed availabilities of X and Y. $X_A + X_B$ must equal X, and $Y_A + Y_B$ must equal Y. The length of each axis measures the fixed quantity of the good it represents; when the two "halves" in panel b are brought together both axes mesh. One thus obtains panel a, Figure 15.2.2.

The point D in panel a indicates the initial endowment of X and

Y possessed by A and B. A begins with $O_A x_A$ units of X and $O_A y_A$ units of Y. Since the aggregates are fixed, B must originally hold $O_B x_B = X - O_A x_A$ units of X and $O_B y_B = Y - O_A y_A$ units of Y.

In a similar fashion, not illustrated in detail, one may construct an Edgeworth diagram for a production problem. The finished product is shown in panel b, Figure 15.2.2. Two goods, X and Y, are produced

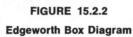

FIGURE 15.2.2

Edgeworth Box Diagram

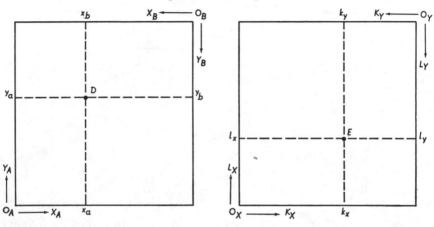

PANEL a--EDGEWORTH BOX DIAGRAM
FOR CONSUMPTION PROBLEM

PANEL b--EDGEWORTH BOX DIAGRAM
FOR PRODUCTION PROBLEM

by means of two inputs, K and L. The two inputs are fixed in aggregate quantity. The origin of coordinates for good X is O_X, for good Y is O_Y. The inputs of K and L used in producing X and Y are plotted along the axes. Accordingly, any point in the box represents a particular allocation of the two inputs between the two production processes. At point E, for example, $O_X k_X$ units of K and $O_X l_X$ units of L are used in producing X. As a consequence, $O_Y k_Y = K - O_X k_X$ units of K, and $O_Y l_Y = L - O_X l_X$ units of L, are allocated to the production of Y.

15.2.b Equilibrium of Exchange

Consider an economy in which exchange of initial endowments takes place. For the moment, production is ignored. If you like, you may think of the problem in the following context. There exists a small country with two inhabitants, A and B, each of whom owns one half the land area. These individuals truly resemble the lilies of the field, for they neither toil nor do they reap. They merely gather and exchange manna which providentially enough falls nightly on their land. Manna of two different types, X and Y, falls nightly; but the two types do not fall uniformly. There is a relatively heavy concentration of Y manna on A's property and, consequently, a relatively heavy concentration of X manna on B's land.

The problem of exchange is analyzed by means of the Edgeworth box diagram in Figure 15.2.3. To the basic box diagram, whose dimen-

FIGURE 15.2.3

General Equilibrium of Exchange

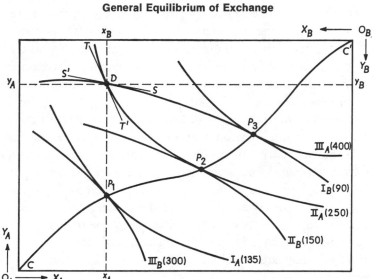

sions represent the nightly precipitation of manna, we add indifference curves for A and B. For example, the curve I_A shows combinations of X and Y that yield A the same level of satisfaction. In ordinary fashion, II_A represents a greater level of satisfaction than I_A; III_A than II_A; and so on. Quite generally, A's well-being is enhanced by moving toward the B origin; B, in turn, enjoys greater satisfaction the closer he moves toward the A origin.

Suppose the initial endowment (the nightly fall of manna) is point D; A has $O_A x_A$ units of X and $O_A y_A$ units of Y. Similarly, B has $O_B x_B$ and $O_B y_B$ units of X and Y respectively. The initial endowment places A on his indifference curve II_A and B on his curve I_B. At point D, A's marginal rate of substitution of X for Y, given by the slope of TT', is relatively high; A would be willing to sacrifice, say, three units of Y in order to obtain one additional unit of X. At the same point, B has a relatively low marginal rate of substitution, as shown by the slope of SS'. Or turning it around, B has a relatively high marginal rate of substitution of Y for X. He may, for example, be willing to forego four units of X to obtain one unit of Y.

A situation such as this will always lead to exchange if the parties concerned are free to trade. From the point D, A will trade some Y to B, receiving X in exchange. The exact bargain reached by the two traders cannot be determined. If B is the more skillful negotiator, he may induce A to move along II_A to the point P_2. All the benefit of trade goes to B, who jumps from I_B to II_B. Just oppositely, A might steer the bargain to point P_3, thereby increasing his level of satisfaction from II_A to III_A, B's real income remaining I_B. Starting from point D, the ultimate exchange is very likely to lead to some point between P_2 and P_3; but the skill of the bargainers and their initial endowments determine the exact location.

One important thing can be said, however. Exchange will take place until the marginal rate of substitution of X for Y is the same for both traders. If the two marginal rates are different, one or both parties can benefit from exchange; neither party need lose. In other words, the exchange equilibrium can occur only at points such as P_1, P_2, and P_3 in Figure 15.2.3. The locus CC', called the *contract* or *conflict curve*, is a curve joining all points of tangency between one of A's indifference curves and one of B's. It is thus the locus along which the marginal rates of substitution are equal for both traders. We accordingly have the following

Proposition: The general equilibrium of exchange occurs at a point where the marginal rate of substitution between every pair of goods is the same for all parties consuming both goods. The exchange equilibrium is not unique; it may occur at any point along the contract curve (for multiple traders, it is more properly called the contract hypersurface).

The contract curve is an optimal locus in the sense that if the trading parties are located at some point not on the curve, one or both can benefit, and neither suffer a loss, by exchanging goods so as to move to a point on the curve. To be sure, some points not on the curve are preferable to some points on the curve. But for any point not on the curve, one or more attainable points on the curve are preferable.

The chief characteristic of each point on the contract curve is that a movement away from the point must benefit one party and harm the other. More generally, suppose there are n people in a society. This society has attained exchange equilibrium (i.e., a point on the contract curve) if, and only if, there is *no reorganization* that will benefit some of the *n* members without harming at least one. Turning the statement around, an organization does not represent a point on the curve if there is any change that will make some people better off and will not make anyone worse off. Every organization that leads to a point on the contract curve is said to be a *Pareto-optimal organization*.

Definition: A Pareto-optimal organization is one such that any change which makes some people better off makes some others worse off. That is, an organization is Pareto optimal if, and only if, there is no change that will make one or more better off without making anyone worse off. Thus, every point on the contract curve is Pareto optimal, and the contract curve is a locus of Pareto optimality.

15.2.c Deriving the Utility-Possibility Frontier

The contract curve is a Pareto-optimal locus in *community space;* it shows all pairs of allocations of *X* and *Y* to *A* and *B* such that the marginal rate of substitution is equal for both parties. This exchange equilibrium locus can be transformed from commodity space to utility space, obtaining what is called the *utility-possibility frontier* relative to the particular endowment aggregate in Figure 15.2.3. The process of derivation is illustrated in Figure 15.2.4.

First consider the point P_1 in Figure 15.2.3. In *A*'s scale of utility measurement, all points on I_A are valued at 135; thus P_1 is associated with a utility value of 135. Similarly, in *B*'s utility scale, all points

FIGURE 15.2.4

**Deriving the Utility-Possibility Frontier
from the Contract Curve**

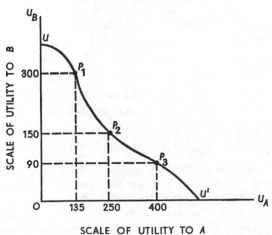

along III_B have the value 300. Now construct a graph, as in Figure 15.2.4, whose coordinate axes are A's and B's utility scales. The point P_1, with coordinates 135 and 300, can be plotted on this graph. Similarly, all other points along the contract curve in commodity space can be plotted in utility space by noting the pair of utility values associated with each point of tangency. Connect all such points by a curve, labeled UU' in Figure 15.2.4. This curve is the utility-possibility frontier.

Definition: The utility-possibility frontier is the locus showing the maximum level of satisfaction attainable by one trading party for every given level of satisfaction of the other. The curve so generated depends upon the absolute endowment of each commodity and upon the aggregate commodity endowment ratio—that is, upon *X, Y,* and *Y/X*.[9]

15.3 GENERAL EQUILIBRIUM OF PRODUCTION AND EXCHANGE

In the model of section 15.2 production does not occur; consumers simply exchange existing stocks or endowments of commodities. We shall now expand by adding a production side to the model. There are still only two consuming units in the society, A and B; there are also only two *producible* commodities, X and Y. But now they must be produced by means of two inputs, K and L. The production functions for X and Y are assumed to be given, and there are fixed, nonaugmentable quantities of the inputs K and L. In other words, the initial endowments in the present model are the fixed input supplies rather than fixed quantities of the two consumption goods.[10]

15.3.a General Equilibrium of Production

The analysis of the general equilibrium of production is precisely the same as that of the general equilibrium of exchange. The only difference is terminology (economic jargon). The fixed endowments of inputs K and L determine the dimensions of the Edgeworth box diagram in Figure 15.3.1. Next, the given and unchanging production functions for goods X and Y enable us to construct the isoquant maps for each, illustrated by curves such as II_X and III_Y.

Suppose inputs are originally allocated between production of X and

---

[9] The student should remember that the utility numbers are purely arbitrary so far as interpersonal utility comparisons are concerned. In particular, 300 for B is not necessarily greater than 135 for A, although to A, 136 is greater than 135.

[10] Note that in contrast to section 15.1 we do not assume a variable labor supply. Both K and L are assumed fixed for purposes of this discussion. By using more mathematics we can account for variable supplies as well as variable outputs.

FIGURE 15.3.1

General Equilibrium of Production

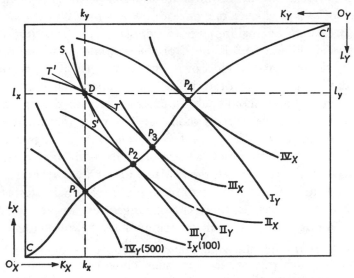

Y so that $O_x k_x$ units of K and $O_x l_x$ units of L are used in making X; the remainder, $O_Y k_Y$ and $O_Y l_Y$ units of K and L respectively, is used to produce Y. This allocation is represented by point D in the Edgeworth box—the point at which II_x intersects II_Y. At the allocation D, the marginal rate of technical substitution of K for L in producing X, given by the slope of SS', is relatively low. The marginal product of K in producing X is high relative to the marginal product of L. The II_x level of production can be maintained by substituting a relatively small amount of K for a relatively larger amount of L. The opposite situation prevails in Y production, as shown by the slope of TT'. The marginal rate of technical substitution of K for L in producing Y is relatively high; thus a comparatively large amount of K can be released by substituting a relatively small amount of L while maintaining the II_Y level of output.

If the producer of X at point D substitutes one unit of K he can, let us suppose, release two units of L. The producer of Y, by employing the two units of L released from X production, can maintain output and release, let us suppose, four units of K. Thus, from a point such as D, input substitution by producers will enable the society to move to P_2, P_3, or any point in between. At P_2, the output of X is the same as at D but the output of Y has been increased to the III_Y level. If the movement is to P_3, the output of X increases with no change in the volume of Y production.

The foregoing discussion establishes a pervasive principle. Whenever the marginal rate of technical substitution between two inputs is different for two producers, one or both outputs may be increased, and neither decreased, by making the appropriate input substitutions. In the example in Figure 15.3.1, the X producer would substitute K for L, decreasing the marginal product of K, increasing that of L, and thereby raising the marginal rate of technical substitution. The producer of Y, on the other hand, should substitute L for K, with the opposite results. Production of one or both goods can always be increased without an aggregate increase in inputs unless the marginal rates of technical substitution between the inputs are the same for both producers.

The locus CC', again called the *contract* or *conflict curve*, is a curve showing all input allocations that equalize the marginal rates of technical substitution—that is, the locus of tangencies between an X isoquant and a Y isoquant. We can accordingly state the following

Proposition: The general equilibrium of production occurs at a point where the marginal rate of technical substitution between every pair of inputs is the same for all producers who use both inputs. The production equilibrium is not unique; it may occur at any point along the contract curve; but each point represents a Pareto-optimal equilibrium organization.

The contract curve is an optimal locus in the sense that if the producers are located at a point not on the curve, the output of one or both commodities can be increased, and the output of neither decreased, by making input substitutions so as to move to a point on the curve. To be sure, some points not on the curve correspond to a greater aggregate output than some points on the curve. But for any point not on the curve there are one or more attainable points on the curve associated with a greater aggregate output.

15.3.b General Equilibrium of Production and Exchange

For any input endowment there are an infinite number of potential production equilibria that are Pareto optimal, that is, any point on the contract curve in Figure 15.3.1. Each point represents a particular volume of output of X and of Y, and thereby dictates the dimensions of an Edgeworth box diagram for exchange (such as Figure 15.2.3). Furthermore, each consumption-exchange box leads to an infinite number of potential exchange equilibria that are Pareto optimal, that is, any point on the contract curve associated with the box in question. Accordingly, there are a multiple infinity of potential general equilibria of production and exchange.

The object of any society is to attain that particular general equilibrium which maximizes the economic welfare of its inhabitants. As we shall see in Chapter 16, there are ways by which either a free enterprise system or a decentralized socialist state may attain the optimum.

15.3.c Deriving the Production-Possibility Frontier or Transformation Curve

The contract curve associated with the general equilibrium of production is a locus of points in *input space;* the curve shows the optimal output of each commodity corresponding to every possible allocation of K and L between X and Y. With the allocation of inputs indicated by point P_1 in Figure 15.3.1, 500 units of Y and 100 units of X are the maximum attainable production. By constructing a graph whose coordinate axes show the quantities of X and Y produced, and plotting the output pairs corresponding to each isoquant tangency in Figure 15.3.1, one may generate the curve labeled TT' in Figure 15.3.2. The curve so obtained is called the *production-possibility frontier* or the *transformation curve.*

The transformation curve is obtained by mapping the contract curve from input space into output space. Fundamentally, this locus depicts the choices a society can make. It shows, in other words, the various (maximum) combinations of X and Y that are attainable from the given resource base (input endowment). No output combination represented by a point lying outside the production-possibility frontier (such as S) can be attained; such a level of output would require a greater resource base. On the other hand, a point lying inside the locus (such as R) is neither necessary nor desirable; it would entail a needless sacrifice of goods attributable to unemployment of available resources. Thus one object of a society is to attain an equilibrium position *on,* not below, its production-possibility frontier.

Definition: The production-possibility frontier or transformation curve is a locus showing the maximum attainable output of one commodity for every possible volume of output of the other commodity, given the fixed resource base. The curve so generated depends upon the absolute endowment of each resource, upon the aggregate input endowment ratio, and upon the "state of the art" (the production functions for both goods).[11]

---

[11] For a numerical example of the derivation of the transformation curve and a simple mathematical formulation, see C. E. Ferguson, "Transformation Curve in Production Theory: A Pedagogical Note," *Southern Economic Journal,* vol. 29 (1962), pp. 96–102.

FIGURE 15.3.2

Deriving Production-Possibility Frontier from the Contract Curve

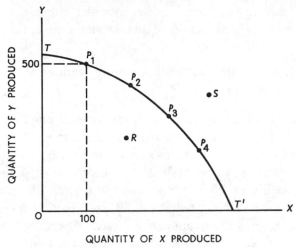

15.4 GENERAL COMPETITIVE EQUILIBRIUM IN A TWO-GOOD ECONOMY

The material of the last two sections opens the way to the analysis of general equilibrium in a two-good, two-input economy. To illustrate how this is done we restrict attention to the case of a fixed coefficient production model where there is no substitution of factors of production. A more general model involving substitution of factors in production parallels the analysis presented here.[12]

15.4.a Production in a Two-Good Economy

We will denote the output of good 1 by Q_1 and the output of good 2 by Q_2. The labor requirements for good 1 are a_{L_1} per unit of output, and the capital requirements per unit of output of good 1 are a_{K_1}. Similarly a_{L_2} and a_{K_2} are, respectively, the labor and capital requirements per unit of output of good 2. The coefficients a_{L_1}, a_{K_1}, a_{L_2}, a_{K_2} are fixed constants. Total labor and capital requirements for good 1 when Q_1 units are produced are

$$L_1 = a_{L_1}Q_1 \tag{15.4.1}$$

---

[12] For a discussion of the more general model the reader may wish to consult Murray C. Kemp, *The Pure Theory of International Trade and Investment* (Englewood Cliffs, N.J.: Prentice-Hall, Inc., 1969), chap. 1.

and

$$K_1 = a_{K_1}Q_1 .$$

Total labor and capital requirements for an output Q_2 of good 2 are

$$L_2 = a_{L_2}Q_2$$

$$K_2 = a_{K_2}Q_2 .$$

(15.4.2)

The total amount of labor and capital available in the economy are assumed fixed at the level L and K, respectively. Hence,

$$L_1 + L_2 \leq L$$

$$K_1 + K_2 \leq K .$$

(15.4.3)

Combining (15.4.1), (15.4.2), and the inequalities in (15.4.3), we get the inequalities

$$Q_1 \leq \frac{K}{a_{K_1}} - \frac{a_{K_2}}{a_{K_1}} Q_2$$

(15.4.4)

and

$$Q_1 \leq \frac{L}{a_{L_1}} - \frac{a_{L_2}}{a_{L_1}} Q_2$$

(15.4.5)

where (15.4.4) represents the capital constraint on output of good 1 when Q_2 units of good 2 are produced and (15.4.5) is the labor constraint on output of good 1 when Q_2 units of good 2 are produced. Hence the production possibility frontier is given by

$$Q_1 = \min \left\{ \frac{K}{a_{K_1}} - S_K Q_2, \frac{L}{a_{L_1}} - S_L Q_2 \right\}$$

(15.4.6)

where $S_K = a_{K_2}/a_{K_1}$ and $S_L = a_{L_2}/a_{L_1}$.[13] The production frontier is shown in Figure 15.4.1. The line DEA is the capital constraint (15.4.4) and shows the maximum Q_1 that can be produced for each output of Q_2 given the fixed capital stock K in the economy. Similarly, the line CEB is the maximum output of Q_1 for each output of Q_2 given the labor constraint. The set of achievable outputs (i.e., combinations of Q_1 and Q_2 that do not violate either the labor or capital constraint) is the area $OCEA$. The production frontier is CEA.

From this description of Figure 15.4.1 we see that the point D is

---

[13] The reader may wish to show that this production possibility frontier can be derived from an Edgeworth box as in section 15.3. The fixed coefficient model production function for Q_1 is $Q_1 = \min\{L_1/a_{L_1}, K_1/a_{K_1}\}$ and for Q_2 it is $Q_2 = \min\{L_2/a_{L_2}, K_2/a_{K_2}\}$. The isoquants are right angles for the fixed coefficient production function. Note that the production functions are linear homogeneous.

FIGURE 15.4.1

Production-Possibility Frontier

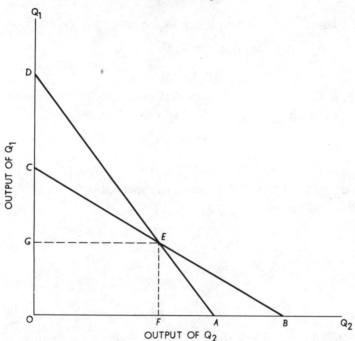

OUTPUT OF Q_1

OUTPUT OF Q_2

K/a_{K_1} and the slope of DEA is $-S_K$. The point C is L/a_{L_1}, and the slope of CEB is $-S_L$. As drawn $S_K > S_L$ and the lines intersect at E.[14] Over the range of output of Q_2 from O to F in Figure 15.4.1, production of Q_1 occurs along CE. Hence, capital is a redundant factor (less than K is needed for production in this range), and accordingly, its price is zero for these outputs. Similarly, over the range FA of output of Q_2 (i.e., output of Q_1 along EA) labor is redundant and its price is zero for these outputs. Only at output OF of Q_2 ($=$ output OG of Q_1) are both labor and capital fully employed.

In the general equilibrium to be discussed we will be interested in determining the prices of goods 1 and 2, the wage rate and the interest rate or rental rate on capital. As in section 15.1, we recognize that only relative prices can be determined, so we pick a *numeraire* commodity and set its price equal to 1. Suppose Q_2 is the *numeraire;* then we need to determine p_1 (the relative price of good 1), the relative wage w, and the relative rental rate on capital r. In a competitive equilibrium,

[14] Other possibilities exist, of course, but for concreteness in the discussion we will stick with this case.

economic profits in industry 1 (which produces good 1) and industry 2 (which produces good 2) will be zero. These zero economic profits requirements can be stated as

$$p_1 Q_1 = w L_1 + r K_1 \qquad (15.4.7)$$
$$Q_2 = w L_2 + r K_2$$

where the first equation says that total revenue equals total cost in industry 1 and the second equation says the same for industry 2. Dividing the first equation by Q_1 and the second by Q_2, we get the conditions[15]

$$p_1 = w \frac{L_1}{Q_1} + r \frac{K_1}{Q_1} = w a_{L_1} + r a_{K_1} \qquad (15.4.8)$$

$$1 = w \frac{L_2}{Q_2} + r \frac{K_2}{Q_2} = w a_{L_2} + r a_{K_2} \cdot \qquad (15.4.9)$$

Now suppose output of Q_2 is in the range F to A in Figure 15.4.1. In this range, output of Q_1 is in the range OG; and since labor is redundant, the wage rate is zero. Setting $w = 0$ in (15.4.8) and (15.4.9) and solving these equations simultaneously, we find $p_1 = a_{K_1}/a_{K_2} = 1/S_K$ and $r = 1/a_{K_2}$ over this range of outputs. When output of Q_2 is in the range O to F in Figure 15.4.1, output of Q_1 is in the range GC and capital is redundant. This means the rental rate for capital, r, is zero. Setting $r = 0$ in (15.4.8) and (15.4.9) and solving, we see that over this range of output $p_1 = a_{L_1}/a_{L_2} = 1/S_L$ and $w = 1/a_{L_2}$.

Combining these results we derive the supply curve of good 1 in Figure 15.4.2. Over the range of output OG the price of good 1 is $1/S_K$ as represented by the horizontal segment $1/S_K A$ in Figure 15.4.2. Similarly over the output range GC the price is $1/S_L$ represented by the horizontal segment BE in this figure. The supply function of Q_1 is thus an increasing step function.[16]

15.4.b Equilibrium in a Two-Good Economy

To complete the analysis of equilibrium in this economy, we must introduce demand curves for good 1 and good 2. Once commodity prices are known we know factor payments. Given factor payments and the

---

[15] Since the production functions are homogeneous of degree 1, these conditions also say that marginal cost equals price because marginal cost and average cost are equal.

[16] A similar supply function for Q_2 can be derived in terms of its *relative* price $1/p_1$.

FIGURE 15.4.2

Supply of Good One

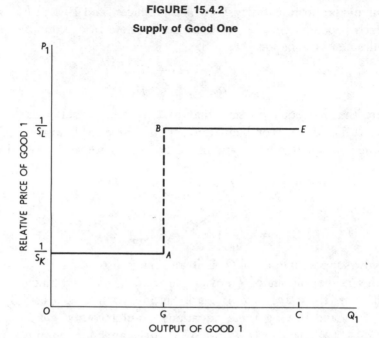

OUTPUT OF GOOD 1

distribution of the community's assets, both total income and its distribution are known. From this information we can in principle calculate the determinants of individual, and hence total, commodity demands. We can thus introduce aggregate demand curves specified as $d_1(p_1, 1)$ and $d_2(p_1, 1)$ for commodities 1 and 2, respectively. We also note that by Walras's Law we can ignore one of these demand functions, say the second, since this market will be in equilibrium if the rest of the markets in the economy are in equilibrium.[17]

If the demand curve for product 1 intersects the supply curve of Figure 15.4.2 in the segment $1/S_K$ A, then, as we have seen, the price of good 1 is $1/S_K$, $w = 0$, and $r = 1/a_{K_2}$. The output of industry 1 is in the interval OG at the point that d_1 intersects the supply curve. If d_1 intersects the segment BE of the supply curve, then output, Q_1, is in the interval GC at the point of intersection of supply and demand. In this case $p_1 = 1/S_L$, $w = 1/a_{L_2}$ and $r = 0$.

When d_1 passes between points A and B as in Figure 15.4.3, output

---

[17] Recall our use of Walras's Law in a related context in section 15.1. Since total income of the economy is given by equations (15.4.7), the consumer budget requirement that total demand equal total income yields

$$p_1 d_1 + d_2 = p_1 Q_1 + Q_2.$$

Hence, if $p_1 d_1 = p_1 Q_1$, it follows that $d_2 = Q_2$. Equilibrium in market 2 is assured by equilibrium in market 1.

of good 1 will be OG and price can be determined along d_1 at this output. In Figure 15.4.3 this price is given by p_1^*. Given this price, equations 15.4.8 and 15.4.9 can be solved for the equilibrium values of r and w. The results are

$$r^* = \frac{S_L p_1^* - 1}{a_{K_2}\left(\frac{S_L}{S_K} - 1\right)}$$

(15.4.10)

and,

$$w^* = \frac{S_K p_1^* - 1}{a_{L_2}\left(\frac{S_K}{S_L} - 1\right)}, \qquad \text{for} \quad \frac{1}{S_K} \le p_1^* \le \frac{1}{S_L}.$$

In our graphical example $S_K > S_L$ and, from equations (15.4.10), this means that an increase in p_1^* increases the interest rate and decreases the wage rate.

15.4.c Factor Intensities and the Relationship between Factor Prices and Commodity Prices

When output in industry 1 is Q_1, demand for labor and capital in that industry are $L_1 = a_{L_1}Q_1$ and $K_1 = a_{K_1}Q_1$. The capital-labor ratio in industry 1 is thus

FIGURE 15.4.3

Supply and Demand for Good One

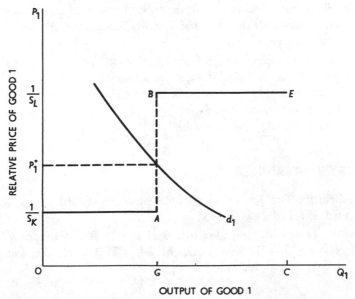

OUTPUT OF GOOD 1

$$\frac{K_1}{L_1} = \frac{a_{K_1}}{a_{L_1}} \cdot \qquad (15.4.11)$$

Similarly, the capital-labor ratio in industry 2 is

$$\frac{K_2}{L_2} = \frac{a_{K_2}}{a_{L_2}} \cdot \qquad (15.4.12)$$

If $a_{K_1}/a_{L_1} > a_{K_2}/a_{L_2}$ industry 1 is said to be relatively capital intensive (and industry 2 is relatively labor intensive). If $a_{K_1}/a_{L_1} < a_{K_2}/a_{L_2}$, then industry 2 is said to be relatively capital intensive (and industry 1 is relatively labor intensive). Using equations (15.4.10), we see that r^* will increase as p_1^* does if $S_L/S_K - 1 > 0$ and w^* will increase as p_1^* does if $S_K/S_L - 1 > 0$. Observe, however, that $S_L/S_K - 1 > 0$ means that $a_{K_1}/a_{L_1} > a_{K_2}/a_{L_2}$, so as p_1^* increases r^* will increase if industry 1 is relatively capital-intensive. Since $S_L/S_K - 1 > 0$ means $S_K/S_L - 1 < 0$, an increase in the price of Q_1 decreases w^*. The reverse would hold if industry 1 were labor intensive. This illustrates what is known as the Stolper-Samuelson Theorem which says that an increase in the price of a commodity gives rise to an increase in the real reward of the factor used relatively intensively in the production of that commodity, and to a decline in the real reward of the other factor.

QUESTIONS AND EXERCISES

1. Using the model of section 15.1, describe the general equilibrium of an economy consisting of a single farmer.
2. Using the model of section 15.1, describe the general equilibrium when one farmer owns all the land (but never works) and the other farmer works but does not own any land.
3. How does the supply curve in Figure 15.4.2 change
   a. When the total capital stock K is increased?
   b. When the total labor force L is increased?
   c. When both a_{K_1} and a_{L_1} double?
   d. When both a_{K_1} and a_{K_2} double?

SUGGESTED READINGS

Fossati, Eraldo. *The Theory of General Static Equilibrium*, pp. 79–183. Oxford: Basil Blackwell, 1957.

Henderson, James M., and Quandt, Richard E. *Microeconomic Theory*, 2d ed., pp. 153–71. New York: McGraw-Hill Book Co., Inc., 1971. [Elementary math required.]

Kuenne, Robert E. *The Theory of General Economic Equilibrium.* Princeton N.J.: Princeton University Press, 1963. Chapter 1 (pp. 3–39) is an excellent statement concerning methodology; here little, if any, mathematics is required of the reader. Otherwise, the level of mathematics is as indicated. Especially relevant are pp. 43–195. [Advanced math required.]

Leontief, Wassily. *The Structure of the American Economy, 1919–1939.* New York: Oxford University Press, 1951. [Advanced math required.]

Walras, Leon. *Elements of Pure Economics* (Jaffe trans.). London: George Allen & Unwin, 1954. [Advanced math required.]

16

Theory of welfare economics

16.1 INTRODUCTION

The general equilibrium conditions of production and exchange, analyzed in Chapter 15, can be used to develop the "marginal" conditions for maximum social welfare and to assess the efficiency of a perfectly competitive economy. It might also help explain why there is only one unique general equilibrium of relevance among the multiple infinity of possible general equilibria that are Pareto optimal.

16.1.a Marginal Conditions for Social Welfare

First return to Figure 15.2.3, which illustrates the general equilibrium of exchange. As you will recall, we proved that a position of equilibrium must occur on the contract curve because if some other distribution momentarily existed one or both trading parties could benefit, and neither be harmed, by moving to a point on the contract curve. Any point on the contract curve satisfies the *optimum conditions of exchange* and gives rise to the first marginal condition for a Pareto-welfare maximum.

Marginal Condition for Exchange: To attain a Pareto maximum, the marginal rate of substitution between any pair of consumer goods must be the same for all individuals who consume both goods.

If this does not hold, one or more individuals would benefit from exchange (without injuring others), as shown by Figure 15.2.3.

The second marginal condition is based upon Figure 15.3.1, which illustrates the general equilibrium of production. With the aid of that figure, we proved that equilibrium must be attained on the contract curve because if a different allocation of inputs momentarily prevailed the output of one or both commodities could be increased, and the output of neither decreased, by moving to a point on the curve. All points on the production contract curve satisfy the *optimum conditions of factor substitution* and lead to the second marginal condition for a Pareto-welfare maximum:

Marginal Condition for Factor Substitution: To attain a Pareto maximum, the marginal rate of technical substitution between any pair of inputs must be the same for all producers who use both inputs.

Otherwise, a reallocation of resources would result in a greater aggregate output, without a reduction in the output of any commodity.

The final marginal condition for a welfare maximum is based upon the *optimum conditions of product substitution*. It is actually a combination of the two previous sets of conditions and may be stated as

Marginal Condition for Product Substitution: To attain a Pareto maximum, the marginal rate of transformation in production must equal the marginal rate of substitution in consumption for every pair of commodities and for every individual who consumes both.

This final proposition is established with the aid of Figure 16.1.1.

The curve labeled TT' is the production-possibility frontier or transformation curve, as derived in Figure 15.3.2. Given full resource utilization, it shows the maximum producible amount of either commodity for every given level of output of the other. The slope of the transformation curve at any point shows the number of units of good Y that must be sacrificed in order to free enough resources to produce one additional unit of good X. With full employment of all resources, more of one good necessarily entails less of another.

Definition: The negative of the slope of the transformation curve is called the marginal rate of transformation of X into Y. It shows the number of units by which the production of Y must be decreased in order to expand the output of X by one unit.

Now suppose a pair of consumers has attained an exchange equilibrium, which means that their marginal rates of substitution in consumption are equal. Further, suppose the common marginal rate of substitution is such that both consumers are willing to exchange two units of Y

FIGURE 16.1.1

Marginal Condition for Product Substitution

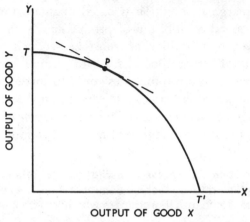

for three units of X. Next, suppose a producer (or producers) has attained an equilibrium of production, in which the marginal rate of technical substitution between each pair of inputs is the same in the production of X as in the production of Y. Finally, suppose this organization of production leads to the point P on the transformation curve TT' in Figure 16.1.1, at which the marginal rate of transformation is 2—that is, by curtailing the output of Y by ½ unit, one additional unit of X may be produced.

Clearly a general equilibrium has not been obtained. By reducing the output of Y, the output of X can be expanded *by more than enough* to keep each consumer on his original indifference curve. Thus if producers shift some resources from Y production to X production, both consumers may be made better off. Consequently, the initial position could not have been one of Pareto optimality.

In the two paragraphs above, it has been shown that if the marginal rate of transformation exceeds the common marginal rate of substitution in consumption, a point of Pareto optimality cannot exist. A similar line of reasoning will show that if the marginal rate of transformation is less than the common marginal rate of substitution in consumption, producers should shift some resources from X production to Y production. Therefore, since an organization cannot be Pareto optimal if the marginal rate of transformation is not equal to the common marginal rate of substitution in consumption, the marginal condition for product substitution is established: a Pareto-optimal organization is achieved only if the marginal rate of transformation is equal to the common marginal rate of substitution in consumption for all pairs of consumer goods.

16.1.b   Welfare Maximization and Perfect Competition

The three sets of marginal conditions developed above state the necessary conditions for welfare maximization in any type of society, that is, for the attainment of a Pareto-optimal equilibrium. We now wish to show, subject to the reservations in section 16.3, that a perfectly competitive, free enterprise system guarantees the attainment of Pareto-optimality. The proof rests upon the *maximizing* behavior of producers and consumers. To recall the dictum of Adam Smith, each individual, in pursuing his own self-interest, is led as if by an "invisible hand" to a course of action that promotes the general welfare of all.

Look just at the marginal condition for exchange, which requires equality of the marginal rates of substitution between every pair of goods for all consumers. As shown in Chapter 2, to maximize satisfaction subject to limited income each consumer must arrange his purchases so that the marginal rate of substitution is equal to the price ratio for every pair of goods. Under perfect competition, prices, and therefore price ratios, are uniform for all buyers. Hence each consumer purchases goods in such quantity that *his* marginal rate of substitution equals the *common* price ratio faced by all consumers. Therefore, the marginal rate of substitution between every pair of goods must be the same for all consumers; the marginal conditions for exchange are a consequence of the price system under perfect competition.

Next consider the marginal condition for factor substitution: the marginal rate of technical substitution between every pair of inputs must be the same for all producers who utilize them. As shown in Chapter 13, each perfectly competitive producer employs inputs in such proportions that the marginal rate of technical substitution (the ratio of marginal products) equals the input-price ratio. He must do this to maximize profit (obtain the least-cost combination of inputs). In a perfectly competitive market input prices are the same to all producers; hence each equates the marginal rate of technical substitution relevant to him to a common input-price ratio. The marginal rates of technical substitution are accordingly equal; and the marginal condition of factor substitution is also a consequence of the price system under perfect competition.

Finally, we come to the marginal condition for product substitution: the marginal rate of transformation in production must equal the marginal rate of substitution in consumption for each pair of goods. The proof in this case requires a slight digression.

As previously said, the marginal rate of transformation shows the number of units by which the production of Y must be curtailed in order to free enough resources to produce an additional unit of X. If the output of X is increased by one unit, the marginal cost of producing X shows how much each additional unit of X costs. But if the output of X is increased, the output of Y must be diminished; hence the marginal cost of producing Y shows how much is saved by reducing Y output one unit. Hence dividing the marginal cost of producing X by the marginal cost of producing Y, one finds the number of units of Y that must be sacrificed to obtain an additional unit of X.[1] Accordingly, the marginal rate of transformation of X into Y equals the ratio of the marginal cost of X to the marginal cost of Y.

Under perfect competition profit maximization is achieved by producing that volume of output for which marginal cost equals price. Thus under perfect competition the marginal rate of transformation of X into Y must equal the ratio of the price of X to that of Y (because both must equal the marginal cost ratio). By previous argument, the marginal rate of substitution of X for Y must equal the ratio of the price of X to the price of Y. As in the two previous cases, the marginal condition for product substitution is a consequence of the price system under perfect competition.[2]

The results of this section may be summarized by the following

Proposition: If the political organization of a society is such as to accord paramount importance to its individual members, social welfare, or the economic well-being of the society, will be maximized if every consumer, every firm, every industry, and every input market is perfectly competitive.

---

[1] Consider point P in Figure 16.1.1. With the output of Y large relative to the output of X, the marginal cost of Y will be large relative to that of X. Suppose the marginal cost of Y is \$10 and the marginal cost of X is \$5. Their ratio is \$5/\$10 or $\frac{1}{2}$. Thus one half of a unit of Y must be sacrificed to produced one additional unit of X.

[2] If X is increased by $\triangle X$ then the increase in cost is $MC_x \triangle X$ where MC_x is the marginal cost of X. The reduction in Y, $\triangle Y$ must reduce cost by the same amount, so $MC_x \triangle X = -MC_Y \triangle Y$ or

$$\frac{MC_X}{MC_Y} = -\frac{\triangle Y}{\triangle X} = MRT_{X \text{ into } Y}.$$

When the price of X and the price of Y equal their respective marginal costs,

$$\frac{P_X}{P_Y} = \frac{MC_X}{MC_Y} = MRT_{X \text{ into } Y}.$$

An interesting extension of this proposition applies to a decentralized socialist society. In the introduction to Part V it was said that the "invisible hand" might more appropriately be called the invisible IBM machine. Neither designation gives much hint to the underlying principle: each individual maximizes in light of *market-determined* (parametric) prices. The functioning of the price system in perfectly competitive markets leads to the social welfare maximum; stated alternatively, when each individual implicitly solves his constrained maximization problem, the result is a set of prices that, given the individual behavior, leads to maximum social welfare. Speaking mathematically, these prices are nothing more than Lagrange multipliers, perhaps ground out by the "invisible IBM machine" in the process of solving the welfare maximization problem.

This invisible IBM machine is not available to a planned socialist society; however a visible, tangible one (or its equivalent) is. The state planning agency (given knowledge of individual preference patterns and production functions) could use the visible machine to solve the now explicit constrained maximization problem. The resulting Lagrange multipliers are "shadow" prices, the equivalent of market-determined prices under perfect competition. Maximum social welfare in this type of society can be attained by following the so-called Lange-Lerner rule:

Proposition (Lange-Lerner Rule): To attain maximum social welfare in a decentralized socialist society, the state planning agency should solve the constrained maximization problem and obtain the shadow prices of all inputs and outputs. Publish this price list and distribute it to all members of the society. Instruct all consumers and all plant managers to behave as though they were satisfaction or profit maximizers operating in perfectly competitive markets.

16.2 INPUT, OUTPUT, AND DISTRIBUTION

We now examine the problem of welfare maximization in greater detail.[3]

16.2.a General Assumptions

The model employed here is identical to that used in the general equilibrium analysis of production and exchange, except that one addi-

---

[3] This section is based upon Francis M. Bator, "The Simple Analytics of Welfare Maximization," *American Economic Review,* vol. 47 (1957), pp. 22–59, esp. pp. 23–31.

tional assumption (*iv* below) is required. Our original assumptions are now recounted and the additional one supplied.

(*i*) There exist fixed, nonaugmentable endowments of two homogeneous and perfectly divisible inputs, labor (*L*) and capital (*K*). Alternatively, one may assume that these inputs are inelastically supplied and the period of analysis is not sufficiently long to permit a change in the given supplies.

(*ii*) Only two homogeneous goods are produced in the economy, fish (*F*) and cabbage (*C*). The production function for each is given and does not change during the analysis. Each production function is smooth (continuous), and each exhibits constant returns to scale and diminishing marginal rates of technical substitution along any isoquant.

(*iii*) There are two individuals in the society, *A* and *B*. Each has a well-defined ordinal preference function yielding indifference curves of normal shape. For convenience, an arbitrary numerical index is adopted for each function, denoted U_A and U_B.

(*iv*) There exists a *social welfare function* that depends exclusively on the positions of *A* and *B* in their own preference scales [for example, $W = W(U_A, U_B)$]. The social welfare function permits a unique preference ordering of all possible situations (hereafter called *states*).[4]

With these assumptions, our problem is to determine the welfare maximizing value of the following variables: the input of labor into fish and cabbage production (L_F, L_C); the input of capital into fish and cabbage production (K_F, K_C); the total amount of fish (*F*) and cabbage (*C*) produced; and the distribution of *F* and *C* between *A* and *B* (F_A, F_B, C_A, C_B).

16.2.b   Retracing Some Steps: From Production Functions to the Production-Possibility Frontier

By assumption (*i*), there are fixed endowments of two homogeneous inputs; suppose the amounts are $\overline{K}$ and $\overline{L}$ of capital and labor respectively. The magnitudes of these endowments determine the dimensions of the Edgeworth box diagram shown in Figure 16.2.1. Next, by assumption (*ii*), the production function for each commodity is given and characterized by smooth isoquants that exhibit constant returns to scale and diminishing marginal rates of technical substitution. These

---

[4] Assumption (*iv*) is heroic and involves some controversy. Clearly, it includes some ethical valuations concerning the relative positions of *A* and *B*. On this thorny problem, see Kenneth J. Arrow, *Social Choice and Individual Values* (New York: John Wiley & Sons, Inc., 1951); Paul A. Samuelson, *Foundations of Economic Analysis* (Cambridge, Mass.: Harvard University Press, 1947), pp. 203–53; and Paul A. Samuelson, "Social Indifference Curves," *Quarterly Journal of Economics*, vol. 70 (1956), pp. 1–22.

FIGURE 16.2.1

**Production Map in Input Space:
Optimum Conditions of Factor Substitution**

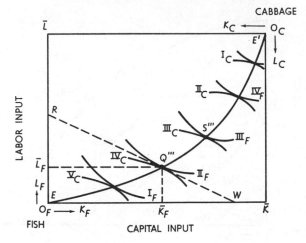

isoquants are plotted as $I_F, \ldots, IV_F$ and $I_C, \ldots, V_C$ in Figure 16.2.1. Satisfying the optimum conditions of factor substitution (equal marginal rates of technical substitution) leads to the contract curve in input space, labeled EE'. As we have already shown in Chapter 15, subsection 15.3.c, the contract curve may be mapped from input space into output space, thereby becoming the production-possibility frontier or transformation curve.

The particular transformation curve associated with the contract curve EE', and therefore directly associated with the fixed input endowments, is plotted as TT' in Figure 16.2.2. As you will recall, the slope of this curve indicates the marginal rate of transformation of fish into cabbage. It indicates exactly how many cabbages can be produced by a marginal transfer of capital and labor from fish production to cabbage production, under the assumption that inputs are optimally reallocated in each production process after the transfer (so as to maintain the optimal conditions of factor substitution). Consequently, the marginal rate of transformation is the marginal cabbage cost of an additional fish, or the inverse of the marginal fish cost of an additional cabbage.

16.2.c Production Possibilities and the Optimum Conditions of Exchange

Select any point on the transformation curve TT' in Figure 16.2.2. Let the point be S, so that the total outputs of fish and cabbage are $O\overline{F}$

FIGURE 16.2.2

Production-Possibility Froniter in Output Space: Optimum Conditions of Exchange

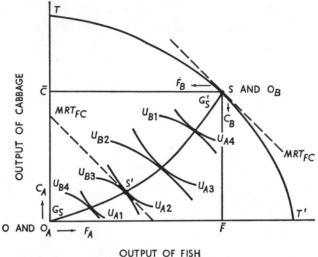

OUTPUT OF FISH

and $O\overline{C}$ respectively. The corresponding point in input space (and the associated allocation of K and L to F and C production) is labeled S''' in Figure 16.2.1.

The outputs $O\overline{F}$ and $O\overline{C}$ determine a particular volume of goods available to A and B; these outputs accordingly determine the dimensions of an Edgeworth box diagram for exchange. This diagram is constructed in Figure 16.2.2. by dropping perpendiculars to the axes from the point S. The original origin O becomes the origin for A, O_A, and the point S becomes B's origin, O_B. By assumption (*iii*) each individual has a well-defined preference function. Thus in the usual way, indifference curves for A and B are constructed in the exchange box. Curves U_{A1}, . . . , U_{A4} illustrate A's preference field and U_{B1}, . . . , U_{B4} show B's. The locus of tangencies, or the *feasible* points of exchange, is the contract curve $G_s G_s'$. The points on this contract curve are feasible because (*a*) an increase in the level of satisfaction of one trading party can be achieved only at the expense of the other, and (b) consumption at any point on the curve precisely exhausts the entire output of fish and cabbage. Thus the contract curve is labeled $G_s G_s'$ to denote it is the curve relative to the point S on the transformation curve; and, as you will recall, it is the locus of exchange possibilities satisfying the optimum conditions of exchange (i.e., it is a locus of Pareto-optimal points).

16.2.d   Retracing Some Steps: From the Contract Curve to the Utility-Possibility Frontier

By observing the utility levels for A and B at each point along the contract curve in Figure 16.2.2, one may generate the utility-possibility curve relative to the output point S, as shown in Chapter 15, subsection 15.2.c. The utility-possibility curve relative to S is plotted as $G_S G_S'$ in Figure 16.2.3. This curve alone does not help us much because it shows an infinite number of Pareto-optimal utility pairs corresponding to each of an infinite number of Pareto-optimal production pairs. We are just where we were at the end of Chapter 15; a multiple infinity of possible equilibria exist. However, we can remove one "infinity" dimension.

The optimum conditions of product substitution require equality between the marginal rate of transformation in production and the marginal rate of substitution in consumption for all pairs of goods and for all individuals consuming these goods. For our particular model, the conditions require equality between the marginal rate of transformation of fish into cabbage and both A's and B's marginal rate of substitution of fish for cabbage.

At the production point S in Figure 16.2.2, the marginal rate of transformation is indicated by the slope of the dashed line tangent to TT' at S, labeled MRT_{FC}. To satisfy the optimum conditions of product substitution, the marginal rate of substitution of both A and B must equal this particular value of the marginal rate of transformation. As

FIGURE 16.2.3

Utility-Possibility Frontier: From Output to Utility Space

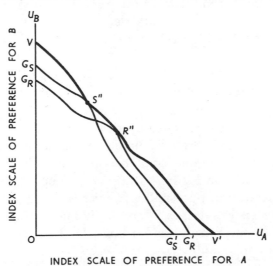

indicated graphically, this condition is satisfied at the unique point S' in Figure 16.2.2. Consequently, while the locus G_8G_8' in Figure 16.2.3 is the utility-possibility frontier relative to S, only the single point S'', corresponding to S' in Figure 16.2.2, is relevant. Relative to the output combination S, S''' in Figure 16.2.1 is the only allocation of inputs that satisfies the optimum conditions of factor substitution. Furthermore, relative to the same output combination S, S'' is the only allocation of fish and cabbage between A and B that satisfies both the optimum conditions of exchange and the optimum conditions of substitution. As a consequence, S'' is the only relevant point on G_8G_8'. One dimension of "infinity" is removed: S'' is the only efficient output allocation relative to S; but S can be anywhere on TT'. One dimension of "infinity" remains.

16.2.e From a Utility-Possibility Point to the Grand Utility-Possibility Frontier

Still using Figures 16.2.2 and 16.2.3, we can generate the "grand" utility-possibility frontier, or the utility-possibility frontier relative to *any* point on the production-possibility frontier. Imagine S moving to a point further down TT'. At the new point there would be more fish and fewer cabbages; a new Edgeworth exchange diagram would be constructed and a new contract curve generated. When mapped into utility space, the new contract curve might look like G_RG_R' in Figure 16.2.3.

Yet at the new output combination point on the production-possibility frontier TT', there would be a unique marginal rate of transformation. Again, the optimum conditions of product substitution would dictate a single relevant point on the contract curve or the utility curve G_RG_R' in Figure 16.2.3. This single relevant point is indicated by R'' in Figure 16.2.3.

As the output combination varies over all points on TT', new Edgeworth exchange boxes and new contract curves are generated. But at each output combination point there is a unique marginal rate of transformation. This unique rate, together with the optimum conditions of product substitution, dictates a unique output allocation between A and B relative to the output combination; and each of these unique points can be plotted in Figure 16.2.3 as a unique utility combination point. The overall utility-possibility frontier is obtained by connecting all these points (points such as S'' and R'' in Figure 16.2.3). This frontier is shown by the heavily shaded line VV'. Each point on this line shows: (a) a unique utility combination for A and B associated with

(b) a unique output allocation between A and B corresponding to (c) equality between the marginal rate of transformation and marginal rate of substitution of F for C (d) at a particular F—C output combination on the production-possibility frontier; furthermore, each F—C output combination dictates (e) a unique allocation of the K—L input endowments between the production of fish and cabbage. Quite a bit is embodied in VV'; but there is still a single infinity of possible solutions (any point on VV').[5]

16.2.f From the Utility-Possibility Frontier to the Point of "Constrained Bliss"

Up to this point the analysis of social welfare has required only assumptions (i)–(iii) in subsection 16.2.a. To reduce the single infinity of possible solutions to a unique solution requires the fourth assumption: there exists a *social welfare function* that depends exclusively on the positions of A and B in their own preference scales.

As previously indicated, this is a heroic assumption. It definitely requires ethical valuations regarding the "deservingness" of A and $B;$ in this respect it is unquestionably an ascientific concept. Furthermore, even the construction of a theoretical social welfare function is a difficult conceptual task, unless the society is ruled by a dictator. In that case the social welfare function is the dictator's individual preference function.

In the absence of a dictator (ironclad adherence to tradition, customs, mores, and such can be a "dictator" for social welfare purposes), how is a welfare function developed? "By direct vote" or "by representative vote through a legislature" would seem logical answers. But either method is likely to fail because of the famous "voting paradox."[6]

The matter may be viewed somewhat differently. Suppose you are A. Your principle interest is $U_A;$ and with given and fully employed resources, the greater U_A the lower U_B. You wish to push as far down and to the right on VV' as possible. You probably want a social welfare function that dictates a position very close to V' (and distant from V). But not necessarily. You are interested in U_A as a *consumer;* you are

---

[5] The mathematically inclined reader will realize that VV' may be derived as the envelope of the utility-possibility curves associated with each point on the production-possibility frontier.

[6] The "voting paradox" cannot be explained here. Basically, it involves the fact that ordering states by voting is likely to cause inconsistent (intransitive) orderings. For somewhat more explanation and bibliography, see C. E. Ferguson, *Macroeconomic Theory of Workable Competition* (Durham, N.C.: Duke University Press, 1964), pp. 10–11.

interested in the social welfare function as a *citizen*. In the latter capacity, you may prefer somewhat less U_A in order for some U_B to exist. This is more or less the situation when a property owner whose son attends a private school votes for a bond issue (and increased property tax) to improve the public school system. Similarly, any contribution to charity is an act that reduces one's satisfaction as a consumer but increases his satisfaction as a citizen.

Nonetheless, a social welfare function is difficult to construct. We merely assume that one exists. Its existence enables us to represent it by a family of social indifference curves, just as an individual's preference function can be represented by a family of consumption indifference curves. A portion of this family of curves is shown by the set W_1W_1', . . . , W_4W_4' in Figure 16.2.4.

The utility-possibility frontier VV' is also plotted in this figure. It shows all possible combinations of utilities to A and B, given the existing resource base, the production functions, and the individual preference orderings. In other words, it shows the utility combinations that are physically achievable. The social indifference curves show utility combinations that result in equal levels of social welfare. The higher the curve, the greater is aggregate social welfare.

For reasons that should now be thoroughly familiar, maximum social welfare is attained at Q, where a social indifference curve is just tangent

FIGURE 16.2.4

Maximization of Social Welfare: From Utility Possibilities to "Constrained Bliss"

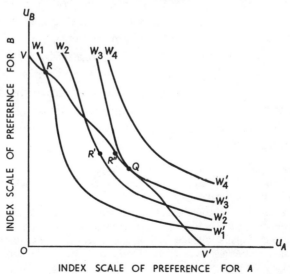

to the utility-possibility frontier. The infinity of possible equilibria has been reduced to a unique equilibrium point by considering the welfare of the society as a whole. This unique equilibrium Q is called the point of "constrained bliss" because it represents the unique organization of production, exchange, and distribution that leads to the maximum *attainable* social welfare. The society, of course, would be more "blissful" on $W_4 W_4'$. But a state on this higher curve is not attainable. The resource endowment and the state of the arts "constrains" the society to a point on VV'. In view of the constraint, society reaches its point of "constrained bliss" at Q.

16.2.g Constrained Bliss and Efficiency

This section begins with a digression to recount the meaning of Pareto optimality or efficiency.

Definition: Any organization (point) is said to be Pareto optimal or Pareto efficient when every reorganization that augments the value of one variable necessarily reduces the value of another.

Some examples should make this definition clear.

The contract curve for exchange is a Pareto-optimal locus. In deriving the locus in Chapter 15, Figure 15.2.3, the following argument was made.

Suppose the original distribution of the initial commodity endowment placed A and B at point D (not on the contract curve). At this point, A is willing to trade a relatively large amount of Y for a unit of X, and B is willing to trade a relatively large amount of X for a unit of Y. Both parties generally benefit from exchange; in the limit, B receives all the benefit, but A is no worse off, if trading moves the distribution to P_2. Similarly, A receives all the benefit, but B does not suffer, if the move is from D to P_3. At any point on CC' between P_2 and P_3, both parties benefit from exchange.

Clearly the point D is not Pareto optimal or efficient. A reorganization from D can benefit both traders (can augment the value of both utility variables). But *all* points on the contract curve are Pareto optimal. For example, a reorganization from P_2 to P_3 benefits A; but it simultaneously places B on a lower indifference curve.

The very same line of reasoning shows that the contract curve for production is a Pareto-optimal locus. If the allocation of inputs initially leads to a point not on the curve, the output of one or both goods can be increased, and the output of neither reduced, by moving to a point on the curve. But once on the curve, a reorganization that increases the output of one good must cause a reduction in the output of another. For example, in Figure 16.2.1, a reorganization from Q''' to S''' increases the output of fish but reduces cabbage production.

This then is the concept of Pareto optimality or efficiency: an organization such that a change that "helps" one must "hurt" another. As we have repeatedly seen, an infinite number of Pareto-optimal points (or organizations) are associated with each problem. One example is the utility-possibility frontier VV' in Figure 16.2.4. An infinite number of points such as R and Q are on this curve. A reorganization from, say, R to Q definitely benefits A because U_A is greater; but B suffers a loss because U_B declines. Thus each point on VV' is Pareto efficient and the entire curve is a Pareto-optimal locus.

Let us now examine a unique characteristic of the "constrained bliss" point Q in Figure 16.2.4. It is the only point of the infinitely many on the utility-possibility frontier that has unequivocal prescriptive significance. It is not only Pareto optimal, it is uniquely associated with maximum social welfare. Pareto optimality or efficiency is a *necessary,* but not *sufficient,* condition for a welfare maximum. The marginal conditions developed in section 16.1 only give the Pareto efficiency requirements; alone they do not guarantee a welfare maximum. For this an explicit welfare function is required.

Furthermore, once a social welfare function is defined the limited importance of "efficiency" becomes clear. The point of "constrained bliss" is, to be sure, Pareto optimal. But compare points R and R'. The former is Pareto efficient inasmuch as it lies on VV'. Yet a reorganization from R to R', a point that is Pareto inefficient, is clearly desirable because a higher level of social welfare is attained. Of course, starting from an "inefficient" point such as R', one or more points on VV' (such as R'' and Q) are socially preferable. But with the single exception of the "constrained-bliss" point Q, for any efficient point on VV' one or more inefficient points are socially more desirable.

16.2.h Inputs, Outputs, Distribution, and Welfare

Using assumptions (i)–(iv) in subsection 16.2.a, a unique constrained-bliss point has been determined by means of Figures 16.2.1–16.2.4. The process may now be reversed to find the *optimizing* values of the 10 variables listed in subsection 16.2.a: the inputs of labor and capital into the production of fish and cabbage (L_F, L_C, K_F, and K_C); the total outputs of fish and cabbage (F and C); and the distribution of fish and cabbage to A and B (F_A, F_B, C_A, and C_B).

The constrained-bliss point Q in Figure 16.2.4 is a unique point on VV'. As shown in subsection 16.2.e, each point on VV' is associated with a unique point on the production-possibility frontier because the marginal conditions for product substitution must be satisfied. Let the point on the production-possibility frontier corresponding to the constrained-bliss point Q be Q' in Figure 16.2.5, where TT' is the transformation curve. Locating the point Q' immediately determines two variables: the general equilibrium and maximum welfare outputs of fish and cabbage are $O\overline{F}$ and $O\overline{C}$ respectively.

Next, return to Figure 16.2.1. The total outputs $O\overline{F}$ and $O\overline{C}$ associated with Q' can be produced efficiently in only one way, by producing at the point on the contract curve EE' corresponding to Q' on TT'. Let this point be Q'''. The organization of production is determined by this point, as are the values of four more variables. The input of capital into fish production (K_F) is $O\overline{K}_F$; labor input (L_F) is $O\overline{L}_F$. Thus the input of capital into cabbage production (K_C) is $\overline{K} - O\overline{K}_F$, and labor input (L_C) is $\overline{L} - O\overline{L}_F$.

The final four variables are determined by constructing the Edgeworth exchange diagram whose dimensions represent the optimizing values of fish and cabbage output. Dropping perpendiculars from Q' in Figure 16.2.5, the box is given by $O\overline{C}Q'\overline{F}$. The contract curve relative to Q', labeled $G_Q G_Q'$, is constructed in the usual way. Finally, imposing the

FIGURE 16.2.5

General Equilibrium: From "Constrained Bliss" to Inputs, Outputs, and Distribution

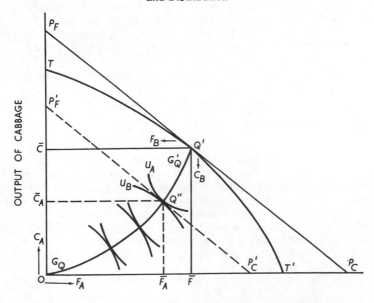

condition that the marginal rate of transformation (given by the slope of $P_F P_C$) must equal the common marginal rate of substitution (given by the slope of $P_F{'} P_C{'}$), one determines the unique point Q'' associated with Q'. Thus A gets $O\overline{F}_A$ units of fish and $O\overline{C}_A$ units of cabbage. B gets the rest: $\overline{F} - O\overline{F}_A$ units of fish and $\overline{C} - O\overline{C}_A$ units of cabbage.

In summary, a unique general equilibrium has been attained and this equilibrium point is uniquely associated with the maximum social welfare attainable by the society from the given resource base.

16.2.i From "Constrained Bliss" to Prices, Wages, and Rent

Subsection 16.1.b contained an informal suggestion of the way the price system under perfect competition leads to the point of maximum social welfare. Our final step is to determine these prices for the two inputs and the two outputs,[7] denoted as p_F (price of fish), p_C (price of cabbage), w (wage rate), and r (capital rent).

Let us first concentrate our attention upon wages and rent (see Figure 16.2.1). To attain the least-cost combination of resources, each producer must employ inputs in such proportions that their marginal rate of technical substitution equals the input-price ratio. Furthermore, the optimum conditions of factor substitution require equality of the marginal rate of technical substitution among all producers using the two inputs in question. This principle establishes the point Q''' in Fig-

---

[7] The social welfare maximum has been called the point of constrained bliss because constraints are imposed by input limitations and the production function. Let $K = \overline{K}$ and $L = \overline{L}$ represent the input endowments; and $K_F + K_C = \overline{K}$ and $L_F + L_C = \overline{L}$. Further, suppose the production functions for fish and cabbage are $F = F(K_F, L_F)$ and $C = C(K_C, L_C)$ respectively. Finally, let the social welfare function be given by $W = W(U_A, U_B)$ where $U_A = U_A(F_A, C_A)$ and $U_B = U_B(F_B, C_B)$, and where $F_A + F_B = F$ and $C_A + C_B = C$.

The constrained maximization problem is represented by the following equations: maximize $W = W(U_A, U_B)$, subject to $K - \overline{K} = 0$, $L - \overline{L} = 0$, $F(K_F, L_F) - \overline{F} = 0$, $C(K_C, L_C) - \overline{C} = 0$. The corresponding Lagrange expression may be written

$$\Lambda = W(U_A, U_B) - r(K - \overline{K}) - w(L - \overline{L}) - p_F(F(K_F, L_F) - \overline{F})$$
$$- p_C(C(K_C, L_C) - \overline{C}),$$

where r, w, p_F, and p_C are Lagrange multipliers. As already indicated, these multipliers are actually prices, so that the solution to the Lagrange problem gives (scale) solutions for the prices of fish and cabbage (p_F and p_C), the wage rate (w), and the rental on capital (r). The solution prices are the maximizing ones whether the economic system is a free enterprise system with perfect competition or a decentralized socialist economy following the Lange-Lerner rule. Smith's "invisible hand" is the market mechanism which, if perfectly competitive, happens to establish w, r, p_F, and p_C. An IBM machine (conceptually) can solve the Lagrange problem to obtain the "shadow prices" w, r, p_F, and p_C.

ure 16.2.1. The common marginal rate of technical substitution is indicated by the slope of the dashed line RW. Since this common marginal rate must equal the input-price ratio, we know that the rent-wage ratio (r/w) must be indicated by the slope of RW.

Next consider Figure 16.2.5. At the maximizing point Q', the marginal rate of transformation of fish into cabbage is given by the slope of $P_F P_C$. The optimum condition for product substitution requires that the marginal rate of transformation in production equal the common marginal rate of substitution in consumption. This principle determines the point Q'' and the marginal rate of substitution given by the slope of the dashed line $P_F' P_C'$. Finally, the optimum condition for exchange requires equality between the common marginal rate of substitution of fish for cabbage and the fish-cabbage price ratio. Hence p_F/p_C is given by the slope of $P_F' P_C'$ (which equals the slope of $P_F P_C$).[8]

Graphical analysis enables us to determine the optimizing input- and output-price *ratios;* absolute values, however, are so far unknown. Given the production functions and input allocation, one principle enables us to relate input prices to output prices: each profit-maximizing entrepreneur must employ units of each resource until the point is reached at which the value of its marginal product equals its (input) price. Denoting the marginal product of input i in producing output j by MP_{ij}, we have

$$r = p_F MP_{KF} = p_C MP_{KC}, \qquad (16.2.1)$$

and

$$w = p_F MP_{LF} = p_C MP_{LC}. \qquad (16.2.2)$$

Now let us take stock. Denote the marginal rate of technical substitution by $MRTS$ and the marginal rate of substitution by MRS. Equality of the marginal rate of technical substitution and the input-price ratio may be represented by

$$r = w(MRTS). \qquad (16.2.3)$$

Similarly, equality between the marginal rate of substitution and the output-price ratio implies

----

[8] Recall that from the theory of the household (Chapter 2, equation (2.2.4)), consumers will equate the ratio of marginal utilities to prices in a competitive market. This means

$$\frac{p_F}{p_C} = \frac{MU_F}{MU_C} = \frac{MC_F}{MC_C} = MRT_{F \text{ into } C} = MRS_{F \text{ for } C}.$$

Accordingly, when the economy is competitive, prices establish the indicated equality between the marginal rate of transformation in production and the common marginal rate of substitution in production.

$$p_F = p_C(MRS) . \tag{16.2.4}$$

Substitute expression (16.2.4) in, say, the first part of expression (16.2.2), obtaining

$$w = p_C(MRS)(MP_{LF}) . \tag{16.2.5}$$

Next, substituting expression (16.2.5) into (16.2.3) yields

$$r = p_C(MRS)(MP_{LF})(MRTS) . \tag{16.2.6}$$

All terms in parentheses in equation (16.2.6) represent *known* values—values determined by the welfare maximizing equilibrium solution. Hence r can be determined once p_C is known. If r is known, equation (16.2.3) can be solved for w. Finally, equation (16.2.4) will give the optimum value of p_F if p_C is known.[9] But there is no equation to determine p_C. Prices, wages, and rents are not unique (although the general equilibrium is). They are determined only as to scale or ratio. One of the prices must be designated as the numéraire of the system; then all other prices will be known. For example, one might specify that the price of one unit of cabbage is unity, $p_C = 1$. Then values of r, w, and p_F, corresponding to $p_C = 1$, can be found.

The reason the price side of the system is determinate only as to scale lies in the fact that our discussion has involved only *real* (nonmonetary) variables. The general equilibrium system can be completed by adding one monetary equation. Then unique (not scale) values can be determined for all input and output prices. For example, Fisher's "equation of exchange" could be added to the system, the familiar $MV = PT$. M is determined by the banking system and is a parameter. V, by assumption, is a psychological determined parameter; and T is given by the (known) real output of goods. Hence the price level P is determined, thereby determining p_C and thus p_F, r, and w. But unless a monetary equation is explicitly introduced, the price side of the model depends upon an endogenous numéraire. Fortunately, ratios are all that are needed for the process of welfare maximization.

16.2.j   Minimum Wages and Pareto Efficiency: A Digression[10]

The usefulness of the models in Chapters 15 and 16 lies in their power as analytical devices. To illustrate, in a simple case, how such analyses proceed, we consider the welfare effects of a minimum wage law.

In section 15.4, we developed a simple two input–two good general

---

[9] The entire manipulation can be turned around to express r, w, and p_C as a function of p_F.

[10] I am indebted to Professor Roy J. Ruffin for suggesting this application.

equilibrium model with fixed production coefficients. Suppose demand conditions in the economy are such that the equilibrium occurs at an output of $Q_1{}^*$ such that the relative price of Q_1 is $p_1 = 1/S_K = a_{K_1}/a_{K_2}$. In other words, the demand curve intersects the supply curve in the range $1/S_KA$ of Figure 15.4.3. Given the assumptions of section 15.4, we know that over this range of output, labor is redundant and the wage rate is zero. The rental rate on capital is $r = 1/a_{K_2}$.

Now suppose a minimum wage law is enacted which sets the minimum wage rate at $\underline{w} > 0$. The zero-profit equations (15.4.8) and (15.4.9) are then two equations in two unknowns, p_1 and r, and can be solved for these values. That is:

$$p_1 = \underline{w}\, a_{L_1} + r a_{K_1}$$
$$1 = \underline{w}\, a_{L_2} + r a_{K_2}$$

can be solved for r and p_1 in terms of $\underline{w}$. The solution is

$$\underline{r} = \frac{1 - \underline{w}\, a_{L_2}}{a_{K_2}}$$

$$\underline{p}_1 = \frac{a_{K_1}}{a_{K_2}} + \underline{w}\left(a_{L_1} - a_{L_2}\frac{a_{K_1}}{a_{K_2}}\right).$$

In Section 15.4, it was assumed that $a_{L_1} - a_{L_2}\, a_{K_1}/a_{K_2} > 0$; hence the relative price p_1 is increased by the introduction of the minimum wage and the rental rate is reduced. This means the demand for good 1 is lower at the new equilibrium price $\underline{p}_1$ than it was before the minimum wage was introduced.[11] Moreover, since good 1 is assumed to be relatively labor-intensive, this reduction in demand for good 1 reduces the employment of labor.

Does the new equilibrium meet the conditions of Pareto optimality? The answer is clearly no. We note that consumers are faced with a relative price of $\underline{p}_1$ that is equal to $a_{K_1}/a_{K_2} + \underline{w}(a_{L_1} - a_{L_2}\, a_{K_1}/a_{K_2})$. However, since the new equilibrium is still in the segment EA of the production possibility frontier shown in Figure 15.4.1, the marginal rate of transformation is unchanged by the minimum wage law. Thus, after the minimum wage is introduced, the marginal rate of substitution is no longer equal to the marginal rate of transformation and one of the conditions for Pareto optimality is violated.[12]

---

[11] Strictly speaking, we must also account for possible shifts in the demand curve that arise from income changes after the minimum wage is introduced. In other words, there may be distributive effects of a minimum wage. Given reasonable assumptions about the utility functions of consumers, it can be shown that the minimum wage does indeed reduce the equilibrium demand for good 1 in our example when these distributive effects are taken into account.

[12] In terms of Figure 16.2.5, the effect of the minimum wage law is to cause the slope of $P_F'P_C'$ to differ from the slope of P_FP_C.

Minimum wage legislation is ostensibly intended to benefit low-wage, low-income individuals. Some individuals no doubt do benefit from minimum wage legislation, but only at the cost of Pareto inefficiency in the economy. For this reason, many economists oppose minimum wage laws and would prefer to solve poverty problems by direct income transfers. Such direct transfers achieve the goal of reducing hardship but do not violate conditions of Pareto optimality. An income transfer is very likely to cause a shift in the point of general equilibrium, but so long as prices are permitted to adjust, the new equilibrium will be another Pareto efficient point.

16.3 EXTERNAL ECONOMIES AND WELFARE ECONOMICS: A FINAL WORD ON FREE ENTERPRISE

Sections 16.1 and 16.2 contain two different approaches to the problem of social welfare; but the conclusion of each is the same. Perfect competition in all markets will lead to a position of Pareto optimality *given* the assumptions that underlie the analysis. If these assumptions are not valid, however, perfect competition may not be so "perfect" after all. The perfectly competitive prices (or the Lange-Lerner Lagrange multipliers) may not be the right ones; or at the set of prices that would properly ration the constrained-bliss outputs, profit-maximizing entrepreneurs will not in fact produce the bliss configuration. If this happens maximum welfare is not achieved, despite the existence of perfect competition in all markets.

To explain this market failure a third approach to welfare maximization is necessary.

16.3.a Social Benefits and Costs

In several instances it has been stated that demand represents the marginal social valuation or the marginal social benefit derived from an additional unit of the commodity in question. The demand for each commodity, in other words, shows the price or marginal resource cost consumers are *willing* to pay for an additional unit. In perfect competition price equals marginal cost; hopefully, marginal cost is the marginal resource cost society *must* incur to have an additional unit produced. Thus by the customary "marginal" argument social welfare is a maximum when marginal social cost equals marginal social benefit, or when the resource sacrifice consumers are willing to make exactly equals the resource sacrifice society must make to secure an additional unit of output.

In certain cases, however, the marginal cost that governs the behavior of profit-maximizing entrepreneurs is not the same as the marginal cost to society as a whole. With obvious definitions, marginal *private* cost does not equal marginal *social* cost. In perfect competition, profit maximization implies that price equals marginal private cost. Maximum social welfare is only attained, however, if marginal private cost also equals marginal social cost, for it is only then that marginal social benefit and marginal social cost are equal.

Definition: An external economy (diseconomy) is said to exist when marginal social cost is less than (is greater than) marginal social benefit.

In this terminology perfect competition does not lead to maximum social welfare if external economies or diseconomies are present.

16.3.b Ownership Externalities[13]

There are three sources of external economies and diseconomies, or three reasons for a divergence between marginal social cost and marginal social benefit. The first is called "ownership externality." An explanation of this source of divergence may make the notion of "externality" somewhat clearer.

The classic example of an external diseconomy involves the poor widow who supports herself by hand laundry, and the factory next door whose smoke blackens the laundry. A more recent and relevant example is smog. The private cost of smoke disposal is the cost incurred in building smokestacks, automobile exhausts, and the like; and the *marginal* private cost to which price is equated is virtually zero. However the social cost is definitely positive when smoke disposal by many factories and automobiles causes smog. Marginal social cost exceeds (the zero) marginal private cost and hence price; social welfare is not maximized.

The externality concept should become even clearer from the following example of an external economy (due to Meade). A beekeeper and an apple orchardist are situated side by side. The production of apples, we may assume, requires only labor; thus the apple production function may be written $A = A(L)$. Now in the course of growing, apple blossoms first appear upon the trees; the apples come later. The bees feed upon the essential apple nectar from the blossoms and subsequently produce honey. The labor of the beekeeper is naturally in-

---

[13] The remainder of this chapter is based upon Francis M. Bator, "The Anatomy of Market Failure," *Quarterly Journal of Economics*, vol. 72 (1958), pp. 351–79.

volved; but so is the availability of apple blossoms and, accordingly, the level of apple production. As a consequence, the honey production function is $H = H(L, A)$.[14]

The marginal private cost of increased apple production depends only upon the (perfectly competitive) wage rate. If one additional unit of labor can produce one additional unit of apples, the marginal private cost of apples is the wage rate. But producing an additional unit of apples entails more apple blossoms and apple nectar; more bees can be fed and more honey produced. The marginal social cost of apples equals marginal private cost *minus* the value of the increment in honey production; the perfectly competitive output of apples is not as great as it "should" be for welfare maximization.

Where is the difficulty? Apple blossoms clearly enter into honey production; they have a positive marginal product and should, therefore, have a positive market price. But the orchardist cannot protect his equity in apple nectar; this scarce factor of production is divorced from his effective ownership. Apple nectar has a zero market price; even a perfectly competitive market fails to impute the correct value to apple nectar. Profit-maximizing decisions therefore fail properly to allocate resources at the margin because scarcity is divorced from ownership. In this situation market failure is attributable to an ownership externality.[15,16]

16.3.c Technical Externalities

A more important source of externalities may be attributable to technology. If production functions exhibit indivisibilities (for instance, can you add one tenth of an IBM machine or of a blast furnace?) or smoothly *increasing* returns to scale, a technical externality exists. The market can fail to achieve the welfare maximum for two reasons. With increasing returns to scale, and perfectly competitive input markets, average cost declines over the relevant range. This is likely to lead, via economic warfare, to monopoly and monopoly price, violating the marginal benefit–marginal cost requirement.

---

[14] We abstract from the bee service of cross-pollenization.

[15] An interesting pedagogical note illustrating the problem of externalities in a simple general equilibrium model is R. J. Ruffin, "Pollution in a Crusoe Economy," *The Canadian Journal of Economics*, vol. 5 (February, 1972), pp. 110–18.

[16] Coase has shown that in some cases, external effects can be properly taken into account by profit maximizing behavior on the part of individuals. Ronald Coase, "The Problem of Social Cost," *Journal of Law and Economics* (October, 1960), pp. 1–44.

If the situation does not lead to monopoly it nonetheless leads to market failure. So long as average cost declines, marginal cost is less than average cost. Equality of marginal social benefit and marginal social cost requires equality of price and marginal cost. But at a price equal to marginal cost a pure loss would be sustained by each producer. Thus the socially correct price would not induce profit-maximizing entrepreneurs to produce the socially correct output.

In summary, a technical externality causes market failure either because it leads to monopoly, in which case price does not equal marginal cost, or because free competitive enterprise is not viable at a marginal cost price.

16.3.d Public Good Externalities

Let us return to the two-person, two-good model: A and B consume X and Y. Let X be available in amount $\overline{X}$. Then X is said to be a public good if both A *and* B can each consume $\overline{X}$ units of X (rather than having $X_A + X_B = \overline{X}$). For example, one person viewing a pyrotechnic display does not preclude another from viewing it as well; concerts may be attended by more than one person; and, to a point, so too may public schools.

Perfect competition establishes equality between the marginal rate of transformation of X into Y and A's and B's common marginal rate of substitution of X for Y. But in the public good case, since A's consumption of X does not restrict B's, the marginal rate of transformation should equal the *sum* of the two marginal rates of substitution. Perfect competition, and perfectly competitive prices, lead to underproduction and underconsumption of public goods.

16.3.e Externalities and Free Enterprise

The existence of externalities places a definite limit on the scope of free competitive enterprise if a (static) social welfare maximum is to be attained. As obviously implied in subsections 16.3.b–16.3.d, public ownership or public control is sometimes necessary. But in a final evaluation one should remember that this analysis is *static;* dynamic considerations are not included, especially considerations of economic growth.

The static theory of welfare economics has been placed on a very rigorous basis and the static criteria for a welfare maximum deduced. But these criteria may not be applicable to a growth economy. One reason is uncertainty of the future. Another, and more important, is that growth itself tends to offset errors of judgment and of management. Doubtless some rate of growth, if sustained in an economy, would allow that economy to violate every static optimality condition with impunity. Therefore, the conclusions of static welfare economics may not afford suitable standards by which to appraise a truly dynamic economy. If free enterprise tends to establish a higher rate of growth than socialized industry, then dynamic arguments are in its favor, even though the free enterprise system may be shot through with oligopoly and monopoly elements. Innovation and growth are more important in the long run.

QUESTIONS AND EXERCISES

1. In 1965 the first hurricane in many years struck New Orleans, causing severe property damage. The government, in the guise of aid to distressed areas, paid property owners for part, and sometimes all, of their losses. What considerations would be uppermost in your mind if you were asked to write a lengthy essay on the impact of these payments upon the allocation of resources and the distribution of income?

2. Excise taxes are said harmfully to distort the allocation of resources in favor of untaxed commodities. Why?

3. Modern welfare economics frequently makes use of the concept of Pareto optimality. Define the concept and explain its role in the theory of welfare economics. Demonstrate the application of the above welfare criterion to a typical welfare problem (e.g., the distribution of income, resource allocation, etc.), and be sure to include in your discussion the problem of evaluating alternative positions from which society may choose.

4. If completely free trade implies maximum economic welfare, does it necessarily follow that any movement toward free trade would *improve* welfare?

5. Show the conditions that ensure efficient distribution of a given combination of products between two consumers. Would the same conditions ensure maximum *equity?*

6. "Resources are misallocated in the television industry since the cost is borne by advertisers rather than by viewers directly." Discuss.

7. It is often asserted that a monopolist generally operates inefficiently, that is, at some point on his average cost curve other than its minimum point, while competitive firms operate at their minimum average cost, and hence operate efficiently. Critically analyze this definition of economic efficiency, and if you find it unsatisfactory, suggest an alternative.

8. How might a community attempt to control a monopoly in the public interest?

9. "A society or firm that is capable of imputing appropriate prices to the factors of production has, in those prices, a tool that can be used to provide efficient direction to its productive activities." Explain.

10. Assume that we now have a socially optimal distribution of factors of production among industries. The imposition of an income tax will not affect this distribution. True or false, and explain.

11. "The government's policies toward agriculture over the last 30 years or so have been basically defective because the policies fail to separate the 'economic' problem of resource allocation from the 'ethical' problem of income distribution." Discuss.

12. "Increasing returns to scale make the achievement of Pareto optimality easier for a society." Discuss.

13. Assume that resources are now allocated optimally within a community. How will the following affect this allocation: (*a*) the imposition of a progressive income tax, (*b*) the imposition of a proportional income tax, (*c*) an industry in the economy becomes monopolized, and (*d*) a new method of producing some product is introduced that has an undesirable by-product (e.g., water pollution)?

SUGGESTED READINGS

Bator, Francis M. "The Anatomy of Market Failure," *Quarterly Journal of Economics,* vol. 72 (1958), pp. 351–79. [Elementary math required.]

———. "The Simple Analytics of Welfare Maximization," *American Economic Review,* vol. 47 (1957), pp. 22–59.

Ferguson, C. E. "Transformation Curve in Production Theory: A Pedagogical Note," *Southern Economic Journal,* vol. 29 (1962), pp. 96–102. [Elementary math required.]

Henderson, James M., and Quandt, Richard E. *Microeconomic Theory,* 2d ed., pp. 254–92. New York: McGraw-Hill Book Co., Inc., 1971. [Elementary math required.]

Kenen, Peter B. "On the Geometry of Welfare Economics," *Quarterly Journal of Economics,* vol. 71 (1957), pp. 426–47.

Reder, Melvin W. *Studies in the Theory of Welfare Economics.* New York: Columbia University Press, 1947.

Samuelson, Paul A. *Foundations of Economic Analysis,* pp. 203–53. Cambridge, Mass.: Harvard University Press, 1947. [Advanced math required.]

Scitovsky, Tibor. *Welfare and Competition.* Homewood, Ill.: Richard D. Irwin, Inc., 1971. [Elementary math required.]

Advanced reading, part V

I. GENERAL EQUILIBRIUM

Kuenne, Robert E. *The Theory of General Economic Equilibrium*. Princeton, N.J.: Princeton University Press, 1963.

Quirk, James, and Saposnik, Rubin. *Introduction to General Equilibrium Theory and Welfare Economics*. New York: McGraw-Hill Book Co., 1968.

II. WELFARE ECONOMICS: GENERAL AND EXPOSITORY

Bator, F. M. "The Simple Analytics of Welfare Maximization," *American Economic Review,* vol. 47 (1957), pp. 22–59.

Baumol, William J. *Welfare Economics and the Theory of the State.* Cambridge, Mass.: Harvard University Press, 1952.

Hicks, J. R. "The Foundations of Welfare Economics," *Economic Journal,* vol. 49 (1939), pp. 696–712.

Kenen, Peter B. "On the Geometry of Welfare Economics," *Quarterly Journal of Economics,* vol. 71 (1957), pp. 426–47.

Lange, Oscar. "The Foundations of Welfare Economics," *Econometrica,* vol. 10 (1942), pp. 215–28.

Lerner, A. P. *The Economics of Control: Principles of Welfare Economics.* New York: The Macmillan Co., 1944.

Little, I. M. D. *Welfare Economics.* 2d ed. Oxford: Clarendon Press, 1957.

Mishan, E. J. "A Survey of Welfare Economics, 1939–1959," *Economic Journal,* vol. 70 (1960), pp. 197–265, with extensive bibliography.

Reder, M. W. *Studies in the Theory of Welfare Economics.* New York: Columbia University Press, 1947.

Rothenberg, Jerome. *The Measurement of Social Welfare.* Englewood Cliffs, N.J.: Prentice-Hall, Inc., 1961.

Samuelson, Paul A. *Foundations of Economic Analysis,* pp. 203–53. Cambridge, Mass.: Harvard University Press, 1947.

III. WELFARE PROPOSITIONS AND THE SOCIAL WELFARE FUNCTION

Arrow, Kenneth J. *Social Choice and Individual Values.* New York: John Wiley & Sons, Inc., 1951.

Burk (Bergson), Abram. "A Reformulation of Certain Aspects of Welfare Economics," *Quarterly Journal of Economics,* vol. 52 (1937–38), pp. 310–34.

Goodman, Leo A., and Markowitz, Harry. "Social Welfare Functions Based on Individual Rankings," *American Journal of Sociology,* vol. 58 (1952–53), pp. 257–62.

Kaldor, Nicholas. "Welfare Propositions in Economics and Interpersonal Comparisons of Utility," *Economic Journal,* vol. 49 (1939), pp. 549–52.

Majumdar, Tapas. *The Measurement of Utility.* London: Macmillan & Co., Ltd., 1958.

Samuelson, Paul A. "Social Indifference Curves," *Quarterly Journal of Economics,* vol. 70 (1956), pp. 1–22.

Scitovsky, Tibor. "A Note on Welfare Propositions in Economics," *Review of Economic Studies,* vol. 9 (1941–42), pp. 77–88.

IV. CONSUMER'S SURPLUS

Henderson, A. "Consumer's Surplus and the Compensating Variation," *Review of Economic Studies,* vol. 8 (1940–41), pp. 117–21.

Hicks, J. R. "The Rehabilitation of Consumer's Surplus," *Review of Economic Studies,* vol. 8 (1940–41), pp. 108–16.

———. *A Revision of Demand Theory.* Oxford: Clarendon Press, 1956.

Hotelling, Harold. "The General Welfare in Relation to Problems of Taxation and of Railway and Utility Rates," *Econometrica,* vol. 6 (1938), pp. 242–69.

Pfouts, R. W. "A Critique of Some Recent Contributions to the Theory of Consumers' Surplus," *Southern Economic Journal,* vol. 19 (1953), pp. 315–33.

V. MARGINAL-COST PRICING

Barone, E. "The Ministry of Production in the Collectivist State," in *Collectivist Economic Planning* (ed. F. A. Hayek), pp. 245–90. London: Routledge & Son, 1935.

Coase, R. H. "The Marginal Cost Controversy," *Economica,* N.S. vol. 13 (1946), pp. 169–82.

Hotelling, Harold. "The General Welfare in Relation to Problems of Taxation and of Railway and Utility Rates," *Econometrica,* vol. 6 (1938), pp. 242–69.

Lerner, A. P. "Statics and Dynamics in Socialist Economics," *Economic Journal,* vol. 47 (1937), pp. 253–70.

Ruggles, Nancy. "Recent Developments in the Theory of Marginal Cost Pricing," *Review of Economic Studies,* vol. 17 (1949–50), pp. 107–26.

———. "The Welfare Basis of the Marginal Cost Pricing Principle," *Review of Economic Studies,* vol. 17 (1949–50), pp. 29–46.

Vickrey, William. "Some Objections to Marginal-Cost Pricing," *Journal of Political Economy,* vol. 56 (1948), pp. 218–38.

VI. IDEAL OUTPUT

Kahn, R. F. "Some Notes on Ideal Output," *Economic Journal,* vol. 45 (1935), pp. 1–35.

Lipsey, R. G., and Lancaster, Kelvin. "The General Theory of Second Best," *Review of Economic Studies,* vol. 24 (1956–57), pp. 11–32.

McKenzie, Lionel. "Ideal Output and the Interdependence of Firms," *Economic Journal,* vol. 61 (1951), pp. 785–803.

VII. EXTERNAL ECONOMIES

Bator, F. M. "The Anatomy of Market Failure," *Quarterly Journal of Economics,* vol. 72 (1958), pp. 351–79.

Baumol, W. J. "External Economies and Second-Order Conditions," *American Economic Review,* vol. 54 (1964), pp. 358–72.

Buchanan, James M., and Kafoglis, Milton Z. "A Note on Public Goods Supply," *American Economic Review,* vol. 53 (1963), pp. 403–14.

———, and Stubblebine, W. Craig. "Externality," *Economica,* N.S. vol. 29 (1962), pp. 371–84.

Davis, Otto A., and Whinston, Andrew. "Externalities, Welfare, and the Theory of Games," *Journal of Political Economy,* vol. 70 (1962), pp. 241–62.

appendix

appendix

A comprehensive examination in microeconomic theory for graduate students

The following questions, furnished the author by Professor Fritz Machlup of Princeton University, constitute a comprehensive and rather exhaustive examination in microeconomic theory for graduate students. The reader will note that some topics covered in the examination are not treated in this text and that welfare economics is not covered explicitly in the questions.

I. QUESTIONS ON THE THEORY OF RELATIVE PRICES

A. The Equilibrium of the Household

1. "Valuation is a subjective process. We cannot *observe* valuation. It is therefore out of place in a scientific explanation." Discuss.

2. Discuss briefly the claims made concerning the methodological superiority of indifference curve theory over marginal utility theory.

3. Present a short outline or organization, in brief sentences or merely in headings for chapters and sections, but not exceeding the space of one page, of a lengthy essay on the question: "Cardinal or Ordinal Utility?"

4. Under what conditions (concerning prices or products) would it be possible for a consumer to be in "equilibrium":
   a. while the marginal utilities of some goods he consumes are zero?
   b. while the marginal utilities of some goods he refuses to purchase are greater than the marginal utilities of some goods he does purchase?

c. while the marginal utilities of all the goods he purchases are exactly proportional to their prices?

d. while the marginal utilities of all the goods he purchases are exactly equal?

5. What does it mean if an indifference curve between goods X and Y (*a*) becomes parallel to the Y axis, (*b*) is positively sloped and has higher indifference curves to its right, (*c*) is positively sloped and has higher indifference curves to its left, (*d*) is negatively sloped and has higher indifference curves to its left?

6. Draw a family of indifference curves between money and commodity X; construct the price-consumption curve; calculate from the graph the corresponding demand schedule and draw the demand curve.

7. Explain the income effect of a price change and connect it with the income elasticity of demand.

8. The slope of income-consumption curves in an indifference map for goods X and Y has definite implications concerning the income elasticities of demand for X and Y, either absolutely or relative to each other; and the slope of price-consumption curves in an indifference map for good X and money (along the Y axis) has definite implications concerning the price elasticity of demand for X. State what these implications are, first, if the income-consumption curve and, then, if the price-consumption curve runs (*a*) to the northwest, (*b*) straight to the north, (*c*) to the north-northeast, (*d*) to the east-northeast, (*e*) straight to the east, (*f*) to the southeast.

9. Explain the concepts of substitutability and complementarity (*a*) in terms of marginal utility theory and (*b*) in terms of indifference curve theory.

10. Pareto thought that the shape of an indifference curve would reflect whether the two goods under consideration were complementary or substitutable. Hicks denied this was the case except under extreme circumstances. J. M. Clark found that the shapes of a family of indifference curves would reflect complementarity or substitutability between the two goods in question.

Present in a few words, with or without the aid of graphical demonstration, the essentials of (*a*) Pareto's opinion, (*b*) Hicks' criticism, and (*c*) Clark's resolution. Then, (*d*) discuss the possibility of expressing or measuring complementarity and substitutability by means of cross-elasticities of demand.

Finally, (*e*) explain what a cross-elasticity of zero may imply concerning the complementarity or substitutability between the two goods if it is known that neither of the goods is inferior, and (*f*) what it may imply if one of them is markedly inferior.

11. If a price reduction of commodity A results in increased consumption of commodity B and in reduced consumption of commodity C, we cannot

know offhand whether this is to be attributed to substitution effects or to income effects.

a. State the possible relations (substitutability, complementarity) among the three commodities that may explain the described changes, assuming that income effects are negligible.

b. Assuming that the three commodities are almost unrelated with one another, how could income effects explain the described changes?

c. How could you in actual fact attempt to ascertain which of the possible explanations is most likely valid?

12. The "diamond case," the "case of speculative demand," and the "Giffen case" are regarded as the most important exceptions to the law of demand. The first two are sometimes ruled out because not all premises of the law are fulfilled; the last is conceded as a real exception.

a. State the law of demand in one sentence.

b. State, in one short sentence each, the three cases mentioned above.

c. State on what ground the first two cases are considered "exclusions" rather than "exceptions" of the law.

d. Give Professor Hicks' explanation of the Giffen case.

13. Hicks, after stating the "reversibility of complementarity" between goods X and Y, warns: "Observe that it is only the substitution effects that are reversible. If a fall in the price of X increases the demand for Y, it does not necessarily follow that a fall in the price of Y will increase the demand for X." Explain.

14. During World War II many consumer goods were rationed; one of the techniques used in rationing was the issuance of books of coupons, in different colors for different commodity groups, and the fixing of "ration-point values" for each commodity. For example, each person had each week a fixed number of "brown ration points," which were good for the purchase of meats and fats. Each person had, so to speak, a fixed weekly "income" of ration points—apart from any money income—and each rationed commodity had a "price" fixed in terms of ration points—apart from its price in terms of money.

In December, 1943, the ration-point values of meats were reduced. This "price reduction" was intended to cause an increase in purchases of meat. Yet it probably caused also an increased demand for butter, although the ration-point values of butter were left unchanged.

a. Would you regard this as a symptom of complementarity between meat and butter? Why or why not?

b. Would you think that butter and meat are more likely substitutes or complements of each other? Why?

c. How can you explain the increased demand for butter in terms of substitution effect and income effect? (Note: These effects refer here to ration points, not money.)

d. Assuming, for the sake of simplicity, that beef and butter are the only things available for brown ration points, draw an indifference map for the two commodities, show the price relation and its change, exhibit the income and substitution effects, and mark the combinations chosen by the consumer before and after the price change. (A rough sketch is sufficient.)

15. Certain "peculiarities of indifference maps involving money" are presented by Hart, particularly (*a*) that all indifference curves will intercept the *Y* axis measuring "money," but not the axis measuring quantities of the good *X* except if the latter were "leisure;" (*b*) that all indifference curves will have lowest points; (*c*) that these lowest points will lie further to the left on higher indifference curves; (*d*) that for given quantities of *X*, if this is not an inferior good, higher indifference curves will be steeper. Explain and comment on all these points.

16. Frank H. Knight states "that we know in general only three facts" about the shape of indifference curves involving money: "They always have a negative slope (within the significant range), they do not intersect (or meet), and they cannot have a uniform slope and vertical spacing for different values of *X*. This third feature would involve zero income elasticity of demand for *X;* and this . . . is conceivable only for a good with a complex utility so arranged that displacement of other goods would exactly offset the diminishing utility of the various component types of satisfaction which it yields." Explain and comment on all these points.

17. Robert L. Bishop discussed seven different concepts of consumer's surplus, and J. R. Hicks presented four concepts (which he interpreted as compensating or equivalent variations). Choose any four of these concepts for a brief exposition, emphasizing the differences between them.

18. Present some of the uses made of consumer-surplus arguments in favor of particular methods of taxation.

B. Production Functions and the Cost of Production

1. Assume that a curve is drawn showing along the abscissa the amounts of a factor *A* employed in combination with a fixed amount of a group of factors called *B*, and along the ordinate the amount of physical product obtainable from these combinations of factors.

a. How can you find (geometrically) the amount of *A* for which the average physical product per unit of *A* is a maximum?

b. How can you find (geometrically) the amount of *A* for which the marginal physical product of *A* is a maximum?

c. Between the two points defined in questions (*a*) and (*b*), will the marginal physical product of *A* increase or decrease as more of *A* is used?

d. Between these two points, will the average physical product per unit of *A* increase or decrease as more of *A* is used?

e. At the point defined (*a*), will the marginal physical product of *A* be higher or lower than the average physical product per unit of *A?* Give reasons.

f. At the point defined in (*b*), will the marginal physical product of *A* be higher or lower than the average physical produce per unit of *A?* Give reasons.

g. How can you find (geometrically) the amount of *A* for which the marginal physical product of *A* is zero?

h. At which point will the average physical product per unit of *B* (the fixed factor group) be a maximum, assuming linear homogeneity?

i. Is it more efficient to work in a phase of increasing returns or decreasing returns? Give reasons.

j. What will determine the proportion between factors *A* and *B* that a producer will choose?

k. Under what condition would he choose the proportion between factors *A* and *B* at which the average physical product per unit of *B* is a maximum?

l. Under what conditions would he choose any of the proportions between factors *A* and *B* in the range between the points defined in (*a*) and (*b*)?

2. Assuming linear homogeneity, prove that according to the laws of return to factors of production combined in varying proportions, (*a*) average product per unit of factor *B* will increase when additional amounts of factor *A* are employed with increasing returns; (*b*) average product per unit of factor *B* will also increase when additional amounts of factor *A* are employed with diminishing returns; (*c*) marginal product per unit of factor *B* will be negative when factor *A* is employed in a proportion that lies within the phase of increasing returns.

3. If engineers prepare a table giving the amounts of product that can be obtained from combining all the necessary factors of production in all possible proportions, can one find a point of "maximum efficiency" or "optimum proportion of factors?" Give reasons for your answer.

4. The law of diminishing returns (or nonproportional output) has been empirically tested and verified for several different factors of production. However, it is said that if "factors of production" are defined in a certain way the "law of diminishing returns" can be logically deduced from that definition and, thus, is an a priori statement. Explain.

5. "That people do not grow all the crops they want in just a few little flower pots is sufficient proof for the existence of diminishing returns." Explain.

6. If the application of auxiliary factors to a fixed factor has been pushed beyond the point where "diminishing returns" set in, does this indicate an inefficient (or uneconomical) proportion of the factors? Give reasons.

7. Under what conditions, if any, might a producer find it preferable to produce within a range of increasing returns?

8. Distinguish the "indivisibility" that may cause a monopolist to employ a variable factor under increasing returns from the "indivisibility" that may be responsible for his monopoly position.

9. While producers may undertake to create or aggravate indivisibilities that might protect their monopoly position, they may at the same time undertake to remove or reduce indivisibilities that force them to produce sometimes under increasing returns. Explain and illustrate.

10. What may be the reason for the fact that early economists believed agricultural production was governed by the law of diminishing returns while increasing returns would prevail in industry?

11. Discuss the essential difference between the laws of proportions and the laws of returns to scale.

12. The same economies of production have sometimes been explained in terms of increasing returns to scale and sometimes in terms of factor substitution. Likewise, the same diseconomies that have been regarded as instances of diminishing returns to scale have alternatively been interpreted as cases of varying proportions among factors. Explain.

13. Draw—on graph paper—a total product curve for combinations of varying amounts of factor A with a fixed amount, say four units, of factor B. Then draw, on the same graph, the total product curves for combinations of varying amounts of A with two units of B and with eight units of B, on the assumption that up to four units of B increasing returns to scale prevail, whereas from this scale upward the returns to scale are constant. It is essential that the three curves reflect the mentioned assumptions.

14. Calculate, on the basis of the productivity curves drawn as directed in the preceding question, the schedules of total cost, average total cost, average variable cost, and marginal cost of production, if factor A costs $1 per unit and is the only variable cost of production, while factor B stands for the equipment of the firm and costs $6.25 per day for each unit installed, whether or not it is used.

a. Assume first that the firm is equipped with four units of B, which are coupled in such a way as to make it impossible to work with less than the entire equipment. (Thus, only one of the three product curves will be relevant for the input-output relations in question.)

b. Now, altering the preceding assumption, assume that the firm is equipped with two sets of four units of B—that is, with eight B units—and that the operation of only two units becomes possible, so that the firm can operate two, four, six, or eight units of B. (Mention for each output volume listed on your cost schedule how many units of B will be operated for its production.)

15. What is the logical relation between increasing returns and decreasing costs?

16. Write a short essay on the concept of "decreasing costs."

17. Fixed costs are often very substantial and real. Is it incomprehensible how the economic theorist can say we should neglect them in the short run and that they don't exist in the long run? Explain.

18. Show the similarities and differences between (*a*) spreading of overhead, (*b*) increasing returns of fuller use of inflexible plant, (*c*) internal economies of large-scale production, and (*d*) external economies of large-scale industry.

19. Considering only elements of internal cost calculations of a firm, explain the situations making for a coincidence of (*a*) decreasing short-run cost and increasing long-run cost; (*b*) increasing short-run cost and decreasing long-run cost; (*c*) increasing short-run cost and increasing long-run cost; (*d*) decreasing short-run cost and decreasing long-run cost; (*e*) constant short-run cost and decreasing long-run cost; (*f*) increasing short-run cost and constant long-run cost.

20. How can the existence of constant short-run marginal cost be reconciled with the law of variable proportions and the U-shaped cost curves that are customarily derived from it?

21. The short-run marginal cost curve of an individual manufacturing establishment is often drawn with a U shape, steeply falling to a minimum point and steeply rising thereafter. The long-run marginal cost curve of the same firm may be drawn much flatter—perhaps falling not less steeply but often moving horizontally over a substantial range and certainly rising much more gradually—than the short-run curve. Sometimes, however, even the short-run marginal cost curve of the firm is drawn horizontally over a considerable range.

Explain the most plausible technological reasons for the conditions pictured in these curves, that is, for (*a*) the steeply U-shaped short-run curve, (*b*) the flat bottom and gentler rise of the long-run curve, and (*c*) the flat bottom of the short-run curve in some instances.

22. "The depreciation of machinery is usually in the short run a fixed cost and in the long run a variable cost; but it may also in the short run be partly a fixed and partly a variable cost." Explain (*a*) depreciation as a short-run fixed cost; (*b*) depreciation as a long-run variable cost; (*c*) depreciation as a short-run variable cost.

23. A student once was asked to show a cost schedule for a firm where "increasing returns" prevail. He gave the following schedule of average total cost:

Output	ATC
60 units	$15
70 units	12
80 units	8

What would you say to the student?

24. Confusion may easily arise in discussing comparisons and variations of cost, even when we deal with only one firm and specify the kind of cost we mean. Contrast, with the aid of graphs, the meaning of the cost variations referred to in the following sentences:

a. "After a certain point diseconomies of large scale may outweigh the economies, and *marginal costs may rise.*" (Joan Robinson, *The Economics of Imperfect Competition,* p. 49.)

b. "The tax . . . may be taken to stand for a *rise in marginal costs* brought about by a rise in wages." (Ibid., p. 82.)

c. "The rise in price due to the imposition of the tax is equal to half the *increase in marginal cost* [which may be equal or more or less than the tax]." (Ibid., p. 77. All italics supplied.)

25. Discuss the comparative difficulties of calculating the total cost, average cost, and marginal cost for a product produced by a multiproduct firm.

26. "When, in a problem of output and price determination, a cost curve is drawn, all problems of factor input and of the technological substitution between factors of production are considered as solved beforehand." Discuss.

27. Explain the differences—regarding the underlying causes—between (*a*) constant costs in the individual firm; (*b*) constant costs in the industry with increasing costs in every single firm; and (*c*) constant supply prices in the industry owing to external economies offsetting the conditions of increasing costs.

28. What are the methodological differences between (*a*) external economies, (*b*) economies due to economic development, and (*c*) economies due to new inventions?

C . The Equilibrium of the Firm

1. Multiproduct firms are more frequently observed in reality; single-product firms are more frequently treated by theory. Give reasons for both these facts.

2. Without revealing your own position, present the strongest possible arguments for and against the view that the principle of profit maximization is merely an empty tautology and useless for any explanatory or predictive purposes.

3. Discuss the alleged dichotomy between maximum profit and security as goals of business conduct in an uncertain world, and the contention that

profit maximization is meaningless as a guide to action where there is uncertainty.

4. Demand curves, in the theory of the equilibrium of the firm, are supposed to describe subjective expectations of future sales possibilities. How does theory allow for the facts (*a*) that such expectations are always uncertain (and usually the more uncertain the more distant the future to which they pertain) and (*b*) that the revenues which can be expected from alternative policies may refer to different points of time?

5. "An entrepreneur will, so we assume, always produce any given output in such a way that the cost to him of that given output is at a minimum. But it is not to his interest to choose from all possible outputs that output whose average cost is least." Explain.

6. State the relation between marginal revenue and elasticity of demand, deriving it by geometrical and algebraic analysis.

7. Can marginal cost and marginal revenue be equal at a volume of output where the average cost curve is intersected by the demand curve? Why or why not?

8. Draw a neat and precise graph according to the following instructions:

a. Draw an average fixed cost curve and mark it *AFC.*

b. Draw a U-shaped average variable cost curve and mark it *AVC.*

c. Construct the average total cost curve and mark it *ATC.*

d. Construct the marginal cost curve and mark it *MC.*

e. Draw a not steeply sloping, straight-line demand curve, cutting the *ATC* curve in its increasing range, and mark it D_1.

f. Construct the corresponding marginal revenue curve and mark it MR_1.

g. Mark the point *K* on the *X* axis to show the chosen output.

h. Mark the point *P* to show the chosen price.

i. Mark and indicate points needed to show quasi rent (the excess of total revenue over total variable cost).

j. Mark and indicate points needed to show net profit (the excess of total revenue over all cost).

k. Draw now another demand curve which, presumably under the influence of newcomers' competition, is so much further downward and to the left that it is a tangent to the *ATC* curve; mark it D_2.

l. Construct the corresponding marginal revenue curve and mark it MR_2.

m. Mark the point *L* on the *X* axis to show the chosen output.

n. Mark the point *T* to show the chosen price.

o. Mark and indicate all points needed to show quasi rent.

p. Mark and indicate points needed to show net profit.

9. Draw a smooth demand curve with some concavity from above and then the corresponding marginal revenue curve, constructing at least three points of the latter with ruler and compass and the rest freehand.

10. "Average cost may be the most important datum for the estimate of long-run demand elasticity." Explain how this can be so and what significance it may have for the explanation of so-called full-cost pricing.

11. Explain how the existence of interventions against "selling below cost" and "profiteering" may be referred to as arguments against the average-cost theory of pricing.

12. "The analysis of the size of the firm in the theory of relative prices relates to problems very different from those with which the theory of growth is concerned." Explain.

13. How is it possible, as is asserted by the theory of monopolistic competition, that firms may possess much "excess capacity" and yet be "undersized?"

14. Prove that for a monopolist faced with a straight-line demand curve and forced to charge a uniform price to all takers, *total revenue* will be maximized if the quantity sold is exactly half the quantity which buyers would take at a price of zero.

15. "It is often said that a monopolist will restrict output by less the greater the elasticity of demand for his product and the more rapid the rate of decreasing cost, or that he will restrict output more the less the elasticity of demand and the more rapid the rate of increasing cost." Mrs. Robinson calls this a "common confusion" and "fallacy" but admits that it "turns out to be correct" in special cases. Explain why the "common view" is incorrect "in general' but correct in special cases, and discuss whether these special cases are very exceptional.

16. "The difference between marginal cost and average variable cost is average rent per unit of output." Prove this proposition for cases of pure competition and show that it does not hold otherwise.

17. An increase in demand for the product of an individual firm may be accompanied by (1) an increase in elasticity; (2) a decrease in elasticity; or (3) no change in elasticity.

State for *each* of the three cases:

a. What may be the actual conditions responsible for the change, or absence of change, in elasticity?

b. What would be the geometric properties of the new demand curve in comparison with the old?

c. What would be the effect upon the selling price of the product if it is produced under constant marginal cost?

d. What would be the effect upon the selling price of the product if it is produced under increasing marginal cost?

e. What would be the effect upon the selling price of the product if it is produced under decreasing marginal cost?

18. An increase in the demand for the product of an individual firm not in an oligopoly position may leave selling price unchanged although marginal cost is not constant.

a. State what condition would account for the unchanged selling price if marginal cost was increasing.

b. State what condition would account for the unchanged selling price if marginal cost was decreasing.

c. Draw a graph picturing the condition under (*b*)—that is, showing the decreasing marginal cost curve, the "previous" (curvilinear) demand curve, and the "new" demand curve that would call for no change of price.

19. Firms are occasionally found to raise prices when trade is bad and the demand for their goods has fallen. The businessmen's explanation usually is that as output has fallen off each unit has to bear a higher share of the overhead cost than before. (*a*) Discuss this explanation. (*b*) Provide another explanation if you reject the first.

20. Can a decrease in the demand for the product of a monopolistic seller induce him to increase his output? If so, under what conditions?

21. Solve the following problem by means of geometrical devices: given are a stretch of a sloping demand curve and a long stretch of a decreasing marginal cost curve, so that you can construct the chosen output volume and selling price. Now demand increases so much that under the given cost conditions and new demand conditions, output will be increased to exactly three times the former volume and price will be maintained at the former level. (*a*) How must the elasticity of demand have changed to bring forth this result? (*b*) Construct the relevant stretch of the new demand curve.

22. "A disappearance of rival firms may just as well increase as decrease the elasticity of demand for the products of the remaining firms." State the conditions that are apt to cause either result.

23. If a firm through efficient advertising succeeds in increasing the demand for its product, will the elasticity of this demand be higher or lower than before? Why?

24. Demand is often conveniently expressed in terms of net prices (average net revenue) received by the seller rather than gross prices paid by the consumer. Different kinds of deductions from the prices paid by the consumers may result in significant differences in the elasticities of the demand curves in terms of average net receipts.

Compare the elasticities of the "previous" and various "new" demand curves (average revenue curves) at (*a*) given net prices and (*b*) given quantities of output, under the following three assumptions: a specific excise tax is introduced (a tax per unit of physical sales); an *ad valorem* excise tax is introduced (a tax as a percentage of price); and a progressive *ad valorem* excise tax is introduced with tax rates increasing with price (with higher percentages of higher prices and lower percentages of lower prices).

[*Note:* For the sake of simplicity assume first that the "previous" demand curve is a straight line. But afterwards examine whether conclusions drawn from straight-line reasoning have to be qualified if the demand curve is concave from above.]

25. Discuss and compare the effects a subsidy given to a monopolist is likely to have upon prices paid by the consumer and upon quantities sold: (*a*) when the subsidy is a fixed sum irrespective of output; (*b*) when the subsidy is a fixed amount on each unit of output produced; (*c*) when the subsidy is a fixed percentage of the price of each unit produced; and (*d*) when the subsidy is progressive (when it increases per unit as the output increases).

26. Draw a graph picturing the situation where the imposition of an excise tax upon a product which a monopolist produces under increasing marginal cost will raise the selling price by more than half the tax. State briefly the essential properties of the curves that account for the result.

27. An individual producer is compelled to raise the hourly wage rates of all his workers by 20 percent. He has been operating under increasing marginal cost.

a. If you expect his marginal cost curve to shift upward in consequence of the wage increase, have you reasons to believe that it will have the same slope, be steeper, or less steep? Why?

b. If wages had been 50 percent of the total variable cost of the output the firm had been producing, would you expect the marginal cost of that same output to rise by 50 percent, 20 percent, 10 percent, something between 10 and 20 percent, or less than 10 percent? Why?

c. If the firm is not in an oligopolistic position and anticipates no change in the demand for its products, will it be apt to raise or lower its output, or leave it unchanged, in consequence of the higher wages? Why?

d. If the demand curve as seen by the firm is a sloping straight line, can you make a statement about the magnitude of the change in the price the firm will charge relative to: the difference between the old marginal cost of the original output and the new marginal cost of any changed output; the absolute change in the marginal cost of the original output; and the percentage change in wage rates?

e. If the demand curve were concave from above, rather than a straight line, how would the answers to the questions in *d* have to be altered?

28. "The problem of the optimal selling effort can be solved independently of production costs, just as the problem of the optimal production technique is ordinarily solved independently of demand and revenue considerations. This solution overcomes the apparent interdependence of cost

and demand curves for a producer whose selling efforts as well as selling prices are variable." Explain.

29. Demonstrate geometrically that recognition of rent as cost will remove "monopoly profit" but increase "monopolistic underutilization of capacity."

30. Product differentiation has "indivisibility" as a logical prerequisite according to Kaldor but not according to Chamberlin. How can there be an unresolved argument about a purely logical inference? Explain the disagreement.

31. Assume that it were possible to achieve standardization of the now differentiated products offered by an industry of many sellers. Discuss the probable effects of such standardization upon prices paid by consumers. Take account of elasticities of demand as seen by the sellers, costs of standardization to sellers and buyers, consumers' reactions to standardization, and sellers' opportunities for collusive arrangements.

32. Discuss the possibility of empirical verifications of propositions asserting that oligopoly or monopoly prevails in a specific situation.

33. "The smaller a seller's share in the market the greater the temptation for him to cut prices in slack times." Discuss.

34. (*a*) Draw a kinked oligopoly demand curve; (*b*) construct the marginal revenue curve; (*c*) show by drawing two marginal cost curves at different levels that price and output need not be affected by a change in the cost of the firm; (*d*) explain in a sentence or two the seller's reasoning pictured by the kinked curve; (*e*) explain why the exhibited insensitiveness of price to the change in cost holds only in cases in which the competitors of the firm are not faced with similar changes in cost.

35. If an oligopolist knows that a given change in production cost will affect not only him but also his rivals, he may assume that the demand for his particular product will be changed. But in which direction and why? Distinguish between several cases: (*a*) he is one of an uncoordinated group of oligopolists; (*b*) he is a price leader; (*c*) he is a price follower, though not a small producer; (*d*) he is an insignificantly small producer; (*e*) he is a member of a quota cartel.

36. "While the 'theory of the firm' can be helpful in analyzing the conduct of a cartel member, it is less helpful in explaining the determination of price in a price cartel." Discuss.

37. State in a very few sentences and without a graph the essential points in Edgeworth's theory of duopoly.

38. What are the essential differences between Cournot's and Edgeworth's theories of duopoly?

39. What is meant by "symmetry" and "asymmetry" in the duopolists' attitudes, and what is the significance of such attitudes in duopoly theory?

40. Is competition among three or four sellers more "competitive" than among only two? Present arguments on both sides of the question.

41. According to Stigler, "Potential competition does not in general exert any influence on duopoly (or monopoly) price." Discuss.

42. Passenger transportation and freight transportation are jointly produced services; eastbound and westbound transportation are also jointly produced services. Does the first or the second of these pairs of joint products more nearly correspond to what some writers call "true" joint products? Give reasons.

43. Whether "joint products" are true products (complementary in their production) or alternative products (substitutes in production) depends often on the degree of utilization of plant capacity. Sometimes they are substitute products in the short run and complementary products in the long run. Explain.

44. Present a graphical demonstration of a monopolist's pricing of a pair of strictly joint products. Assume that demands are not interrelated; that the two markets cannot be subdivided; that the disposal of unsold output is not without cost (make it a constant cost).

45. Assume a case of inseparably joint production in a firm selling under monopolistic conditions. The two joint products, A and B, need some separate processing before they can be marketed. State what effects upon the prices of the two products you would expect in the short run (a) if a processing tax is imposed on A; (b) if the real property tax of the firm is increased; (c) if the demand for A rises; (d) if the demand for B is found to be less elastic than has previously been assumed; (e) if a rival develops and offers a close substitute for A. Consider each of the five cases separately, giving reasons for all answers.

46. State under what conditions price discrimination is (a) possible, and (b) profitable.

47. State the circumstances under which, according to Mrs. Robinson, price discrimination will restult in a higher output than nondiscriminating monopoly, and the reasons she believes these circumstances are more likely to exist than are conditions making for a smaller output under discrimination.

48. Present graphically, with precise construction of all relevant points and curves, a case in which a profit-maximizing monopolist who sells in two separate markets with unrelated demand will increase his production when he is prohibited from practicing price discrimination.

49. Assume that a monopolist is able to divide his market into two separate markets independent of each other; thus, he has the power to engage in price discrimination of the third degree.

a. What may be the properties of the relevant curves accounting for the following situations: (*i*) He finds it most profitable to charge the same price in both markets. (*ii*) He finds it most profitable to charge different prices, but not to change his output. (*iii*) He finds it most profitable to charge different prices and to increase his total output.

b. Concerning the second situation, state which of the markets will be charged increased or reduced prices and will receive reduced or increased deliveries.

c. Concerning the third situation, state whether and why it is possible or impossible that: both markets are charged increased prices; both markets are charged reduced prices; or one market is charged an increased price, the other a reduced price, but both markets receive increased deliveries.

50. Milk cooperatives usually charge a higher price for milk in the "fluid" market (for direct consumption) than in the industrial market (for butter and cheese). Why? What assumptions does this imply about the demand in these two markets? Can you give reasons why those assumptions prevail in fact?

51. Marshall discusses four conditions determining the elasticity of derived demand. State the rules (in any order you like) and tell which of these rules, if any, help explain the following instances of price discrimination:

a. Railroads usually charge higher freight rates for materials that have a higher value per ton than for materials of lower value.

b. Utility companies often charge higher rates to consumers of electricity for lighting than to consumers of electricity for heating.

c. A producer of plastics sells the same material at high prices to dentists and dental technicians for use as dentures and at lower prices to other industrial users.

d. A producer sells aluminum ingots at higher prices than aluminum made into cable.

e. A producer sells plate glass in large sheets at higher prices than glass cut into small pieces.

52. Pigou stated that under price discrimination of the "first degree . . . no consumers' surplus was left to the buyer."

a. What is price discrimination of the first degree?

b. What is consumers' surplus, broadly speaking, without distinguishing between the dozens of different definitions?

c. Is one particular definition or measurement of consumers' surplus implied in Pigou's quoted statement; if so, which one?

d. What is Knight's opinion on this particular definition or measurement?

D. The Equilibrium of the Industry

1. Discuss purposes and definitions of the concept of the "industry."

2. "If the world were such that perfect competition were possible, it would be such that the demarcation of commodities would present no difficulty." Explain. (In order to specify the meaning of "perfect competition" it is necessary to reveal that the statement is by Mrs. Robinson.)

3. Explain why the notion of a supply curve is not very meaningful except for a perfectly polypolistic industry.

4. Discuss Chamberlin's statement of "group equilibrium" where a large number of producers offers, with different selling efforts, products of different quality to buyers with different preferences. Place major emphasis on the various effects of advertising upon sellers outside the group as well as on those within, upon the scale of production, and upon the prices paid by consumers.

5. "The supply curve of a commodity produced under perfect competition is the curve of average costs including rent." Is this proposition based on empirical evidence or is it a tautology? Show how and from which facts, assumptions, or definitions the proposition is derived.

6. "If we include the economic rents in our average total cost we can show that the minimum average total cost of *all* firms, not merely of the marginal firm, will be equal to the price of the product when an industry is in equilibrium." Explain and prove this proposition.

7. Discuss, connect, and compare the following three statements by Mrs. Robinson:

"Normal profits is that level of profit at which there is no tendency for new firms to enter the trade, or for old firms to disappear out of it." (*P. 92.*)

"The level of normal profits must be defined in respect to the particular industry. . . . The level of normal profits in trades which are easy to enter . . . are likely to be low relatively to the normal profits of industries requiring a very large initial investment or peculiar efficiency or peculiar facilities of various kinds. . . ." (*P. 93.*)

"Indeed it is when profits are abnormally high (because new firms are failing to enter the industry to a sufficient extent to keep profits at the normal level) that the firms are of more than optimum size." (*P. 97.*)

8. Discuss the nature and significance of divergent profit calculations by insiders, outsiders, and disinterested economists.

9. Explain briefly the theory of "equilibrium with excess capacity."

10. It is stated that with perfectly easy entry into the industry the demand curves will be tangent to average cost curves of all individual firms. What is meant? What would absence of the "tangency condition" imply? What forces are supposed to bring about the tangency?

11. How could it be said that "competition" could result in production at the lowest possible cost?

12. Prove that firms under monopolistic competition, in an industry into which entry is easy, will be of less than optimum size.

13. Newcomers' competition may increase cost by forcing individual producers to operate with more excess capacity, to reduce specialization, to pay higher factor prices, and probably in some other ways. May one conclude that newcomers' competition is wasteful? Argue both sides of the case without revealing your own opinion.

14. Explain the distinction and relation between "cost at the margin" and "intensive marginal cost."

15. "The fact that when entrepreneurship is a scarce factor intramarginal firms are larger than what . . . would be called their optimum size merely shows that the differential advantages of entrepreneurs whose efficiency cost is relatively low are being fully exploited, so that the marginal cost of their output is not less than the marginal cost of the outputs of more expensive entrepreneurs." Explain and discuss.

16. "If the statisticians assure Mr. Sraffa that he is right, and that almost every industry works under conditions of constant costs, the task of the monopoly analysis will be much simplified. But it will lose none of its validity and will gain considerably in charm." Explain and discuss every part of this statement by Mrs. Robinson, including the reasons for Sraffa's view that constant costs prevail in almost every industry.

17. According to Mrs. Robinson, "A rising supply curve of the factor to an industry is not a sufficient condition, although it is a necessary condition, for the existence of rent from the point of view of that industry." (*a*) Explain why it is a necessary condition. (*b*) Explain why it is not a sufficient condition.

18. Explain the difference between rent from the point of view of an industry and rent from other points of view.

19. Whether a factor of production earns rent in an industry will depend, among other things, on the extension of the group of firms that one chooses to regard as a separate industry. Explain and discuss.

20. Boulding states: "There is no rule which will tell us *a priori* whether the rent in a firm will rise or fall when the price of the variable input rises. . . . Probably rents will tend to rise in low-cost firms and fall in high-cost firms." Boulding's statement refers to firms in an industry where competition is pure and perfect; and it takes account of "industry effects" as well as "firm effects." Explain the statement.

21. When Marshall in Book V of his *Principles of Economics* resorts to the highly fictitious assumption "that a meteoric shower of a few thousand

large stones harder than diamonds" fell on the earth, what principles does he try to illustrate?

22. If the supply of factors of production is fixed and there are no economies of a large-scale industry, one may say that "for any commodity considered separately there is rising supply price, because an increase in the output of any commodity turns the relative factor prices against itself." Explain both the proposition and its presuppositions; then comment on the significance of the statement within the theory of relative prices and output as contrasted with the theory of aggregate output.

23. What is the significance of the distinction between external economies depending on reductions in the prices of products furnished by other industries, and external economies depending on improvements in services rendered by factors of production?

24. Discuss the similarities and differences between increasing transfer costs of productive factors, seen as external diseconomies of an industry, and decreasing costs due to external economies of large-scale industry.

25. "When economies [of large-scale industry] are present it is no longer true that marginal cost of the industry, excluding rent, is equal to the cost of the additional factors employed when output increases. The cost of the additional factors employed, or cost at the margin, must necessarily be equal to supply price, but marginal cost to the industry, excluding rent, is now less than the supply price by the amount of the induced economies." Elucidate.

26. Under conditions of constant cost due to absence of economies of large-scale production and absence of any scarce factors to the industry, monopoly output is smaller than competitive output. By how much (*a*) if the demand curve is a sloping straight line; (*b*) if it is concave from above; (*c*) if it is convex from above?

27. Making the four general assumptions on p. 98 in Mrs. Robinson's *Economics of Imperfect Competition,* that (1) cost conditions are not a function of time but only of volume of output and size of establishment, (2) all firms adjust immediately to changes and reach equilibrium positions without delay, (3) cost curves of individual firms are independent of changes in the number of firms in the industry, and (4) all firms—old as well as newly entering—have identical cost and selling conditions; and further assuming that (5) all sellers in the industry are in positions of monopolistic competition, but (6) there is perfect newcomers' competition, and that (7) an increase in the number of firms by reducing average transportation costs will increase the elasticity of all demand curves; how will an increase in total demand affect (*a*) the selling price, (*b*) the volume of output of each firm, (*c*) the number of firms, and (*d*) the relative change in the number of firms compared with the relative change in the output of the whole industry?

28. Demonstrate Mrs. Robinson's contention that "when there is a scarce factor for which the full rent is not paid, and at the same time there are

economies of large-scale industry . . . it is possible that monopoly output may be greater than competitive output."

29. According to Mrs. Robinson, "An increase in the total demand for the commodity, when the market is imperfect, is far more likely to lower the average cost curves of the firms than when the market is perfect." Her reason for this statement is the "reservoir of potential economies of large-scale industry" likely to exist under imperfect competition because of a retarded process of specialization. Explain.

30. The theory of derived demand was formulated as a part of the analysis of the equilibrium of the industry; with minor adaptations it is used also in the analysis of the firm. Besides these uses in the theory of relative prices it is also employed in the theory of relative incomes. Discuss the adaptations, the changes in emphasis, and the differences in purposes.

31. Marshall distinguishes four conditions "under which a check to the supply of a thing that is wanted not for direct use, but as a factor of production of some commodity, may cause a very great rise in its price." These four conditions resulting in inelasticity of derived demand relate to the technological substitutability of the factor of production, the demand for the product, the portion of the total expenses of production that consists of the cost of this factor, and the supply of other factors of production. Discuss the ways in which these conditions are related to the elasticity of the derived demand.

32. Graphs of the sort of Marshall's knifeblade-handle diagram must necessarily oversimplify one of the conditions that is often the most essential for the elasticity of derived demand. Which condition? Why can more realistic assumptions about this condition not be dealt with in the diagrammatical representation?

33. A product, X, is made from three "ingredients" or factors of production, A, B, and C, all of which are necessary and can be used only in a fixed proportion. Total output of X is 1,000 units per unit of time; the product sells at a price of $100 per unit. The factor costs per unit of product are $60 for A, $30 for B, and $10 for C. The supplies of A and B are perfectly elastic to the industry. The demand for X has an elasticity of minus two. The industry is competitive both in its buying and in its selling.

Assume that the quantity of C available to the industry is reduced by 20 percent. Calculate the elasticity of the industry's derived demand for C. Show your reasoning step by step.

34. Change the assumptions of Problem 33 in that the elasticities of supply of A and B to the industry are plus four and plus two, respectively. Then make the calculation again.

35. Change the assumptions of Problem 33 in that the supplies of B and C to the industry are perfectly elastic and that it is the quantity of A which is reduced by 20 percent. You are now asked to calculate the elasticity of the industry's demand for A.

36. If a commodity is jointly demanded with others, the elasticity of the market demand for it tends to be low. Why?

37. "When charcoal was generally used in making iron, the price of leather depended in some measure on that of iron; and the tanners petitioned for the exclusion of foreign iron in order that the demand on the part of English iron smelters for oak charcoal might cause the production of English oak to be kept up, and thus prevent oak bark from becoming dear."

Explain first the economic relations between (*a*) oak charcoal and English iron, (*b*) oak bark and English leather, (*c*) oak charcoal and oak bark, (*d*) foreign iron and English iron; and then (*e*) explain how the price of leather was affected by the price of iron and therefore by the importation of iron.

38. Discuss and compare the usefulness of alternative "measurements" of the degree of monopoly, including the indexes of concentration, profitability, price flexibility, and price-marginal-cost discrepancy.

E. Equilibrium of the Market

1. Discuss the concept and definition of the "perfect market" as distinguished from the various concepts of pure or perfect competition.

2. To what extent is the existence of reservation prices compatible with a "perfect market"?

3. The cobweb theorem as an illustration of an unstable equilibrium rests on the assumption that the adjustment of supply lags behind the movement of market price." Explain.

4. Assuming that adjustments of supply lag behind the movements of market price, draw three sets of supply and demand curves, the first such that an accidental disturbance of equilibrium will result in dampening oscillations of market price with a gradual return to the initial equilibrium position; the second such that an accidental disturbance of equilibrium will result in perpetual and constant oscillations of market price around the initial equilibrium position; and the third such that an accidental disturbance of equilibrium will result in oscillations of ever-increasing amplitude.

5. It s conceivable that demand and supply curves may both have negative slopes and intersect each other several times. Some of the intersections are regarded as defining positions of "stable equilibrium," and others of "unstable equilibrium." According to Marshall, "It will be found to be a characteristic of stable equilibria that in them the demand price is greater than the supply price for amounts just less than the equilibrium amount, and vice versa." Other writers—for example, J. R. Hicks—took exception to this statement. Discuss.

6. Prove geometrically that Hicks' "excess-demand curve" must have the same properties as Wicksteed's demand curve, differing from it only by a constant.

7. "The only possible case of instability [of exchange between X and Y] is when . . . the sellers of X will . . . be much more anxious to consume more X when they become better off than the buyers of X are." Explain.

8. Explain Hicks' concepts of perfectly stable and imperfectly stable market systems.

9. For the equilibrium price to be attained in a market certain types of reaction to disequilibrium positions must occur. What kinds of reactions?

II. QUESTIONS IN THE THEORY OF INCOME DISTRIBUTION AND GENERAL EQUILIBRIUM

A. General Equilibrium Theory

1. Describe in words, without using any symbols, Walras's system of general equilibrium, stating the essential asumptions, the variables assumed to be given, and the unknown variables to be derived.

2. How does the Walras system of general equilibrium, as first presented by him and usually reproduced by his expositors, deal—explicitly or implicitly—with the following: (*a*) the law of diminishing returns (or of nonproportional output); (*b*) the law of returns to scale; (*c*) the optimum size of the firm; (*d*) the degree of competition; (*e*) the homogeneity or heterogeneity of productive resources; (*f*) the mobility of productive resources; (*g*) the profits of entrepreneurs; (*h*) the elasticity of supply of labor; (*i*) the liquidity preference; (*j*) the supply of money; (*k*) the time structure of the production process; (*l*) the accumulation of capital?

3. In any general equilibrium model certain restrictive assumptions are made. Some of them simplify the system only slightly and can be dropped without difficulty while others simplify the system so much that dropping them would unduly complicate the analysis; others are indispensable and could not be dropped without wrecking the model. Put each of the assumptions below into one of these three categories and explain why. State also whether the particular assumption was in fact made by Walras or any other model builder of whom you know.

Assumptions: (1) There are only three or four factors of production. (2) All labor is perfectly homogeneous. (3) Labor is perfectly mobile. (4) Labor responds only to pecuniary rewards. (5) The supply of factors of production is fixed and perfectly inelastic. (6) The coefficients of production are fixed. (7) The production functions are homogeneous of the first degree. (8) All sellers and buyers operate under pure competition (as perfect polypolists and perfect polypsonists, respectively). (9) Entry into all trades is easy (there is perfect pliopoly and perfect pliopsony). (10) All available factors of production are fully empoyed. (11) The elasticity of price expectations is equal to unity. (12) Receipts and outlays balance for every firm and household.

B. Derived Demand

1. After formulating his "law of derived demand" Marshall set forth four conditions determining the elasticity of derived demand. State each of these conditions, alternatively (*a*) expressing the independent variation as "a check to the supply" of the factor of production in question and the dependent variation as "a rise in its price," and expressing the "conditions" likewise without using the term "elasticity"; (*b*) expressing the independent variation as "a reduction in the price" of the factor of production in question and the dependent variation as "a rise in its employment," and expressing the "conditions" likewise without using the term "elasticity"; and (*c*) expressing the "conditions" as well as the general relation between independent and dependent variations in terms of "elasticities."

2. Marshall's "third condition" determining the elasticity of derived demand—sometimes referred to as "the importance of being unimportant"—has been found by Mrs. Robinson to hold only under certain circumstances.

a. State the condition without Mrs. Robinson's qualification.

b. Give an example of its practical significance in economic life.

c. State Mrs. Robinson's qualification. [You need not reproduce the proof.]

3. If the elasticity of demand for the product is infinitely elastic, the elasticity of derived demand for a factor of production, say labor, will be $\frac{\sigma + ke}{1 - k}$ where σ is the elasticity of substitution between labor and non-labor, e is the elasticity of supply of nonlabor, and k is the proportionate share of labor in the value of the product. Prove that, when the quantity of nonlabor is fixed, a certain relation between σ and k will gurantee that the absolute share of labor will increase as the quantity of labor increases, even if its relative share is reduced.

C. Marginal Productivity and Substitution

1. If a product X is made out of factors A and B, both of which are perfectly divisible, the chosen proportion between the amounts of factors employed will ordinarily be such that diminishing returns will prevail with regard to both factors. Yet increased employment of A would permit an in-

creased average product per unit of B. Is this not inconsistent with diminishing returns? Explain your answer.

2. "If the proportion between the amounts of factors A and B employed were such that the employment of A could be increased with increasing returns—that is, increasing average product—the average product per unit of B would also be increased when the employment of A is increased. The marginal product of B, however, would be negative." Assuming linear homogeneity of the production function, is the first sentence of the statement correct? Why or why not? Is the second sentence correct and consistent with the first? Why or why not?

3. Given is the total product curve for combinations of varying amounts of A with four units of B. If you want to construct a total product curve for combinations of varying amounts of B with eight units of A, you will be able to compute the needed values provided constant returns to scale prevail and both factors are perfectly divisible. Show how you would compute the product of (a) $1B$ and $8A$; (b) $3B$ and $8A$; (c) $6B$ and $8A$; (d) $8B$ and $8A$; (e) $16B$ and $8A$.

4. The phases of increasing and diminishing returns within the law of variable proportions are often defined in terms of average product but sometimes in terms of marginal product. Discuss the differences in demarcations between the two phases under the two definitions, indicating the geometrical techniques of finding the exact locations of the phases, their relative lengths, and so on.

5. Assume a production surface that depicts total physical output of a certain product (P) as a function of two factors of production (A and B).

a. What geometrical operations with this surface will best aid in a demonstration of the laws of variable proportions? The laws of scale? The elasticity of substitution?

b. What factual conditions determine whether the surface will have a peak or extend upwards without limits?

c. What factual conditions determine whether there will be any increasing returns to scale?

6. "It is possible that both marginal physical product and the marginal gross revenue product are zero and, nevertheless, the marginal net revenue product is positive."

a. Under what conditions will the marginal physical product be zero?

b. Under what conditions will the marginal gross revenue product be zero while the marginal physical product is positive?

c. Under what conditions will the marginal net revenue produce be positive although the marginal gross revenue product is zero?

7. Define or explain the concept of elasticity of substitution as it is used by Mrs. Robinson. Is "technical" substitution or "total" substitution involved in Mrs. Robinson's concept? What is the difference between the two?

D. Wages of Labor

1. "The marginal productivity theory of wages is of a naïve unrealism. How can one say that wages are determined by the marginal productivity of labor when it is obvious to all but the blind and deaf that in our society wage rates are the result of bargaining; and that the employer, where he need not bargain but can dictate his terms, will surely fix wage rates well below the marginal productivity of labor?"

a. List the parts of the above statement that you would select for criticism and indicate (in one brief sentence each) your line of attack.

b. Explain briefly the relation between wage bargaining, contractual wage rates, and marginal productivity.

c. Explain briefly the relation between employer-dictated wage rates and marginal productivity.

2. "The marginal productivity theory of wages is unsatisfactory for several reasons: first, the separation of a certain physical product attributable to the 'marginal laborer' is impossible; second, employers try to pay less than the marginal product, however it be computed, unless they are pressed by powerful labor organizations; third, in times of large unemployment employers can easily succeed in reducing wage rates below the marginal product, even if there is collective bargaining." Explain and discuss point by

3. "The wage rate is determined by the marginal productivity of labor." If someone offers this statement as a formulation of the "marginal productivity theory of wages," what corrections or amendments will you offer?

4. Theorists hold that in any trade or industry the wage rate, or marginal factor cost, tends to be equal to the marginal productivity of labor. How can this be reconciled with the fact that wage rates of several kinds of workers have increased over the decades while their output per hour has hardly changed at all? Think of the "productivity" of house painters who use, by and large, the same techniques they used half a century ago but receive wage rates that have increased as much, if not more, than those of workers whose output per hour has doubled several times. Explain the apparent paradox.

5. To what extent will wage differentials prevailing between different occupations, different geographic areas, and different industries reflect differences in the qualifications or efficiencies of the various types of workers?

6. How, if at all, does the marginal productivity curve (marginal net revenue product curve) of a factor employed in a given firm reflect; (*a*) the operation of diminishing returns? (*b*) the possibility of technical substitution? (*c*) the elasticity of demand for the product? (*d*) the elasticity of supply of the factor? (*e*) the elasticity of supply of other factors?

7. Mrs. Robinson states that "for full equilibrium it is necessary that the marginal cost of labor (the wage) should be equal to average net productivity." Explain.

8. Mrs. Robinson states, "When the supply of labor to the individual unit is perfectly elastic . . . the double condition of equilibrium can only be fulfilled when the wage is equal to the value at which the marginal and average net productivity curves cut."

a. Under what conditions is the supply of labor to the firm perfectly elastic?

b. Under these conditions what will the marginal cost of labor be in comparison with the average cost of labor?

c. What is meant by "the double condition of equilibrium?" Answer first in terms of general principles and then in terms of net productivity and cost of labor.

d. At what value of the average net productivity curve will this curve be cut by the marginal net productivity curve? Does this depend on perfect competition? On profit maximization? Or on what else?

e. Why, under the conditions cited in the statement, must the wage be equal to the value of net productivity at which the marginal and average curves intersect?

f. Give a graphical presentation of the situation to which the statement refers.

9. Assume that men and women are equally efficient in a certain occupation but the conditions of supply of men and women workers are different. It is possible for the employer to pay different wage rates to men and women; there are no trade unions. With the marginal net productivity curve and the two labor supply curves given, show in a graph the wage rates the employer will pay and the number of men and women he will employ. (Exact geometric construction is essential.)

10. "Professor Pigou once defined exploitation of laborers as the compensation of labor at a rate below the marginal product. If marginal product stands here for the value of the marginal physical product, then, indeed, exploitation is almost generally practiced in industry, though perhaps the relative 'underpayment' is not substantial in the majority of cases. If, however, marginal product stands for marginal value product, then exploitation seems to be less frequent. Labor scarcity, on the one hand, and oligopolistic peculiarities in selling the product, on the other hand, appear to be the most important reasons for such exploitation." Explain all parts of this statement.

11. The gap between the value of the marginal physical product and the wage rate has been attributed for one part to monopolistic exploitation and for another to monopsonistic exploitation; in some cases a third part is attributed to imperfect divisibility. Show these three parts of the "gap" on a graph and point out the facts behind each.

12. What can a trade union do to prevent (*a*) monopolistic exploitation, and (*b*) monopsonistic exploitation?

13. Explain and discuss the "shock theory" of wage-rate boosts, according to which increased productivity will be induced by successful wage pressures by unions.

14. What theoretical arguments or empirical evidence can be adduced to support or refute the contention that trade unions have succeeded in increasing the share of labor in the national income at the expense of profit?

15. Discuss the case for and against wage increases in proportion to the increase in productivity in those industries which, because of lower production cost, can afford to pay higher wages without charging higher prices.

16. It may be possible for a trade union to raise the wage rate and yet increase employment in an industry faced with unchanged demand for its products and unchanged supply of all factors of production. How, why, and under what conditions?

17. "From the point of view of a whole industry, the supply of a certain type of skilled labor may be scarce and, at the same time, of infinite elasticity from the point of view of each single firm within the industry." Explain.

18. Discuss the probability of a negative elasticity of the supply of labor (*a*) to the individual firm, (*b*) to the industry, and (*c*) in the economy as a whole.

19. Explain the possibility of a backward-rising supply curve of labor (*a*) in terms of the income elasticity of demand for leisure, (*b*) in terms of the elasticity of demand for income in terms of effort, and (*c*) in terms of the substitution effects and income effects of changes in the price of labor.

20. Dennis H. Robertson divides the effects that "an artificial raising of the wages" is apt to have upon employment into two analytically separable reactions—first, "a movement along the existing [marginal productivity] curve," and second, "a cumulative lowering of the curve." Explain the two reactions and indicate what assumptions concerning other factors of production, especially capital, are involved.

21. Assuming that workers have the possibility of varying by small amounts the total of labor or effort they supply, and that the elasticity of their demand for income in terms of effort is smaller than unity, what effect will the imposition or increase of an income tax have upon the amount of labor supplied? Show how your answer can be deduced from the definitions of the term employed and show how the assumption concerning the "elasticity of demand for income in terms of effort" can be translated into "price elasticity of supply of labor."

E. Rent of Land and Scarce Resources

1. In his discussion of "differential rents versus scarcity rents" Marshall makes the following statement (*Principles of Economics,* p. 424): "The opinion that the existence of inferior land, or other agents of production,

tends to raise the rents of the better agents is not merely untrue. It is the reverse of the truth." Explain and discuss. Distinguish between rent from the point of view of the industry and rent from the point of view of the economy.

2. Develop a statement on "sufficient and necessary conditions" for the existence of a positive land rent by discussing imaginary situations in which all existing land is (*a*) of equal fertility and equal locational advantage, (*b*) of equal fertility but different locational advantage, (*c*) of different fertility and locational advantage but not subject to diminishing returns.

3. "Rent is equal to the difference between marginal cost and average cost, multiplied by output." (*a*) Prove this proposition with the aid of a graph. (*b*) Is the proposition true also if competition is not pure? Why, or why not? Explain with a graph. (*c*) If a tenant-farmer pays full rent to the landowner and considers this rent a fixed cost, what will be the relation between average total cost and marginal cost? Explain.

4. Ricardo says, in "On Rent," *Principles of Political Economy and Taxation:* "If the high price of corn were the effect and not the cause of rent, price would be proportionately influenced as rents were high or low, and rent would be a component part of price. But that corn which is produced by the greatest quantity of labor is the regulator of the price of corn; and rent does not and cannot enter in the least degree as a component part of its price." Discuss.

5. Explain the relation between society, the law of diminishing returns, and rent.

6. What will you expect to be the effect on the rent of land: (*a*) if a new type of fertilizer is developed, capable of increasing the productivity of land of all qualities by 10 percent? (*b*) if a flood makes all low-grade land uncultivatable, spoiling all "marginal" and "submarginal" land and leaving only the land that had been called "superior" available for cultivation?

Note: Distinguish also (*a*) rent per unit of output, (*b*) rent per acre of land under cultivation (perhaps divided between land of different quality), and (*c*) total rent.

7. Give the meaning of all terms listed below and indicate their place in the general theory of rent: (*a*) explicit and implicit rent; (*b*) intensive and extensive margin; (*c*) differential and scarcity rent; (*d*) inelastic factor supply; (*e*) imperfect homogeneity of the factor supply; (*f*) quasi rent.

8. Decide the following argument between Mr. A and Mr. B:

A: The rent of an office in these high houses and skyscrapers is much higher than the rent of equal space in smaller uptown houses.

B: Of course, that's why the skyscrapers were built.

A: But it is surely the high building cost and high land value that makes for high rent in high houses.

B: No, high land values are not the cause but the effect of high rents.

A: But, anyway, the high rents are due to the high houses, and, in particular, to the cost of building high houses.

B: No, people have built high houses because of the high land values, so as to economize on the scarce land.

A: You have it all twisted. If the cost of building these skyscrapers were lower, rents would be lower wouldn't they?

B: I stick to my position that rents are the result of demand, not of costs.

A: You are being dogmatic. If building costs fall, rents will fall. Likewise, if site values fall, rents will fall.

B: Well, let's ask the student who has just completed his course in economic theory. He will explain just what the relation is between height of houses, height of rents, height of building costs, and the height of site values.

9. "Rent is not the income of some particular factor of production, but merely an aspect of the income of any factor of production." Explain.

10. Take that old phrase about rent not entering into cost and (*a*) explain what it means; (*b*) state to what extent it is true (or under what conditions it aids in explaining observed facts); and (*c*) discuss the advantage or disadvantage of making it true by definition.

11. Classical "pessimism" generally expected that the increase in population and the increase in the supply of capital would result in ever-increasing land rents. State the conditions under which this expectation would or would not come true; refer also to the history of the last 150 years.

12. "Rent, like all prices, is a test, even though an imperfect one, of social need: its payment roughly ensures the most economical distribution of land between different uses; and its remission, by a land-owning state, to those in a position to pay it, whether private persons or public enterprises, would in general promote waste." Explain every part of this statement.

F. Interest on Capital

1. If you expect a certain piece of land to yield a yearly net rent of $1,500, what will its present value be (*a*) at a current rate of interest of 3 percent, (*b*) at a current rate of interest of 6 percent?

2. Explain how and why individuals and business firms might react to an increase in the market rates of interest. Divide your answer into these parts: (*a*) consumption, (*b*) production, (*c*) securities, and (*d*) cash.

3. "The schedule of marginal rates of time preference may be represented either as a consumption function or as a saving function with the interest rate as a variable and income as parameter."

a. Sketch such functions, labeling the axes precisely, and explain their meaning and significance.

b. Contrast these functions for low and high incomes.

c. What would be the meaning of a negative rate of time preference?

d. Could the marginal rate of time preference be negative if the same individual's marginal rate of liquidity preference is positive? Why or why not?

4. Explain the relation betwen expected future changes in interest rates and present liquidity preference.

5. Explain the relation between the interest rate and the demand for durable goods.

6. *a.* State how a change in liquidity preference affects the rate of interest and how a change in the rate of interest affects the rate of liquidity preference. Explain how it works.

b. State how a change in time preference affects the rate of interest and how a change in the rate of interest affects the rate of time preference. Explain how it works.

c. State how a change in the marginal efficiency of investment affects the rate of interest and how a change in the rate of interest affects the marginal efficiency of investment. Explain how it works.

7. How are "hoarding" and "dishoarding" accounted for (*a*) in the loanable-funds theory of interest and (*b*) in the liquidity-preference theory of interest?

8. A certain government bond carries a stated rate of interest of 3 percent per year.

a. If the market rate of interest is 3½ percent, will the bond sell above or below par value? Why?

b. If the market rate of interest rises to 4 percent, will the price of the bond rise or fall? Why?

c. Would this rise or fall be smaller or greater for a bond that matures in 10 years or for one that matures in 15 years?

d. What can you learn from the above relations that might be relevant to the explanation of demand conditions for durable equipment, houses, and such?

e. Bond yields are usually affected by people's expectations concerning future changes in the interest rate. How and why?

9. "If depreciation allowances are included among the sources of supply of investment funds, the marginal efficiency of capital will have to refer to gross-investment rather than net-investment." Explain.

10. (*a*) How are capital values affected by changes in the rate of interest? Explain your answer. (*b*) How and why does the reaction of present values of future income series to given changes in interest rates depend on the length of these future income series?

11. The following quotation is taken from Marshall (*Principles of Economics,* p. 412): "That which is rightly regarded as interest on 'free' or

'floating' capital, or on new investments of capital, is more properly treated as a sort of rent—a quasi rent—on old investments of capital. And there is no sharp line of division between floating capital and that which has been 'sunk' for a special branch of production, nor between new and old investments of capital; each group shades into the other gradually." Explain.

12. Accountants are often bewildered by the economic theorist's treatment of interest as cost. The theorist dealing with short-run output neglects interest on investment as a cost even if interest is actually paid out to creditors. The theorist dealing with long-run output includes interest in cost even if there are no debts and no interest is paid out to anybody. Explain all three ways of treating interest: (*a*) in accounting, (*b*) in short-run theory, and (*c*) in long-run theory.

13. Explain why the long-term interest rate (*a*) can never fluctuate as widely as the short rate; (*b*) may move temporarily contrariwise to the short rate; and (*c*) will usually be higher than the short rate, but may sometimes be lower.

14. Explain what is meant by the "marginal efficiency of money measured in terms of itself" and contrast it with the "marginal efficiency of capital."

15. What are the essential differences between the "supply of money," the supply of "loanable funds," the "supply of liquidity," and the "supply of finance," as conceived by the economists making use of these concepts?

16. "Thus the rate of interest is what it is because it is expected to become other than it is; if it is not expected to become other than it is, there is nothing left to tell us why it is what it is. . . ." Explain this statement by first stating concisely the theory it criticizes and then discussing the main point of the criticism.

17. What is the difference, if any, between Keynes' "marginal efficiency of capital" and Lerner's "marginal efficiency of investment"?

18. State the three grounds on which Böhm-Bawerk bases his explanation of the existence of interest and discuss whether each or any of them constitutes a necessary and/or sufficient condition for the existence of interest. (You may avoid committing yourself to the arguments expressed by attributing them to "some writers.")

19. Reasoning along the lines of Böhm-Bawerk's capital theory, assume that land is abundant and that there are two, and only two, alternative ways of using labor in the production of consumers' goods: one without any roundabout ways and the other with an average investment period of one year. With the latter method labor is 20 percent more productive than with the former.

From these assumptions one might conclude: (*a*) that the rate of interest will be 20 percent; (*b*) that the interest rate will be zero and wages will be determined by the productivity of labor used in the more productive way;

(*c*) that the rate of interest might be anything between zero and 20 percent; (*d*) that the rate of interest might be well above 20 percent. Discuss each of these alleged possibilities and state any additional assumptions needed for it to be realized.

20. Without indicating your own opinions or inclinations, present both sides in the controversy between Frank H. Knight and the "Austrians" with respect to the following points: (*a*) that all capital is conceptually perpetual or conceptually nonpermanent; (*b*) that economic progress may result in a "shortening" of the investment period; (*c*) that an increase in the supply of capital need not change the production period of any single product; and (*d*) that it is not possible to identify the contributions of the original factors of the remote past.

21. State the reasons for which certain theorists prefer not to regard capital as a factor of production in models constructed for the analysis of the economy as a whole and examine whether these reasons would hold for models constructed for industry and firm analysis.

2. "The quantity of capital as a value magnitude, no less than the different investment periods, are not data but are among the unknowns which have to be determined." Explain.

23. Give a brief exposition of Hayek's explanation of the causes of the productivity of investment.

24. What are the chief differences between the capital theories of Böhm-Bawerk and Hayek?

25. Explain Hayek's concept of an "intertemporal equilibrium" and the use to which it is put.

26. In a sense capital theory is inherently dynamic; yet Knut Wicksell presents what he calls a "static theory of capital" (*Lectures on Political Economy* vol. 1, p. 165). Discuss briefly the "static" features in Wicksell's theory and then reconcile their use with the "inherently dynamic" character of capital theory.

27. Knut Wicksell wrote (*Lectures on Political Economy,* vol. 1, p. 164): "The capitalist saver is thus, fundamentally, the friend of labor, though the technical inventor is not infrequently its enemy. The great inventions by which industry has from time to time been revolutionized at first reduced a number of workers to beggary, as experience shows, whilst causing the profits of the capitalists to soar. There is no need to explain away this circumstance by invoking 'economic friction,' and so on, for it is in full accord with a rational and consistent theory. But it is really not captial which should bear the blame; in proportion as accumulation continues, these evils must disappear, interest on capital will fall and wages will rise—unless the laborers on their part simultaneously counteract this result by a large increase in their numbers." Explain Wicksell's reasoning.

28. In a footnote (*Lectures* vol. 1, p. 164), Wicksell observed that "capital investment undoubtedly tends to disturb the conditions under which labor and land are able to replace each other at the margin of production. It may therefore happen in exceptional cases that wages alone reap the benefit of a growth of capital, whilst rents fall; or vice versa." Explain and discuss.

29. Explain how Wicksell related the rate of interest to the marginal productivities of labor and land.

30. On p. 208 of his *Lectures,* vol. 1, Wicksell quotes the following statement by Gustav Cassel: "A man who attaches the same importance to future needs as to present ones, if he expects to be able to provide for his needs in the future just as easily as he does now, has no reason for setting aside anything of his present income." According to Wicksell, "Cassel is not quite correct," inasmuch as his "argument actually presupposes the absence of any rate of interest." Explain.

31. Theorists distinguish two basic concepts of fixed capital: the *net* depreciated value of the stock of productive plant and equipment—that is, its value taking account of its remaining service life—and the *gross* value of that stock, without regard to depreciation, constituting productive capacity available for complementary use with current inputs of other productive factors. Discuss the rationale of the distinction; indicate the problems for which either concept proves useful; and comment on the bearing obsolescence may have on either or both of the concepts.

G. Profit of Enterprise

1. Discuss the difference between "economic profit" and profit in the business or accounting sense.

2. Define profit, interest, and rent; and explain the essential differences between these concepts.

3. Discuss the problems that arise if profit is defined as the income of "entrepreneurship" or "enterprise."

4. Discuss the arguments for and against regarding "enterprise" as a factor of production.

5. Contrast various profit theories with some of the empirical studies of business profits and discuss the mutual relevancies.

6. "A positive aggregate net profit above all losses means a bias on the side of caution, while a preponderance of the spirit of adventure will entail net loss on the whole." Explain this statement and give the essentials of the profit theory on which it is based.

7. Evaluate whatever role in the explanation of profit can be assigned to the following factors: (*a*) differential ability or talent, (*b*) innovating drive

of entrepreneurs, (*c*) immobility of resources, (*d*) indivisibility, (*e*) economic change, (*f*) impediments of entry, (*g*) insurable risk, (*h*) uncertainty.

8. Discuss the possibility of long-run profit (in an industry or firm) that cannot be characterized as a rent.

9. Compare the usefulness of considering profit as an *ex ante* or as an *ex post* concept.

10. What place may windfall profits arising from an increase in inventory valuations have in the theory of profits?

11. Explain the concept of normal profit, show its role in value theory, and discuss its place in theory of income distribution.

12. Discuss the lack of parallelism in the profit rates and the profit margins of various industries.

13. Discuss the relativity of profit from the points of view of the insider, the outsider, and the economist; then comment on the relevance of these notions for the theory of income distribution.

H. Relative Shares, Total-Product Distribution

1. Economists dealing with the theory of distribution often refer to a theorem by the mathematician Euler. (*a*) State the theorem without any reference to economics. (*b*) Explain its connection with the theory of distribution. (*c*) Reasoning in terms of the theorem, show what significance the phenomenon of "increasing returns to scale" has for the distribution of income. (*d*) Indicate how Mrs. Robinson attempts to solve the "contradiction" involved.

2. State and discuss Kalecki's theory of income distribution, giving special emphasis to his method of defining the "degree of monopoly" as the "ratio of sales going to gross profit" and of explaining the distributive share going to nonlabor as determined by the "average degree of monopoly."

3. According to Kaldor, "no hypothesis as regards the forces determining distributive shares could be intellectually satisfying unless it succeeds in accounting for the relative stability of these shares in the advanced capitalist economies over the last 100 years or so, despite the phenomenal changes in the techniques of production, in the accumulation of capital relative to labor and in real income per head." Discuss (*a*) the facts in question, (*b*) the claim that a hypothesis is needed to account for the facts, and (*c*) the hypothesis or hypotheses proposed by Kaldor.

4. Discuss the meaning of "relative stability of relative shares," especially the reference of the first of the two "relativities."

5. "It would be nice to have a single aggregative bulldozer principle with which to crash through the hedge of microeconomic interconnections

and analogies." Explain (*a*) the general idea expressed in this sentence, (*b*) the meaning of the "single aggregative bulldozer principle," and (*c*) the meaning of "the hedge of microeconomic interconnections and analogies."

6. Assuming an aggregate production function for two factors, labor and capital, and constant returns to scale, "how different from unity need the elasticity of substitution be in order that it convert a strong trend in the capital/labor ratio into a strong trend in relative shares"? Before you attempt an answer, explain (*a*) the issue to which this question refers, (*b*) the implied causal connections between the three variables mentioned in the quotation, and (*c*) the significance of the question for the problem under discussion.

7. "If it were possible to separate out the part of nominal wages and salaries which is really a return on investment, the share of property income in the total might be found to be steadily increasing." Explain all parts of this comment by Solow.

Indexes

Author index

A

Ackley, G., 339 n
Alchian, A. A., 122
Alderson, 339 n
Allen, R. G. D., 29, 291
Antonelli, G. B., 16 n
Arrow, Kenneth J., 28 n, 216, 458 n, 480

B

Bacon, Nathaniel T., 331 n
Bailey, Martin J., 121, 339 n
Barone, Enrico, 366, 481
Bastiat, Frederic, 423
Bator, Francis M., 457 n, 473 n, 477, 479, 481
Baumol, William J., 122, 339 n, 479, 481
Becker, Gary S., 86 n
Bertrand, Joseph, 334
Borts, George H., 177, 216
Brehm, C. T., 74 n
Brown, Murray, 393 n
Buchanan, James M., 7, 481
Burk (Bergson), Abram, 480

C

Carlson, Sune, 216, 395
Cartter, Allan M., 364 n, 365 n, 394, 416 n, 420
Cassells, John M., 177, 216, 321, 325
Chamberlin, Edward H., 313, 317, 322–23, 326–28, 337–38, 343, 347, 361, 406, 421
Chapman, S. J., 384 n
Charlesworth, James C., 7
Chenery, Hollis B., 216
Clark, J. M., 143, 215
Clark, John Bates, 365–66, 383–85, 395
Coase, Ronald H., 474 n, 481
Cohen, K. J., 327
Coombs, C. H., 4 n
Cournot, Augustin A., 331, 334
Curran, William J., 348 n
Cyert, R. M., 327

D

Davis, Otto A., 481
Debreu, Gerard, 21 n
de Cani, John S., 393 n

Dewey, Donald J., 5
Dirlam, Joel B., 354
Douglas, Paul H., 394, 421
Dunlop, John T., 364 n

E

Edgeworth, Francis Y., 16 n, 334–37
Edwards, Ward, 79 n
Ehrlich, Isaac, 86 n
Eisenhower, Dwight D., 220
Engel, Christian Lorenz Ernst, 40, 104

F

Fama, E., 50, 116 n
Fellner, William, 361
Ferguson, C. E., 89, 102, 120, 122,
    137 n, 143, 151 n, 169 n, 173 n,
    177, 211 n, 215–17, 328, 374 n,
    389 n, 392 n, 393 n, 394, 404 n,
    406 n, 414 n, 421–22, 443 n,
    463 n, 477
Fisher, Irving, 16 n
Fossati, Eraldo, 450
Friedman, Milton, 6, 80 n, 121–22,
    249 n
Frisch, Ragnar, 102, 121

G

George, Henry, 365–66
Georgescu-Roegen, Nicholas, 23 n, 89,
    120–22
Goodman, Leo A., 480
Gossen, H. H., 16 n

H

Harberger, Arnold, 308 n
Harrod, R. F., 7, 321, 327
Hayek, F. A., 481
Healy, James J., 364 n
Henderson, A., 480
Henderson, James M., 28, 51, 89, 122,
    143, 178, 215, 258, 450, 477
Herstein, I. N., 80 n
Hicks, John R., 28–29, 51, 89, 120–
    22, 174 n, 178, 291, 361, 366,
    385, 387 n, 389 n, 390, 394,
    420–21, 479–80
Hirschleifer, Jack, 86 n, 309 n
Hotelling, Harold, 29, 120, 313, 337 n,
    361, 377 n, 480–81
Houthakker, H. S., 121
Hurwicz, Leonid, 7

I–J

Ichimura, S., 121

Jevons, W. Stanley, 16 n, 366
Johnson, W. E., 395
Jureen, Lars, 120

K

Kafoglis, Milton Z., 481
Kahn, R. F., 321, 325, 481
Kaldor, Nicholas, 480
Kaplan, A. D. H., 354
Kemp, Murray C., 444 n
Kendrick, J. W., 389 n
Kenen, Peter B., 477, 479
Kennedy, John F., 220
Knight, Frank H., 7, 121, 137 n, 143,
    258, 312–13
Koopmans, T. C., 7
Krupp, Sherman Roy, 7
Kuenne, Robert E., 122, 451, 479

L

Laffer, A., 116 n
Lancaster, Kelvin, 481
Lange, Oscar, 479
Lanzillotti, Robert F., 339 n, 354
Leontief, Wassily, 451
Lerner, A. P., 339 n, 479, 481
Leser, C. E. V., 105
Lindman, Harold, 79 n
Lipsey, R. G., 481
Little, I. M. D., 480
Longfield, Mountifort, 365

M

MacAvoy, Paul W., 254–55
Machlup, Fritz, 6, 143, 216, 258, 291,
    328, 331, 361
McKenzie, Lionel, 481
Majumdar, Tapas, 480
Malinvaud, E., 347 n, 361
Markowitz, Harry, 122, 480
Marshall, Alfred, 28, 119, 312, 321,
    325, 366, 375 n, 381–82 n, 385
Martindale, Don, 7
Metzler, Lloyd A., 122
Miller, M., 50
Milnor, John, 80 n
Minhas, Bagicha, 216
Mishan, E. J., 177, 216, 480
Morgenstern, Oskar, 7, 80, 122, 340–
    41, 345 n, 346
Morishima, M., 121
Mosak, Jacob L., 421
Mossin, Jan, 86 n

N–O

Nelson, P., 358 n
Nixon, Richard M., 220
Ozga, S. A., 122

P

Pareto, Vilfredo, 16 n
Pfouts, Ralph W., 30 n, 421, 480
Pindyck, Robert S., 254–55
Polasek, Metodey, 102

Q–R

Quandt, Richard E., 28, 51, 89, 122, 143, 178, 215, 258, 450, 477
Quirk, James, 479
Raiffa, Howard, 4 n
Reder, Melvin W., 477, 480
Robinson, Joan, 119, 291, 313, 328, 405 n, 406, 420, 422
Rothchild, K. W., 361
Rothenberg, Jerome, 480
Rowe, D. A., 102
Ruffin, Roy J., 334 n, 470 n, 474 n
Ruggles, Nancy, 481

S

Samuelson, Paul A., 28, 51, 89, 120–22, 178, 217, 251, 291, 394, 458 n, 477, 480
Saposnik, Rubin, 479
Sato, Ryuzo, 389 n
Savage, Leonard J., 79 n, 80 n, 122
Saving, Thomas R., 74 n, 169 n, 177, 211, 215–16, 374 n, 394, 404 n, 421
Schneider, Erich, 395
Schultz, Henry, 102–3, 120–21, 421
Scitovsky, Tibor, 477, 480
Shephard, Ronald W., 217
Shubik, Martin, 361
Simkin, C. G. F., 291

Slutsky, Eugen, 29
Smith, Adam, 2, 208, 220, 423–24, 455, 468 n
Smith, Richard Austin, 353 n
Smithies, Arthur, 328
Solow, Robert M., 216
Sraffa, Piero, 313
Staehle, Hans, 89, 121
Stigler, George J., 28, 61 n, 217, 258, 313, 327, 340, 361, 376 n, 394, 422
Stone, Richard, 102
Strotz, Robert H., 122
Stubblebine, W. Craig, 481
Swan, P. L., 309 n
Sweezy, Paul, 338–40, 361

T

Telser, L. G., 347 n, 358 n
Thrall, R. M., 4 n
Triffin, Robert, 328

V

Vickrey, William, 343 n, 481
Viner, Jacob, 215, 217
Von Neumann, John, 80, 122, 340–41, 345 n, 346
Von Thünen, T. H., 365

W

Walras, Leon, 16 n, 366, 451
Walters, A. A., 217
Weston, J. F., 339 n
Whinston, Andrew, 481
Wicksteed, Philip, 366, 383–85, 395
Wilcox, Clair, 353–54 n
Wold, Herman O. A., 102, 105, 120
Wood, Stuart, 366

Y–Z

Yeager, Leland B., 121
Zeuthen, F., 262 n, 313

Subject index

A

Acreage controls, 220
Acreage restriction programs, 308
Advertising, 222, 357–59
Aggregate demand; *see* Market demand
Agriculture
  government regulation of markets, 220
  implements industry, 354
  output, 125
  price supports, 306–8
  production, 124
Allis-Chalmers, 353
Allocation of resources, 1–2
  efficiency of, 219, 221
  oligopoly, 359
  profit maximization, role of, 221
Alternative cost of production, 180–81
Aluminum Company of America (Alcoa), 261
American Tobacco Company, 314
Antitrust decisions, cross-elasticities in, 65
Antitrust regulations, 220–21
Arc elasticity, 98 n

Automobile market, 358
Average cost
  defined, 206 n
  long-run, 198–201
    changes in, 211
Average cost curves; *see* Cost curves
Average fixed cost, 190–91
Average product, 130–32, 137–38; *see also* Production function
  defined, 131, 134
  maximum value of, 135
Average product curve, 191
  geometry of, 133–36
Average total cost, 192
Average total cost, minimum, changes in, 211–12
Average variable cost, 191; *see also* Cost curves

B

Bayesian decision making, 79 n
Bee service of cross-pollenization, 473–74
Bilateral monopoly, 288–89
  collective bargaining as, 364

Box diagram; *see* Edgeworth box diagram
Budget line, 31, 35–36
 clockwise movement, 34
 counterclockwise movement, 34
 definition, 32
 ordinate intercept, 31, 33–34
 parallel shift, 33–34
 shifting of, 33–34
 slope of, 31, 33
 steeper slope of, 34
Budget map, information from use of, 67
Budget space, 32, 34–35
 definition, 32
 indifference map and, 35
 mathematic definition, 32 n

C

Camel cigarettes, 314
Capital equipment, 124, 128
Capital-labor ratio, 149–50, 386–87, 391–92, 449–50
Cardinal measurement of utility, 16–17, 21
Cartel marginal cost curve, 348–49
Cartels, 220–21
 collapse of, 352–53
 defined, 348
 forms, 348
 great electrical conspiracy, 352–53
 ideal, 348–51
 loose, 349–50
 marginal cost curve, 348–49
 market sharing, 348–52
 nonprice competition, 349–50
 open collusion, 348
 price fixing, 348
 profit maximization, 348
 quota system, 350–52
 sales allocation, 349–52
 secret collusion, 348
 secret price concessions, 352
 services performed by, 348
 short and turbulent life of, 352–53
 typical, 352
Cellophane, 261
CES function, 137 n
Ceteris paribus assumptions, 62
Chamberlin solution, 337–38
Changes in money income, 39–44
 Engel curves, 40–42
  income elasticity of demand and, 42–44

Changes in money income—*Cont.*
 income-consumption curve, 39–40
Changes in price, 44–48
 demand curve, 45–46
 elasticity of demand, 46
  price-consumption curve and, 47–48
 price-consumption curve, 44–45
  elasticity of demand and, 47–48
Chesterfield cigarettes, 314
Cigarette taxes, 293 n
Circular flow of economic activity, 424–25
Clark-Wicksteen product exhaustion theorem, 383–85, 395–96
Classical microeconomic theory, 312
Cobb-Douglas function, 137 n, 141
Coefficient of price cross-elasticity of demand, 103–4
Coefficient of price elasticity, 97, 99
Coin tossing, 79
Collective bargaining as bilateral monopoly, 364
Collusion; *see* Cartels
Collusive behavior, 220
Collusive oligopoly, 330–31
Commodities
 defined, 11
 nature of, 11–12
Commodity bundle, 13
 cardinal measurement of utility of, 16–17, 21
 numerical value assigned to, 14–16
 ordinal measurement of utility of, 16, 20–21
 rank ordering of, 13–14, 34
Commodity classification, cross-elasticity approach to, 62–65
Commodity market, monopoly in, 397–406
Commodity market organizations, types of, 407
Commodity outputs of manufacturers, 377
Commodity outputs of mining operations, 377
Commodity space, 21, 35, 439
Commodity supply curves, 377
Community preference rule, 28
Comparative static changes, 33
Competition; *see also* Monopolistic competition; Perfect competition; *and* Perfectly competitive markets
 absence of; *see* Monopoly

Competition—*Cont.*
  nonprice, 323–24, 349–50, 357–58
  oligopoly markets, 357–58
  potential, 260–61
  price, 322–23
Competitive industry; *see* Perfectly
    competitive markets
Complementary goods, 62–65, 92–93
  demand surfaces, 65
Conflict curve; *see* Contract curve
Constant cost industries
  long-run equilibrium in perfectly
      competitive market, 248–51
  lump-sum taxes, effects of, 300
  unit tax, effects of, 297
Constant expected utility indifference
    curves, 82–85
Constant returns to scale, 140–41, 204,
    208
Constant-sum games, 341, 346
Constant utility contour, 18
Constrained bliss; *see* Welfare eco-
    nomics, constrained bliss
Consumer behavior; *see also* Consumer
    demand
  analogy with producer behavior, 175
  assumptions necessary for analysis
      of, 12–14
  theory of, 9 ff., 29 ff.
Consumer demand, 52–89; *see also*
    Consumer behavior
  complementary goods, 62–65
  consumption and saving over the
      life cycle, 75–78
  cross-elasticities, 62–63
  geometric illustrations, 63–65
  Giffen's Paradox, 59–61
  income effect, 53–54, 57–58, 61–62
  indifference curve analysis, applica-
      tions of
    index numbers, economic theory
        of, 65–69
    leisure and income, choice be-
        tween, 69–75
  inferior goods, 58–62
  normal goods, 53–58
  risk, choices involving, 78–84
  risk, decision making in, 84–87
  substitute goods, 62–65
  substitution effect, 52–57, 61–62
  superior goods, 53–58
  time preference, 75–78
Consumer equilibrium, 34–39
  marginal rate of substitution, 37

Consumer equilibrium—*Cont.*
  mathematical expression of, 37–39
  maximizing satisfaction subject to a
      limited money income, 36–39
  point of, 37
  price ratio, 37
  relevant part of commodity space,
      35
Consumer-laborer, farmer as, 430–32
Consumer Price Index, 68 n
Consumer-worker equilibrium, 72
Consumers, 9
  assumptions underlying decisions of,
      12, 14
  commodities consumed by, 11–12
  knowledge pertaining to decisions of,
      12, 14, 224–25
Consuming unit, derivation of satisfac-
      tion of, 12–13
Consumption
  laws of, 104
  life cycle, period of, 75–78
Continuous production function, 147–
    50
Contract curve, 438–39, 442, 452–53,
    465–66
  welfare maximization, 461–62
Corner solutions, 94
Cost curves
  average, 194–97
    long-run, 200–202, 208–11
    short-run, 199–200, 208
  average total cost, 195
  average variable, 191–92, 195
  individual firm, 241
  long-run average, 200–202, 208–11
    shape of, 208–11
  marginal, 192, 194–97, 201
    long-run, 201–2
  short-run, 197–98
    average, 199–200
    shape of, 208
  typical set, 197
  unit, 195
Cost elasticity, 205–8
Cost function, 179
Cost of production, 219
  alternative, 180–81
  average, 206
    changes in long-run, 211
    long-run, 198–200
  average fixed cost, 190–91
  average product curve, 191
  average total cost, 192

Cost of production—*Cont.*
  average variable cost, 191
  curves; *see* Cost curves
  diseconomies of scale, 208–11
  economies of scale, 208–9
  efficient entrepreneur behavior as
      factor, 179
  elasticity and function coefficient,
      204–8
  envelope curve, 200
      expansion path and, 203–4
  explicit, 181–82
  factors determining, 179
  fixed, 187–88
  implicit, 181–82
  long-run, 179, 183–85, 198–204
      changes in factor price and, 211–
          12
      production function and, 183–85
      short-run and, 198–200
      theory of, 198–204
  marginal cost, 193–94, 206 n
      changes in long-run, 211–12
      long-run, 201–2
  marginal product curve, 194
  monopoly, 266–70
  opportunity, 180–81
  optimal adjustment, 202
  planning horizon, 187, 198
  private, 181–82
  production function as factor, 179
  resource prices as factor, 179
  short-run, 179, 183, 185–98
      long-run and, 198–200
      production function and, 185–87
      theory of, 187–98
  social, 180–81
  suboptimal adjustment, 202
      expansion path and, 203
  theory of, 123 ff., 179–215
  total, 206 n
  total short-run, 188–90
  variable, 187–88
Cost schedule, 179
Cournot case, 331–34, 337
Cross-elasticities
  demand, 62–63
  price, 62–63, 103
Curves; *see* Cost curves *or other specific
    type*

D

Decentralized socialist society, 457
Decision making

Decision making—*Cont.*
  risky situations, 84–87
  two-outcome or two-state model, 84
Deduction, 4
Deductive method, 4–5
Definitions; *see specific terms*
Demand, 219; *see also* Consumer de-
      mand *and* Market demand
  cross-elasticities, 62–63
  determinants of, 91–93
  elasticities of, 96–105
  income elasticity of, 42–44, 103–5
  market demand in relation to, 93–96
  money income as determinant, 91,
      93
  monopoly, 263–66
  preference as determinant, 92–93
  price of commodity as determinant,
      91, 93
  price cross-elasticity of, 103
  price elasticity of, 46, 48, 62–63,
      97–98
  price inelastic, 46, 48
  price of related commodities as de-
      terminant, 92–93
  shifting determinants of, 92
  theory of, 9 ff.
  transition to market demand, 90–96
  unitary elasticity, 46, 48, 99
  variable productive service, 367–77
      individual demand curves, 371–
          75
      market demand for, 376–77
      one variable, 367–71
      several variables, 371–75
Demand curves, 45–46, 52
  defined, 45
  determination of, 29
  perfectly competitive firm, 115–17
  proportional, 315–17
  several variable inputs, 375
Demand functions, derivation of, 12
Demand and supply analysis
  monopoly, 266–70
  perfectly competitive market equi-
      librium, 239–42
Demand surfaces
  complementary goods, 65
  geometric illustrations, 63–65
  substitute goods, 64
Design differences, 358–59
Dictator, 463
Die tossing, 78–79
Differential demand function, 115 n

Differentness, cost of, 322–23
Diminishing marginal physical returns, law of, 133
Diminishing marginal rate of technical substitution, 156–57
Discrete production function, 147
Diseconomies of scale, 208–11
Diseconomy; *see* External economies
Distribution
   marginal productivity theory of, 365–96
   perfectly competitive markets, 365–96
   relative factor shares and, 385–94
   theory of, 363 ff.
Division of labor, 208–9, 424
Doctors' associations, code of ethics of, 349–50
Duopoly, 407
   cartels, 348–53
   Chamberlin solution, 337–38
   Classical solutions, 331–47
   competition in, 357–58
   Cournot case, 331–34, 337
   defined, 329
   Edgeworth case, 334–37
   games-theory models, 331, 340–47
   homogeneous products, 330
   kinked demand-curve hypothesis, 338–40
   labor unions, effects of, 418–19
   market solutions, 347–57
   mutual recognition of market interdependence, 337–38
   nature of market, 330
   price leadership in, 353–57
   price theory in, 329–61
   product differentiation, 330
   stability in, 337–40
   Sweezy solution, 338–40
   welfare effects of, 359–60
Duopoly theories, 312
du Pont de Nemours, E. I., & Co., 261, 350
Durable goods, 11

E

Eastman Kodak Company, 261
Economic activity, circular flow of, 424–25
Economic agents
   goals of, 2
   types, 9

Economic equilibrium; *see* General economic equilibrium
Economic region of production, 158–60
   ridge lines defining, 167–68
Economic welfare; *see* Welfare economics
Economics
   allocation of resources, 1–2
   defined, 1
   entrepreneur's role, 182
   large scale, 2–3
   models, 3–5
   policy, 3
   scope, 1–2
   small scale, 2–3
   tasks of, 5
Economies of scale, 208–9
   concentration of effort, 208–9
   division of labor, 208–9
   specialization, 208–9
   technological factors, 209
Edgeworth box diagram, 434–36, 440, 442, 445 n, 458, 462, 467
   consumption problems, 435
   production problem, 436
Edgeworth case, 334–37
Edgeworth model, 357
Elasticity of cost, 205–8
Elasticity of demand, 46, 96–105
   defined, 46
   income, 103–5
   linear demand curve, ranges for, 100–101
   price, 97–99
   price-consumption curve and, 47–48
   ranges for linear demand curve, 100–101
   unitary, 46, 48
Elasticity of production function, 395
Elasticity of substitution, 387–88
   changes in relative factor shares and, 388–89
Electrical equipment industry, market-sharing cartel in, 353
Electrical power companies, 262
   monopoly position of, 260
Empirical testing, 5
Employment; *see also* Productive service *and* Variable productive service
   equilibrium price and, 405
   monopoly, 397–406
   monopsony, 407–19

Engel curves, 40–42
  defined, 40
  derivation of, 40
  importance of, 40
  income elasticity of demand and, 42–44
Entrepreneurs, 9
  efficient behavior as cost factor, 179
  farmer as, 427–29
  role of, 182
Envelope curve, 200
  expansion path and, 203–4
Equilibrium
  consumer, 34–39
  consumer-worker, 72
  consumption and saving over life cycle, 75–78
  general economic; *see* General economic equilibrium
  income and leisure, 70–72
  long-run
    comparisons of, 324–26
    firm, 324–25
    industries, 325–26
    monopolistic competition, 320–21, 324–26
    monopoly, 279–84, 325
    perfectly competitive markets, 242–53
    product groups, 325–26
  market period, 226–28
  monopoly, 270–84
  output and expansion path, 168–69
  perfectly competitive markets, 226–28, 242–53
    industry in market period, 226–27
    price as rationing device, 227–28
  short-run
    monopolistic competition, 317–20
    monopoly, 270–79
    perfect competition, 315–17
    perfectly competitive markets, 228–42
Equilibrium budgets, 40
Equilibrium combinations, 39
Equilibrium price and employment, 405
Examination in microeconomic theory for graduate students, 485–518
Excess capacity, concept of, 321–24
Exchange of two or more goods
  Edgeworth box diagram, 434–36
  equilibrium of, 436–39, 442–43

Exchange of two or more goods—*Cont.*
  marginal condition for, 452–53, 455
  production and, 442–43
  utility-possibility frontier, 439–40
  welfare maximization, 459–60
Excise taxes in competitive industry, 293–98
  constant cost industry, effects on, 297
  long-run effects, 295–97
  short-run effects, 293–95, 297
Expansion path, 166–71
  changing output and, 168–69
  defined, 169, 205 n
  envelope curve and, 203–4
  expenditure elasticity, 169–71
  isoclines, 166–68
  long-run total cost schedule in relation to, 185
  suboptimal adjustment and, 203
Expected utility, 82
  constant, 82–83
  value of, 83–84
Expected utility hypothesis, 80–81
Expected value, 78–79
Expected value of a game, 345–46
Expected value of utility and utility of expected value distinguished, 81
Expenditure elasticity, 169–71
  defined, 169
  factor classification, 170–71
  formula for, 170
Explicit costs, 181–82
Exploitation
  monopolistic, 406, 414
  monopsonistic, 414–16
External economies, 472–76
  defined, 473
  free enterprise and, 475–76
  ownership externalities, 473–74
  public good externalities, 475
  social benefits and costs, 472–73
  technical externalities, 474–75

F

Factor intensities, 449–50
Factor of production
  defined, 170
  expenditure elasticity of, 169–71
  inferior, 173–74
  long-run cost and changes in, 211–12
Factor-price ratio, 166, 169

Factor substitution, 459
  marginal condition for, 453, 455, 468
Fair trade laws, 350
Family members, 9
Farm economy, 427
Farmer
  consumer-laborer, 430–32
  entrepreneur, 427–29
Featherbedding, 289
Federal Pacific, 359
Federal Power Commission, 253–54
Federal Trade Commission, 348 n
Firm organization, theory of, 219 ff.
Fixed costs, short-run, 187–88
Fixed input, 125
  defined, 126
Fixed proportions production, 127–28
Fixed proportions production functions, 150–54
  isoquant map for, 151, 153
Florida Power and Light Company, 353
Ford Motor Company, 358
Free enterprise
  externalities and, 475–76
  price system, 424
Free market, 220
Function coefficient, 204–5, 395

G

Game theory, 331, 340–47
  chance, games of, 341
  constant-sum games, 341, 346
  defined, 341
  expected value of, 345–46
  matching pennies, 344–46
  minimax solution, 341–42, 346–47
  nonstrictly determined games, 343–47
  object of, 340
  payoff matrix, 341–45
  players, 341
  rules of, 341
  strategies, 341–47
  strictly adversary games, 341
  strictly determined game, 341–42, 346
  theory of the core, 347 n
  zero-sum games, 341
General assistance payments, demand for, 74–75
General economic equilibrium
  constrained bliss, 466–68
  contract or conflict curve, 438–39, 442

General economic equilibrium—*Cont.*
  Edgeworth box diagram, 434–36
  exchange between two or more goods, 434–40
    production and, 442–43
  factor intensities, 449–50
  factor prices in relation to commodity prices, 449–50
  farm economy, 427
  farmer as consumer-laborer, 430–32
  farmer as entrepreneur, 427–29
  fixed coefficient production model, 444
  one consumption good, 426–34
  Pareto-optimal organization, 439, 442
  production, 440–42
    exchange and, 442–43
  production-possibility frontier, 446
    derivation of, 443–44
  simple two person economy, 427
  theory of, 423 ff.
  transformation curve, 443–44
  two-good economy, 434–40, 444–50
  utility-possibility frontier, derivation of, 439–40
  wage rate, 432–34
  Walras's Law and, 432–34, 448 n
General Electric Company, 353
General Motors Corporation, 358
  allocation of resources by, 1
General Motors v. *UAW,* 364
Geographical quotas, 350
German *Kartelle,* 348
Giffen's Paradox, 90, 93, 96, 263
  defined, 60
  illustration of, 60
  inferior goods and, 59–61
Goals of economic agents, 2
Golf club market, 358
Goodyear Tire and Rubber, 354
Governmental activities, 124
Governmental involvement, 5–6
Governmental regulation, 220–21
Grand utility-possibility frontier, 462–63
Great Depression, 348
Guaranteed minimum income, 74–75
Gulf Oil, 354

H

Heterogeneous products, 314
Hicks-Marshall money, 47
Homogeneous of one degree, 140

Homogeneous product, 224, 330
  industry producing, 226
Homogeneous production function,
  386–87
Hotelling case, 331
Households
  demand decisions by, 10
  derivation of satisfaction from com-
    modities, 12–13
  task confronting, 11
Hydrogen-nitrogen-ammonia illustration of production, 127–28
Hypothesis testing, 5

I

IBM machine, invisible, 2, 424, 457,
  468 n
IBM machines, 262
Ideal output, concept of, 321–23
Imperfect competition; *see* Duopoly;
  Monopoly; *and* Monopsony
Imperial Chemicals, 350
Implicit costs, 181–82
Income tradeoff with leisure; *see* Lei-
  sure-income tradeoff
Income change, index of, 67
Income constraint, 71
Income-consumption curve, 39–40
  defined, 40
  Engel curves derived from, 40
Income earners, 9
  allocation of resources by, 1
Income effect, 53–54, 171
  defined, 57
  inferior good not subject to Giffen's
    Paradox, 61–62
  normal good, 57–58
  price decrease, 55
Income elasticity of demand, 42–44,
  103–5
  defined, 104
  negative, 105
Increasing cost industries, 251–53
Increasing returns to scale; *see* Returns
  to scale
Indeterminacy of purest competition,
  251
Index numbers
  budget map, information from, 67
  economic theory of, 65–69
  income change, 67
  indicators of individual welfare
    changes, 67–69
  Laspeyre index, 68

Index numbers—*Cont.*
  Paasche index, 68
Indifference curve, 18–21
  characteristics of, 21–23, 26
  commodity space, passing through,
    21
  concave, 94–96
  convex, 22–23, 94–95
  defined, 19
  derivation, 12
  downward sloping, 21
  intersection, 21–22
  partial set of, 19–20
  state preference analysis and, 82–84
  transitive relation, 22
Indifference curve analysis
  index numbers, economic theory of,
    65–69
  labor supply, 378–80
  leisure and income, choice between,
    69–75
Indifference map, 19–20, 34, 36
  budget space and, 35
Individual behavior, 2–3
Individual demand; *see* Consumer demand *and* Demand
Individual welfare changes, index numbers as indicators of, 67–69
Industry
  constant cost, 248–51
  defined, 226, 315
  equilibrium in market period, 226–
    27
  increasing cost, 251–53
  long-run adjustment of, 244–47
  long-run equilibrium, 325–26
  perfectly competitive, 247–48
Inferior factors of production, 173–74
  defined, 174
Inferior goods, 42
  defined, 43, 58–59
  Giffen's Paradox and, 59–61
  illustration of, 59
  income effect for, 61–62
  negative income elasticities, 105
  substitution effect for, 61–62
Ingredient inputs, 128
Input demand curves, 404
Input price, 161–62, 363
  changes in, 171–74
  isocost curves, shift in, 171
  output effects, 172–73
    inferior factors and, 173–74
  substitution effect, 172–73

Input-price ratio, 164–65, 386, 469
Input ratios, 127
Input returns, marginal productivity theory of, 381–85
Input space, 443, 459
Input substitution, 146, 154–60
  marginal rate of technical substitution, 154–56
  diminishing, 156–57
Inputs, 123–24
  average product of, 130–32
  ingredient, 128
  least-cost combination of, 386–87
  long-run, 126–27
  marginal expense of, 407–9
  marginal product of, 130–32
  one variable, 125–43
  short-run, 126
  two variables, 144–78
Intermediate goods, 377
  supply curve of, 377, 380
International Business Machines; *see* IBM machine, invisible *and* IBM machines
International markets, 350
Inverse demand curve, 110 n
"Invisible hand" doctrine, 2, 424, 455, 457, 468 n
Isoclines, 166–69
  defined, 167
Isocost curves, 162–63
  shift to show increase in price of labor, 171
Der isolierte Staat, 365
Isoquant map, 149
  fixed proportions production function, 151, 153
  homogeneous production function, 386–87
  product curves for different types of, 160
  range of production and, 158–59
Isoquants, 146, 149–50
  defined, 149
  kinked line, 152–53
  ray of, 150
  smooth, 153–54
  typical set of, 150
  variable proportions production function, 153–54
ITE, 353

K

Kinked demand-curve hypothesis, 338–40
Kinked isoquant line, 152–53
Knowledge of consumer, 12, 14, 224–25
Kroger Grocery, 354

L

Labor, 125–26, 128, 144–46; *see also* Labor supply *and* Variable productive service
  marginal productivity theory of demand for, 366–67
Labor supply, 377
  indifference curve analysis of, 378–79
  supply curve of, 378–81
Labor unions
  economic effects of, 416–19
  monopsony and the economic effects of, 416–19
Lagrange multipliers, 457, 469 n, 472
Land, 125, 144–46
Lange-Lerner rule, 457, 468 n, 472
Laspeyre index, 68
Lawyers' associations, code of ethics of, 349–50
Least-cost combination of inputs, 146, 386–87
Least-cost combination of variable inputs, 411–14
Lectures on Political Economy, 365
Leisure-income tradeoff, 69–75, 426
  consumer-worker equilibrium, 72
  demand for general assistance payments, 74–75
  equilibrium, 70–72
  graph, 70
  income constraint, 71
  overtime rates, 72–73
Leontief function, 151 n, 152 n
Life cycle of individuals, consumption and saving decisions over, 75–78
Liggett and Myers, 314
Limited money income, 30–32, 34
  maximizing satisfaction subject to, 36–39
Linear demand, ranges of elasticity for, 100–101
Linear demand curve, 110–11
Linear homogeneity, 140

Linearly homogeneous production functions, 140–41, 169, 386–87
Long-run, 126–27
  costs, 179, 183–85, 198–204; *see also* Cost of production
  defined, 183, 198
  excise taxes, effects of, 295–97
  lump-sum taxes, effects of, 300–301
  total cost schedule, 185
Loose cartels, 349–50
Lucky Strike cigarettes, 314
Lump-sum taxes in competitive industry, 299–302
  constant cost industry, effects on, 300
  long-run effects of, 300–301
  short-run effects of, 299–300
  size distribution of firms and, 301–2
Luxuries, 42 n, 104

M

MacAvoy-Pindyck estimates of natural gas industry shortages, 254
MacGregor golf clubs, 358
Macroeconomics, 2
Manufacturing industries, 377
  production in, 124
Marginal conditions for social welfare, 452–57
Marginal cost, 193–94, 472–73; *see also* External economies
  defined, 206 n
  long-run, 201–2
  changes in, 211–12
Marginal cost curves; *see* Cost curves
Marginal expense of input, 407–9
  defined, 410
Marginal expense of variable input, 268–70
Marginal physical returns, diminishing, law of, 133
Marginal product, 130–32, 137–38
  defined, 131, 137
  maximum value of, 135, 137
  variable productive service, 369
Marginal product curve, 194
  geometry of, 134–37
Marginal productivity
  Clark-Wicksteed product exhaustion theorem, 383–85, 395–96
  demand for a variable production service, 367–77
  input returns, 381–85
  labor, demand for, 366–67
  long-run analysis, 383–85

Marginal productivity—*Cont.*
  origin of theory, 365–67
  principle of, 366
  product exhaustion theorem, 383–85, 395–96
  quasi rents, 381–83
  short-run fixed inputs, 381–83
  supply of a variable productive service, 377–81
  technological progress, 390–93
  theory of distribution in perfectly competitive markets, 365–96
  wages, determination of, 365–66
Marginal rate of substitution, 23–26, 37
  defined, 24
  diminishing, 25–26
Marginal rate of technical substitution, 154–56, 164, 169, 386–87, 452–55
  defined, 155–56
  diminishing, 156–57
Marginal revenue, 105–11
  calculation of, 106–8
  defined, 106
  geometry of determination of, 109–11
  monopoly, 263–66
  negative, 108
  positive, 108
  price elasticity of demand and, 113–15
Marginal revenue curve, 110–11
Marginal revenue product
  defined, 399–400, 410
  monopoly, 398–401
Marginal revenue product curve in single productive service, 400–401
Marginal utility, 37
  defined, 24 n
Market demand, 219
  characteristics of, 90–119
  defined, 10, 96
  demand in relation to, 93–96
  determination of, 93–96
  transition from individual demand to, 90–96
  variable productive service, 376–77, 405
Market demand curve in monopoly, 263–66
Market-determined prices, 457
  equivalent of, 457

Market equilibrium, 226–28
demand-supply analysis, 239–42
industry, 226–27
price as rationing device, 227–28
profit or loss, 238–39
short-run, profit or loss, 238–39
variable productive services, price of, 381–82
Market failure, 472; *see also* External economies
Market franchises, 262–63
Market organization; *see also* Duopoly; Monopolistic competition; Monopoly; *and* Perfectly competitive markets
theory of, 219 ff.
types, 407
Market period
defined, 226
equilibrium in, 226–28
Market sharing, 348–52
nonprice competition, 349–50
quota system, 350–52
Market supply curve, 226
Marshall-Hicks approach to distribution, 366–67
Matching pennies, 344–46
Maximization of output for given cost, 163–65
Maximization of profit, 2, 166, 182, 221, 426, 455–56
cartels, 349
multiplant monopoly, 277–79
price discrimination and, 286
short-run equilibrium under monopoly
marginal revenue–marginal cost approach, 230–31, 272–74
total revenue–total cost approach, 228–30, 270–72
variable productive service, 367–71
Maximization of satisfaction, 2, 13, 29, 34–35, 90, 426, 455
limited money income, subject to, 36–39
Methodology, 3–5
Microeconomics, 2
Mineral springs case, 331–33
Minimax game solution, 341–42, 346–47
Minimization of cost subject to given output, 165–66
Minimum wage, 470–72
Mining operations, 377

Minnesota Mining and Manufacturing Company (Three M), 262
Model analysis, 3–5
Money income
changes in, 39–44
demand determinant, 91, 93
limited, 30–32, 34, 36–39
Money prices of goods, 32 n
Monopolist, market power of, 260
Monopolistic competition, 407
appraisal of, 326–27
characteristics of, 321–24
excess capacity, 321–24
historical perspective, 312–13
ideal output, 321–23
long-run equilibrium, 320–21, 324–26
nonprice competition, 323–24
price theory, 312–28
product differentiation, 313–14, 326
product groups, 315
short-run equilibrium, 317–20
welfare aspects, 326
Monopolistic exploitation, 405–6, 414
Monopoly, 220–21, 407
absence of direct competition, 259, 261
assumptions underlying analysis of, 270
bases of, 261–63
bilateral, 288–89
commodity market, 397–406
cost under, 266–70
defined, 259–61
demand for several variable services, 403–4
demand for single variable service, 401–3
demand-supply analysis, 266–70
demand under, 263–66
employment in, theory of, 397–406
equilibrium, 270–84
factors leading to establishment of, 261–63
indirect competition, 260–61
industry, 315
input-control, 261
long-run equilibrium, 279–84, 325
multiplant, 282–84
perfect competition compared, 281–84
single plant, 279–82
marginal expense of variable input, 268–70

Monopoly—*Cont.*
marginal revenue, 263–66
marginal revenue product, 398–401
market demand curve, 263–66
market demand for variable productive service, 405
market franchise, 262–63
multiplant
long-run equilibrium, 282–84
short-run equilibrium, 277–82
natural, 262
number of firms in, 312
patents, 260–62
perfect competition distinguished,
259
potential competition, 260–61
price controls in, 304–6
price discrimination, 284–87
price-output policies, 260–61
price theory, 259–91
product quality and, 309–11
profit maximization
marginal revenue–marginal cost
approach, 272–74
total revenue–total cost approach,
270–72
short-run equilibrium, 270–78
marginal revenue–marginal cost
approach, 272–74
total revenue–total cost approach,
270–72
single plant, long-run equilibrium in,
279–82
specialized inputs, 266
substitute goods, 260–61
supply under, 266, 270
short-run, 276–79
suppression of inventions in, 309–11
Monopsonist, 266 n
Monopsonistic exploitation, 414–16
Monopsony
defined, 407
employment in, theory of, 407–19
labor unions, effects of, 416–19
least-cost combination of variable
inputs, 411–14
marginal expense of input, 407–9
one variable input, 409–11
several variable inputs, 411–14
supply of input curve, 407–9
Moonlighting, 70 n
Moral suasion, 220
Multiplant monopoly; *see* Monopoly
Municipal waterworks, 262

Mutual recognition of market interdependence, 337–38

N

Nanosecond, 183
National Steel, 354
Natural gas industry, 253–54
cost of service policy, 254–55
deregulation policy, 254–55
MacAvoy-Pindyck estimates of short-
ages, 254
price controls, 253–54
regulatory status quo policy, 254
shortages in, 253–54
total reserves, 255
Natural monopoly, 262
Natural resources, 377
supply curves of, 377, 380
Necessities, 42 n, 104
Newsprint industry, 354
Nixon administration, 302
"No profit" situation, 248
Nominal prices, 32 n, 34
change in, 52
Nondurable goods, 12
Nonferrous alloys industry, 354
Nonprice competition, 323–24, 349–
50, 357–58
advertising, 357–58
design differences, 358
quality differentiation, 358
Normal goods, 39–40, 42
defined, 43–58
income effect, 57–58
substitution effect as to, 53–57
Norms, 3
NRA codes, 348
Numeraire commodity, 427, 446

O

Office of Price Administration (OPA),
353
Oligopoly; *see* Duopoly
Oligopsonist, 266 n
Oligopsony defined, 407
"One-mill" town, 288
Opportunity cost of production, 180–81
Optimal adjustment, 202
Optimal combination of resources, 160–
66
input prices and isocosts, 161–62
maximization of output, 174
for a given cost, 163–65

Optimal combination of resources—
Cont.
minimizing cost subject to given
output, 165–66
Optimum conditions
exchange, 452, 459–60
factor substitution, 453, 459, 468
product substitution, 453
Ordinal measurement of utility, 16, 20–
21
Ordinate intercept, 31, 33–34
Output; see Production
Output effect
inferior factors and, 173–74
input price changes, 172–73, 372–73
monopoly demand for variable pro-
ductive service, 404
Output elasticity of productive services,
396
Output-price ratio, 469
Output restrictions, 307–8
Overtime wages, 72–73
Overview of book, 5–6
Ownership externalities, 473–74

P

Paasche index, 68
Pareto efficiency; see Pareto-optimal
organization
Pareto-optimal organization, 439, 442,
452–54, 465–66
defined, 465
minimum wages and, 470–72
welfare maximization, 461–63
Pareto optimality; see Pareto-optimal
organization
Paris a century ago, 423
Parity-price programs, 220
Part-time employment, 70 n
Patents, 260–62
Payoff, 79–80
Payoff matrix, 341–45
Perfect competition
assumptions underlying analysis of,
270
auctioneer parable, 223
concept of, 222
defined, 222–23, 225
free mobility of resources, 224
homogeneous product, 224
industries, 315
monopoly distinguished, 259
monopoly long-run equilibrium compared

Perfect competition—*Cont.*
multiplant, 283–84
single plant, 281–82
number of firms in, 312
perfect knowledge, 224–25
price taking demanders and suppliers,
223–24
proportional demand curve, 315–17
short-run equilibrium, 315–17
welfare maximization and, 455–57
Perfect knowledge, 224–25; *see also*
Knowledge of consumer
Perfectly competitive markets, 407
demand curve for, 115–17
distribution, theory of, 395–96
equilibrium in market period, 226–
28
industry, 226–27
price as rationing device, 227–28
excise taxes, 293–98
labor union, effects of, 417
long-run equilibrium, 242–53, 325–
26
constant cost industries, 248–51
established firm, 242–44
increasing cost industries, 251–53
industry, 244–47
perfectly competitive industry,
247–48
lump-sum taxes, 299–302
Marginal productivity theory of distribution, 365–96
market equilibrium, short-run, profit
or loss, 238–39
model in practice, 253–55
output restrictions, 307–8
perfect competition concept; *see* Perfect competition
price controls, 302–4
price floors, 306–7
price system, functioning of, 457
short-run equilibrium, 228–42
demand-supply analysis, 239–42
profit or loss, 233–34, 238–39
proof of, 231–33
short-run profit maximization
marginal revenue–marginal cost
approach, 230–31
total revenue–total cost approach,
228–30
short-run supply curve, 234–38
theory of price in, 222–58
Planning horizon, 187, 198

Plant size, long-run adjustment of, 242–44

Point elasticity, 97–98
  computation, 100
  graphical measurement, 99–101

Policy, 3

Positive economics, 3

Potential competition, 260–61

Preferences
  assumptions about, 12–14, 21
  demand determinant, 92–93
  determination of order of, 13
  quantification of, 14–16
  theory of, 12–14

Price; *see also* Nominal prices *and* Relative price
  changes in, 44–48
  cost factor, 179
  demand determinant, 91, 93
  duopoly, theory in, 329–61
  function of, 227
  goods, 363
  input; *see* Input price
  monopolistic competition, theory under, 312–28
  monopoly, theory in, 259–91
  oligopoly markets, theory in, 329–61
  perfectly competitive markets, functioning in, 457
  perfectly competitive markets, theory in, 222–58
  rationing device, 227–28
  related commodities, as demand determinant, 92–93

Price ceilings; *see* Price controls

Price competition, 322–23

Price-consumption curve, 44–45
  defined, 45
  elasticity of demand and, 47–48

Price controls
  competitive industry, 302–4
  monopoly, 304–6
  shortages resulting from, 253–54, 304, 306

Price cross-elasticity of demand, 62–63, 103
  coefficient of, 103–4
  defined, 103

Price discrimination
  market conditions leading to, 284–85
  monopoly, 284–87
  profit maximization with, 286

Price elasticity of demand, 46, 48, 62–63, 97–99

Price elasticity of demand—*Cont.*
  coefficient of, 97, 99
  defined, 97
  direct, 97
  estimated numerical values of, 101–2
  factors affecting, 101–3
  importance of, 101
  marginal revenue and, 113–15
  number of uses to which a good may be put, 102
  point, 97–101
  substitute goods, availability of, 102
  total revenue and, 111–14
  unitary, 99

Price fixing, 348
  vertical agreements, 348 n

Price floors, 306–7

Price inelasticity of demand, 46, 48, 99

Price leadership, 353–57
  dominant firm, 355–56
  lower cost firm, 354–55

Price ratio, 37

Price supports; *see* Price floors

Price system, 5

Price takers, 300 n

Price taking demanders and suppliers, 223–24

Price wars, 357

Private cost of production, 181–82

Private enterprise, abolition of, 326

Probabilities, 78–79

Process materials; *see* Raw materials

Producer behavior, analogy with consumer behavior, 175

Product demand, 219

Product differentiation, 313–14, 326, 330, 357, 406

Product exhaustion theorem, 383–85, 395–96

Product groups, 315
  long-run equilibrium, 325–26

Product quality and monopoly, 309–10

Product substitution, marginal condition for, 453–56

Production, 123
  agricultural, 124
  capital equipment required for, 124
  cost of; *see* Cost of production
  defined, 123
  economic region of, 158–60
  examples of, 123
  fixed proportions, 127–28
  input substitution, 146, 154–60

Production—*Cont.*
  long-run organization of, 127
  manufacturing industries, 124
  one variable input, 125–43
  optimal combination of resources, 160–66
  private cost of, 181–82
  raw materials required for, 124
  revenue side of, 219
  short-run theory of, 126
  social cost of, 180–81
  technical conditions of, 219
  theory of, 123 ff.
  three stages of, 138–40
  two variable inputs, 144–78
  variable proportions, 127–28, 132
Production equilibrium, 440–42
  exchange and, 442–43
  two-good economy, 444–47
Production function, 128–33
  average product, 130–32, 137–39
  average product curves, geometry of, 133–36
  continuous, 147–50
  cost factor, 179
  defined, 129
  diminishing marginal physical returns, law of, 133
  discrete, 147
  elasticity of, 395
  fixed proportions, 150–54
  homogeneous, 386–87
  linearly homogeneous, 140–41, 386–87
  long-run costs and, 183–85
  marginal product, 130–32, 137–39
  marginal product curves, geometry of, 134–37
  short-run costs and, 185–87
  total output or product, 129–30, 137–39
  variable proportions, 153–54
  welfare maximization, 458–59
Production isoquants, 149–50
Production-possibility frontier, 446, 453–56, 467
  defined, 443
  derivation of, 443–44
  welfare maximization, 458–60
Production surface, 146–54
  continuous case, 147–49
  discrete case, 147
  fixed proportions production functions, 150–54

Production surface—*Cont.*
  production isoquants, 149–50
Production table, 144–46
Productive service; *see also* Marginal productivity *and* Variable productive service
  exploitation of, 406
  marginal revenue product curve for, 400–401
  output elasticity of, 396
  supply curve for, 407
Professional associations, 348
  code of ethics of, 349–50
Profit maximization; *see* Maximization of profit
Profit maximizing effect
  monopoly demand for variable productive service, 404
  variable productive service, 374
Progress and Poverty, 365
Proportional demand curve, 315–17
Psychological perception threshold, 23 n
Public good externalities, 475
Public utilities
  natural monopolies, 262
  regulation of, 220
Public welfare, regard for, 220; *see also* Welfare economics
Pure monopoly; *see* Monopoly

Q

Quality differentiation, 358–59
Quasi rents, 381–83
  defined, 381 n, 382 n
  determination of, 382–83
Quota system, 350–52
  geographical division as base, 350
  statistical base, 350

R

Rank ordering of commodity bundles, 13–14, 34
Rationing, price as device of, 227–28
Raw materials, 124, 126
Real world, model analysis of, 3–5
Regression relation, 174 n
Relative factor shares
  biased technological progress and, 392–93
  distribution and, 385–94
  elasticity of substitution and changes in, 388–89
Relative price, 32 n, 34
  change in, 52

Rent
controls, 302
defined, 381
Research and development, 359–60
Resource owners, 9
Resources
allocation of; *see* Allocation of resources
free mobility of, 224
optimal combination of, 160–64
Returns to scale; *see also* Constant returns to scale
decreasing, 204, 208
increasing, 204, 208, 474
Revenue function; *see* Marginal revenue
Reynolds Tobacco, 314
Risk
choice among alternative situations of, 80–81
choices involving, 78–84
decision making in, 84–87
expected utility hypothesis, 80–81
expected value, 78–79
indifference curves, 82–84
probabilities, 78–79
state preference analysis, 82–84
Risk aversion, 81
Risk, Uncertainty, and Profit, 313
Rohm and Haas, 350

S

Sales allocation, 349–52
Satisfaction, 12; *see also* Maximization of satisfaction
Savings, 30 n
life cycle, period of, 75–78
Scotch Tape, 262
Service trades, 124
Sewage disposal system, 262
Shadow prices, 457, 468 n
Sherman Antitrust Act of 1890, 220–21, 331, 348 n
Short-run, 126
defined, 183
excise taxes, effects on cost, price and output, 293–95, 297
fixed inputs and marginal productivity, 381–83
lump-sum taxes, effects of, 299–300
Short-run cost curves, 197–98
Short-run costs, 179, 183, 185–98; *see also* Cost of production
Short-run equilibrium in perfectly competitive market, 228–42

Short-run supply curve in perfectly competitive industry, 234–38
Short-run supply in monopoly, 276
multiplant, 277–79
Shortages, 304, 306
natural gas industry, 353–54
Single-plant monopoly, 279–82
Size distribution of firms and lump-sum taxes, 301–2
Smog, 473
Social benefits and costs, 472–73
Social consciousness, 220
Social cost of production, 180–81
Social responsibility, 220
Social welfare, 2–3; *see also* Welfare economics
Social welfare function, 458, 463
absence of a dictator, 463
construction of, 464–65
unique preference ordering of states, 458
Soil bank programs, 307–8
Spaulding golf clubs, 358
Specialization, 208–9, 424
State of the art, 124, 129, 375, 443
States of nature, 82
Statistical method, 4–5
Statistical quotas, 350
Statistical testing, 5
Steel industry, 354
Stolper-Samuelson Theorem, 450
Strategies
defined, 341
game theory, 341–47
mixed, 345–47
optimal mixed, 346
pure, 343
Strictly adversary games, 341
Students' allocation of study time, 1
Study on the Pure Theory of Production, A, 395
Suboptimal adjustment, 202
expansion path and, 203
Substitute goods, 62–65, 92, 260–61
availability as price elasticity factor, 102
demand surfaces, 64
Substitution, elasticity of; *see* Elasticity of substitution
Substitution effect, 52, 78, 171
defined, 54
inferior good not subject to Giffen's Paradox, 61–62

Substitution effect—*Cont.*
  input price changes, 172–73, 372–73
  monopoly demand for variable productive service, 404
  normal good, 53–57
  price decrease, 55
  price rise, 56
  superior good, 53–57
Superior goods, 39–40, 42
  defined, 43, 58
  substitution effect as to, 53–57
Supply; *see also* Demand and supply analysis
  monopoly, 266, 270
    multiplant, 277–79
    short-run, 276–79
  variable productive service, 377–81
Supply conditions, 219
Supply curves
  intermediate goods, 377, 380
  labor, 378–81
  natural resources, 377, 380
  productive services, 407
Sweezy solution, 338–40

T

Tariffs, 220
Taste; *see* Preferences
Technical externalities, 474–75
Technological progress
  biased, 391–93
  capital-using, 390–93
  classification of, 390–92
  defined, 390
  labor-using, 391–93
  neutral, 390–91, 393
  relative factor shares, 392–93
Technology, 124, 129, 375
Telephone companies, 262
Theorie der Production, 395
Theories; *see specific topic or type*
Theory of the core, 347 n
Theory of Games and Economic Behavior, The, 80, 340
Theory of Wages, 385
Thermofax Copier, 262
Time preference, 75–78
Total cost
  defined, 206 n
  elasticity of, 206–7
  short-run, 187–90
Total effect of price change, 53–54, 58
  defined, 53

Total output, 129–30, 137–39
Total products, 137–39
Total revenue, 105, 107–8; *see also* Marginal revenue
  measurement of, 106
  price elasticity of demand and, 111–14
Total variable cost, 187
Trade associations, 348
Tradeoff between leisure and income; *see* Leisure-income tradeoff
Transformation curve; *see* Production-possibility frontier
Transportation services, 262

U

Unions; *see* Labor unions
Unit tax; *see* Excise taxes in competitive industry
Unitary elasticity of demand, 46, 48, 99
Universal law of wages, 365
Universities, allocation of resources by, 1
Utility, 12, 378 n
  cardinal measurement of, 16–17, 21
  ordinal measurement of, 16, 20–21
  theory of, 11 ff.
Utility of expected value and expected value of utility distinguished, 81
Utility function
  continuous, 21 n
  function of, 15–16
  geometric representation of, 17
  use of, 14
Utility-possibility frontier
  derivation of, 439–40
  grand, 462–63
  to point of constrained bliss, 463–65
  welfare maximization, 461–63
Utility surface, 16–18
  constant utility contours and, 18–20

V

Ad valorum taxes, 293 n, 297–98
Value
  marginal product, 369
  theory of, 363
Variable costs, short-run, 187–88
Variable inputs, 125
  defined, 126
  least-cost combination of, 411–14
  marginal expense of, 268–70
  one, 125–43
  two, 144–78

Variable productive service
  classification of, 377
  demand for, 367–77
    determinants of, 375
    individual demand curves, 371–75
    intermediate goods, 377
    labor, 377
    market demand for, 376–77, 405
    market equilibrium price, 381–82
    monopoly demand for, 401–4
      several variables, 403–4
      single variable, 401–3
    natural resources, 377
    one variable, 367–71, 401–3
    output effect, 372–73
    profit maximizing effect, 367–71, 374
    several variables, 371–75, 403–4
    substitution effect, 372–73
  supply of, 377–81
  value of marginal product, 369
Variable proportions production, 127–28, 132
Variable proportions production function, 153–54
  isoquants for, 153–54
Von Neumann-Morgenstern theory, 80–81, 84
Voting paradox, 463

W–Z

Wage-price freeze of 1971, 220
  Phase I to Phase IV policies, 220, 302
Wage rate equilibrium, 432–34
Wage-rent ratio, 386, 389
Wages
  marginal productivity theory of determining, 365–66
  minimum, 470–72
  overtime, 72–73
  universal law of, 365
Walras's Law, 448 n
  defined, 434
  general economic equilibrium and, 432–34
Wealth effect, 78
Welfare criteria; *see* Welfare economics
Welfare economics, 2–3, 452–77
  citizen, interest as, 464

Welfare economics—*Cont.*
  constrained bliss
    defined, 465
    efficiency and, 465–66
    to inputs, outputs, and distribution, 466–68
    to prices, wages and rents, 468–70
    from utility-possibility frontier to, 463–65
  consumer, interest as, 463
  contract curve, 461–62
  decentralized socialist society, 457
  efficiency in, 465–66
  exchange, 452–53, 455
  external economics and, 472–76; *see also* External economies
  factor substitution, 453, 455
  general assistance payments, 74–75
  general assumptions, 457–58
  Lagrange multipliers, 468 n, 472
  Lange-Lerner rule, 457, 468 n, 472
  macroscopic criteria, 326
  marginal conditions for, 452–57
  maximization of profits, 455–56
  microscopic criteria, 326
  minimum wages, 470–72
  monopolistic competition, 326
  oligopoly, 359–60
  optimum conditions of exchange, 459–60
  Pareto-optimal organization, 465–66
  perfect competition and, 455–57
  product substitution, 453–56
  production functions, 458–59
  production-possibility frontier, 458–60
  static theory of, 475–76
  theory of, 423 ff.
  utility-possibility frontier, 461–63
    grand, 462–63
    to point of constrained bliss, 463–65
Welfare maximization; *see* Welfare economics
Welfare norms, 3
Westinghouse, 353
Wilson golf clubs, 358
World War II, 261, 302
Zero-sum games, 341

This book has been set in 12 and 11 point Garamond #3, leaded 1 point. Part numbers and titles are 24 point Helvetica. Chapter numbers are 30 point Helvetica and chapter titles are 18 point Helvetica. The size of the type page is 27 by 45¾ picas.

330.01 Ferguson, Charles
FERGUSON E.

Microeconomic
theory

$16.50

350

DATE		
Joseph-Grover		

WITHDRAWN